PENGUIN BOOKS

SIX FRIGATES

Ian W. Toll has been a Wall Street analyst, a Federal Reserve financial analyst and a political aide and speechwriter. A lifelong sailor, Toll's research into British and American naval history dates back to the early 1990s, when he was first introduced to the historical novels of Patrick O'Brian. *Six Frigates* is his first book.

SIX FRIGATES

*How Piracy, War and British
Supremacy at Sea gave
Birth to the World's Most
Powerful Navy*

Ian W. Toll

PENGUIN BOOKS

PENGUIN BOOKS

Published by the Penguin Group
Penguin Books Ltd, 80 Strand, London WC2R 0RL, England
Penguin Group (USA) Inc., 375 Hudson Street, New York, New York 10014, USA
Penguin Group (Canada), 90 Eglinton Avenue East, Suite 700, Toronto, Ontario, Canada M4P 2Y3
(a division of Pearson Penguin Canada Inc.)
Penguin Ireland, 25 St Stephen's Green, Dublin 2, Ireland (a division of Penguin Books Ltd)
Penguin Group (Australia), 250 Camberwell Road, Camberwell, Victoria 3124, Australia
(a division of Pearson Australia Group Pty Ltd)
Penguin Books India Pvt Ltd, 11 Community Centre, Panchsheel Park, New Delhi – 110 017, India
Penguin Group (NZ), 67 Apollo Drive, Rosedale, North Shore 0632, New Zealand
(a division of Pearson New Zealand Ltd)
Penguin Books (South Africa) (Pty) Ltd, 24 Sturdee Avenue, Rosebank, Johannesburg 2196, South Africa

Penguin Books Ltd, Registered Offices: 80 Strand, London WC2R 0RL, England

www.penguin.com

First published in the United States of America by W. W. Norton & Company 2006
First published in Great Britain by Michael Joseph 2006
Published in Penguin Books 2007
1

Frontispiece: USS *President* entering the harbour of Marseilles. Watercolour by
Antoine Roux, *c*. 1805. New York Public Library. Page 1: "Preparation for war to defend commerce."
The USS *Philadelphia* under construction in Joshua Humphrey's shipyard, 1800. New York Public Library.
Page 145: USS *Constitution*. Watercolour, 1819. Artist Unknown. The Mariners' Museum, Newport
News, Virginia. Page 255: USS *Philadelphia* on the rocks off Tripoli, October 31, 1803. Coloured
lithograph, P. S. Duval Son & Co., undated. The Mariners' Museum, Newport News, Virginia.

Printed in England by Clays Ltd, St Ives plc

ISBN: 978-0-141-01456-2

To my parents

CONTENTS

DEBTS OF GRATITUDE

This book would have required at least twice as much time to write—and it might be more truthful to say it would not have been written at all—if not for the painstaking efforts of the Department of the Navy, beginning in the 1920s and continuing to this day, to collect, transcribe, and publish large numbers of early naval records, documents, journals, and letters. Three series merit special mention. *Naval Documents Related to the Quasi-War Between the United States and France* (7 vols.) is invaluable not only as a documentary history of the Quasi War, but for its attention to the construction and fitting out of the first frigates. *Naval Documents Related to the United States Wars with the Barbary Powers* (6 vols.) reaches back to the earliest debates of the 1780s, when American ships first fell prey to the Barbary corsairs, and provides a comprehensive day-to-day history of Commodore Edward Preble's 1803–04 campaign against Tripoli. *The Naval War of 1812: A Documentary History* (3 vols. with a fourth in process) addresses not only the naval war itself but the Anglo-American disputes that preceded the war. The third volume, released in 2004, provides a wealth of newly published material on the 1814 operations in the Chesapeake Bay, including the invasion and destruction of Washington. Additional naval records and letters are kept at the National Archives, Record Group 45; and several collections of officers' correspondence can be found at the New-York Historical Society and the Historical Society of Pennsylvania. The latter is the repository of Joshua Humphreys's letter and account books, an essential source both for debates over the design of the frigates and for the construction and fitting out of the frigate *United States*.

 American State Papers (38 vols.) provides many vital documents, particularly in the volumes for Foreign Relations, Finance, Commerce and Navigation, Military Affairs, and Naval Affairs. *Annals of Congress* provides a record of debates in the House. The Library of Congress Web site provides scanned original images of the Thomas Jefferson Papers, much of it text-searchable, with transcriptions by Paul Leicester Ford. (The Library's site, at http://memory.loc.gov, also provides full-page access to *American State Papers*, *Annals of Congress*, and several other essential sources.) *The Papers of Thomas Jefferson*, an ongoing project at Princeton University Press, is the preferred source for Jefferson's early career. Also useful are *The Adams-Jefferson Letters* (Lester J. Cappon, ed.) and *The Republic of Letters: The Correspondence Between Thomas Jefferson and James Madison 1776–1826* (James Morton Smith, ed.). Most trade, economic, and fiscal statistics have been drawn from the U.S. Census Bureau's *Historical Statistics of the United States, Colonial Times to 1970* (2 vols.). Of the contemporary newspapers, the most essential are the Philadelphia *Aurora General Advertiser* (excerpted at length in Richard N. Rosenfeld's *American Aurora*, 1997), the *Niles' Register*, *The Times* of London, and the British *Naval Chronicle*.

For naval policy debates and politics during the pre–1815 era, two books merit special mention: Marshall Smelser's *Congress Founds the Navy* (1959) and Craig Symonds's *Navalists and Anti-Navalists* (1980). The importance of American merchant shipping interests is emphasized in Robert G. Albion and Jennie Barnes Pope's *Sea Lanes in Wartime* (1942). The best overall work on the early American merchant marine is William Armstrong Fairburn's *Merchant Sail* (1945–55). Howard Chapelle remains the leading American authority on ship design issues in the age of sail, even if most of his books are more than half a century old. I have particularly relied on *The History of the American Sailing Navy: The Ships and Their Development* (1949). Virginia Steele Wood's *Live Oaking: Southern Timber for Tall Ships* (1981) relates the little-known history of the use of live oak as a ship's timber. For ship-handling and seamanship, the best modern work I have found is John Harland's *Seamanship in the Age of Sail* (1984).

Several naval biographies deserve mention. The best I have read from this era is Christopher McKee's *Edward Preble: A Naval Biography* (1972). Also important are David F. Long's *Ready to Hazard: A Biography of Commodore William Bainbridge, 1774–1833* (1981), Albert Gleaves's *James Lawrence* (1904), Eugene Ferguson's *Truxtun of the Constellation* (1959), and Linda Mahoney's *Captain from Connecticut: The Life and Naval Times of Isaac Hull* (1986). Two biographies of Stephen Decatur, Jr., were published in 2004: *A Life Most Bold and Daring*, by Spencer Tucker, and *A Rage for Glory*, by James Tertius De Kay. Of the political biographies, I have relied particularly on David McCullough's *John Adams* (2001), Dumas Malone's *Jefferson and His*

Time (1948–70), and Joseph Ellis's several excellent works on the founders. For the politics of the 1790s, no single work is more comprehensive than Stanley Elkins and Eric McKitrick's monumental *The Age of Federalism: The Early American Republic, 1788–1800* (1994). Two important sources on the Quasi War are Michael A. Palmer's *Stoddert's War* (1987) and Alexander DeConde's *The Quasi War: The Politics and Diplomacy of the Undeclared War with France, 1797–1801* (1966).

For general histories of the navy during the pre–1815 period, a seminal modern work is Christopher McKee's *A Gentlemanly and Honorable Profession: The Creation of the U.S. Naval Officer Corps, 1794–1815* (1991). Tyrone Martin's *A Most Fortunate Ship: A Narrative History of Old Ironsides* (1980) is the definitive work on the frigate *Constitution*, written by one of her former commanders. William Fowler's *Jar Tars and Commodores* (1984) is a good narrative history of the era between the Revolution and the War of 1812. For the Barbary Wars, there are several histories; none is more thorough than Glenn Tucker's *Dawn Like Thunder: The Barbary Wars and the Birth of the U.S. Navy* (1963). Two accounts of captivity in Tripoli by members of the crew of the *Philadelphia*, one written by a surgeon and one by a sailor, appear in *White Slaves, African Masters: An Anthology of American Barbary Captivity Narratives* (Paul Baepler, ed., 1999).

For the political history of the Jeffersonian period, the essential point of departure is Henry Adams's magisterial nine-volume *History of the United States of America During the Administrations of Thomas Jefferson and James Madison*, published in the last decade of the nineteenth century. Spencer Tucker and Frank Reuter's *Injured Honor* (1996) is the indispensable source for the *Chesapeake-Leopard* encounter of 1807. For the War of 1812, Theodore Roosevelt's *The Naval War of 1812* (1882) and Alfred T. Mahan's *Sea Power in Its Relation to the War of 1812* (1905) have done remarkably well at standing the test of time. I have also relied on Donald R. Hickey's *The War of 1812: A Forgotten Conflict* (1989) and Wade Dudley's *Splintering the Wooden Wall: The British Blockade of the United States, 1812–1815* (2003). For the British perspective, no one interested in the subject should ignore William James's *Naval Occurrences of the War of 1812* (1817). A good modern treatment, with contributions by several British historians, is *The Naval War of 1812* (Robert Gardner, ed., 2001); and a neglected classic is C. S. Forester's *The Age of Fighting Sail: The Story of the Naval War of 1812* (1956), a work of non-fiction by the author better known for the "Horatio Hornblower" series of historical novels.

Thanks to Burt Logan, Sarah Watkins, and the staff of the USS Constitution Museum for their enthusiastic support for this project. The officers and crew of the *Constitution* generously allowed me to be conducted on an extended tour of the frigate. Richard Whelan of the Naval Historical Center (NHC) Detachment Boston, who is responsible for looking after the *Constitution*, showed me around both the frigate and the adjoining repair and maintenance facilities. Thanks too to Michael Crawford, Charles Brodine, and the staff of the NHC's Early History Branch at the Washington Navy Yard for allowing me access to their excellent research facilities and for taking the time to discuss the project. I would also like to acknowledge the efforts of the professional archivists and librarians at the National Archives, the Library of Congress, the Historical Society of Pennsylvania, the American Philosophical Society, the Phillips Library (Salem, MA), the New-York Historical Society, the New York Society Library, and the New York Public Library. For assistance, advice, and support, I must thank, in no particular order, Peter Neill, Phil Kopper, Jay Iselin, Ralph Carpenter, Admiral Paul Engel, Nick Stevens, Kate Sheekey, Chris Vroom, Illya Szilak, Jim Woolsey, William Luers, David McCullough, and finally McKay Jenkins, who was a die-hard advocate of this project before the first word was committed to paper. Others who have helped along the way are Dan Hollins, Roy Penny, and Bill Schenck; also Dorothy Brown, Emmet Curran, and Ed Ingebretsen. For their kindness and generosity when I was struggling through the middle chapters, I would like to thank Frank, Kay, and Montgomery Woods. At Janklow & Nesbit, I would like to thank Mort Janklow, Tif Loehnis, Dorothy Vincent, and particularly Eric Simonoff, who has been a gentleman, a consummate professional, and a friend. At W. W. Norton, thanks to Morgen Van Vorst, Louise Brockett, and especially my editor, Starling Lawrence, who unknowingly started me down the path that led to this book when he made the decision, almost fifteen years ago, to publish the novels of Patrick O'Brian in the United States.

No research assistants were employed in this project, but several family members provided invaluable (and unbillable) assistance. My father, among other things, hunted down several obscure eyewitness accounts of the sea actions of 1812. My mother read and critiqued the manuscript, and her comments have been extremely useful. My brother, Adam, explored and turned up sources in Halifax (during his honeymoon, no less). Kathryn, my wife, often helped me talk through the outlines and provided excellent critical feedback on the early drafts of the manuscript. George Orwell once said: "Writing a book is a horrible, exhausting struggle, like a long bout of some painful illness." For love, inspiration, and support, I am grateful, above all, to Kathryn.

War is the tao of deception.

Therefore, when planning an attack, feign inactivity.

When near, appear as if you are far away.

When far away, create the illusion that you are near.

If the enemy is efficient, prepare for him.

If he is strong, evade him.

If he is angry, agitate him.

If he is arrogant, behave timidly so as to encourage his arrogance.

If he is rested, cause him to exert himself.

Advance when he does not expect you.

Attack him when he is unprepared.

—SUN-TZU, *THE ART OF WAR*
CA. 4TH CENTURY B.C.

NOTE ON LANGUAGE AND NAUTICAL TERMINOLOGY

The era of wooden sailing ships produced a vast and highly specialized vocabulary, and few of us living today are able to decipher it without the constant use of a reference guide. It is tempting to adopt the rule that one should simply avoid jargon as often as possible. On the other hand, the language of the maritime past is part of the essential DNA of modern English. When we hear it said that Smith's marketing report was "by and large" encouraging, or that Jones was "taken aback" by the sales forecasts, or that Smith is a marketing man "through and through," or that Jones is a "loose cannon," or that Smith has let "the cat out of the bag," or that Smith and Jones are "at loggerheads," how likely are we to pause and reflect that these are faint echoes of a language that time and progress have rendered obsolete? To be interested in nautical jargon is to be interested in English itself.

But if jargon is to be employed and not avoided, how much of it should be defined in the text? To include no definitions risks leaving the reader mystified. The alternative, defining every unfamiliar term, results in prose that reads like a glossary. In these pages, I have attempted to steer a middle course, using or quoting nautical terms and phrases when the narrative context sheds light on their meaning, and only rarely pausing to insert a definition or explanation. All direct quotations, nautical or otherwise, are taken from the original sources verbatim; I have occasionally modernized spelling or punctuation for the sake of clarity or readability.

PART ONE

To Provide and Maintain

CHAPTER ONE

On October 21, 1805, an English fleet commanded by Admiral Lord Horatio Nelson hunted down and annihilated the combined fleets of France and Spain in an immense sea battle off Cape Trafalgar, near the Spanish coast. The Battle of Trafalgar, as it came to be known, crowned the British Royal Navy as undisputed sovereign of the world's oceans and confounded Napoleon's last hope of a cross-Channel invasion of England.

Napoleon, campaigning against the Austrians and Russians in the east, was angered and disgusted by the news. But he was hardly surprised. Since the outbreak of war in 1792, the Royal Navy had methodically and ruthlessly burned, sunk, or captured nearly every enemy warship that had come within range of its guns. To the French and all the other European peoples who had been punished by British seapower—the Spanish, the Russians, the Dutch, the Danes—it seemed as if the English were inherently more skillful, more resourceful, and more in their element while at sea, in the same way that a seal or a shark is inherently a better swimmer than a horse or a bear.

It would be no exaggeration to say that England's naval supremacy in the early years of the nineteenth century was unlike anything the world had ever seen before, or has since. The Romans had won complete control of the Mediterranean twenty centuries earlier, but rarely did they venture in force out into the Atlantic, and of the more distant oceans they knew nothing. In our own time, the United States might be capable of defeating all the world's other navies combined, but that claim has never been tested in war, and there are many other functioning navies afloat. But Britain, after Trafalgar, forced every other great power virtually to abandon the sea and seek refuge in its harbors. Though remnants of the French navy survived in some French ports, they were imprisoned there by blockading squadrons of British warships that maintained a constant presence from the Scheldt estuary to Toulon. The Danish navy had ceased to exist after the British assault on Copenhagen; the Dutch navy had never recovered after being routed at Camperdown. The Russian tsar ordered his ships not to leave their moorings in his Baltic seaports. Spain's seapower had been mortally wounded at Cape St. Vincent and put out of its misery at Trafalgar; after that its days as a global empire were numbered, and Spain would never fulfill its ambition of recapturing Gibraltar.

Britain's gigantic fleets held sway over the Atlantic, the Pacific, the Indian, the Caribbean, the North Sea, the Baltic, and the Mediterranean. Its bases were far-flung, strategically located, and unassailable; the Royal Navy sailed out of Chatham, Sheerness, Plymouth, Portsmouth, Kinsale, Gibraltar, Port Mahon, Malta, Halifax, Bermuda, Jamaica, Barbados, Antigua, Capetown, Bombay, Calcutta, Trincomalee, Jakarta, Pelu Penang, and New South Wales. England had huge seaports and dockyard complexes on its southern and western coasts, with a large and highly developed infrastructure to build, fit out, and provision ships of every kind. The nation could draw upon a broad population of experienced seamen who had learned their professional skills in service on merchant ships, fishing dories, coastal traders, and men-of-war. Britain's far-flung colonies brought wealth—wealth that it in turn reinvested in defending the trade routes that linked it to those colonies.

British warships were kept constantly at sea, on convoy duty, on blockade duty, in commerce-raiding cruises, in shuttling troops and dignitaries from place to place. They put into port for short, furious bursts of work—with little or no shore liberty for the crews, who were kept constantly busy in refitting and reprovisioning—and then hurried back out to sea. A captain who kept his ship in port too long was diminished in the eyes of his colleagues and superiors. The long months at sea were the best possible training for officers and crew, working them into a high state of efficiency and readiness. With constant repetition and practice, every maneuver became second nature. The men learned to work together, to anticipate one another, to carry out the countless finely timed and intricate procedures involved in sailing and handling a wooden ship. Foreign naval officers who visited British warships—or were taken aboard as prisoners of war—were dismayed by what they saw. The contrast with their own ships was palpable and stark. British ships were simply far more trim, more highly disciplined, and better handled than their own.

British naval hegemony was founded on the leadership of great commanders, and none was greater than Nelson, who is still revered as a kind of god in England. His stone likeness, three times larger than life, gazes down on Whitehall, the British Admiralty, and the Houses of Parliament from a 165-foot-high column at the geographic center of London. The third son of a country parson, he was a small, harmless-looking man, who stood five feet six inches tall and weighed 130 pounds. His features were gentle and pubescent, even feminine. He was as passionate and tender as a poet in springtime, pouring his heart out to the women he loved—above all to Emma Hamilton, the beautiful young wife of the British ambassador to Naples, whom he loved adulterously and publicly. He wrote impassioned love letters to her, addressing her as "my dearest beloved Emma," "Fair Emma, Good Emma, Great Emma, Virtuous Emma," and "the dear friend of my bosom," and he adored their illegitimate daughter, Horatia, whom he called "my dearest angel." He was full of warmth and kindness and praise for all of his colleagues in the navy. He called them his "Band of Brothers"—a reference to *Henry V*, his favorite play—and he was gracious and thoughtful and generous to them all. He had a magnetism that drew his fellow officers to him and made them compete for his approval.

But Nelson had a darker side. Behind the gracious and sensitive exterior there was a cold resolve, a ruthlessness, even a kind of savagery. His personal courage was extreme to the point of recklessness. He had seen so much action that it is incredible, in retrospect, that he survived as long as he did. In a 1794 attack on Corsica, a shell had exploded nearby, blasting sand and dirt into his face. He lost the sight of his right eye as a result, and for the rest of his life both the pupil and the iris had a uniformly cloudy blue tone that made his gaze unnerving, especially when he was angry. In an attack on the Canary Islands in 1797, his right elbow had been shattered by a musket ball, and his arm had to be amputated without anesthetic. He did not complain when the surgeon sawed through the bone, but he thought the use of a cold knife to cut through the flesh caused unnecessary pain, and instructed that all future amputations should be performed with a heated blade. At age thirty-nine, Nelson was required to submit to his government a memorial summarizing his service record. He wrote, in part:

> Your memorialist has been in four actions with the fleets of the enemy, in three actions with frigates, in six engagements with batteries, in ten actions in boats employed in cutting out of harbors, in destroying vessels, and in the taking of three towns. . . . He has assisted in the capture of seven sail of the line, six frigates, four

corvettes, eleven privateers of different sizes, and taken and destroyed near fifty sail of merchantmen. [He] has been actually engaged against the enemy upwards of one hundred and twenty times, has lost his right eye and arm, and been severely wounded and bruised in his body. . . .

This he had written in 1797, when his three greatest sea battles—Aboukir Bay, Copenhagen, and Trafalgar—had not yet been fought.

Nelson's approach to war at sea was simple, effective, and brutal. He had little regard for clever maneuvering, and no patience for complicated battle tactics. He thought it a waste of time to try to outsail an opponent in the hope of winning an advantageous position, and he thought it a waste of ammunition to fire at an enemy from long range. Nelson chose to take his ships directly and quickly into close-range action, where they would pulverize the enemy with broadside after broadside from his main weapon, the "great guns" or heavy cannon. His notion of how a naval action should be fought, which he put into practice at Trafalgar, was to fight the enemy "yardarm to yardarm," to position his ships parallel to those of the enemy—so close that their hulls were literally touching—and to order his gun crews to fire and reload and fire again as quickly as they possibly could. "The best and only mode I have found of hitting the enemy afloat," he told a colleague, "is to get so close that whether the gun is pointed upwards or downwards, forward or aft, it must strike its opponent." His officers could not fail to understand his wishes. On the eve of Trafalgar, he wrote them: "In case signals can neither be seen nor perfectly understood, no captain can do very wrong if he places his ship alongside that of an enemy." And in case that wasn't clear enough, once the battle was joined he flew his trademark signal from the flagship *Victory*'s masthead: *Engage the enemy more closely*.

Warships of this era were armed with a battery of so-called great guns, colossal iron weapons with barrels nine or ten feet long, each weighing 2 tons or more. The caliber of a gun was based on the weight of the round shot it fired. Battleships and frigates carried 18- or 24-pounders, weapons three and four times heavier and more destructive than the standard 6-pounder field-piece used by the army during the same period. On firing, the gun bellowed with a noise that was "like some awfully tremendous thunderstorm, whose deafening roar is attended by incessant streaks of lightning." It discharged enormous billowing clouds of white, acrid smoke, and recoiled with a force that would kill a man who was caught in its way. As the gun came to rest at the end of its breeching, the gun crew—as many as ten or twelve men to a weapon—began a rapid and precisely timed series of movements to reload and fire again. The bore hole was sponged out with a swab; the gunpowder, bound in a cloth cartridge, rammed down into the muzzle; a wad was rammed in on top of the powder; and then the cannon ball and another wad were rammed down on top of that. The cloth of the cartridge was pierced and some priming powder poured into the touch hole; the gun crew ran the monstrous weapon out through its port by heaving in unison on the gun tackle; the captain of the gun adjusted his aim and gave the order to fire. A match was touched to the primer. The gun roared, recoiled, and the process began again.

The British were happy to trade blows at point-blank range, to fight "ball for ball," because their gunnery was superior to that of their enemies. The potency of British gunnery owed nothing to the weapons themselves, for the French and Spanish ships were armed in much the same way. Nor was it the aim of the British gun crews, for even when their aim was superior it was rarely decisive. The single most important factor was the *rate* of fire. A British warship would fire three broadsides to every two fired by an enemy ship—if that enemy ship was particularly well manned, well led, and well practiced. More often, the British would get off two or three broadsides to the enemy's one, and the ratio would continuously improve in their favor as the battle wore on toward its inevitable conclusion.

The Royal Navy owed its advantage in gunnery to its commitment to intensive training. The gun crews drilled and drilled endlessly as their officers timed them with stopwatches and corrected their mistakes. Crew was pitted against crew in competition. Wagers were placed. Rewards were offered: double rum rations or light duty assignments. The men strove to improve and took pride in perfecting their skills. Practice and team spirit transformed the British gun crews into well-oiled fighting machines. When English and French warships met in battle, the French ships commonly suffered much greater casualties, even when the ships were evenly matched. Remarkable discrepancies in the number of killed and wounded were common. One example of such a rout—and there are many—was the single-ship action between the *Monmouth* and the *Foudroyant* off Cartagena in 1758, when the French enjoyed a 2.6 to 1 advantage in combined weight of ordnance, but surrendered with losses of four and a half Frenchmen dead for every Briton killed. During the long period of war from 1793 to 1815, the British lost 17 frigates to the French (9 of which were subsequently recaptured), while in the same period the French lost 229 frigates to the British.

The heavy round shot was the standard ammunition, and its main advantage was its ability to concentrate the force of the weapon on a single point. It was useful for smashing a hole in the enemy's hull at the waterline, for example; this might cause seawater to pour in, slowing the ship down, impairing her ability to maneuver, drawing her men away from the fight to man the pumps, and eventually even sinking her. If aimed high, it might cause a mast to fall, or knock away a few yards, bringing down the enemy's sails and preventing the vessel from running away. But the British were generally content to simply fire on the level, directly at the opposing ship's gun deck, where her gun crews worked. The heavy iron shot might pierce the hull and maul the men working on the other side. When fired on a lighter ship, a shot might penetrate "through and through," passing all the way through both sides of the ship and disappearing into the ocean on the far side. If the enemy's hull was strong enough to stop the ball, an eruption of splinters on the inside wall would mutilate any men working within a 10- or 15-foot radius. So great was the force of the big naval guns that surgeons swore they had seen men killed by the wind of a passing shot; on examination, their corpses were found to be completely unmarked. But when a cannon scored a direct hit on a man, it did not leave a pretty picture. It was not at all uncommon for a ball to blow a man's head off, splattering his mates with blood and brains and tiny fragments of bone and tissue. Men had their hands or arms taken cleanly off by passing balls. One sailor recalled seeing the top half of another man's head cut off by a round shot. He was surprised at how neat and symmetrical the wound was, as if someone had swung a very sharp broadax in a wide horizontal arc and struck the unlucky man on the bridge of his nose. Both earlobes had been left on his lower cheeks.

Abovedecks, the British ships were armed with carronades, named for the town of Carron, Scotland, where they were first cast. The carronade was a kind of snub-nose cannon, shorter and lighter than the long gun. Because it was lighter, it could be carried high above the waterline and fired and reloaded more rapidly. The carronade was not effective at long range, but in the close action favored by the British captains it was deadly. The French, who bore the brunt of their immense destructive power, called them "devil guns." The largest carronades were bored for enormous 68-pound balls that required 5.5-pound cartridges of gunpowder to fire. But they were most pernicious when loaded with shrapnel-like types of ammunition such as grape or canister shot. Grape shot were fist-sized iron balls bound in canvas bags that blew apart when fired. Canister shot were cylindrical cases containing pistol balls that became a kind of airborne Claymore mine as they were fired. There was also chain shot and bar shot, both designed to cut up the enemy's rigging, but both equally capable of cutting a man in half. Before being fired, they were sometimes heated in the galley fires until they glowed bright orange. In the tops, the platforms positioned high on the masts, the marines would fire down onto the enemy decks with their smooth-bored rifles and muskets. Their objective was to kill the officers—to break down the command structure and send their crews into confusion. If a ship did not surrender after being battered by the British long guns, carronades, and snipers, the officers gave the order to "board and carry her." A swarm of seamen, often with their faces blackened with soot to horrify the enemy, leapt across to the enemy deck armed with cutlasses, boarding pikes, axes, swords, and pistols, and slaughtered any man who dared to resist.

The point-blank engagements favored by Nelson and his fellow officers were horribly destructive, but they left Britain's enemies—and France especially—not only beaten on the sea but utterly demoralized. England held its enemies under a spell of invincibility that seemed to preordain the result of every battle. In the days before Trafalgar, the French and Spanish officers in the combined fleet were gloomy and pessimistic. Many favored remaining in the safety of the harbor at Cadiz, where at least the fleet would be preserved. They put to sea because they had no choice. In August 1805, Napoleon had demanded that his fleet win command of the English Channel long enough for France's armies to mount an invasion of England. His orders were direct and unambiguous: "Sail; do not lose a moment; enter the Channel with my assembled squadrons; England is ours." When they hesitated, the emperor came close to calling his admirals a pack of traitors and cowards. Their goal was not even to win, but to lose honorably, to prove to themselves and the world that they could still fight bravely. They sailed into a desperate battle against a more powerful foe, knowing they would be not only beaten but annihilated.

The battle was fought exactly as Nelson had wished. His flagship, *Victory*, engaged the French flagship so closely that when the guns were run out, they came into contact with the enemy hull. *Victory*'s officers were concerned that the fire from their guns would engulf both ships in flames. To prevent this, a man at each gun threw buckets of water into the holes made in the enemy's side by each shot. One officer aboard the *Victory* recalled the scene: "There was fire from above, fire from below . . . the guns recoiling with violence, reports louder than thunder, the decks heaving and the sides straining. I fancied myself in the infernal regions, where every man appeared a devil. Lips might move, but orders and hearing were out of the question: everything was done by signs." A sailor stationed on the lower decks of the 110-gun *Royal Sovereign* told his

"Honoured Father" that he felt fortunate in having lost only three fingers in the battle. "How my fingers got knocked overboard I don't know," he confessed; "but off they are, and I never missed them till I wanted them."

The victory of the British fleet at Trafalgar was perhaps the most decisive in naval history. Eighteen French and Spanish ships were captured or destroyed. Six thousand French and Spanish sailors were killed or wounded, and twenty thousand taken prisoner. British casualties amounted to 1,700; and the Royal Navy did not lose a single ship. Napoleon, after Trafalgar, was forced to admit that he could never hope to lead an invasion of England. He turned his energies to the east, to military conquest by land, a path that would eventually end with his disastrous invasion of Russia and his final defeat a decade later at Waterloo.

Nelson's officers urged him not to wear his medals and orders and full-dress admiral's uniform while exposed on the *Victory*'s quarterdeck. He turned a deaf ear to their pleas. Almost at the same moment *Victory* broke the enemy line, he was shot through the chest by an enemy sniper. When the doctor rushed to his side, Nelson declared the wound to be mortal and rejected any further medical attention. He asked his flag captain to kiss him as he lay dying. He asked to be remembered to Emma and Horatia. "I have done my duty," he said at last, "thank God for that." In England, news of the British victory and the death of Nelson arrived simultaneously. Joy over the victory was swamped by the outpouring of mass grieving at the loss of the beloved admiral. "The only signs of a great victory," remarked a Londoner, "are endless posters saying 'alas, poor Nelson.'" A foreign visitor wrote: "It was as if a great calamity had befallen the land." The sailors of the navy were "useless for duty for days," wrote one seaman. "Chaps that fought like the devil sat down and cried like wenches."

For three days, Nelson's body lay in state at Greenwich, in a casket carved from the mainmast of the French battleship *Orient*, viewed by thirty thousand mourners who passed in long, hushed queues. On January 8, 1806, the body was taken up the Thames on a funeral barge, followed by a procession of vessels two miles long, to Whitehall Stairs in London. A vast funeral pageant carried him into the whispering chamber at St. Paul's, where the great dome overhead was lit by the spectral glow of several thousand candles. Forty-eight sailors from the *Victory* carried the flagship's ensign. A scuffle broke out between them at the cathedral door; the flag was torn to pieces and each man ran off with a fragment of red, white, or blue.

Before the slain hero was lowered into the crypt and sealed in his sarcophagus, the mourners sang the patriotic anthem that was always sung on such occasions—"Rule, Britannia." And what did Britannia, that "Blest Isle, with matchless beauty crown'd," rule? "Britannia rules the waves," answered the refrain, and therefore, "Britons never, never, never will be slaves." Though the words had been written before he was born, "Rule, Britannia" was Nelson's song—or rather, he had made it his own. The words that had once been merely rhetorical were now made literally true by the man they were laying to rest.

THE *ANN ALEXANDER*, an American square-rigged merchantman with a cargo of flour, tobacco, salt fish, and apples, was eighteen days out of New York when she met the British fleet off Trafalgar a few hours after its victory. That there had been an enormously destructive battle was apparent from the sea-litter floating across many miles of the ocean. Bobbing on the surface were huge sections of spars and rigging, torn pieces of sailcloth, and dead seamen who would soon slip beneath the waves. Nelson was already dead and embalmed. His head had been shorn, his arms and legs folded in a fetal position, and his body sealed head-down in a cask of brandy, camphor, and myrrh. Most of the British ships were still too battered to sail, and their uninjured crews were working to repair the damage while also caring for hundreds of wounded British sailors and thousands of wounded French and Spanish prisoners. A boat from the *Victory* came across to the *Ann* to inquire if any stores could be purchased to aid in the repairwork. As luck would have it, *Ann* was carrying a deckload of lumber, which her master was happy to sell, along with some flour and apples. He received a fair price and was paid in English gold.

It was a minor footnote to the Battle of Trafalgar, and not a significant event in itself. But it was typical of the presence of the Americans on the sea in those years. Merchant vessels sailing under the Stars and Stripes were ubiquitous on the high seas, but rarely was an American warship ever seen. The first three American presidents—Washington, Adams, and Jefferson—had gone to great lengths to stay out of the conflict raging in Europe. The only exception had been a brief, undeclared naval war with France in the Caribbean a few years earlier, but that was a small-scale, regional conflict, fought more against French privateers than against the French navy, and it had come to a quick, negotiated end. The truth was that America did not want war, least of all a sea war, because its merchant marine was making money hand over fist in the "carrying trade," a role it could continue to exploit only so long as its government remained neutral.

In 1805, the United States was not much more than a narrow strip of sparsely populated beachfront real estate. In time the west would open up, and its receding frontier would lure millions away from the coast. But in the opening decade of the nineteenth century, the lands beyond the Appalachians were remote, little known, poor, and dangerous. Half of the country's 6 million inhabitants lived within a day's journey of the vast, gray, tumultuous ocean to the east—an ocean that served both as a defensive barrier against the rest of the world and as a highway to it. Centers of population were strung out along the coastline like a chain of islands, enclosed on one side by the sea and on the other by a sea of woods. Roads were roads only in name—they were tentative wagon tracks through a seemingly interminable wilderness, and when not awash in mud they were everywhere obstructed by stumps and fallen trees. Coach and wagon drivers were constantly stopping and descending from the driver's seat, ax in hand. Every stream crossing was an adventure; every river was impassable when the ferryman was drunk or in bed. Travelers were happy to put twenty miles behind them without losing their way in the woods.

The biggest American towns—Boston, New York, Philadelphia, Baltimore—were all Atlantic seaports, with large communities of professional seamen and all the essential supporting industries needed to build, fit out, provision, and repair ships. In every town, the waterfront was a maze of warehouses, ropewalks, boatbuilders' sheds, countinghouses, and sail lofts. The shipyards drew from a broad pool of expert laborers and master craftsmen, including carpenters, caulkers, joiners, painters, sparmakers, woodcarvers, coopers, ropemakers, smiths, and sailmakers. Shipwrights used crude hand tools and manually operated wooden lathes to turn out masts, spars, bowsprits, tops, and blocks. Planking was sawed, steamed, shaped, and fitted by skilled craftsmen using adzes, broadaxes, and planes. No precision instruments then existed, but a skilled hewer could lift a broadax and split a piece of timber precisely along a pencil line. Shipyard workers worked from sunrise to sunset, six days a week, and were paid the same daily wage in the long days of June as they were during the shorter days of the fall and winter months. All day long, the yards were filled with the sounds of saw, adze, broadax, and caulking mallet sawing and chipping and tapping away at the timbers. Day after day, all up and down the coast, newly built ships rumbled down the ways and plunged into the sea. Every launch of a new ship made room on the stocks for a new keel to be laid.

Fast little fore- and aft-rigged Baltimore schooners ran the English blockades into French, Dutch, and German ports, carrying grain, flour, kiln-dried corn in barrels, dried fish, salted meats, rice, cheese, and other foodstuffs to feed the war-torn Continent. Big square-rigged blue-water sailors out of Salem and Boston rounded the Cape of Good Hope bound for the East Indies, or chanced the grueling passage round Cape Horn to the South Pacific and on to Whampoa Roads and the burgeoning China trade. American ships were seen taking on pepper in Sumatra; tea, coffee, silks, and spices in China; ivory and sandalwood and strange, beautiful lacquer boxes in Malaysia. Weather-beaten whaling ships out of Nantucket and New Bedford were seen north of the Arctic Circle and deep in the heart of the South Pacific. The sailing stock-yards of New England and Pennsylvania shipped cargoes of oxen, sheep, cattle, horses, and swine along with an abundant supply of shovels. In a gale the terrified animals were apt to be injured or killed and would have to be swayed up through the hatchways and heaved over the side.

New York merchantmen rode every tide down the Narrows, outbound for Caribbean destinations, laden with flour, salmon, brandy, dried hams, barrels of salted pork and beef, peas, candles, soap, pots of butter, herring, claret, glassware, oil, juniper berries, cheese, indigo, spruce and hickory hoops. They might return home with rum, coffee, sugar, pimento, molasses, and muscovado; or they might continue on the long, stormy transatlantic run to Europe. Drab little sloops, brigs, snows, cutters, ketches, and other rigs for the coastal trade sailed out of Portsmouth, Newburyport, Ipswich, Bristol, New London, Baltimore, Charleston, and a hundred other American seaports. They were laden with sugar, flour, cotton, rice, corn, tea, sausages, almonds, sweetmeats, earthenware, varnish, pig iron, oak staves, liquor, shoes, tanned leather, looking glasses, playing cards, books, perfumes, hair powder, and a thousand other cargoes.

A Marylander marveled at the number of American ships and sailors he encountered in the West Indies, where Europe's sugar colonies subsisted largely on foodstuffs imported from the United States. "When I see our numerous fleets constantly passing these islands, it looks as if our vessels sprung out of the forests, ready equipped," he remarked—"and . . . like Cadmus's soldiers, the men seem to spring up out of the ocean instead of the earth."

From the American merchantman's point of view, Napoleon's world war made the seas far more hazardous, but at the same time rendered them far more lucrative. So long as the United States avoided being dragged into the war, its merchant marine would reap windfall profits. The disparities between prices of goods in different ports widened; a barrel of flour that cost $8 in New York might be sold for $18 in Amsterdam; a bale of cotton that cost $11 in Savanna might fetch $23 in Brest. The wider the price spreads, the more fantastic the profits. With every other major maritime nation at war, competition fell off drastically. Ships sailing under the colors of the warring nations were subject to immediate capture by their enemies, and neutral ships

became the safest means of importing and exporting goods that might otherwise never reach their destinations. American neutrality was big business: it
set off an explosion in American exports, shipping tonnage, and overseas
commerce. As Napoleon made his bid for mastery of the Old World, the
good times were rolling in the new one.

Merchants, shipowners, and sea captains found that it was easier to make
money than ever before. A 250-ton merchantman—a ship with the capacity
of about six modern ocean cargo containers—would cost $15,000 to $20,000
to build, fit out, and provision. One successful voyage in the war years would
clear that much in profit for the owners. When a single six-month voyage
would pay for an asset with a useful life of twenty years, the economic incen-
tives driving men to trade on the sea were irresistible. Merchants built
handsome, columned Georgian mansions, comfortable and airy but not
ostentatious, their grounds demarcated by discreet black wrought-iron
fences. Their offices were in countinghouses near the wharves, second-story
rooms whose windows were blocked with heavy drapes; rooms with deep,
musty chairs and couches that smelled of brandy and cigars. They surrounded
themselves with charts, globes, oil paintings, model ships, and curiosities
from distant parts of the world. Their heavy walnut desks were piled with
paperwork and their shelves lined with ledger books. Had they wished, these
men could have gone out and thrown fistfuls of gold coins into the street.
Money washed into port as predictably and relentlessly as the incoming tide.
Every returning ship brought another payday, and at the height of the season,
in summer and early fall, 250 ships entered American seaports every day.

No one had any illusions. Business was booming because Europe was at
war, and for no other reason. Peace would bring an end to the boom; so
would an end to American neutrality. One New York merchant had shown his
hand in 1787, two years before the French Revolution and five years before
war broke out in Europe. He had written to a West Indian business partner:
"Should a war (O, horrid war!) take place between Great Britain and France,
will not your ports be open to us, and our commerce with you as neutrals be
an object of consideration?" From the outbreak of war in 1792 to 1807, two
years after Trafalgar, American exports (and re-exports) more than quintu-
pled, to $108 million per year. They would not touch that level again until
1835, when the nation's population had more than doubled. In the same
fifteen-year period the size of America's merchant marine nearly tripled, to
well over 1 million metric tons—more than 10,000 vessels, manned by about
69,000 seamen. This did not include the untold numbers of "tramp
traders"—American vessels that plied the waters between foreign ports with-

out ever returning home. Flour exports alone would fill four hundred ships a year. In active tonnage and cargoes, the United States—a small country, and isolated—had surpassed every other maritime power save Great Britain. And if the trend held, as it might, the United States—with no colonial empire and no navy to speak of—would overtake Britain as the nation with the largest merchant shipping fleet in the world.

AMERICAN NAVAL HISTORY had begun thirty years earlier, with the American Revolution. It was not a proud beginning. General George Washington and the Continental Army endured and eventually prevailed. The Continental Navy, with few exceptions, was a wasteful and humiliating fiasco.

In 1775, the Continental Congress, assembled at Philadelphia, appointed a "Marine Committee" and charged its seven members with the task of organizing a navy. The committee met each evening in a private chamber on the second floor of the City Tavern, a block from the Philadelphia waterfront. Huddled in front of a fire, with the noise of a boisterous taproom rising through the floorboards, this handful of audacious neophytes invented the American navy. John Adams, a thirty-nine-year-old delegate from Massachusetts, later remembered these meetings as "the pleasantest part of my Labours for the four Years I spent in Congress," but he was also painfully aware of the committee's collective inexperience, not least his own. "It is very odd that I, who have . . . never thought much of the old ocean, or the dominion of it, should be necessitated to make such inquiries," he told his good friend Elbridge Gerry. "But it is my fate and my duty, and therefore I must attempt it."

From the outset, the committee struggled to reach consensus on the most basic strategic and tactical questions. Would the navy be used to defend the nation's shores? For convoys? For commerce raiding? To deliver diplomatic ministers to Europe? What kind of ships? Should they be bought or built? How should they be armed and manned? Officers' commissions were dealt out according to a spoils system in which political influence was more important than seamanship or other pertinent qualifications. Only time and experience would expose the officer who was inept, cowardly, corrupt, or insubordinate, and many of the earliest American naval officers combined several of these qualities. On some ships, drunkenness and desertion were as common among the officers as among the enlisted men. Wardrooms were fractured by rivalries and personal enmity. Lieutenants and midshipmen feuded and dueled and pilfered one another's personal possessions. European officers who had been cast off from other navies arrived in America and finagled commissions. Influential men lobbied their congressional delegates to take unruly sons and nephews off their hands. Officers feuded publicly, even publishing broadsides against their rivals in the newspapers. Adams remarked that Congress was besieged by officers who were "scrambling for rank and pay like apes for nuts."

The first men-of-war to sail under American colors were converted merchant vessels, weakly constructed and easily overwhelmed in action. In late 1775, the committee authorized the construction of thirteen light frigates, based upon designs proposed by two Philadelphia shipwrights, John Wharton and Joshua Humphreys. Because Britain had discouraged the construction of warships in the colonies, American shipbuilders generally lacked relevant experience, and they made costly and time-consuming mistakes. None of the Continental frigates was completed on time, but as it turned out the construction delays did not really matter. Once the ships were launched, they all lay at anchor or dockside for a year or more, awaiting ordnance, rigging, provisions, and crews. Arming them posed a serious problem. Britain had forbidden the manufacture of heavy cannon in the colonies, and there were no domestic foundries capable of smelting, refining, and casting big naval guns. The Continental frigates that did get to sea were often so poorly fitted out that they were quickly forced back into port for repairs. Many were stepped with rotten masts that snapped in a gale. Fine imported English or Russian sailcloth was in short supply, and the navy resorted to hemp and jute-blended sails derisively labeled "Hessians," which were too heavy to provide driving power in light breezes.

Critics pointed out that the revolutionary cause would be better served by having no frigates than by having half-completed or damaged frigates lying idle in American harbors. A port-bound frigate had to be guarded against attack by British raiding parties. Washington was exasperated by constant requests for troops to guard the Continental warships. He believed, not unreasonably, that the navy should exist to support the army, and not the reverse. In July 1777, when a British invasion force was advancing toward Philadelphia, he urged that the frigates lying in the Delaware River be scuttled to prevent capture. Congress could not bring itself to swallow such a bitter pill, but the issue was settled when enemy cruisers and gunboats attacked up the Delaware and the Continental Navy's entire force on the river was destroyed, either by the British or by their own crews. Of the thirteen American frigates built during the Revolution, seven were captured and taken into the Royal Navy, and another four were destroyed to prevent their falling into enemy hands.

Only in Europe did the rebel navy achieve any degree of success. When

France entered the war in 1778, its Channel ports were thrown open to American warships and privateers, providing good bases within a day's sail of England's busiest sea-lanes. Benjamin Franklin, serving as American envoy in Paris, pledged to "insult the coasts of the Lords of the Ocean with our little cruisers." The best-remembered naval hero of the American Revolution was a Scotsman, John Paul Jones, who captained two successful hit-and-run cruises in British coastal waters in 1778 and 1779. Raiding isolated seaports in England and Scotland, taking dozens of prizes, defying the Royal Navy cruisers dispatched to hunt him down, Jones robbed the British people of their sense of peace and security at home. "Paul Jones resembles a Jack O'Lantern, to mislead our marines and terrify our coasts," said the *Morning Post* in London: "He is no sooner seen than lost." He was branded a "desperado," "a daring pirate," a "vile fellow." Jones's reputation was capped by a truly remarkable naval victory on September 23, 1779. As captain of a converted French Indiaman, the 40-gun *Bonhomme Richard*, Jones engaged the British 50-gun frigate *Serapis* off Flamborough Head on the east coast of England. After a close-action battle of four hours, in which the *Serapis* lost about half her crew, the Englishman surrendered. One of the *Richard*'s midshipmen said that the surviving men in his division were wearing no more than the collar of their shirts, and that the "flesh of several of them dropped off from their bones and they died in great pain." The *Bonhomme Richard* sank before she could be brought into port; Jones transferred his crew into the *Serapis* and navigated her under American colors into the Texel.

The American privateering war dealt a heavy blow to British trade. Privateers were privately owned and financed ships of war that were licensed to prey on enemy shipping. Captured vessels and cargoes became the property of the owners, who awarded the officers and crew a share of the prizes taken during each cruise. The Continental Congress and the states distributed about two thousand privateering commissions during the war; a thousand were distributed in Massachusetts alone. The mania for privateering was stimulated by a blend of patriotism and greed, but the latter was understood to dominate. Most American merchants and shipowners transferred their wartime capital into the privateering industry. Swarms of privateers attacked the British supply convoys off the American coast; others cruised the English Channel and sent captured prizes into French ports. The success of their efforts was measured in rising maritime insurance premiums paid by British mercantile interests.

Americans had their French allies to thank for the decisive naval campaign of the Revolutionary War. A twenty-eight ship fleet under the command of

Rear Admiral François de Grasse cut off General Charles Cornwallis's escape by sea from Yorktown in September 1781, forcing the surrender that effectively brought the war to an end. When a messenger brought Washington the news that de Grasse's fleet had anchored in Lynnhaven Bay, off Cape Henry, the commander in chief leapt off his horse and waved his hat over his head in celebration. On September 5, off the Virginia Capes, de Grasse's fleet engaged a British fleet under the command of Admiral Thomas Graves. No ships were captured or sunk on either side, but the British fleet withdrew and returned to New York, abandoning Cornwallis's army to its fate. The Battle of Virginia Capes, twenty-four years before Trafalgar, was the last time the French would ever defeat the Royal Navy in a major fleet engagement.

In the first flush of independence, what little remained of the Continental Navy was taken entirely out of service. The ships were sold at auction, the officers decommissioned, and the men discharged, often without receiving the back pay they were owed. A recently launched battleship, the largest built in America up to that time, was presented as a gift to the French. American seamen went back to their familiar peacetime pursuits on merchant vessels, coasters, and fishing dories. The country was broke and heavily in debt; Congress under the Articles of Confederation had no power to raise funds; the public was weary of war. There was a widespread fear that if the armed forces were permitted to remain intact they might be tempted to seize power and impose a military autocracy on the infant republic. If naval protection was needed, Americans reasoned, their French allies would come to the rescue once again.

The very last ship in the Continental Navy was the frigate *Alliance*. "This ship is now a mere Bill of Costs and I do not think we have the Means to fit her out," wrote Robert Morris, the revolutionary financier who served as Superintendent of Finance in the postwar period. She was sold to a private buyer in 1785 and later abandoned on a mud bar in the Delaware River, where her sagging hulk remained until the 1920s.

Adams was stung by the magnitude of the failure. "In looking over the long list of vessels belonging to the United States taken and destroyed, and recollecting the whole history of the rise and progress of our navy, it is difficult to avoid tears," he told a congressional committee in 1780. Vast funds and huge commitments of manpower had been exhausted in the construction, arming, and victualling of warships that never inflicted any serious blow against the enemy. Robert Morris said there was no use keeping a navy afloat if the American people were unwilling to bear the financial burden. "Until Revenues for the Purpose can be obtained it is but vain to talk of Navy or Army or anything else. . . . Every good American must wish to see the United

States possessed of a powerful fleet, but perhaps the best way to obtain one is to make no Effort for the Purpose till the People are taught by their Feelings to call for and require it. They will now give money for Nothing."

INDEPENDENCE WAS EXPECTED to open lucrative new markets for shipping and trade. Once free of British taxes and trade restrictions, revolutionary pamphleteers had promised, commerce would boom and Americans would prosper beyond their wildest dreams. In 1778, David Ramsey imagined a postwar world in which American ships would "no longer be confined by the selfish regulations of an avaricious stepdame" but would "follow wherever interest leads the way." Thomas Paine, in *Common Sense*, said: "Our plan is commerce, and that, well attended to, will secure us the peace and friendship of all Europe, because it is the interest of all Europe to have America a free port." American food exports, he added, "will always have a market while eating is the custom of Europe." The cover of a popular 1782 almanac depicted an allegorical scene entitled "America Triumphant and Britannia in Distress." America was represented as a woman, sitting on a shore on the left side of the picture. A caption described her as "holding in one hand the Olive branch, inviting the ships of all nations to partake of her commerce; and in the other hand supporting the cap of liberty." In the harbor at her feet were ships flying the flags of France, Spain, and Holland. On the right side of the picture, sitting on the opposite shore, was Britannia. The harbor at her feet was deserted, and she was "weeping at the loss of the trade of America."

These hopes were quickly dashed. American trade had always depended, above all, on access to England's West Indian colonies. The hungry Caribbean Islands, with their huge slave populations and their narrow economies devoted entirely to cultivation of sugar and coffee, had once consumed more than two thirds of American food exports. In 1783, however, a British Order in Council debarred any American ship from entering any British West Indian seaport. The measure was final, sweeping, and devastating. Cut off from their traditional markets, prices of flour, beef, pork, salted fish, naval stores, bar iron, and other mainstays of the American export economy fell 30, 40, or 50 percent. By 1788, ship arrivals from the British West Indies had fallen to half of what they had been before the Revolution. With Europe at peace, the vast opportunities offered by the wartime carrying trade would not be available until several years later.

In the seaports, unemployed seamen and shipwrights loitered around the wharves and slept in the streets. Warehouses stood half empty. Entire families threw themselves on the mercy of the churches and poor relief rolls. Creditors foreclosed on homes and farms. A British official said that the New England merchant marine had "suffered more by the Act of Independence than any part of the Country, from the decay of their shipbuilding and the effect which the dismemberment of the Empire has produced on their oil and fish in foreign markets." With their traditional markets for salted fish cut off, boats that had once fished cod and mackerel on the Grand Bank now rotted on the beaches. An unknown number of New England fishermen emigrated to Nova Scotia, where their catch could be lawfully sold in British markets. "Our West Indies business is ten times worse than it was before the war and God only knows that was bad enough then," wrote one merchant. "Trade and commerce is almost at a stand." Merchants called in their debts to inland farmers and forced many into debtor's jails. In late 1786 in western Massachusetts, rebellious farmers united behind the leadership of Captain Daniel Shays, a veteran of the Revolution. They attacked and shut down debtor's courts in Northampton, Worcester, Concord, Taunton, and Great Barrington, and eventually stormed a federal arsenal in Springfield. Before "Shays' Rebellion" was suppressed in 1787, it left many American conservatives wondering whether democratic government was tenable.

Prior to the Revolution, British merchants had contracted to have their ships built in America, where timber was cheap and plentiful; they would sail for England on their maiden voyages, to be entered into British registry. After the war, British commercial regulations banned the practice. Lumbermen, draftsmen, shipwrights, yard workers, and every class of specialized craftsmen who depended upon shipbuilding were thrown on hard times. A French traveler reported that in the Cape Ann town of Newburyport, three ships were launched in 1788; at the industry peak, sixteen years earlier, there had been ninety. The same traveler found Portsmouth "in ruins, women and children in rags . . . everything announces decline." In a petition to Congress, Boston shipwrights complained that the decline of shipbuilding had left "a numerous body of citizens, who were formerly employed in its various departments, deprived of their support and dependence." The Bostonians warned that agriculture would share the same fate as commerce, "as the impoverished state of our seaports will eventually lessen the demand for the produce of our lands."

Enterprising merchants sought out new trading partners in exotic parts of the world. For the first time, ships sailing under the Stars and Stripes were seen in the Indian and Pacific Oceans. In 1785, the *Empress of China*, a 360-ton New York merchantman, sailed round the Cape of Good Hope to Canton, and returned the following year with a cargo of silks, nankeens, teas, china plate, and cassia. The voyage turned a profit of $37,000 on an investment of $120,000. Many followed in her wake, laden with native North American ginseng for the Chinese market. The Bengali government, still independent, offered most-favored-nation trade status to American ships in the East India Company's outposts. New markets were found in the Baltic and the Mediterranean. Churchgoing Rhode Island and Massachusetts merchants, their consciences apparently untroubled, outfitted new ships with ring bolts spaced at intervals of a few inches on the lower decks. These specially constructed vessels sailed for the Guinea coast, laden with hogsheads of rum to be bartered for cargoes of human beings.

A LEADING OBJECTIVE of America's post-revolutionary foreign policy was to secure access to new export markets. Trade consuls were dispatched to nineteen foreign ports. France offered the greatest hope of replacing the lost British markets, both because of the size of its economy and its colonial empire (especially the French West Indies) and because it remained America's major ally. In 1784, Thomas Jefferson, author of the Declaration of Independence and wartime governor of Virginia, was appointed as a "Minister Plenipotentiary" and charged with negotiating new commercial treaties with European trading partners. He sailed from Boston in a packet, the *Ceres*, on July 5, 1784. It was his first time at sea.

Jefferson was six feet two and a half inches tall, his figure bony and loose-jointed but "well formed, indicating strength, activity, and robust health." His skin was flushed and freckled; his eyes hazel, his hair reddish-blond. Though he found the nineteen-day transatlantic voyage uncomfortable, Jefferson kept meticulous daily records of latitude and longitude, the direction and strength of the winds, the temperature, and his sightings of gannets, petrels, sheerwaters, sharks, and whales. The *Ceres* landed at West Cowes on the Isle of Wight; a week later, Jefferson crossed the Channel to Le Havre in a small boat, sleeping in a cabin that he could enter only by crawling on his hands and knees under a low beam.

At the court of Versailles, Jefferson acted in the role of a commercial attaché, promoting American exports of whale oil, furs, ships, naval stores, potash, grain, livestock, and tobacco. In return, he said, French manufactured goods could be imported into the United States, replacing those previously imported from England. Louis XVI's foreign minister, the comte de Vergennes, was sympathetic, but powerful French mercantile interests were determined to oppose any relaxation of trade barriers. When an August 1784 decree opened the French West Indies to American ships, the competition evoked a furious response from French shipowners. Thus torn, the Vergennes ministry tended to vacillate. "The Ministry are disposed to be firm," Jefferson told James Monroe, but "there is a point at which they will give way." As he predicted, American privileges were soon whittled down by countervailing decrees.

Some of the smaller European powers were willing to expand trade links with the new nation. New agreements were signed with the Dutch, the Swedes, and the Russians. Frederick II of Prussia signed a trade agreement with the United States in July 1785, though he privately said he did not expect the American union to last. Negotiations with Austria and Portugal dragged on for years. In any case, none of these agreements could replace the loss of the British markets. It was increasingly clear that the United States would have to grasp for concessions from its recent enemy. This responsibility fell to John Adams, who received the news that he had been appointed the first American minister to the Court of St. James's in May 1785.

The London press greeted the arrival of an ambassador from the former colonies with a chorus of boos. Adams was said to be "pretty fat and flourishing," an "imposter," and a "pharisee of liberty." "An Ambassador from America!" exclaimed the *Public Advertiser*: "Good heavens what a sound! . . . This will be such a phenomenon in the Corps Diplomatique that 'tis hard to say which can excite indignation most, the insolence of those who appoint the Character, or the meanness of those who receive [him]."

Incensed by the attacks on her husband, Abigail Adams vented her spleen in letters to Jefferson. She characterized one newspaper report as "false—if it was not too rough a term for a Lady to use, I would say false as Hell, but I will substitute one not less expressive and say, false as the English." She was appalled by the boxing matches she witnessed in the streets of her neighborhood, where she had "been repeatedly shocked to see Lads not more than ten years old striped and fighting untill the Blood flowed from every part, enclosed by a circle who were clapping and applauding the conqueror, stimulating them to continue the fight, and forcing every person from the circle who attempted to prevent it." She associated the brutality of the street hooligans with the invective of the English newspapers. "Bred up with such tempers and principles, who can wonder at the licentiousness of their Manners, and the abuse of their pens?"

Jefferson commiserated: "I would not give the polite, self-denying, feeling, hospitable, goodhumored people of [France] for ten such races of rich, proud, hectoring, swearing, squibbing, carnivorous animals as those among whom you are." He proposed a tongue-in-cheek explanation for this supposed difference in French and English manners: "I fancy it must be the quantity of animal food eaten by the English which renders their character insusceptible of civilization."

Shortly after his arrival, Adams was escorted by the thirty-three-year-old Lord Carmarthen, Minister of Foreign Affairs, to be presented to George III at St. James's Palace. Observing protocol, Adams bowed once upon entering the court chamber, a second time as he reached the middle of the room, and a third time as he stood directly before the king. Adams delivered a short speech, declaring it a "distinguished honor [to] stand in your Majesty's presence in a diplomatic character," and said he hoped his mission would restore the "old good nature and the old good humor between people who, though separated by an ocean and under different governments, have the same language, a similar religion, and kindred blood." The king was visibly emotional, and the meeting was "as gracious and agreeable as the reception given to the Ministers of any other foreign powers."

But Adams soon learned that the government of twenty-four-year-old Prime Minister William Pitt had no intention of letting America back into the British trading system. In one of his early meetings at 10 Downing Street, Adams pressed into Lord Carmarthen's reluctant hands a proposed "Treaty of Commerce," which would have established reciprocal rights of access for British and American ships. The ministers did not refuse the proposal outright. They stalled, and seemed content to go on stalling indefinitely. Adams began to suspect a conspiracy to reassert British sovereignty over the former colonies. "There is a strong propensity in this people to believe that America is weary of her independence," he wrote in August, "that she wishes to come back; that the states are in confusion; Congress has lost its authority; the governments of the states have no influence; no laws, no order, poverty, distress, ruin, and wretchedness. . . . This they love to believe."

But England's trade restrictions were founded on something more than spite. They were founded on a cogent understanding of seapower, and its contribution to the prosperity and security of the British Empire. A vast maritime trading establishment—British-built ships manned by British seamen engaged in the overseas "carrying trade"—was understood to be the wellspring from which England's naval power was drawn. Strict exclusion of foreign ships from British ports, argued Lord Sheffield in one of his many essays on the subject, was the "basis of our great power at sea . . . if we alter that act, by permitting any state to trade with our islands . . . we sacrifice the marine of England." Even Adam Smith, the free market visionary, accepted the principle of commercial exclusion in *The Wealth of Nations:* "The defence of Great Britain depends very much on the number of its sailors and shipping."

The British carrying trade, Adams realized, was the priority that trumped all others at Whitehall. "The words 'Ship and Sailor' still turn the Heads of this People," he told Jefferson. "They grudge to every other People a single ship and a single seaman. . . . They seem at present to dread American Ships and Seamen more than any other." British resistance to free trade measures, he told Massachusetts governor James Bowdoin, was founded on military rather than economic considerations. "Seamen, the navy, the power to strike an awful blow to their enemies at sea, on the first breaking out of a war, are the ideas that prevail above all others."

PEACE WITH BRITAIN had removed the threat posed by the Royal Navy to American merchant ships, but it had also left them without the umbrella of protection the Royal Navy had provided before 1776. For the first time, the Stars and Stripes were seen on the high seas and in foreign seaports—but the flag was seen flying only on richly laden and defenseless merchant vessels, never on ships of war. Greedy eyes studied the ships of this new nation the way wolves study sheep. The British let it be known that the Americans no longer enjoyed their protection. The wolves were hungry; the sheep were fat, numerous, and slow; and there was not a shepherd in sight.

The first attacks took place in the Mediterranean, where piracy had been practiced since the beginning of recorded history. The pirates in this case were from the four Barbary States of Tripoli, Tunis, Algiers, and Morocco, whose corsairs operated out of ancient seaports along the North African coast. Since the Islamic conquest of North Africa in the eighth century, these dusty, sun-drenched little city-states had pledged nominal allegiance to the Sultan of Turkey, but they were largely autonomous. Nested on the edge of the Mediterranean, with their backs to the North African desert, the Barbary States had little agriculture or industry to sustain them. Their traditional livelihood was piracy, and their traditional victims were the foreign merchant vessels that plied the Mediterranean trade routes close to their shores. Captured crew members were transported back into port in chains, where they were imprisoned, put to hard labor, or sold at slave markets. Women faced the prospect of being raped or sold into private harems. Prisoners who disobeyed or attempted to escape might be burned alive or impaled. That sub-

Saharan Africans were subjected to the same cruelties by white masters in America did not prevent the news of such attacks from creating a sensation in the United States, where they inspired a genre of lurid fiction and plays.

Because the Barbary societies worshipped Allah and prayed to Mecca five times per day, and because the corsairs often claimed to be at war with all infidels, the conflict was often cast in religious terms. But the real impetus behind Barbary piracy was not religious or political, but economic. The Bashaw of Tripoli freely admitted as much. If he forbade slave raiding, he told an American diplomat, his people would be ruined and he would most likely lose his head. "I do not fear war," he declared. "It is my trade."

By the late eighteenth century, the major European powers could have snuffed out piracy in the Mediterranean without much trouble. Even acting alone, Britain could have put all four Barbary States out of business with two or three powerful naval squadrons combined with the threat of invasion by land. But the Barbary States and their corsairs were tolerated, perhaps even encouraged. From the mid-seventeenth century, a protection racket had evolved, whereby the nations that wished to ensure safe passage for their ships paid annual tribute to each Barbary ruler. In most cases, the decision to pay simply reflected a cold calculation that tribute was cheaper than the cost of constantly defending the vital Mediterranean trade routes. But Britain was playing a more devious game. It saw the ever present threat of Barbary piracy as a check against the growth of economic competition from smaller maritime rivals.

By the mid-1780s, 100 American ships and 1,200 American sailors carried 20,000 tons of sugar, flour, rice, salted fish, and lumber to ports in the Mediterranean each year, returning with cargoes of wine, lemons, oranges, figs, opium, and olive oil. In July 1785, two American ships, the *Maria* and the *Dauphin*, were seized by Algerian corsairs. Twenty-two crewmen were transported to Algiers and thrown into dungeons among the slaves of other nations. They were dressed in coarse cloths, given a single dirty blanket each, and fed a daily ration of 15 ounces of bread. Most were set to work as ship riggers, longshoremen, porters, and draft animals. Some were forced to carry rocks and timber along a nine-mile path into the hills outside the city, dragging their chains and manacles behind them on the ground. They were often beaten or whipped, and always in fear for their lives. American leaders came under pressure to strike back at the pirates, to rescue their enslaved countrymen, and to prevent further attacks.

The captives wrote to Thomas Jefferson, while he was stationed in Paris, begging him to raise funds to ransom them. "Our sufferings is beyond our expressing or your conception," one wrote. "Hoping your Honor will be pleased to represent our grievances to Congress. Hoping they will take such measures as to tend to our speedy redemption." The plight of the captives, wrote Jefferson, left him "absolutely suspended between indignation and impotence." He asked the French government for assistance. Vergennes agreed to mediate with the Dey of Algiers, but insisted that America would have to follow the example of all the European maritime powers and pay tribute to the Barbary States. And since America had no naval force in the Mediterranean to protect its shipping, Vergennes added, that price was likely to be high: "Money and fear are the only two agents at Algiers."

Negotiations did not bear fruit. The Dey of Algiers demanded a huge payment in exchange for a peace treaty (the amount was never actually fixed, but would have run to hundreds of thousands of dollars) and a separate ransom of $59,496 for the release of twenty-two Americans held as prisoner. The sums demanded seemed impossibly large, and would be followed by similar demands from the other Barbary powers. Congress was unlikely to authorize such enormous sums; it was doubtful that the Congress could scrape up that much cash even if it wished. Negotiations dragged on; the captives remained enslaved; and American ships steered clear of the Mediterranean.

Although Algiers was the largest and most powerful of the Barbary powers, the Mediterranean would not be safe for American ships unless there were bilateral peace treaties with each of the four rulers. In February 1786, Adams met with the Tripolitan ambassador in London. The meeting was a farce, Adams told Jefferson, but he could not resist sharing his amusement as "the Ridicule of it was real and the Drollery inevitable." Knocking on the door of the residence one evening, intending only to leave his card, Adams was greeted by a servant who announced that the ambassador was at home and would receive Adams at once. He was shown into a drawing room, introduced to the ambassador, and seated in an armchair before a fire. The ambassador spoke no English, but the two men were able to communicate in broken Italian and French. While they were getting comfortable, a servant brought two pipes. The stem of the pipe offered to Adams was two yards long—"fit for a Walking Cane"—and to smoke it he was obliged to rest the bowl on the floor. In this position he

Smoked in aweful Pomp, reciprocating Whiff for Whiff with his Excellency, untill Coffee was brought in. His Excellency took a Cup after I had taken one, and alternately Sipped at his Coffee and whiffed at his Tobacco, and I wished he would take a Pinch in turn from his Snuff box for Variety; and I followed the Example with Such Exactness and Solemnity that the two secretaries appeared in Raptures, and the superiour of them who speaks a few Words of French cryed out in Ecstasy, "Monsieur, vous êtes un Turk!"

With the initial courtesies behind them, the ambassador turned to business. America and Tripoli, he said, were at war. Adams, holding his cool, replied that he was "Sorry to hear that. . . . [I] had not heard of any war with Tripoli." The ambassador explained that Tripoli considered itself at war with all Christian nations until a bilateral peace treaty had been signed between them. Such a peace could be arranged, he added, at the bargain price of "30,000 Guineas for his Employers and £3,000 for himself . . . and this must be paid in Cash on the delivery of the treaty signed by his sovereign."

Though he was able to laugh at the rituals of tribute diplomacy, Adams reached the sober opinion: "it to be wisest for Us to negotiate and pay the necessary Sum, without Loss of Time." Fighting the corsairs, he told Jefferson, would only compound the economic losses to the United States: "We might at this hour have two hundred ships in the Mediterranean, whose Freight alone would be worth two hundred Thousand Pounds, besides its Influence upon the Price of our Produce." Recalling America's recent naval debacle, Adams doubted the Congress would vote to send warships to the Mediterranean. The tribute system, he reminded Jefferson, had been in place long before the United States arrived on the scene: "The Policy of Christendom has made Cowards of all their Sailors before the Standard of Mahomet. It would be heroical and glorious in Us to restore Courage to ours. I doubt not we could accomplish it, if we should set about it in earnest. But the Difficulty of bringing our People to agree upon it has ever discouraged me."

But Jefferson was taking a different tack. He told Adams he believed that "it would be best to effect a peace through the medium of war." He laid out his reasons: "1. Justice is in favor of this opinion. 2. Honor favors it. 3. It will procure us respect in Europe, and respect is a safe-guard to interest." Based on the best intelligence he could obtain, Jefferson estimated Algiers's aggregate fleet strength at no more than twelve xebecs and four galleys, and Algiers was the strongest of the four powers. The corsairs' vessels, designed for quick strikes against lightly armed merchant ships, would be easily overpowered by conventional European warships. Algerian crews could be captured and perhaps exchanged for the American captives. Jefferson proposed building a fleet with aggregate force of 150 guns, estimating the initial cost at £450,000 and the subsequent annual expenses at £45,000.

Responding three weeks later, Adams acknowledged that Jefferson's arguments were "great and weighty." But Adams did not believe the American people or their leaders were ready either to rebuild the navy or to fight a war in the Mediterranean. "We ought not to fight them at all," he wrote, "unless we determine to fight them forever. This thought is, I fear, too rugged for our People to bear." The more likely outcome, Adams predicted, would be that the United States would fight for years at great expense, only to pay for peace in the end. He concluded with the pessimistic thought that the entire debate was irrelevant. Congress was so weak and indecisive, he told Jefferson, that it would not be capable of doing anything at all about the Barbary threat: "I perceive that neither Force nor Money will be applied . . . your Plan of fighting will no more be adopted than mine of negotiating." No effective response to the problem was possible, short of sweeping constitutional reform to correct the deficiencies of American government.

WRITING YEARS LATER, John Quincy Adams—John and Abigail's son, sixth president of the United States—stressed the historical importance of the partnership between Thomas Jefferson and James Madison. "The mutual influence of these two mighty minds upon each other," he wrote, "is a phenomenon, like the invisible and mysterious movements of the magnet in the physical world, and in which . . . the future historian may discover the solution of much of our national history not otherwise easily accountable."

Known to his family and longtime friends as "little Jemmy," Madison was barely five and a half feet tall and weighed less than 140 pounds. He habitually dressed all in black, giving him the look of a physician or a schoolmaster. He spoke in a low voice and carried himself with a grave scholarly reserve. Those who did not know him well found him cold and uninteresting, but in small groups of trusted friends, he revealed a dry wit and even a fondness for off-color humor.

Born into one of the oldest and wealthiest families in Virginia, Madison had grown up on a 5,000-acre tobacco plantation in Orange County. Before turning eleven, he finished every book in his father's private library. A Scottish tutor was hired to live on the plantation and teach him Latin, Greek, French, mathematics, history, philosophy, theology, and law. Late in life, remembering his tutor, Madison would pronounce: "All I have been in life I owe largely to that man." At age nineteen he traveled north to the college at Princeton, New Jersey, where he compressed three years of work into two, graduating in September 1771. Returning to Virginia, Madison was elected to the convention that declared the state independent of Great Britain, and became a close friend and adviser to Governor Thomas Jefferson. He was elected to the Continental Congress in March 1780. When sworn in, he was its youngest member.

Like many eighteenth-century intellectuals, Jefferson and Madison regarded politics and government as tedious work, a duty rather than a calling. They were dedicated members of the international "republic of letters," and passionately devoted to the study of science, philosophy, history, and the arts. They stood for reason, empiricism, free speech, and a free press; for scientific inquiry, self-governance, individual rights, and a secular state. In their own eyes, they were the advance guard of a world revolution that was being waged, as Jefferson would later put it, "against every form of tyranny over the mind of man." It was a revolution that had not yet been won, and might yet be lost—or, as Immanuel Kant had put it, in 1784: "We are not living in an enlightened age. We are living in an Age of Enlightenment."

While in Paris, Jefferson offered to act as Madison's literary purchasing agent, choosing "such books as may be either old and curious or new and useful." He spent hours browsing in the bookshops and stalls along the Seine, "turning over every book with my own hand and putting by everything related to America, and indeed whatever was rare and valuable to every science." His first letter to Madison from Paris was accompanied by a shipment of 45 books, including 37 volumes of the *Encyclopédie méthodique*; a single "literary cargo" in 1785 included 207 books. Madison, deeply engrossed in his campaign to replace the Articles of Confederation with a new constitution, was especially interested in "whatever may throw light on the general Constitution and [laws] of the several confederacies which have existed." He would be happy to have books by the "historians of the Roman Empire during its decline," "Pascal's provincial letters," "Ordinances Marines," Amelot's "travels into China," and "such of the Greek and Roman authors where they can be got very cheap, as are worth having and are not on the common list of School classics."

The Virginians' transatlantic correspondence mostly ranged over subjects unrelated to politics or diplomacy. In a typical letter, politics and public affairs would receive attention only after long discussion of more interesting subjects; and even then, the dreary business was likely to be relegated to a half-apologetic postscript. Pages were devoted to Buffon's theory of the central heat of the earth; to the "grinders of the Incognitum which were found in Brasil and Lima"; to animal magnetism; to hot air ballooning; to the Aurora Borealis; to the Maison Carrée at Nîmes, which Jefferson pronounced "the most beautiful and precious morsel of architecture left us by antiquity"; and to the reported discovery of a subterranean city in Siberia, with "an equestrian Statue around the neck of which was a golden chain 200 feet in length." Madison sent Jefferson a pamphlet on the language of the Mohicans, to assist his friend in his project of collecting "all the vocabularies I can of the American Indians, as of those of Asia, persuaded that if they ever had a common parentage it will appear in their language."

Jefferson sent Madison curiosities and gadgets not yet generally available in America: a pocket compass, a box of phosphorous matches, a pedometer, a retractable telescope, and an Argand cylinder lamp, which was said to generate light equal to that of six or eight candles. Madison in turn sent Jefferson dozens of specimens of North American flora, which Jefferson hoped to transplant; the shipments included paccan nuts, pippins, apple and sugar maple trees, cranberry plants, plum trees, live oaks, candleberry myrtles, standing American honeysuckles, three-thorned acacia, rhododendrons, and dogwood trees. He also offered to send samples of North American "animal curiosities." "I can without difficulty get the skins of all our common and of some of our rarer quadrupeds," he promised, "and can have them stuffed if desired. It is possible also that I may be able to send some of them alive." In a letter of June 1786, Madison opened with a paragraph on political developments in Virginia and then continued: "For want of something better to fill the remainder of my paper, I will now add the result of my examination two days ago of another of our minor quadrupeds. I mean a Weasel." The description of the animal and its internal organs filled eight long paragraphs. Thirty-eight different anatomical measurements were recorded in an appended table.

Madison was one of the recognized leaders of the "nationalist" movement, which championed a more muscular constitution to strengthen Congress's powers of legislation and taxation. Jefferson's letters from France, describing the frustrations and failures of diplomacy in Paris, London, and other European capitals, lent strong anecdotal support to the cause. The European powers were adept at exploiting the jealousies between the individual American states, Jefferson wrote, and the situation would only grow worse until "with respect to every thing external we be one nation only, firmly hooped together." Foreign policy must be the exclusive province of a supreme central government, while "interior government is what each state should keep to itself." It was essential, he told Madison, to arm American negotiators with powers of commercial retaliation that could be enforced in every seaport, regardless of the laws or policies of the individual states. "I think it possible that England may ply before them. It is a nation which nothing but views of interest can govern."

At Madison's urging, Virginia planned a national conference in Annapolis, Maryland, in September 1786, inviting the other states to send delegates "for the purpose of forming such regulations of trade as may be judged necessary to promote the general interest." One of the delegates sent by the state of New York was Alexander Hamilton, Madison's former colleague in the House of Representatives. Thus began one of the most indispensable partnerships in early American history.

In an era preoccupied with details of birth and lineage, Hamilton had entered the world as a bastard from a broken home. Born on Nevis, raised on St. Croix, Hamilton had started out in life as a lowly clerk in a small British West Indian merchant shipping firm. Emigrating to New York in 1772, he had earned a degree at King's College (later Columbia), joined the Continental Army in 1775, and served as an aide-de-camp to General Washington. He had led a daring assault on a British redoubt at Yorktown, retired from the army with the rank of colonel, married into New York's powerful Schuyler family, studied law, joined the bar, served in both Congress and the New York State Assembly, and was, by 1786, an elite Wall Street lawyer and one of the nation's leading critics of the "feebleness" of the Articles of Confederation. Hamilton's ascent from humble beginnings had been extraordinary, and his greatest achievements still lay ahead of him.

His hair was a sandy, reddish strain of blond; his complexion pale, smooth, and prone to freckling. His eyes were gray-blue and bordered across the top by straight, delicate eyebrows. He dressed impeccably in tailored suits, knee breeches, and waistcoats, with polished brass buttons and silver buckles on his shoes. He kept his hair long, as his son James described it, "plaited, clubbed up, and tied with a black ribbon [in back]. His front hair was pomatumed, powdered, and combed up and back from his forehead." In his engraved portrait on the modern ten-dollar bill, Hamilton's unsmiling expression projects confidence, aggressiveness, and restless energy, but there is also a suggestion of warmth and wit at the corners of the eyes and mouth.

Hamilton's career as an American nationalist had begun during the vicious winter of 1777–78, when the Continental Army hunkered down at Valley Forge, Pennsylvania, snowbound and nearly starving. History has made Valley Forge a symbol of the rebel army's will to endure awful deprivation, but contemporaries dwelled less on the heroism of the troops and more on the neglect and incompetence of the civil authorities in Philadelphia, less than twenty-five miles away. Washington said that some of his troops "might have been tracked from White Marsh to Valley Forge by the blood of their feet." Half-naked, half-frozen, half-starved, huddled like bear cubs in a winter den, the soldiers subsisted on meager rations while the Continental Congress debated how to persuade the states to provide more funds to support the war effort. In Hamilton's view, it was plain that the men had been failed by Congress, which had dithered and debated and exposed the men "frequently to temporary want, and to the danger of a dissolution, from absolute famine." The delegates had consistently maneuvered on behalf of the parochial interests of the individual states, when the war effort demanded that they serve "the common interests of the confederacy."

Just five states attended the Annapolis convention, and in the absence of a quorum no reform could be enacted. But the convention agreed on a resolution, written by Hamilton, acknowledging "important defects in the system of the Federal Government" and calling for a Constitutional Convention to take place the following year in Philadelphia. Madison, returning to Virginia, visited Mount Vernon, and persuaded George Washington to throw his immense prestige behind the cause.

Delving into the books that Jefferson had acquired for him in Europe, Madison made an exhaustive legal and historical study of confederations and ancient republics, and he arrived at the Philadelphia convention prepared. He framed the debate with a paper entitled "Vices of the Political System of the United States." He and his fellow Virginia delegates prepared fourteen resolutions, collectively known as the "Virginia Plan." Washington, elected president of the convention, let it be known that he favored the plan, and his support was critical. On September 17, 1787, the convention approved a new constitution and sent it to the Continental Congress, which ten days later sent it to the states for ratification.

References to a navy in the proposed constitution were limited to a few broad clauses: Article I granted Congress the authority to "provide and maintain a Navy" and to "make Rules for the Government and Regulation of the land and naval Forces"; Article II designated the president as "Commander in Chief of the Army and Navy of the United States." Equally important was Congress's power, also in Article I, to "lay and collect Taxes, Duties, Imposts and Excises," because a great deal of money would be needed to "provide for the common Defence and general Welfare of the United States."

Ratification was up against heavy odds, not least of which was the presence of strongly anti-federal sentiment in Hamilton's and Madison's home states of New York and Virginia. It was Hamilton's idea to publish a series of essays urging ratification, and he threw himself into the work with characteristic intensity, penning fifty-one individual essays in four months. Madison added twenty-nine and New Yorker John Jay, who was ill, managed five. All were published under the pseudonym "Publius." Printed in four New York newspapers between October 1787 and May 1788, they were collected in a book entitled *The Federalist* in the spring of 1788.

Hamilton's *Federalist* essays made a ringing case for "active commerce, an extensive navigation, and a flourishing marine" (No. 11). It was America's destiny to trade by sea, and "the little arts of the little politicians" could never "control or vary the irresistible and unchangeable course of nature." The major European powers were determined to suppress the growth of American trade—to "clip the wings by which we might soar to a dangerous greatness." If America was serious about asserting its maritime rights and protecting its hard-won independence, "we must endeavor, as soon as possible, to have a navy" (No. 24). Madison pointed to the vulnerability of the nation's long, unfortified coastline. Those living near the sea, north and south, should be "deeply interested in this provision for naval protection" (No. 41). Without a navy to defend them, they were vulnerable to the "predatory spirit of licentious adventurers," and would sooner or later be "compelled to ransom themselves from the terrors of a conflagration, by yielding to the exactions of daring and sudden invaders."

Opponents of ratification warned that a navy would expand the power of the federal government to the detriment of the states; that it would increase the public debt; that it would lead to higher taxes; and that its expense would fall on the small farmer of the impoverished interior of the country, who might never even lay eyes on the sea. The proposed navy, declared William Maclay, a Pennsylvanian, was merely a pretext to raise taxes and hire "a host of revenue officers" to collect them—and then, "farewell freedom in America." An old soldier in Massachusetts pointed out that no foreign fleet could invade the territories of the United States, because "they cannot bring their ships on the land." Some argued that America's destiny lay to the west, and that the country should not waste its time or treasure building fleets to fight for control of the ocean. "No, sir," said James Jackson of Georgia, "to the agricultural interest—to the hardy sons of the West—to the American yeomanry we shall appeal, and we shall there find support." The time for a navy would come far in the future, said William Grayson of Virginia, when the United States had populated its enormous inland territories. Only then, "half a century hence," would it be wise "to talk of measures for a navy."

On October 27, 1787, the first of the *Federalist* essays was published in New York. On December 7, Delaware became the first state to ratify the Constitution, followed in quick succession by Pennsylvania, New Jersey, Georgia, Connecticut, and Massachusetts. In the ensuing six months, Maryland, South Carolina, and New Hampshire ratified. That summer, the two largest states in the country, Virginia (June 25, 1788) and New York (July 26, 1788), voted to ratify by narrow margins: 89–79 in Virginia and 30–27 in New York. The new government took effect on March 4, 1789.

In New York City, a great victory celebration was held under the direction of the French architect and designer Pierre L'Enfant. A huge parade, the largest the nation had ever seen, meandered through the streets in a procession stretching a mile and a half long. The procession was led by a Grand Marshal who wore a blue coat with a red sash, followed by thirteen deputies who wore white coats and blue capes, each representing a state. The trade guilds were represented by delegations marching under banners identifying them as blacksmiths, joiners, pressmen, cordwainers, tanners, coopers, ironmongers, glassmakers, and so on. Farmers marched under a banner that read: "God Speed the Plough." Captains of merchant ships carried one that said: "Our Exports Exceed Our Imports." The bakers carried a gigantic loaf of bread, identified by a banner as the "Federal Loaf." An artillery company marched with their fieldpieces in tow; the students and faculty of Columbia College brought up the rear. The whole was borne along by the music of marching bands. Newspapers estimated the number of marchers at more than five thousand. At the end of the parade, on the grassy expanse of Bowling Green, the assembly shared in a banquet of bullock, mutton, and ham, served under an enormous canvas tent. A scroll hung at the entrance, with the words "Independence, Alliance with France, and Peace."

The most impressive feature of the parade, observers agreed, was a house-sized model frigate on wheels. Built by New York's shipwrights, this early version of the modern-day parade float was 27 feet long on the keel and 10 feet on the beam, stepped with three towering masts, fully and accurately rigged with shrouds, stays, and miniature sails; armed with thirty-two miniature cannon that fired salutes; and manned by a crew of thirty sailors and uniformed officers. She was drawn through the streets by ten white horses. Her figurehead was a likeness of the New Yorker for whom she was named, the man who had been a dedicated promoter of the merchant marine, and who had almost single-handedly secured New York's ratification of the Constitution. His name was carved across her transom: "HAMILTON."

CHAPTER TWO

On October 8, 1793, the U.S. minister to Portugal, David Humphreys, addressed a circular letter "To All Governors, Magistrates, Officers Civil, Military & others concerned, in the United States of America." Copies were to be carried by vessels sailing from Lisbon for every point on the compass. It was short and to the point:

> You are earnestly desired, as speedily as possible, to give a universal alarm to all Citizens of the United States concerned in navigation, particularly to the southern parts of Europe, of the danger of being captured by the Algerines. . . . A truce for twelve Months is concluded between Portugal and Algiers. In consequence of which a fleet of Algerine Cruizers passed through the Straits into the Atlantic on Saturday night last.

It was, to be specific, a fleet of eight vessels, comprising "four frigates, three Xebecks, and a Brig of 20 guns," and its undoubted objective was "to cruise against the American flag."

As the awful intelligence spread throughout the Mediterranean, American merchants and sea captains panicked. Their letters betrayed a breathless terror. "I have not slept since Receipt of the news of this hellish plot—pardon me for such Expressions—Another corsair in the Atlantic—God preserve us—," wrote Edward Church, U.S. consul in Lisbon, to Thomas Jefferson, who was now serving in Philadelphia as the nation's first Secretary of State. Through the rest of October and early November 1793, the limitations of eighteenth-century communications left the maritime community in suspense. A month after the warning had gone out from Lisbon, no credible report of the whereabouts of the Algerian fleet had arrived in any of the major Portuguese, Spanish, or Mediterranean seaports. Every American vessel bound for Lisbon, Cadiz, or the Straits of Gibraltar was a potential victim.

Finally, in mid-November, hard news arrived from Algiers itself. A consul who lived in the hostile seaport under diplomatic protection reported that "the Algerine cruisers have captured in the latter end of October ten American Vessels, the Masters & Crews to the number of 110 Men is brought into Algiers and is made Slaves of this Regency, these and all the other American Captives is in a distressed and naked situation." Among the captured ships were the *Hope* of New York, bound from Rotterdam to Malaga in ballast; the brig *George* of Rhode Island, inbound to Lisbon laden with grain and Indian corn; and the *Dispatch* of Petersburg, Virginia, bound from Cadiz to Hamburg with sugar, indigo, and sarsaparilla.

The tactics employed by the Algerian corsairs against merchantmen were simple, effective, and brutal. They sailed lateen-rigged ships, xebecs, polacres, and feluccas that were fast enough to overtake most prey under sail, but could also be rowed in a calm. Running down a fleeing merchantman, they dropped their long lateen yards across the victim's rail. Ferocious men armed with pistols and cutlasses swarmed aboard and slaughtered any who resisted. The captives were beaten, stripped, and chained together belowdecks, and then returned to Algiers, where they were imprisoned or sold into slavery.

The Algerians allowed some of the captured Americans to write home, perhaps in the hope of obtaining ransoms from their families. David Pierce had been master of the schooner *Jay* of Colchester, captured in the Atlantic, four days out of Malaga and bound for Boston with a cargo of raisins, figs, grapes, and wine. "On our landing," he wrote,

> we were all put into Chains without the least distinction and put to hard labor from daylight until night with only the allowance of two small black loaves and water & close confined at night. . . . When they boarded us they even took the clothes from our backs & brought us on board almost naked in this situation they put us into the Cable Tier without any thing, not even a blanket to Cover us where we remained until our arrival here without even a shirt to shift us. Death would be a great relief & more welcome than a continuance of our present situation. . . . We think ourselves happy if we escape through the day being beat by our driver, who carries a stick big enough to Knock a man down, and the innocent often suffer with the guilty as they say we are all Christians.

American vessels had once been ubiquitous in the Mediterranean. Now, in a matter of weeks, they vanished. Seamen who had braved the most awesome winter gales the North Atlantic had to offer were paralyzed by the fear of enslavement in North Africa. Vessels bound for the Straits of Gibraltar could not be manned at any rate of pay. Maritime insurance premiums doubled and then tripled, U.S. government bond prices collapsed, and merchant houses were bankrupted.

The closing of the Mediterranean to American commerce was a particularly bitter setback because Europe, in 1793, was once again at war—and war, as always, brought the hope of windfall profits. There was intense demand for imported foodstuffs and naval stores beyond the Straits of Gibraltar. Tens of thousands of British soldiers and sailors were posted at bases in Gibraltar, Minorca, Malta, and Sicily, and their supply officers would pay generously for "all manner of eatables and drinkables." Great fortunes were there to be made. "If we had but the free navigation of the Mediterranean," David Humphreys lamented, "what an extensive market would be open for our produce!"

Some Americans saw evidence of English treachery. Britain's merchant interests regarded Americans and other neutrals as economic rivals to be foiled by any means necessary. The British government had mediated the October truce between Portugal and Algiers, which had allowed the Algerines to break out of the Mediterranean. English diplomats had reportedly gone so far as to lobby Queen Maria of Portugal to deny naval convoys to American vessels. The combined powers appeared to be setting up a proxy war against American commerce. "England and Spain seem to be plotting in what way they can most effectually clip our Eagle's Wings," wrote Edward Church. "They are both extremely envious of her soaring."

NEWS OF THE CAPTURES appeared in the Philadelphia newspapers in mid-December. As Christmas and New Year's came and went, and the winter ice closed the river to navigation, the Algerian emergency commanded the city's rapt attention.

In 1793, Philadelphia was to the United States as London was to England or Paris was to France: simultaneously the nation's political, economic, and cultural capital. With a population of some fifty thousand, it was by far the largest city in North America. In the English-speaking world, only London was larger. Travelers agreed that Philadelphia had America's best theaters, libraries, inns, and taverns. It was home to the nation's most eminent scientists, philanthropists, poets, physicians, and artists. Its newspapers were the most famous, or the most infamous, but in either case the most widely circulated. Behind paned windows overhung with brightly colored awnings, its rows and rows of shops displayed the greatest variety of imported luxuries. Its real estate was the most expensive on the continent. In contrast to the gloomy, labyrinthine alleyways of New York and Boston, Philadelphia's streets were broad, sunny, and straight, intersecting at right angles to form a perfectly symmetrical rectilinear grid. They were paved with cobblestones and shaded by precisely spaced trees, and at night they were lighted by four-paned whale-oil lamps erected on elegant wrought-iron poles. High walkways paved with brick or flagstones allowed women to go out on foot without collecting filth on the hems of their dresses. Many of the more lavish row houses were adjoined by private gardens planted with rose bushes, azaleas, magnolias, or English ivy. Wallpaper, ice cellars, walk-in closets, and indoor lavatories were luxuries only the rich could afford, so the rich made a point of having them.

Philadelphia was a multicultural, multi-religious, polyglot society, and by eighteenth-century standards the city was uncommonly tolerant of its own diversity. Journeymen and mechanics in leather aprons and homespun jackets shared the sidewalks with expensively dressed merchants, lawyers, and clergymen. Fifth-generation Anglos co-existed comfortably with newly arrived Palantine Germans, Swedes, Welsh, Scots-Irish, Irish, and French royalist exiles. Free blacks, American Indians, buckskin-clad frontiersmen, and dangerous-looking sailors did not warrant a second glance.

Most important, Philadelphia was the seat of the federal government. Four and a half years had passed since the ratification of the Constitution, and George Washington was commencing his second term as president of the United States. His opulent cream-colored carriage, drawn by six white horses and attended by four footmen in livery, was a familiar sight in the streets of the city. Serving in his administration were several of the ranking statesmen of the founding generation, a circle that later came to be known, collectively, as "the founding fathers." John Adams was the first vice president, Thomas Jefferson the first Secretary of State, Alexander Hamilton the first Secretary of the Treasury, and former Continental Army general Henry Knox the first Secretary of War. Congress met in a plain two-story red brick building known as Congress Hall, just west of the Pennsylvania State House on Chestnut Street between Fifth and Sixth. The two buildings were adjoined by a public yard where, in mild weather, the senators and representatives lounged on benches or napped in the shade of a weeping willow. The yard was enclosed by a seven-foot brick wall broken only by a high arched gate that opened onto Walnut Street, and faced the ominous edifice of the Walnut Street prison.

Even before the Algerian captures, the president and his advisers had worried about the nation's ability to defend itself in what seemed to be an increasingly lawless world. The French Revolution, now entering its fourth year, had taken a savage and radical turn. King Louis XVI, whose troops, ships, and money had helped America win its independence, had been guillotined in Paris on January 21, 1793, his severed head brandished before a jeering mob. Shortly thereafter, leaders of the radical faction known as the Jacobins seized power and began a bloody campaign of terror against their domestic enemies. That same month, news arrived from Europe that Great Britain, Spain, and the Netherlands had declared war against France with the avowed purpose of restoring the Bourbons to the throne. The entire continent was mobilizing for war.

Even at that early date, in the fall of 1793, it was evident that this new war would be something unprecedented in European history. The conflict between Revolutionary France and its enemies would be, arguably, the first true world war—a war fought on many continents and many oceans. It would be a test of strength between irreconcilable political philosophies. When the fighting was finished, Europe would be ruled either entirely by revolutionaries or entirely by monarchs. It would be longer and more savage than the earlier imperial wars of the eighteenth century, foreshadowing a future in which conflicts would be fought not between kings and their armies, but between and against entire peoples.

Washington had embraced a policy of strict neutrality, embodied in his historically famous "Neutrality Proclamation" of April 1793. Neutrality may have been the only realistic choice for a nation with seven hundred farm boys in uniform and not a single armed ship afloat. On the other hand—and this is the largely forgotten dimension of Washington's policy—there was everything to be gained from allowing the nation's merchant marine to flourish in the wartime carrying trade. Northern merchants would prosper and southern planters would command better prices for their exportable produce. Surging customs duties would generate revenue for the federal government, which was essential to the entire fiscal and economic program crafted by Alexander Hamilton.

And yet, in the late months of 1793, it was not clear that neutrality could even be managed. Neither the French nor the British were wholly satisfied with American neutrality, and each preyed upon American shipping under the pretense of blocking shipments of wartime contraband to enemy ports. War brought chaos, especially on the high seas, where lawlessness was endemic; American vessels were increasingly at the mercy of any sea robber who wished to prey upon them. New reports of captures by British, French, and Algerian ships poured in all at once. By land, reports of Indian attacks on frontier settlements (presumably incited by Great Britain) gave the impression that the western frontiers were crumbling. It was hardly far-fetched to imagine that Philadelphia could be invaded and occupied by redcoats, as it had just fifteen years earlier. In a world at war, it seemed, American defenselessness would only provoke aggression. Hamilton's warning in *Federalist* No. 11 now loomed as prophecy: "A nation, despicable by its weakness, forfeits even the privilege of being neutral."

BEFORE THE ALGERIAN CRISIS, there had not been much serious talk of building a navy. Even proponents tended to accept the judgment that the federal government, still groaning under the weight of its Revolutionary War debts, could not afford one. The administration's only tangible proposal had been to organize American seamen into a kind of naval militia—"to register all actual seamen, and to render those of a certain age amenable to service, if demanded within a given period." But Congress had not even acted on that half-step. In a typical pre-1793 resolution, the Senate endorsed the idea of a new American navy—but only "as soon as the state of the public finances will admit."

News of the Algerian attacks changed the politics of the issue in one stroke. On January 2, 1794, a closely divided House enacted a resolution proclaiming that "a naval force adequate to the protection of the commerce of the United States, against the Algerine corsairs, ought to be provided." A select committee was appointed to study the intelligence reports and determine what class of warships should be built. The committee, weighted with congressmen from northern seaports who were themselves merchants and ship owners, reported its findings on January 20:

> By the best information the committee could obtain, it appears that the naval force of the Algerines consists of light vessels, of different size and force . . . carrying in the whole two hundred and eighty-two guns. . . . The vessels (except two or three) are slenderly built, smaller in size than vessels belonging to the Christian Powers, carrying the same number of guns, and principally manned with people little accustomed to the management of large ships.

Concluding that a small squadron should be more than adequate to deal with Algiers, the committee recommended that Congress appropriate funds to acquire a squadron of six warships. The estimated cost of construction, victualling, and three months' pay for officers and crew was $600,000. It was an estimate that would seem preposterous in retrospect.

House debate on the proposed squadron began on February 16 and dominated the chamber's attention for a month. The debate was remarkable for its scope and complexity, ranging across diplomacy and foreign affairs, military strategy and tactics, fiscal policy and taxes, the benefits of foreign trade, and the meaning of national honor. It exposed, along the way, fundamental questions about America's national identity. Should the United States build a navy? Should it join the Europeans in paying protection money to the Barbary States? Or should the commercial maritime interests be left to fend for themselves? Would a navy bankrupt the country? Would it plunge the nation into Europe's war? Shouldn't America instead channel its resources and energies into internal development?

Congress was not yet divided along formal party lines. The very concept of a political party had not yet become respectable. But the ideological schism that lay beneath the party system had already opened, and every member knew it. Individual senators and congressmen were lining up behind one or the other of the two dominant personalities in Washington's cabinet, Secretary of State Jefferson and Treasury Secretary Hamilton, who cordially hated one another and took the opposing sides of every important issue that came before the president. The followers of Hamilton called themselves "Federalists," a term that had its origins in the constitutional debates. The followers of Jefferson were beginning to get comfortable with the term "Republicans" and in time they would embrace it as a party label.*

Although Jefferson was recognized as the ultimate leader of the Republicans, James Madison was in fact the party's chief organizer, tactician, and the source of much of its energy. He was a third-term member of the House, and although the congressional leadership system had not yet emerged, there was no doubt that he controlled the Republican voting bloc in the House and possibly in the Senate as well. Madison and the Republicans argued that a navy was hopelessly unaffordable to a nation still groaning under the weight of its Revolutionary War debts. Once started, they warned, a navy would become a self-feeding organism, demanding greater and greater sums as it grew. Even Alexander Hamilton, in *Federalist* No. 34, had asserted that fourteen of every

---

* The modern Republican Party originated in a later period, and does not claim any direct historical lineage to the Jeffersonian Republicans.

fifteen shillings in taxes collected in Great Britain was required to service the national debt it had run up to support its navy. The French Revolution had been preceded by a financial crisis brought about, in large part, by the cost of the *ancien régime*'s vast naval establishment. Like the European naval powers, they argued, the United States would be forced to levy higher taxes on its people. Wasn't that what had caused the American Revolution?

The Republicans were obsessed with restraining the size and reach of the federal government, and their campaign against the navy was one face of that obsession. Government institutions were in Federalist hands and therefore a source of Federalist influence and patronage. As the partisan rupture widened, Republicans began to speak fearfully of the growth of a Federalist military establishment—of row after row of party loyalists in uniform and under arms. With the memory of marauding British troops so fresh in mind, the revolutionary generation felt a deep loathing for standing armies. While a navy could never pose an equivalent threat to inland farms and homes and villages, it was not difficult to imagine boats loaded with heavily armed sailors and marines descending upon rebellious coastal regions and occupying the seaports.

Regarding militarism as the close cousin of despotism, Republicans were inclined to regard navies as the playthings of kings and tyrants. William Maclay, the Republican senator from Pennsylvania, who was an ardent anti-navy man, kept a detailed and frequently acerbic running commentary on the debate in his private journal. "This thing of a fleet has been working among our members all the session," he grumbled. "I have heard it break out often." He was convinced the Federalists were exaggerating the danger in order to maneuver the Congress into a declaration of war, for "war is often entered into to answer domestic, not foreign purposes." Maclay detested the thought that Americans might "forego our republican innocence, and, like all other nations, set apart a portion of our citizens for the purpose of inflicting misery on our fellow mortals. This practice is felony to posterity."

Early congressional debates were notoriously chaotic. Members leapt to their feet in no particular order, launching new lines of argument, rebutting opinions that had been offered days or weeks earlier, or reiterating arguments that had already been presented. Even so, the Federalist performance in the navy debate was far more disciplined and coordinated than that of their rivals.

The first part of the pro-navy case was grounded in the simple arithmetic of costs and benefits. The Republicans had objected to the cost of building a navy, but what did they have to say about the cost of not building one? Protecting the sea-lanes, argued the Federalists, was in the entire nation's interest. In the spring of 1794, marine insurance premiums on ships sailing for transatlantic destinations had risen to 25 percent of the total value of ship and cargo. This would impose an additional cost on trade of some $2 million per year. The burden would be carried not just by merchants, but by farmers who exported their produce and by consumers of imported goods. Take the case of salt, said the Federalists. The threat of piracy would raise the cost of imported salt by at least a dollar and as much as two dollars per bushel. In the first year alone the added costs would equal three to six times the total cost of the proposed squadron. The Federalists' second thrust was a rousing appeal to national honor, and this was the feature of their argument that had the most rhetorical power and the most resonance beyond the capital. Didn't the Republicans have any national pride? Hadn't America recently won a war against the most powerful nation on earth?

When the House vote was cast on March 10, 1794, an Act to Provide a Naval Armament passed by a margin of 50–39. Passage in the Senate followed quickly on a voice vote and Washington signed it into law on March 27. The act authorized the War Office either to buy or build six frigates. Four would be rated for 44 guns and two for 36 guns. The bill set the numbers, grades, and ratings of officers and men, laid out details of pay and rations, and gave the president authority to appoint six captains, each of whom would supervise the construction and launch of one ship. The then-colossal sum of $688,888 was appropriated to fund the program.

Republicans managed to work their will in one respect. They added a provision stipulating that the sole purpose of the frigates was to police the Mediterranean against piracy. Should a truce be successfully negotiated with Algiers, the building program would come to an immediate standstill and the navy, such as it was, would cease to exist.

The House did not vote on strict party lines. Several Republicans from northern coastal and urban districts, where pro-navy sentiment was strong, cast their votes with the Federalists. The result hinted at the latent rivalry between North and South, but also at the antagonism in every part of the country between the maritime seaboard and the agrarian interior. Even so, these two embryonic political parties had found, in the navy, a hard ideological line to divide and define them. The Federalists had become (and would remain) the party of the navy. Republicans had embraced anti-navalism as a core ideology, and a generation would pass before they began to change their minds.

Among the 39 "no" votes recorded on March 10 was that of the de facto Republican floor leader, James Madison. This was one of those twists of historical fate that often passes unnoticed. If the Virginian had found another 6 votes, he would have blocked construction of the same six frigates that would play such a momentous part in his own presidency, twenty years later.

CONGRESS HAD ACTED; the authorization had been given; very large sums of money were ready to be poured out of the federal treasury. All eyes now turned to Secretary of War Henry Knox, whose office would bear the principal responsibility for getting the frigates built and launched.

Knox, who had started out in life as the proprietor of a Boston bookshop, had served under Washington as the Continental Army's chief artillery officer in the early days of the Revolution, rising eventually to the rank of major general. He had pulled off one of the most important logistical feats of the early Revolution in the winter of 1776, when he oversaw the transport of fifty-nine heavy cannon from Fort Ticonderoga, on Lake Champlain, to Boston. The guns were dragged on sleds, mile by bitter mile, over the Berkshire Hills. When rebel artillery emplacements appeared unexpectedly on Dorchester Heights, with the enemy positions well within their range, the British were forced to withdraw from Boston, never to return.

The War Office was on the corner of Chestnut and Fifth, diagonally across from the State House and Congress Hall. From this cramped suite of rooms, heated by the warmth of a single fire, General Knox and a half dozen clerks managed the entire defense establishment of the United States. Knox, who dearly loved food and drink, had ballooned to a weight of nearly 300 pounds. He carried a gold-headed cane which he waved theatrically as he spoke. He was cheerful and high-spirited by temperament; but he was also in the habit of being obeyed, and when irritated with a subordinate he was liable to burst into profanity in a voice that was strong and "deep as a thunder-growl."

Congress had charged Knox with considering the problem from the standpoint of the ships themselves—design, armament, personnel, construction, and cost. The technical and logistical problems involved in building frigates were daunting. It would be a vast and complex undertaking. It was only natural for Knox to feel overwhelmed and perhaps a bit intimidated by the duty that had descended on him. He was the son of a sea captain but had spent his entire career ashore, and by his own admission he could not begin to grasp the intricacies of naval architecture. Knox's instinct was to reach out to friends, acquaintances, and colleagues who knew more than he did about the subject. In this, he was fortunate in the location of the capital.

Surrounded in every direction by rich, arable farmlands, Philadelphia was the land-to-sea link for the entire Delaware River basin. Water and Front

Streets, running parallel to the river for miles along the waterfront, were given wholly over to the maritime industry. The bowsprits of the square-riggers extended 50 or 60 feet above the storehouses adjoining the wharves. Elaborately carved and garishly painted figureheads gazed down at the pedestrians on Front Street. Despite its location, 100 miles up the river from the open sea, Philadelphia was by far the largest seaport in North America, and it was almost certainly the largest freshwater port in the world. More than a quarter of the nation's total exports—nearly $7 million worth in 1793—passed through its wharves. More to the point, Philadelphia was the largest shipbuilding center in the United States. In 1793, more than 8,000 tons of shipping were built at Philadelphia—twice the tonnage of any other shipbuilding center in the United States. The city was home to many of the country's most respected ship architects and builders. Knox reached out to this community of experts, invited them to his office, toured their shipyards, and pored over their plans. He did everything short of strolling along the Philadelphia waterfront and stopping strangers at random to ask for their opinions.

The city's leading ship architects were, almost to a man, members of the religious sect known as the Society of Friends, more commonly called "Quakers." The "Greene Country Towne" on the western bank of the Delaware River had been founded by William Penn just over a century earlier, as a refuge for Quakers fleeing religious persecution in Europe. By the late eighteenth century, immigration had reduced the sect to about a fifth of the city's population, but their virtues of frugality, humility, and egalitarianism were deeply rooted in the city's laws and customs.

Quakers believed in the "inner light," or the essential goodness of each human being. No one person, they believed, was more or less capable of spiritual enlightenment than any other. They embraced the subversive idea that the plain teachings of the Christian gospel should be applied literally and in every aspect of daily life. No one could distinguish a rich Quaker from a poor one, because they all dressed in plain, homespun clothes without lace, ribbons, or silver buckles. Women wore bonnets and plain white or blue skirts with handkerchiefs high and tight around their necks. Men wore broad-brimmed hats, plain gray mulberry coats, breeches with white stockings, and square-toed shoes. Quakers would not lift their hats, bow to a magistrate, or swear oaths. They had no churches and no clergy. Disdaining the notion of a "hireling priesthood," they met in plain, wooden meetinghouses where no person occupied a place of authority and where any man, woman, or child could speak at will. The Quaker doctrine of social equality was two centuries ahead of its time. Women and men, rich and poor, servants and employers,

Indians and Europeans, blacks and whites were essentially alike in the eyes of God—they were all "Friends"—and therefore deserving of the same rights and courtesies as any other. Quakers were among the first Americans to petition for the abolition of slavery, and when their efforts failed, they took direct action by buying slaves and setting them free.

A South Carolina congressman, William Loughton Smith, likened the union of the states to a troubled marriage. "We took each other, with our mutual bad habits and respective evils, for better, for worse," he said. "The northern states adopted us with our slaves, and we adopted them with their Quakers."

One facet of Quaker doctrine, above all others, brought them into conflict with their fellow citizens. This was the "peace testimony," which condemned war or any kind of "warlike preparation." Quaker pacifism was absolute and unconditional: no exception was allowed for defense against invasion. Not only were Quakers expected to refuse to serve under arms, but they were to refrain from any act that would enable others to do so. In practice, this meant that Quakers could not assist in the building of fortifications or barracks; they could not pay any tax levied to pay for measures of collective defense; they could not contribute to any aspect of military provisioning or logistics. Strictly speaking, Quaker doctrine even ruled out providing medical care to wounded soldiers, if doing so would free others to take up arms.

Critics charged that the Quaker peace testimony was camouflage for cowardice and even greed. "They are not Men of Arms," one wrote, "but a herd of silly insignificant People, aiming rather to heap up Riches in Obscurity, than to acquire a Fame by an heroick Undertaking." Anger against the sect rose during the Revolution, when many Quakers purported to agree with the justice of the cause but refused to join the fight. Conscientious objectors were fined and jailed. As a codicil to his essay *Common Sense*, Tom Paine (who was himself a Quaker, born and raised in London) included an address to the "Religious Society of the People called Quakers." Pacifism, he wrote, was a gift to all tyrants because it had "a direct tendency to make a man the quiet and inoffensive subject of any and every government which is set over him."

> We fight neither for revenge nor conquest; neither from pride nor passion; we are not insulting the world with our fleets and armies, nor ravaging the globe for plunder. Beneath the shade of our own vines are we attacked; in our own houses, and on our own lands, is the violence committed against us. . . .
>
> If the bearing [of] arms be sinful, the first going to war must be

more so, by all the difference between willful attack and unavoidable defence. Wherefore, if ye really preach from conscience, and mean not to make a political hobby-horse of your religion, convince the world thereof by proclaiming your doctrine to your enemies, for they likewise bear ARMS.

Not all Quakers failed to be impressed by the arguments against the peace testimony, and the revolutionary experience opened a rift within their ranks. When news of the battle at Lexington and Concord reached Philadelphia in April 1775, thirty young Quaker men formed themselves into a militia and began drilling on the public greens. Others enlisted in the Continental Army or aboard privateers. Major General Nathanael Greene, who served under Washington as Quartermaster General and later as commander of American troops in the South, had been raised as a Quaker in Rhode Island. Many Quakers who chose to fight were "read out of meeting"—the equivalent of excommunication. Some managed to have themselves reinstated; others never did.

One of these renegade Quakers was a forty-two-year-old Philadelphian shipbuilder named Joshua Humphreys. He had been born in Marion Township (now Haverford), in the backcountry west of Philadelphia. At age fourteen he had traveled to Philadelphia to be apprenticed to Jonathan Penrose, then one of the city's leading shipwrights. At some point in his late adolescence, for reasons not known, he transferred his apprenticeship to another Quaker shipwright, John Wharton. When Wharton died in 1771, Humphreys, then just twenty years old, became a young master shipwright with his own yard. He was an early and ardent supporter of the American Revolution and the Revolution, in turn, helped him to achieve success in his profession. Brushing aside pacifist objections, he outfitted more than a dozen privateers for Philadelphia customers, and he built the *Randolph*, one of the thirteen original Continental frigates. In postwar Philadelphia, Humphreys was one of the busiest and most-sought-after shipbuilders in the city. His main shipyard complex was located on the waterfront south of town, in the neighborhood of Southwark, adjacent to an old Swedish Lutheran church.

Like many professional shipbuilders, Joshua Humphreys had never been to sea, and by his own admission he had never even seen one of the great European battleships. But he had designed, built, or repaired perhaps three hundred merchantmen in the course of his thirty-year career, and he knew far more about marine architecture than the captains who took his creations to sea. Whether motivated by patriotism, or a pecuniary interest in navy contracts, or simple professional enthusiasm, Humphreys threw himself into the subject of designing the new frigates. He devoured every book on naval architecture he could get his hands on. He was always ready to let loose a torrent of words whenever the subject of designing and building warships came up. Humphreys's command of the subject seems to have dazzled Secretary Knox, who eagerly sought his advice.

To convey the ingeniousness of the Humphreys design requires a brief discussion of the three broad categories of warship then afloat. The largest was the battleship, known by contemporaries as a line-of-battle ship or a ship of the line. Battleships were huge, heavy, and relatively slow, usually carrying guns on two fully armed gun decks, with additional weapons mounted on the quarterdeck and forecastle. They generally carried at least 74 guns, and their frames, or "scantlings," were so massive that they could withstand heavy enemy fire. The frigate was an intermediate class of warship. Every frigate mounted her principal battery of guns on one fully covered gun deck, though she often mounted additional weapons (as with the battleship) on the quarterdeck and forecastle. Frigates might carry as many as 40 to 50 guns, or as few as 20; most carried between 28 and 38. The third category incorporated a wide variety of "unrated" vessels—smaller ship-rigged (three-masted) sloops and brigs, generally carrying fewer than 20 guns, all on the upper deck. They were commanded by lieutenants or recently promoted captains.

The frigate represented a compromise between power and speed. She was lighter and of shallower draft than a battleship, but she mounted enough firepower to overawe any merchantman or privateer. She was a good open-ocean sailing ship and versatile in her uses. The frigate could range ahead in search of the enemy, drop over the horizon, nose into bays and harbors, run up rivers, and carry intelligence back to the flagship. Nelson called frigates "the eyes of the fleet." The frigate was also suited to long, solitary cruises, seeking action with other enemy frigates, seizing enemy commerce, or carrying dignitaries to distant posts. But a frigate rarely engaged an enemy battleship, if she could avoid it, because in such an action she would be cruelly outgunned.

During the Revolution, American shipwrights had been dismayed by the special challenges involved in building frigates. They had to be much larger and stronger than merchant vessels. Being so much heavier than merchantmen, they had to carry a much larger rig—towering masts and spars—to drive them through the water at speed. A frigate's chief purpose was to serve as a floating battery, or a transportable platform for heavy naval cannon. This platform was most effective when placed high above the sea. Guns on the upper decks could be fired at a great distance; they could be worked in heavy weather; they could be fired to leeward even when the ship was pressed with sail and heeling severely; they could be fired down onto a smaller enemy's decks. But guns placed high above the waterline also raised the vessel's center of gravity and thus compromised her stability. An unstable ship would have a long, sickening roll that would bury her mainchains in the foam. In heavy weather she would ship big seas through her hawseholes, gunports, and even over her bulwarks. The tremendous strain on her overall structure would cause her to deteriorate rapidly. Because of her need to carry heavy guns, a frigate's instability was her birthright, the inevitable consequence of her reason to exist. In designing a frigate, the ship architect's greatest challenge was to resolve this inherent weakness as best he could.

Joshua Humphreys proposed, in short, to build exceptionally large, heavily armed, fast-sailing frigates—ships weighing well over 1,000 tons, with a deck length of not less than 175 feet, mounting a battery of thirty 24-pounder long guns on the gun deck and a smaller battery of carronades on the upper deck. "They are superior to any European frigate," Humphreys wrote of the design he had in mind, "and if others should be in [the enemy's] company, our frigates can always lead ahead and never be obliged to go into action, but on their own terms, except in a calm; in blowing weather our ships are capable of engaging to advantage double-deck ships." In another formulation, he proposed "such frigates as in blowing weather would be an overmatch for double-deck ships, and in light winds evade coming into action."

The frigate Humphreys envisioned would be powerful enough to overwhelm a lone enemy cruiser because of her unusually heavy battery of 24-pounder long guns, weapons that had been known to drive a ball through two feet of solid oak planking at a range of 1,000 yards. When pitted against a battleship, the American frigate would enjoy one of the most important advantages that any warship can ever have: the option to either fight or flee, to outrun or outgun. In heavy weather, when an enemy battleship would be obliged to house her lower deck guns to avoid being swamped, Humphreys's frigate might have the temerity to attack the larger ship and overpower her. In milder conditions, when a battleship could bring all of her guns into action, his frigate would be fast enough to make sail and "clean outrun" the larger ship.

Algerian piracy was the immediate impetus for the frigates, but Humphreys was thinking of the potential for a confrontation with one of the warring superpowers of Europe. Britain and France had each been responsible for depredations against American shipping, and each had vital interests in North America that might bring them into conflict with the United States. The potential for a war at sea with the British or French was a politically sensitive topic—there was still strong anti-navy sentiment in Congress, and the fear that American warships would drag the nation into an unwelcome war was one reason for it. Humphreys was aware of these sensitivities, and he wrote in veiled terms. But laced throughout his letters was his conviction that the frigates should be designed to fight a naval war with one or more of the great European naval powers.

Over several generations, the English had developed a rating system that organized all battleships and frigates into six "rates." A ship's rate was determined, nominally, by how many guns she carried. The Royal Navy included ships of many different sizes and designs, some new and some long afloat, and many that had been built in France, Spain, or Holland and later captured. For decades, the sprawling British fleets had been anything but homogeneous, and the rating system was intended to impose order on the chaos. The first-, second-, third-, and fourth-rates were the battleships. The fifth- and sixth-rates were, respectively, the heavy and light frigates. But in the closing years of the eighteenth century, the six-rating system was fast becoming an anachronism. The British fleet was increasingly dominated by two types of warship: the 74-gun battleship and the 36- or 38-gun frigate. These accounted for virtually all new construction, while ships of other rates, whether larger or smaller, were liable to be rebuilt or taken out of service. The reasons for these changes were complex. In part, they were a tactical response to corresponding changes in the enemy fleets; in part, a means of alleviating the manpower shortage in the Royal Navy; in part, to economize on shipbuilding costs. Whatever the reasons, however, the important fact was that the British fleet and to some extent the French and Spanish fleets as well were evolving toward a binary combination of 74-gun battleships and much smaller frigates.

As a small, underpopulated country, the United States had no hope of achieving numerical parity with the major European naval fleets for two generations at the very least; meeting them with their own types of ships would not do. In proposing very heavy frigates—frigates with keels, frames, and scantlings akin to those of a 74-gun ship—Humphreys was essentially proposing to build a hybrid between the frigates and battleships of the Royal Navy. His unique insight was that the Europeans, with their binary fleets composed of battleships and smaller frigates, had failed to grasp the advantage of ships that combined qualities of both. Moreover, the very failure of the European navies to recognize the merits of such a hybrid exposed a tactical weakness that could be exploited by the Americans in the event of a naval war.

Although he did not say it, Humphreys might have added that if the United States should ever fight another naval war with Great Britain, the English frigate captains would be driven by their own hubris to attack the more powerful American ships. Their pride and contempt would act as a powerful gravitational field, drawing them inexorably into fights they could not win.

THE PROFESSIONAL SHIPWRIGHT of the period was conservative by tradition and temperament. His conservatism was a natural consequence of the grave responsibility he bore. When evaluating an unproven innovation in ship design or construction, he could easily picture himself cringing before the accusing stares of widows and orphans. He had entered his vocation by serving a long apprenticeship to an older man, an established master builder who had himself been schooled in much the same way. His craft was an heirloom that had been handed down from generation to generation. If it evolved at all, it did so only gradually, little by little, in fits and starts. In 1794, a newly launched ship was not much different from one still afloat after fifty years of service.

The Humphreys frigate was unconventional, and therefore controversial. According to a rival Philadelphia shipwright, the proposed design was "rejected by the unanimous voice of all the principal shipbuilders from Swedes Church to the upper part of Kensington."

The criticism leveled against Humphreys may not have been entirely impartial. His professional colleagues were all members of a small, fractious circle of local Quaker shipbuilders. They were business rivals who had no doubt been manhandled by Humphreys in fair competition and who resented his rapid ascent to the summit of the profession. And there was an enormous amount of federal spending at stake. Their principal objection was to the ship's great size. Some believed that the heavy frame and long keel would cause structural weakness. Others maintained that the weight and number of the guns should be reduced. Concerns were raised about the deep draft. But the essence of the case against the design was simply that frigates of that size did not exist anywhere else in the world. If England and France chose not to build such frigates, they asked, then why should the United States? Why not trust in the wisdom that could only come through centuries of experience?

In February 1794, as the frigates bill was still working its way through Congress, Humphreys was summoned to the War Office on Chestnut Street to discuss his proposed design. On arriving, he found that one of his competitors, Jonathan Penrose (the son of the Penrose to whom Humphreys had first been apprenticed), was already sitting with Secretary Knox in his office. Penrose was pressing Knox to choose a more orthodox design—to build smaller, lighter 36-gun frigates. An argument ensued. As Humphreys recalled it, Penrose charged that his dimensions were "extravagant, and that the ships, if built by them, would be useless, as they could not be built sufficiently strong." Humphreys defended his model. "Building the frigates of extended dimensions," he argued, "would give us a superiority over any of the European frigates and would render all their frigates of little or no effect in a contest with us. It would give us a lead in naval affairs that no smaller dimensions would afford us." Knox asked the two master shipbuilders to try to agree upon a compromise, but they were unable to do so.

Penrose had another young Quaker shipwright living under his roof. This was Josiah Fox, a well-to-do, thirty-year-old Englishman who had traveled to the United States in 1793 in order to survey American timber resources. He had been engaged to teach Penrose's sons the art and science of drafting. Fox had completed his apprenticeship in the Royal Dockyard at Plymouth, and as such, claimed to be the only ship architect in America "who had served his apprenticeship under the best architects and shipyards of that period in England, and the English navy was recognized as the finest in the world." He also claimed that he alone was able to produce models "formed to combine buoyancy with fast sailing."

Humphreys asked Fox for a formal assessment of his design, probably in mid-April. Fox's reaction was blunt. His view was that in the Humphreys frigate the wales were placed too low; the bow and stern were too sharp; and there were too many large hollow spaces in the hull, which would contribute to the weakness of the hull's structure. The design ought to include more rake (the stem and stern should rise at a smaller angle from the keel). Fundamentally, Fox was concerned that the Humphreys frigate was too long in proportion to her beam. The resulting structural weakness was so great that the ship might even break her back on launching.

The historical record of the debate over the frigate design is fragmentary and incomplete. Since the key players were all residing in Philadelphia, they exchanged their views in face-to-face meetings at the War Office, and no paper trail was created. It seems clear that Knox solicited the advice of several of Philadelphia's leading ship architects, and attempted to herd them toward consensus. He drew upon the expertise not only of Humphreys and Fox, but also of John Wharton and perhaps to a lesser extent the younger Penrose.

Knox was troubled by the lack of consensus among his advisers. Writing to John Wharton in May, he asked about several aspects of the Humphreys design, and his questions provide some indication of the objections that were being raised. He asked:

Whether the model has too much or too little raising, and whether it is too sharp or full forward and abaft? Whether the proportion of the depth of hold, to the depth of beam, is just? What is your opinion as to the length of the ship? And what are the advantages and disadvantages of such long length?

If the principal objection to Humphreys's design was that it was different from what had prevailed in Europe, Humphreys's response was to say that the United States could not afford to imitate its rivals. "It is determined of importance to this country to take the lead in a class of ships not in use in Europe, which would be the only means of making our little navy of any importance. It would oblige other powers to follow us intact, instead of our following them. . . . It will in some degree give us the lead in naval affairs."

On April 15, little more than two weeks after the passage of the frigates bill, Secretary of War Knox sent his recommendations to the president. He advocated building frigates based on the Humphreys design, writing that they would "combine such qualities of strength, durability, swiftness of sailing, and force, as to render them equal, if not superior, to any frigate belonging to any of the European Powers." The president gave his assent the next day and urged that the work begin as quickly as possible.

By the end of the month, Humphreys had provided the War Office with a half model of the hull for the 44-gun frigates. The dimensions were 147 feet on the keel, 43 feet of beam, and 14 feet depth of hold. In June, Humphreys was informed that he had been appointed "Master Constructor of the United States." He would serve as a full-time salaried employee of the federal government, devoting all of his time to the construction of the frigates. Because Humphreys had not been compensated for the months of work he had already done on the building program, his date of employment was backdated two months, to May 1, 1794.

Knox had also been impressed by the young Englishman with the Royal Dockyard credentials who had criticized the dimensions of Humphreys's frigate. In July, the War Office employed Josiah Fox to serve as a draftsman to the man whose design he had disparaged. In spite of their professional differences, Humphreys at first professed to hold Fox in high regard, acknowledging that the younger man's training in England had made him "a first rate draftsman." But the arguments continued. Humphreys soon accused his colleague of drafting the models "according to his own opinion, so foreign to my own," and reassigned him to the inglorious work of "making moulds for cutting timber." The two Quaker shipwrights eventually came to hate one another so fervently that neither man could stand to be in the presence of the other. When Fox identified himself by the title "Naval Constructor" in a letter of July 1797, Humphreys detonated. "Sir," he replied,

> I cannot receive hereafter or attend to any directions from you, although directed by the Secretary of War, while you style yourself "Naval Constructor." You must know that my station in the service of the United States requires no directions from a "Naval Constructor." You also know that I am at the head of that Department, and when you direct a letter to me let it be done in style as "Clerk of the Marine Department." Whenever the Secretary deems my services no longer necessary, you may then to other persons assume such title as your vanity may suggest.

This response was addressed to "Mr. Josiah Fox, Clerk in the Marine Department, War Office."

THE QUICKEST AND LEAST EXPENSIVE way to obtain the frigates would be to purchase and convert existing merchantmen. The second option—to construct new ships—would clearly take longer and cost more. From the very beginning, however, the president and his advisers preferred building and launching to buying and converting. Building new ships would enable the War Office to enforce rigorous quality controls, and it would give Humphreys the opportunity to test his design theory from the laying of the keel to the crossing of the yards.

Washington wanted the six frigates built in six different seaports, to be chosen based on "wealth and populousness," both to spread the financial benefits and to ensure that a handful of Philadelphia Quakers would not become the nation's exclusive source of expertise in the construction of ships of war. Knox proposed to build the four larger ships specified in the act of Congress—the 44-gun frigates—in Boston, New York, Philadelphia, and Baltimore. Joshua Humphreys would build Philadelphia's 44-gun vessel in his Southwark shipyard. The two 36-gun frigates would be built in Portsmouth, New Hampshire, and Norfolk, Virginia. Washington ordered one change. He desired that one of the 44s be built in Norfolk, in his home state of Virginia. Baltimore would instead build one of the smaller ships.

Just a few years earlier, opponents of the Constitution had argued that no central government could effectively govern a territory the size of the original thirteen states. The building of the frigates would test that hypothesis. The largest procurement program in the brief history of the federal government would sprawl across the map in a 600-mile arc. Messages would take weeks or months to pass between the capital and the more distant sites.

Philadelphians were disappointed. They had evidently hoped that the entire building program would be carried out in the capital. A local sea captain complained that building the frigates in six cities appeared to "be going great lengths for the gratification of a few individuals." Writing to Knox, he pointed out that the War Office plan would require six separate agents and six master builders, and predicted (with impressive foresight) that the communication intervals would lead to time-consuming delays. Knox replied flatly that the president's decision would stand, adding that "it is just and wise to proportion . . . benefits as nearly as may be to those places or states which pay the greatest amount to its support" and that saving "a few thousand dollars in expenses will be no object compared with the satisfaction a just distribution would afford." It was an early example of pork barrel politics, before that term had even been coined.

The government tried to retain as much control over the far-flung building program as could reasonably be expected. The War Office did not merely parcel out contracts to private shipbuilding firms. It leased shipyards in each of the six seaports, transforming them into federal installations and calling them "Navy Yards." Master shipwrights, superintendents, clerks, craftsmen, and yard workers were hired as full-time salaried employees who were individually and directly accountable to the War Office. Merchants who were assumed to have the best knowledge of local vendors were engaged to act as procurement specialists or "agents." They would be paid a commission on all materials and supplies they purchased for the building program.

The master builders in each city received their instructions in July. They were told that they must "undeviatingly adhere" to the drafts and models sent from Philadelphia. To keep the program under budget, they were warned to "observe the highest degree of economy . . . whether of materials, or labor of the workmen." On the other hand, they would be personally responsible for making certain that "no materials, of any sort, enter into the construction of the said ship, but of the best quality."

Knox closed with a dangling carrot. Each seaport's performance in building its frigate would guide the War Office in "ascertaining where similar work may in future be done to most advantage . . . and the place where the business shall be best performed may derive permanent and great benefits."

WORD THAT A NEW NAVY was being assembled set off a frenzy of job seeking. Washington and the War Office were inundated with letters requesting officers' commissions for a son, a nephew, or a friend. The scenario was familiar. In the early years of the republic, the clamor for government patronage was relentless. From the day of his inauguration Washington had been under siege. The rich, the wellborn, and the politically connected naturally assumed they were entitled to special consideration, and they did not hesitate to ask for what they wanted. Friends, colleagues, relatives, and acquaintances begged to be appointed as postmasters, clerks, customs inspectors, and judges. They wrote the president directly, and they expected to hear back directly, with a personal reply written in his own hand. Responding to such letters consumed much of Washington's time.

The president was sensitive to the deep-rooted distrust of federal institutions, particularly in his home state of Virginia, where ratification of the Constitution would not have been possible without his support. In the hope of consolidating the prestige and authority of the government he had helped create, Washington always insisted upon exacting standards of merit and good character in all federal appointments. When he did not know an office seeker personally he consulted with trusted third parties, sometimes approaching the senators representing the candidate's state. He rejected applications even when it was socially or politically awkward to do so.

As a military man who had witnessed at firsthand the debacle of the Continental Navy, the president was aware that the quality of the naval officer corps was more important by far than the quality of the frigates. Good officers and bad ships would make a better navy than good ships and bad officers. When Washington was importuned in March by an old friend on behalf of his son, he responded bluntly: "It is impossible he can be contemplated by me as commander of one of the Frigates. . . . The most that can be done for your Son would be to make him a second or third Lieutenant, and even here I would not, at this time, be under any engagement until the matter is more unfolded than it is at present."

Congress had authorized the recruitment of a full complement of naval officers for each of the six frigates. At first, however, only six men—the captains—would be appointed. Each was to be employed to oversee the construction of one frigate. First on the captains' list was a naval veteran of the American Revolution, John Barry, who had commanded the Continental frigates *Raleigh* and *Alliance* in 1778–81. Barry was a Philadelphian who had many friends in Congress, and Washington relied on his advice in naming the other five captains. Barry reported to a friend that in spite of "powerful interest made here to get men appointed Captains in the Navy . . . the President from the first was determined to come as near to justice as was in his power. The appointments have given general satisfaction." Barry's influence was likely decisive in the selection of the five men who followed him. The question of seniority and relative rank was, as usual, a powder keg. Hoping to avoid internecine feuding, the War Office fixed the captains' order of seniority by the dates of their commissions in the earlier war. The last and lowest-ranking man on the list seems to have been appointed almost as an afterthought. Alone among them, he had never held a naval commission, although he had commanded several successful privateers in the Revolution. He was Thomas Truxtun, a native of Hempstead, Long Island—and although no one could have known it at the time, he would do more to shape the culture of the new officer corps than any of the men who stood above him on the roster.

Truxtun set out for Baltimore to prepare a shipyard for the construction of a 36-gun frigate. The road ran through Newark, Delaware, to a hamlet known as Head of Elk. There he was forced to change horses, because the Elk River crossing was via a small boat that the passengers pulled across, hand-over-hand, by hauling on a rope that was strung across the stream. From the far bank, it was a single long day's ride to the outskirts of Baltimore.

The city's principal shipbuilding district was concentrated in the area around Fells Point, but Truxtun preferred David Stodder's yard, a mile downriver, where more space could be had on reasonable terms. The yard was situated near the mouth of Harris Creek, in a wooded, secluded area east of town, but not so far that laborers could not be induced to join the work rolls. The facilities on the site seemed equal to the needs of a naval shipyard: there was a large and well-appointed blacksmith shop, sheds for the boat builders and mastwrights, and a serviceable road running into the town. Just across the Patapsco was Whetstone Point and the crumbling remains of a fortress that had been built during the Revolution. The yard was situated on the perimeter of a natural basin that would provide ample depth for the launch of a large ship.

Truxtun betrayed a northerner's instinctive disdain for the maritime and shipbuilding capabilities of the southern seaports. He told the War Office that Baltimore offered "no choice of Artificers, Labourers [are] scarce and indolent, every article [is] higher in point of price than in the other parts of the United States northeast of this." He estimated that the same ship could be built in Philadelphia for 20 percent less. Worse, Truxtun heard whispers circulated through the yard that the Master Constructor, David Stodder, had informed his subordinates that he did not like the Humphreys design and would ignore the draft that had been sent from Philadelphia. Truxtun, characteristically, confronted the man face-to-face and Stodder tamely retracted all he had said.

The first step in preparing the yard was to shore up the foundation for the keel blocks. Sand and gravel were dumped into holes dug in the soggy bank of the Patapsco. Massive wooden pilings, spaced about five feet apart, were driven into the holes. An oak "cap" was affixed to the top of each piling, with the grain in the wood running in the same direction as the slipway, to form a keel block. Together, these blocks would have to bear the weight of more than 1,000 tons of oak, pine plank, copper sheathing, and iron bolts. They were positioned in such a way as to slope toward the water at about one inch per foot. As the first keel timbers were delivered to the yard, they would be "scarfed" together in a series of carefully cut and precisely fitted joints, fixed in place with wedges and bolts. Once the keel was completed and faired, the framing of the ship could begin.

NORTH AMERICA WAS RICHLY ENDOWED with the raw materials needed for shipbuilding. Its forests seemed to offer a limitless supply of the world's most prized ship's timbers—northern white oak for planking and frame pieces, pine and spruce and cedar for masts and spars and deck beams. Navigable rivers provided access to the heavily forested interior and a means of transporting raw timber down to the sea. Hemp was grown for cordage, jute for caulking material, flax for sailcloth. Mines and blast furnaces produced pig iron for the blacksmiths, who turned out the wrought-iron bolts, hooks, bands, nails, spikes, pintles, gudgeons, and chain plates.

Washington and his advisers were in no mood to economize. The frigates would be built to last. The builders and yard workers, who had been conditioned to turn out vessels for merchants who wanted the work done quickly and cheaply, would have to unlearn some of their bad habits. Once the keels were laid down, the master builders, agents, and superintending captains at each building site would hold joint responsibility for quality control. But before construction work could even begin, the building materials—the timbers—had to be selected, cut out of the forests, and transported to the yards.

Humphreys was exacting in his specifications. The beams and decks should be made of Carolina pine, he wrote, and the planks of red cedar. But most important—here he was both explicit and insistent—key pieces of the frame, including the futtocks, knight heads, hawse pieces, bow timbers, stanchions, knees, transoms, and breasthooks, must be made of live oak.

Quercus virens, the southern live oak, is found only in the southeastern United States, and only in a twenty-mile-wide coastal zone stretching from southern Virginia to East Texas. It makes a dramatic and beautiful sight. John Muir, who knew what he was talking about, called it "the most magnificent planted tree I have ever seen." An early European naturalist wrote that live oak had "the appearance of a large apple or pear tree, [with a] . . . spreading picturesque top, and delicate olive shaped leaves of a deep shining green . . . one of the most magnificent and delightful shade trees in the world." A mature tree stands 40 to 70 feet high, but its branches can spread to a radius of 75 feet or more and its shade can cover half an acre. The trunk is enormous, reaching 20 feet in circumference, but it divides into branches 5 to 18 feet from the ground, giving the tree a squat, stocky appearance. The limbs separate from the trunk at right angles and extend horizontally, often low enough for a man standing on the ground to reach up and touch. As it grows, the live oak's vascular system is plugged up with a thick, viscid gum, making it dense and heavy—as heavy as 75 pounds per cubic foot, the heaviest oak there is. It seems impossible that the trunk can support the weight of so many huge branches, each weighing in the tons and each reaching outward at right angles. One only has to look at the tree—to contemplate its peculiar geometry—to gain some idea of its tremendous strength.

Not long after Europeans settled in North America, shipwrights recognized the potential of the live oak as a building material. Its extraordinary tensile strength and its resistance to both salt air and rot made it ideal for the key load-bearing sections of a ship's frame. In the joints formed between the trunks and limbs could be found angled pieces that served perfectly for the "short timbers"—the knees and futtocks on which so much of the ship's structural integrity and longevity depended. Carpenters prized its uniformity of substance, its straightness of fiber, its smooth consistency, its fine grains. Properly seasoned, it was said to have a life span five times that of white oak. But the shipyard workers also dreaded the extra work it took to cut, shape, and manipulate live oak, and they rolled their eyes whenever a new load of raw timber sections was brought into the yard. A nail driven into it was nearly impossible to extract. Axes bounced off it and saws moved back and forth across it again and again, making little or no discernible progress. Nothing took the sharpness out of a ship carpenter's tools as quickly as well-seasoned live oak.

In Philadelphia, Fox was busy producing the "moulds" which the cutting parties would use to match the size and shape of the timbers to the dimensions of the frigates. Molds were life-sized, three-dimensional models of each unique timber section, constructed of light wooden battens. The dimensions of each piece, taken from the original plan, were chalked onto the smooth, dark, painted floorboards of a "moulding loft," typically the second floor of a large warehouse. The dimensions were then taken off the floor, the battens cut and carefully numbered, and the entire package shipped unassembled to the forest. The cutting parties assembled the molds and used them to measure and cut the logs.

Obtaining the timber for the frigates would prove far more difficult, expensive, and time-consuming than anyone might have expected. Several hundred live oak trees were needed for each of the six ships. Because of the great size of Humphreys's model, the frame pieces could only be cut from the largest and oldest trees. To find the specified timber, the cutting parties would have to journey into the most remote and inhospitable part of the live oak's range—the uninhabited coastal islands of Georgia.

A Boston shipwright named John T. Morgan agreed to lead the first timber-cutting expedition. As a reward for taking on the arduous assignment, he hoped to be appointed master constructor of one of the frigates. The entire building program depended on his success. Arriving at St. Simon Island off the Georgia coast in early August 1794, Morgan was aghast at the conditions he found. The workmen, who had not yet arrived, would have to live in lean-tos on the edge of a swamp, pelted by never-ending rain, wallowing in mud, tormented by mosquitoes. "I have received the moulds," he wrote to Humphreys, "but have no hands, and if I had, it would not have been in my power to cut one stick as yet, for I have not seen ten fair days since I left you. . . . Never was so much rain known in this country." All the provisions would have to be sent in by sea. The expedition would need to be supplied with regular cargoes of food, blankets, and medical supplies. To haul the timber out of the forests, they would need to bring in heavy wagons, teams of oxen, and hay and grain to feed the animals.

On September 23, ninety "sober and industrious Axe-men and Ship-carpenters" sailed from New London, Connecticut. They arrived at St. Simon in mid-October. Within a week of their arrival, many of the New Englanders were prostrated with illness, probably malaria. A visitor compared their camp to an army field hospital after a battle. Of the men who survived, all but three decided that no amount of money could induce them to stay, and shipped out before Christmas. Morgan was among the sick. "I have been all but dead since the 4th of September," he complained to Humphreys in October. "I lost a fine lad, an apprentice, last Saturday with the fever. I have it now. Everybody is sick here and if I am to stay here 'til all the timbers is cut, I will be dead."

"If you was here," he added, "you would curse live oak."

In late October, Captain John Barry, who had been appointed commander of the yet-to-be-built Philadelphia frigate, took passage on the brig *Schuylkill* from Philadelphia to assess the state of affairs on St. Simon Island. The vessel anchored off the north shore and the captain went ashore at Gashayes Bluff. He found Morgan "with his two boys sick and not a man with him nor a stick of wood cut." Barry sent for reinforcements. Sixteen slaves were brought from the mainland (with wages presumably paid to their owners) and set to work clearing a road from the camp into the interior of the island.

As if his other problems were not enough, Morgan was concerned that he would not find live oak specimens large enough to satisfy Humphreys. "These moulds frighten me they are so long," he confessed. It was the "compass pieces"—the sharp-angled knees and breasthooks—that presented the greatest difficulty. Only the largest live oak trees—perhaps one in fifty—would serve the need. But the largest specimens were often the hardest to get at. The live oak stands were located along creeks and on the margins of swamps in the remote corners of the island. When cut timber could not be floated out, the logs had to be "baulked" by teams of oxen over the roots and underbrush. By December, Morgan reported that "all but four of the oxen have died."

Humphreys received his first load of live oak more than six months after work on the Philadelphia frigate had purportedly commenced and four months after Morgan had first set foot on St. Simon. He was "pleased with the timber generally." But he was less satisfied with the next shipment, which arrived two weeks later along with a box of native Georgia oranges for Mrs. Humphreys. "Your letter and box of oranges came safe to hand," he wrote Morgan, "but the oranges were so soured by the most infamous stem piece you sent that their flavor is lost. I am sure you must never have seen it otherwise you would not have sent it, for the most ignorant negro you have employed would have had sufficient understanding to know it would not do."

AT THIS EARLY STAGE, the ships were designated only as "Frigates A, B, C, D, E, and F." Because they were progeny of the new federal government, each of the proposed names on a list prepared by the War Office embodied an institution or symbol of the U.S. Constitution. Washington (perhaps thinking it was not a very important point) simply chose the first five names on the list: *United States*, *President*, *Congress*, *Constitution*, and *Constellation*. The sixth frigate, which would be built in Norfolk, Virginia, would later be christened *Chesapeake*.

As 1794 drew to a close, Secretary Knox prepared a progress report. Taking a defensive tone, he asked Congress to keep in mind that "few or no materials of any sort, either for construction or equipment, existed in their proper shape. That everything, if not to be created, was to be modified. That the wood of which the frames were to be made was standing in the forests; the iron for the cannon lying in its natural bed; and the flax and hemp, perhaps, in their seed." Promising that "the materials will soon be collected, and the building vigorously pushed," Knox predicted that the frigates would be completed within twelve months. As to the likely expense involved in completing the ships, he would make no prediction.

The final dimensions were not taken off the loft floors until the summer of 1795, and by the end of that year, no frigate was more than half-finished. Humphreys's Philadelphia frigate, the *United States*, was only partially framed, although nearly all of the needed timbers had arrived and been stored in the yard. Truxtun's Baltimore frigate, the *Constellation*, was merely a collection of timber lying here and there on the ground, roughly laid out in the manner in which it would be scarfed and bolted into the frame. It took an educated eye to see how this sculpture garden of raw, roughly shaped logs would be assembled into a structure resembling a ship. Knox faced the embarrassing task of informing Congress that, for the second consecutive year, twelve more months were needed to complete the frigates.

In February 1796, diplomatic negotiations with Algiers at last bore fruit. President Washington asked the Senate to ratify a treaty which, he said, would bring a "speedy peace and the restoration of our unfortunate fellow-citizens from a grievous captivity." The Algerian peace would cost Americans nearly a million dollars in bribes, ransom, and payments of tribute. Particularly humiliating was a stipulation that the United States would build a 32-gun frigate for the Dey and deliver it to him as a gift. The cost of the treaty was equivalent to 13 percent of the total annual expenditures of the federal government in that year. The Senate ratified it without debate.

On the same day, Washington sent a second message to Congress. A Republican amendment to the original law authorizing the frigates had required the building program to come to an immediate halt in the event of a truce with Algiers. The president now asked Congress to continue the work or risk "the derangement in the whole system." Congress chose to give him half of what he asked for. The three frigates that were most advanced—*United States* (Philadelphia), *Constellation* (Baltimore), and *Constitution* (Boston)— would be completed and launched. The remaining three would be left to rot on the stocks; eventually, perhaps, to be broken up for firewood.

CHAPTER THREE

On Saturday, March 4, 1797, the morning skies above Philadelphia were overcast and gray. John Adams, the newly elected president of the United States, left his lodgings at the St. Francis Hotel a little before noon and climbed into the new carriage he had recently purchased for a price of $1,500. The carriage, he told Abigail, was elegant enough for a president, but it was distinctly unpretentious when compared to his predecessor's luxurious coach, which had been pulled through the streets of the capital by a team of six horses and attended by liveried foot servants. Adams satisfied himself with two horses who were "young, but clever."

As he arrived at Congress Hall, the sun was breaking through the haze; the afternoon would be clear and brisk. He entered the first-floor chamber of the House of Representatives and took a seat on the dais next to Thomas Jefferson, who had just been sworn in as vice president. The closely packed crowd in the chamber and galleries waited for a moment in tense silence. After a pause, Washington entered, resplendent in a black velvet suit, trailing a cavalcade of clerks and servants, with an expression on his face that was, Adams wrote, "as serene and unclouded as the day."

Spectators and participants remarked upon the almost overpowering emotional intensity of the scene. Adams later said of the ceremony: "Everybody talks of the tears, the full eyes, the streaming eyes, the trickling eyes." The three men on the dais—the retiring president, the incoming president, and the incoming vice president—were the three most prominent American statesmen of the revolutionary generation. The ceremony would mark the nation's first peaceful transition of power. It was, Adams later said, strange and affecting to witness this essential ritual of democracy—to see the "sight of the sun setting full-orbit, and another rising (though less splendid)."

Washington's departure from office was the cause of great anxiety. For eight years, his imposing presence had been a comfort to his countrymen, who regarded him as the one man who could float above the increasingly bitter partisan warfare in the capital, and they feared for the survival of constitutional government in his absence. Adams and Jefferson were old friends but also political rivals; they had opposed one another in the election and Adams's victory had been narrow. The result thrust Jefferson into the inelegant position of acting simultaneously as vice president and leader of the opposition.

The issue that divided them was France. Two decades after the Declaration of Independence had been signed on this very spot, the United States faced its most dangerous foreign policy crisis since the Revolution. The government of Revolutionary France, angered by what it saw as American favoritism toward Great Britain, had begun licensing privateers to attack American shipping. The State Department had collected sworn statements detailing the seizure of three hundred American merchant ships, and reports of new captures were arriving every day. France had refused to recognize or accept the new American ambassador when he presented himself in Paris in December 1796. The French minister in Philadelphia, Pierre Adet, had publicly denounced the new American president as favoring an alliance with England.

Adams wore a pearl-gray broadcloth coat with a sword hanging from his belt and a cockaded hat under one arm. He did not wear a wig, as they were passing out of fashion. His thinning hair was powdered and pulled neatly back. He was five feet seven inches tall, about average height for a man of that era—but in company with Washington and Jefferson, each of whom stood more than six feet tall, he seemed shorter and fatter than he was. His detractors were in the habit of sneering at Adams's physique. But if it was true that Adams was overweight, it was also true that he was no stranger to hard physical labor, and he had a pair of farmer's thick, muscular wrists to prove it.

He had not slept well the previous night. He was visibly shaken and his hands trembled badly; he was concerned that he might even faint. He was no great orator and knew it. But he delivered his 2,300-word inaugural speech in a voice that was steady and filled with conviction.

The great danger to American independence, Adams said, came from abroad—from "the profligacy of corruption, and the pestilence of foreign Influence." Foreigners were plotting to manipulate the American democratic process, he warned, and if they were not resisted it would be they "who govern us, and not we, the people, who govern ourselves."

He spoke only briefly on the looming crisis with France. His tone was moderate and his sentiments balanced. He felt "a personal esteem for the French nation, formed in a residence of seven years, chiefly among them, and a sincere desire to preserve the friendship which has been so much for the honor and interest of both nations." But it was his "inflexible determination" to preserve American neutrality in the European war, and American shipping must be protected against the depredations of the belligerent nations.

Adams knew the crisis with France would define his presidency, his odds of winning reelection, and his place in history. He placed his first hope in a course of diplomacy and negotiation. A new treaty with France would, at a single stroke, avert a maritime war with the former ally and calm the waters of domestic politics. Adams was a veteran ambassador, however, and he knew the practical limits of diplomacy. A peaceful settlement might be unattainable. At a minimum, France must consent to a version of American neutrality that permitted Anglo-American trade to continue unmolested. Beyond that limit Adams would not go; he would not be bullied into offering unjust concessions. Writing that month, he confided in his son, John Quincy: "My entrance into office is marked by a misunderstanding with France, which I shall endeavor to reconcile, provided that no violation of faith, no stain upon honor, is exacted. But if infidelity, dishonor, or too much humiliation is demanded, France shall do as she pleases, and take her course. America is not *scared.*"

FRANCE WAS AMERICA'S FIRST ALLY. Its troops and ships and money had helped America win its independence. The French Revolution had seemed like a reflection and a vindication of the American Revolution. To many Americans, it was almost inconceivable that France could become an enemy. And yet, in 1796, the United States stood on the verge of fighting its first war, as a sovereign and independent nation, against none other than France. How could it have come to this?

In pledging its blood and treasure to the American revolutionary cause, as it did in 1778, France was chiefly interested in striking at Great Britain. Louis XVI and his ministers could not have been eager to establish the precedent of a successful rebellion against a sovereign. But it also is true that there was a powerful emotional and ideological bond between the two nations. France had been the cradle of many of America's revolutionary ideals, while America, to a generation of young and idealistic French aristocrats, was a kind of Arcadia that promised to remake and redeem civilization. The marquis de Lafayette was revered in America as a hero of the Revolutionary War. Lafayette, in turn, so loved Washington that he insisted upon referring to himself, in broken English, as "the General's son"; and he named his own son George Washington Lafayette. No American captured the French imagination like Benjamin Franklin, who, during his nine-year diplomatic sojourn in Paris, was adored by the French as a living symbol of New World innocence and integrity. He would later be exalted as a kind of patron saint of the French Revolution. A popular slogan was: "He snatched lightning from the sky and the scepter from tyrants."

In the summer and spring of 1789, American newspapers carried the first news of the revolutionary turmoil in Paris. First came the meeting of the Estates-General in May, then the National Assembly in June, and then the fall of the Bastille in July. In August, the *Declaration of the Rights of Man and Citizens* was ratified, and Americans could not fail to note its resemblance to the Declaration of Independence and the Bill of Rights, upon which it was largely based. In its early, temperate stages, from the spring of 1789 through the fall of 1791, the French Revolution was greeted with near-universal rejoicing in America. The beloved Lafayette was conspicuously at the center of the events unfolding in Paris, where he served as vice president of the National Assembly and commander of the revolutionary militia. He sent George Washington the key to the Bastille, engraved with the words: "It is a tribute which I owe to you, as a son to my adoptive father, as an aide-de-camp to my General, as a Missionary of Liberty to its Patriarch." On the streets of American cities and towns, a rush of nostalgia brought back all of the old symbolism and music and pageantry of the American Revolution. Liberty poles were erected in town squares, just as they had been in 1776; men wore liberty hats, just as they had in 1776. At festivals and civic feasts, the Stars and Stripes appeared alongside the new Tricolor of Revolutionary France: a red, white, and blue flag designed by Lafayette himself to replace the royal white banner of the Bourbons.

Beginning in mid-1792, however, there were disturbing reports of mob savagery on the streets of Paris. In August, a crowd gathered outside the Palace of the Tuileries, where the royal family was being held in closely guarded splendor, and howled for the king's head. They slaughtered some five hundred of the king's Swiss Guards and paraded their severed heads on pikes. Lafayette was denounced and forced to flee across the border, where he was captured by the Austrians and thrown into jail. In September, as foreign armies massed on the border, rumors of a domestic counterrevolutionary plot circulated among the *sans-culottes* of the Parisian mobs. More than a thousand prisoners, among them women, children, and priests, were dragged virtually at random from their cells and hacked to pieces. The princesse de

Lamballe, a friend and confidante of the queen, was raped, murdered, and mutilated; her head was exhibited on a pike beneath Marie-Antoinette's window. The duc de La Rochefoucauld, the man who had first translated the Declaration of Independence, was snatched from his carriage and stoned to death as his wife and aging mother watched helplessly.

The details of the massacres were so outlandish that many Americans refused to believe them. Jefferson maintained that they should be dismissed as English propaganda. But in late March 1793, shortly after Washington was sworn in for his second term as president, news arrived in Philadelphia that could not be so easily ignored. Louis XVI had been sent to the guillotine in the public square named for his father. As his severed head was lifted from the basket into which it had fallen, cries of "Vive la Republique!" had resounded through the streets of Paris and "every hat was in the air."

Republicans justified the act. Madison said that if Louis "was a Traytor, he ought to be punished as well as another man," and Jefferson agreed that monarchs should be "amenable to punishment like other criminals." On the streets of American cities, liquor-fueled demonstrations provided entertainment to those who would otherwise pass their leisure hours in boredom. French revolutionary anthems such as *La Marseillaise* and *Ça Ira* were performed nightly in the theaters. Men and women addressed one another as "Citizen" and "Citess." Philadelphians lined up to see an exhibit in which a wax likeness of Louis was shoved into a mock-up of the guillotine. The audience was thrilled to watch "the knife fall, the head drop and the lips turn blue." In Boston, twelve men armed with cleavers performed a ritualistic slaying of an "Ox of Aristocracy." The animal's head and horns were erected on a pike in Liberty Square.

Washington, Hamilton, and the Federalists worried that this upsurge of pro-revolutionary sentiment would alienate Britain and pull the United States into the war. Popular demonstrations were mostly harmless, but some of the demonstrators were threatening to take direct action. Democratic societies passed resolutions deploring "the cruel and unjust war carried on by the combined powers of Europe against France" and declaring that "America is implicated in the fate of the French republic." Francophile militias drilled on public greens and primed their old artillery fieldpieces. John Adams wondered if there were more rounds fired in America to celebrate the French victory at Valmy than the French army itself had fired in battle. In the seaports, sea officers and shipwrights outfitted privateers to sail against British merchantmen. The British ambassador warned that if American harbors were converted into bases for French privateering, the Royal Navy would retaliate.

Washington's answer was the historically famous Neutrality Proclamation of April 22, 1793, which decreed that American citizens must observe "a conduct friendly and impartial towards the belligerent powers." Any American found "committing, aiding, or abetting hostilities" against either side in the conflict would be prosecuted.

Before the ink on the proclamation was dry, however, a new ambassador named Edmond-Charles Genet arrived from France with a sheaf of three hundred privateering commissions. Disembarking at Charleston, Genet commissioned four privateers within a week of his arrival. They were christened the *Republican*, the *Sans-Culotte*, the *Anti-George*, and the *Patriote Genet*. They would be manned and officered by American citizens. Genet empowered Charleston's French consul to condemn and sell any British prizes that might be brought into port. A week later, the French frigate *Embuscade* dropped anchor at Gray's Ferry in the Delaware River with a captured British merchantman, the *Grange*, in company. Jefferson described the scene to James Monroe: "Upon her coming into sight, thousands & thousands of the yeomanry of the city crowded & covered the wharves. Never before was such a crowd seen there, and when the British colours were seen reversed, and the French flag flying above them they burst into peals of exultation."

Though the Secretary of State was sympathetic to the French cause, the *Grange* had been captured within American territorial waters, and he had no choice but to inform Genet that the vessel must be restored to her owners. Genet grandly announced that he would do as Jefferson asked, but only as a voluntary gesture "to convince the American government of our deference and friendship." The Treaty of 1778, he said, gave him the right to carry on privateering operations against Britain, and he intended to do just that. On July 6, the governor of Pennsylvania reported that a French privateer, the *Little Democrat*, was making ready to sail from Philadelphia. Secretaries Hamilton and Knox favored erecting a battery of guns on Mud Island, manned by men from the Pennsylvania militia, to prevent her from dropping down the river. Before such action could be taken, however, the *Little Democrat* weighed anchor and dropped downriver to Chester. When Jefferson asked Genet to stop the ship from sailing, he refused.

In the cabinet meetings that followed, it was decided to call upon the French government to recall the minister. The point, as it turned out, was moot. The Girondin faction which had sent Genet to America was driven from power by a *coup d'état* engineered by the rival Jacobins. When the news arrived in America, Genet asked for—and received—permission to remain in exile in the United States.

With the Jacobin "Grand Terror" in the autumn of 1793, France surrendered to its worst demons. The Jacobins saw their enemies everywhere, and their answer was judicial mass murder. Everyone was suspected; anyone could be denounced. Summary executions at the guillotine were a daily event. Records gave proof of the mechanical efficiency of the device. On one occasion, thirty-two heads were struck off in twenty-five minutes; on another, twelve heads in five minutes. In Paris, the corpses piled up in the streets and the blood overflowed the gutters, posing a sanitary emergency. In Lyon, the Jacobins grew impatient with the pace of the guillotine. The condemned were simply lashed together and bombarded with cannon fire. The executioners then moved in and finished off the survivors with knives, bayonets, and swords.

American conservatives recoiled in disgust. The French Revolution, they argued, had spiraled into a meaningless cycle of terror and counterterror that would end in autocracy. "Danton, Robespierre, Marat, etc. are furies," John Adams wrote his son. "Dragon's teeth have been sown in France and will come up as monsters." The so-called Whiskey Rebellion of 1794, an abortive tax revolt led by a ragged band of impoverished frontiersmen in western Pennsylvania, seemed to confirm Federalist fears that the turmoil was being imported into America by homegrown radicals. To put down the insurrection, Washington raised an army of thirteen thousand militiamen, a force far larger than any he had commanded in the American Revolution. The rebellion petered out before the army arrived on the scene, but the episode reinforced the Federalists' premise that anarchy was endemic to democracy. "We might have seen the banks of the Delaware covered with human carcasses and its waters tinged with blood," warned a Federalist editor; " . . . and even the head of our admired and beloved President rolling on the scaffold."

Fearing and reviling what the French Revolution had become, Federalists hoped to reduce the growth of French influence in America. Whatever its flaws, Great Britain offered the chief alternative. Conservatives found much to admire in Britain's example of a constitutional government that balanced the interests of monarch, nobles, and commoners. John Jay went to London as Washington's envoy in the hopes of negotiating a treaty that would avert war and reduce Anglo-American hostilities at sea. The Jay Treaty was an act of submission that in effect recognized British naval supremacy and set out the rules by which American vessels could prosper in the carrying trade. News of the treaty sparked a political brushfire. Jefferson derided it as a "monument of venality," and Madison said it had been forced on the nation by a formidable combination of interests: "the exertions and influence of

Aristocracy, Anglicism, and mercantilism," directed by "the Banks, the British Merchants, the insurance Companies." Jay was burned in effigy in cities and towns throughout the nation. When Hamilton defended the treaty at a riotous meeting in New York, a protester threw a rock which struck him in the head. Washington supported the treaty, ensuring its ratification in the Senate in August 1795.

Though the Jay Treaty headed off a rupture with Great Britain, it guaranteed that there would be a rupture with France. The French interpreted the treaty as a formal alliance that broke the letter of the old 1778 Franco-American alliance, and as a personal betrayal of the most base and insidious kind. The Directoire, the latest revolutionary government of France, decreed in the summer of 1796 that France would "treat neutral vessels, either as to confiscation, as to searches, or capture, in the same manner as they shall suffer the English to treat them." The American minister in France, James Monroe, was informed of the decree five days after it had taken effect. The French policy, he was told, would be one of simple parallelism. America was no longer the ally it had once been; therefore, the new policy would be to treat America as no different from any other neutral, and to deal with the nation as it had consented to allow the enemy to deal with it. As an added measure of hostility, the French ambassador to American was recalled and none other appointed. Diplomatic relations were broken off completely.

The real crisis, however, was not in France's official policy toward the United States, but the avarice of its privateers and the corruption of its prize courts, both in France and in the French West Indies. Essentially, the French practiced high-seas piracy, thinly disguised as national policy. Secretary of State Thomas Pickering reported that in the year 1795, French privateers had captured 316 American merchantmen. He protested in vivid terms the treatment of captured American seamen, of embargoes illegally laid upon American shipping by local authorities in Bordeaux, and of the non-payment of bills run up by colonial officers in the West Indian colonies. The French depredations were increasing both in frequency and in violence. As the privateersmen realized that they had nothing to fear from an American naval force, they drew closer to U.S. shores. When the spring sailing season commenced in 1797, privateers were hovering just off the coast, even sailing into rivers and bays, and taking ships within sight of land. Hostile privateers were hove to at the mouth of Delaware Bay; in the waters just off Sandy Hook in New Jersey; in the placid waters of Long Island Sound; and in the lee of Block Island. There was nothing the United States could do to stop them.

THE CONFLICT WITH REVOLUTIONARY France was more than a foreign policy crisis. It was a domestic political crisis that polarized the American public and threatened to end in disunion or even civil war. In the minds of Jefferson and his followers, the years 1776 and 1789 would be forever linked in history. The two revolutions constituted a break from the feudal past, a rejection of all tyrants and their supplicants. Other nations would inevitably follow. "This ball of liberty, I believe most piously, is now so well in motion that it will roll around the globe," wrote Jefferson. He saw England as "the dead hand of the past"—a fortress of corruption, repression, militarism, privilege, and monarchy. Though he did not advocate entering the war on France's side, Jefferson advocated a pro-French version of American neutrality, and held the Federalists responsible for provoking French aggression by their evident preference for England in the war raging in Europe.

Adams, by contrast, felt little affection for the French and no confidence in their revolution. He found them passionate, erratic, and undependable. He had experienced at firsthand the subterfuge and doublespeak that seemed to permeate French diplomatic culture, and had concluded that corruption and cynicism were endemic to French society. He held a common prejudice against their Catholicism. He had always been skeptical of the French Revolution, even in the heady days of 1789 and 1790, and construed its later, bloodstained excesses as a vindication of his original instincts. Most of all, he was persuaded that the French were incapable of self-governance, and that their revolution would end in despotism. "The French are no more capable of a republican government than a snowball can exist a whole week in the streets of Philadelphia under a burning sun," he told Elbridge Gerry.

Adams had hoped that he and Jefferson would put aside their political differences and make good their old friendship. He would be disappointed. Jefferson foresaw that the French crisis would destroy Adams politically. "I know well that no man will ever bring out of that office the reputation he carries into it," he wrote. "The honeymoon would be as short in that case as in any other, & its moments of ecstasy would be ransomed by years of torment & hatred." Washington had been a stabilizing force; his stature and universal popularity had allowed him to soar above the partisan rift. With his retirement, Jefferson predicted, "the next president of the United States will only be the president of a party." He and Madison planned to have nothing to do with the new administration. They would bide their time and wait for the political windstorm to blow Adams away.

————

HAD THE NEWLY SWORN PRESIDENT felt an urge to take in the Philadelphia skyline that March, he could have crossed the courtyard to the State House and climbed three sets of stairs and two ladders to the top of the belltower. From that altitude he would have looked down on an urban landscape of steeply canted shingled rooftops and brick chimneys, interrupted here and there by a white wooden church steeple. A quarter mile to the west, the city petered out into a neighborhood of brick kilns and burying fields, and beyond that a bucolic suburb of meadows, ponds, and orchards. To the north, beyond the low hills of the Northern Liberties, the marshlands were spanned by a long causeway, often crowded with Conestoga wagons bringing farm produce into the city from the backcountry north of Germantown. To the south was Moyamensing Township, the future site of South Philadelphia—a long, rolling stretch of wheat fields and pastures enclosed by post-and-rail fences and dotted with farmhouses.

To the east was the wide, lazy, muddy river. From Federal Street all the way up to Shackamaxon, where it shoaled and turned east, scarcely a yard of riverfront was left vacant. Ships docked yardarm to yardarm at the wharves, their crosstrees perched above the windowless storehouses along Front Street. The roadstead beyond was congested with other ships riding to the tide in eight-fathom water. Cutters, barges, shad boats, and two-masted shallops plied the waters in the main anchorage, selling provisions directly to the larger merchantmen riding at anchor in the stream.

The less valuable real estate at the southern extremity of the riverfront was the shipbuilding district, known as Southwark. Frames and hulls in various stages of advancement stood on the stocks, perpendicular to and inclined toward the river, and evil-looking columns of thick, black smoke rose from the tar pits. The largest hull by far was the enormous shape of the frigate *United States*. Though her keel had been laid down almost two and a half years earlier, she was still on the stocks, looming like a cathedral over the rooftops of the surrounding houses and taverns. Her hull, now completely planked, was braced upright by heavy stanchions and enveloped in scaffolding. Her bulwarks rose 60 feet above Swanson and Christian Streets—about the same height as Adams's putative vantage point in the State House belltower. From that distance—about a mile and a half—she would have appeared pale and gleaming in the afternoon sun. This was Saturday, a work day, so teams of caulkers and carpenters would have been swarming over her.

Joshua Humphreys's yard was the scene of feverish activity. Supplies needed to complete the frigate were brought through the gate in drays, carts, stages, and wagons; materials were unloaded onto the dock from shallops, barges, and flat-bottomed durham boats. Humphreys made meticulous daily records in his account books: buckets of paint and pitch; sheets of copper; assorted cables, blocks, and anchors; buckets of bolts and nails; racks of iron hooks and assorted fasteners; lengths of canvas and assorted cordage. As the storehouses overflowed, newly arrived equipment and supplies were dumped in makeshift heaps in any vacant corner of the yard.

Caulkers were hard at work sealing the hull. Fragments of discarded rope ends were smeared with hot tar, then pounded with mallets into the seams between the strakes, and finally paid with layers of hot pitch. Others were hurrying to complete the frigate's inboard works—installing the interior decks and bulkheads, planking over the ceilings, fairing the exposed edges of the frame timbers. Twelve white oak "diagonal riders" were being seated in the keel and through-bolted to the interior of the hull. This was another of Humphreys's controversial innovations, which he believed would add longitudinal strength to the hull and diminish the amount of "hogging" (downward sagging of the bow and stern, which would cause the ship's midsection to arch upward like a hog's back) that would occur after the launch.

The *United States* was one of the city's most popular sightseeing destinations. From the High Street Wharf, pedestrians walked a mile south along the river on Front Street and arrived at the entrance to the yard, where her bows towered above their heads like the wall of a medieval castle. She was by far the largest ship ever built in Philadelphia. Seamen and travelers could boast that they had seen larger—but even a 2,000-ton English ship of the line would cut a smaller profile when she was afloat, with her keel three or four fathoms beneath the waterline.

Given that the *United States* was the single most expensive military asset in American history, security was amazingly slack. Tourists strolled into the yard as if they owned the place. They mounted the scaffolding, climbed into the inboard works, and chatted with the tradesmen. The danger of sabotage did not escape Joshua Humphreys's imagination. One phosphorous match, struck in the right place, would reduce the entire project to an enormous heap of ashes. The War Office sent a detachment of soldiers to stand guard over the frigate, but Humphreys was not satisfied. The guards, he noted, seemed to spend most of the day drinking. Instead of holding back the civilian hordes that descended on the yard each day, they simply collected and pocketed payments of admission. When they grew too bored or too drunk to stay at their posts, they wandered off. That March, Humphreys wrote the secretary to complain:

It is with great regret I have to inform you of the many irregularities in the guard placed for the safety of the frigate. . . . Last Saturday morning I found several of them drunk. This led me to watch their conduct closely. That evening, about nine o'clock, the sentinel was found asleep. About ten no one [was] on duty, he had left his post for a relief, tho' contrary to a late struck order. Between eleven and twelve o'clock, no one [was] on duty, the musket then left in the duty box, which I brought up to the house, where it now remains. This conduct, my duty would not permit me to pass in silence.

Among the curious were many of Philadelphia's most prominent citizens. Humphreys was always on hand to conduct guided tours for the many federal officials, members of Congress, and assorted grandees who visited the yard. Among his best-known guests were George and Martha Washington, and later John Adams. Humphreys was an unabashed Federalist partisan. His loyalty might have had something to do with his pecuniary interests, since the Federalists were the party of the navy as well as the party in power. But Humphreys's instinctive deference to high-ranking officials was also typical of the era in which he lived. In the 1790s, there was no broadly accepted notion of a "loyal opposition," and it was not anomalous for Humphreys, or others like him, to regard critics of the commander in chief as essentially treasonous. It was against this backdrop of partisan acrimony that the beating of Benjamin Franklin Bache took place on April 5, 1797.

Bache, a maternal grandson of Benjamin Franklin, was editor of the notorious opposition *Aurora General Advertiser*, published six days a week in a two-story print shop at 112 High Street. The newspaper's subscriber base of 1,700 did not begin to quantify its influence, because Bache's editorials were reprinted to the letter in other opposition newspapers throughout the country. Bache had ridiculed President George Washington's imperial style—his "pompous carriages, splendid feasts, and tawdry gowns"—as the "apish mimicry of Kingship." He wrote that Washington's military incompetence during the Revolution would have lost the war, had Bache's illustrious grandfather not persuaded the French to intervene. He went so far as to accuse Washington of having committed battlefield atrocities during the French and Indian War, four decades earlier. During the 1796 presidential campaign, Bache supported Jefferson over Adams, mocking the latter's "sesquipedality of belly." Federalists reserved a special loathing for Bache, whom they derided as "Young Lightning Rod"—an "infamous scoundrel" and purveyor of "malignant falsehoods."

On the afternoon of April 5, a month after Adams's inauguration, Bache and two friends walked to Southwark and were given permission by the guard to go aboard the *United States*. They climbed the scaffolding and stepped onto the gun deck, stopped to admire the view of the river from the stern galleries of the captain's cabin, and then climbed up the companionway to the quarterdeck. At that moment someone struck a bell, and at the signal, "some 12 or 15 of the workmen came upon the deck . . . and stood along the gunwale." Bache did not see the attack coming:

> I was thus standing, alone as I thought, still looking at the bell, when I felt a violent blow on my head. My first thought was that something had fallen on me; I then received a second blow, and immediately after, perceived the cowardly ruffian behind me in a menacing attitude. Stunned as I was with the violence of the two blows, which must have struck from behind, I was unable to defend myself against a third, much less to return them. . . . The perpetrator of this act of cowardly assassination, I have since been informed, is HUMPHREYS, son of the builder of the frigate.

The beating had been administered by Clement Humphreys, Joshua's oldest son and apprentice. Bache's friends, heavily outnumbered, carried the injured journalist from the yard. He spent the next two days at home in bed, convalescing.

DURING THE FINAL WEEKS before launch, work on the frigate accelerated to an almost frantic pace. Painstaking bookkeeping was essential to prevent equipment and supplies from walking out of the yard, and Humphreys's account books recorded the distribution of an extraordinary array of materials and supplies to the working parties. Nails and spikes and twopenny jacks were distributed by the thousands, along with scupper pumps, barrels of pitch, caulking thrumbs, hides of leather, assorted chizzles and gimblets, pails of putty, and panes of glass. The books made note of which tools were handed out each morning—mauls, beveling hammers, claw hammers, caulking mallets, screw augers, and smoothing planes—and which were checked back in at night. The carpenter and his mates went to work installing shelves and lockers in the gun room and drilling holes on the orlop deck for the hooks from which the seamen's hammocks would swing. The sound of hammers striking nails began a little after daybreak each day and scarcely let up until nightfall, as the men nailed lining on the air ports, canvas on ladders, cleats to secure the kentledge (iron ballast), and tin lining to the freshwater pumps. Four stop-blocks and two pounds of spikes were distributed to secure the figurehead; ten pounds of spikes were distributed "for the purpose of securing guns in a gale of wind."

As the days grew longer and warmer, sightseers descended on the yard in ever greater numbers. Again Humphreys complained to the War Office:

> It will be absolutely necessary to have the wharf kept clear of the inhabitants. I know of no other way than by increasing the guard, which in my opinion ought to consist of at least forty [men], with good officers. I wish you will please take the matter into your consideration and order such force as you may think proper.

He informed the War Office that he intended to launch the *United States* at high water on the afternoon of May 10. The great hull now had a clean, finished look: the wooden trunnels had been trimmed and capped, so that the strakes ran fair and smooth all round the ship. Two huge iron anchors had been sunk into the ground and secured to the frigate with cables lashed through the hawseholes and hove taut to the capstan. All the launching accoutrements—the bilge ways, blocking cross pieces, fore and aft wedges—were primed and fitted.

The launch would be one of the greatest spectacles that the city of Philadelphia had ever seen. At daybreak on the tenth, dozens had already shown up to lay claim to the best vantage points around the yard, and by late morning the streets south of town were choked with an "immense concourse of spectators." They came on foot, on horseback, in carriages—a crush of humanity pressing south on Front and Water Streets, lining the wharves, clambering over the rooftops, craning their necks from every patch of unoccupied grass along the riverbank. The uniformed companies of the Pennsylvania militia were on parade, and a park of artillery was ready to fire a salute as the ship entered the river. Some reports put the crowd at more than thirty thousand. Whatever the number, it was certainly one of the largest ever assembled in North America.

On the river, riding at anchor a short distance off the bank, was a fleet of private yachts and pleasure boats, some colorfully decked out with flags and bunting. The brig *Sophia* had sailed down the river with three cabinet officers—the secretaries of State, War, and Treasury—all aboard.

Humphreys had good reason to be anxious. Launching a hull the size of the *United States*, even under the best possible conditions, brought daunting physical forces into play. Since it had never been done before, at least in Philadelphia, the procedure was almost by definition an experiment. He worried about the strangely low level of the water: a strong northwest breeze had prevented the whole volume of the flood tide from coming up the river. If he had erected the slipways at too steep an incline, the ship might descend too rapidly and strike the riverbed. On the other hand, if the slipways were too green, or not greased amply with tallow and oil, or if the air was too humid, the frigate might stick to the ways and refuse to budge. Success depended on an exact sequence of perfectly timed events involving more than a hundred men stationed on the ground, under the hull, and on the spar deck. A failure, witnessed by virtually the entire population of Philadelphia, including most of the ranking officers of the federal government, would be a calamity and a personal humiliation from which the Quaker shipwright might never recover.

A few minutes after one o'clock, at the very height of the tide, Humphreys ordered the restraining blocks removed from under the keel. Almost at once, prematurely, the 1,500-ton mass of oak, iron, and copper shifted and began to travel toward the river. Spectators let out a cheer and the militia fired an abortive salute. At that instant Humphreys grasped that there was nothing he or any other mortal being could do to arrest the launch—the frigate wanted to go, and she *was* in fact going. The critical thing was to knock away the remaining spur shores before they could damage the hull, and he shouted for this to be done. The men on deck, understanding that the launch was underway, sprinted with their axes to cut away the lashings. About thirty workmen were stationed under the keel blocks—they lay down and hugged the ground as the great shape of the hull rumbled over them. None was injured. The frigate plunged into the river, pushing a wave of water out into the stream, and the spectator boats must have heaved and strained at their moorings.

Humphreys announced that he was delighted with the launch. After going aboard and taking measurements, he found, to his "unspeakable satisfaction," no more than one and a quarter inches of hogging—far less than the two feet that was common for ships of that size. His report did not mention—and the spectators apparently did not notice—that the frigate had indeed struck the riverbed on launching, severely damaging her keel and rudder braces.

A full hour after the launch, a newspaper reported, Front and Second Streets were still choked with crowds returning to the city.

DEVOTED AS PRESIDENT ADAMS was to the navy, he was more devoted to the first lady. He skipped the launch of the *United States* because he expected Abigail to arrive that day from Massachusetts. Leaving the capital early in the morning, he met her that afternoon on the road about twenty-five miles north of the city. She climbed down from her carriage and climbed up into his; they stopped for dinner in Bristol and rolled into the city at sunset.

Distressing news from Europe had arrived in the weeks after his inauguration. The French Directory had formally abrogated the Treaty of 1778. An American ambassador, Charles Cotesworth Pinckney, had been expelled from the country. Several new decrees had expanded the French war against American commerce. Any English goods found aboard an American ship, contraband or not, would be confiscated. American vessels were required to carry a *rôle d'équipage*—a list, in a specified format, of all crew members. If a skipper could not produce the list, or if it was not formatted perfectly, the ship and her cargo would be confiscated. Any American sailor found serving on an enemy ship could be hanged as a pirate. French warships and privateers could now seize American vessels on any one of several flimsy pretexts, no matter what their cargoes or their destinations. They would be brought into French harbors where notoriously corrupt Admiralty Courts would condemn them in cursory proceedings. France had effectively declared a worldwide, all-out *guerre de course*—a war against American trade.

Adams found his options limited. Events were moving quickly. A declaration of war against France might be justified, but even with one of the frigates afloat at last, it would be months before she could be fitted for sea. The *United States*, formidable as she might be, did not comprise a navy. Moreover, even if the nation had been prepared for war militarily, it was not close to being prepared politically. There was still no national consensus in favor of war with France, and Republicans were convinced that the entire crisis had been manufactured as a means of maneuvering the country into an alliance with Great Britain. A premature declaration of war would probably prompt a secession movement in the south and west.

Adams sought and received the advice of his Federalist cabinet, all holdovers from Washington's administration. Each of the secretaries recommended the same course of action: to make one last, public attempt at a diplomatic reconciliation. (Their advice was unanimous because they had all sought and received guidance from Alexander Hamilton, now a New York lawyer in private practice.) The president was persuaded. A fresh diplomatic overture, if successful, would end the crisis; if it failed, it would nurture popular sentiment for a fight. While awaiting the outcome, the nation could get itself on a war footing.

With his chosen policy in hand, Adams called Congress back to the capital for a special session to begin on May 15. From every state, north and south, legislators slogged back to Philadelphia over roads that had been assaulted by heavy spring rains; as the date approached they straggled into town, exhausted and dirty. On the appointed day, Congress was still short of a quorum; but by the sixteenth, enough members had arrived. Adams delivered his opening address at noon.

France, Adams declared, had "inflicted a wound in the American breast." Its refusal to receive an ambassador "is to treat us neither as allies, nor as friends, nor as a sovereign state." It and the rest of the world must be persuaded that "we are not a degraded people, humiliated under a colonial spirit of fear and a sense of inferiority, fitted to be the miserable instruments of foreign influence, and regardless of national honor, character, and interest."

A three-member bipartisan peace commission would sail for France immediately to make one last attempt at negotiation. In the interim, the country should strengthen its armed forces. The militia should be reorganized into a provisional army and three new permanent regiments should be established—one each of cavalry, infantry, and artillery. But the greatest effort and expense, Adams said, must be reserved for the navy:

> Our seacoasts, from their great extent, are more easily annoyed and more easily defended by a Naval force than any other. With all the materials our country abounds; in skill, our naval architects and navigators are equal to any; and commanders and seamen will not be wanting. . . .
>
> . . . it appears to me necessary to equip the frigates, and provide other vessels of inferior force to take under convoy such merchant vessels as shall remain unarmed.

If Adams's inaugural ceremony two months earlier had created a feeling of bipartisan amity, the special session broke the spell. Republicans, dismissing the significance of the peace mission, were convinced that the president was pushing for a naval buildup as a means to provoke the French into a full-scale war. The speech, Bache wrote in the *Aurora*, was a war cry let out by "a man divested of his senses." He wondered if Adams had "fed upon pepperpot these three weeks past in order to bring his nerves to a proper anti-Gallican tone." Referring to the narrow electoral margin of the previous November's election, he doubted whether "the President by Three Votes" had a mandate to drag the country against its will into war—and reverting to one of his favorite themes, he mocked Adams as "His Rotundity."

As one of the three diplomatic commissioners, Adams chose his old friend Elbridge Gerry, a man who still commanded the respect and trust of Jefferson and the Republicans. Writing to Gerry, Adams denied the Republican charge that he was pushing the country toward war. "As to going to war with France lightly, I know of nobody who is willing for it—but she has already gone to war with us lightly. She is at war with us, but we are not at war with her."

THE PRESIDENT'S NAVAL PROGRAM sailed through the Federalist Senate, but the House was still closely divided. The nominal breakdown of Federalists and Republicans was 56–48, but some members were almost always absent and others had a bent for crossing party lines. House Republicans, counting heads, saw they did not have the votes to deny Adams his navy outright, so they resorted to parliamentary delaying tactics and crippling amendments in the hope of accomplishing much the same thing.

James Madison had relinquished his seat and gone home to Virginia, leaving a void that no other Republican seemed to have the intellectual powers or political clout to fill. But a second-term congressman from western Pennsylvania was emerging as his natural successor. Albert Gallatin was a native-born Genevan who had emigrated to America in the hope of making his fortune. He had first set foot in Boston, in 1780, at the age of nineteen, and shortly thereafter migrated to western Pennsylvania. He had entered politics as a delegate to the Constitutional Convention in Harrisburg, where he was an opponent of ratification. Elected to the House in 1794, Gallatin's signature issue was his insistence upon a rapid pay-down of the national debt, which he regarded as the root of all political evil. He set up the Ways and Means Committee as a counterweight to the treasury, and with his formidable grasp of finance he was able to throw light on Hamilton's obfuscation of the true extent of federal borrowing.

On June 24, Gallatin rose to his feet and objected to the completion and arming of the frigates. To maintain them would cost some $350,000 a year, and to man them would cost the treasury another $500,000 per year. The nation, said Gallatin, could ill afford these tremendous expenses. Calculating that six or even ten frigates could not convoy more than 5 percent of American merchant trade, Gallatin argued that "they could, therefore, be of little use, but might be the means of producing the greatest evil to the country." Republicans moved to have the entire question of the navy referred to a committee where it could be studied and debated, perhaps forestalling action until the fall session. When that tactic was defeated, they offered an amendment to limit the deployment of the frigates to American territorial waters, which also failed.

"An Act providing a Naval Armament" was signed into law on July 1. The bill passed the House by the apparently commanding margin of 78–25, but the Republican amendments had knocked out the president's request for nine sloops of war and imposed a one-year time limit on the law. The legislation authorized the fitting out and manning of three frigates and spelled out details of personnel, pay, and rations. Congress appropriated $200,000 to complete and arm the frigates and $100,000 for pay and provisions. Federalists were disappointed. After all the talk of a major defense buildup, the measures adopted that summer seemed anticlimatic. The British minister in Philadelphia said that "every measure of warlike preparation or internal defence has been adopted with an excess of caution, and provided for with a niggardly hand."

As the recess approached, the heat settled in oppressively and the city became, in the first lady's words, a "bake house." The partisan bitterness reached new heights. When John Adams learned at third hand that his vice president was criticizing his policy toward France, he exploded: "It is evidence of a mind soured, yet seeking for popularity and eaten to a honeycomb with ambition, yet weak, uninformed, and ignorant." Jefferson professed to regret the general decline in civility: "Men who have been intimate all their lives cross the street to avoid meeting and turn their heads another way, lest they should be obliged to touch their hats."

AFTER THE GROUNDING of the *United States* on launch, Secretary of War James McHenry was concerned that the mishap might be repeated in Baltimore. The War Office ordered Humphreys to tear himself away from his duties for a few days to travel south and "consult on the best Method to be pursued in Launching the Frigate *Constellation* into the Water (so as to float) without Sustaining injury by the Operation."

Work on the 36-gun Baltimore frigate had progressed under the autocratic supervision of Captain Thomas Truxtun. She was still on the stocks, but she was fully caulked and the shipwrights were at work sheathing her hull in a thin copper skin. A ship with an unprotected wooden hull would become a virtual reef within months of entering salt water. Colonies of barnacles and shellfish and other marine organisms would attach themselves below the waterline, impairing the vessel's speed and maneuverability. Worse, the *teredo*, a wood-eating ship worm, could eat through a hull completely. Copper sheets bolted to the hull would deter most sea organisms, and they were known to repel the *teredo* altogether. Humphreys had insisted that "it is important to a Nation that all their ships of War shall be coppered," and since the American copper-rolling industry was in a primitive state, thousands of four-foot sheets were imported, at great cost, from England.

On Humphreys's arrival in Baltimore, he and the Baltimore master, David Stodder, took soundings in the basin at the end of the slipway. They found 16 feet of water deepening to 30 feet further from shore. The *United States* had drawn 19 feet on launch. The shipwrights took some comfort in the thought that high tide would add another three feet of depth, that the *Constellation* was a smaller ship than her Philadelphian sister, and that the soft mud bottom of the Patapsco would be more forgiving than the Delaware's firmer riverbed. Even so, no ship the size of the *Constellation* had ever been launched into the Patapsco, and the depth of water adjacent to the yard left no margin for error.

Truxtun, who was finding it hard to obtain enough skilled workers in Baltimore, asked that as many Philadelphians as could be spared be sent south to assist in launching the *Constellation*. Humphreys promised to send "as many hands as I possibly can," but warned that it would be difficult because "many have objections to Baltimore."

News of the planned launch was reported in a Baltimore newspaper: "Wind, weather and tide permitting, the United States Frigate CONSTELLATION will be LAUNCHED on THURSDAY, the 7th of September." As in Philadelphia, the launch drew an enormous crowd, probably more than ten thousand, most of whom traversed on foot the quarter-mile stretch of sandy marsh separating Stodder's yard from the city. An army guard was detached from nearby Whetstone Point and local militia companies paraded in their colorful uniforms. Sentries on the ground kept the crowds back, while others were posted on deck, where they would remain as the ship entered the river. As in the Delaware four months earlier, a fleet of colorfully decorated private boats dropped their anchors a short distance from the bank.

Constellation was about 20 percent smaller (by tonnage) than the *United States*, but she was still a tremendous vessel when compared to the brigs and schooners that Baltimore shipwrights were accustomed to launching, and her gigantic hull must have been an extraordinary sight. She was held upright by a file of heavy oak stanchions that rose, like flying buttresses, from the ground to her wales. The new copper sheets under the waterline would turn green and greasy after a few months at sea, but now they shone a deep, polished bronze. One hundred and twenty dollars' worth of tallow had been applied to grease the ways. Truxtun stood on the quarterdeck in full-dress uniform; he would ride his ship into the Patapsco.

Two hundred workmen were engaged in the difficult operation—all of them, Stodder warned, must be ready to obey his instructions "at the instant directed." A drummer stationed by his side emphasized his orders. At high water, a few minutes after nine o'clock in the morning, the signal was given and the men all around the ship swung their mauls in unison and struck the heavy wedges under the hull "with as much exactness and precision as the manual exercise by a regiment of veterans." The coordinated blows lifted the weight of the hull imperceptibly from the keel blocks.

At Stodder's word, the stanchions were removed, the stops knocked away, and the lashings cut. The frigate lurched, glided down the slipway, and plunged into the river. The thousands cheered. The cannons in the yard roared. The infantrymen in the waist of the ship, now afloat, fired a 16-gun salute, one for each state in the Union. The process had seemed as natural and effortless as a duck sliding off a log.

Truxtun was relieved. "A Better Launch I never Saw," he told Humphreys. "The Ship Cleared the ways without touching or Meeting with the Smallest Accident . . . did not strain in the least, or straiten her sheer." "Nothing could surpass the proud and stately movements of the ship," a witness reported; "—she seemed conscious of the occasion, and passed on to the embrace of her destined element with an air of dignity and grandeur, inconceivable."

EVERY JULY AND AUGUST, relentless summer heat and eighteenth-century standards of sanitation made urban life unbearable. Philadelphians, like city dwellers everywhere, heaved their household garbage into the sunken gutters that ran along the streets outside their homes. Manure, animal carcasses, and fishheads baked in the sun and permeated the city with a putrefying stench. Rainstorms were welcomed because they washed the streets clean, but during the long summer droughts, accumulated heaps of refuse fed the dogs, pigs, and goats that ran wild in the streets.

Like all the big seaports, Philadelphia was susceptible to late summer outbreaks of the viral disease known as yellow fever. Just four years earlier, in the early fall of 1793, nearly one in ten Philadelphians had died in the city's worst ever epidemic. Eighteenth-century physicians imagined that the fever was brought about by "a particular construction of the atmosphere"—deadly "fetid humors" and "mephitic vapors" that emanated from the ground. Few suspected that the real perpetrator was the *Aedes aegypti*, a mosquito borne up the river in ships arriving from the tropics. Introduced into the city's densely populated waterfront districts during the sweltering summer months, when windows were thrown open to bring in a breeze, the mosquito and the deadly virus it carried gained easy entry into Philadelphian homes.

On August 1, 1797, three weeks after Congress had adjourned and left the city, the physician Benjamin Rush was called to the bedside of a storekeeper near the Penn Street wharf. The patient complained of wrenching headaches, dizziness, chills, and nausea—symptoms that might have indicated any number of common summertime illnesses. In the next five days, however, he progressed through a cycle of advanced hemorrhagic symptoms that marked him as a terminal victim of yellow fever. He became severely dehydrated; his skin turned flushed and leathery, his eyes jaundiced and shot through with thick, red veins. In the last two days, if his case was typical, he would have begun to bleed freely though the eyes, nose, ears, and anus. Blood might even have seeped like sweat from his pores. His tongue would have taken on a dry, polished texture, turning sallow and then darkening to black. He would have vomited seemingly impossible quantities of a black, granular material that had the appearance and consistency of coffee grounds. He would have descended into an unconscious delirium, tormented by hallucinations, shouting at imagined demons, possibly even rising to attack his attendants.

On the fifth day, the storekeeper died. In the following week, several other inhabitants of the neighborhood took sick. The numbers of dead and dying rose rapidly. Soon there would be fifty new cases per day. With the memory of the 1793 epidemic in mind, the public was quick to assume the worst. The panic intensified with the publication of official warnings and a plan to rope off infected neighborhoods. The roads out of the city were choked with refugees, a series of squalid tent cities sprung up in vacant fields west of Broad Street, and a temporary hospital was set up in the Wigwam Tavern on the Schuylkill. The federal government was effectively shut down as officeholders and clerks joined the exodus. By the end of August, an estimated 35,000 inhabitants had evacuated. Those few that remained were awed by the city's eerie, post-apocalyptic stillness.

One of the worst afflicted neighborhoods was Southwark, where the frigate *United States* was still secured at the Humphreys Wharf. To repair the damage she had sustained to her bottom on launching, the ship had been careened, or "hove down," so that teams of workers could gain access to her keel. This long, painstaking process had required all of her gunports and hawseholes to be stopped up and made watertight, planks to be nailed to her strakes to provide footing for the workers, and her lower masts rigged up as derricks. With the means of numerous hawsers run ashore, the great hull had been heaved down, inch by inch, until the spar deck was nearly vertical and the men could get at the damage on the ship's bottom.

In late August, Captain Barry reported that the difficult repairs had been completed, and the ballast and water casks brought aboard and stowed, and asked the War Office for permission to take the ship to her moorings lower down the river. The captain was anxious to move the frigate away from the riverfront, where there had been, as he reported, several cases of the "bilious unremitting fever." Most of the riggers and craftsmen who had been hired to fit out the ship for sea were packing up their families and fleeing for their lives.

Joshua Humphreys had retreated to his country house in Haverford Township. The master builder sheepishly informed the War Office that letters addressed to him could be "left at the Buck Tavern at Turnpike Road kept by Mrs. Chilling, which is within a mile and half of my house." At first, he hoped that the fever would subside, allowing the ship to be made ready for sea before winter. By late September, however, with the dead still being piled on carts to be buried in mass graves, he was less confident:

> I was in hopes of soon returning to the City, and until yesterday was very sanguine of having [the frigate] completed, to sail before the river closed this season, but the unfortunate report of the contagion, and the number of deaths in the vicinity of the yard, will prevent for the present, my return there. The number is much greater than in the year 93. I know of no family that has escaped. The Clerk of the Yard was taken sick in the Country House and is now dead.

While Humphreys was rusticating in safety, unhappy news arrived from Boston. The launch of the 44-gun frigate *Constitution* had failed. When the stanchions and blocks were knocked away, she had traveled 27 feet toward Boston Harbor and then stopped, stuck fast to the launch ways. Especially galling was the news that one of the thousands of disappointed spectators had been President John Adams. The Boston builder, Colonel George Claghorn, made a second attempt two days later. The frigate had traveled another 31 feet and again stopped short, and another crowd had gone home disappointed.

"I cannot help feeling for the situation of the Frigate, as well as for Col. Claghorn whose situation must be mortifying," Humphreys wrote the War Office. "If you should consider that I could offer any services to the Builder, I shall cheerfully obey your order." Since Humphreys had suffered his own mortification in launching the *United States* into the ground, one suspects he was secretly pleased. Not surprisingly, he suggested that the mishap must have been due to unauthorized alterations in his design.

In the ensuing weeks, the Boston yard workers increased the angle of descent of the launch ways, re-tallowed them, and cut away an adjoining wharf. The third attempt to launch the *Constitution*, a few minutes past noon on October 21, attracted a much smaller crowd. They were rewarded by the sight of the great frigate rumbling down the ways and plunging into the water, pushing a wave across the harbor.

COLD WEATHER BROUGHT AN END to the yellow fever, as it always had in the past. Beginning in late October, refugees straggled back into the city—tentatively at first, and then in growing numbers. Windows were unshuttered and shops opened their doors. Ships that had lain at anchor at Marcus Hook for weeks finally got underway and rode the tides up to the city wharves. Federal officials and their staffs trickled back into town, congressmen and senators began arriving for the second session of the Fifth Congress, and the government gradually resumed its routines of daily business.

Adams had hoped to send the *United States* to sea before the river froze and trapped her for the winter, but as the fever abated and the workmen returned to Southwark, it was painfully clear that the frigate would not sail in 1797. The careening had placed great stress on her entire frame, and the seams on her decks and topsides had broken open. Caulking gangs would have to replicate much of their earlier work. Having taken in her ballast, she had been warped out into the fairway; from Southwark she would have been a distant shape on the river, a bare hull without topmasts or rigging. She had no guns, no provisions, and no crew to speak of. An acting lieutenant of marines had been ordered to begin enlisting men to fill his complement; as the new recruits came aboard, they relieved the army guard that had been detached from Fort Mifflin. Twenty men were berthed aboard a ship designed to carry a crew of more than four hundred.

The War Office kept up a steady drumbeat of pressure to finish arming, fitting out, and victualling the three frigates that were finally afloat. In a typical ultimatum, Secretary McHenry urged David Stodder to complete the fitting out of the *Constellation* "in the shortest possible time" and to "put her in a situation to leave Baltimore by the most prompt, full and undivided exertion of your whole time, talents and force. . . . Should she suffer by any want of Industry or exertion upon your part, it will necessarily and justly be ascribed to you."

But yellow fever also struck in Fells Point, Baltimore, interrupting work on the *Constellation*. She would pass the winter of 1797–98 in the Patapsco's shallow channel, with ice all around her, and, after the thaw, resting on the riverbed at low tide. Stodder worried that the *Constellation*'s moorings might not be strong enough "during heavy Squalls or Spurts of wind." There was apparently no anchor to be found in Baltimore heavy enough to secure the 1,200-ton vessel. The mental picture of the ship being thrown back onto the bank of the Patapsco was enough to move the War Office to have a heavy anchor sent to Baltimore from Portsmouth, New Hampshire.

Humphreys and Captain Truxtun clashed over the proper height, diameter, and placement of the masts and spars. There was no well-established principle to guide shipwrights in the masting and sparring of ships, and the result tended to vary from vessel to vessel according to the whim of the builder. It was a technical question, but a vital one. In view of the great size of the frigates, all could agree that exceptionally large rigs were needed to provide sufficient driving power; but if the masts and spars were *too* large, they would render the ship unseaworthy.

The War Office was inclined to defer to Truxtun, who was never happier than when taking up his pen to instruct others on the finer points of seamanship, and who had given a great deal of thought to the subject. "To find the length of the main-mast," he wrote, "I take twice the breadth of the beam, and one-sixth of the sum, and add them together; and to find the length of the main yard, I take twice the breadth of the beam." Truxtun's formula, when applied to the *Constellation*, would result in towering masts and a heavy top-hamper (combined weight aloft). He suggested that his dimensions be reviewed by the other captains. "I mention sea officers," Truxtun added, "because it is almost impossible that any other description of men, who have not had an opportunity of being often at sea, can form a proper judgment on this important subject." By this he meant to imply that naval architects—Joshua Humphreys, specifically—should not have the final word.

Humphreys reacted mildly to the gibe. The two had known one another for years, and Humphreys had built and repaired ships for Truxtun in the past. He might even have interpreted Truxtun's remark as lighthearted and therefore essentially harmless. Moreover, in their highly ranked society, the naval captain stood a rung or two above the shipbuilder. Acknowledging his "worthy friend's great experience as a sea officer," Humphreys pointed out that he himself had a great deal of experience in "building, repairing, strengthening vessels many of which cases never came under [Truxtun's] notice." He thought the captain's mast plan was too large, and warned that the frigates, if overmasted, would be unstable in heavy seas.

The War Office took the easy way out by authorizing each captain to choose mast and spar dimensions for the frigate under his command, according to his own judgment. Humphreys lost the point, but his judgment would be vindicated.

THERE WAS STILL NO WORD FROM PARIS on the progress of diplomatic negotiations. With war raging on land and sea, the three American envoys had worried that their dispatches might be intercepted. As a precaution, they sent them by circuitous routes, and contrary winds delayed them further still. Even by contemporary standards, the delays were frustrating. Congress found itself with little to do. The question of war or peace depended upon the news from France, and there was no news from France.

At a quarter past noon on November 23, 1797, Adams delivered the opening address to the second session of the Fifth Congress. Whatever the outcome of the Paris talks, he said, the United States must have a navy. In a world in which "pride, ambition, avarice, and violence have been so long unrestrained," the nation's maritime commerce could not survive without naval protection. And commerce, said Adams, was essential to the American people: "The genius, character, and habits of the people are highly commercial; their cities have been founded and exist upon commerce; our agriculture, fisheries, arts, and manufactures are connected with, and must depend upon it. In short, commerce has made this country what it is, and it cannot be destroyed or neglected without involving the people in poverty and distress."

But when House leaders moved a resolution to provide additional funds for the completion of the three frigates, Republicans objected—and this time they were joined by several Federalists who were exasperated by the seemingly endless delays and cost overruns. One member remarked that Congress might as well throw the money into the sea. Instead, the House voted to appoint a special committee to investigate the "apparently enormous expenses and unaccountable delays" since 1794. Why were the frigates several years over schedule and hundreds of thousands of dollars over budget? How could a $200,000 appropriation provided just six months earlier have run out? How could Humphreys have disbursed the extraordinary sum of $7,000 in a single month? Who was to blame and whose heads were going to roll?

Secretary McHenry's defense was a long report with an impressive sheaf of accompanying documents and tables of data. Much of the information was evidently provided by Joshua Humphreys for McHenry's signature; entire passages were lifted word for word from Humphreys's earlier letters to the War Office. The report referred to the difficulties encountered in cutting the live oak out of the forests, the logistical challenges of delivering supplies to six different building yards, and the delays caused by the yellow fever outbreaks in Philadelphia and Baltimore.

Humphreys, a stiff-backed Quaker businessman, privately fumed at the accusations of waste and corruption that had been raised against him in Congress. "When we came to calculate on expense, I have in my Yard exploded everything that was unnecessary," he had earlier written Captain Thomas Truxtun: " . . . For my part I feel no kind of criminality attached to my conduct, but am ready to look any accuser fully in the face and ready to answer any pertinent interrogations without a *blush*."

On March 4, exactly a year to the day since Adams had taken his oath of office, a packet of dispatches arrived at the offices of the State Department at Fifth and Chestnut Streets. Secretary of State Timothy Pickering deciphered the first few paragraphs, then hurried to the president's house to brief Adams on their contents. The decoding would take weeks, and the whole story was learned only by degrees. But as the particulars emerged, Adams realized that the dispatches were incendiary. It was not just that the mission had failed, or that the government of France had shown little interest in negotiations. During their months in Paris, the three American envoys had been repeatedly insulted, threatened, and humiliated. They had even been told they would be required to bribe the foreign minister, Charles-Maurice de Talleyrand-Périgord, as the price of direct negotiations.

Talleyrand was one of the great political survivors of all time, a man who somehow managed to adapt to nearly every change in regime throughout the most turbulent period of French history. Horace Walpole compared him to "a viper who has cast his skin" and Napoleon would later call him "a pile of shit in a silk stocking." He had honed his talents as a financier, administrator, and Machiavellian tactician while serving as a Catholic bishop in the last years of the *ancien régime*. In 1795 and early 1796, while living as an exile in western Massachusetts, he had made a fortune speculating in commodities and real estate. An American who knew him during this period recalled "his pas-

sionless, immovable countenance, sarcastic and malicious even in his intercourse with children. . . . But who does not know, or rather, who ever did
know Talleyrand?"

If the American envoys hoped that the foreign minister's sojourn in
America would leave him disposed toward peace, they were soon disappointed. France needed money to finance its continuing war against the Royalist coalition, and the privateering system was a lucrative source of revenue.
Talleyrand himself needed money, both to support his extravagant lifestyle
and to fund the system of graft that kept him in power. After an extraordinary
series of battlefield victories won by the young Corsican general Napoleon
Bonaparte, France was growing accustomed to treating the rest of Europe
with the arrogance of a proven conqueror. Why shouldn't the United States
be reduced to the status of yet another vassal state, whose payments of bribes
and tribute would buy it the right to exist?

Upon their arrival in Paris, the American envoys had been kept waiting
for weeks. When admitted into Talleyrand's presence at last, he seemed bored
and impatient and escorted them to the door almost immediately. A few days
later, three of Talleyrand's agents—Jean-Conrad Hottinguer, Pierre Bellamy,
and Lucien Hauteval—approached the envoys and said there could be no
treaty without the payment of a bribe (douceur) of £50,000 sterling to Talleyrand personally. "I will not disguise from you," one of these would-be bag-
men said, " . . . you must pay money. You must pay a great deal of money."

Congressional Republicans, still ignorant of the explosive contents of the
dispatches, hoped that they would provide some evidence that the French
government had been willing to negotiate. The trap was laid, and the Republicans stepped into it. On Monday, April 2, with the support of Federalists
who may have had some inkling of their content, the House voted to demand
full copies of the dispatches and the original instructions provided to the
envoys. Adams, putting aside his reservations, delivered a complete, unedited,
and fully decoded copy of the dispatches to Congress Hall the next morning.
He withheld only the names of Talleyrand's agents, who were identified as
"X, Y, and Z." As a result, the whole imbroglio passed into history as the
"XYZ Affair."

The House cleared the galleries, locked the doors, and went into closed
session for three days. Twelve hundred copies were printed. Not surprisingly,
a few were soon leaked to the newspapers. Having hoped that the dispatches
would furnish them with rhetorical ammunition to use against the president,
the Republicans suddenly learned that France's treatment of the envoys had
in fact been far worse than Adams had let on. Now the entire nation would

know the whole sordid tale. Abigail Adams observed that the Republicans were "struck dumb, and opened not their mouths." Fenno, in the *Gazette of the United States*, wrote that the revelations had acted upon them "like the shock of some vast explosion," and that Jefferson "stands an awkward and misplaced colossus."

Adams ordered the envoys to return home at once, and the State Department named Clement Humphreys as the diplomatic courier who would carry the president's instructions to Paris. Humphreys had been indicted and convicted for assaulting Benjamin Franklin Bache on the deck of the *United States* a year earlier, but his fine had been paid by Federalist sympathizers. Republicans interpreted the appointment as a reward for extralegal violence against an anti-government editor. Jefferson wrote in his journal: "The President . . . has chosen as bearer of [dispatches] one Clement Humphreys, the son of a ship carpenter, ignorant, underage, not speaking a word of French, most abusive of that nation, whose only merit is having mobbed & beaten Bache on board the frigate built here, for which he was indicted & punished by fine." Republican editor James Callender charged that "the case of Humphreys demonstrates how gladly those who professed to applaud his intended murder and who paid his fine would butcher if they dared."

But Adams was enjoying a surge of public support. On April 10, a huge crowd gathered outside his house to attend his weekly levee. Two days later, prominent Philadelphia Federalists met at Dunwoody's Tavern on High Street to approve a series of resolutions supporting the president's policy. Joshua Humphreys was among them. A much-repeated toast was: "To John Adams. May he, like Samson, slay thousands of Frenchmen with the jawbone of Jefferson."

Secretary McHenry asked Congress to mobilize for war. French privateers, he warned, were hovering in the sea-lanes off every major American seaport. To offer no resistance would "exhibit to the world a sad spectacle of national degradation and imbecility." The administration's defense program called for warships, harbor fortifications, ordnance, small arms, gunpowder, and other military stores. Within two weeks, Congress had given the president authorization to arm, man, and deploy twelve additional vessels. This legislation triggered a round of new merchant ship conversions, and this in turn expanded the number of ships available to the navy and allowed the big frigates to cruise with smaller ships in company. Congress also appropriated $400,000 to equip, man, and provision the frigates.

Republicans would oppose the president, Albert Gallatin pledged, even if "branded with the usual epithets of Jacobins and tools of foreign influence."

He rose to his feet, day after day, to decry the rush to build a navy. Citing statistics to prove that American commerce had grown and prospered year after year, even while being plundered by the warring powers, he argued that "a commerce can be protected without a navy, whilst a nation preserves its neutrality." A navy would be a sop to the merchants of the northern seaports, but its costs would fall heavily on the rural interior. And if taxes were inadequate, the nation would run up its national debt, borrowing at 6 percent interest from the same northern merchants and moneymen who had demanded a navy in the first place. The Federalists, Gallatin said, were cooking up a war scare to "increase their power and to bind us by the treble chain of fiscal, legal and military despotism."

But the political balance had tipped decisively in the government's favor. Several House Republicans joined the Federalists in supporting the naval measures, which passed handily. "The question of war & peace," Jefferson wrote Madison, "depends now on a toss of cross & pile."

AS THE FIRST SPRING thaw arrived in March 1798, and the ice covering the surface of the Patapsco shifted and began to break up, the War Office instructed Thomas Truxtun to "repair with all due Speed on board the Ship *Constellation* lying at Baltimore . . . no Time [should] be lost in carrying the Ship into deep Water, taking on board her Cannon, Ammunition, Water Provisions & Stores of every kind, completing what Work is yet to be done, shipping her Complement of Seaman & Marines, and preparing her in every Respect for Sea."

Born in Hempstead, Long Island, Truxtun was the only son of a country lawyer. Defying his father's wishes that he should study law, he had escaped to the sea at age twelve to pursue a brilliant and lucrative career in the merchant marine. Before the Revolution, he was briefly pressed into the Royal Navy, where he was offered a midshipman's warrant, which he declined. By 1798, Truxtun was a wealthy merchant sea captain, and one of the leading lights of his profession, with thirty years of experience at sea. He had been three times around the Cape of Good Hope, having commanded two highly profitable voyages to China and one to India. He had probably earned enough money to provide for his ten children without ever making another voyage, and certainly had no need for the $120 a month in salary and rations that the federal government was paying him. Money, he declared, no longer held his interest. "Does any man enter into [naval service] for the sake of subsistence?" he asked. "Are not glory and fame the grand incentives?"

Truxtun had collected all of the books, charts, and tables published in Greenwich by the British Commissioners of Longitude, and he had mastered the difficult art of determining longitude by "lunars"—a process requiring precise celestial observations and arduous logarithmic calculations. Many sea officers despaired of ever mastering the system. In the hope of reducing the process to manageable proportions, Truxtun had published a book on the subject, entitled *Remarks, Instructions, and Examples relating to the Latitude & Longitude*. He supplied copies to the U.S. War Office, suggesting that each of his fellow captains be assigned to read it.

Truxtun held stanch views on the importance of choosing lieutenants and midshipmen carefully. "Without officers what can be expected from a navy? The ships cannot maneuver themselves," Truxtun lectured McHenry. "If we are to have a navy, we must make officers to manage that navy." Though he had spent most of his career in the merchant service, he was wary of men who had learned the ropes aboard merchantmen. The life of a naval officer, he said, was a life of unremitting toil, close attention to detail, and intense devotion to excellence in every aspect of his duty and deportment. The slack discipline that prevailed in the merchant service would not do. "Every citizen in private life is his own master," he said, "but when he enters into the navy or army he is no longer so, for he must submit to strict subordination."

The hope of the American navy would lie in its first generation of midshipmen, the young officers at the bottom rung of the promotion ladder. These "young gentlemen" would enter the service with little or no experience at sea; they would learn their profession in the navy. They would have to prove themselves worthy of promotion, or be pruned out of the service. Those with ambition, Truxtun warned, would have to avoid the destructive influences and habits that were so prevalent among sea officers in the merchant marine.

> If the dunces who are [a midshipman's] officers or messmates are rattling the dice, roaring bad verses, hissing on the flute, or scraping discord from the fiddle, his attention to more noble studies will sweeten the hours of relaxation. He should recollect that no example from fools ought to influence his conduct or seduce him from that laudable ambition which his honor and advantage are equally concerned to pursue.

Truxtun also watched over the critical process of recruiting 220 common seamen to fill out the frigate's complement. The War Office had authorized him to enlist men who were older than eighteen, younger than forty, and "five feet six Inches high without shoes." The surgeon should be on hand to certify that each sailor was "well-organized, healthy, robust, and free from scorbutic and consumptive Affections." They should be engaged for a term of one year and paid a monthly wage of ten dollars for ordinary seamen and fifteen dollars for able seamen. A sailor could be paid an advance equal to two months' pay if his officers were confident he would not run away with the money. Advances lost to deserters would be deducted from the responsible officer's own salary.

Naval service, the War Office emphasized, would be strictly voluntary. There would be no English-style impressment of sailors; nor would there be any of the ruses so commonly used to trick or coerce them: "It being important that those who enlist should feel an Inclination for the service, no indirect means are to be used in inveigling them, and therefore no Individual must be enlisted while in a state of intoxication, nor must he be sworn until 24 hours after signing the enlistment." It would not be easy to recruit enough prime seamen to fill the *Constellation*'s large complement. Baltimore, like the other major American seaports, was booming. Vessels were departing every day, and the merchant houses were competing for the best, most experienced seamen by bidding up their wages. Most sailors preferred a two- or three-month West Indian voyage to a year's term of enlistment on a warship. Many had served in the Royal Navy and wanted no more of that kind of discipline.

Truxtun placed his second lieutenant, John Rodgers, in charge of overseeing recruiting for the *Constellation*. A native of Havre de Grace, Maryland, Rodgers was a big man, tall and dark-haired, with heavy bones in his face. Though he was only twenty-five years old, he had commanded his first merchant voyage while still in his teens. Before accepting his naval commission, he had lost a merchant vessel to a French privateer. He would emerge as one of the dominant personalities in the early American navy, wearing the uniform for forty years, serving in three wars, and eventually serving as president of the Board of Navy Commissioners.

Truxtun ordered Rodgers to open a "Rendezvous" at Cloney's Tavern in the maritime district of Fells Point. He was to be careful in managing costs. "Every expence attending the rendezvous for fire, candle, Liquor, house rent, &c &c must not exceed one dollar for every man actually entered & received on board," the captain warned. On the other hand, the recruiting station, which would be located on a busy street, should reflect well on the ship and on the navy. Truxtun consented that "a reasonable allowance will be made you for music to indulge and humour the Johns in a farewell frolic." Each sailor who took the oath would be provided with a set of "slops," or sailor's clothing. He would receive one woolen hat, one coat, one vest, two pairs of woolen overalls, two pairs of linen overalls, four shirts, four pairs of shoes, four pairs of socks, one stock and clasp, and one blanket. In addition, the *Constellation* would ship a supply of heavy wool watch coats, which would be distributed to the men of the watch who had to stand unsheltered on the deck in cold weather.

Rodgers remained at Fells Point every day for five weeks, but the recruiting progressed slowly. Often he passed an entire day without signing a single man. Even after the War Office authorized an increase in wages, Rodgers was only able to enlist a hundred men, less than half the number needed. The rest would have to be found in other seaports further down the Chesapeake Bay.

On April 22, with the wind blowing hard, the *Constellation* cast off her moorings and got underway, navigating down the Patapsco's main ship channel, well north of the shoals off Rock Point and the dramatic white rocks that guard the head of the bay. There she entered Chesapeake Bay, one of the largest and most magnificent estuaries in the world, a brackish soup fed by the collective discharge of forty rivers and a twice-daily surge of salt water from the Virginia Capes. *Constellation* sailed by Cape St. Clair and the smart little harbor of Annapolis on the south bank of the Severn River; by the pale line of bluffs on the western shore, with no safe harbor for miles; by the long, timbered shoreline of Tilghman and Sharp's Islands on the eastern shore; by the stands of loblolly pines, some 100 feet high; by low marshlands choked with cordgrass and wild rice; by endless mudflats littered with heaps of spent oyster shells and rafts of deadwood and worked over by teal, pintails, and great blue herons; by Cove Point; by Drum Point. And here the ship came to anchor in the mouth of the Patuxent River, where she would complete her provisioning before dropping still further down the bay.

Her officers reported that the ship handled beautifully on her first passage. Sailing under double-reefed topsails, courses, jib, and staysails, she "ran ahead of everything that was in company, going down with their light sails set." She steered easily, "like a boat."

A SHELL OF ICE COVERED the Delaware in January and February 1798, but when the spring thaw opened the river to navigation, the War Office informed Captain Barry that the *United States* "incommodes in her present Station the Merchant Vessels in coming in and going out," and directed that the frigate be taken downriver to an anchorage opposite the ropewalks, south of the city.

The warmer weather played havoc with the ship's caulking. Fluctuations in temperature and humidity continued to work the seams open, allowing rainwater to leak into the berth and orlop decks. Joshua Humphreys, who would have liked to be done with the seemingly endless recaulking of the *United States*, was told that "the Decks, topsides, and other parts of the ship are much opened & the oakum loosened, and those parts will require caulking previously to her leaving the Delaware."

She may have leaked, but the *United States* was beginning to wear the unmistakable appearance of a fully rigged ship of war. Miles of freshly laid hemp cordage had been brought aboard for the setting up of the lower rigging, and the newly enlisted hands were employed each day in worming, serving, splicing, hitching, bending, grafting, seizing, and parceling. Barry was overseeing the work of the sailmakers, who were cutting a new suit of sails from bolts of patent English canvas imported a year earlier. Painters were putting the finishing touches to the figurehead, an elegant female figure whose accessories had allegorical significance: "Her hair escaped in loose, wavy tresses, and rested upon her breast. . . . In her right hand she held a spear and belts of wampum—the emblems of peace and war. In her left was suspended the Constitution of the Union. . . . On the base of the tablet were carved the eagle and national escutcheon, and the attributes of commerce, agriculture, the arts and sciences."

The difficulty in obtaining suitable cannon was a source of great frustration. The War Office had hoped to foster the development of domestic foundries, but the casting of heavy ordnance was an intricate process that no American ironmonger had yet mastered. The navy purchased dozens of weapons from the Cecil Foundry, located between Philadelphia and Baltimore near the head of the Elk River, only to learn that many were unsound. Captain Barry warned the War Office that shoddy cannon were liable to explode in battle. Not only could such accidents kill or maim six or a dozen men, but they tended to terrify and demoralize the survivors, who would shrink from firing the other weapons. Better to sail with twenty dependable guns, Barry wrote, than a hundred that were "in the least suspected."

As a last resort, terrestrial cannon were transferred from coastal fortifications to the frigates. Barry persuaded New York governor John Jay to part with twenty-six 24-pounder cannon from the fortress on Governors Island. They were sent by sea and taken aboard the *United States* in May. For the spar deck, a battery of 12-pounders was removed from the fort at Whetstone Point in Baltimore and transported by sea to New Castle, where they were mounted on newly built oak gun carriages and hoisted aboard the frigate.

The *United States*'s armorer stowed an impressively diverse inventory of munitions, shot, and small arms. There were stools of grape and canister shot, double-headed chain shot, braces of pistols, muskets and blunderbusses, flints, flannel powder cartridges, portfires, priming tubes, matchstuff, cutlasses with scabbards, boarding pikes, and lynch stocks. Some of the smaller items were cheap and readily obtainable, others not so. The War Office hoped to import 500 tons of saltpeter from Calcutta to be used in manufacturing gunpowder. Secretary of State Pickering requested the necessary clearances from the British ambassador, promising that the material would be used to wage war "against the inveterate and inexorable enemy of Great Britain."

From Philadelphia it was 100 miles downriver to the open ocean and a 100-foot drop in elevation. The *United States* went down the river in stages, anchoring first at Mud Island, then at Marcus Hook, then off the town of Chester. At each anchorage she settled deeper into the water as she took on men, arms, stores, and fresh water.

Working a big ship down a tidal river was the ultimate test of seamanship. The sounding lead was in constant use and the anchor was carried cockbilled, hanging from the cathead, ready to drop at a moment's notice. If the wind was working moderately against the tide, the ship could drift broadside to the stream. But when the tide set to leeward, maneuvering was almost impossible. Though the frigate could rush headlong down the river, she would have no steerageway at all. With her deep draft, she could easily be lifted onto a shoal. She might be obliged to drop anchor and await a change in wind or tide.

On June 13 the frigate lay at Chester, where she took on water casks to complete her ration for a cruise of three months. The added weight settled her deeper into the river; she was observed to draw almost 21 feet abaft. Her anxious pilot asked that she take on no more stores until she had dropped down to New Castle, at the head of the Delaware Bay.

FROM BOSTON CAME THE DISAPPOINTING NEWS that the 44-gun *Constitution* was nowhere near ready for sea. Well-manned merchantmen were clearing for destinations all over the world, but the big frigate lay at anchor in Boston Harbor, short of men. Recruiting handbills had been posted throughout the waterfront districts, urging "the brave and hardy seamen of New England" to present themselves at a rendezvous on Fore Street, "where they shall be kindly received, handsomely entertained, and may enter into immediate pay." Not enough had responded to the call.

The Boston Navy Agent, Stephen Higginson, blamed the officers. Captain Samuel Nicholson, he told the War Office, was "a rough, blustering tar merely," a man whose "noise & vanity is disgusting to the sailors." As for the second lieutenant, "he is said to be intemperate & he looks like it." The surgeon was "the opposite of what he ought to be in Morals, in politics, and in his profession. There is not a man in this Town who would trust the life of a dog in his hands."

A nephew of the Secretary of State, who had won a contract to supply the *Constitution,* complained that "wet provisions" (casks of salted beef or pork) had been sitting in a storehouse for four months awaiting the paperwork necessary for them to be taken on board the frigate. He feared they would turn rancid and go to waste. The War Office, he told his uncle, was not up to the challenge of outfitting a frigate, let alone a fleet:

> Till there is some system—a Department, and proper agents under & dependent on it I despair of our receiving any benefit, at least, from *this* Frigate. I believe there has been a Scandalous waste of property in building her; owing, I conceive, to the *entire ignorance* of the [War Office]. . . . What can be done, I know not. It is to be regretted, that So fine a Ship should lie uselessly at her anchors.

The War Office was the target of mounting criticism from many quarters. John Barry placed much of the blame for the delays in the outfitting of the *United States* on Secretary McHenry, commenting acidly that "there ought to be some allowance made for young beginners." Even Alexander Hamilton, McHenry's patron and mentor, was forced to admit that the man was "loaded beyond his strength." The most devastating assessment of his job performance may have been the gentle admonition he had received from President Washington two years earlier. The commander in chief had urged him "to deliberate materially, but to execute promptly and vigorously, and not to put things off until the morrow which can be done, and require to be done, today."

As early as March 1798, when called upon to defend his management of the frigates, McHenry had admitted that he was overburdened and asked to be relieved of some of his responsibilities. In the post-XYZ environment, Congress was in a mood to spend liberally on a naval mobilization. But its members were also painfully aware that the added funding, if funneled through the War Office, would likely be squandered. Over Republican opposition, a bill to establish a new cabinet-level Department of the Navy passed and was signed by the president on April 30. Adams and his advisers began searching for a candidate to assume the new job of Secretary of the Navy.

THAT SPRING, Philadelphia was in the grip of war fever. In Southwark, a hotbed of Federalist militancy, Joshua Humphreys hosted a raucous banquet at Jim Cameron's Tavern. To accommodate the crowd, tables were set up in an alley outside, sheltered by two sails. President Adams attended as the guest of honor. Toast after toast was drunk; the liquor flowed freely; the guests "roared like a hundred bulls." Glasses were raised to "the infant navy of the United States—Like the Infant Hercules, may it even in its cradle strangle the serpents which would poison American glory." Soon after: "Death to Jacobin principles throughout the world." And then: "May the Atlantic be a Red Sea to all who shall attempt to invade our country." A Republican editor reported that "These hundred staunch Federalists drank no less than thirty-two staunch toasts, to each of which they gave exactly 9 cheers . . . each of which was accompanied with the tossing of hats, caps & wigs in the air, merry-andrew jumps . . . [and] other irregularities and violent movements."

When the orchestra at the New Theater on Chestnut Street struck up once popular French revolutionary anthems such as the "Marseillaise" and "Ça Ira," theatergoers shouted in protest. A Federalist editor condemned the songs as "Gallic murder-shouts . . . that grate and torture the public ear." With the first lady in attendance, the singer Gilbert Fox sang a new rendition of the patriotic song "Hail Columbia" to such wild acclaim that he was called back to the stage to sing it four more times. When some of the musicians refused to play the song, perhaps because they were tiring of it, they were pelted with missiles by Federalist rowdies who (as Bache reported in the *Aurora*) "created some alarm in the citizens in every part of the house, who imagined that these men had broken out of the Lunatic Hospital."

Federalists took to wearing black "cockades," or rose-shaped ribbons similar to those worn by American soldiers during the Revolution. The black cockade was intended as an answer to the red or tricolor cockades that Republicans had worn since 1789 in support of the French Revolution. These variously colored emblems of political affiliation held the capital in the grip of what one Republican labeled "COCKADEROPHOBIA." In some neighborhoods, a person wearing the wrong color risked being assaulted. A congressman recalled witnessing a scuffle between two women on the steps outside a church as they attempted to "violently pluck the badges from one another's bosoms."

Pro-government militias were forming up all over the city. Young men lined up at recruiting stations to join the Troops of Horse, the Grenadiers, or the MacPherson's Blues. The ranks of the Blues swelled to over six hundred.

Abigail Adams was delighted by this sudden dam burst of martial enthusiasm. "This city," she wrote, "which was formally torpid with indolence and fettered with Quakerism, has become *one* military school, and every morning the sound of the drum and fife lead forth, 'A Band of Brothers Joined.'"

Her husband was showing signs of the immense pressure he was under. He had lost weight; he was pale and haggard; he had lost several teeth and Abigail worried that he was smoking too many cigars. John Adams had never been especially popular with the American people. He always avowed that he was indifferent to public approbation, so long as he was right. But he was warmed by the outpouring of popular support for his policy, and urged his supporters to mobilize for war. "To arms, then, my young friends," he wrote to a group of young Bostonians who had offered themselves as volunteers; "To arms, especially by sea!"

Republicans were threatened with mob violence. On May 7, after the city's assembled militia companies had passed the president's house in review, groups of young men spread out through the streets, fired with patriotic emotion and fueled by liquor. Some knocked down lampposts and smeared mud on the statue of Benjamin Franklin on the steps of the Philadelphia Library. After dark, a mob gathered outside the home of Benjamin Franklin Bache, where Peggy Bache, five months pregnant, was alone with their three young children. A few proposed to set the house on fire, but they confined themselves to battering on the door and breaking some of the windows. Drunken gangs were out all night, carousing in the streets and singing patriotic songs beneath the windows of imagined traitors. The sleep-deprived inhabitants of Carter's Alley complained that one such "Band of Brothers" had insisted on singing until four o'clock in the morning, and hoped they would find some other place to "warble their wood notes wild."

Deborah Logan, a Philadelphia Quaker, later recalled the hostile climate: "Friendships were dissolved, tradesmen dismissed, and custom withdrawn from the Republican party. . . . Many gentlemen went armed that they might be ready to resent any personal aggression." Leading Republicans were shadowed by Federalist spies. Jefferson, finding himself "dogged and watched in the most extraordinary manner," traveled by circuitous routes in order to be certain he was not being followed. Agents of the Federalist-controlled Post Office opened and read his private letters. Many Republicans, finding they could no longer endure the climate of oppression in the capital, departed for their homes while Congress was still in session. "No one who was not a witness to the scenes of that gloomy period can form any idea of the afflicting persecutions and personal indignities we had to brook," Jefferson wrote years later.

High Federalists encouraged the public to believe that foreigners were conspiring with native-born traitors to prepare for a French invasion of the American mainland. A recruiting advertisement for a Federalist militia in Philadelphia read: "Your country, my boys, is threatened with invasion! Your houses and farms with fire, plunder, and pillage! and your wives and daughters with ravishment and assassination by horrid outlandish sans-culotte Frenchmen!" The Hamiltonian *Gazette of the United States* asked: "Is it not high time to enquire who are these traitors, who have sold their country and are ready to deliver it to the French? . . . Whose houses are the resort of Frenchmen, and who are always in French company?"

Federalists in Congress moved to enact the Alien and Sedition Acts, perhaps the most infamous series of laws in American history. The latter empowered federal magistrates to prosecute journalists and authors who published news or editorial opinions that could be interpreted as "false, scandalous, and malicious" or that might tend to "excite against government officials the hatred of the good people of the United States." Bache warned that "the good citizens of these States had better hold their tongues and make tooth picks of their pens."

From his suite of rooms at the St. Francis Hotel, Jefferson laid down the opposition party's lines of defense. The XYZ revelations, he told Madison, had produced "such a shock on the republican mind, as has never been seen since our independence." Several House Republicans had retreated from the capital, and others had crossed the aisle to join the pro-war party. "All, therefore, which the advocates of peace can now attempt," Jefferson wrote, "is to prevent war measures externally, consenting to every rational measure of internal defence & preparation."

But the opposition no longer had the votes to deny the Federalists their naval and military buildup. A new slogan, often repeated in toasts and promulgated widely in the newspapers, was: "Millions for defense, but not a cent for tribute." From April through mid-July, Congress passed twenty separate laws to put the nation on a war footing. The 1798 navy budget would reach $1.4 million, exceeding naval spending in all past years combined, and comprising 30 percent of non-interest federal spending that year. Adams ordered a general embargo on trade to France and its colonies and signed a formal declaration abrogating the Treaty of 1778. French diplomatic representatives were stripped of their credentials and American naval vessels were authorized to capture any armed ship sailing under French colors, in American territorial waters or out of them. A provisional army was being raised and coastal fortifications were being built up and down the coast. In the seaports, agents had begun the work of purchasing, converting, arming, outfitting, and manning new ships of war. It seemed likely that the country would be engaged in a full-scale naval war before the summer was out.

Madison, who now represented his home district in the Virginia state legislature, had never shared an intimate friendship with Adams (as Jefferson once had) and his loathing for the New Englander was now palpable. The Federalists, he said, had plotted to inflame public opinion to serve purely domestic political purposes. They were conjuring the specter of a French invasion in order to justify punitive measures against their rivals. "Perhaps it is a universal truth that the loss of liberty at home is to be charged to provisions against danger, real or pretended, from abroad."

CHAPTER FOUR

O n the Fourth of July, 1798, at the same hour Congress was debating the Alien and Sedition Acts, *Constellation* was in latitude 32° 18′ N by longitude 73° 42′ W, about 370 miles off the coast of South Carolina, laboring in heavy seas and gale-force easterlies that rose all through the afternoon and evening. Captain Truxtun ordered close reefs in the topsails, then sent the hands aloft to strike the topgallant yards. At eight o'clock the next morning, the wind backed abruptly into the north—"blowing a violent Hurricane, with much Rain"—and now the ship scudded under bare poles. The wind backed still further into the west northwest, where it continued to blow hard with a "high and cross Sea running."

Constellation was weathering her first storm, and Truxtun was not entirely pleased with her. Though the guns were housed and "all was made as snug as possible," the vessel was taking on more water than Truxtun would have liked. He blamed shoddy caulking in her upper decks. The ship was uncomfortably wet, but there was no real danger. When the hands rigged the chain pumps, they pumped water out faster than it came in. Truxtun and the other veteran seamen on board the *Constellation* had endured far worse conditions at sea.

All the next day the frigate ran under bare poles before "Hard Gales" out of the west southwest, with "the Sea running very Cross." In the evening the wind finally began to subside, and the crew bent the mizzen and mizzen staysail, and then a close-reefed fore topsail. Truxtun gave the order to wear ship, and the *Constellation* stood into the west northwest, making sail in the rapidly moderating weather. The hands carried their wet clothes and hammocks on deck to dry in the sun, and went to work "repairing sundry small Matters that got rubbed, chafed, and out of Order in the Gale."

The captain was relentless in his demands for combat readiness. He insisted that "every Article, at any Time, Night or Day, be ready for Action in a Moment's Warning." Even when the weather turned ugly, the hands were obliged to drill at the cannon and small arms. The gunner and his mates filled cartridges of powder for muskets, pistols, blunderbusses, howitzers, and the heavy cannon. Imperfections on the surface of the 24-pound round shot were chipped clear and flakes of rust were removed from the cannon bores. Truxtun urged special attention to the training of men who would be stationed aloft, ordering that midshipmen and sailors practice the "use of, loading, pointing down on a Ship's decks, of the Howitzers . . . which if well managed, have often cleared the decks of an enemy in a Short time." A sharp lookout must be kept at all times, he told his lieutenants, and "Whenever a Sail is in Sight, I must be immediately informed, Night or Day." All were collectively engaged in a mission to invent a new American institution. "We have an Infant Navy to foster and to organize, and it must be done."

On her maiden voyage, *Constellation* had been ordered to patrol from Cape Henry, at the entrance to Chesapeake Bay, to the nation's southern border, the St. Mary's River between Georgia and Spanish Florida. She was to hunt French privateers and provide "all possible Protection to the Vessels of the United States." In the busy shipping lanes off the Carolina coast, the *Constellation* hailed as many as a dozen ships per day. But none had seen or heard of any enemy privateers. As the days passed, a tone of frustration crept into Truxtun's journal entries.

TUESDAY, JULY 3: Saw two Sail to the North West, gave Chace, and at seven PM spoke the armed Ship *Sterling* of Boston from Edenton, North Carolina, bound to Surinam, with a Schooner in Company from the same Place; these Vessels had been out 36 Hours, and seen no Cruizers.

WEDNESDAY, JULY 11: At 9 saw a Ship to Leeward in the North North West, got to Quarters, and bore down upon her; at 10 spoke the Ship *South Carolina*, John German, Master, from Charlestown bound for Philadelphia, out two days, had seen no Cruizers.

MONDAY, JULY 16: At 2 PM saw a Sail to the Northward, Gave Chace, and at 6 spoke the Schooner *Peggy* from Martinica, bound to Charleston; this Vessel . . . has seen no Vessel of War of any Sort.

THURSDAY, AUGUST 2: At 10 AM saw a Sail in the South West, gave Chace . . . she proved to be the *Eliza* from Savannah, bound to Boston, out two Days, and had neither seen or heard of any french Cruizers.

The afternoon of August 5 found the *Constellation* fifty miles off Cape Roman, South Carolina, when a whale suddenly surfaced alongside the ship and blew off "a tremendous Water Spout." Truxtun, who had heard stories of whale strikes that had smashed the hulls of vessels not much smaller than *Constellation*, ordered the cannon fired in hopes of frightening the creature away. Before a gun could be run out, however, the whale sounded. A few minutes later it resurfaced at a more comfortable distance and spouted again. The skies opened the next afternoon, and Truxtun wrote of "a Flood of Rain pouring down in Quantities that equalled, and perhaps surpassed, whatever before fell in the same Space of Time in any Quarter of the Globe. In Fact our Scuppers could not carry it off the Decks as fast as it fell, the Consequence of which was, that it run over the Gunwales in immense Quantities."

Regretting that he had failed to meet an enemy vessel, Truxtun decided it was time to take the *Constellation* back to port for water and provisions. On August 15, she doubled Cape Henry and entered Chesapeake Bay. At noon the next day she rode the tail of the flood into Hampton Roads and anchored under Sowel's Point, with the cluster of rooftops known as Hampton Town visible through the trees on the north shore. Two of the gunner's mates, having "behaved exceeding ill . . . and in a mutinous Manner," were clapped in irons and sent to the jail in Norfolk.

WHILE THE *CONSTELLATION* was shaking down at sea, the first Secretary of the Navy was taking up the duties of his office. President Adams's choice for the office was Benjamin Stoddert, a successful forty-seven-year-old merchant from the burgeoning little port of Georgetown, at the head of navigation on the Potomac River. In appointing Stoddert, Adams had reasoned that a merchant, experienced in outfitting ships for foreign trade, was best qualified to oversee the naval mobilization of 1798. A merchant would be practiced in the arts of bargaining with shipwrights, in managing the details of manning and provisioning, in the dull rigors of accounting, and in judging the reliability of sea officers. The instinct to manage costs for profit ran in every merchant's blood—who better to watch over the public purse?

Stoddert was a former cavalry officer and a Revolutionary War veteran who had been wounded at Brandywine. He had prospered by purchasing tobacco from producers in the Potomac basin and exporting it to business partners in Europe. From the windows of his mansion on the Potomac bluffs, he could watch the slow-moving river take its long, lazy turn to the south. Further east was a lowland wilderness that was, implausibly, the predetermined site of the new Federal City, to which Congress and the federal government planned to relocate in another year.

Arriving in Philadelphia on June 12, 1798, Stoddert set up the new department in two adjacent offices at 139 Walnut Street, where his staff consisted of one chief clerk, four assistant clerks, and a messenger boy. A crushing workload awaited him. His desk was piled high with applications for clerkships and officers' commissions that McHenry, in the last days of his naval stewardship, had ignored. As Stoddert took office, the entire U.S. naval fleet—three frigates and assorted schooners, brigs, and sloops of war—amounted to a dozen vessels officered by fifty-nine men. Two years later, the fleet would include forty-nine vessels, altogether carrying more than a thousand guns, and the officer corps would number more than seven hundred men.

Stoddert despaired of making sense of the incomprehensible accounts he had inherited from his predecessor. A rapid fleet mobilization depended on prompt and efficient day-to-day administration—approvals of provisioning requisitions, payments of salaries, orders to move weapons and ammunition, and constant balancing of accounts with a far-flung network of craftsmen and contractors. The drudgery of bookkeeping may not have been the most thrilling aspect of naval business, but Stoddert understood that it was indispensable. He asked Congress for authorization to hire clerks at a salary greater than the $500 per annum first authorized, and Congress, having come to appreciate the value of good accounting as a means of maintaining control over its own appropriations, assented.

In negotiating with naval contractors, Stoddert treated the public's money with as much care as if it were his own. In August, he was directing the purveyor, Tench Francis, to "buy the whole of the 130 or 140 Tons of Hemp on board the *Voltaire*, and all the duck [canvas] you can get from the owner, on Terms you think reasonable." He urged his agents not to be taken in by the shrewd negotiating tactics of naval contractors. When victuals delivered to the *United States* were found unfit to eat, Stoddert upbraided the Treasury Department clerk who had signed a contract with the supplier. "How come the Bread & Fish turn out so very bad? Ought not the man who Sold the Bread, no doubt for very fine, take back what remains on hand? I think he ought, and that you insist upon his doing so. Or if he will not, he should be sued for fraud on the public."

Stoddert named Joshua Humphreys Chief Naval Constructor of the United States, and authorized him to oversee naval shipbuilding operations throughout the country. But Humphreys's efforts to impose his authority on shipwrights in other cities met with strong resistance. Different techniques, styles, and designs prevailed in the various seaports, and much of the terminology had evolved into regional dialects that outsiders found unintelligible. To ask a master builder to take direction from another master builder, in another region, was contrary to every tradition of the profession. Humphreys now proposed to bring openness and transparency to an enterprise that had always been shrouded in the medieval secrecy of the craftsmen's guild. Shipbuilding is a "noble art," he told a colleague. "I consider it my duty to convey to my brother builders every information in my power."

Work was resuming in New York, Norfolk, and Portsmouth, New Hampshire, on the second three of the six frigates. Humphreys's former assistant, the English immigrant Josiah Fox, was appointed master constructor of the 38-gun frigate to be built in Norfolk, the ship that would soon be christened the *Chesapeake*. Her keel was laid on December 10. In New York, builder Foreman Cheesman laid the keel for the 44-gun *President*. She was to be built on the same lines as the *United States* and the *Constitution*. Humphreys encouraged Cheesman to learn from the expensive mistakes committed during the construction of her sisters. "It is the opinion of many of the officers of the frigate *United States* that her foremast is too far forward," wrote Humphreys. "In order to remedy this in your frigate, I think it will be best to place yours about two feet further aft." He also urged Cheesman to raise the *President*'s gun deck about two inches, which would provide enough room for a port on either side of the wardroom, allowing an additional gun aft in the gun deck battery while also adding "immeasurably to the health and convenience of the officers."

THE *UNITED STATES* had sailed from the Capes of Delaware on July 13, in company with the 20-gun *Delaware*. Their orders were to rendezvous in Boston with another sloop of war and a revenue cutter. From there the little squadron was to sail for the Caribbean.

During the passage to Boston, *United States* ran the *Delaware* hull-under in a few hours and had to shorten sail repeatedly in order to allow the smaller ship to remain in company. Captain Barry wrote Humphreys to say he was delighted with the speed and handling of the big frigate. "No ship ever went to Sea answers her helm better, and in all probability will surpass every thing afloat." The sailing master, James Morris, added that the ship steered beautifully ("one spoke and a half of the wheel is all she wants"); she was fast ("we have been going 12 knots at the same time we could have carried a great deal of more sail"); and she was weatherly ("I saw Mr. Barron carry a lighted candle fore & aft when she was going 9 knots by the Wind"). Barry's only complaint was that the frigate was "rather tender," meaning that she carried too much weight above her center of gravity, and as a result heeled excessively. This was, he admitted, partly due to the unseamanlike way in which her firewood and spare lumber had been stacked between decks, instead of in the hold. He would rectify the fault by stowing the wood properly and adding 20 or 25 more tons of iron kentledge ballast.

Truxtun's review of the *Constellation*'s first performance at sea was more measured. He had never been a great believer in Joshua Humphreys's theories of ship architecture, and was not willing to alter his judgment after six weeks at sea. He believed the *Constellation* was too long in relation to her beam, and noted that she had "hogged" perceptibly. He complained that her narrow beam limited the amount of space in her hold for stowage of provisions: "Three or four months' full allowance of provisions and water is as much as this ship will carry, and then she will be very much down in the water for sailing fast." Truxtun also criticized the frigate's 22-foot draft, which would render her all but worthless in shoal waters.

But when Truxtun read Barry's praise of the *United States*, his competitive impulses came to the surface. He told Stoddert not to believe Barry's "Bombastical Nonsense" about the Philadelphia-built frigate. The *Constellation*, Truxtun predicted, would prove faster than her sisters. "[I]n no Instance of Chase during our Cruize, was half our Canvass necessary, to overhawll the fastest sailing Vessel we met, some of which were termed before Flyers. Should we therefore meet the *United States* and *Constitution*, you need not be surprized if you hear that in going by or large, she outsails them both. . . . [*Constellation*] is in every Situation the easiest Ship I ever was in."

Though they were reluctant to admit it, the captains and officers had themselves to blame for the uneven performance of the frigates in their early cruises. They tended to favor very large masts and spars and very heavy, high-caliber cannon. Towering masts and spars, they reasoned, would allow a ship to spread more canvas, presumably giving her more speed. More and bigger guns would give her added hitting power in combat. But these advantages came at a cost to a vessel's seaworthiness. In heavy weather, an overloaded frigate would ship big waves through her gunports and hawseholes. When pressed with sail, she would heel sickeningly to leeward, her deck sloping like the roof of a house, her mainchains burying themselves in the sea. British naval officers, with their hard-earned experience, tended to avoid overmasting and overarming their men-of-war. The Americans had not yet learned the lesson.

John Barry was the most culpable of the captains. He had been determined to outfit the *United States* with a huge rig, and the War Office had indulged him. After her shakedown cruise, Humphreys urged that the ship be brought back up the Delaware to be refitted with smaller masts. "It is the opinion of almost all the officers except Capt Barry that the *United States* is overmasted," he told a colleague; "I am of opinion it will be best to reduce them." Barry had even gone so far as to have a wheelhouse constructed on his ship's quarterdeck, an addition that his colleagues judged superfluous.

Truxtun lectured the Baltimore Navy Agent, who was at work converting merchantmen into sloops of war, on the "great Folly" of overarming. Mounting excessively heavy guns, he warned, rendered a warship "laboursome and crank . . . and after all these Disadvantages, it has been often proved that much greater Execution is done by a few Pieces of Artillery well served, than by many. . . ." Truxtun was not yet ready to admit that the *Constellation*, with her battery of 24-pounders—each gun was eight feet long and weighed 4,500 pounds—was herself too heavily armed.

AFTER A BRIEF INTERLUDE at Norfolk, Truxtun got the *Constellation* back to sea. His orders were to sail to Cuba in order to rescue a fleet of sixty to eighty stranded American merchantmen. Reports had indicated that Havana was blockaded by an armada of some thirty or forty French privateers, evidently preparing to seize the American vessels the moment they put to sea. When *Constellation* arrived in Cuban waters after an uneventful passage, however, there were no enemy vessels in sight. She brought home a large convoy of American vessels, weathered a fierce Atlantic gale, and anchored safely in Hampton Roads on October 27. Truxtun told Stoddert, with a shade of disappointment, that every vessel he had spoken off the North American coast had "neither seen or heard of any French Cruizers. . . . [T]hat they are therefore all to the Southward . . . you may depend."

Stoddert had already reached the same conclusion: the French privateers that had posed such a menace in the spring had obviously withdrawn from the North American coast. Although the earliest naval patrols had captured less than half a dozen enemy privateers, they had secured the sea-lanes out of the major American seaports. Their success could be quantified in the falling premiums for marine insurance. For voyages departing to the West Indies, premiums had fallen from a peak of 30 percent to a range of 10 to 20 percent. As the year 1798 drew to a close, pro-navy Federalists could argue with some justification that the navy had already paid for itself.

Stoddert had a more ambitious operation in mind for the next stage of what would come to be called the Quasi War. He planned to establish a permanent American naval presence in the Leeward Islands. This would convert the conflict from a defensive operation on the American coast into a war of aggression against the bases of French privateering. It would also demonstrate that the navy was something more than a private marine police force whose deployments could be dictated by merchant interests in Salem, Philadelphia, and New York. Inundated with requests for convoys to more distant regions of the world, such as the Mediterranean and the Baltic, Stoddert refused them all. His priority was to suppress privateering in the Caribbean, and substantially all his forces would be concentrated there. "It seems in vain to guard our Merchants' vessels on our own Coasts, if we suffer them to be taken about the Islands," Stoddert wrote Adams, who was summering in Quincy. "By keeping up incessant attacks upon the French Cruisers on their own ground, they will in a degree at least be prevented from coming on ours."

The main focus of a southern deployment, Stoddert said, should be the French island colony of Guadaloupe. "From information which cannot be doubted, the French have from 60 to 80 Privateers out of the little Island of Guadaloupe. That Island is plentifully supplied with Provisions by means of the Captures they make." Several nearby islands remained in English hands, and could serve as bases from which American warships could provide southbound and northbound convoys for American merchantmen.

The big American frigates were too heavy to chase small privateers into shoal water, and would therefore have to be supported by smaller armed vessels. Truxtun proposed outfitting a fleet of shallow-draft schooners that could pursue a fleeing privateer close inshore, and could be propelled with sweeps (oars) in a calm. A few such vessels dispatched to cruise between Matanzas and Havana, he wrote, would have "ten Times the Chance of a Frigate, or any other large Ship in making Captures . . . it will knock up the Privateering System altogether."

Stoddert had overseen the conversion of several small merchantmen and sloops of war, and there would be an adequate number of smaller vessels to suit the purpose. But the frigates would fulfill a vital purpose in the West Indies as well. Only the frigates could demonstrate to the privateers that the American force was a real navy, akin to that of Great Britain or France itself. Moreover, there were persistent rumors of French frigates operating in the Leewards. Two were said to be outfitting in one of the harbors of Guadaloupe. If Truxtun could confirm these reports, Stoddert said, he should attempt to bring an enemy frigate to action, for "it would be glorious if you could devise a plan for capturing these frigates."

Truxtun would take command of a small squadron comprising the *Con-*

stellation and three smaller warships. He would set up a base of operations on the island of St. Christopher's (better known by the nickname the English had given it: "St. Kitts"), and cruise "as far Leeward as Porto Rico, paying attention to St. Martins and that Group of Islands called the Virgin Gorda; and wherever else between St Christophers & Porto Rico your judgment shall direct you." Truxtun was ordered to coordinate with John Barry, who would command a larger squadron consisting of the *United States*, the *Constitution*, and "several ships of considerable force" to be based further south, in the Windward Islands, at Prince Rupert's Bay in the island of Dominica.

Captured French privateersmen were entitled to all the same rights as prisoners of war. In the West Indies, however, the distinction between a privateer and a pirate was sometimes doubtful. Any crew of an armed vessel unable to produce a privateering commission would be considered as pirates, and the penalty for piracy was known throughout the seafaring world. "Nothing is said in your instructions respecting pirates," Truxtun's orders read. "You know how to treat them."

TRUXTUN WAS NOT SURPRISED when a delegation of Norfolk merchants asked for permission to attach their vessels, like barnacles, to the outbound *Constellation*. In the six months since her shakedown cruise, the ship had never once sailed from any port without a convoy of merchantmen in her wake. This was the heart of winter, however, and only a few hardy merchantmen were sailing—the convoy would number four vessels. The frigate and her little fleet put to sea late in the afternoon on the last day of the year 1798. "We bade farewell to the United States with three hearty cheers, [and] resolved to conquer the French, or die," wrote ship's cooper Elijah Shaw. As the New Year dawned, with fresh breezes and a head sea, *Constellation* swayed up her topgallant masts, unbent her cables, stowed her anchors, housed her guns, and signaled the convoy to sail in close order.

The weather was uncharacteristically mild for the season, with variable winds and "smooth water." Truxtun grew frustrated with the sluggish merchantmen in the *Constellation*'s wake. On January 10, 1799, reaching the end of his patience with the incompetent maneuvers of the schooner *Little John*, he "gave Directions to the Officer of the Watch to inform him, if he did not make more Sail, and pay Attention to our Motions, I would fire into him."

Thirteen days out of Norfolk, the *Constellation*'s lookout raised the island of Antigua. Truxtun hailed the British man-of-war *Concorde* and learned from her captain that two French frigates had been seen in the harbor at Guadaloupe. On January 17, having parted ways with the convoy and struggled against adverse winds, the *Constellation* arrived at Basseterre Roads, St. Kitts. She dropped her anchor in ten fathoms of water, about half a mile from the town.

Basseterre was a typical Caribbean landscape. Windswept palm trees leaned over beaches littered with coconuts. A brilliant sapphire bay met an almost blinding expanse of white sand. The town was a low cluster of stone buildings just beyond the beach, backed by a patchwork of cane fields and plantation houses further up the hill. A tropical forest, inhabited by a noisy army of monkeys, rose steeply up to the 3,792-foot peak of Mount Liamuiga, a dormant volcano. St. Kitts was one of Horatio Nelson's old haunts. As a young captain commanding the Royal Navy's Leeward Islands Squadron in 1787 he had rendezvoused in this very harbor, and he had married his wife, Fanny, on the adjacent island of Nevis.

Basseterre Roads was not a good natural harbor. It was little more than a dent in the otherwise smooth coastline that ran along the western side of the island. There was no pier—visitors were obliged to run their boats directly onto the beach, sometimes surfing in on waves that broke heavily as they reached the shore. Basseterre had been chosen as Truxtun's rendezvous because of its proximity to the privateering hub at Guadaloupe. Were it not for the strategic location of St. Kitts, the commodore would certainly have preferred English Harbour in neighboring Antigua.

At some point shortly before or after his arrival, Truxtun learned of the capture of the U.S. naval schooner *Retaliation*. The *Retaliation* had been commanded by Lieutenant William Bainbridge, a twenty-four-year-old native of Princeton, New Jersey. She had been cruising just to the east of Guadaloupe at dawn on November 20 when her lookout sighted three sails in the east southeast. By their towering pyramids of canvas it was obvious that two of the strangers were frigates. Bainbridge mistakenly assumed them to be English ships that were known to be operating in the Leewards. He did not take evasive maneuvers until the *Retaliation* was directly under their guns. They were the French frigates *Le Volontaire*, 40 guns, and *L'Insurgente*, 36 guns. When *L'Insurgente* fired into the much lighter *Retaliation*, Bainbridge realized he was hopelessly outgunned, and hauled down the colors. It was the first time since the end of the Revolutionary War that an American man-of-war had surrendered to an enemy. Her officers were held as prisoners on board the French frigates and her crew thrown into a "loathsome prison" in Guadaloupe.

From the British governor, who invited him to dine, Truxtun learned that *Le Volontaire* was still at Guadaloupe, and that *L'Insurgente* had sailed. *L'Insurgente* was thought to have set out for France with the deposed governor of Guadaloupe, Victor Hughes, but this report would soon prove false.

———

TRUXTUN SPENT HIS FIRST WEEKS in the Leeward Islands arranging the details of the convoy system. Barry's squadron would provide convoys to American merchantmen from the Windward Islands to a safe anchorage in St. Kitts. From there, Truxtun's squadron would assume responsibility to convoy them to the relatively safe waters north of the Bahamas. All of the warships under Truxtun's command would be deployed in convoy duty, but whenever left idle they would cruise the Leeward passages and hunt enemy privateers.

Within three weeks of his arrival on the station, Truxtun had dispatched three convoys to the north. Although the convoys were effective in securing the sea-lanes, Truxtun was impatient for action, and was not content to keep his frigate at anchor. *Constellation* cruised north for a few days, to the waters around Antigua, St. Eustatius, St. Bartholomew, and St. Martin; and then to the south of Montserrat. She circumnavigated the island of Guadeloupe, flying her colors, keeping carefully out of range of the enemy guns, but close enough to tempt them.

With a few exceptions, *Constellation*'s lieutenants and midshipmen had been serving under Truxtun since the frigate's maiden cruise the previous summer. In the commodore's view, there should no longer be any confusion about what was expected of each officer. Now, when an officer disappointed Truxtun, he was rebuked in strong personal terms. A young midshipman named John Dent received this jolt from Truxtun as the *Constellation* was patrolling off the coast of Guadaloupe:

> You have paid so little Attention to the Rules and Regulations of the Navy, and to the general Duty assigned you in your Station, on Board this Ship as a Midshipman, that I have almost been induced to send you Home . . . you have been so very inattentive to Orders, and your own Improvement, and even Careless in your Person, that I have been ashamed to see you on the Quarter Deck.
>
> Was my own Son . . . to act as you have done, contrary to Example, and the most wholesome Advice, I should not only dismiss him from the Service, but I believe I should disinherit [him], and let him shift for himself.

Midshipman Dent remained on the ship, however, and his performance must have improved, because he was soon promoted to lieutenant, and would eventually rise to the rank of captain.

On February 2, with the winds "baffling and light," *Constellation* tacked into St. Pine Harbor on Guadaloupe, hugging the southern shore so as to remain out of range of the French harbor guns. The battery opened fire, lobbing a few heavy iron balls into the sea, all of which splashed short of the target. Truxtun counted the shot and waited for the battery to fall silent. Then the *Constellation* answered with exactly twice the number of guns, her shot also falling short. While this ineffectual exchange was taking place, the lookout hailed the deck to report a convoy of seven sail away to the south southwest, and Truxtun ordered the *Constellation* to make sail in chase. The first ship in the convoy proved to be a British man-of-war, the *Elliot*, bound for Liverpool; she was very kindly convoying a number of Americans out of hostile waters. *Constellation* had been diligent in running down every sail on the horizon, but all were American or British, none French. Her run of bad luck seemed relentless. She returned to St. Kitts for water and provisions.

The *United States* was in the passage from Barbados to Martinique with a convoy of ten sail in her wake. That morning at eight, she bore off to chase a schooner sighted to leeward, and by three in the afternoon had almost overtaken her. The chase proved to be a 6-gun privateer, *L'Amour de la Patrie*, which made a reckless attempt to escape by hauling her wind and sailing directly under the frigate's guns at pistol-shot range. The *United States* fired three 24-pound balls at the fleeing schooner. The third passed "through and through," blasting holes through both of the schooner's sides. *L'Amour de la Patrie* rapidly filled with water and began to sink. One of the officers aboard the *United States* recalled that the privateersmen "set up the most lamentable howl I ever heard; and though it's said [the French] have abolished all religion, they have not forgot the old way of imploring the protection of the omnipotent, with gestures, professions, and protestations." Boats were lowered and all sixty of the crew were saved.

The *Constellation* returned to sea on February 6. On the eighth, Truxtun noted in his journal: "Very squally disagreeable Weather all these twenty four Hours, with Rain and a Head Sea." The crew was set to knotting and splicing as the frigate stood on her tacks between Barbuda and St. Bartholomew's, with no vessels in sight. For two days the horizon was strangely clear of any sails; but at midday on February 9, about five or six leagues northeast of the island of Nevis—Alexander Hamilton's birthplace—the lookout hailed the deck to report that he could see a single ship in the south, hull down and standing to westward. The *Constellation* immediately hauled her wind and gave chase. Scrutinizing the stranger through his long glass, Truxtun could see that she was a very large ship, with a soaring pyramid of canvas. In his journal he noted: "I take her for a ship of war."

At half past twelve, just minutes after she was sighted, the stranger altered course, bringing the wind onto her quarter and standing to the north-west. She soon passed under the *Constellation*'s lee, at a distant of about five leagues. With aggressive maneuvering it was within Truxtun's power to bring her into action. He did not know what ship she was—she could be English or even one of the *Constellation*'s sister frigates—but he was determined to close to signaling distance, if not closer.

Although Truxtun did not yet know it, the chase was the French 36-gun frigate *L'Insurgente*, the ship that had fired into and captured the American naval schooner *Retaliation* in November. She was reputed to be one of the fastest ships in the French navy. Rather than sailing for Europe as Truxtun had been led to believe, she had sailed north into the Bahamas to hunt British merchantmen. Three weeks earlier, she had been chased by the *Constitution*, but managed to escape.

Her captain, Michel-Pierre Barreàut, called for his glass, went aloft, and stood on the foretopsail yard to have a look at his pursuer. That she was a frigate, the Frenchman had no doubt. What he did not yet know was whether the pursuer was American or English. In either case, he had no intention of closing with her, and every intention of avoiding an engagement even if it required him to flee. The French were numerically inferior in the West Indies and their priority was to preserve what naval force they had on the station. A frigate could do more for France's cause by destroying enemy commerce than by engaging an enemy man-of-war.

An hour after hauling off in chase, *Constellation* had closed to within signaling distance. Truxtun ordered his signal officer to make the British private signal: blue flag at the fore topmast and a red, white, and blue flag at the main topmast. To this the unidentified frigate made no answer, but ran the American ensign up to the mizzen peak. *Constellation* made the private signal for the U.S. Navy. Again there was no response.

Truxtun ordered the *Constellation* cleared for action and the bosun beat to quarters. As if to respond, *L'Insurgente* lowered the American colors, raised the Tricolor, and fired a shot to windward in affirmation.

The bosun's whistle sounded and the frigate came alive with the sounds of men scampering to their stations. Muskets, pikes, hatchets, and blunderbusses were served out to the men in the waist. Hammocks were brought up from the berth deck and stacked in the nettings to raise the bulwarks. Marines and topmen leapt into the shrouds and went up the ratlines to the tops. The carpenter and his mates swept away the bulkheads on the gun deck to make a clean sweep, fore and aft. Gun crews gathered around their weapons, and the captains stood by with their handspikes.

L'Insurgente initially stood to the northwest to fetch the passage between St. Kitts and Saba. But now the Frenchman bore up and sailed close-hauled, eight points free of the wind on a starboard tack, perhaps hoping to gain the weather gauge—that is, engage the enemy from windward—and thus an advantage in battle. *Constellation*, passing south of the shoals off the south headland of Nevis, shaped a course to cut her off. It would be a long, grueling chase.

Though the wind was coming up, Truxtun ordered his crew to make all sail in chase, and a "crowd of canvas was then spread on the *Constellation*." Truxtun was driving the frigate to the very limit; pressed heavily with sail in the stiffening breeze, she could easily have carried away a spar. One can imagine the *Constellation* tearing through the water with the wind on her beam; the foam surging back along the lee rail in a deep, plunging run; the spray thrown up at the bows and into the faces of the foremast jacks; the top yards flexing visibly under the strain; the audible hum of the rigging.

Constellation was gaining on the chase, but the wind was rising steadily and the sky took on an ominous, hazy texture. To windward was the characteristic low-lying bank of thick, ugly clouds, moving rapidly over a mottled sea, that every seamen recognized as the immediate prelude to a squall. Each captain was forced to choose whether to shorten sail and risk losing headway or to keep up a full press of canvas and risk carrying away a mast or spar, which would likely bring the chase to an end. It was a test of the strength of each ship's rigging, as well as a test of seamanship for the respective crews. Pursuer and prey each kept up a press of sail, their captains hoping for the best.

As the wall of wind and rain enveloped the *Constellation*, she lurched violently to leeward. All hands let fly all the sheets, and the din of flapping canvas was added to the roar of the squall. All the masts and spars survived except one—the studding sail boom, which carried away with (as one of her crew later said) "such a cracking and snapping [as] I never heard before." But if a spar had to be lost, better a boom than a topmast or a yard. As the squall passed over, the crew of the *Constellation* sheeted home her sails and the frigate resumed tearing through the warm Caribbean water "like a race horse."

Some distance ahead, the squall also closed over *L'Insurgente*. Barreaut ordered the crew to take in her topgallants, but as the men were out on the yards, a wall of wind struck the ship and the main topmast snapped by the cap and came down, covering the deck with a tangled mass of spars, rigging, and sails. The crew raced with cutlasses and axes to clear away the wreckage. It was a devastating loss, and Barreaut understood that his ship now had almost no hope of escape. At first he attempted to bear away and run for the safety of St. Eustatius, but then hauled his wind and stood on a starboard tack, eight points off the wind, waiting for the *Constellation* to range up. Barreaut later told his government that the loss of the topmast was the "sole source of our misfortunes."

As *Constellation* closed the gap with the fleeing *L'Insurgente*, the great weight of her 24-pounder guns caused her to heel excessively to leeward. To keep his ship upright, Truxtun was forced to run out the windward guns and keep the leeward guns housed behind closed ports. Here was a dramatic proof of the dangers of overarming. The *Constellation* held the weather gauge—could engage the enemy from windward—and tactical doctrine dictated that Truxtun must conserve this valuable advantage. Yet, doing so would require him to bring his leeward battery into action. With the *Constellation* a cable length astern of the French vessel, Truxtun decided to surrender the weather gauge by crossing the *Insurgente*'s wake and running under her lee.

At a quarter past three, with the two frigates a few leagues west of Nevis, the *Constellation* closed to within pistol-shot range. The French captain was plainly visible now at *L'Insurgente*'s taffrail, shouting for a parlay. For once in his life Truxtun had nothing to say, and he refused even to reply. In his mind it was evident that a state of war existed between America and France, even if undeclared. Licensed French privateers were hunting American merchant-men throughout these waters, and French men-of-war had captured Ameri-can men-of-war. *L'Insurgente* could either fight or strike her colors; there would be no discussion and no negotiation. When the aftermost gun on the *Constellation* could bear on the enemy, Truxtun gave the order for the star-board guns to fire in rotation.

The 24-pounders fired, one by one, forward to aft; each jumped, made a stabbing flash of light, and expelled a cloud of thick, white smoke that was instantly carried away by the wind. The American gun crews fired their can-non in the English fashion, directly into *L'Insurgente*'s hull. They were double-shotted, and wrought terrible devastation, killing or wounding per-haps a score of Frenchmen in the first half-minute of the engagement.

L'Insurgente at once responded with a broadside of her own, firing up at the *Constellation*'s masts and rigging. The fore topmast was struck just above the cap, and seemed to teeter on the verge of coming down. An eighteen-year-old midshipman named David Porter, stationed in the foretop with the marines and small arms men, attempted to hail the deck. Unable to get Trux-tun's attention over the clamor of the battle, he climbed up and cut away the slings, allowing the yards to fall and removing pressure from the injured mast, which was saved.

L'Insurgente's decks were littered with dead and dying men, and her officers seemed to be losing control of the remaining crew. Many of them ran from their guns, some even rushing into the captain's cabin. Barreaut, perhaps sensing that his vessel was outgunned, called for boarders and ordered the helmsman to run aboard the *Constellation*. But his ship was losing way, and the maneuver failed. It was a costly failure, for it allowed the *Constellation* to range ahead, cross the Frenchman's bows, and fire a ferocious, double-shotted, raking broadside. The *Constellation* passed to windward of the traumatized *Insurgente* and wore round on a parallel course. The gun crews of both ships ran across their respective decks to serve the guns on the other side. *Constellation*'s larboard gunports swung open, the muzzles ran out, blazed, roared, and vanished behind a curtain of smoke. *L'Insurgente*'s starboard battery answered, and now the two frigates hauled close to the wind and fought a running battle, trading ball for ball.

On *Constellation*'s gun deck, a member of one of the gun crews was overcome with panic and ran from his gun. The lieutenant who commanded his division was Andrew Sterrett, a twenty-one-year-old native of Baltimore. Sterrett drew his sword, chased the terrified man through the ship, cornered him, and killed him. He later boasted to his brother: "One fellow I was obliged to run through the body with my sword, and so put an end to a *coward*. You must not think this strange, for we would put a man to death for even looking pale on board *this* ship."

One of the *Constellation*'s 24-pound balls smashed through *L'Insurgente*'s hull, dismounting a gun, damaging the carriage of a second gun, and killing several men. According to an account published shortly after the battle in *Claypoole's American Daily Advertiser*, the spent ball rolled along the gun deck until it was stopped and picked up by a French officer, who took it as proof that *L'Insurgente*, with her 12-pounders, was outgunned, and carried the ball aft to show to Barreaut.

For a time, the two ships drew apart. The French sailors were set to work re-reeving the running lines that had been cut by the *Constellation*'s fire. The American frigate had suffered little damage, and at a few minutes after four in the afternoon, Truxtun maneuvered the ship into a position directly athwart *L'Insurgente*'s stern, setting up another raking broadside. *Constellation*, said John Rodgers, "should certainly have sent her to the infernal regions had we fired whilst in that position."

Barreaut had to admit that his ship was in a pitiful state. The main topgallant sail had fallen over the maintop, and was now draped like a veil over the men stationed there. The spanker was "completely riddled and torn," and

Barreaut ordered his men to lower it in order to relieve the wounded mizzen-mast. The main and mizzen topmasts had been shot away, and now lay uselessly across the deck. Several of the cannon had been dismounted. The braces and bowlines of the foresails were cut to pieces, and innumerable rope ends hung limp from aloft and trailed in the sea. His casualties were heavy: scores of dead and wounded were strewn along the decks and rivulets of blood were running in the seams between the deck planks. The bosun was not on deck, nor any of the petty officers; the captain could see only one man left standing in the forecastle.

Looking across at the *Constellation*, Barreaut saw a ship that appeared largely intact. She had a few minor injuries—her rigging was shot up, she had lost a foremast yard, and there were holes in her sails where balls had passed through—but she could maneuver properly and her guns were still well manned. Though he could have fought on, Barreaut later said, "sooner or later, in my position, I should have to strike to a superior force." *L'Insurgente* was, he said, "totally unrigged . . . a hulk, having for her entire defense a battery of 12's." He went forward over the gangway and told his first lieutenant he intended to surrender the ship. The lieutenant answered: "Do as you will." At a quarter past four in the afternoon, the Tricolor was hauled down from the mizzen peak.

On the quarterdeck of the *Constellation*, Truxtun summoned Lieutenant Rodgers and ordered him to gather a prize crew of one midshipman and eleven seamen. A boat was lowered and the party was rowed across. As Rodgers came up over the side to take possession of the captured ship, he was privately thrilled by the sight of the carnage the enemy had suffered. "Although I would not have you think me bloody minded," the bloody-minded lieutenant wrote Stoddert, "yet I must confess the most gratifying sight my eyes ever beheld was seventy French pirates (you know I have just cause to call them such) wallowing in their gore, twenty-nine of whom were killed and forty-one wounded."

Barreaut and his first lieutenant were sent across to the *Constellation*. The French captain hoped to have possession of the defeated frigate restored to him. Although he was certainly aware of the intense privateering campaign carried on by French West Indian colonies against American commerce, he also knew that war had never been declared by either nation. As he came up over the *Constellation*'s side, he said to Truxtun: "Our nations are not at war. Why have you fired on our national flag?" Truxtun's attention was on the challenge of managing two disabled frigates and several hundred prisoners in strong winds with night coming on, and he refused to enter into a debate. He asked Barreaut's name and the name of the captured ship, and then said: "You, sir, are my prisoner." Barreaut and the lieutenant were stripped of their side arms and sent below.

Three of the *Constellation*'s topmen had been hit by cannon or small arms fire. One was killed outright, and a second died later of his wounds. The fourth casualty was Neil Harvey, the man Lieutenant Sterrett had executed for running from his gun. "I send you a list of the killed and wounded on board the *Constellation*," wrote Midshipman Porter to his father; "in the fore-top, John Andrews, shot through both of his legs—George Water, back broke by the wind of a cannon ball—Samuel Wilson, leg shot off, died of his wound—one man killed for cowardice."

In the hours after the action, the wind continued to rise. It was deemed too dangerous to ferry the *L'Insurgente*'s prisoners and casualties across a heaving sea in the rapidly oncoming darkness, so Rodgers and his small prize crew were obliged to navigate the jury-rigged frigate back to St. Kitts with 173 prisoners in the hold. There was not even enough time to deal with the dead. The bodies were left on deck wherever they had fallen. The gratings that would otherwise have been lashed down over the hatches had been thrown over the side by the prisoners, so a man had to stand guard over each of the hatchways, armed with a blunderbuss, a cutlass, and a brace of pistols, "with orders to fire, if any of the prisoners should attempt to come upon deck, without having previously obtained his permission."

Sailing for two days and three nights into the teeth of gale-force winds, *L'Insurgente* was finally brought to anchor under the guns of Bluff Point, at the northern end of Basseterre Roads. If the English colonists in the town had wondered at the identity of this unfamiliar frigate, a glance through a long glass would have answered the question: an American ensign flew above the Tricolor at the mizzen peak.

CAPTAIN BARREAUT TOLD TRUXTUN that the diplomatic conse-quences of the battle would be severe. When the news reached Paris, he said, the French government would issue a declaration of war. Truxtun pointed out that *L'Insurgente* had herself taken part in the capture of the American naval schooner *Retaliation* a few months earlier; that *L'Insurgente*'s own logbook proved she had seized several American merchant vessels; and that his orders, in any case, instructed him to attack any French armed ship he met at sea. "The french Captain tells me, I have caused a War with France," Truxtun wrote Stoddert. "If so I am glad of it, for I detest Things being done by Halves."

The new governor of Guadaloupe, General Etienne Desfourneaux, adopted the same tone of shock and indignation. Communicating with St. Kitts by a vessel dispatched under a flag of truce, the governor demanded, "in the name of the Republic," the return of *L'Insurgente* and her crew. Replying two days later, Truxtun rejected the demand, and declared that he would continue to attack any French armed ship he found operating in the West Indies, "untill ordered to the Contrary by the President of the United States." The American people, Truxtun added, "wish Peace with France and all the World on fair and honorable Terms, but on any Other we disdain it. Yes Sir, we spurn at the Idea."

Truxtun proposed a prisoner exchange, but Desfourneaux flatly denied that there were any imprisoned Americans on Guadaloupe, an assertion he must certainly have known to be false. The governor's refusal posed a dilemma, because the small American squadron did not have the means to provide for the prisoners taken in *L'Insurgente*. Truxtun solved the problem by transferring the French seamen to English jails on St. Kitts, and allowed the fifty-two French officers to sail in a cartel to Guadaloupe, each having signed a parole agreement pledging not to "take up Arms against the . . . U. S. of America by Sea or Land." Though Captain Barreaut had protested the taking of his ship, he was grateful for the humane treatment he and his fellow prisoners received. "You have united the two Qualities which characterize a Man of Honor—Courage and Humanity," he wrote Truxtun. "Receive from me the most Sincere Thanks, and be assured, I shall make it a Duty to publish to all my fellow Citizens the generous Conduct which you have observed towards us." Barreaut presented Truxtun with a plume from his hat, which the American commodore in turn gave to his nephew as a gift.

Lieutenant Rodgers was promoted to the rank of acting captain of *L'Insurgente*, pending the Navy Department's approval. Throughout February and early March 1799, he supervised repairs to the damaged ship, abiding by the commodore's wishes to "be as frugal as possible in the Outfit." According to the navy's prize regulations, every officer and seaman of the *Constellation* would receive a share of her value, and Truxtun suspected that the government might deduct the cost of repairs. Thirty-one officers and seamen were transferred from the *Constellation* to *L'Insurgente*. With additional men from other vessels in the squadron, her crew would amount to 124, less than a third of her complement—there would be enough hands to navigate the ship home, but not enough to defend her against an opponent of comparable size. For safety, the two frigates would sail to North America in company.

Barry and the *United States* returned home in early April, leaving the

Leeward Island passages largely undefended. With American merchant vessels arriving in the West Indies in ever greater numbers, Truxtun felt it was necessary for the *Constellation* and her consorts to remain in the south as long as possible, but the squadron was running short of stores and provisions, and the one-year enlistments of the *Constellation*'s crew were expiring. By May 7, having received no new orders from Stoddert, the commodore concluded that he had no choice but to sail. After a quiet two-week passage, the *Constellation* and *L'Insurgente* both arrived in Hampton Roads on the afternoon of Monday, May 20, anchoring in the bight of Craney Island. Truxtun ordered Rodgers to hoist the French Tricolor beneath the American flag at *L'Insurgente*'s mizzen peak, "and gratify our Countrymen with that Sight for three Days."

Norfolk was overjoyed to be the first port of call for the victorious frigate and her prize. The mayor and other civic officials prepared a welcome dinner for the captain and his officers, preceded by a parade of local militia companies and a sixteen-round rifle salute. All up and down the eastern seaboard, the newspapers were full of admiring reports of the *Constellation*'s victory, the theaters performed hastily written sketches and songs, and vendors sold ornaments and memorabilia commemorating the battle, including "brave Truxtun cock'd & round hats, in the Military and Naval stile." A widely quoted toast, first given at a banquet in New Hampshire, alluded to Talleyrand's rejection of American diplomatic overtures: "Captain Truxtun: our popular Envoy to the French, who was accredited at the first interview." Alexander Hamilton attended a dinner given in the captain's honor at the Tontine Coffee House in New York. A group of English merchants and underwriters at the London Exchange raised 500 guineas to commission a silver urn for Truxtun, in thanks for the blow he had struck against the common enemy.

In Philadelphia, leading Republicans predicted that the capture of *L'Insurgente* would lead to an escalation of the conflict, but President Adams was pleased. "I wish all the other officers had as much zeal as Truxtun," he told Stoddert. " . . . If you correct [his] ardor a little, as you ought to do, I pray you to do it very gently and with great delicacy. I would not have it damped for the world."

Truxtun's ardor would be on full display in his campaign to collect the prize money he and his crew were owed. Captured enemy vessels were required to be sold at auction or purchased by the federal government, and a share of the proceeds paid to every officer and seaman aboard the victorious ship. Each man was paid according to a formula based on his rank, with the captain taking the largest share (three twentieths of the total). If the prize was of lesser force than the capturing ship, the crew received half the proceeds and the federal government retained the other half. If the prize was equal or superior in force to the capturing ship, the prize was declared "the sole property of the captors," and the crew was paid the entire amount of her value. The relative force of *Constellation* and *L'Insurgente* was therefore a question of pressing interest to Truxtun and the men who had served under him.

Truxtun maintained that *L'Insurgente* was superior. His accounting dwelled on her crew, which he reckoned at 409, compared with 316 on the *Constellation;* and also on the number of guns she carried: 40, as compared to the *Constellation*'s 38. But these figures were misleading, perhaps deliberately so. The Frenchman carried more than fifty passengers, who had made little or no contribution to the fighting. More to the point, *L'Insurgente* was nearly 30 percent lighter than *Constellation* by tonnage, and she carried 12-pounders as her main battery of weapons, whereas the *Constellation* carried 24s. By any objective measure the prize was of lesser force than the *Constellation*. But Truxtun and his officers employed a combination of bluster and obfuscation to convince their countrymen (and perhaps themselves) that the *Constellation* had triumphed over a more powerful opponent.

An Admiralty Court, assembled at Norfolk in June, took sworn testimony from First Lieutenant John Rodgers. Rodgers cited the bare numbers of guns and men on each ship, but the court did not press him (and he did not volunteer) to give details about the calibers of the weapons or the overall size and weight of the two frigates. Based on this testimony, the court ruled that *L'Insurgente* was the stronger ship. A panel chaired by Navy Agent William Pennock subsequently examined *L'Insurgente* and assessed her value at $120,000.

The Rules and Regulations of the Navy, then in draft form, decreed that any officer "who shall execute, or attempt, or countenance any fraud against the United States . . . shall on conviction be cashiered and rendered forever incapable of any future employment . . . and suffer such other punishment as a court martial shall inflict." By law, all money raised by the government in prize cases was to be deposited into a fund to support disabled officers, sailors, and marines. Rodgers thus tried to defraud the navy, and to do so in a way that would deprive disabled veterans of their pensions. Though Truxtun did not testify, he supported the court's judgment and attempted to collect the entire $120,000. Captain Alexander Murray, also stationed in Norfolk, believed Truxtun's powerful influence was at work behind the scenes. "There is one thing Certain, that his Word is a Law here," he wrote the secretary, "which may not be his fault, as Mankind will sometimes be Blinded in the radiance of Glory."

Stoddert was not fooled. Although he had not seen *L'Insurgente* with his own eyes, he had received a survey report with her dimensions from Josiah Fox. He knew she was inferior in force to the *Constellation*, and he also knew $120,000 was a high estimate. "The sum fixed on by the Gentlemen at Norfolk is far beyond her value, in my opinion," he told Truxtun. "She is, I presume, seven or nearly seven years old, a rough-built Vessel, much the worse for wear. Her copper it seems will soon want shifting." The secretary asked Joshua Humphreys to provide his fairest estimate of her value, "no more, no less." Based on Fox's plans and detailed survey notes, Humphreys arrived at an estimate of $84,500. Stoddert also considered appealing the Admiralty Court's ruling that *L'Insurgente* was the stronger of the two frigates into a federal district court, but that would involve "the disagreeable circumstance" of litigation between the Navy Department and the country's most celebrated naval hero. So Stoddert made Truxtun an offer: 100 percent of Humphreys's reduced estimate of $84,500. "I hope this offer will be agreeable," he wrote. "You know the principle upon which I make it, & I really think it ought to be satisfactory. I cannot exceed it."

Truxtun, perhaps suspecting the judgment concerning the relative force of the two frigates was unlikely to hold up in court, accepted the offer. His share, after agent's commissions and expenses, would amount to more than $8,000. It was a fortune—the modern-day wage equivalent would be about $2 million. Many of the *Constellation*'s enlisted men, however, failed to collect their shares of the settlement, having naively sold them to speculators for a fraction of their value.

GEORGE WASHINGTON HAD AGREED to come out of retirement to serve as commander in chief of the 10,000-man "new provisional army." On November 10, 1798, dressed in full military regalia and accompanied by a calvary company, the old general rode into Philadelphia to an ecstatic welcome.

The decision to bring Washington back was, Abigail Adams said, "one of those strokes which the prospect and exigency of the times required, and which the President determined upon without consultation." But John Adams had no real enthusiasm for the mobilization of land forces, and his preference for the navy grew stronger as the Quasi War entered its second year. "Floating Batteries and wooden walls have been my favorite System of Warfare and Defense for this Country for Three and Twenty years," he wrote in reply to an address by the Boston Marine Society. News of a great British fleet victory over the French off the coast of Egypt the previous August (Nelson's Battle of the Nile) helped convince Adams that the mobilization of a new American army was expensive and unnecessary. "At present there is no more prospect of seeing a French army here than there is in heaven," he told McHenry.

There was a second factor working in the president's mind. Against his wishes, Adams had nominated Alexander Hamilton as second-in-command of the army. His hand had been forced by Washington, who had threatened to refuse command of the army if he could not choose his own subordinates. Major General Hamilton had taken effective control of the force, distributing officers' commissions and placing his loyal lieutenants in command of key regiments. Adams began to understand that Hamilton harbored ambitions of conquest—that he would, if given the opportunity, lead an "army of liberation" to conquer Louisiana and Spanish Florida, perhaps even continuing through Mexico and into Central and South America. With the cooperation of the British navy, St. Domingue and France's other remaining West Indian colonies could be wrested away. When his conquests were secure, Hamilton would return to America as the archetypical man on horseback with a victorious army on foot.

It was a well-traveled route through history. Great republics had often been subverted by their own successful generals. It was the route traveled by Julius Caesar, when he crossed the Rubicon; it was the route that was being traveled at that very moment by Napoleon Bonaparte, returning to Paris after his great victories over the Austrians in northern Italy. At the last extremity, Hamilton's personal ambition might climax in an upheaval of the same constitutional government that he had done so much to create and nurture. The domestic political turmoil of the 1790s had left Hamilton and the so-called High Federalists with profound doubts that the Constitution *could* be saved, and perhaps even whether it was worth saving.

Abigail had once warned that Hamilton would "become a second Buonaparty" if ever given the opportunity, and Adams was now inclined to agree. "The man is stark mad or I am," he said. Elbridge Gerry recalled a conversation in which Adams said he "thought Hamilton and a party were endeavoring to get an army on foot to give Hamilton the command of it, and thus to proclaim a regal government and place Hamilton as the head of it, and prepare the way for a province of Great Britain." Years later, Adams told a correspondent: "I have always cried Ships! Ships! Hamilton's hobby horse was Troops! Troops! With all the vanity and timidity of Cicero, all the debauchery of Marc Anthony, and all the ambition of Julius Caesar, his object was the command of fifty thousand men. My object was the defense of my country, and that alone, which I knew could be effected only by a navy." At about the same time Adams began to understand that his cabinet, all holdovers from the Washington administration with the exception of Navy Secretary Stoddert, were personally loyal to Hamilton. Cabinet deliberations were being relayed to Hamilton in detail, and perhaps even guided by him at a distance. Adams began to keep his own counsel, sharing nothing with his department heads but what was absolutely essential.

Even after Talleyrand's blundering attempt to extort a bribe from American diplomats in the fall of 1797, Adams was willing to engage in negotiations with the French. In late 1798, while many Federalists in Congress were clamoring for a declaration of war, Adams had announced to the Congress that his government would resume diplomatic engagements should France promise not to repeat the humiliating treatment of the American envoys. If the French government would first take the "requisite step" of providing such assurances, Adams said, he would send a second delegation to Paris.

France had good reasons to pursue a peaceful accommodation with America. The Directory observed the warming trend in Anglo-American relations with growing apprehension, and feared for the security of French colonial possessions in the Caribbean and the North American mainland. For all the harassment of merchant vessels by French privateers, France depended upon neutral maritime powers, particularly the United States, to carry goods and foodstuffs between Europe and the islands. When Talleyrand learned of the firestorm created in the United States by the XYZ revelations, he understood that he had overreached himself. As a conciliatory gesture, he issued direct orders demanding the liberation of American prisoners in the West Indies. Adams learned of these measures, and other indications of a French eagerness to renew diplomatic contacts, through American envoys in other European capitals.

On February 18, 1799, without consulting his cabinet and without any warning, Adams sent a message to the Senate. It was read by a surprised Jefferson, sitting in his capacity as president of the Senate: "Always disposed and ready to embrace every plausible appearance of probability of preserving or restoring tranquility, I nominate William Vans Murray, our minister resident at the Hague, to be minister plenipotentiary of the United States to the French Republic."

High Federalists, many still hankering for a formal declaration of war, were thunderstruck. "Had the foulest heart and ablest head in the world been permitted to select the most embarrassing and ruinous measures," said Senator Theodore Sedgewick of Massachusetts, "perhaps it would have been precisely the one which has been adopted." Abigail Adams observed with satisfaction that the New England war party was "like a flock of frightened pigeons; nobody had their story ready." Secretary of State Pickering told colleagues that he had had nothing to do with the decision, and openly opposed it. "The only negociation compatible with our honor or safety," he said, "is that begun by Truxtun in the capture of *L'Insurgente*."

Hamilton advised that it would be politically unwise to oppose Adams outright, but urged his followers to expand the mission to include two other envoys with harder-line credentials. The Senate endorsed a three-headed delegation consisting of William Vans Murray; Chief Justice Oliver Ellsworth; and William R. Davie, governor of North Carolina.

Pending the result of this new round of negotiations, Adams told Stoddert, naval operations should be carried out with undiminished energy. "Nor do I think we ought to wait a moment to know whether the French mean to give us any proofs of their desire to conciliate with us," he wrote. "I am for pursuing all the measures of defense which the laws authorize us to adopt, especially at sea." One frigate must be spared, however, to deliver Ellsworth and Davie across the Atlantic. That important assignment would fall to Captain John Barry and the USS *United States*.

BENJAMIN STODDERT HAD MOVED his wife and seven children from Georgetown to Philadelphia, and the family settled into a comfortable house on Chestnut Street between Ninth and Tenth, not far from the Navy Office. The new secretary was performing well on the job. He had earned the confidence of the president, who relied upon him to direct all Quasi War operations during Adams's seven-month sojourn in Massachusetts through the spring, summer, and early fall of 1799. Stoddert was, in fact, the only member of the cabinet who was not allied with Hamilton against Adams in the Federalists' increasingly heated intraparty struggle. "Mr. Stoddert is a man of great sagacity, and conducts the business of department with success and energy," wrote Treasury Secretary Oliver Wolcott in late 1799.

While managing the Quasi War deployments, Stoddert also planned for the long-term development of the navy, arguing (without success) for building a fleet of battleships, and developing procedures to limit the chaos, waste, and mismanagement that had been the blight of naval building programs since 1794. Above all, the secretary placed great emphasis on the importance of recruiting and promoting midshipmen who were capable of rising to command rank. Without an officer corps characterized by "zeal & spirit," he said, the navy "had better burn its vessels."

The lack of American bases and supply depots in the West Indies complicated the Quasi War deployments. In the late spring of 1799, the *United States*, *Constitution*, and *Constellation* each returned home, leaving the theater of operations without much of a naval presence at a time when large numbers of merchantmen were sailing from American ports. Stoddert hoped that the *Constitution* would return to the south by June 1, but she did not manage to leave Boston until July 23. Painful experience would teach Stoddert that six to eight weeks in port were needed to refit, reprovision, and man the big frigates. Moreover, the navy was an all-volunteer force, and recruiting was an omnipresent consideration. As a merchant and shipowner, Stoddert knew how the game was played. The sailors must be paid off and allowed to spend every last dollar on shore. "I think it will be best for you to discharge as many of your men as can be spared from the necessary services on board, whose times expire in this month and next," Stoddert wrote Captain Barry in May, as the *United States* lay in the Delaware, preparing to sail on her truce mission to France. "The sooner they are discharged, and have an opportunity of spending their money, the sooner they will enter for another year."

The success of the navy, in mid-1799, was reflected in the sharply declining numbers of American merchantmen captured by French privateers. In the waters surrounding Guadaloupe, where eighty-nine American vessels had been captured the previous year, only thirty-eight were taken in 1799. Overall, the number of American ships lost to the French in 1799 fell by nearly two thirds. A congressional study concluded that the navy had saved the nation more than $9 million in shipping losses. Naval deployments had proven that America was capable of defending its maritime trade against a major European power, and may have persuaded the Directory not to escalate the conflict by issuing a formal declaration of war.

Rivalries among naval commanders continued to roil the waters. Stoddert was called upon to settle a rancorous dispute concerning the rank and seniority of Captains Truxtun, Dale, and Talbot. Truxtun's had been the sixth and last name on the 1794 captain's list, and he was the only man who had not served in the Continental Navy during the Revolution (he had commanded a privateer). But when work had halted on three of the six frigates in 1796, Richard Dale and Silas Talbot (who had ranked third and fifth, respectively) had been released from duty. Their commissions had lapsed, and each man had returned to private life as a merchant captain. Did Truxtun, the most efficient and successful officer in the navy, who had returned from the Leeward Islands with a captured enemy frigate, still rank behind Talbot and Dale? Or had he superseded them? Each of the parties was especially interested in the decision because there was talk in Congress of creating the rank of admiral, and each man's seniority would influence the likelihood of his promotion.

"This avarice of Rank in the infancy of our Service is the Devil," Stoddert remarked in a letter to Alexander Hamilton, and he refused to pay any attention to the Truxtun-Dale-Talbot quarrel for almost a year. By midsummer of 1799, however, it was no longer possible to postpone a decision. Silas Talbot was serving as captain of the *Constitution*, which was provisioned, outfitted, and ready to sail from Boston Harbor. Early in July, Talbot informed Stoddert that he would resign and leave the ship unless his commission indicated that his original 1794 rank remained intact. Stoddert resented the ultimatum and was inclined to side with Truxtun, but he referred the decision to President Adams, who sighed: "We shall never get the *Constitution* to sea, by any means that I know of."

Because Adams was summering in Quincy, ten miles south of Boston, Talbot was in a position to lobby the president in person. On the morning of the fourteenth, the *Constitution*'s barge transported him from Nantasket Roads to Braintree, a passage of less than eight miles. A short ride delivered him in person to the doorstep at Peacefield. The stratagem succeeded. In a long conference in the president's parlor, Talbot reviewed his career and pressed his claim. Without allowing Truxtun a similar opportunity, Adams decided in Talbot's favor. The captain returned to his ship with his commission signed and dated by the president's own hand.

Right or wrong, the decision got the *Constitution* to sea. "After a detention of nine days by contrary winds," Adams wrote Stoddert on July 23, "the *Constitution* took advantage of a brisk breeze, and went out of the harbor and out of sight this forenoon, making a beautiful and noble figure amidst the joy and good wishes of thousands of good federalists." Although his decision on Talbot's rank was "irrevocable," he added, he hoped Truxtun would not resign. "Far be it from me to depreciate the merits, services, or talents of Captain Truxtun. I respect, I esteem, and, especially since his late glorious action, I love the man."

Truxtun had taken the *Constellation* to New York, where her battery of 24-pounder long guns was being replaced with 18-pounders and 32-pounder carronades. On August 1, he received Stoddert's letter informing him of the president's decision. Stoddert urged him to "Take at least one day to consider before you answer this Letter," but Truxtun mailed his commission back to Philadelphia the same afternoon. Shortly afterward, he told the officers of the *Constellation*: "It as little becomes my character to yield my rank . . . as it would my Ship to an enemy unequal in force. I have therefore thought proper to quit."

Truxtun set out on the half-day overland journey to Pleasant View, his estate in Perth Amboy, New Jersey. His house stood at the end of a long driveway lined with Lombardy poplars, surrounded with gardens that sloped down to the shore of Raritan Bay, with views across the water to Staten Island and the lighthouse at Sandy Hook. He told his friends he was reconciled to a peaceful retirement ashore, at home with his large family. With the *Insurgente* prize settlement added to his already considerable fortune, he was rich enough to live the rest of his life without earning another dollar.

Within days, however, Truxtun began to regret his abrupt decision. Having spent more than half his adult life at sea, he felt oppressed by the quiet, domestic routines of his country estate. "I must confess," he told a friend, "that it mortifies me to be Idle in a moment like the present, when every mind and every hand should be employed to save our country." In August, Truxtun learned that another French frigate had been seen at sea and might be in the vicinity of the American coast. In letters to friends and acquaintances, the former captain poured out his resentments against Adams and Talbot, but he also expressed a desire to "have another touch at those Frenchmen."

Secretary Stoddert was willing to have his best commander back in the service. From Philadelphia he wrote to say that Truxtun's resignation had never been formally accepted, and that his commission could be returned to him at any time. Letters arrived at Perth Amboy from friends and colleagues, urging him to reconsider. In September, George Washington invited him to visit Mount Vernon. No record was made of their conversation, but Truxtun afterward hinted that he would return to duty if asked.

In October, Stoddert offered Truxtun a choice of two commands: He could have the USS *President*, still on the stocks at the Brooklyn Navy Yard, almost ready for launch. She would be a powerful 44-gun ship, built on similar lines to the *Constitution* and the *United States*. Alternatively, the captain could resume command of the *Constellation*, which was back in Norfolk, and almost ready to sail for the West Indies. His commission would be returned to him without loss of seniority, and the secretary promised that the *Constellation* would not serve on the same station at the *Constitution*, so that Truxtun's hated rival, Silas Talbot, could never command him.

As tempting as the *President* was—she was larger and more powerful than *Constellation*—the new frigate would not sail until late spring at the earliest, and Truxtun was impatient to get back to sea. He caught a coasting sloop for Hampton Roads and reassumed command of the familiar *Constellation* in late November. No record was made of any speech he gave to the crew, but he might as well have repeated the words he had used the previous June: "On the ocean is our field to reap fresh laurels. Let the capstan, then, be well-manned, trip cheerfully our anchor, spread the sails, give three cheers, and away to hunt up our enemies, as we have done before, until we find them." On Christmas Day, 1799, the *Constellation* cleared Cape Henry and stretched away to the south, once again bound for St. Kitts.

A PASSAGE OF TWENTY-SIX DAYS brought the *Constellation* into the now familiar waters of the Lesser Antilles. On January 20, 1800, she came to anchor in Basseterre Roads. Moored securely in the harbor were most of the vessels of the Leeward Islands Squadron, now under Truxtun's sole command: the *John Adams*, the *Adams*, the *Baltimore*, the *Pickering*, and the *Eagle*.

The presence of so many American men-of-war in the port was not a welcome sight. Stoddert's orders had dwelled on the importance of keeping the squadron "constantly cruising," because the sea-lanes could only be made safer by vessels actively patrolling at sea. "You cannot be too adventurous," Stoddert had written. "We have nothing to fear but from want of enterprise." The secretary had also urged Truxtun to dispatch the vessels to cruise independently, rather than in groups or pairs, so that they could patrol a wider expanse of sea. "Nothing fills the President with more disgust," he had warned, "than the paragraphs frequently seen in our Papers giving an account of three or four of our Vessels having sailed from some port in the West Indies on a cruise . . . when there is no prospect of meeting an Enemy equal to the smallest of them."

Shortly after arriving at St. Kitts, Truxtun received intelligence that two French warships were anchored at Guadeloupe—a 44-gun frigate and a 28-gun corvette. He planned to take the *Constellation* into the offing and "give them a fair challenge to come out" and do battle. The ship was heavily laden with stores, lumber, and provisions for the squadron, and these had to be transferred to Clarkson's Yard in town. Truxtun was confident, verging even on boastfulness. He ordered the *Constellation*'s carpenter to clear the orlop deck of every extraneous item, and "not to leave a rope yarn in the way, as in one week . . . he was determined to have five hundred prisoners on board."

Constellation sailed from St. Kitts on January 30, with the ship "in excellent trim for sailing," and tacked into the unceasing southeast trade winds. The next morning she hailed *L'Insurgente*, Captain Alexander Murray, escorting a convoy of merchantmen to the north. There were very few sails on the horizon that afternoon, but as the sun rose on February 1, the lookout caught sight of a big ship about two leagues distant in the southeast. Truxtun at first assumed she was an English frigate, and the *Constellation* hoisted the British ensign; but the stranger continued on her course, made no attempt to answer signals, and flashed out studding sails in an apparent attempt to gain speed. Truxtun studied her for a while through his long glass, and concluded that "she was a heavy French frigate mounting at least 54 guns."

He was right. The stranger was the powerful frigate *La Vengeance*, 54 guns. In addition to her regular crew of 320, she carried 80 passengers (mainly French soldiers), 36 American prisoners, and a large sum of money. She was homeward-bound for France, and her captain, F. M. Pitot, had no wish to meet any enemy man-of-war. He put his ship before the wind and packed on sail, hoping to stay ahead in a long run to leeward.

Constellation cleared for action and continued in hot pursuit through freshening winds in the afternoon, proceeding with "every inch of canvas being set, that could be of service." Evening came on, the battle lanterns were lit, and the *Constellation* continued gaining on the chase. The hands remained at their battle stations for twelve consecutive hours. They talked in low voices, ran their guns in and out, tested the handspikes, and a few passed the hours "combing out their hair like Spartan sons of old." An hour after darkness had fallen, the *Constellation* reached extreme hailing range, and Truxtun took a speaking trumpet forward to the lee gangway. At about eight o'clock, he leaned over the rail and shouted at Pitot "to demand the surrender of his ship to the United States of America."

The hail was answered by a cannon fired through the Frenchman's stern ports, and Truxtun abandoned the attempted parley. The *Constellation* did not return fire immediately, as Truxtun wanted to get the ship into a position from which the entire broadside would bear on the enemy. Orders were sent forward to all the division commanders "not to throw away a single charge of powder and shot, but to take good aim, and fire directly into the Hull of the enemy . . . to cause or suffer no noise or confusion whatever; but to load and fire as fast as possible, when it could be done with certain effect."

La Vengeance hauled her wind and came up on a larboard tack, her guns bearing on *Constellation*, and fired a broadside. Her guns were aimed high, at the *Constellation*'s rigging. *Constellation* also turned into the wind, took a parallel course to the enemy, and ranged up on her quarter. A half moon hung low in the west. Visibility was poor: each ship appeared to the other as a vague shape across the water.

As *Constellation*'s guns came to bear, at a range of about 300 yards, Captain Truxtun gave the order to fire. It was a well-aimed, double-shotted broadside. *La Vengeance* responded, and then the gun crews on both ships continued firing and reloading as quickly as they could. There was little maneuvering. The frigates ran on parallel courses, trading broadsides from middle range, pounding each other relentlessly. It was, Truxtun wrote, "as sharp an action as ever was fought between two frigates."

La Vengeance was larger and heavier than *L'Insurgente*, and *Constellation* carried lighter cannon than she had in the earlier encounter. Under the French vessel's heavy fire, *Constellation* took severe punishment, particularly to her rigging. Her foresails were completely shot away, and the American ship lost the ability to maneuver while her crew worked to rig new stays. *La Vengeance* made sail and attempted to escape; the *Constellation* chased and resumed a battle of running broadsides. Twice the ships seemed on the verging of coming into contact, and both captains called for boarding parties. At a critical point in the action, said a witness aboard the *Constellation*, Captain Pitot "manned his rigging and quarters, to have boarded us," but the small arms fire of the American marines and topmen "so well received them, that [the French crew] fell back and damned the cause."

An hour into the battle, the French vessel's decks were strewn with dead and wounded. Captain Pitot had his speaking trumpet shot out of his hand— the ball continued past him and took off the arm of a lieutenant standing nearby. It is possible (reports are contradictory) that Pitot attempted to surrender, but in the darkness it was not clear whether the Tricolor had been struck, and the action continued.

At one o'clock in the morning, five hours after the first shot was fired, the French ship was silenced. Truxtun assumed she had surrendered. At that moment, however, the *Constellation*'s mainmast, which had been struck many times by cannon fire, was on the verge of going by the board. Most of the stays and shrouds that supported it had been shot away. Attention now turned to saving the mast: the crew raced to rig stoppers, and tried to repair the damaged shrouds and get up temporary stays—but the frigate was rolling on the sea, and the mast was losing its footing. Finally it broke, just above the deck, and fell over the side, into the sea, among a raft of wreckage. The topmen went with it, and all but one were drowned. Among the dead was thirteen-year-old Midshipman James Jarvis of New York. On the deck, a marine was caught beneath the mast as it fell. He was pinned under it, and could not be rescued for several hours. The *Constellation* was now, said surgeon Isaac Henry, "the most perfect wreck you ever Saw."

The moon had set, and the night was nearly pitch-black. A few hours after the battle, the lights of the Frenchman's lanterns could be seen in the distance, but she soon disappeared from view. At four in the morning, her signal guns were heard. Several hours were required to clear the wreckage on the *Constellation*'s deck, the men hacking at it with their hatchets and allowing most of the ruined spars, sailcloth, and rigging to slip over the side.

The injured *Constellation* had little hope of making any progress to windward, and St. Kitts was now 150 miles upwind. Truxtun ordered a course set for Jamaica, 700 miles to the west, beyond the hostile islands of San Domingo and Cuba. The frigate's casualties amounted to fifteen dead and twenty-five wounded. In the aftermath of the battle, Isaac Henry performed six "Amputations of Limbs" and treated "a number of very severe flesh wounds." All thought of *La Vengeance* was now pushed aside as Truxtun's chief concern was to save his jury-rigged ship and the lives of his exhausted crew.

The long run down to Jamaica took a week. Not until February 8 did the injured frigate creep into Port Royal, where the British gave them "a kind and friendly reception." Admiral Hyde Parker came aboard the *Constellation* as a guest. Nine severely wounded men were transferred to the hospital on shore.

Still there was no word of the fate of the French ship. "It is hard to conjecture," Truxtun wrote Stoddert, "whether she sunk, or whether she got into St. Thomas or Curacao. If she is still above water, she must be irreparable in the West-Indies. Her loss of men must have been prodigious in an action of five hours, with 600 men on board. My fire was directed principally at her hull." Several of the *Constellation*'s officers believed they had seen the French vessel sinking. Her pumps had been working hard when she parted company with the *Constellation*.

Truxtun and his officers oversaw the repairs to their ship. The most pressing was the replacement of the mainmast. Stores and supplies were in short supply in the West Indies, however, and the British could not or would not spare an extra spar. The repair of a Yankee frigate was not a priority. *Constellation* would have to make her way back to an American port under a jury-rig. She sailed from Jamaica on March 1, a week after the action, with a convoy of fourteen American merchantmen in her wake.

Not until the *Constellation* was safely home in Hampton Roads did Truxtun learn the fate of *La Vengeance*. As he had guessed, she had made for the Dutch island of Curacao, off the coast of modern-day Venezuela. The action had left her in a sinking condition, with six feet of water in her hold and an estimated two hundred shot holes in her hull. Civilian passengers were employed in bailing water from the ship, some armed with "buckets and wooden bowls." The American prisoners, who had been permitted to go below during the fighting, helped pump the water out and plug the shot holes. *La Vengeance* limped across the Gulf of Mexico "in a most distressed situation, without a Mast standing except the lower Fore and Mizen Masts, and not an original rope to be seen except the fore and bobstay that was not knotted or spliced."

Arriving at Curacao, Pitot deliberately ran his disabled ship onto the beach near town rather than attempt to navigate the entrance to the harbor. Eyewitness reports described the French ship as "shattered"—her shrouds and ratlines "were cut up so, you could scarce see any of them for stoppers. In short, there appears no place that has escaped a shot." Her remaining masts were "perforated with round and double-headed shot in such a manner as to surprise a person how they could hold together." In thanks to the American prisoners who had helped save the ship, Captain Pitot allowed them to go free.

Though *La Vengeance* was slightly smaller than *Constellation* by tonnage, she mounted a significantly heavier broadside: a total of 559 pounds versus 372 pounds in combined weight of metal. The *Constellation* had engaged an adversary that outgunned her by some 50 percent, but the French had suffered far worse in the fight. Captain Pitot reported 28 killed and 40 wounded, but some reports in Curacao estimated the combined casualties at 160. If true, *La Vengeance* had suffered four casualties for every one suffered by the *Constellation*. This could be attributed, in part, to the traditional French tactical preference for firing high into the rigging rather than into the hull. But the efficiency and speed with which the American gun crews did their work was the most critical factor. By Captain's Pitot's own account, *La Vengeance* had discharged 742 rounds in the course of the action, while the *Constellation*, with fewer guns, had discharged a total of 1,229. The American gun crews had worked twice as fast as their adversaries.

CAPTAIN TRUXTUN'S RECEPTION was much as it had been the year before. Banquets, songs, toasts, poems greeted the officers and enlisted men of the *Constellation*. Few questioned that the ship was the victor even if the enemy had escaped. Congress voted to cast a gold medal for Truxtun.

Republicans, however, charged that Truxtun had endangered prospects of a negotiated peace, and even some supporters of the navy believed that Quasi War operations should be confined to providing convoys and protecting commerce, not to seeking out battle with French men-of-war. The battering of *La Vengeance*, the *Aurora* editorialized, was a "hideous transaction." "Whence comes this madness for killing foreigners and for getting one's fellow countrymen killed," Pierre du Pont de Nemours asked Jefferson, "when it is evident that both nations are reconciled or arbitrating?"

Hampton Roads was crowded with frigates, each in need of attention from the overworked Gosport Navy Yard. The Norfolk-built *Chesapeake* had been launched the previous December, and her mostly bare hull was anchored in the Elizabeth River. *L'Insurgente* had recently arrived from the West Indies, having sprung her foremast in a storm off Cuba. And on February 24, a month before the arrival of the *Constellation*, the Portsmouth-built *Congress* had crept into the lower Roads, storm-beaten and completely dismasted, without a single spar standing. Her officers were feuding openly and her crew was verging on mutiny.

Congress had sailed from Newport, Rhode Island, on January 6, in company with the Salem-built subscription frigate *Essex*. Their destination was the East Indies, where they were ordered to fetch home a convoy of stranded American merchant vessels. Except for the short coastal run to Newport from Portsmouth, New Hampshire, where the *Congress* had been launched the previous August, the passage to Asia would be her maiden voyage. She was under the command of Captain James Sever, a native of Portsmouth who had received his naval commission in 1794.

The first five days out of Newport were wintry and bitter cold, with a northerly wind sending snow and hail down on deck. On the eleventh, however, the wind veered into the south and blew a very hard gale, bringing warm rain and heavy seas. *Congress* and *Essex* lost contact. The *Congress*'s standing rigging had been set up during the New England winter, and the sudden rise in temperature caused the tarred-hemp ropes to stretch and go visibly slack. Supporting tackles were set up and the ship hove to, but to no avail. On the morning of the twelfth, the mainmast began to give way, about eight feet above the deck. Fourth Lieutenant Nathaniel Bosworth raced up the shrouds to the maintop, followed by a crew of five sailors. The men worked furiously to cut away the topmast, in the hope of saving the lower mast, but before they could do so the entire mainmast gave way and plunged into the sea, taking the mizzen topmast with it. Bosworth drowned, while the others clung to the wreckage and were rescued. With the loss of so many sails and such a great part of her rigging, Captain Sever wrote, the *Congress* was left "laying in the trough of the Sea, Laboring very much." At half past noon the fore topmast went over the side, and a few minutes later it was discovered that the bowsprit was badly sprung. At 3:30 p.m. the bowsprit was lost; soon afterwards the rest of the foremast went, leaving the unfortunate frigate completely dismasted and "entirely at the mercy of the winds and waves."

For the next several days, the crew of the *Congress* fought to save the crippled ship. Immense waves crashed over the spar deck. The jolly boat was torn from the stern davits and swept into the sea. Many of her crew assumed all was lost. A full ten days were required to rig the jury mast, and eventually the ship managed to limp back toward the North American coast. After a six-week ordeal, on February 22, the *Congress* and her exhausted crew reached the safety of Cape Henry and the Chesapeake Bay. As if to add insult to injury, her jury mast was lost over the side as the ship attempted to run up to Hampton Roads; she was obliged to anchor in the channel and rig another.

The frigate had been saved, but discipline had collapsed. Captain Sever demanded the court-martial of First Lieutenant John Cordis for insubordination. Cordis, in turn, charged Sever with gross incompetence. Before the dismasting of the *Congress*, the lieutenant had recommended that she run or "scud" before the storm. While the shrouds and stays on the weather side were kept taut by the wind, he said, the slack could be taken out of the lee rigging. The ship could then wear, bringing the wind onto her opposite quarter, and the procedure could be repeated. Sever had overruled the suggestion, saying, "I, sir, am the best judge," and the *Congress* instead lay close-hauled against the gale. If Sever had accepted his advice, Cordis told Secretary Stoddert, "we should have reserved the masts." (The lieutenant's position was vindicated when it was learned that the *Essex*, smaller and more lightly built than the *Congress*, had done just as Cordis had advised and survived the gale with masts and rigging intact.)

Stoddert's instinct was to side with the commanding officer, but there were other indications that Captain Sever had lost the confidence of his junior officers. Marine Lieutenant Benjamin Strother wanted out of the ship. "The Service is to me in every way disgusting, & I think you would perfectly agree with me if you [served aboard the *Congress*] for one week only," he told Major Commandant William Burrows. He gave as his excuse a proneness to seasickness—"I have been almost continuously seasick & I believe I should remain so if I sailed for a year"—but he also referred, obliquely, to "many other reasons." In March, a gang of sailors attempted to seize control of the frigate while she lay at anchor in Hampton Roads. They were arrested and confined. On April 9, Lieutenant Cordis traded fisticuffs with a sailor, Patrick Brown, who would not back off until the other officers threatened to shoot him.

In mid-April, Midshipman John Duboise applied to the Navy Office for a transfer. Stoddert replied: "You soon shall be separated from Sever. If he goes in the *Congress*, you shall be removed. But do not mention this to the other Midshipmen, as there is too much disorder and uneasiness on board of the *Congress* already." Before receiving this reply, Duboise fought a duel with a fellow midshipman, Samuel Cushing, and "shot his antagonist through the neck, which put an immediate period to his Existence." Fearing arrest on a murder charge, Duboise fled.

With so many injured frigates competing for attention from the small Norfolk shore establishment, Naval Constructor Josiah Fox and his gang of shipwrights and laborers were pressed to full capacity. There were simply not enough men on hand to do all the needed work. In March, Stoddert ordered that priority should be given to the *Congress*, since she was fully manned, with her officers and crew drawing wages. Fox apparently preferred to continue fitting out the *Chesapeake*, a ship he had designed and built himself. On March 20, Stoddert amplified the order. "The *Congress* is full of men," he told Fox. "The *Chesapeake* has not a seaman aboard. You will take every man from the *Chesapeake* that can be in any measure useful . . . and pay no attention to any other object to the prejudice of [the *Congress*] until it is accomplished."

When *Constellation* arrived in Hampton Roads a few days later, however, Captain Truxtun was in no mood to wait for the mainmast he had been unable to obtain in Jamaica. "You will proceed with all the dispatch that is in your power to make the mainmast for the *Constellation*," he told Fox, brushing aside Stoddert's order. "You should procure a proper gang to make the *Constellation*'s spars . . . I desire that you proceed to obey this order, and that I hear no excuse in future."

Whatever the order of priority for frigate repairs, Stoddert was only too willing to delegate authority to his favorite captain. The various complaints emanating from the Norfolk station had already demanded far too much of the secretary's time and attention. Though Truxtun was expected to assume command of the USS *President*, launched in New York on April 10, Stoddert asked that he remain in Hampton Roads until the "disorders" aboard the *Congress* could be sorted out. He encouraged Truxtun to "assume all the authority belonging to your rank at Norfolk, which is as much as if you were already an Admiral . . . or as if you had the Command of the whole Navy." Truxtun did not have to be asked twice. He moved quickly to extend his autocratic rule over every aspect of naval business. A marine lieutenant on the station described him a "tyrant," a man "accustomed to receive homage . . . without bounds," who demanded "abject submission to his supreme will." The commodore signed an order: "Thomas Truxtun, Vested with the powers of Commander in Chief of the Navy of U.S."

The dismasting of the *Congress* called Sever's seamanship into question, but the public charges of mutiny, incompetence, and insubordination among her officers and crew threatened to turn the entire service into a laughingstock. Truxtun told Stoddert he intended "to put an End to such Conduct as the officers of the *Congress* have exhibited here & with as little noise & trouble to the Public as possible," in order to protect the standing and reputation of the navy.

On April 29, a court of inquiry convened in the greatcabin of the *Chesapeake* as she lay anchored in the Elizabeth River. Truxtun and two other captains presided. Captain Sever arrived promptly at 9:00 a.m., his logbook under his arm, accompanied by his sailing master and several lieutenants. His chief accuser, First Lieutenant Cordis, did not appear: the court minutes stated that he was "unwell and not able to attend." A letter signed by Cordis was read aloud. It flatly contradicted his earlier assertions, and corroborated Sever's version of events in every important detail. The court quickly rendered its verdict: "We unanimously acquit [Captain Sever] with honor of any charge of negligence, and are of the opinion that he used all his skill and endeavors to prevent the accident," which was caused by "the Badness and insufficiency of the Masts." Sever was judged "a very Attentive, Modest, and firm officer, and a gentleman who possesses materials well worth cultivating in the Navy of the United States."

The entire proceeding had been orchestrated in advance. Working behind the scenes, Truxtun had arranged a deal with Lieutenant Cordis. In exchange for reversing his testimony, Cordis (whom Truxtun deemed "a good seaman") was allowed to transfer into the *Chesapeake*, where he would retain his rank under Captain Samuel Barron. Several of the officers and most of the crew of the *Congress* would go with him. The would-be mutineers were condemned to be "flogged with a cat of Nine tails at the gang way," with sentences ranging from forty-eight to a hundred lashes each. The ringleaders, after suffering the punishment, were to be "discharged as unworthy of ever serving in future on board of any ship belonging to the United States."

With the *Chesapeake* now fully manned and the *Congress* nearly empty, Truxtun prodded Fox to shift his focus to the former. On May 22, the Norfolk-built frigate put to sea for the first time. "As her sails filled, a band of music on the quarterdeck played the President's March," the *Norfolk Herald* reported. "As she passed the shipping that lay in the harbor, she fired a salute of 13 guns, which was handsomely returned by every vessel. . . . The wharves and houses next to the river were lined with people, who with three cheers welcomed her as she passed the town point. . . . Thus, from the *Chesapeake*, the navy of the United States receives no small addition of strength."

Pushing the *Congress* out of port would prove more difficult. Few sailors were willing to serve under Sever. "I fear some difficulty in manning [the

Congress]," said Truxtun, "—the prejudices against Captain Sever are very great. Indeed I fear his Idea of discipline is not correct. Discipline is to be effected by a particular department, much easier than by great Severity." Despite many sharply worded orders from Washington, the *Congress* did not sail from Norfolk until July, after a six-month hiatus in port. Even then, the ship remained unhappy. Captain Alexander Murray, after visiting her in October, told Stoddert he was "sorry to say that the same kind of discontent prevails yet aboard the *Congress.*" Captain Sever, he said, "is a well-informed gentleman but has not the practical knowledge of a Seaman."

THE HAMILTONIAN FACTION, including several members of the president's cabinet, had done their utmost to capsize Adams's decision to send a second peace delegation to Paris. They believed the policy would leave America looking weak and craven in Europe, and feared a rupture with England. But there was a critical subtext to the issue: the fate of the army. Adams did not disguise his view that the new army was superfluous and expensive. "Regiments are costly articles everywhere," he told McHenry, "and more so in this country than any other under the sun." If it were up to him, he said, the army "should not exist a fortnight."

His intraparty rivals took advantage of Adams's long absence from the capital in the spring, summer, and early fall of 1799. The ever loyal Stoddert warned him, in letters written confidentially and "entirely in a private character," that conspiracies were afoot to prevent the peace mission from sailing, and that "artful designing men might make such use of your absence" to subvert the president's chosen policy. At last awakening to the magnitude of the opposition arrayed against him, Adams rode out of Quincy on the last day of September. Two weeks later, he reached Trenton, where the federal government had decamped in order to escape Philadelphia's annual yellow fever epidemic. The town was choked with refugees, and the president was fortunate to obtain a small two-room suite at a local boardinghouse.

General Hamilton, whose headquarters were located in nearby Newark, called on Adams directly in order to press his case against the mission. They met at Adams's boardinghouse, presumably in the small parlor attached to his bedroom, and spoke for several hours. According to Adams, Hamilton's "eloquence and vehemence wrought the little man up to a degree of heat and effervescence." Hamilton argued that England was likely to prevail over France in the great European war; that it would be contrary to American interests to conclude an early peace with France. He even predicted that

Louis XVIII and the Bourbons would be restored to the French throne by Christmas. Adams later said he was taken aback by Hamilton's "total ignorance" of the state of affairs in Europe. "I heard him with perfect good humor, though never in my life did I hear a man talk more like a fool."

The following day, Adams rendered his decision. The mission would sail at the earliest possible date. "The President has resolved to send the commissioners to France," Hamilton wrote Washington, who had returned to Mount Vernon. "All my calculations lead me to regret the measure."

It was Adams's particular wish that Chief Justice Ellsworth and Governor Davie should sail for France in the frigate *United States*. Her captain, John Barry, may not have been the navy's most active or efficient commander, but he was the highest-ranking officer in the service, and the *United States* was (with *Constitution*) one of the two largest and most powerful ships in the fleet. The frigate would be closely observed in whatever French port she disembarked her distinguished passengers—L'Orient, Le Havre, Cherbourg—and Adams thought it important that she make a formidable impression. Stoddert tried to persuade the president to send a smaller vessel, so as to avoid diverting "so great a proportion of our force for so long a time," but Adams was adamant. He would only concede to allowing the *United States* to return after delivering the envoys, rather than remain in a French port pending the result of the negotiations.

John Barry, aging and in poor health, was developing a reputation as a commander who liked to keep his ship in port for excessive lengths of time. Stoddert's letters on the subject grew more pointed. He asked Barry to consider the poor example the *United States* would set for the other vessels of the navy by remaining so long at her moorings while needing no obvious repairs. "Let me therefore urge you to hasten your departure," he wrote on June 17, while the *United States* was lying in the Delaware. "If anything on my part is necessary to accelerate it, inform me, and it shall instantly be done. I hope you will be able to sail in the course of this week."

The envoys would meet the ship in Newport, Rhode Island. Stoddert urged Barry to be ready to sail the moment they arrived: "it will be proper that you take in without delay such Provisions, Stores etc etc such as you stand in need of that you may be ready in a moment to proceed to Sea." Stoddert took a direct hand in arranging the details of hospitality and accommodations for the ministers and their suite, consisting of two secretaries and two servants. They should be, he told Barry, "liberally but not profusely supplied with the best provisions for the Voyage . . . erring rather on the side of too much than too little." Arriving in Newport on October 31, Ellsworth and

Davie made a point of praising "the most ample and satisfactory preparations for our accommodation on board the *United States.*"

United States sailed on November 3, reaching the port of Lisbon three and a half weeks later. There her troubles began. A strict quarantine had been laid on all vessels arriving from America because of "the terrible and Mortiferous Contageon the Yellow fever which lays waste and destroys that country." Detained several weeks in the Tagus by contrary winds, *United States* finally sailed for L'Orient on December 21. Barry had predicted a passage of seven or eight days, but on Christmas Eve, in the Bay of Biscay, a ferocious gale rose out of the north and blew relentlessly until January 2. When celestial observations again became possible, it was discovered that the ship had drifted far out into the Atlantic.

Ellsworth and Davie, whose enthusiasm for sea travel was diminishing rapidly, asked to be landed anywhere on the continental European coast. They would travel overland to Paris. On January 11, 1800, the *United States* made landfall near La Coruña in northern Spain, but new gale-force winds forced her to strike her topmasts and seek refuge in the Bay of Ares. There she lost two anchors when her cables broke, and the big frigate was nearly lost. The envoys hailed a small fishing vessel, which landed them at the village of Puentes d'Eume, from which they could travel to La Coruña overland, and from there to Paris.

In La Coruña they learned of the *coup d'état* of 18 Brumaire, in which the thirty-three-year-old Napoleon Bonaparte had proclaimed himself First Consul and the effective military dictator of France. Bonaparte was eager to isolate Britain by cultivating good relations with America and other neutral states. In December, he had proclaimed that French-American relations would be governed by Louis XVI's Treaty of 1778. Talleyrand, who had managed to survive and regain his seat as foreign minister, sent passports to the American envoys with assurances that the new regime wished to receive them with full diplomatic honors. Their presence in Paris was urgently requested.

Hostilities were brought to a close by the Convention of Mortefontaine, signed on October 3. A grand celebration was held north of Paris, at the chateau for which the treaty was named. The event was "the most splendid occasion of its kind since the beginning of the French Revolution." Speaking to an audience of several hundred dignitaries, Napoleon described the three-year Quasi War as a "family quarrel." Gifts were exchanged, and toasts brought back the old familiar rhetoric of Franco-American amity and alliance.

The first rumors of peace reached America in November 1800; a copy of the treaty arrived in Washington in mid-December. Though it did not require France to pay indemnities for an estimated $12 million in cumulative maritime spoliations, it released the United States from obligations to France under the Treaty of 1778. The terms were welcomed by merchants and shipowners, who had never held out much hope of receiving compensation for past losses and who were chiefly interested bringing hostilities to an end. Pending ratification, Stoddert circulated orders to all naval commanders to cease preemptive attacks on French armed ships. Convoy operations continued. As news of the treaty spread, hostilities in the Caribbean relaxed and attacks on American shipping declined in frequency. By early spring of 1801, they had all but ceased. The Quasi War was over.

The result was a great vindication for John Adams. His controversial decision to send a second delegation to Paris had preserved American neutrality and restored peace. He had pulled the country back from the brink of dissolution and civil war. He had, as he said, "steered the vessel . . . into a peaceable and safe port." In so doing, he sacrificed his hopes of reelection, as the Hamiltonian faction flared up in open opposition and the Federalist Party splintered.

Two decades earlier, Adams had been closely associated with the disappointments of the Continental Navy. As president, he engineered a "second commencement" of the navy that managed to avoid the worst mistakes and misadventures of the earlier experience. In the Quasi War, the nation had demonstrated to itself and to Europe that it was capable of projecting military force far from North American shores. The United States had built a small but respectable fleet of warships and a shore-based infrastructure to keep them at sea. The 44-gun frigates *United States*, *Constitution*, and *President* were the most powerful ships of their class in any navy in the world. Good officers had planted their feet firmly on the lowest rungs of the promotion ladder, and in time they would inherit command of a thoroughly professional service.

In retirement, ex-President Adams would continue to press his campaign for naval power. "The counsel which Themistocles gave to Athens, Pompey to Rome, Cromwell to England, DeWitt to Holland, and Colbert to France, I have always given and shall continue to give to my countrymen," he wrote Truxtun in 1802—"That the great questions of commerce and power between nations and empires must be determined by sea . . . [and therefore] all reasonable encouragement should be given to a navy." Letters from Quincy repeated the same catchphrase, again and again, like a mantra: "The trident of Neptune is the scepter of the world."

PART TWO

To the Shores of Tripoli

CHAPTER FIVE

The presidential campaign of 1800 pitted Adams against the man who was both the sitting vice president and leader of the opposition, Thomas Jefferson. It was almost certainly the most bitterly fought election in American history. The political culture of the young democracy was still evolving, and there was not yet an established boundary between acceptable rhetoric and outright slander. The result was a campaign of personal vilification, rumormongering, and mudslinging not quite like anything the American people had ever seen before, or have since.

Arch Federalist and Yale College president Timothy Dwight warned his congregation that if Jefferson won the election, "The Bible would be cast into a bonfire, our holy worship changed into a dance of Jacobin frenzy, our wives and daughters dishonored, and our sons converted into the disciples of Voltaire and the dragoons of Marat." A Federalist newspaper in New York predicted that a Republican victory would bring a flood of French and Irish revolutionaries, "the refuse of Europe," who would launch a Jacobin-style reign of terror against "all who love order, peace, virtue, and religion." For the first time, rumors surfaced that a slavewoman who lived at Monticello, Sally Hemings, had borne Jefferson's children.*

The Republicans, on their part, struck back, reiterating all their favorite charges against the president. Adams, a campaign handbill proclaimed, was an "avowed friend of monarchy" who was plotting to "saddle you with Political Slavery." He was a warmonger, a plutocrat, and a secret agent of the Eng-

---

* Comparisons of Y-chromosome DNA samples taken from descendants of Jefferson's male relatives and Sally Hemings's sons have established, beyond a reasonable doubt, that the rumors were true.

lish crown. Some of the more scurrilous Republican broadsheets called attention to the indisputable (if not particularly relevant) fact that Adams was a fat, toothless old man. But what was especially galling for Adams was that he was taking fire from two sides. His decision to send a second peace delegation to France had turned the High Federalists intractably against him. The intraparty attack on Adams climaxed with a hostile pamphlet entitled *Letter from Alexander Hamilton Concerning the Public Conduct and Character of John Adams, Esq., President of the United States*. Hamilton concluded this strange and incoherent essay with a reluctant endorsement of Adams's reelection, on the basis that a Jefferson presidency was unacceptable. But the damage was done: Adams himself recognized that the rupture with Hamilton would cost him the election.

In the sixteen-state electoral college, Jefferson polled 73 votes to Adams's 65. The pivotal state had been New York, where the Federalist influence was strong—the efforts of the Republican vice-presidential candidate, Aaron Burr, ensured a narrow victory in the popular vote. But a flaw in the original version of the U.S. Constitution (corrected in 1804 by the Twelfth Amendment) brought about a perverse result. There was no separate line on the presidential ballot for a vice-presidential candidate: the Constitution merely ruled that the candidate receiving the second largest number of electoral votes would become vice president. Burr had won 73 electoral votes, the same number as Jefferson. The Republican running mates were tied in the electoral college. Although it was understood by all that Jefferson had run for president and Burr for vice president, the question of which man would occupy the highest office was thrown into the House of Representatives, which was still controlled by the Federalists.

Instead of casting his support to Jefferson, the unscrupulous Burr maneuvered for a deal that would secure the top office for himself. House Federalists, hating both men equally, plotted to void the election results and elevate the president pro tempore of the Senate to the presidency. Separately, Hamilton and Adams each sought to obtain Jefferson's assurances on several issues (including a pledge to "maintain the navy") as the price of Federalist support, but Jefferson refused to bargain for the office he had rightfully won. Ballot after ballot ended in deadlock. A constitutional crisis loomed. The Republican governor of Pennsylvania threatened to send his state's militia to march on Washington.

At last, Hamilton intervened to resolve the impasse. With confessed reluctance, he urged his followers in the House to choose Jefferson over Burr, because (he said) Burr was a truly dangerous man, while "a true estimate of

Mr. J's character warrants the expectation of a temporizing rather than a violent system." On February 17, 1801, with the thirty-sixth ballot, the House voted to elect Thomas Jefferson the third president of the United States.

Two weeks later, shortly before noon on March 4, Jefferson left his boardinghouse at New Jersey Avenue and C Street and trudged up the muddy, rutted road to the unfinished Capitol, which was surrounded by brick kilns, construction sheds, and workmen's shanties, and littered with "mud, shavings, boards, planks, & all the rubbish of building." Pools of dirty water had collected in holes where clay had been dug out of the ground to be used in manufacturing bricks. Horses and carriages were parked wherever their drivers could locate a patch of vacant grass. Except for the main dirt road, which skirted north of the Capitol, the entire hill was overgrown with brush and briars and could be traversed only on footpaths. The north and south wings of the Capitol were coupled by a boardwalk, covered by a makeshift wooden roof, that allowed members to pass from one to the other without sinking into the mud. The unfinished south wing, where the House of Representatives met, was a poorly ventilated, oval-shaped brick structure that members had nicknamed "the oven." The Senate Chamber in the north wing was more or less completed, so this was where the inaugural ceremony would be held. The senators had crowded into one side of the chamber to make room for their House colleagues, many of whom remained standing in order to allow the ladies to sit. There was thought to be as many as a thousand people in the chamber. A witness recalled that the room "was so crowded that I believe not another creature could enter."

The outgoing president had caught the 4:00 a.m. stage to Philadelphia, where he would be reunited with Abigail for the long journey back to Quincy and retirement. Adams's absence was condemned by Republicans as a crowning act of petulance, and a missed opportunity to signal that the Federalists would remain loyal to the Constitution while in opposition. Adams and Jefferson would not return to speaking terms for a dozen years.

Jefferson had always been a reluctant orator. He disliked being thrust in front of a large crowd, and he spoke in a low, tentative voice. Only a handful of people seated directly in front of the rostrum could hear him—the others would have no idea what was said until a printed version was passed out at the end of the ceremony. But whatever the quality of the original performance, Jefferson's first inaugural address was one of the most important public statements of his career, ranking alongside the Declaration of Independence as a justification of the American democratic experiment, and cast in phrases that managed simultaneously to seduce and command. The United States, Jefferson said, was "a rising nation, spread over a wide and fruitful land, traversing all the seas with the rich productions of their industry, engaged in commerce with nations who feel power and forget right, advancing rapidly to destinies beyond the reach of mortal eye." Self-government, as practiced in America, was "the world's best hope"—and self-government had been given a fighting chance by the fortunate presence of a great ocean separating America "from the exterminating havoc of one quarter of the globe." He introduced the axiom that has been so often quoted by advocates of an isolationist foreign policy, and so often misattributed to George Washington: "Possessing a chosen country, with room enough for our descendants to the thousandth and thousandth generation," the people of the United States would seek "honest friendship with all nations, entangling alliances with none."

The partisan bitterness and repression of the 1790s, said Jefferson, had been an aberration, a distant echo of "the throes and convulsions of the ancient world." Now, all would be forgiven. In the line that was best remembered and most often quoted, the new president offered a truce to his political enemies: "Every difference of opinion is not a difference of principle. We have called by different names brethren of the same principle. We are all republicans, we are all federalists."

Jefferson exited the Capitol without fanfare and returned to his lodgings at Conrad & McMunn's boardinghouse. As he and his thirty or so fellow boarders sat down in the dining hall, Jefferson took his habitual chair, furthest away from the fire, declining to be seated at the head of the table in recognition of his new rank. He would continue to live at the boardinghouse for the first two weeks of his administration, conducting the business of the federal government from a private parlor adjoining his bedchamber, from which he enjoyed sweeping southern views of the "thick & noble wood" along the banks of the Potomac.

THE NEW PRESIDENT WAS FIFTY-SEVEN YEARS OLD, but he was as healthy and vigorous as a man half his age. He was six feet two inches tall and "straight as a gun-barrel," recalled Edmund Bacon, who worked at Monticello for many years: "He was like a fine horse—he had no surplus flesh. He had an iron constitution, and was very strong." With advancing years, his shoulder-length hair had gone completely gray, and his face showed the ruddy color and peeling skin of a man accustomed to long hours of outdoor exercise. He had keen, friendly eyes that were either gray, blue, or hazel, according to the contradictory opinions of his friends and relatives. His most striking feature, evident to posterity only in images that depict him in profile (such as busts, reliefs, or silhouettes), was his cartoonishly strong chin.

Jefferson had a pleasant, easygoing manner that seemed to refute the barrage of Federalist propaganda that had been launched at him from the hustings. Margaret Bayard Smith, wife of the editor of the Washington *National Intelligencer* and a shrewd chronicler of early Washington society, had been raised by Federalist parents who taught her to believe that Jefferson was "an ambitious and violent demagogue, coarse and vulgar in his manners, awkward and rude in his appearance." She described how a visit from an anonymous guest, shortly after the election, had changed her mind:

> I was one morning sitting alone in the parlour, when the servant opened the door and showed in a gentleman who wished to see my husband. The usual frankness and care with which I met strangers were somewhat checked by the dignified and reserved air of the present visitor; but the chilled feeling was only momentary, for after taking the chair I offered him in a free and easy manner, and carelessly throwing his arm on the table near which he sat, he turned towards me a countenance beaming with an expression of benevolence and with a manner and voice almost femininely soft and gentle, entered into conversation on the commonplace topics of the day. . . .
>
> I know not how it was, but there was something in his manner, his countenance and voice that at once unlocked my heart, and in answer to his casual enquiries concerning our situation in our new home, as he called it, I found myself frankly telling him what I liked or disliked in our present circumstances and abode. I knew not who he was, but the interest with which he listened to my artless details . . . put me perfectly at my ease; in truth so kind and conciliating were his looks and manners that I forgot he was not a friend of my own, until on the opening of the door, Mr. Smith entered and introduced the stranger to me as Mr. Jefferson.
>
> I felt my cheeks burn and my heart throb, and not a word more could I speak while he remained. Nay, such was my embarrassment I could scarcely listen to the conversation carried on between him and my husband.

The last week of March, Jefferson moved into the executive mansion, which stood on a hilltop a mile and a half west of the Capitol. The big white sandstone house, which would not be called the White House until decades later, was rectangular in shape, with a series of four engaged Ionic columns on the north side, facing Pennsylvania Avenue and President's Square. The south-facing windows commanded a sweeping view of the Potomac and the port of Alexandria in the distance. The mansion, like all of Washington, was a work in progress, and the grounds were crowded with construction sheds, stacks of lumber, and stonecutters' huts. A visitor complained that "in a dark night, instead of finding your way to the house, you may, perchance, fall in a pit, or stumble over a heap of rubbish."

The twenty-three rooms were cold, drafty, unfurnished, and smelled of fresh paint and plaster. Jefferson lived in the southwest corner on the main floor, working and living in two rooms where his books and personal papers were piled up on tables, and in which he kept his treasured "scientific instruments, maps, globes, and gardening tools." Adjoining his study was an antechamber that Jefferson used as a sitting room, and an oval drawing room where he received visitors. The East Room had originally been intended for public receptions. Abigail Adams had used it as a space to hang clothes out to dry. Now it was partitioned into a combined bedchamber and office for the president's private secretary, Meriwether Lewis.

Jefferson remarked that he and Lewis lived in the great house like a pair of mice in a church. In fact, they were well looked after by a staff that included a steward, a coachman, a French chef, a footman, a valet, and a varying number of scullions and maids. "We find this a very agreeable country residence," Jefferson wrote his son-in-law shortly after moving in; "Good society, and enough of it, and free from the noise, the heat, the stench and the bustle of a close-built town."

Jefferson was never out of bed later than dawn. In the cold months, a servant kept a box in his room well supplied with dry firewood, and the president began his day by building and stoking a fire with his own hand. From five until nine, he worked without interruption at the green baize–covered portable writing desk that he had had built to his own design in 1776, the same desk on which he had written the Declaration of Independence. He sat in an ingeniously contrived ergonomic revolving chair, also built to his own design. He wrote quickly and with little or no editing, and it was in these letters that most of the substantive work of his presidency was done. After nine, he was willing to receive cabinet officers, members of Congress, and others; but if no one appeared, he continued to write. He wrote 116 letters during his first month in office and 677 letters in his first year, taking care to keep a copy of each. In November, he could report that his daily routine had "got to a steady and uniform course. It keeps me from 10 to 12 and 13 hours a day at my writing table, giving me an interval of 4 hours for riding, dining and a little unbending."

Jefferson's daily ramble on horseback was his main form of exercise, and his cherished escape from the duties of his office. Every afternoon at exactly one o'clock, he quit his desk and went down to the stables, where his Irish coachman and riding agent, James Dougherty, would already have saddled and bridled one of the president's horses. Jefferson's tastes ran to imported plated stirrups and leopard-skin saddles. He was an expert rider. "You saw at a glance," said his grandson, Thomas Jefferson Randolph, "from his easy and confident seat, that he was master of his horse, which was usually the fine blood horse of Virginia. The only impatience of temper he ever exhibited was with his horse, which he subdued to his will by a fearless application of the whip, on the slightest manifestation of restiveness."

Long hours on the rutted carriage roads and bridle paths of the District of Columbia allowed him to survey the capital city at firsthand. Its French designer, Pierre L'Enfant, had envisioned a "system of larger and lesser centers widely dispersed over the terrain," interconnected by expansive avenues that reached out diagonally, like the spokes of a wheel, from the major public edifices. It was a grand vision, and Jefferson was smitten with it. But it was only that, a vision—the reality, in 1801, fell far short. It was not just that L'Enfant's city was not yet finished. Skeptics doubted that it could *ever* be finished. The ambitious street plan had contemplated a great city, a major population center, and a nexus of commerce and the arts. What was actually there was a mostly uncultivated lowland wilderness in which one might find, here or there, an isolated public building or a half-deserted, tumbledown hamlet.

Valuing his solitude, Jefferson did not allow a servant to accompany him on his daily rides. He rode east or west along Pennsylvania Avenue, the District's main thoroughfare, named as a consolation to the state from which the capital had been transferred. The road started in Georgetown, crossed the Rock Creek bridge at M Street, passed through the little village that had sprung up around the White House, crossed Goose Creek by a stone bridge at Second Street, cut through the little village that surrounded the Capitol, then turned south on New Jersey Avenue and ran through a hilly backcountry all the way to the Navy Yard on the Eastern Branch of the Potomac. This was, at least, the theoretical route. In 1801, the best parts of the road were still littered with stumps, while the worst stretches appeared to peter out into the surrounding wilds. One bridge across Rock Creek had collapsed into a heap of stones, and the stretch between the creek and the executive village passed over a steep hill that was virtually impassable to carriages and wagons.

Between the White House and Capitol Hill, a rutted causeway traversed the "Tiber swamp," a soggy lowland overgrown with brambles, hawthorns, blackberries, and wild rose bushes. A flagstone walkway had been started from the White House toward the Capitol, and a footpath strewn with stone chips had been started from the Capitol toward the White House, but both had been abandoned before they ever met. At high tide, Pennsylvania Avenue was often flooded, and a traveler trying to reach Capitol Hill from the west would be obliged to take a long, circuitous detour along the highlands to the north, or float down the Potomac in a boat.

Visitors compared the District to the ruins of an ancient city, once great and populous, now half-buried and overgrown. L'Enfant's street plan appeared to bear little or no relationship to the actual landscape. Major intersections could be reached only by cow paths, and were marked only by stones half-hidden in the underbrush. One could walk or ride for miles through bogs, copses, and meadows and never encounter another person. The District had been a financial graveyard for every major real estate speculator who had bet on its future, and the economic devastation was evident in the dozens of half-built and abandoned buildings, many occupied by vagrants. One still wore a bold red sign: HOTEL. On the arrival of the federal government in 1800, there were only 109 houses built of native brick or stone in the District. Most permanent residents lived in rude wooden huts or hovels. Congressmen and senators were content to live in boardinghouses like prep school boys crammed together into dormitories.

"Figure to yourself," wrote a Virginia congressman in 1807, after he had fallen from his horse on Pennsylvania Avenue between the White House and Capitol Hill, "of a man almost bruised to death, on a dark, cold night, in the heart of the capital of the United States, out of sight or hearing of human habitation, and you will have a tolerably exact idea of my situation."

According to a story told many years later by his grandson, Jefferson was returning from his daily ride one afternoon, accompanied by several acquaintances whom he had invited to dinner. The horses and riders were spread out along the bridle path, some ahead and some behind. As the president's horse reached the edge of one of the District's many small streams, a stranger who was on foot asked if he could be carried across. Jefferson gave the man a hand up and allowed him to ride behind, and then let him down on the far side.

The gentlemen in the rear coming up just as Mr. Jefferson had put him down and rode on, asked the man how it happened that he had permitted the others to pass without asking them? He replied, "From their looks I did not like to ask them. The old gentleman looked as if he would do it, and I asked him." He was very much surprised to hear that he had ridden behind the President of the United States.

THERE WAS NEVER ANY QUESTION who the major figures in Jefferson's administration would be. James Madison would serve as Secretary of State and Albert Gallatin as Secretary of the Treasury. They were the recognized leaders of the Republican Party; they possessed intellectual and political talents on a par with the president's; they held Jefferson's total and implicit confidence. So completely did they dominate the administration that Jefferson's presidency has been depicted as a triumvirate. The addition of two New Englanders gave the cabinet an appearance of geographic balance. Levi Lincoln, a Massachusetts lawyer, was appointed Attorney General, and Henry Dearborn, from the northern district of Massachusetts (later Maine), Secretary of War.

Finding a candidate to occupy the office of Navy Secretary presented a potentially serious problem. From the day the first frigate's keel had been laid in 1794, the Republicans had complained without interruption about waste and overspending in the naval accounts. During the campaign they threatened to do away with the navy altogether. It could come as no surprise to Jefferson that no high-ranking Republican was eager to preside over an institution marked for downsizing and possibly even termination. And few politically reliable Republicans had the requisite maritime experience to run the Navy Office. "Republicanism is so rare in those parts [regions] which possess nautical skill," Jefferson observed, that qualified Republican candidates were scarce.

Between December 1800 and March 1801, the job was offered to—and refused by—Robert Livingston of New York, Congressman Samuel Smith of Baltimore, John Langdon of New Hampshire, and finally William Jones of Philadelphia. Jefferson jokingly remarked to Gallatin that "we shall have to advertise for a Secretary of Navy." His appeals grew more pointed as the rejections mounted. In March, the president again turned to Congressman Smith, who had refused the job in December, and pressed him to reconsider. Smith had a "moral duty," Jefferson told him: "if you refuse, where are we to find a substitute?"

Samuel Smith agreed to a temporary arrangement. Keeping his seat in Congress, he would oversee the day-to-day affairs of the Navy Office, acting nominally under the authority of the Secretary of War. It was not until July 15 that Jefferson finally identified a suitable candidate. Samuel Smith's brother, Robert, who had a flourishing admiralty law practice in Baltimore, agreed to take the job. Robert Smith was a Revolutionary War veteran who had seen combat, like his predecessor, at the Battle of Brandywine. He had lived in Baltimore from the age of two and was, like Madison, a graduate of Princeton University. Smith was apparently a controversial choice—he made a poor first impression on several of his colleagues, who seemed to doubt his capabilities. It was understood that a major benefit of the appointment was that it would bind the Smith family—a powerful Republican family, influential in Maryland politics—to the Jefferson administration.

Incoming Treasury Secretary Gallatin was intent on undoing the entire Hamiltonian legacy of internal taxes, funded debt, and centralized government institutions, and he threw himself into the task with ferocious energy. "To fill that office in the manner I did, and as it ought to be filled, is a most laborious task and labor of the most tedious kind," he later recalled of his first two years. "To fit myself for it, to be able to understand thoroughly, to embrace and to control all its details, took from me . . . every hour of the day and many of the night, and nearly brought a pulmonary complaint."

Gallatin's first objective was to eliminate the national debt, which stood at $83 million in 1800. Amounting to about $15 for every American man, woman, and child, the debt was by no means excessive. As the population and economy expanded, the burden diminished steadily even if the principal outstanding did not. But what Hamilton had called a "national blessing" the Jeffersonians denounced as a "moral canker." Public debt begat high taxes, corruption, and repression. It gave rise to a parasitical class of financial speculators. It would cause America to duplicate, as Jefferson wrote, "the English career of debt, corruption and rottenness, closing with revolution." In his first report to the president, Gallatin proposed to pay down the national debt at a rate of $7.3 million per year, which would reduce the principal by a total of $32.3 million in the span of two presidential terms, leaving a balance of $45.6 million in 1808. If the policy was continued, it would cut the balance to zero by 1817.

It was an aggressive timetable, considering that the total revenues of the federal government amounted to less than $11 million per year. It also raised a second question: What should be done about taxes? As much as they hated public debt, the Jeffersonians abhorred taxes, especially internal excise and property taxes, which fell upon land and individual citizens. With roots in the revolutionary movement against England, anti-tax ideology had a powerful hold on the American imagination. Both Washington and Adams had been forced to call out troops to put down tax rebellions. Republicans had used the issue to great effect during the 1800 campaign; taxes, said the Jeffersonians, were "hostile to the genius of a free people."

Carried into office on the wings of Republican anti-tax rhetoric, Jefferson was tempted to eliminate all excise and property taxes in one dramatic stroke. Gallatin was not unsympathetic to this view, telling the president that "if this Administration shall not reduce taxes, they never will be permanently reduced." But he was concerned that tax cuts would interfere with his still more important priority to pay down the national debt. The Jeffersonians were forced to confront a paradox in their arithmetic—their goals of tax reduction and debt reduction were at odds, unless federal spending could be rolled back to a bare minimum.

In his first inaugural, Jefferson promised "a wise and frugal Government, which . . . shall not take from the mouth of labor the bread it has earned." In private letters, he made the point more sharply: the Republicans would "reform the waste of public money, and thus drive away the vultures who prey on it." Using presidential authority whenever congressional authorization was not needed, Jefferson and his cabinet simply dismissed federal office-holders they considered superfluous. The State Department closed all foreign embassies except those in Madrid, Paris, and London. The Treasury Department's internal revenue inspectors were fired en masse. "We are hunting out and abolishing multitudes of useless offices," Jefferson told his son-in-law in June; "striking off jobs, etc., etc." The magnitude of federal waste they were finding, he told James Monroe, was even greater than the Republicans had expected: "agencies upon agencies in every part of the earth, and for the most useless or mischievous purposes, and all of these opening doors for fraud and embezzlement far beyond the ostensible profits of the agency. These are things of the existence of which no man dreamt, and we are lopping them down silently to make as little noise as possible."

In the first full year of Jefferson's presidency, there were 6,479 uniformed and civilian personnel on the rolls of the army, navy, and marine corps, amounting to more than 70 percent of all federal employees. Inevitably, the budget ax would fall on the armed forces. Apart from the Jeffersonian aversion to standing armies and navies, the end of hostilities with France had weakened the case for military spending. The day before Jefferson had taken office—literally less than twenty-four hours before his inaugural ceremony—John Adams had signed into law a Peace Establishment Act authorizing his successor to order a massive naval demobilization. The lame duck Congress had enacted the law as an act of preemption, hoping it would forestall even more drastic action by the incoming Republicans, some of whom had threatened to eliminate the navy.

At the height of the Quasi War, the service had swollen to 700 officers commanding 49 ships, most of which were converted merchantmen and galleys. The Peace Establishment Act would reduce the officer corps to 9 captains, 36 lieutenants, and 150 midshipmen. Of the fleet, only thirteen frigates would be kept in the service, and seven of these would be "laid up in ordinary"—stripped of their armament and rigging and stored under specially constructed sheds. All of the smaller vessels in the navy—brigs, schooners, galleys—would be sold back to private owners and returned to the merchant service from which they had been drawn. Hundreds of officers would be discharged and paid a severance equivalent to four months' salary. Of those officers retained, the ones not immediately employed on active duty would be reduced to half pay. Outgoing Navy Secretary Benjamin Stoddert remarked that the officer layoffs would be "a most painful Duty—fortunately for my feeling it will not fall on me." In the early weeks of the new administration, Stoddert's successor, acting Secretary Samuel Smith, wrote to approximately two thirds of all active duty naval officers with the news that they were no longer needed. "The act providing for naval peace establishment has imposed on the President a painful duty," he wrote Captain Sever of the *Congress*, in a typically worded termination letter:

> It directs him to select from among the Captains in the Navy nine Gentlemen to be retained in service, & to permit the remaining Gentlemen of that grade to retire. . . . I have deemed it a duty as early as possible to inform you that you will be among those whose services, however reluctantly, will be dispensed with. . . . You will please settle your accounts for pay & subsistence with the Purser of the *Congress*. . . . Be assured that the President has a just sense of the services rendered by you to your Country.

Assuming politics would enter into the process, some naval officers declared fealty to the Republican Party. But Smith denied there was any partisan element to his decisions. "Permit me here to remark that you are mistaken, when you suppose that the Politics of the Party will be the criterion by which the selection of officers will be made," he told a lieutenant who had written to plead for his job. "Merit & services & a deep proportion for each state will be a better criterion. They will govern this Department, & this rule cannot fail to meet your entire approbation & that of every good American."

Jefferson was determined to consolidate the entire naval shore establishment in the District of Columbia, at the Washington Navy Yard on the Eastern Branch of the Potomac (known today as the Anacostia River). "I shall really be chagrined," he wrote Samuel Smith on April 17, "if the water in the Eastern Branch will not admit our laying up the entire seven [frigates] there in time of peace, because they would be under the immediate eye of the department, and would require but one set of plunderers to take care of them." The transfer of the ships to the Potomac was bitterly resented by the (largely Federalist) maritime interests of Philadelphia, Baltimore, and New York, but they were powerless to prevent it. Keeping the frigates in Washington, Jefferson told Congress, was the fairest and most economical policy. "Besides the safety of their position, they are under the eye of the executive administration, as well as of its agents, and where yourselves also will be guided by your own view. . . . They are preserved in such condition . . . as to be at all times ready for sea at a short warning."

In 1801, the Washington Navy Yard was nothing more than a cluster of huts, storehouses, and wharves on an isolated bank of the Eastern Branch, separated from Capitol Hill by a thick forest. The grounds of the yard had been enclosed by a "good tight board fence" that would soon be replaced with a stone wall. Inside the yard was a two-story brick house for the superintendent, a stone kitchen, a frame stable, a carriage house, and a hayloft. The channel was only accessible by a small portion of the waterfront, so the shallows at the river's edge were being filled in with excavated soil and detritus. A timber wharf extended well out into the channel on a series of piles. Storehouses lined the eastern side of the yard, about 20 feet from the wharf. A row of adjacent huts housed the shops—among them the blockmaker, sail loft, armorer, tinman, blacksmith, cooper, and boat builder. Nothing was permanent: the entire premises was a construction site. Nearly every structure was in the process of being built, torn down, expanded, or otherwise improved. Fifty marines were ordered to report to the yard at five o'clock every morning, where they would assist the Master Constructor in preparing the frigates for long-term storage. The Marine Barracks was still under construction, so the marines would have to spend the summer living in tents and lean-tos.

Decommissioning the frigates would require them to be navigated through the so-called Kettle Bottoms—a treacherous section of the lower Potomac River, near Maryland Point. A pilot took soundings and reported that he could confidently take any ship drawing less than 20 feet over the shoals. Fully laden, a 44-gun frigate had been observed to draw as much as 23 feet, so it would be necessary to remove her provisions, start her fresh water (dump it overboard), and shift her ballast forward in order to "trim her by the head." As each ship approached the mouth of the Eastern Branch, her captain was to prepare a complete inventory of the ship, her stores, her boats, her furniture, and all of her supplies and rigging. Once at the wharf, she would be stripped of all her rigging, cordage, cables, sails, and all other stores; and the crew paid off. Each decommissioned ship would be manned by a skeleton crew of some sixteen men. The annual cost to maintain each ship in ordinary, including pay and rations for the crew, was estimated at $15,300, or less than one tenth the cost of keeping her in active service.

The *United States*, at anchor in the Delaware River near Chester, sailed for the Virginia Capes on May 17 and arrived in the Eastern Branch on June 6. Her boatswain, William Whitehead, reported that the frigate's bottom copper was probably beyond repair. "I have frequently, on heaving in the Cable, seen it very much cut by the copper, particularly when the Ship has been ahead of her anchor. I have seen the Yarns shaved as if cut by a knife." The *Constellation*, under the command of Captain Alexander Murray, was also in the Delaware River, two miles below the battery at Mud Island, just downriver from Philadelphia. In need of repairs, she was to be brought alongside a dock south of the Humphreys Shipyard. Since the *Constellation* was to be laid up in ordinary, Smith wrote Murray on April 11, "no unnecessary expence must be incurred in her repairs."

At 1:00 a.m. on the night of the twelfth, however, the ship suffered a catastrophic accident. With a strong northwest wind building to gale force, the *Constellation* began to drag her bower anchor. Drifting to the leeward, she ran aground. Fatefully, the grounding occurred at almost exactly high water, and "before timely assistance could be afforded, the Tide Ebbed so fast that she lay down almost on her Beam ends." As the ship careened, her crew rushed to seal the ports, but the river poured in through the hatchways so suddenly that the officers had no time to rescue their possessions from the wardroom. The crew worked to strike the yards and topmasts and remove as much of the ship's stores as they could before the lower decks were completely flooded. But the damage was done. The frigate lay half sunk in the river, just a few hundred feet from the Southwark waterfront where her sister, *United States*, had been launched four years earlier.

For three weeks, Joshua Humphreys, Captain Murray, and the crew worked to right the *Constellation*. They stripped her rigging and tackle and removed all of her stores, which they laid out on the wharf to be dried in the sun. On May 3, they successfully floated her and hauled her to the wharf, where teams of unskilled laborers would "cleanse her of the Mud & filth collected since the misfortune." There she lay, with her rigging "promiscuously scattered about . . . and a good deal of it cut & otherwise abused." It was soon clear that the *Constellation* was not going to leave the Delaware that year. In

December, Murray wrote Smith to say the passage should not be attempted because of the hazards posed by winter storms. Smith, reluctantly, was forced to agree with the captain's logic. Why employ a crew to navigate the frigate all the way to Washington, as Murray had asked in an earlier letter, when she could simply remain at Philadelphia at her "good snug Wharf at the expence of only $3 per day wharfage?"

Jefferson had been warned by shipwrights that vessels laid up in ordinary were prone to rapid decay. There was a risk that the frigates dismantled and moored in the Eastern Branch might "be entirely rotten in 6 or 8 years, or will cost us 3 or 4 millions in repairs." The added costs of repairing the ships could well exceed the funds saved in placing them in caretaker status. A potential solution was to build an enormous dry dock on the banks of the Potomac, which would allow the fleet to be placed, the president said, "in a state of perfect preservation, so that at the beginning of a subsequent war it shall be as sound as . . . when laid up." Infatuated with the dry dock concept, Jefferson collaborated with Benjamin Henry Latrobe, the English-born architect and engineer who was serving as Surveyor of the Public Buildings, to prepare a design. They envisioned cutting a great basin on the river's bank, enclosed by a lock and fed by a source of running water—either Rock Creek, Tiber Creek, or the upper Potomac. Eight hundred feet long and 275 feet wide, sheltered from the elements by a vast roof, the basin would be large enough to accommodate twelve frigates—in other words, the entire navy. Once dry-docked, the vessels would be scrubbed with fresh water, then drained and ventilated. Advocates maintained that they could be left stored in that manner for a century without deteriorating. Although the claimed benefits were exaggerated, there was no question that dry docking significantly elongated the life of a wooden ship.

Jefferson had a scale model of the dry dock built and exhibited in the White House. He estimated that the project would cost about $1 million and require a year to complete. He pitched the concept to Congress in his annual message, first in 1801 and again in 1802, urging the logic of "saving what we already possess." But the idea never won funding. Anti-navalists were not persuaded the dock would reduce long-term maintenance costs, and the navalists were unwilling to give Jefferson the means of taking the entire fleet out of service.*

* The nation's first dry dock was built at the Norfolk Navy Yard and placed in service in 1833.

———

"ALMOST EVERY OTHER AMERICAN STATESMAN might be described in a parenthesis," Henry Adams wrote of Jefferson, in his great nineteenth-century history of the nation's third presidency. "A few broad strokes of the brush would paint the portraits of all the early Presidents . . . but Jefferson could be painted only touch by touch, with a fine pencil, and the perfection of the likeness depended upon the shifting and uncertain flicker of its semi-transparent shadows."

Henry Adams (John and Abigail's great-grandson) might have been the first historian to puzzle over Jefferson's contradictions, but he would not be the last. In the past two decades, especially, scholars and biographers have given emphasis to a pattern of hypocrisy and duplicity in the president's life and career. Affecting the modesty and frugality of a simple country farmer, Jefferson's private tastes ran to fine food, fine wines, fine homes, and fine horses. He criticized government waste, overspending, and public debt, but his profligate spending habits kept him buried under a mountain of personal debt all his adult life. He was enthralled by mechanical contrivances and innovations, but an enemy of industrialization. He denounced financial speculators while speculating aggressively in real estate. Deploring the smear tactics that were so pervasive in the 1790s, he arranged to have his political adversaries smeared. He declared that "If I could not go to heaven but with a party, I would not go there at all," but he was the first acknowledged leader of a major American political party. Jefferson was his country's greatest spokesman for liberty—swearing "eternal hostility to every form of tyranny over the minds of men"—and also the deeded owner of more than two hundred men, women and children, some of whom were his blood relations. As Dr. Samuel Johnson had asked: "How is it that we hear the loudest yelps for liberty among the drivers of negroes?"

With this in mind, it is hardly surprising to find that Jefferson's words and deeds on the subject of seapower are dissonant. While serving as minister to France in the 1780s, he had argued in favor of building frigates to patrol the Mediterranean, offering several reasons: "1. Justice is in favor of this opinion. 2. Honor favors it. 3. It will procure us respect in Europe, and respect is a safeguard to interest." Fifteen years later, campaigning for president at the head of a fiercely anti-navalist Republican Party, he declared himself in favor of "such a naval force only as may protect our coasts and harbors from such depredations as we have experienced; and not for . . . a navy, which, by its own expenses and the eternal wars in which it will implicate us, will grind us with public burthens, and sink us under them." He took a direct hand in disseminating an anti-navy treatise, Thomas Cooper's *Political Arithmetic*, endorsing the view that John Adams's naval buildup had served the interests of northern merchants and shipowners while "the consumer, the farmer, the mechanic, the laborer, they and *they alone* pay." To Joseph Priestley, the English clergyman and political theorist, he ranted that the Federalists were "running navigation mad, & commerce mad, & navy mad, which is worst of all."

In Jefferson's mind, as in the minds of most Americans, the navy was subordinate to a larger problem: How much should be risked to protect shipping and trade? Jefferson believed America's destiny lay in the west, in the settlement and cultivation of the interior. If foreign trade had to be tolerated, it was to be tolerated only as a necessary evil. He distrusted the merchants of the northern seaports, thought them inherently less patriotic than many of their countrymen, and was determined to reduce their influence in politics. "Merchants have no country," he later wrote. "The mere spot they stand on does not constitute so strong an attachment as that from which they draw their gains." When living in Paris in 1786, Jefferson had been asked to assist the editors of the *Encyclopédie méthodique* in preparing the entries on the American states. His comments on Rhode Island had been uncharacteristically blunt, possibly because he feared any ambiguity would be lost in translation:

> The cultivators of the earth are the most virtuous citizens and possess most of the *amor patriae* [love of country]. Merchants are the least virtuous, and possess the least of the *amor patriae*. The latter reside principally in the seaport towns; the former in the interior country. Now it happened that of the territory constituting Rhode Island and Connecticut, the part containing useful seaports was erected into a state by itself and called Rhode Island, and that containing the interior country was erected into another State called Connecticut, for though it has a little seacoast, there are no good ports in it. Hence it happens that there is scarcely one merchant in the whole state of Connecticut, while there is not a single man in Rhode Island who is not a merchant of some sort.

Because it was not much more than 1,000 square miles and had hardly any agriculture, Jefferson added, Rhode Island did not deserve the status of a state. He predicted that it would eventually be expelled from the Union or merged into Connecticut.

But Jefferson denied that he was an enemy to all commerce, or that he wanted every American to take up farming. On this point he was never as dogmatic as his critics charged. Like any southern planter, he understood the importance of exporting America's huge agricultural surplus, and conceded that ships were needed to carry those exports to foreign markets. In his inaugural address he promised the "encouragement of agriculture, and of commerce as its handmaid." While farmers were undoubtedly "the most valuable, the most vigorous, the most independent, the most virtuous" of all citizens, it was not for political leaders to decree how their constituents should earn a living. Americans had inherited from the mother country "a decided taste for navigation and commerce"; they were "determined to share in the occupation of the ocean"; and their elected leaders were therefore duty-bound "to preserve an equality of right . . . in the transportation of commodities, in the right of fishing, & in the other uses of the sea."

Jefferson was never aligned with the most extreme anti-navalists in his own party. He was willing to concede the need for an American navy, on three conditions. First, that its purpose, design, and deployment must be *defensive*. Second, that it must not be exploited as a source of patronage and corruption by the maritime and shipbuilding interests (who were, not coincidentally, aligned with the Federalists). Third, and most important, it must be affordable.

In practice, the last condition left the United States with no realistic hope of building a navy large enough to contend with the great powers of Europe because the cost of such a fleet would exceed the value of the commerce it protected. "To aim at such a navy as the greater nations of Europe possess would be a foolish and wicked waste of the energies of our countrymen," Jefferson had written in his *Notes on the State of Virginia*. "It would be to pull on our own heads that load of military expence which makes the European labourer go supperless to bed, and moistens his bread with the sweat of his brows." A small navy, on the other hand—one capable of policing sea-lanes against piracy—was within the country's means. It was on this basis that Jefferson had first advocated naval action against the Barbary pirates in 1786, and he had never wavered. It was a consistent thread in a career that has since become famous for its inconsistencies.

ON MARCH 13, 1801, nine days after his inauguration, Jefferson received a disturbing set of dispatches from the Mediterranean. Yusuf Karamanli, the Bashaw of Tripoli, had summoned U.S. Consul James Cathcart to his palace and threatened to send his corsairs out to attack American shipping. The attacks could be averted, Cathcart was told, if the U.S. government would present Tripoli with a cash gift of $225,000 immediately and $25,000 in future annual tribute. In the interest of peace, the Bashaw added, he would wait six months for the American president's response.

Yusuf's ultimatum was a flagrant breach of the treaty governing U.S.-Tripolitan relations. Negotiated in 1796 and ratified by the Senate the following year, the treaty had established a "firm and perpetual Peace and friendship" between the two nations, to be guaranteed by the Dey of Algiers. In exchange for a onetime cash payment of $56,000, which he had received upon signing the treaty, Yusuf had pledged not to allow his corsairs to attack American vessels plying the lucrative Mediterranean trade routes. Article 10 had stipulated that "no pretence of any periodical tribute or farther [sic] payment is ever to be made by either party." But the Bashaw now brazenly denied that he had ever agreed to any such thing, insisting that "for the Peace we had paid him it was true, but to maintain the Peace we had given him nothing."

Cathcart responded bravely, telling Yusuf that "the meanest of our Citizens would expend their last dollar and lose their last drop of blood before they would ever consent to become tributary to the Regency of Tripoli." In the past, however, American ministers had used equally brave rhetoric just before agreeing to new and larger payments to the Barbary powers. Why should the Bashaw assume this case would be any different?

The dispatches had been written five months earlier, in mid-October 1800. Even if Jefferson had wanted to reply before the threatened deadline, there was not enough time. The new president could only assume Tripolitan cruisers would be hunting American ships through the Mediterranean in another month's time, if they were not doing so already. He ordered circulars distributed in the major seaports advertising the danger to vessels bound for the Straits of Gibraltar and beyond.

Jefferson's predecessors had managed the problem of Barbary piracy with a combination of flattery, promises, bribes, and occasional threats. The earlier Algerian treaty of 1795—the treaty that had triggered a momentary suspension of the frigate-building program that year—was supposed to have been the key to maintaining peace throughout the Mediterranean. As the largest and most powerful of the Barbary regencies, Algiers was thought to hold great sway throughout Islamic North Africa, and it was hoped that the patronage of the "most potent and exalted" Dey of Algiers would allow American envoys to deal with the other three powers—Morocco, Tunis, and Tripoli—from a position of strength. On this premise, George Washington championed—and the Senate ratified—a treaty that was expensive, humiliating, and served to prop up the system of piracy and blackmail that had been practiced by the Islamic societies of North Africa for three centuries.

An American envoy, William Eaton, left a colorful description of his first meeting with the Dey of Algiers:

> We were shown to a huge, shaggy beast sitting on his rump upon a low bench covered with a cushion of embroidered velvet, with his hind legs gathered up like a tailor, or a bear. On our approach to him, he reached out a forepaw as if to receive something to eat. Our guide exclaimed: "Kiss the Dey's hand!" The consul general bowed very elegantly, and kissed it, and we followed his example in succession. The animal seemed in that moment to be in a harmless mood. He grinned several times but made very little noise. . . . Can any man believe that this elevated brute has seven kings of Europe, two republics, and a continent tributary to him when his whole naval force is not equal to two line-of-battle ships? It is so.

The settlement with Algiers had cost the United States almost a million dollars in a combination of cash payments and sundry gifts. Among the 122 Americans who had been taken hostage by the Algerian corsairs in the prior decade, 85 were released; the others had died in captivity. Among the gifts was a newly built light frigate, the *Crescent*. Designed and built by Joshua Humphreys, the *Crescent* was admired as a very fine ship—dry, weatherly, and fast. There was no doubt she would be fitted out as a corsair to attack the shipping of Europe's lesser maritime powers. The treaty further committed the United States to deliver annual tribute in the form of naval stores, weaponry, and ammunition, specified as "powder, lead, bullets, bombshells, masts, poles, yards, anchor chains, cables, sailcloth, tar, pitch, boards, beams, laths, and other necessities." The annual cost of this cargo of maritime stores was initially estimated, in 1795, at $21,600, but as markets tightened the actual cost proved three or four times higher. The United States thus found itself supplying the vital inputs for a system of state-sponsored piracy.

A provision in the treaty required the Dey of Algiers to keep secret the enormous settlement he had extorted. It had been inserted by the American negotiators in the hope that Tripoli and Tunis would not demand similarly extravagant sums. (Morocco, having signed a treaty in 1786, was deemed relatively benign.) At first, the strategy seemed to pay off. American envoys obtained treaties with Tripoli and Tunis for the relatively modest sums of $56,486 (November 1796) and $107,000 (August 1797) respectively. Almost immediately after signing the treaties, however, the Bashaw of Tripoli and the Bey of Tunis began to suspect they had been duped. American vessels were entering the Mediterranean in ever larger numbers. The commercial wealth of this distant and relatively unknown nation was obviously much greater than they had been led to believe. Rumors of the lavish sums paid to Algiers reached their ears. They demanded more money, more presents, more naval stores.

Stalling for time, U.S. consuls in the Mediterranean offered magnificent gifts to the Barbary rulers: silver snuff boxes, diamond rings, jewel-encrusted gold watches, ornamental swords, rubies, emeralds, lengths of fine silk and linen, and (especially) firearms. The renowned English gunsmith H. W. Mortimer was commissioned by the U.S. government to design and build a gold-barreled musket to be presented as a gift to the Bey of Tunis. Mortimer's invoice of £525 included a description of the weapon:

> A most Superb Gun, Elegantly mounted in solid Gold barrel & lock, richly & beautifully Embossed with gold ornaments & with the furniture finished in a manner never before attempted in this Kingdom. Ornaments on the Stock, Barrel & Lock consisting of matchless designs. Warlike Trophies formed of Helmets, Caps, Coats of Mail, Battleaxes, Battering rams, Pikes, Swords, Scimitars, Drums & Fifes, Trumpets & Bugle horns, Halberds, Bows with Quivers of Arrows, Flags, Cannons, Shields, etc. etc. etc. Fruits & Flowers of various kinds forming a most beautiful assemblage, in neat Mahogany Case lined with Crimson Velvet.

The Dey of Algiers's influence with the other Barbary powers was not as great as had been advertised. Tripoli and Tunis envied Algiers and dreamed of extorting similar sums from the United States. The Bey of Tunis, upon learning that Algiers had taken delivery of the *Crescent*, insisted that Tunis should have a new frigate as well. Thanking Jefferson for "all the military and naval stores, as well as the superb jewels," he got quickly to the point: "I avow to you, with frankness . . . that it would have been infinitely agreeable to me if you had also made me a present of a vessel of war." Most worrying was the fact that the Dey, whose steady friendship the United States had counted upon, would not stay bought. He was constantly irritated, either because his tribute was late, or judged deficient, or both. If he so much as lifted a finger to help the Americans, he expected fresh compensation. After sending a letter to Tripoli on behalf of American interests in January 1801, he turned to the American consul in Algiers, Richard O'Brien, and demanded presents. Pleading lack of funds, O'Brien scraped together $500 to buy two pieces of muslin, twelve lengths of fine cloth, two handkerchiefs, two caftans, two pieces of Dutch linen, a 40-pound loaf of sugar, and a sack of coffee. Poking through these admittedly tawdry offerings, the Dey complained: "No watch? No ring?," but kept them nonetheless.

In September 1800, a 32-gun converted merchantman named the *George Washington* sailed from Delaware Bay to carry that year's annual tribute—money, naval stores, various other presents—to Algiers. She was the first American warship ever to enter the Mediterranean. Her captain was William Bainbridge, who had won promotion from lieutenant in spite of his surrender of the schooner *Retaliation* to *L'Insurgente* in the West Indies two years earlier. While she was anchored in Algiers Harbor, within easy range of more than two hundred shore guns, the Dey sent word that he expected the *George Washington* to carry the Algerian ambassador and his entourage to the Ottoman Porte (or court) in Constantinople. The entourage would consist of a hundred men, women, and children, and it would bear various presents, including a petting zoo of antelopes, horses, parrots, sheep, ostriches, and (if the record can be believed) four lions and four tigers. When Bainbridge refused the voyage, the Dey threatened to tear up his American treaty and have the American ship blown out of the water. "You pay me tribute," he reportedly told Bainbridge. "By that you become my slaves."

Believing the Dey's threats, Bainbridge submitted. His humiliation was complete when the Algerians demanded that the Stars and Stripes be lowered. The vessel named for America's recently deceased first president would be obliged to sail under the Algerian Crescent. Bainbridge later defended his conduct by insisting he had no realistic alternative. "I hope I shall never again be sent to Algiers with tribute," he wrote, "unless I am authorized to deliver it from the mouth of our cannon."

"I AM AN ENEMY to all these *douceurs*, tributes & humiliations," Jefferson confided to Madison shortly after taking office. "I know that nothing will stop the eternal increase of demand from those pirates but the presence of an armed force, and it will be more economical & more honorable to use the same means at once for suppressing their insolences."

The Peace Establishment law gave the president authority to keep six frigates in service: he was at liberty to send them to the Mediterranean, if he chose to do so. Jefferson issued orders for a squadron to rendezvous at Hampton Roads. The New York–built 44-gun frigate *President* would serve as flagship, with two privately built subscription frigates, *Philadelphia* and *Essex*, in company. A naval schooner, the *Enterprise*, would be attached to the squadron to perform as a tender. The squadron was directed to take on provisions and men and ready itself for sea by May 1, 1801.

Aware that the decision to send the squadron could lead to war, Jefferson waited to consult with his full cabinet before issuing sailing orders. Gallatin did not arrive in town until May 13, and the meeting took place at the White House two days later. Jefferson put two questions to his department heads, recording their answers in his own handwritten notes. First: "Shall the squadron now at Norfolk be ordered to cruise in the Mediterranean?" If so: "What shall be the object of the cruise?" The cabinet decided unanimously in favor of sending the frigates with orders "to superintend the safety of our commerce, and to exercise our seamen in nautical duties." It would be characterized as a "squadron of observation," with peaceful intentions. However, if it was discovered that Tripoli was waging war against the United States, the squadron would be authorized to retaliate against Tripolitan ships and even to attack Tripoli itself.

Jefferson and his advisers agreed that Thomas Truxtun, hero of the Quasi War, remained the single most capable officer in the navy. Though he was known to be a staunch Federalist, they were inclined to offer him command of the squadron. Summoned to the capital by outgoing Navy Secretary Stoddert, Truxtun arrived two days after Jefferson's inauguration and called upon the new president at Conrad & McMunn's. The meeting, Truxtun said, was cordial and pleasant. But the brash captain continued to press his claim to seniority over Silas Talbot, and his indefatigable lobbying campaign soon strained the patience of the new administration. Truxtun made the tactical error of appealing to Vice President Aaron Burr, an old friend, apparently failing to understand that Burr was the president's hated rival and commanded no influence in the administration. His next move, circumventing the chain of command, was to appeal directly and personally to Jefferson himself, who brusquely rejected Truxtun's claim on the grounds that the question had been put to rest by former President Adams, "an authority equally competent with myself."

Frustrated and resentful, Truxtun announced that he would decline command of the Mediterranean Squadron, ostensibly because "peace can afford no field for me on the ocean." Smith acquiesced, placing Truxtun on half pay and ordering Richard Dale, another of the original six captains appointed by George Washington, to report to Norfolk and assume command. As Dale arrived aboard the *President* on May 22, Truxtun assured him she was "the finest frigate that ever floated on the waters of this Globe." On June 1, the squadron sailed for the Straits of Gibraltar.

CHAPTER SIX

During his diplomatic service in France two decades earlier, Jefferson had repeatedly been warned that the Barbary States were perfectly situated to blackmail any nation desiring access to the Mediterranean trade routes. Their proximity to passing ship traffic, the difficulty of blockading their harbors, their lack of maritime commerce upon which to retaliate—all of these factors united to make war against the Barbary powers expensive and frustrating. The only realistic military options were large-scale naval operations or troop landings, and both alternatives were more costly and more risky than the time-worn path of bribery and tribute.

Though he had been fairly warned, it seemed as if Jefferson was destined to learn these lessons the hard way. The conflict with Tripoli was no closer to resolution in 1803 than it had been in 1801. As devoted as he was to strict economy in government, Jefferson could not fail to notice that the funds spent to keep a squadron active in the Mediterranean had surpassed the highest estimates of what it would take simply to bribe Yusuf off. After two years in office, the president appeared willing to reconsider the wisdom of his hawkish policy.

The first two years of the U.S.-Tripolitan War proved the rule that good officers are more important than good ships. Three months were required to carry dispatches from Washington to Gibraltar and back. The voyage between Gibraltar and Tripoli added another three weeks, at least. When a commodore sailed from the American coast, he might as well have been transported to another planet. If he proved complacent, inefficient, or incompetent, there was no way to correct the error until months had passed.

Commodore Richard Dale's tour began with a stormy transatlantic passage in which the *President* and her consorts labored through violent head seas and heavy squalls. The flagship's deck seams opened and she leaked badly into her lower decks. When the battered squadron crept into Gibraltar Bay on July 1, 1801, Dale learned that Tripoli had indeed declared war on the United States six weeks earlier. Complying with his orders, Dale dispatched most of his squadron to blockade Tripoli. From the start, however, the attempted blockade was feeble and intermittent. The unfamiliar harbor was protected by uncharted reefs and rocks, and the deep-draft American frigates could not safely approach the main channel. Frequent gales sent a heavy swell on shore, requiring the blockading vessels to gain sea room or risk being thrown onto the enemy's beach. The nearest safe harbor was on the island of Malta, two or three days' sail against the prevailing winds. The squadron was not numerous enough to maintain a constant presence in the offing; its vessels needed to rotate back into port frequently for reprovisioning and refitting.

Discouraged by the difficulty of the blockade and fearful of losing his ships, Dale concentrated his efforts on providing convoys to American merchantmen. The only fighting of his tour took place on August 1, when the schooner *Enterprise*, commanded by Lieutenant Andrew Sterrett (the same Sterrett who had served under Truxtun on the *Constellation*, and who had executed an American sailor for cowardice during the *L'Insurgente* action), engaged a Tripolitan 14-gun galley commanded by Admiral Rais Mahomet Rous. In a three-hour battle, the outgunned galley lost sixty men, while the *Enterprise*, incredibly, lost none. The Tripolitans twice lowered their colors, only to resume fighting when the Americans approached to take possession of the surrendered vessel. Sterrett, believing that he did not have authorization to make the galley a prize, ordered her masts cut away and her guns thrown into the sea. Thus crippled, she was permitted to return to Tripoli. Yusuf, infuriated, ordered the ship's admiral beaten and forced to ride backward on a donkey through the streets of the city while wearing a necklace of sheep entrails.

In his first annual message to the Congress in December 1801, Jefferson acknowledged that "some difference of opinion may be expected to appear" among the Republicans with regard to naval operations, but that "a small force will probably continue to be wanted for actual service in the Mediterranean." In February 1802, Congress granted authority to "subdue, seize and make prize of all vessels, goods and effects, belonging to the Bashaw of Tripoli, or to his subjects." The navy was authorized to recruit American seamen for terms of up to two years. Secretary Smith ordered a relief squadron, including the frigates *Constellation* and *Chesapeake*, to sail for the Mediterranean. Dale's ships would return to the United States, discharge their crews, and undergo needed repairs and refitting.

The administration continued to regard Truxtun as the navy's most talented officer, and in January 1802 Secretary Smith offered him the command of the relief squadron preparing to sail from Hampton Roads. Accepting the commission, Truxtun traveled to Norfolk to prepare the *Chesapeake* for sea. The *Chesapeake* was the smallest of the original six frigates, and Truxtun deemed her too humble to serve as his flagship. He would have preferred his old command, the *Constellation*, or one of the 44s—but for various reasons none was available. *Chesapeake*'s lieutenants were young and untrained, and it looked at if he would have to promote one or more midshipmen to fill out their ranks. The inexperience of his officers would force Truxtun to involve himself deeply in the tedious details of readying the frigate for sea.

The answer to his problems, Truxtun decided, was for Smith to send him a flag captain—an officer who stood below him on the captain's list and who would direct everything pertaining to the *Chesapeake* and her crew, freeing the commodore to attend to the squadron and the war. Truxtun did not ask for a flag captain. He demanded one. Informing the Navy Secretary that "I have a reputation to lose which I am very tenacious of," the malcontented commodore presented an ultimatum. If no flag captain could be found to sail with the *Chesapeake*, "I must beg leave to quit the service."

The threat to resign may have been a bargaining ploy. But Smith had reached the end of his tolerance for Truxtun's Olympian ego and his high, whining tone. No flag captain was available for the *Chesapeake*, Smith replied on March 13, and therefore: "I cannot but consider your notification as absolute." Without giving Truxtun a chance to respond, Smith struck his name off the navy rolls and ordered Richard Valentine Morris to travel immediately to Norfolk to assume command of the *Chesapeake* and the relief squadron.

Had Smith foreseen the consequences of appointing Morris, he might have gone to any lengths to appease Truxtun. Morris (nephew of Gouverneur Morris, the famous financier and diplomat of the American Revolution) was a disastrous choice. Against advice he chose to bring his pregnant wife and young son along for the cruise. Sailing from Norfolk on April 14, the *Chesapeake* was tossed in heavy seas and sprang her mainmast. On her arrival in Gibraltar in late May, Morris reported: "I never was at sea in so uneasy a ship; in fact, it was with the greatest difficulty we saved our masts from rolling over the side." For much of the next seven months, Morris would keep the frigate in port, undergoing long and leisurely repairs.

Morris's orders had directed him to "place all our naval force under your command before Tripoli." From the start, however, Morris showed little or no interest in blockading Tripoli. The junior officers came to believe that Mrs.

Morris was the real source of authority on board, and clandestinely referred to her as the "Commodoress." Her principal interest seemed to be to keep the flagship in port as much as possible. Mrs. Morris gave birth to a baby boy in the hospital at Malta, while the *Chesapeake* lay at anchor for five consecutive months in the Grand Harbor of Valetta. As a gesture in the direction of his orders, Morris sent Captain Alexander Murray and the *Constellation* to blockade Tripoli; but Murray soon realized that the deep-draft *Constellation* was no more suitable for operating in the uncharted shoal waters off Tripoli than her sister, the *President*, had been under Commodore Dale. Tripolitan galleys and gunboats were able to slip out of the harbor by sailing along the shore, using their superior knowledge of the passages through the shoals.

Jefferson and his cabinet were rapidly losing faith. The failure of the blockade was not the worst of it: Morris's dispatches were so obtuse that the president and his secretaries found it difficult to piece together what was happening in the Mediterranean. "I have for some time believed that Commodore Morris's conduct would require investigation," Jefferson told Gallatin. "His progress from Gibraltar has been astonishing." In September 1803, Morris was recalled to the United States, where he would face a court of inquiry and be summarily dismissed from the navy.

Thus far, all that the United States had accomplished was to make a show of naval force in the Mediterranean. The galleys and feluccas of the Barbary fleets were no match for the big American frigates, and they dared not challenge them directly. But naval superiority would not matter in the end. The corsairs could sally out from the harbors, seize unprotected merchantmen, and retreat to safety before the squadron could react. These tactics would never pose a direct threat to the American frigates, but—as a Tunisian minister told William Eaton, the American consul in Tunis—"though a fly in a man's throat cannot kill him, it will make him vomit!"

But there was another, more important consideration. The futility of American naval operations had eroded American prestige in the Mediterranean. The United States, its envoys warned, was on the verge of becoming a general laughingstock throughout the region, and the result might weaken the American bargaining position in future negotiations with the other Barbary powers. Eaton expressed his concern to Madison in August 1802: "Our operations of the last and present have produced nothing in effect but additional enemies and national contempt. If the same system of operations continue, so will the same consequences. . . . The [Tunisian] minister puffs a whistle in my face, and says; 'we find it is all a puff! We see how you carry on the war with Tripoli!'"

Bribing Yusuf began to look like a more palatable option. "I sincerely wish you could reconcile it to yourself to empower our negotiators to give . . . an annuity to Tripoli," Gallatin wrote the president that August; "I consider it no greater disgrace to pay them than Algiers." Stressing debt reduction above all other objectives, the Treasury Secretary urged Jefferson to consider it as a "mere matter of calculation whether the purchase of peace is not cheaper than the expense of a war." In a cabinet meeting the following May, Jefferson put the question to his department heads: "Shall we buy peace with Tripoli?" The response was unanimously in the affirmative.

But Jefferson was not quite ready to pull his frigates back from the Mediterranean. He would continue to pursue—as he put it to Madison in his reticent way—"a steady course of justice aided occasionally with liberality." To put it differently, the navy would continue to make a show of force in the Mediterranean, but American diplomats would not be slow to offer bribes, ransom, and tribute when it appeared that peace could be bought on reasonable terms. The Bashaw of Tripoli would be offered a financial settlement in exchange for renewing the peace. Until a deal was done, however, the war would carry on.

Two commodores had disappointed Jefferson's hopes. Secretary Smith was determined that the third, Edward Preble, should succeed where his predecessors had failed.

ON THE MORNING OF MAY 21, 1803, Boston Harbor was swept by breezes under cloudy skies. It was the busiest month of the year, with vessels of every description preparing for sea and taking on cargoes. At her moorings was the USS *Constitution*, the 44-gun frigate that had been launched from nearby Hartt's Shipyard six years earlier. Joshua Humphreys had never laid eyes on her, but she was his ship, his design. Built on the same lines as the *United States*, she was 204 feet long from her Hercules figurehead to her taffrail; she displaced more than 2,000 tons of water. She was almost certainly the largest ship in the harbor that day.

Having been laid up in ordinary for more than ten months, she would have looked lonely and bare, stripped of her guns, masts, boats, anchors, and most of her men. Originally, her hull had been painted ochre with a black wale strake, her two uppermost panels vibrant blue and red, and her taffrail gold; but now the paint was faded and peeling, contributing to the overall impression that she had been neglected and unloved. She would need a good deal of work to be made respectable, let alone seaworthy.

Her new captain, Edward Preble, was from Falmouth (later Portland), a small seaport town in the northern, non-contiguous district of Massachusetts (later Maine). Preble was a small, wiry man, with the sharp, prominent nose and cold, piercing eyes of a bird of prey. His coloring was "that of a fair-skinned man who had spent many years at sea," and his hair was close-cropped and combed forward in front, giving him the look of an ancient Roman general. He suffered from ulcers that kept him in a bad temper for weeks at a time; his subordinates quickly learned that he was prone to explode without warning into fits of rage.

As an adolescent, during the Revolution, Preble had served as a midshipman in the Massachusetts state navy. When his ship, the 26-gun *Protector*, was captured in May 1781, it was Preble's bad luck to be imprisoned in the notorious prison ship *Jersey*. The *Jersey* had once been a 64-gun Royal Navy battleship, but in 1781 she was a blackened and rotting hulk, permanently anchored in Wallabout Bay in New York's East River, near the present-day site of the Manhattan Bridge. Mortality rates for prisoners of war in the *Jersey* almost certainly exceeded 50 percent; an estimated eleven thousand American prisoners died while confined in her lower decks. The stench of waste and death was so powerful that boats would not approach her from leeward. Newly arrived prisoners inoculated themselves against smallpox by making a small cut in their arms and massaging in a bit of blood or pus taken from one of the sick. One survivor told the editor of the *Niles' Register* that "the hardest battle he ever fought in his life was with a fellow prisoner on board of the *Jersey*; and the object of contention was the putrefied carcass of a starved rat." Each morning the guards opened the hatches and shouted down to the living to turn out the dead. Burial details took the bodies in boats to the beach, heaved them into shallow trenches, and threw a layer of sand over them. Heads and limbs were left jutting from the surface. When it rained, bodies sometimes washed into the river and floated out to sea.

Preble was fortunate. His imprisonment in the *Jersey* lasted only two months before a parole was negotiated and he was permitted to move to lodgings in New York. During those weeks, however, he nearly died of typhoid fever, and he continued to suffer from bad health for the rest of his life.

In the postwar years, Preble served as master or supercargo on several merchantmen. At the outset of the Quasi War, in April 1798, he received a naval lieutenant's commission and a year later was promoted captain. As commander of the USS *Essex* in 1799, he sailed to Jakarta to fetch home a convoy of stranded merchantmen. It was the longest voyage that had ever been made by an American naval vessel, and the first beyond Cape Hope.

Preble had hoped to have the *Constitution* at sea in three weeks, but an inspection of the hull using iron rakes and boat hooks showed that the copper sheathing was "ragged and full of small holes with a quantity of grass and sea moss." The original panels, imported from England at great cost in 1797, would have to be torn off and replaced. The careening and coppering operations would require a minimum of seven to eight weeks.

Within days of his arrival, Preble had whipped the Boston naval establishment into a paroxysm of activity. While the *Constitution* lay in ordinary, her guns had been loaned to the shore battery at Castle Island, which guarded the approaches to Boston's inner harbor. The huge iron weapons would have to be transported, one by one, up the harbor to Charlestown Wharf. An inspection of the rigging and stores, laid up in the Charlestown warehouses, was discouraging. Examining the huge coils of tarred hemp, Preble judged that some of it was in passable condition but much was decayed and useless. The ship would need new anchor cables, and most of her old powder would have to be discarded. New blocks and rigging would have to be built and fitted.

On May 28, in a dead calm, the ship was warped across the harbor to Colonel Mesa's Wharf, where she would be hove down for the replacement of her copper sheathing. It was a complicated and costly operation. But the replacement copper, at least, would not have to be imported from Europe, because high-quality copper sheets were now being manufactured at a local mill owned by an entrepreneur named Paul Revere. Revere's copper, Preble wrote, was "good, and of proper thickness."

Revere was respected as a master silversmith and a Revolutionary War veteran, but he was not particularly well known outside Massachusetts. If a time traveler from the future had told him that his name would one day be on the lips of every schoolchild in America, he would have laughed. He was just a tradesman—a glorified platemaker. But in January 1861, more than forty years after his death, the *Atlantic Monthly* would publish a poem by Henry Wadsworth Longfellow that began:

> *Listen, my children, and you shall hear*
> *Of the midnight ride of Paul Revere.*
> *On the eighteenth of April, in Seventy-five;*
> *Hardly a man is now alive*
> *Who remembers that famous day and year.*

They listened, with drawn breath and wide eyes, to the story of the covert plan to warn of the coming British attack by means of lanterns placed

Nelson's Funeral Procession on the Thames, January 9, 1806. Oil on canvas by Daniel Turner, 1807. National Maritime Museum, London.

Henry Knox by Gilbert Stuart, c. 1805. The Granger Collection, New York.

Above: The southern live oak, *Quercus virens*. This native North American hardwood was a highly prized shipbuilding timber. Artist unknown, c. 1872. The Mariners' Museum, Newport News, Virginia. *Below Left*: John Adams by Gilbert Stuart, c. 1800–15. Gift of Mrs. Robert Homans, National Gallery of Art, Washington, D.C. *Below Right*: Thomas Jefferson by Rembrandt Peale, 1805. Painted in the middle years of Jefferson's presidency. Library of Congress.

Above: USS *Constellation* capturing French frigate *L'Insurgente*, February 9, 1799. Watercolor by Irwan John Bevan. The Mariners' Museum, Newport News, Virginia. *Below Left:* Thomas Truxtun. Oil on canvas by Orlando S. Lagman (after Bass Otis), 1965. U.S. Naval Historical Center, Washington, D.C. *Below Right:* Edward Preble, c. 1805–07. Artist unknown. U.S. Naval Academy, Annapolis, Maryland.

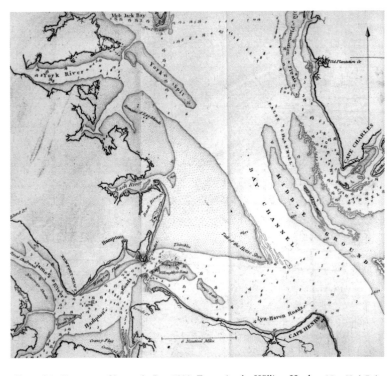

Chart of the Entrance to Chesapeake Bay, 1822. Engraving by William Hooker. New York Public Library.

William Bainbridge by John Wesley Jarvis, c. 1814. U.S. Naval Academy, Annapolis, Maryland.

City of Washington, D.C. Colored lithograph by Peter Anderson, 1838. The Mariners' Museum, Newport News, Virginia.

USS *Philadelphia* on the rocks off Tripoli, October 31, 1803. Colored lithograph, P.S. Duval & Son, undated. The Mariners' Museum, Newport News, Virginia.

Stephen Decatur, Jr. Oil on canvas by Orlando S. Lagman (after Gilbert Stuart), 1965. U.S. Naval Historical Center, Washington, D.C.

Above: Burning of the USS *Philadelphia* in Tripoli Harbor, February 16, 1804. Nicolino Calyo (attributed), c. 1804. The Mariners' Museum, Newport News, Virginia. *Below*: *Preparation for War to Defend Commerce*. The USS *Philadelphia* under construction in Joshua Humphreys's shipyard, 1800. This hand-colored engraving by Thomas Birch significantly understates the actual dimensions of the vessel. New York Public Library.

Stephen Decatur in hand-to-hand combat with a Tripolitan gunboat captain, August 3, 1804. Engraving, 1857. The Mariners' Museum, Newport News, Virginia.

USS *President* entering the harbor of Marseilles. The New York–built ship was deemed the fastest and finest of America's early frigates. Watercolor by Antoine Roux, c. 1805. New York Public Library.

in the belfry of the North Church—"One if by land, two if by sea"—and of Revere's dead-of-night gallop through the countryside to Lexington and Concord, rousing the militiamen from their beds to fight the battle that would begin the American Revolution. After the publication of "Paul Revere's Ride," Revere's name was as familiar to posterity as those of Benjamin Franklin or Samuel Adams. History would forget two other men who rode alongside Revere: William Dawes and Samuel Prescott. Their names did not rhyme with "hear."

During the Adams administration, Benjamin Stoddert had preached the importance of fostering a domestic copper sheet-rolling industry, and had promised to finance Revere's start-up operations by lending him $10,000 from the federal treasury. With Jefferson's election, Revere at first assumed that the loan would be canceled, but after a tenacious lobbying campaign he managed to obtain the money, which he paid back in full by the end of 1802. In 1803, Revere's mill generated revenues of $14,610 from sales of copper sheathing, bolts, spikes, and nails. Revere's largest customer was the U.S. Navy, but his highest-profile customer (literally) was the Bulfinch State House in Boston, for which he manufactured 6,000 feet of copper sheets to cover the dome. Demand expanded rapidly, and production was limited only by a scarcity of raw copper. Working through agents in New York, Philadelphia, and Providence, Revere bought whatever copper could be found on the American market. He also suggested that the old copper sheets "Stripped off Ships belonging to the government, should be reserved to be worked over again," and that the American warships departing for the Mediterranean should be ordered to call at Smyrna, where high-quality copper could be purchased and carried back to Boston as ballast.

On June 11, 1803, under hazy skies and a soft rain, the *Constitution* was hove down until the keel was completely out of the water: "The mast did not complain although the ship hove out very heavy." The larboard copper was torn off and Revere's new panels bolted to the hull, and then the hawsers were slackened, a few inches at a time, and the ship was allowed to right herself. On June 21, all hands manned the capstan and the big ship was hove down again, this time with the keel raised to starboard. The operation was repeated. By June 25, the difficult work was done: "At five in the afternoon, the copper being entirely finished, the carpenters gave nine cheers and were answered by the caulkers and seamen."

Constitution had an authorized complement of more than four hundred, and filling out her crew would be a challenge. The Navy Secretary had authorized a monthly wage of $10–$12 for an able seaman. This was one third lower than the wage offered during the Quasi War, in 1798. If market wages for sea-men had declined, they had not declined enough, and on June 26, Preble reported that he could not recruit a full crew without raising the rate of pay. The Boston labor market was tighter; the fishermen had all gone to sea, and many merchant vessels had already advanced wages to the best seamen. Able seamen, Preble reported, would not enlist for less than $13 per month and a two-month advance. While awaiting Smith's reply, the commodore sent a lieu-tenant to New York and another to Providence in search of good men.

During the final preparations for sea, the *Constitution* lay alongside Boston's Long Wharf, an enormous pier that began at the foot of State Street and thrust out into the harbor for a distance of nearly half a mile. As men came aboard they were mustered and divided into watches, and life aboard the frigate began to take on the familiar disciplined daily routine of naval service. A Sergeant's Guard was kept constantly on duty, with sentinels at each gangway. The crew was kept busy setting up the rigging, taking on bal-last and water, and recaulking the deck seams. On July 29, it was found that the gun carriages were "so badly constructed that it is absolutely necessary to send them on shore to be altered." On August 4, the logbook noted: "We are lumbered from morning till night with provisions and stores and surrounded all day with lighters."

At dawn on August 12, *Constitution* sailed down the main channel, threading between the dozens of little green islands separating the harbor from the sea—Bird Island, Governor Island, Castle Island, Spectacle Island—and anchored between President Roads and the Narrows, eight miles below Boston. Next morning, with the wind blowing fresh, the ship put to sea under double-reefed topsails, clearing the lighthouse a little after 8:00 a.m. Preble was pleased with her: "The ship sails well, is perfectly tight, and the officers and crew healthy."

Light and unfavorable winds made for a long, uneventful crossing, but Preble was grateful to escape the punishing weather that had tormented his predecessors. During the passage Preble imposed his will on the flagship's officers and crew. He was, like Truxtun, an uncompromising disciplinarian, quick to reprimand his subordinates for seemingly minor infractions. But whereas Truxtun had been calm and pedagogical, Preble was prone to sarcas-tic outbursts and humiliating tirades. The younger officers, many of whom were accustomed to a more collegial shipboard environment, chafed under the new regime.

Passing the hours in the *Constitution*'s spacious greatcabin, Preble wrote out 107 standing orders. The officers would be censured if they should "suffer the most trifling thing under them to be executed with indifference." In their treatment of the common seamen, they were to set an example of probity and good manners: "Blasphemy, profanity, and all species of obscenity or immorality are peremptorily forbid," and the officers were not to tolerate "such disorderly and despicable practices amongst the men." Like Truxtun, Preble insisted that the officers do the enlisted men the courtesy of learning their names. Preble could even sound like an anxious mother, as when he ordered that the crew should not be allowed to wear "their best clothes" when cleaning the ship. When the hands were washing the deck, the officers were "to make them pull off their shoes and stockings and tuck their trousers up."

On September 6, Cape St. Vincent was sighted from the masthead. The *Constitution* was entering the long funnel between Spain and Morocco, and the land closed in from both sides as the ship coasted along toward the Straits. Just eight miles wide at its narrowest point, separating two continents and two oceans, the Straits of Gibraltar are enclosed by the two great rocks known since antiquity as the Pillars of Hercules—Jabal Musa to the south and the Rock of Gibraltar to the north. The Straits are a notoriously difficult passage to navigate. A powerful hydraulic current draws water in from the Atlantic along the surface, always setting to the east, and counterbalanced by a cooler subsurface current setting to the west. The prevailing westerly winds build to gale force as they enter the long, steep-sided funnel. When a rare easterly wind sets against the current, a nasty chop kicks up in the channel and the sea "boils like a pot."

On the tenth, a dark and hazy night, *Constitution*'s watch officers noticed that a strange ship, evidently large enough to be a warship, had suddenly come within close range. The commodore was quickly alerted, and he hurried up on deck. Midshipman Charles Morris, in his autobiography, described the incident that followed:

> The crew were immediately but silently brought to quarters, after which the Commodore gave the usual hail, "What ship is that?" The same question was returned; in reply to which the name of our ship was given, and the question repeated. . . . Again the question was returned instead of an answer, and again our ship's name given and the question repeated, with no other reply than its repetition, "What ship is that?"
>
> The Commodore's patience now seemed exhausted, and, taking the trumpet, he hailed and said, "I am now going to hail you for the last time. If a proper answer is not returned, I will fire a shot into

you." A prompt answer came back, "If you fire a shot, I will return a broadside." Preble then hailed, "What ship is that?" The reply was "This is His Britannic Majesty's ship *Donegal*, 84 guns, Sir Richard Strahan, an English Commodore. Send your boat on board." Under the excitement of the moment, Preble leaped on the hammocks and returned for an answer, "This is the United States ship *Constitution*, 44 guns, Edward Preble, an American Commodore, who will be damned before he sends his boat on board of any vessel." And turning to the crew, he said, "Blow your matches, boys."

The conversation here ceased and soon after a boat was heard coming from the stranger, and arrived with a lieutenant from the frigate *Maidstone*. The object of this officer was to apologize for the apparent rudeness which had been displayed. He stated that our ship had not been seen until we had hailed them; that it was, of course, very important to gain time to bring their men to quarters, especially as it was apparent we were not English, and they had no expectations of meeting an American ship of war there; and that this object had induced their delay and misrepresentation in giving the ship's name. The excuses were deemed satisfactory, and the ships separated.

The *Constitution*'s young officers were surprised and impressed with Preble's handling of the exchange. During the passage from Boston they had resigned themselves to serving under a humorless curmudgeon, a man prone to sudden "ebullitions of temper," whose hectoring would make life aboard the ship unbearable. Now they saw a man who was obviously spoiling for a fight. If Preble intended to carry on the war against Tripoli in the same spirit, the officers would gladly endure the occasional ebullition—and all at once the "unfriendly feelings" that had sprung up between the commodore and his officers were "mitigated greatly." The ship's company had just taken an important step toward becoming a cohesive fighting force. That the *Constitution* had nearly fired on a British frigate within a few miles of one of the Royal Navy's primary naval bases did not seem to bother either Preble or any of the junior officers.

At 1:00 p.m. the next day, *Constitution*'s lookout hailed the deck to report the Rock of Gibraltar bearing northeast by north. The frigate entered the bay at half past three, anchored in 23 fathoms water, and saluted the garrison with fifteen guns. The salute was returned by an equal number of guns from the battery.

Gibraltar was the linchpin of British naval supremacy in the Mediterranean, and Britain was not taking any chances with it. The Rock was the most heavily fortified stronghold on the face of the earth. To the men looking up from the deck of the *Constitution*, it must have been an awesome sight, a dramatic exhibition of British military power. Deep galleries had been blasted out of the stone to serve as artillery casements. Hundreds of heavy cannon could fire down from a great height on enemies approaching by land or sea. To reach these embrasures from the harbor, one had to ride a mule up a long, precarious, steeply ascending series of switchbacks. No enemy could ever hope to take those positions by force. They could be taken only by starving the defenders out, and the defenders were plentifully supplied with powder, ammunition, and provisions.

In Gibraltar Bay, Preble found one of the ships attached to his squadron, the U.S. frigate *Philadelphia*, under the command of William Bainbridge. The *Philadelphia* had three smaller vessels moored under her guns. One was an American merchant brig, the *Celia* of Boston. The second was the *Mirboka*, a Moroccan corsair of 22 guns, which had reportedly captured the *Celia* and was escorting her into Tangier when the *Philadelphia* ran them both down. Another Moroccan vessel, the *Meshouda*, was also in custody; she had been run down and captured several months earlier, while attempting to run the American blockade into Tripoli.

On board the *Mirboka*, Bainbridge had found the equivalent of a smoking gun: an order authorizing the capture of all American vessels. Had Morocco, traditionally the most benign of the Barbary States, declared war on the United States? If so, Preble faced the unwelcome prospect of fighting two wars simultaneously.

But it was not yet clear that Morocco really had declared war. At first, the Moroccans aboard the *Mirboka* denied any hostile intent toward American shipping. When confronted with the translated order, which had not been signed, the Moroccan captain admitted that he had been given the authorization by the governor of Tangier—but added that the country's sovereign authority, the emperor of Morocco, had no knowledge of the order and would probably disavow it. The American crew of the *Celia* attested that they had not been harmed, and had only been obliged to hide themselves below when the *Philadelphia* hove in sight. Evidently, there was confusion and dissent among the Moroccans.

Preble hoped that the affair could be settled quickly, through a deft combination of diplomacy and a show of naval force at Tangier. Needing a free hand to deal with Tripoli, the commodore had no wish for hostilities with Morocco. He settled on his course of action. The Moroccan captain and six of his officers taken in the *Mirboka* would be transferred to the *Constitution*. The remaining crew of the *Mirboka*—ninety-two men in all—would be left aboard a prison ship in Gibraltar. The *Mirboka* herself would be left at anchor in Gibraltar Bay, manned by a lieutenant and a five-man prize crew.

Bainbridge and the *Philadelphia* would be sent off to the east with orders to do what Preble's predecessors had been roundly condemned for failing to do—maintain a rigorous blockade of Tripoli. When she sailed, the *Philadelphia* would convoy all of the eastbound American merchant vessels that had gathered in Gibraltar Bay and nearby Malaga on the Spanish coast. Once the Moroccan situation had been dealt with, the *Constitution* and the remaining vessels in the squadron would set sail for Tripoli to rendezvous with the *Philadelphia*.

Less than forty-eight hours after the *Constitution*'s arrival, two more American light frigates arrived from the east: the *John Adams*, commanded by Truxtun's former first lieutenant aboard the *Constellation*, John Rodgers; and the *Adams*, commanded by the returning Commodore Morris. Both ships were homeward-bound, calling at Gibraltar only for provisions and to await favorable conditions for passing through the Straits. Morris and Rodgers agreed that their ships would accompany the *Constitution* to Tangier, so as to make a greater show of force.

Tangier was only thirty miles from Gibraltar, but ships passing westward through the Straits often found it difficult to make headway. "I find it hard sailing against wind and current," Preble wrote on September 22. Reaching Tangier at last on the twenty-fifth, Preble learned that the emperor and his court were camped in the backcountry on the far side of the Alcassar River. Heavy rains had raised the river to such a height that it could be crossed only "on Goat Skins filled with Wind." As night fell, the men on the deck of the *Constitution* were treated to a dramatic spectacle. Huge signal fires were lit along the peaks of the Rif Mountains, to give the alarm to the villages along the Moroccan coast.

For two weeks the squadron cruised between Cape Trafalgar (Spain) and Cape Spartel (Morocco), returning twice to Gibraltar. The Moroccan prisoners aboard the *Constitution* were treated as honored guests on a pleasure cruise. The two highest ranking among them, the captain of the *Mirboka* and a "priest" or mullah, shared Preble's cabin. For the first few days after coming aboard, all of the Moroccans dined each day at the commodore's table, and "after this they messed under the half deck and had the Commodore's servants to attend them." Writing to a female cousin with barely concealed mirth, Midshipman Henry Wadsworth told her that he had made friends with the Moroccan captain, who "invites me (after the War) to go home to Sallee with him and says he will give me four wives."

On October 6, the squadron returned to Tangier Bay after a short passage aided by light easterly breezes. From the appearance of the harbor it was obvious that the emperor had returned. Twenty-five hundred troops had formed up along the beach. At half past one in the afternoon they commenced a march with "innumerable volleys of small arms, toward the town and Castle." When the American colors were hoisted over the consul's house, the harbor batteries opened with a salute of 18 guns and an equal number were returned by the *Constitution*.

As these salutes were exchanged, Preble later learned, the emperor was himself at the fortress at the end of the harbor mole, studying the *Constitution* through a telescope. He was impressed with her size and armament. Tangier's fortifications were ancient and decrepit; many of the cannon had not been fired in years. According to Midshipman Ralph Izard, the Moroccans "were trembling in their shoes for fear we should batter down their town, which can very easily be done. For you can have no idea of the miserable situation their batteries are in. They have several Guns it is true but the carriages they rest upon are so rotten that three times firing will render them perfectly useless." The emperor seemed interested in keeping the peace. As a gesture of goodwill, he presented the squadron with a gift of ten head of cattle, twenty sheep, and four dozen fowls.

The morning of October 10, Preble and a party of diplomats and officers went ashore under a flag of truce. Passing through a long, narrow passage lined with the emperor's guards, they were escorted into an outdoor court adjacent to the castle walls. A moment later the emperor himself appeared and sat down on the steps. The Moroccans lowered their heads all the way to the ground, and the Americans removed their hats. Midshipman Izard described the scene:

> I had connected with the idea of Emperor of Morocco something grand, but what was my disappointment at seeing a small man, wrapped up in a woolen *heik* or cloak, sitting upon the stone steps of an old castle in the middle of the streets, surrounded by a guard with their arms covered with cloth. . . . We stood before the Emperor with our Caps in hand & the conversation was carried on by means of an interpreter. The Emperor said he was very sorry that his governor had behaved so much amiss & said he should punish him "more than to our satisfaction."

The emperor regretted the misunderstanding and said that he had ordered all American vessels that had been taken to be restored to their owners. He assured Preble that Morocco wished to remain at peace with the United States, and asked that the *Mirboka* and *Meshouda* be restored to him as a favor and a gesture of goodwill.

It was that easy. Moroccan governors and ship captains were enjoined against any further hostile action against American shipping, on penalty of "severe punishment." The emperor reaffirmed his commitment to abide by the American treaty that had been signed by his father in 1786.

Preble had already decided to return the *Mirboka*, which, he said, was "such a miserable piece of naval architecture that I do not believe we have an officer in our service that would be willing to attempt to cross the Atlantic in her for ten times her value." He was more reluctant to part with the *Meshouda*, since she had been (by all reports) a Tripolitan vessel. The commodore suspected that the emperor was angling for the best bargain he could get, but Preble finally agreed to let Morocco have her as a "gift," with the stipulation that she remain in port for as long as the conflict between the United States and Tripoli continued. In his report to Secretary Smith, Preble justified the concession by pointing out that the emperor "has such an extensive seacoast on the Atlantic, and is so advantageously situated on the Straits for annoying our commerce, that it is very much in our interest to be on good terms with him."

Parting company with the homeward-bound vessels, the *Constitution* ran back through the Straits before "fresh Gales and Rain." On the morning of October 15, she steered into Gibraltar Bay for the fourth time in a month, coming to anchor in 15 fathoms of water. The commodore had every right to be pleased. He had neutralized the Moroccan threat, and he had done so in the space of three weeks, without firing a single shot in anger. Now he had nothing standing between him and Yusuf, and could bring his entire force to bear against Tripoli.

WHILE PREBLE WAS AWAY SETTLING affairs with the Moroccans, twenty-five-year-old Lieutenant Charles Stewart of Philadelphia had been left in Gibraltar as the senior American officer on the station. He commanded the sloop of war *Siren*, with the *Mirboka* and *Meshouda* anchored under her guns.

Gibraltar was thought to be a safe shelter for the U.S. Navy. Britain and America were at peace; the narrowly averted exchange of broadsides between the *Constitution* and *Maidstone* had been laughed off; Preble had visited the senior civil and military officers of the place, and been politely received. With a few exceptions, English officers were instinctively courteous toward their former countrymen, with whom they shared a language, a culture, and a profession. Most of the American officers, in turn, were Federalists who favored closer Anglo-American relations, and said so. British dockyards and shore establishments in the Mediterranean welcomed the American frigates because they were paying customers and good for business.

But while *Constitution* was away in Tangier, a quarrel had broken out over the issue of deserters. On October 7, three British-born sailors who were enlisted in the American squadron, and assigned temporarily to the captured *Mirboka*, had gone ashore for provisions. While in town they had deserted and enlisted aboard the *Medusa*, one of several English frigates anchored in the bay. Lieutenant Stewart wrote a formal protest to the captain of the *Medusa*, John Gore, and demanded the return of the three men, whom he branded "as Felons and Deserters." Gore's response was courteous in tone; but he refused to return the men on the grounds that they were "subjects of his Britannic Majesty and have returned to their duty and allegiance."

In the following days, Stewart and Gore exchanged several more letters, and with each exchange the rhetoric escalated. Not only did Gore refuse to return the deserters, who "having again placed themselves under the Flag of their Liege Sovereign cannot possibly be given up either to the United States or any other Foreign power," he demanded two other seamen serving on board the *Mirboka* who were, he said, known to be British-born. More alarming, one of Gore's lieutenants passed on a spoken threat that the captain presumably did not dare put into writing: If every British sailor serving in the American squadron was not given up, they would be seized by force.

The expanding European war had raised the scarcity value of professional seamen—men who spoke English no worse than the next man and who could hand, reef, and steer without being taught. Neither the British nor the American Navy cared much about the nationality of the sailors they enlisted. Sailors were frequently induced to desert one service and reenlist in the other, and every man bearing a grudge against his officers could be expected to make the attempt as soon as he saw the chance.

On Preble's return, Stewart provided the commodore with copies of his correspondence with Captain Gore, adding that "you will perceive that we are liable to great inconvenience and contention with the Officers of the British Navy." The *Medusa* had put to sea, but she was expected to return in a few days. Preble prepared a strongly worded letter to be delivered to Gore on the ship's return. If the three men were not restored at once, Preble wrote, he would appeal to the British admiral on the station and also make "a representation" to the U.S. government. "The Officers of our Navy have invariably given up deserters from the British Navy or Armies, on the first application; and have a right to expect the same liberality on your part."

Preble knew full well that the squadron under his command employed large numbers of British-born sailors. It was an open secret among the American officers. Stewart had worried that if the Royal Navy made a policy of demanding all British-born seamen, "many of our men may be claimed on the same principle." Preble could hardly claim that none of the common seamen under his command had been born in England, Scotland, or Ireland. Instead, he told Gore—in language artfully contrived to evade the point—that "I know of no such person as a *British Subject*, on board any of the Ships of the Squadron under my command: I know them only as *Citizens* of the United States, who have taken the Oath of Allegiance to our Government, and have volunteered their Services."

The point that Preble evaded was this: Did British-born sailors have a right to be naturalized as American citizens? The American government asserted that they did; the British government insisted that they did not. With lawyerly prudence, Preble did not actually admit that some of his men were British-born American citizens. His immediate goal was to recover the deserters and shut off a route of desertion he knew more men were likely to try. Captain George Hart of the *Monmouth* offered an exchange: all American seamen to be returned from British ships, with "a like number of British seamen" given up in return. This Preble could not do. The U.S. Navy was a volunteer service, and sailors could not be simply handed over to a foreign navy against their will. To do so, Preble realized, would represent a breach of faith with the men under his command.

In his report to Secretary Smith, Preble pointed out the obvious: that the British government claimed rights and privileges it would not recognize in others. "The British make a practice of taking from our Merchant Vessels every man that has not a Protection [a certificate of American citizenship], and very often those who have. What would be said if our Ships of War were to take by force even Americans out of English Merchant Ships? . . . And why have we not as good a right even to impress from their Ships English Men when destitute of Protections, as they have Americans from Ours?" The answer, as Preble himself knew, was that England had eight hundred ships of war afloat, while the United States, after the downsizing of 1801–02, had fewer than ten.

Midshipman Wadsworth wrote that the English frigates deliberately moored close to the *Constitution*, as an invitation to deserters. On November 12, a sailor enlisted on the *Argus* dove into the bay and swam toward the British ship *Donegal:* a boat picked him up and returned him to the *Argus*, where he was confined in irons. When junior officers of the two navies met in town, harsh words were exchanged; a British officer reportedly said it was the Royal Navy's policy to "afford protection to every man who has an opportunity to claim it, and will say he is an Englishman." On the evening of the nineteenth, a group of American officers from the brig *Siren* encountered a group of English officers at Bernard's Tavern. "Some misunderstanding" occurred; but (as one of the Americans reported to his commander) there was "no riot, or other improper conduct . . . it was confined to the room in which it originated, and has since been amicably and honorably adjusted."

In the last week before sailing, Preble decided to move the squadron to the opposite side of Gibraltar Bay, near the Spanish town of Algeciras, safely out of swimming range of the British fleet. Here the *Constitution* lay at anchor for several days under strong breezes and rain, the crew employed in cleaning the ship between the decks.

As the commodore submerged himself in the tedious details of victualling and preparing the squadron for sea, he made an important decision. Previously, Preble had intended that his base of operations would be Malta, because of its proximity to Tripoli. But Malta, like Gibraltar, was a British naval base—and "at Malta the Ships lay so near the shore that it will be impossible to prevent [desertion], which has determined me to make Syracuse . . . the General rendezvous of the Squadron. It is an excellent harbor, safe and easy of access." When the *Constitution* hove up her anchor on the morning of November 14, her destination was Sicily.

CHAPTER SEVEN

After parting with the *Constitution* in the Straits, the *Philadelphia* had run up the Spanish coast as far north as Cabo de la Não, and then hauled off to the east, passing south of Majorca and Minorca, through the approaches to the Bay of Tunis, and arriving at the Grand Harbor of Valetta at Malta on October 3, 1803—a passage of fourteen days.

Preble's orders to Captain William Bainbridge had emphasized that he was to take the *Philadelphia* to Tripoli as swiftly as she would sail. Once there, he was to maintain a rigorous blockade of the harbor until relieved by the flagship or other vessels in the squadron. He was to remain at Malta no longer than twenty-four hours. Preble was aware that his predecessors had squandered weeks and months in port, and he was determined to keep the squadron at sea as long as possible, especially during the summer months when commercial traffic in the Mediterranean was heaviest.

Philadelphia was reckoned a very fine ship. At 1,240 tons burden, she was a heavy frigate, though not so heavy as the *Constitution*. Though she was not one of the original six frigates, she might as well have been. She was one of the "subscription" ships, commissioned in a private contract by the merchant community of the city for which she was named, built in 1799–1800 by Joshua Humphreys in the same yard that had launched the *United States*, and offered as a kind of gift to the navy. In the Quasi War she had captured five French privateers in the West Indies. After the *Constitution*, she was the largest ship in the Mediterranean Squadron, representing about a third of its total strength.

Bainbridge was twenty-nine years old, six feet tall, and heavyset. His thick, fleshy face was framed by an impressive pair of muttonchops that fell from his ears halfway down his jawline to his chin. He had been born in

Princeton, New Jersey, to parents who had remained loyal to England during the Revolutionary War; his father, a physician, had served as a surgeon to a British regiment. Just eight years old at the end of the war, Bainbridge was too young to fully understand his father's choices and their consequences, but he learned what it meant to have been a loyalist when his family's property was confiscated after the Peace of Paris.

Among his brother officers, Bainbridge was well liked and respected, both as a gentleman and as a talented seaman. But he was unpopular with the enlisted men. He was a ruthless disciplinarian, even by the standards of the era; he readily admitted that he regarded seamen as inveterate miscreants, unworthy of the slightest courtesy. Once approached by a man who tried to address him respectfully, Bainbridge cut him off, saying: "I don't allow a sailor to speak to me at all." In a letter to Preble, he summed up his view of the men who served before the mast. "I believe there never was so depraved a set of mortals as sailors are. Under discipline they are peaceable and serviceable—divest them of that and they constitute a perfect rabble."

From his first days at sea Bainbridge had used physical intimidation to enforce shipboard discipline. On most ships, the captain's dirty work was carried out by the boatswain and his gang of mates; Bainbridge did not hesitate to beat a troublemaker with his own fists. In 1802, Bainbridge had been assailed in print as "a man destitute of reason and humanity" by one John Rea, an ordinary seaman who had served under him in 1800 on the *George Washington*. If Rea's twenty-four-page pamphlet was to be believed, Bainbridge had injured a drunken sailor during the voyage by striking him on the head with his sword. Not only did the attack split the unlucky man's head open, fracturing his skull and sending him into violent convulsions, but the blow was dealt while the victim's hands and feet were confined in irons. Not satisfied, Bainbridge had afterward ordered the bleeding man seized up at the gangway and flogged. As the punishment was meted out, the captain had allegedly remarked: "I have no compassion on such a damned rascal."

But Bainbridge's unpopularity with his men seems to have been founded on something more than his reputation for brutality. It was known throughout the navy that Bainbridge had surrendered the *Retaliation* to the French in 1798, and then been forced to navigate the *George Washington* under an Algerian flag in 1800. In both cases he had been subsequently exonerated by courts of inquiry. But seamen were notoriously superstitious, and Bainbridge was dogged by the belief that he was terminally unlucky. To be lucky or unlucky was no small matter in the eyes of a sailor—all sought to sail with a lucky captain, and all would go to great lengths to avoid serving under an unlucky one.

The belief that Bainbridge sailed under a dark star—that mishaps, defeats, and ill fortune would inevitably follow him and any ship he commanded—seemed to be widely held among the enlisted men of the navy. Indeed, Bainbridge himself seems to have accepted his unluckiness as inevitable; he often referred to himself as a "child of adversity," and admitted to Edward Preble that "misfortune has attended me throughout my naval career."

Philadelphia hove in sight of Tripoli the morning of October 31 (then, as now, the day held special meaning to the superstitious). In the first light of dawn, the lookout sighted a native vessel standing to the east, close inshore with the town, and Bainbridge gave orders to make sail in chase. At eleven, seeing that the fleeing vessel was coming within the extreme range of the frigate's guns, Bainbridge ordered the bow chasers to open fire. For another hour the chase continued. The leadsmen were kept busy, constantly casting the lead and reporting a depth that varied from seven to ten fathoms. At half past eleven, with the walls and rooftops of Tripoli in plain sight, the *Philadelphia* entered the shoal waters that guarded the entrance to the harbor, and Bainbridge gave up the chase and ordered the helmsman to put the ship up into the wind.

The *Philadelphia*, unknown to her captain and crew, was already in mortal danger. With her head put into the wind and her speed at 7 or 8 knots, she all at once lurched, shuddered, and came to rest. Her bow was canted six feet out of the water and her deck was suddenly as fixed and motionless as a patch of dry ground. When the men on deck leaned over the side, they saw the green and greasy copper undersheathing of the hull resting on a reef just below the surface. The *Philadelphia* had run hard aground. Worse, she had struck with such force that the lip of the reef was directly beneath her fore chains. A full third of her length had been thrown on top of the shoal. Later charts would identify it as "Kaliusa Reef," but the *Philadelphia*'s charts showed no such reef in that position, and Bainbridge later said that the grounding was "as unexpected to me as if it had happened in the middle of the Mediterranean Sea."

Immediately Bainbridge ordered the sails laid aback and the guns run aft to lift the bow. The sounding lead was heaved from the taffrail and the leadsman reported an ample depth of water astern for the ship to float, if the *Philadelphia* could be backed off the reef. But the wind was blowing stiffly onto the starboard beam, and the sea was setting with it. When the weight of the guns was transferred to the stern, the bow was lifted from the reef just as Bainbridge had intended—but the wind and waves only drove the hull further onto the shoal. Two hours after grounding, the entire length of the frigate had come to rest and she was heeling severely to larboard, with water beginning to pour through her leeward gunports.

With the ship "immovably grounded on rocks," Bainbridge called his officers back to the quarterdeck for a hurried conference. All agreed that the *Philadelphia*'s situation was desperate enough to justify an extreme measure: they would heave the guns into the sea and start the fresh water out of the hold.

In the *Philadelphia*'s distressed position, she was plainly visible from the town. Tripolitans raced down to the harbor to man the gunboats. Nine vessels put out from the harbor and by midafternoon they had approached to within cannon-shot range of the stranded frigate.

All but a few of the *Philadelphia*'s guns were thrown over the side, and the few that remained were mounted on her stern. Because of the awkward angle at which the ship was heeling, these guns could be brought to bear only with difficulty. The Tripolitan gunboat crews soon realized they could approach with impunity. Armed with 18- and 24-pounder brass guns, they kept up a steady fire on the *Philadelphia*, aiming chiefly for the masts in order to prevent her escape. The frigate's situation, said Bainbridge, was like that of "one man tied to a stake attacked by another with arms."

As the afternoon wore on, the crew of the *Philadelphia* took increasingly desperate steps to lighten the ship. Men with hatchets cut away the foremast and all its supporting rigging. Casks of water and provisions were hoisted up through the hatchways and thrown haphazardly over the side. The anchors, one by one, were cut free and allowed to splash into the sea. "All that seamanship could dictate was acted upon to relieve us from the rocks," Bainbridge later wrote—"but all proved in Vain!"

Four hours after the grounding, the captain called his exhausted officers together for a second conference. All agreed that the *Philadelphia* was doomed. Nothing more could be done to get her off the reef. Nor was there any hope of bringing the frigate's few remaining guns to bear on the Tripolitan gunboats. Further resistance would end in the slaughter of the crew. For the third time in his short naval career, Bainbridge gave the fateful order to haul down the American colors and surrender his ship "to an enemy whom chance had befriended."

In the last minutes before the Tripolitans came aboard to take possession, the crew took measures to scuttle the ship. The carpenter took his mates below to bore holes through the ship's bottom. The gunner drowned the magazine by "turning the cock and securing the key," allowing a rush of cold seawater to pour into the hold. Cannon shot was thrown into the pumps to render them useless. Bainbridge himself tore the signal book into pieces and handed them to a midshipmen to be burned or thrown overboard. At six, with darkness falling, the victorious corsairs clambered over the side to seize the prize that had fallen so unexpectedly into their hands.

There seems to have been little discipline among the Tripolitans. According to ship's surgeon Jonathan Cowdery, a quarrel between some of the Tripolitan officers and their own men escalated into a melee. The officers drew their swords and "cut off the hands of some, and it is believed several were killed."

Communicating with the prisoners using gestures and a few phrases from the amorphous *lingua franca* of the Mediterranean—an amalgamation of French, Spanish, Italian, and Arabic—the Tripolitans instructed the prisoners to climb down into the gunboats, where they would be transported to the town. In the confusion that followed, many of the Americans were beaten and robbed. Tripolitans rifled the prisoners' pockets, tore off their clothes, and stripped them of their watches, money, books, pocket handkerchiefs, and gloves. Dr. Cowdery was robbed of his surgical instruments and a silver pencil. "The treatment we received from these Savages was such as raised our utmost indignation," said Bainbridge. "Nothing was sacred or escaped their prying search. . . . Our swords were snatched from us, our pockets searched and emptied; some of us had our boots pulled off, to examine if something was not concealed there, and some had their very coats pulled off their backs, which the barbarians exultingly put upon themselves, and as if the rewards of some signal Exploit; they seemed to triumph in acquiring what fortune alone had obtained them."

As the overcrowded boats reached the inner harbor, some of the prisoners were thrown into the sea and forced to swim or wade ashore. The boat carrying Bainbridge and several of his officers landed at a pier at the foot of the Bashaw's Castle. They were driven through the streets—"amidst the shouts and acclamations of the rabble Multitude"—to a passageway "lined with terrific janissaries, armed with glittering sabers, muskets, pistols and tomahawks." Hurried along through "various turnings and flights of stairs," they were escorted into an opulent hall, where the walls were made of enameled porcelain and the marble floors covered with luxuriant Turkish carpets. The prisoners were compelled to sit in a half circle before an elevated throne.

After a short delay, Yusuf Karamanli himself entered, trailing an entourage of councilors and guards. At thirty-five years old, the Bashaw was in the prime of his health. He was tall and athletic, with a long, dark beard and a "manly, majestic deportment." He wore a long robe made of cerulean silk and embroidered with gold lace. A gold sword hung from his diamond-encrusted belt, and his head was crowned with a magnificent white turban. As he gazed down on the prisoners from his throne, Bainbridge later wrote, "a gracious smile appeared upon his countenance, expressive of his inward satisfaction."

Yusuf seemed willing to treat his prisoners as honored guests, and after a short audience the officers were served a sumptuous dinner at a table "set in the European style." The servants appeared to be Maltese and Neapolitan slaves. The incongruity of the lavish setting must have heightened the officers' sense of shock and dislocation. They must have known that few prisoners taken by the Barbary States were ever restored to freedom. None kept a record of any conversation that passed between them during the meal, but it is not difficult to picture them eating in stunned silence.

After dinner, the officers were escorted out of the castle by a retinue of armed guards. Walking for a short distance through the city, they arrived at the former residence of James Cathcart, the last American consul who had lived in Tripoli before the war. This house, they were told, would serve as their quarters for the duration of their captivity. It was large and pleasant, with a spacious interior court and an imposing portico lined with ancient marble pillars, but it had stood empty for years and its many rooms contained no furniture. On the first night, Bainbridge and the others made themselves as comfortable as they could, sleeping on "mats and blankets spread upon the floor, which was composed of tiles."

Most of their personal belongings—"everything but what we had on our Backs & even part of that"—had been stolen. It was unclear whether their captors would provide them with food or other essentials. The Tripolitans offered to sell the officers their own trunks of clothing (which had been recovered from the still-grounded *Philadelphia*) for the exorbitant price of $1,200, but the Americans did not have that kind of money and would not pay it even if they did.

Relief came on the second day, when the Danish consul, Nicholas Nissen, brought mattresses, blankets, and baskets of pomegranates, dates, and oranges. Nissen, prompted by nothing more than simple charity, offered to assist the American officers in making their captivity as comfortable as possible. He introduced Bainbridge to local bankers and assisted him in negotiating an order for 300 Spanish dollars "which will serve his wants as well as those of his officers." Bainbridge also borrowed 500 dollars from the Tripolitan foreign minister, Sidi Mohammed Dghies, at 15 percent interest.

The Tripolitans were familiar with the European military custom of the parole of honor, and agreed to a generous degree of personal freedom in exchange for a pledge that no American officer would try to escape. On November 5, Dghies sent his personal secretary to the officers' house with a parole written in French. Each man signed it. The guards relaxed and the prisoners were permitted to climb a stairway that led to a terrace at the top of the house, which "commanded a handsome prospect of the harbor, the sea, the town, the Palace, and the adjoining country." They were irked to see many Tripolitans "running about town with our uniform coats and other clothing on."

Bainbridge lost no time in laying the foundation of his defense. Having consulted with his officers before surrendering the *Philadelphia*, he now asked them to put in writing their approval of his conduct. They complied, each signing a statement that expressed "our full approbation of your conduct concerning the unfortunate event of yesterday . . . believe us, sir, that our misfortunes and sorrows are entirely absorbed in our sympathy for you."

In his official letters, Bainbridge's anguish was palpable. "Sir," he wrote Secretary Smith the day after the capture; "Misfortune necessitates me to make a communication, the most distressing of my life, and it is with the deepest regret that I inform you of the loss of the United States frigate *Philadelphia* under my command by being wrecked on Rocks between four and five miles to the Eastward of the Town of Tripoli." Anticipating the criticism that he should have fought rather than surrender, he told Captain Preble: "Some Fanatics may say that blowing the ship up would have been the proper result. I thought such conduct would not stand acquitted before God or Man, and I never presumed to think I had the liberty of putting to death the lives of 306 Souls because they were placed under my command."

As if the loss of the *Philadelphia* was not bad enough, on either November 1 or 2, a westerly gale raised a heavy sea, and with the help of the *Philadelphia*'s own carpenter and his mates, the damaged frigate was lifted off the shoal and brought triumphantly into Tripoli's inner harbor. Over the next several days, divers free-dove the reef and successfully retrieved many of the guns and much of the other equipment that had been thrown overboard. Having first assured his superiors that the *Philadelphia* was a complete loss, Bainbridge was now forced to admit that he had been wrong. "We were not Gods to foresee the Wind, and to know that the Sea would so rise; and had we been apprised of it all, it could have availed us nothing."

Although he maintained a cool outward demeanor, Bainbridge's private letters written during this period suggest he was borderline suicidal. He assumed that when the news of the loss of the *Philadelphia* reached America, he would be condemned as an incompetent, perhaps even a coward. Isolated by his rank, Bainbridge was mostly left alone by his subordinate officers, and he passed the long, uneventful hours imagining what his countrymen were thinking of him and saying about him. Unless liberated, he would never even have the opportunity to defend himself and his decision to surrender his ship. He told his wife, Susan, "These are the mere reveries which daily pass through my heated brain. . . . These impressions, which are seldom absent from my mind, act as a corroding canker at my heart."

Writing on November 1 to Susan, Bainbridge exclaimed that "it would have been a merciful dispensation of Providence if my head had been shot off by the enemy, while our vessel lay rolling on the rocks." Only his certainty that she would always love him, in spite of his disgrace, gave him a will to go on living: "If the world desert me, I am sure to find a welcome in her arms—in her affection, to receive the support and condolence which none others can give."

FOR THE OFFICERS, captivity in Tripoli was shaping up to be something like an extended vacation in a tropical seaside resort. The midshipmen amused themselves by catching scorpions in the courtyard, while the lieutenants accepted an invitation to lunch with Nissen at the Danish consulate. The enlisted men of the *Philadelphia* were not nearly so fortunate. Their plight was recorded by an ordinary seaman named William Ray, a thirty-four-year-old native of Salisbury, Connecticut, whose career had included failed stints as a shopkeeper, a schoolmaster, and a newspaper editor. Published in 1808, his account was entitled *Horrors of Slavery, or the American Tars in Tripoli*.

Hours after the surrender of the *Philadelphia*, the sailors were taken under heavy guard to a damp cell within the walls of the castle. The chamber, which would house more than two hundred prisoners, was 50 feet long and 20 feet wide. Light entered through a narrow aperture in the ceiling and two grated windows. "Not a morsel of food had we tasted," Ray wrote, "and hunger, like the vulture of Prometheus, began to corrode our vitals." Eventually, each man was given a small, unsatisfying loaf of coarse white bread. They slept that night on the floor, which was cold, damp, and "planted with hard pebbles." A few were lucky enough to have salvaged some flimsy, tattered fragments of sailcloth; the others rolled up their shirts as pillows. As the room was not nearly large enough for all the men to stretch out, some slept while sitting and others spent the night on their feet.

In the morning, the prisoners were awoken before sunrise by "the horrid clanking of huge bolts." They were divided into smaller groups and taken off to different parts of the city to be put to work. Those who were slow to comply were beaten by the guards. Some were forced to carry stone, dirt, lime, and mortar to a construction site; others carried buckets of water from a well to the castle. A few were rowed out to the *Philadelphia*, where they remained all night, working to bring her off the reef.

On returning that night, a scuffle broke out as men tried to force their way into the cell in front of their mates, hoping to stake out enough space on the floor to get a night of sleep. They were fed a meal of couscous, which they had never seen before—Ray described it as "barley ground very coarse, and neither sifted nor bolted"—and small loaves of coarse black barley bread, which the ravenous prisoners "seized with avidity." Accustomed to the harsh conditions of naval service, the seamen showed a remarkable ability to adapt to the grim routine. Ray observed with admiration that his fellow prisoners, "in the most despondent aspect of times, . . . would caper, sing, jest, and look as cheerful, many of them, as if they had been at a feast or wedding."

On the third day, while at a work site, some of the Americans managed to sneak away from their overseers and wander into town in search of liquor, which was purveyed by some of the city's Jews and Christians. Most of Tripoli's streets were alleyways abutted by the walls of the houses, so narrow that pedestrians had to walk in a single file. Homes were built of materials apparently scavenged from ancient ruins, including fragments of marble with "engravings and inscriptions, mostly defaced," in Greek and Latin. Beginning just inside the city's main gate, which was festooned with the severed hands of accused thieves, a long line of low brick huts served as a market. At the door of each shop, a proprietor sat cross-legged on the ground, wrapped in a blanket. One could buy or barter for "pumpkins, carrots, turnips, scallions, oranges, lemons, limes, figs, etc. etc. with a thousand trinkets, and haberdashers' wares."

When caught, the sailors who had deserted their work site were sentenced to suffer a "bastinado." Ray described the punishment:

The instrument with which they prepare a man for torture is called a *bastone;* it is generally about four or five feet long, and as thick in the middle as a man's leg, tapering to the ends. At equal distances from the center, it is perforated in two places, and a rope incurvated, the ends passed through the holes, and knotted. This forms a loop. The person is then thrown on his back, his feet put through the loop, and a man at each end of the stick, both at once, twist it round, screw his feet and ankles tight together, and raise the soles of his feet nearly horizontal. A Turk sits on his back, and two men, with each a bamboo, or branch of the date tree, as large as a walking staff and about three feet in length, hard and very heavy, strip or roll up their sleeves, and with all their strength and fury, apply the bruising cudgel to the bottoms of the feet. In this manner they punished several of our men, [who were] writhing with extreme anguish, and cursing their tormentors.

Among the *Philadelphia*'s crew were a number of British-born men. Some hoped to win release by declaring themselves loyal subjects of the king of England and asking for the intervention of the British consul. Captain Bainbridge endorsed the idea on grounds of "Interest and Humanity." But several of the *Philadelphia*'s renegade Britons had nothing but contempt for the idea, saying that "they would not be released by a government which they detested, on account of its tolerating the impressment of seamen, and swearing that they would sooner remain under the Bashaw than George the third." No prisoner was ever claimed by the British government, and Lord Nelson himself was said to have remarked that he would sooner "have the Rascals all hung" than intercede on behalf of men who had turned their backs on England to enlist in a foreign navy.

There was another way to escape captivity, and that was to "turn Turk"—to agree to convert to Islam. Muslims could not be enslaved in Tripoli, and any captive who agreed to undergo the conversion was usually emancipated. Owners sometimes tried to block such conversions so that they would not be divested of their slaves.

On November 8, one of the *Philadelphia*'s crew expressed an interest in conversion. He was John Wilson, formally the captain's coxswain (the man who piloted the captain's barge) aboard the *Philadelphia*. He had been born in Germany and had learned the Mediterranean *lingua franca*. He apparently invented stories in the hope of gaining Yusuf's ear, falsely reporting to the Tripolitans that Captain Bainbridge had thrown nineteen boxes of gold dollars and a large bag of gold overboard before surrendering the *Philadelphia*, and later warning of a plot among the prisoners to rise up and take over the town. As a reward for his cooperation, Wilson was promoted to overseer of his former crewmates. He was, Ray said, a "perfidious wretch." On November 20, a second of the *Philadelphia*'s seamen, a seventeen-year-old Rhode Islander named Thomas Prince, also agreed to convert to Islam. He was allowed to leave the prison and was taken to the palace, where he would be employed by the Bashaw as a private servant.

Ten weeks after the loss of the *Philadelphia*, the Tripolitan harbor batteries fired a salute to mark the end of the fast of Ramadan. Mosques and houses were illuminated and people turned out in their best clothes to rejoice in the streets. Captain Bainbridge was invited to a celebratory feast with the Bashaw and the entire diplomatic corps. Along with all the other vessels in the harbor, the *Philadelphia* was dressed in bright flags and colors, and her guns were fired to join the general salute.

PREBLE LEARNED OF THE LOSS of the *Philadelphia* on November 24 from the captain of the Royal Navy frigate *Amazon* (38 guns), when she spoke the *Constitution* at sea a few miles southwest of Sardinia. The Commodore wrote in his private diary that he had received "melancholy and distressing Intelligence of the loss of the US ship *Philadelphia* . . . the loss of that ship and capture of the Crew with all its consequences are of the most serious and alarming nature to the United States. . . ." Preble feared that Algiers and Tunis would seize the opportunity to declare war. He dreaded the prospect of expanded hostilities at a time when his squadron's effective strength had been diminished by some 30 to 40 percent. "I most sincerely pity the cruel fate of poor Bainbridge," Preble wrote his wife, Mary; "I know not what will become of them. I suspect very few will ever see home again."

Preble put the *Constitution* on a course for Malta, where he hoped to gather more intelligence about the appalling event. On November 27, the flagship was just off the Grand Harbor of Valetta, lying to under freshening breezes from the north. Preble chose not to take the *Constitution* into Valetta, an English port, fearing another spate of desertion. A lieutenant took a boat with a handpicked crew and sailed into the harbor, returning a few hours later with a sheaf of correspondence from Captain Bainbridge. Not only did the letters confirm the capture of the *Philadelphia* and her crew, but Preble now learned that the Tripolitans had floated the ship and were busy refitting her in Tripoli's inner harbor. The latter news effectively doubled the pain of the loss. A powerful weapon had been subtracted from Preble's fighting strength and added to that of the enemy.

The wind came up all through the afternoon. Soon after the lieutenant had returned from Valetta and the boat safely hoisted back onto the davits, the *Constitution* was laboring in gale-force northerly winds and "tremendous seas in the channel." Preble put her into the teeth of the gale, under reefed courses and staysails, and she had a rough time of it for the next twenty-four hours, finally fetching the lee of Sicily on the twenty-ninth. Moored in the harbor at Syracuse were two other squadron vessels, *Enterprise* and *Nautilus*, and a storeship recently arrived from America, the *Traveler*.

Preble landed and waited upon the governor, Marcello de Gregorio, who was obviously delighted to welcome the squadron. The U.S. Navy had money to spend, and its presence would discourage the Barbary cruisers from operating in waters near the Sicilian coast. The squadron was generously allowed the use of the arsenal, which provided covered shelter for boats, spars, "and very excellent Magazines that will contain five thousand Barrels of provisions; and all these free of expence!" Syracusians put out in boats from the quays to tour the *Constitution*, and the local nobility vied to invite the officers into their homes as guests. Preble felt his decision to move the rendezvous from Malta was vindicated: "The Inhabitants are extremely friendly and civil, and our Sailors cannot desert."

The squadron lay moored in the harbor for two weeks, as Preble attended to the tedious details of refitting and provisioning. Ugly weather delayed the transfer of several hundred casks of fresh water aboard the *Constitution* and her consorts, as well as the landing of the *Traveler*'s cargo ashore. *Constitution* prepared a new suit of sails, and the *Enterprise* was newly rigged from stem to stern.

Preble was known as a "hard horse"—a harsh disciplinarian—and he lived up to his reputation while the squadron harbored at Syracuse. Floggings were a near-daily event aboard the *Constitution*. On November 29, several seamen were given two or three dozen lashes each for crimes that included "drunkenness, neglect of duty, and stealing rum from the ship's stores." As commodore, Preble had the right to punish seamen serving aboard any vessel under his command, and it was a right he did not hesitate to exercise. On December 1, Lieutenant Stephen Decatur, Jr., commander of the *Enterprise*, received the following curt note: "Your men on shore for the purpose of fitting your Rigging were this Afternoon most of them drunk. This must undoubtedly have happened in consequence of the negligence of the Officers in charge of them. I request you to make the necessary inquiry respecting this Neglect on their part, as I shall most certainly take notice of it. One of your men is in Irons on board this ship for impertinence to me."

Preble planned to get the squadron underway for the coast of Tripoli, where he would try a winter blockade. His predecessors had tried and failed to blockade the port continuously, even during the milder summer months, but Preble believed they had bungled the logistical aspects of the operation and that he could succeed where they had failed. On the other hand, he admitted to Secretary Smith that the loss of the *Philadelphia* "distresses me beyond description, and very much deranges my plans of operation for the present."

He asked to be reinforced with two more frigates. With such a squadron under his command, he promised, he would bring Yusuf to his knees.

As news of the *Philadelphia*'s capture spread through the Mediterranean, Bainbridge came in for savage criticism, just as he had known he would. "How glorious it would have been to have perished with the Ship," wrote James Cathcart from Leghorn on the Italian coast to Secretary of State Madison, with a civilian's enthusiasm for the romance of dying in battle: " . . . while humanity recoils at the idea of launching so many souls into eternity, everything great, glorious, and patriotic dictates the measure [blowing up the ship], and our national honor and pride demanded the sacrifice." The junior officers of the squadron were hardly more sympathetic. Midshipman Wadsworth's disgusted view was that "one of our Finest Frigates was deserted, without even making a defense to be expected from an American cockboat."

Preble expressed a variety of opinions on the subject, depending on whom he was addressing. In his letters to Bainbridge (sent to Tripoli in care of the Danish consul, Nissen), he expressed nothing but sympathy and reassurance. "I feel most sensibly for the misfortune of yourself, your Officers, and Crew," he wrote December 19. "Your situation is truly distressing, and affects your friends too powerfully to be described." Doubting not for a moment that Bainbridge had done everything within his power to save the *Philadelphia*, Preble said that what he most regretted was losing the services of such a "valuable commander."

In his official letters to the Navy Department, Preble took a different tone. "I shall not hazard an opinion on the subject of the loss," he wrote Secretary Smith, and then offered one: "Would to God that the Officers and crew of the *Philadelphia* had one and all determined to prefer death to slavery; it is possible such a determination might have saved them from either!" He added, caustically, that he was surprised the ship had not been properly scuttled before she was delivered into the hands of the enemy.

THE NIGHT BEFORE CHRISTMAS EVE, the *Constitution* was in the offing near Tripoli, running south toward the African coast in company with the *Enterprise*. Soon after first light, the lookout at the masthead sighted land to the southwest, and a few minutes later hailed the deck again to report a sail on the horizon in the same direction.

Preble ordered the British ensign hauled up to the mizzen peak. The hands were turned out to make sail and the *Constitution* gave chase. The wind soon veered into the southwest, bringing the stranger dead to windward, and she might have escaped into Tripoli Harbor had she been handled with determination. Evidently, however, the crew did not suspect that the English colors were a ruse, and since they had no reason to fear the Royal Navy, they made no effort to escape. At 10:00 a.m., nine miles northeast of Tripoli, the vessel submitted to a shot fired across her bow.

She was ketch-rigged, about 60 tons burden, and flying Tripolitan colors. Her name was *Mastico*. A moment after her captain had stepped onto the quarterdeck of the *Constitution*, Preble ordered down the British ensign and up the Stars and Stripes, at which "the People on board the vessel appeared to be in the greatest confusion." Directly under the guns of a 1,500-ton frigate, however, the little ketch did not have the slightest hope of escape.

Questioning the captain and officers through a translator, Preble learned that *Mastico* had sailed from Tripoli the evening before for Constantinople. Her crew included a Turkish master, seven Greeks, four Turks, two Tripolitan officers, ten Tripolitan soldiers, and forty-two sub-Saharan African slaves—men, women, and children—who were to be given as tribute to the Grand Ottoman Turk. Though she had been flying a Tripolitan ensign when captured, *Mastico*'s captain insisted that she was an Ottoman vessel. The presence of several Turks in her crew made it difficult for Preble to dismiss the claim out of hand. The last thing Preble needed was a quarrel with the Ottoman Empire. The ketch's papers were written in Arabic and would require some time to be translated properly. The commodore decided to send her into Syracuse with a prize crew so that her national identity could be definitively ascertained. He would decide what to do with her later.

The officers and crew were taken aboard the *Constitution* as prisoners, and the prize set off to the north under convoy with the *Enterprise*. It was Christmas Eve. *Constitution* at first stood in toward Tripoli Harbor, but the sky appeared menacing, with "every appearance of strong breezes from the north," wrote Sailing Master Nathaniel Haraden in the ship's log. Plans for a winter blockade were for the moment abandoned, and Preble put the frigate into the wind to gain a safe offing against the coming gale.

The storm came on Christmas morning. Every resource of seamanship was needed to claw the *Constitution* off a lee shore that was also, as it happened, enemy territory. The prisoners lined the rail and seemed to will the ship to be wrecked: "The Horrors of ship wreck added to irretrievable slavery make this coast very dangerous in the winter," Haraden observed.

For several days, *Constitution* labored through heavy seas and rain under close-reefed topsails and reefed courses, her topgallant masts and yards struck down on deck. She clawed her way north, mile by bitter mile, at last over-hauling the *Enterprise* and *Mastico* near Malta. The *Mastico* was so battered that she was no longer capable of sailing, and the *Constitution* took her in tow. On December 30, the weather-beaten squadron arrived at Syracuse and anchored in five fathoms water, just outside the mole.

In Syracuse, the case against the *Mastico* was reinforced by an Italian doctor from Malta who identified two of her officers as high-ranking Tripolitans, swearing "that one of them was a principal officer of the Bashaw and that the other held high rank in his troops." Even more damning, Preble learned from an English pilot who had been in Tripoli on October 31 that *Mastico* had taken part in the capture of the *Philadelphia*. The ketch had been moored in Tripoli's inner harbor that day under Ottoman colors. When it was obvious that the American frigate was grounded and distressed, the *Mastico* "took on board upwards of One hundred Tripolines armed with muskets, sabers, etc, slipped his cables, hauled down the Turkish and Hoisted Tripoline Colors, and proceeded to the Attack of the *Philadelphia*."

If any doubt remained in Preble's mind, it was dispelled when articles belonging to the officers of the *Philadelphia*, including a sword and belt Preble recognized as belonging to Lieutenant David Porter, turned up in the possession of the *Mastico*'s crew. Whether she was Tripoline or Ottoman was beside the point, said Preble: "If a Tripoline, she is a prize; if a Turk, a pirate."

The *Mastico* was not a valuable prize. A panel of American officers estimated her worth at no more than $1,800. But her economic value was not important. As the officers and men of the squadron celebrated the new year, 1804, Preble had an important mission in mind for the little ketch—a mission that promised, if successful, to bring him one long step closer to winning the war.

SHOULD THE OFFICERS AND CREW of the *Philadelphia* be ransomed? The suggestion could not be dismissed out of hand. There was a precedent for it in the recent past: the U.S. government had paid a huge ransom to recover American seamen taken by Algiers. Even before the loss of the *Philadelphia* was known in Washington, the president's cabinet had voted to authorize a new payment to the Bashaw of Tripoli. Jefferson and Madison were not adamantly opposed to paying for peace in the Mediterranean; they just wanted to be sure of getting value for the American people's money.

Months would pass before the dispatches could be carried back to America, digested by Jefferson and his advisers, and new orders carried back to

Syracuse. Preble could not afford to keep the squadron idle as he awaited new instructions. To do so would risk bringing on himself the same censure that had ended his predecessor's naval career. He had no choice but to proceed as best he could.

American diplomatic consuls were stationed in most of the major ports of the Mediterranean. They were an unruly and fractious group, often operating with little or no supervision from their putative boss, Secretary of State Madison. They blended public duties with private business affairs in ethically troubling ways, and they seemed to devote much of their time to feuding among themselves. For all their flaws, however, the members of this embryonic diplomatic corps knew better than anyone else how to get things done in the Barbary States.

Working independently and through backchannels, several of the consuls sounded out the Bashaw's ministers on the cost of ransoming the officers and crew of the *Philadelphia*. In mid-December, James Cathcart, the former consul to Tripoli, told Madison that "if government concludes to redeem our fellow citizens immediately and sue for peace on the Bashaw's own terms, it will cost us $300,000 at least, exclusive of consular presents and annuity (tribute) of $10,000 or $15,000. . . ." Richard O'Brien, the former consul to Algiers, came up with the similar figure of $282,800, based upon a price of $600 for each sailor and $4,000 for each officer. Peace, he said, would require an additional onetime payment of $100,000. Tobias Lear, the current consul at Algiers, weighed in on Christmas Eve, estimating the ransom at $1,000 per head ($307,000) and peace at about $150,000.

Naturally, such a settlement would only be reached at the end of long negotiations. The Bashaw's initial demand would be something like $3 million. "A pretty good asking price," Preble commented dryly.

If half a million dollars would wash away America's troubles in the Mediterranean, the Bashaw's terms might have been deemed a bargain. But there were other variables to consider. As a new country, placed on the opposite side of the great western ocean, America was a bit of an enigma; the Barbary powers had not yet decided, as James Cathcart put it, "how to rank us among the nations of the earth." Was the United States a formidable military power to be treated with deference, like England and France? Or was it a nation to be preyed upon and blackmailed, like Naples, Portugal, Holland, Denmark, and Sweden? Or was it something in between? The outcome of the Tripolitan War would provide the answer. A large peace settlement would be interpreted by Tunis and Algiers as a fatal sign of weakness, and tempt them to escalate their own demands. Worse, they might take the view that

long-term war against a nation so obviously rich and defenseless was prefer-
able to peace at any price.

O'Brien reminded Preble of another important consideration. The
Bashaw of Tripoli had reneged on an earlier U.S. treaty. Why should he be
trusted not to do so again? For appearance's sake, he might keep the peace for
a year or two, meanwhile turning his corsairs loose on other second-rate
commercial powers. But "after they bowed to his caprice it would be our turn
again. The result of course will be more frigates in this sea."

From a variety of sources, Preble gathered intelligence on the nature and
extent of Tripoli's harbor fortifications. By January 1804, the commodore had
pieced together a reasonably accurate picture of what he was dealing with.
Numerous batteries, altogether comprising 115 guns, commanded various
approaches to the harbor. It was said that many of the harbor guns and their
carriages were ancient and decrepit, and some were in such a poor state that
they could not be fired, even in a salute. Tripoli had always relied upon its
fleet of gunboats to defend the harbor, but its gunboats were unrigged and
hauled up onto the beach for the winter. The Bashaw evidently did not expect
an American attack before the spring.

Using a telescope, William Bainbridge had surveyed Tripoli's harbor
defenses from the roof terrace of the officers' prison house. Writing in cipher,
and forwarding the letters through Consul Nissen to Malta, he warned that
the town could not be taken from the sea. "Nature has strongly guarded the
Harbor of Tripoli by Rocks and Shoals—the Town is too well fortified for our
shipping, by an attack, to make an impression on it . . . ," he wrote on January 14. "[Yusuf] is only vulnerable to the United States one way; that is by
eight or ten thousand men landing near his Town, which in my Opinion
would soon become an easy conquest."

Preble did not have eight or ten thousand men; he did not have a thousand. Total American forces in the Mediterranean amounted to one frigate,
one brig, and three schooners—comprising in all about 100 guns and seven
hundred men. And the brig, *Argus*, was stationed at Gibraltar, where she was
needed to protect American merchant vessels passing through the Straits.
The commodore did not know when—or whether—reinforcements would
appear on the western horizon. But Preble's self-appointed advisers in the
diplomatic corps seemed convinced that the commodore was somehow able
to call upon vast reserves of ships, manpower, and weaponry, and they offered
him their unsolicited tactical advice on how to batter Tripoli into submission.
O'Brien envisioned gigantic floating batteries capable of carrying heavy cannon into the inner harbor, where they would "fire on the Town, rake the

Marine Sea Battery, and flank the Bashaw's Palace or Castle." He urged that Preble ask the government to lose no time in building 74-gun ships, as well as six more large frigates.

Added to Tripoli's defenses was the frigate *Philadelphia* (soon to be renamed *Gift of Allah*), now anchored in the main channel about three fourths of a mile from shore. Most of her guns had been retrieved from the shallow waters into which they had sunk and remounted on the gun and spar decks. It was doubtful that the Tripolitans were capable of rigging and manning the great frigate, and the Bashaw was known to have advertised her for sale to Tunis or Algiers. But so long as she lay in the enemy's harbor, the Tripolitan ensign at her mizzen peak, her guns mounted and charged, the *Philadelphia* would serve as a powerful and strategically positioned fortress. Worse, her very existence was a humiliating symbol of American powerlessness in the Mediterranean.

The idea to destroy the *Philadelphia* seems to have occurred independently to several American officers. Years later they would disagree on who had been the first to propose it. Preble said he resolved to do it the moment he first learned of her capture. "I shall hazard much to destroy her," he had written Smith in December; "—it will undoubtedly cost us many lives, but it must be done." From his prison in Tripoli, Bainbridge urged that a small crew of men be sent into the harbor in boats, armed with combustibles. The boats should approach the target surreptitiously, under cover of darkness; if the Tripolitans were surprised, Bainbridge predicted, the firing of the ship "could be easily effected." Twenty-five year-old Lieutenant Stephen Decatur, commander of the schooner *Enterprise*, volunteered to take a hand-picked crew and do it himself, and several colleagues later corroborated his claim that the mission had been his initiative.

A FELLOW OFFICER, when interviewed by a biographer years later, attempted to put his finger on the elusive quality that set Stephen Decatur apart. "In Decatur I was struck with a peculiarity of manner and appearance, calculated to rivet the eye and engross the attention. I had often pictured to myself the form and look of a hero, such as my favorite Homer had delineated; here I saw it embodied." Born in a log cabin in Tidewater Maryland and raised in maritime Philadelphia, Decatur was tall, trim, broad-shouldered, and athletic, with curly dark hair and large, proud brown eyes. His physical magnetism was famous—upon entering a room, resplendent in his blue and gold-laced naval uniform, his mere appearance had been said to cause young women to actually collapse and lose consciousness. No officer of the period better personified the eighteenth-century ideal of the romantic hero. To Decatur, the object of war was personal and national glory, and he sought after both with a single-minded intensity.

There is no doubt that Decatur volunteered to lead the dangerous mission, but he was not the only officer to do so. Among the junior officers of the Jefferson-era navy, the only realistic hope of promotion was to be distinguished in combat, and the Tripolitan War had thus far provided little opportunity. The mission to destroy the *Philadelphia*, if successful, would transform its participants into national heroes, and the officers could count on being rewarded with rapid promotions. Predictably, Preble was inundated with volunteers. In choosing Decatur to command, the commodore was expressing his confidence that the young lieutenant was capable of leading the expedition to success. But he was also making the implicit judgment that Decatur was worthy of promotion to higher rank—of entering that select society of officers who would make a lifelong career of the navy, and inherit responsibility for its institutional success.

Preble had briefly considered the possibility that the *Philadelphia* might be "cut out"—recaptured, hastily made ready for sea, and navigated safely out of Tripoli Harbor. But he was deterred by the intelligence he had received of the state of the ship, the harbor defenses, the difficulty of the channel. "I was well informed that her situation was such as to render it impossible to bring her out," Preble later wrote Secretary Smith, "and her destruction being absolutely necessary to favor my intended operations against that city, I determined the attempt should be made."

The captured *Mastico* would carry the raiding party into the enemy's harbor. No other vessel in the American squadron would do, said Preble, because "our frigates and schooners are so well known, that they create alarm the moment they are seen." But the native-rigged Tripolitan ketch looked no different from a thousand other small merchantmen that plied the North African coasting trade. She could easily pass for a common trading vessel, inbound to Tripoli to embark a cargo of provisions for the British garrison at Malta. If the ruse succeeded, her approach would arouse no suspicions. She was given a new name, chosen by Preble himself: *Intrepid*.

On January 30, 1804, Preble ordered the prisoners transferred from the *Intrepid* to the flagship. The damaged ketch was towed into the inner harbor at Syracuse for repairs. She took on thirty days' allowance of fresh water and provisions for a crew of seventy-five men.

The commodore wrote out his orders on January 31. Decatur was to transfer his crew from the *Enterprise* into the *Intrepid*. The *Intrepid* would sail in company with the brig *Siren*, commanded by Lieutenant Charles Stewart, to a rendezvous north of Tripoli. As *Siren* waited in the offing, *Intrepid* and the *Siren*'s boats would steal into the harbor under cover of darkness. "Board the Frigate *Philadelphia*, burn her, and make your retreat good," wrote Preble. Before escaping to safety, Decatur must be certain that the ship had been completely and utterly destroyed. The raiding party was to ignite combustibles in the gun room, berth deck, and cockpit storerooms. "After the Ship is well on fire, point two of the 18-pounders shotted down the Main Hatch and blow her bottom out."

"The destruction of the *Philadelphia* is an object of great importance," Preble added. "I rely with confidence on your Intrepidity & Enterprize to effect it."

The expedition sailed from Syracuse the evening of Friday, February 3, in moderate breezes and pleasant weather. As a precaution against leaks, the enlisted men had not previously been told the purpose of the mission. The crew of the *Siren* was called aft and a letter from the commodore, explaining all the details, was read aloud. Afterward, the seamen "were pleased to express their satisfaction, by three hearty cheers." When the officers asked for volunteers to join the raiding party, every man on board raised his hand.

Intrepid was a slow sailor, and she was taken in tow by the *Siren*. The weather was unseasonably mild for the first several days of the passage, but as the two vessels reached the offing north of Tripoli on the night of the seventh, the skies were threatening. Another winter gale, much like the one that had nearly done in the *Constitution* six weeks earlier, was gathering in the north. The *Intrepid* and *Siren* anchored in six fathoms of water abreast a line of rocks that formed the outer barrier to Tripoli Harbor. The night was "dark & hazy." A pilot took a small crew in one of the boats and went to reconnoiter the channel. On returning, he said that "if we attempted to go in we would never come out again for the breakers were tremendously high owing to the late gale." Decatur decided to sail the *Intrepid* back into the offing before sunrise, so that she would not be discovered by the Tripolitan lookouts. *Siren*'s crew tried and failed to win her larboard bower anchor, which was wedged in a rocky bottom—several men were knocked down by the capstan bars and "much injured." With dawn fast approaching, and the *Siren* rolling her gunwales under the waves, Stewart finally ordered the cable cut and the anchor sacrificed, and the brig followed the ketch back out to sea, to a distance offshore of about ten miles.

For five days they lay to against the worst conditions the Mediterranean had to offer, carrying scarcely any canvas at all. Owing to her small size and "frail construction," the *Intrepid* was wet, overcrowded, and miserable. Pitching and rolling in heavy seas, the crew suffered terribly from seasickness, and even those who could stomach their food were made sick by "an accidental supply of putrid provisions." The hold was infested with rats and vermin. Morale suffered: some of the men thought the mission was doomed. Because they had shown themselves off Tripoli, they whispered, the enemy was on guard against their attack. Throughout the ordeal, Decatur maintained an appearance of absolute confidence and resolve. By all accounts, his leadership during those wretched five days kept the crew from descending into a state of total despair.

When the gale finally abated on February 12, the *Siren* and the *Intrepid* had been separated and driven far to the east. Each vessel navigated back to Tripoli by identifying features of the North African coast—especially Mount Togura, a few miles east of the city. On the fifteenth, the two vessels rendezvoused, and a council of officers was held aboard the *Intrepid*. Decatur decided the operation would be attempted the following night. Nine men from the *Siren*, armed with cutlasses, pistols, and muskets, went across in the cutter to join the raiding party aboard the *Intrepid*.

February 16 dawned with clear and pleasant weather. A fresh breeze sprung up in the afternoon, and *Intrepid* began her approach to the harbor, flying English colors. No more than six or eight men showed themselves on deck, all disguised in native Maltese clothing. Steering and handling the ketch in a careless and lethargic fashion, they created the illusion that she was a common merchantman—so much so that answering colors were raised over the town's British consulate. When it seemed as if the *Intrepid* might reach the harbor before nightfall, Decatur ordered that ladders, buckets, and spars be towed astern to act as drags, slowing her progress. At dusk the wind fell off, the ketch's speed dropped to 2 knots, and the drags were taken back on board. The *Siren*, meanwhile, had fallen far behind in the failing breeze, and her boats were late in reaching the mouth of the harbor. Decatur decided that the *Intrepid* would carry on alone.

She wafted down the channel, pushed along by an almost imperceptible breath of wind on her larboard quarter. Hours passed. The huge stone walls of the Molehead Battery and the Bashaw's Castle rose up on either side, dimly lit by a crescent moon hanging low in the west. Eighty men were crammed aboard the little ketch, all but a few concealed belowdecks or stretched out prone behind the weatherboards. They were armed to the teeth, silent as the dead.

From the *Philadelphia*, moored ahead in the channel, the Tripolitan guards scrutinized the approaching vessel. They had no reason to suspect the *Intrepid* was not exactly what she seemed to be—an ordinary Maltese merchantman. But the *Siren* had been seen earlier, far out in the offing, and the sight of her had put them on edge.

When the *Intrepid* came within hailing distance, her Maltese pilot, Salvador Catalano, called out to the guards in Arabic. He told the story that Decatur had invented. The ketch had come to Tripoli to ship a cargo of livestock for the British garrison at Malta. She had suffered badly in the gale, losing both her anchors, and she needed assistance. Could she have permission to make fast to the frigate for the night?

The guards relaxed and assented. The water in the harbor was as smooth as glass, and the wind had all but died off. It did not seem as if the ketch could reach the frigate without being hauled in by a line. A boat was lowered from the *Philadelphia* and a hawser taken in hand to be rowed out to the ketch. A boat simultaneously put out from the *Intrepid*. The two boats met and the hawsers were made fast. Men aboard the *Intrepid* began hauling on the line, hand-over-hand, drawing the ketch closer to the target.

It was the moment of maximum danger. The *Philadelphia*'s gunports were open and the tompions had been taken out of the guns—she could easily have blown the *Intrepid* out of the water. As the distance narrowed, the Tripolitans on board the *Philadelphia* could look down onto the deck of the ketch. One noticed that she had not lost her anchors, as Catalano had claimed—and another caught sight of one of the armed men lying prone on the deck. He cried out: "Americanos!"

Catalano lost his nerve and shouted to Decatur to give the order to board. The lieutenant, seeing there was still a gap between the vessels, answered firmly: "No order to be obeyed but that of the commanding officer." The crew restrained themselves for a few critical seconds as the *Intrepid* drifted closer. The guards seemed confused—some shouted that it was a trick, but others remained uncertain. When the ketch was directly alongside, just under the *Philadelphia*'s forechains, Decatur shouted: "Board!"

"The effect was truly electric," Surgeon's mate Lewis Heermann later recalled. "Not a man had been seen or heard to breathe a moment before; at the next, the borders hung on the ship's side like cluster bees; and, in another instant, every man was on board the frigate."

The rail was 10 or 12 feet higher than the *Intrepid*'s, so the men had to climb the hull as if scaling a rampart. Decatur leapt first and clung to the fore chains: eighty men were just behind him. So quick and tightly choreographed was the assault that by the time the commander slipped over the bulwark, the frigate's decks were already swarming with attackers. Some came over the rail; others darted in through the gun ports. To keep the noise to a minimum, they worked with edged weapons only: swords, pikes, and knives. No shots were fired.

The battle for possession of the *Philadelphia* was short and savage. Taken by surprise, the Tripolitans made a feeble and halfhearted defense. Some ran to the forecastle and others to the starboard rail, "whooping and screaming" as they went. A dozen or so scrambled into a boat and rowed to safety. Most simply leapt overboard and swam toward the beach. About twenty men turned on their attackers and fought. As a reward for their courage, they were slashed, hacked, and stabbed, and their ruined bodies thrown into the harbor. The raiding party took only one prisoner, and he was so badly lacerated that he was not expected to live through the night. One American was slightly wounded, none killed.

In ten minutes the fighting was over, and Decatur gave the order to destroy the *Philadelphia*. Like every other aspect of the mission, the firing of the ship had been meticulously planned in advance. The raiding party separated into squads, each assigned to set fire to a different section. Each squad carried a single lighted lantern and each man a three-inch length of spermaceti candle soaked in turpentine. Combustibles were passed from the *Intrepid* up to the deck of the *Philadelphia*. The squads took them below and planted them in the storerooms, gun room, cockpit, and berth deck. All was ready in minutes. Decatur walked back along the spar deck from forward to aft, pausing at each hatchway to shout: "Fire!" Each man lit his candle at the lantern and ignited the combustibles.

The conflagration spread so rapidly that the men had to scramble up the ladders to escape. The lower decks, said Heermann, were soon "enveloped in a dense cloud of suffocating smoke." One officer was nearly trapped on the orlop deck when flames spread across the berth deck, above his head, and filled the after hatches with smoke. He ran toward the bow and went up the forward ladders. Decatur waited until the last of his men had climbed down to the deck of the *Intrepid*, and then followed. Flames were roaring out of the hatchways "in volumes as large as their diameters would allow."

As soon as the lieutenant was aboard, the men worked frantically to fend off before the ketch was consumed. The bow hawser was thrown off and the *Intrepid* began to fall astern, with her main boom running afoul of the frigate and her jib sail flapping dangerously close to the flames. The stern hawser jammed and men raced to cut it with their swords. Long oars were brought up to be used as poles to fend the vessel off, but the fire sucked in air from every direction and the *Intrepid* was repeatedly drawn back. Finally, Decatur sent a crew to take one of the boats ahead to tow the ketch's bow around. Her sails filled and she began to make way.

An alarm had gone up through the harbor. The *Intrepid* was taking small arms fire from two xebecs moored nearby, and soon the guns in the castle and harbor batteries came to life. The Americans were fortunate. The enemy cannonade was wildly inaccurate—only one shot came close to hitting the fleeing ketch, and that passed through her topgallant sail. Men laid hold of the oars and rowed her down the channel. Once out of range of the enemy guns, they laughed, joked, sang, and paused to watch the spectacle of the still-blazing *Philadelphia*.

None of them would ever forget the sight. The walls of the castle and city were bathed in a warm, orange, spectral light. As the flames reached the frigate's tar-saturated rigging, they raced up to the mastheads and "presented a column of fire truly magnificent." At 11:00 p.m., the masts and tops, still burning brightly, fell majestically into the harbor. The cannon, as they were heated by the flames, fired in succession—some casting their shot at the castle. At midnight the cables burned through and the floating inferno drifted in toward shore. By six the next morning, the men on the deck of the *Siren*, forty miles out to sea, could still see the light of the distant fire on the southern horizon.

CHAPTER EIGHT

———————•———————

William Bainbridge and the incarcerated officers of the *Philadelphia* were roused from their beds by "the most hideous yelling and screaming from one end of the town to the other, and a firing of cannon from the castle. On getting up and opening the window which faced the harbour, we saw the frigate *Philadelphia* in flames." Bainbridge himself had urged that the ship be destroyed, so he must have welcomed the event. Whatever elation he felt, however, was tempered by his concern for the safety of the officers and crew. Would the Bashaw retaliate against the prisoners?

Bainbridge had good reason to be anxious. From the windows of his palace, Yusuf was watching in a rage of impotence as the *Intrepid* retreated to safety amid the inept cannonade of his batteries. Before the *Philadelphia* had burned all the way down to the waterline, the consular house in which the officers were lodged was surrounded by a heavy guard. Their liberties were summarily revoked, and they were told they would be allowed no more visitors or mail until further notice. Surgeon Jonathan Cowdery, who was treating dozens of Tripolitan patients—including members of Yusuf's own family—was told he would no longer be permitted to make his rounds. The guards intimated that the officers would soon be moved to a prison within the castle walls. Not daring to strike directly at the officers for fear of retaliation against high-ranking Tripolitan prisoners held in Syracuse, Yusuf took his anger out on the common seamen of the *Philadelphia*, ordering that they be forced to carry out "an additional portion of labor."

Bainbridge protested to Minister Dghies. The Americans had had nothing to do with the raid, he said. They had sent no information to Preble that could be useful in planning or executing the operation. (This was a lie.) The parole of honor signed by the officers, Bainbridge said, was sufficient to guarantee that they would not try to escape. He added that no change in treatment of the American prisoners would "prevent the Commodore's acting in every Warlike manner. . . . His Excellency will find the Americans true friends in time of Peace but active Enemies in War."

In response, the minister visited Bainbridge and assured him that the officers would continue to be treated as high-ranking prisoners of war. He offered to allow them to send and receive letters from their families and friends, so long as these were first sent to Dghies, who would "peruse them."

On March 1, the American officers were taken under guard from the consular house and moved into a securely guarded suite of rooms within the castle. Cowdery described the lodging as "very dark and smoky, having no light but what came through the skylight." The officers complained of stifling air and "noxious reptiles." The complaints were probably exaggerated: Bainbridge said only that "our situation is not as comfortable as it has been."

In defiance of the tighter net that had been drawn around him, Bainbridge was able to continue his highly effective espionage campaign, which he dryly termed "magical aid." It is likely that he bribed the drogermen and guards to smuggle his letters. Shortly after the destruction of the *Philadelphia*, he sent a short note to Preble warning of a potential counterattack on the squadron at Syracuse. Writing in cipher, he warned that the Tripolitan crews planned to disguise themselves as merchantmen from a Christian country. "Our cruisers should examine every description of Vessels . . . and not trust to any Colours or dress of the Crews and should not consider themselves secured from attack at Anchor. Most may happen when least expected."

In the days after the raid, the bodies of three slain guards washed up on shore between Tripoli and Mesurat. They were riddled with stab wounds. The Bashaw and his ministers were convinced Decatur's raiding party had executed the men after they had surrendered. On March 5, Dghies wrote Bainbridge to lodge a protest, asking: "How long has it been since Nations massacred their Prisoners?"

Bainbridge promised to inquire with the commodore about the circumstances of the killings, but added that he was sure they would "not merit the appellation of *Massacre*. . . . You may be assured, Sir, that it is an incontrovertible fact, that the Americans always treat their Prisoners with the greatest humanity and give quarters the moment opposition ceases."

Was there any truth in the charge of a prisoner massacre? The allegation is corroborated in an affidavit given in April 1828 by a member of the raiding party, Surgeon's Mate Lewis Heermann. Heermann testified that after the attackers had gained possession of the *Philadelphia*, but before setting her ablaze, lookouts were posted on her starboard bow to watch for any attempt to recapture the frigate. The lookouts reported "in quick succession the approach of enemy's boats, and their retreat, with an interval of time just sufficient to execute the order which grew out of it—*of killing all prisoners*, and draw from the ketch part of a supply of ammunition, small arms, and pikes, for the defence of the ship."

In subsequent letters to Bainbridge and Dghies, Preble categorically denied the charge. The Tripolitans, he said, had "a right to expect their fate from the opposition they made, and the alarm they endeavoured to create. . . . People who handle dangerous weapons in War, must expect wounds and Death, but I shall never countenance or encourage wanton acts of Cruelty." He invited Dghies to send a representative under flag of truce to interview the one Tripolitan prisoner taken alive from the raid, who was wounded badly in the action, "but from the kindness and attention he has received is now well in health."

PREBLE WAS OVERJOYED by Decatur's success. The surrender of the *Philadelphia* and her crew the previous November had almost convinced him to sue for peace. Now he spoke with renewed bravado about forcing Yusuf to terms. "I hope before the end of next summer to make him give me the Officers & Crew of the late frigate *Philadelphia* without a ransom," he told Smith. Preble planned to attack the city in late June or July, when milder weather would enable the squadron to cruise safely in the offing. Throughout March and April 1804, the *Constitution* and her smaller consorts lay at their moorings in Syracuse as the commodore planned the summer campaign.

Preble was convinced that Syracuse was perfectly suited as a naval base for the U.S. Mediterranean Squadron, but his officers were no great admirers of the ancient city. Midshipman Ralph Izard told his mother he found Syracuse so "detestable" that he had not set his foot on shore for six weeks. Washington Irving, who visited the following winter, recorded his impressions: "Streets gloomy and ill-built, and poverty, filth, and misery on every side. No appearance of trade or industry. . . . All is servility, indigence, and Discontent." When the officers walked the streets, they were trailed by a parade of beggars; after dark they had to fight off would-be thieves. Even the aristocracy was impoverished. A high-ranking nobleman, Baron Cannarella, was caught trying to pocket two silver spoons at a dinner party given by Stephen Decatur. A watchful steward held out a tray and said: "When you have done looking at them, Sir?"

Because the classics were held to be the bedrock of every young man's education, most of the American officers had at least a nodding acquaintance with Latin and Greek, and none could fail to be impressed by the city's magnificent ancient ruins. The *Constitution* filled her freshwater casks at the ancient spring-fed Fountain of Arethusa on the edge of the harbor. Officers on liberty visited the famous Temple of Minerva, transformed into a Roman Catholic cathedral; the remains of Diana's temple; the Roman amphitheatre; and the sites of Tyche, Neapolis, and Achradina. They found fragments of broken marble apparently scavenged from ancient sites, many "full of engravings and inscriptions, but most of them defaced and spoiled." The legendary Mount Etna, encrusted in snow from summit to base, dominated the view to the north. Preble, who was a bit of a history buff, regretted that his workload did not allow him more leisure for sightseeing. He told his wife he hoped to return someday as a tourist.

In the eyes of many of the officers, however, the city's glorious past only emphasized how far it had fallen. Ancient history recorded that Syracuse had once been home to a quarter of a million people. In 1804, its population was just twelve thousand. "It is truly melancholy to think of the dismal contrast that [Syracuse's] former magnificence makes with its present meanness," wrote Purser John Darby of the *John Adams*. What had once been a powerful and opulent city-state, possessing "fleets and armies that were the terror of the world," was now despoiled and forgotten, and did not "deserve the name of a nation."

The U.S. Navy had dollars to spend—a lot of dollars. The squadron's presence was a powerful boost to the local economy. New inns, taverns, and shops opened. Cash circulated. Merchant vessels from other ports in the Mediterranean crowded into Syracuse in the hope of unloading their cargoes. Syracusian women were fond of the American officers and their money, and they were not shy. John Darby observed that in Sicily "a breach of the marriage vow is no longer looked upon as one of the deadly sins"—and Sicilian women, whether married or not, preferred "the American officers to any other nation in the world, their own not excepted." Officers frequented the opera, said to be the best in Sicily, and threw money on the stage as a gesture of appreciation to their favorite performers. It was said that the prima donna Cecilia Fontana Bertozzi was provided for "in a very handsome manner" by Lieutenant John H. Dent, commander of the *Scourge*.

The American officers were high-handed and arrogant toward the Syracusian civil authorities. All understood that Syracusian prosperity depended upon the continued presence of the squadron. "We do as we please," boasted one young midshipman. Objecting to a public health law that required vessels inbound from Malta to perform an eight-day quarantine, officers either bribed the quarantine authorities to turn their heads or brusquely refused to comply at all. In April, Stephen Decatur sent an armed boat to seize a deserter off the deck of a French privateer anchored in the harbor. Protesting that the act violated Sicilian neutrality, Governor Marcello de Gregorio ordered the city gates closed, detaining nine American officers who were in Syracuse that night. Two Neapolitan officers put out from the harbor in boats to the *Constitution* to inform Preble that the gates would not be opened until the disputed sailor was restored to the French. When told what the governor had done, the commodore exploded. "You know he is not a man who commands his temper," wrote Henry Wadsworth. "So in the rage the tables and chairs and Neapolitan officers' hats flew about the cabin, and when the light was again brought in it was some time before these unfortunate messengers could be found. They were detained on board all night frightened out of their senses."

Gregorio reversed himself and opened the gates without insisting upon the return of the deserter. His capitulation confirmed that the Americans could impose their will on the civil authorities. They grew steadily more haughty and abusive. "Although we had great power at Syracuse before, yet now we are uncontrolled," Wadsworth boasted. "We disarm their guards, and open their gates, and break their laws with impunity." When Preble was absent in Malta for several weeks, Gregorio begged him to return: "It is with the utmost regret I am constrained to acquaint you that the discipline which you enforced is no longer maintained, for which reason continual applications of the inhabitants here are made to me for redress."

Preble realized that his manhandling of the governor had set a bad example for the younger officers. He was concerned for the reputation of the navy and its officers, and later warned his successor, Commodore Samuel Barron, to crack down on the worst abusers. "I suspect you will find it necessary to make an example, and the sooner the better."

YOUNG HOTHEADS WITH GUNS, uniforms, and an overcharged sense of personal honor: in 1804, it was a formula for frequent "affairs of honor" or "interviews"—the favorite euphemisms for the practice of dueling.

Dueling was rife among aristocratic men in society at large—this was the same year Alexander Hamilton would be shot dead by Aaron Burr in Weehawken—but among the officers of the navy and marines it approached the proportions of an epidemic. By one historian's count, there were thirty-six naval officers killed in eighty-two duels between 1798 and 1848, and half of these killings occurred in the period before 1815. The U.S. Congress passed a law outlawing duels among army officers in 1806—but perhaps because most naval duels occurred overseas, out of American civil jurisdiction, the ban was not extended to the navy until almost sixty years later. Powerful figures in the naval establishment and Congress held the view that dueling, though deplorable, was an essentially private affair that the government had no business regulating. Official acquiescence allowed the custom to take root in the culture of the officer corps. The predictable result was almost constant gunplay, especially among the midshipmen and young lieutenants who represented the navy's future.

Dueling had its roots in the medieval practice of "judicial combat," and had evolved through the centuries as a means of resolving disputes between individual members of the gentry. The actual face-off between men armed with swords or pistols was not an end in itself, but a final resort after all non-violent alternatives had been exhausted. It was preceded by a ritualistic process of negotiation carried on through intermediaries, or "seconds." Purported insults might be parsed, elucidated, or otherwise explained in a manner that satisfied the aggrieved party. If no such resolution was possible, the seconds negotiated the time, place, weapons, and conditions of the duel. They acted as coaches, advocates, witnesses, and referees.

Duels were governed by principles that had changed very little over the centuries, known collectively as the *code duello*. The version most widely adopted in America was the "Clonmel Code," a set of twenty-six specific rules that had been published by a group of Irishmen in 1777 and "prescribed for general adoption throughout Ireland." The rules specified when and in what cases a challenge could be made; how weapons and distances were to be chosen; how many shots must be fired for each type of offense; and in what cases it was permissible to avert a duel. Among the rules were the following: challenges were to be delivered on the morning after an insult—not on the same evening, "for it is desirable to avoid all hot-headed proceedings." When one gentleman calls another a liar, the accuser "must either beg pardon in express terms; exchange two shots previous to apology; or three shots followed up by explanation; or fire on till a severe hit be received by one party or the other." In certain cases, according to the Clonmel rules, a duel *must* take place, as when one man strikes another: "As a blow is strictly prohibited under any circumstances among gentlemen, no verbal apology can be received for such an insult."

Dueling was the target of criticism and even ridicule by Enlightenment-era philosophers. Nearly all of the major American political figures of the founding era deplored the practice as a relic of the medieval past. Benjamin Franklin said duels were a "murderous practice . . . they decide nothing," and Jefferson condemned them as "the most barbarous of appeals." Washington's distaste for the custom was more influential because he was a military man: he discouraged dueling among his subordinate officers in the Continental Army, and for the most part his wishes were respected. Even Alexander Hamilton, the most notorious dueling casualty in American history, professed to take a dim view of the practice. Hamilton had lost his oldest son, Philip, to a duel in 1802; the young man had fought, poignantly, to avenge an insult against his father. When challenged to a duel in June 1804 by his political rival, Aaron Burr, Hamilton avowed a reluctance to fight, considering himself "strongly opposed to the practice of Duelling." He agreed to the meeting after concluding that it was "impossible to avoid" without bringing on himself the contempt of his peers. To resolve the dilemma, he wrote, he planned "to reserve and throw away my first fire." Burr, on the other hand, did not miss.

Leading political figures seemed to unite in professing their aversion to dueling, but the message transmitted to the young officers of the navy and marines was, at best, a mixed one. Old war heroes like Washington might have deplored the practice, but they had earned the privilege of doing so because they had already proven their personal courage in battle. And deploring the practice was not the same as denouncing it, much less forbidding it. Rarely did a duelist who had killed his adversary find himself prosecuted. A typical view was expressed by Captain Arthur Sinclair when he referred to the killing of one of his subordinates as "one of those imperious cases which frequently occurs among military men, where life must be hazarded to save what is far more valuable, his reputation." A naval officer who engaged in duels did not suffer negative career consequences; in fact, the reverse was often true, because a man who had proven that he could "stand fire" without flinching was enhanced in the eyes of his colleagues and superiors.

Predictably, it was the youngest and lowest ranking of the commissioned officers who did most of the dueling in the Mediterranean. Among the eighteen dueling fatalities in the pre-1815 navy, twelve were midshipmen and four were lieutenants. Many of the young men who entered the U.S. Navy—or were pushed into it by their families—were restless, defiant characters who seemed unlikely to thrive in a more sedentary, landlocked career. Like the eighteen-year-old who sought a midshipman's commission because he was "tired of the inactivity of the business . . . as unsuitable to the energy of his desires," many officers were drawn into the service by a deep yearning for a life of adventure. Once aboard, however, they found the routine even more monotonous than life ashore. Close confinement, hard work, boredom, lack of privacy—the wardroom was an environment that provided few outlets for supercharged adolescent hormones.

The problem reached its peak in the First and Second Mediterranean Squadrons of Commodores Richard Dale and Richard Morris in 1801–03. As captain of the *Philadelphia* in July 1802, Captain Samuel Barron reprimanded his lieutenants for failing to maintain discipline among the frigate's midshipmen. "I have great cause to complain of the conduct of the midshipmen of this Ship," he wrote.

> They are young men totally regardless of any order they receive and pay no kind of attention to their duty, answer no purpose on board but to create noise and confusion, and set an ill example to the people. . . .
>
> It has already been ordered that officers of the watch are not to engage in any conversation on deck but what relates to their duty and not to appear without side arms. Both those orders have been disregarded. On the contrary, they are generally in the group or riding on the gunwale, at the gangway, lolling on the binnacle or capstan or on the guns of the quarterdeck, but more generally around a table on the gun deck, making use of such language as any decent sailor would be ashamed of. They absolutely keep the ship in an uproar; the boys and others imitate their example; and no greater scene of disorder and confusion can possibly exist than at times does on board this ship.

The most trivial disagreement was liable to trigger a challenge. One midshipman was offended when another entered the wardroom wearing a hat. Another challenged a messmate because the offender had spilled some water on a letter he was writing. A pair of midshipmen nearly dueled after arguing whether a bottle was green or black. "I can't omit one piece of disagreeable information," Captain James Barron wrote his brother from Malta in January 1803; "namely the situation of Mr. Vandyke, who is now laying momently expecting death to his relief from a most horrid wound which he received in a duel from Mr. Osborne, lieutenant of marines. Two days will end his voyage through this life, and all for the preference in a simple game of billiards."

In some cases, no one seemed to recall the original disagreement. It did not matter. Once the mechanisms of a challenge were set in motion, it was nearly impossible for the adversaries to extricate themselves without leaving a stain on their reputations. "I at present am unable to acquaint you of the origin of the quarrel of these two young men," John Rodgers wrote of a duel that killed a junior officer. "But, from the information I have been able to collect . . . it was something of a very trivial nature. Indeed, it would appear that they went out rather from motives of bravado than anything else, and after getting on the ground were ashamed to return without fighting."

One of the strangest duels in the early navy was set in motion by an exchange of friendly banter between Stephen Decatur and Richard Somers in 1798, when both were midshipmen serving on the *United States* under Captain Barry. The two young men were, by their own reckoning, inseparable friends, and as they were joking in the wardroom one day, Decatur laughingly called Somers a "fool." Neither man thought anything of it until the next day, when several of their fellow officers refused to share the wardroom table with Somers. Having talked it over among themselves, they had agreed that Decatur's use of the term "fool" constituted an insult, and that Somers must either issue a challenge or be ostracized as a coward. Somers and Decatur protested that their bantering had been harmless. Decatur had not meant to suggest that Somers was literally a fool, and Somers had not taken offense at the remark. Decatur offered to host the entire wardroom at a dinner in which the exchange would be explained in fuller detail. Their messmates refused the invitation.

Somers's exasperated response was to issue a challenge, but not to Decatur. Nominating Decatur as his second, he challenged the other officers to fight him in sequence. The multiple challenge was accepted. In the first duel, Somers took a ball in his pistol arm; in the second, he took a ball in the thigh. Decatur offered to take his friend's place for the third duel, but Somers refused. Bleeding heavily, Somers sat on the ground while Decatur propped up his pistol arm. After the third exchange of gunfire, all agreed that Somers had resolved any doubts about his courage, and the business was called off.

The duel was a ritual that was supposed to uphold each adversary's honor and reputation through a demonstration of personal courage. But some were fought under conditions so lethal that it was a virtual certainty one or both men would be killed. The two ranking marine officers of the *Constellation*—Captain James McKnight and Lieutenant Richard Lawson—fought such a duel at Leghorn, Italy, in October 1802. Lawson proposed large-caliber, smoothbore flintlock pistols at the murderous distance of three paces. When McKnight's second refused the terms, Lawson circulated a written statement among the *Constellation*'s officers boasting that he had "proved the famous duellist a coward." McKnight then agreed to fight with a brace of pistols at the distance of six paces. In the unlikely event that both men should miss, they would throw down the firearms and fight on with cutlasses. At the first exchange, Lawson shot his captain though the heart and killed him.

One of McKnight's fellow officers took the body to the coroners at Leghorn, where he "was witness to a scene I shall ever remember, that have been obliged to see a brother officer's heart cut out, that I might certify that the ball had passed through the center of it. . . . I left them up to their armpits in blood." He collected contributions from the wardroom of the *Constellation* to pay for a decent burial. The frigate's captain, Alexander Murray, was one of the navy's most vocal critics of dueling; he suggested that McKnight's headstone be inscribed with an epitaph stating that the dead man "had fallen a victim to a false idea of honor."

Since dueling was also common in the Royal Navy, and because American and English officers came into contact at Gibraltar, Malta, and other Mediterranean seaports, it was perhaps inevitable that the friction between them would lead to duels. The tug-of-war over deserters was, as Preble had discovered in Gibraltar, a constant problem in any ports shared by British and American warships. It is also true that the American Revolution loomed large in recent memory, and there were undoubtedly English officers who resented the very existence of the United States and thought its puny navy laughable. But for every hostile English officer, there was another who greeted his American equivalent with genuine warmth. In some cases, officers of the two services got on well; in others, not at all. "The envy & jealousy of the British officers is excited by our fine Ships & handsome maneuvering," wrote Midshipman Wadsworth in March 1804; "we meet on shore but to fight & insult each other." Yet at almost that same moment Preble was being wined and dined in Malta as a guest of Governor Sir Alexander Ball, Admiral Sir Richard Bickerton, and the colony's various other high-ranking military and civil officers. The British, Preble reported, "have given every assurance of being friendly disposed towards the United States."

Nor was cordiality confined to the upper ranks. Midshipman Melancthon Woolsey recalled that a group of midshipmen from the frigate *Boston* had gone ashore in Malta to celebrate the Fourth of July in 1802. On the streets of Valetta, they encountered another set of midshipmen from the Royal Navy ship *Tigre*. One might have expected hostile words to pass between them, as the Americans were celebrating a holiday that marked a major British defeat. Instead, they all went "arm in arm" to a coffee shop for an ice cream. The next day, the *Boston's* midshipmen invited their new friends to dine aboard the

American frigate. Arriving at noon, the *Tigre*'s midshipmen did not leave the *Boston* until ten o'clock that night, leaving their American hosts (as Woolsey said) "nearly as independent as we had been the day before."

Six months later, however, a different group of American midshipmen were at liberty in Malta. They were attached to the frigate *New York*, anchored in the Grand Harbor at Valetta. On a night late in January 1803, they went ashore to attend an opera at the Marsamuscetto Theatre on St. Mark's Street. While seated at the performance, a young American officer named Joseph Bainbridge—William's younger brother—heard an English voice say: "Those Yankees will never stand the smell of [gun]powder."

Bainbridge (if the American version of events is to be believed) chose to ignore the remark, as it had not been directed at him. In the lobby, during an intermission, the same stranger passed by him and brushed him rudely with his shoulder. Bainbridge ignored this second insult, so the stranger came in for another pass and brushed him again, at which point Bainbridge made a fist and smashed his antagonist in the face. The stranger proved to be John Corcoran, a civilian clerk in the British Commissariat Department. He sent his challenge the next day.

Bainbridge chose Stephen Decatur as his second. Decatur pointed out that Corcoran was older, more experienced, and a better shot. To compensate for Bainbridge's disadvantage, Decatur proposed that the two adversaries fight at a distance of four paces. Alternatively, he offered to fight Corcoran in Bainbridge's place at a more conventional range. The Englishman agreed, reluctantly, to fight the younger man at four paces. On the second exchange, Bainbridge's shot hit Corcoran in the face. He fell to the ground, blood gushing from his mouth, and died a few minutes later.

In his journal that day, Henry Wadsworth observed that "this morning a duel was fought between Mr. Bainbridge, midshipman of the *New York* and Mr. Cochran [sic]—an Englishman residing at Valletta: the latter received the ball in his head and instantly died: they fought at four paces distance and exchanged two shots: with pleasure I observe that Mr. Bainbridge was clearly in the right and behaved honorably throughout the affair."

Governor Ball ordered a judicial inquiry, and may have demanded that Bainbridge and Decatur be turned over to the civil authorities to face trial. Commodore Morris refused, and sent them both back to America. The affair seems to have blown over quickly, for both officers were back in the Mediterranean by the following summer, and Governor Ball was warmly entertaining Morris's successor.

Not surprisingly, the frequency of dueling appears to have been inversely related to the frequency of naval combat. The junior naval officer, done up in his high standing collar and gold lace, was as testy and vain as a fighting gamecock. He prayed for war as a farmer would pray for rain and a lawyer would pray for lawsuits. War was his profession: it offered the most practical outlet for his aggression and the best hope for his advancement. For the junior officers of the Mediterranean Squadron, there had not been enough war to go around. Commodore Preble, as he planned the summer campaign, was determined to set that right.

COMMUNICATIONS BEING WHAT THEY WERE in 1804, Preble's dispatches reporting the surrender of the *Philadelphia* and her crew arrived in Washington on March 19—a month after Decatur's successful expedition to destroy her at her moorings. President Jefferson and his cabinet were thus made aware of the abysmal intelligence that Yusuf had 307 American prisoners and a new 44-gun frigate in his clutches, but did not yet have the slightly reassuring news that the frigate, at least, had been removed from the equation.

Jefferson and his department heads were dismayed. The Tripolitan War was virtually the only blemish on their first-term foreign policy record. In every other respect, the Republican administration could congratulate itself. The United States was at peace with all the major European powers. The rupture of the abortive Peace of Amiens in May 1803, and the resumption of war between Britain and France, had brought a predictable surge in American exports and shipping clearances. Most important, the recently completed purchase of the Louisiana Territory had, at a single stroke, doubled the size of the country and resolved a major potential source of international conflict on the western frontier. Against all of this, the extortionist city-states of the North African coast were merely an irritant, but they were proving more irritating than expected.

A day after receiving Preble's dispatches and Bainbridge's official letter, Jefferson forwarded the entire package to Congress. In the past he had tended to defer to Congress's judgment on the size and costs of Mediterranean naval operations, but now he was unambiguous and resolute: he wanted more ships and more men. "[T]his accident renders it expedient to increase our force, and enlarge our expenses in the Mediterranean, beyond what the last appropriation for naval service contemplated."

Even worse than the actual loss of the frigate and her crew, Jefferson and Madison agreed, was the impetuous behavior of the American ambassadors in Europe—those in Paris and Moscow, especially—who had taken it upon themselves to ask their host governments to intercede with the Bashaw on the prisoners' behalf. "I have never been so mortified as at the conduct of our foreign functionaries on the loss of the *Philadelphia*," Jefferson wrote Navy Secretary Smith on April 27. "They appear to have supposed that we were all lost now, & without resource: and they have hawked us in *forma pauperis* begging alms at every court in Europe." Jefferson had no wish to see Napoleon or the tsar of Russia claim credit for persuading Yusuf to free the prisoners—"Our expedition will in that case be disarmed, and our just desires of vengeance disappointed, and our honor prostrated." He was anxious to show the world that the United States was capable of forcing Tripoli to terms without the intervention of other powers. It was essential, he instructed Smith, "to strike our blow . . . without a moment's avoidable delay."

Another source of embarrassment was the various attempts by friends and family members to ransom individual officers. Private ransom offers, Madison explained to a Philadelphian, ran the risk of raising the Bashaw's expectations and thus "thwarting the negotiations of the Executive," which might then "protract the sufferings of those unhappy men."

The Republican-controlled Congress responded quickly to Jefferson's desire for reinforcement. It required just six days to pass "An Act Further to protect the commerce and seamen of the United States against the Barbary Powers," which gave the president broad powers to carry on operations against Tripoli as he chose, including "equipping, officering, manning, and employing such of the armed vessels of the United States, as may be deemed requisite. . . ."

To the vital question of costs, Congress's answer was a new *ad valorem* tax of 2.5 percent on all imported goods. Revenues would be set aside in a dedicated "Mediterranean Fund." Since 1801, Secretary Gallatin and the fiercely anti-tax Republican rank and file had complained of rapidly escalating naval expenses. The Mediterranean Fund was their sine qua non; from that point forward, the Tripolitan War would be underwritten by the shipping and commercial interests it benefited.

Jefferson ordered four additional frigates manned and readied for sea. Three were among the original six: *President*, *Congress*, and *Constellation*. The fourth was the Salem-built subscription frigate *Essex*. A storeship, the *John Adams*, would sail laden with provisions for the squadron, including (among many other things) 6 tons of suet, 70 tons of bread, 450 bushels of peas, and 1,500 gallons of molasses.

In appointing commanders to the relief squadron, the Navy Office was thrown onto the horns of an unwanted dilemma. Edward Preble had done, in Secretary Smith's words, "all that a sound mind, an ardent Zeal, and daring valor could achieve." But if four frigates were to sail for the Mediterranean, four captains would have to sail with them, and it was impossible for Smith to find that many officers who stood junior to Preble in order of seniority. By tradition and rule, the seniormost captain would automatically become the new commodore on his arrival in the Mediterranean station. Preble could not be reinforced without being simultaneously demoted. It was yet another example of how the navy's rigid adherence to the rule of seniority impaired its operational effectiveness. Smith hoped Preble would remain in the Mediterranean as commander of the *Constitution*, but he must have known the proud down-easter was unlikely to suffer relegation with composure.

The new commodore would be Samuel Barron, a thirty-nine-year-old Virginian and son of a merchant sea captain. Barron was reputed to be a fine seaman, but he had nearly died during a bout of yellow fever in 1799 and suffered chronic health problems that seemed to worsen whenever he put to sea. He would command the *President* as his flagship. His younger brother, James, was also a captain and would command the *Essex*. The remaining two captains, John Rodgers and Hugh Campbell, would command the *Congress* and *Constellation*, respectively. The morning after Jefferson's message to Congress requesting reinforcements, Smith told a lieutenant at the Washington Navy Yard that "the Frigates *President* and *Congress* must be prepared for Sea with all practicable dispatch. On this occasion we require the exertions of your most strenuous efforts."

The mostly bare hulls of the *President* and *Congress* were moored on the edge of the channel, stripped of their blocks, tackle, rigging, and spars, all of which had been carefully stored in dry sheds. Their tops and caps had been removed from the lower masts, and large "tents" of well-tarred canvas had been stretched above their decks. For months, the yard's permanent staff had been left mostly idle, whiling away their hours sleeping and drinking. Now, a furious burst of labor was required to return the ships to service. As usual, there was a critical shortage of skilled workmen to be found in Washington, and more would have to be recruited from the maritime centers of Baltimore and Philadelphia. On April 7, Smith received word that Joshua Humphreys had hired fifteen or sixteen men in Philadelphia and expected to hire five or six more in Baltimore. Because of the war-related boom in shipping, wages were high everywhere, and workers would migrate to the wilderness capital only because the federal government offered to overpay them.

By the first week of June, both frigates had anchored in Hampton Roads, where the *President* was to receive a new bowsprit. Most of the commercial center of Norfolk had been destroyed in a fire four months earlier; more than three hundred buildings, including storehouses, shops, and private houses, had been reduced to ashes. A witness had described the catastrophe as "a most awful sight to see . . . the columns of smoke, the bursting out of the flames, the cries of those that were on the streets saving their little properties, exposed to a most terrible, drifty and snowing night." Jefferson had given $200 in charitable relief for the sufferers. With Norfolk's maritime industries still reeling from the disaster, the navy's patronage was more important than ever before to the city's economy.

Congress began taking on spars and cordage from the Gosport Navy Yard, and also recruited some additional seamen (Rodgers wrote) "in the place of that Number of Miserable Wretches . . . shipped in Baltimore, all of whom I shall be obliged to discharge, being totally unfit for service." Having taken a careful inventory of the ship's stores, the captain found that the *Congress* was missing "many Articles which are of the Utmost Importance." He was convinced he had been swindled by one of the tradesmen at the Washington Navy Yard. Writing the man directly, Rodgers promised to report him to the Navy Office—but then added, characteristically, that he planned to mete out justice himself when he returned to the capital after his Mediterranean tour. "It is your Interest to pray that my Head may be Knock'd off before I return," he wrote, "for be assured if you are not punished before that period I will revenge the Injury you have done me, with my own hands."

The *Congress*, Rodgers optimistically reported, "can be made ready for Sea in 24 Hours." Even if it were true, it would make no difference, because the other frigates in the squadron were lagging behind. The *President* was at the wharf in Norfolk, getting in her bowsprit. *Essex* was anchored at Maryland Point in the Potomac River. *Constellation* remained in Washington, awaiting an anchor cable, and only a series of urgent notes from the Navy Office got her underway by June 13.

On June 19, Commodore Barron charged one of the *President*'s ordinary seamen, Robert Quinn, with circulating a letter "calculated to excite a general mutiny." He asked the second-ranking captain in the squadron, John Rodgers, to convene a court-martial.

Rodgers's first commanding officer, Thomas Truxtun, had preached that flogging was a last resort, to be used rarely and with great reluctance. But Rodgers was as bloody-minded a disciplinarian as any officer in the navy, and the court's sentence reflected his taste for imaginative brutality. Quinn was sentenced to have his head and eyebrows shaved and the word "MUTINUS" cattle-branded across his forehead. Then he would be "flogged through the fleet." Bound to an upright grating in a boat, wearing a white cap with the word "MUTINY" written across it in bold letters, he would be rowed through the squadron's anchorage, coming up alongside the hull of each vessel in turn. At every stop a new boatswain would climb down with a new cat-o'-nine-tails and give him a new flogging. In all, he would receive 320 lashes, a quantity that had in other cases been tantamount to a death sentence. In the British service, there were instances in which the punishment continued even after the offender had expired.

The punishment was carried out at 8:00 a.m. on June 25. Quinn survived but was severely maimed. He was "drummed on shore under a gallows in a boat towed stern-foremost . . . as unworthy of serving under the flag of the United States." A week and a half later, on a hazy day, *President* made the signal to weigh anchor. At 3:45 p.m., four frigates were underway for the Straits of Gibraltar.

BASHAW YUSUF WAS ENRAGED by the destruction of the *Philadelphia*, but he was also perplexed. Who were these Americans, who seemed so intent upon persisting in a costly and unproductive war? Hadn't his ministers made it clear that Tripoli would return the prisoners and sign a new treaty in exchange for a moderate amount of money—say, $200,000 or $300,000? Wasn't that sum reasonable when compared to the million-dollar peace settlements paid by countries like Portugal and Sweden? And wasn't it far less than what the United States was obviously spending to maintain its Mediterranean Squadron?

At home in his palace, Yusuf's rhetoric was as brave and bellicose as ever, but he simultaneously sent out new peace feelers. His agent on Malta approached Preble and offered a five-year truce, to begin immediately with no payment of money. Preble refused: he would accept nothing less than a return of the prisoners and a "solid Peace." He also doubted the offer was real. Yusuf might merely be playing for time, or his agent might be negotiating without the Bashaw's full authority. Preble was not averse to ransoming the *Philadelphia*'s crew, if the sum could be haggled down to $100,000 or so. But he would pay nothing for peace and no tribute. "If it was not for the situation of our unfortunate Country Men," he told Smith, "I should be sorry to have a peace with Bashaw, until we could oblige him to beg for it as a favour, and sign any treaty that might be dictated to him."

When news of the *Philadelphia*'s loss reached Paris, the American ambassador to France, Robert Livingston, had asked the government of First Consul Bonaparte to intervene with Yusuf to secure the release of the prisoners.

Because Bonaparte's Foreign minister was none other than Talleyrand, the American government was thus thrown into the position of begging assistance from the same man whose attempt to extort a bribe from an earlier group of American envoys had been the immediate cause of the Quasi War, five years earlier. In 1803, however, in the friendly afterglow of the recently completed Louisiana Purchase, the French government was apparently inclined to use its influence on the Americans' behalf. Talleyrand sent instructions to the French minister in Tripoli, Bonaventure Beaussier, to mediate the negotiations, and to make Yusuf understand "the ardent desire of the First Consul that a Peace settled on advantages to both parties would shortly put an end to the War which divides them."

But Captain Preble never trusted Beaussier; and when the French consul told him that peace would cost the United States between $250,000 and $500,000, Preble responded sharply: "The Bashaw's pretension to the enormous sum you mention is, on his part, a vain one; nor will he ever obtain a tenth part of it for ransom. The negotiation for ransom and Peace must be separate, as we will not pay one dollar for Peace."

Preble was showing new interest in a scheme that had been under discussion among America's Mediterranean envoys for several years. The idea was to lend financial and military support to Yusuf's exiled older brother, Hamet, who had a competing claim to the throne of Tripoli. Yusuf had seized power in the same way that previous generations of Karamanlis had—by slaughtering all his rivals, and not sparing his blood relatives. Hamet had been lucky to escape with his life. In June 1795, Yusuf had tricked his older brother into leaving the city on a gazelle-hunting expedition, and then seized power in a *coup d'état* and closed the gates against Hamet's return.

With American support, Hamet now promised to march overland before an army of Arabs and Mamelukes who would seize Derna, then Benghazi, and then attack Tripoli from the lightly defended inland side. "Through these instruments," wrote William Eaton, the plan's most energetic sponsor, "I firmly believe the enemy may be taken from his sofa at the same instant that our fellow citizens are rescued from their chains." Yusuf would be hanged from the city walls and the Americans could name the terms of a new treaty. Perpetual peace without ransom or tribute? Naturally. High-ranking Tripolitan hostages to be held in American custody as a guarantee against future aggression? Done. Could the United States install a permanent garrison in one of the principal batteries guarding Tripoli Harbor? Agreed. Would Tripoli free all its Christian slaves—not just Americans, but all the Maltese, Italians, and Europeans of every nation? Hamet, with nothing to lose and everything to gain, agreed.

Hamet's Maltese agent told Preble what was needed: five hundred barrels of gunpowder, six brass artillery pieces, and 80,000–90,000 Spanish gold dollars. Preble was paying attention. "I wish earlier notice had been taken of this man and his views," he told Smith in January 1804.

James Madison had admitted some scruples two years earlier, when the scheme was first proposed. Could the world's lone democracy, in good conscience, subvert a corrupt, repressive, and unfriendly regime, only to replace it with a corrupt and repressive regime that was friendly to American interests? And yet, the Secretary of State reasoned, it was Yusuf who had declared war against the United States, in flagrant violation of the treaty he had signed a few years earlier. "Although it does not accord with the general sentiments or views of the United States to intermeddle in the domestic contests of other countries," Madison had written Eaton, "it cannot be unfair . . . to turn to [our] advantage the enmity and pretensions of others against a common foe." But from the moment the United States committed itself to Hamet, Madison warned, the country would have to protect his interests. It would be dishonorable to use him as a negotiating chip to be thrown onto the pile. If Hamet's campaign to regain the throne should ultimately fail, the United States would have to "treat his misfortune with the utmost tenderness, *and to restore him as nearly as may be to the situation from which he was drawn*," perhaps even insisting upon a favorable treaty provision in a final settlement with Yusuf. Beaussier, meanwhile, told Yusuf that the Americans were plotting to bring his brother back to the throne. Yusuf professed unconcern, as his brother was "without means, inclined to drunkenness, and incapable of acquiring partisans."

A formal alliance with Hamet—the money, particularly—would require more explicit instructions from Jefferson and the approval of the Congress. In the interim, Preble continued to plan and prepare for his summer operations. What he needed most of all were shallow-draft gunboats. Three years of war had demonstrated beyond any doubt that a fleet composed of frigates and brigs was poorly suited to attacking Tripoli. Preble had known of this deficiency even before his arrival in the Mediterranean. While outfitting *Constitution* in Boston in July 1803, he had asked Secretary Smith for authority to purchase or charter gunboats "constructed and rigged in a manner peculiar to the Mediterranean," which could be used "for the purpose of capturing or destroying the Tripoline Merchant Vessels, and distressing their coast." Smith had acknowledged the merit of the concept but pointed out that Congress had not authorized it.

Now Preble renewed the call: "If you will allow me to expend $100,000 in such additional naval force as I think proper, I will take Tripoli or perish in the attempt. I am confident that it may easily be destroyed or taken in the summer with gun and mortar boats protected by our cruisers." Nor was Preble willing to await legislative approval. So confident was he of success that he was sure Congress would retroactively agree to reimburse his expenses. In fact, though he would not know it until later, Congress had already acted. The March 26 legislation authorizing a relief squadron and setting up the Mediterranean Fund had given the president authority "to hire or accept on loan in the Mediterranean sea, as many gun boats as he may think proper."

The same day Congress gave its authorization, Bainbridge sat down at a desk in his cell to write Preble a letter in lime juice. The juice-ink was undetectable to the eyes of the Tripolitan censors, but became legible when heated with a candle. Bainbridge assured the commodore that a shallow-draft flotilla, well armed and manned, could puncture Tripoli's harbor defenses. "I am clearly of Opinion that if you could arm about 18 or 20 ship's boats you can destroy all the Gun Boats, which would be attended with the most favorable consequences towards a peace; the Gun Boats carry about 25 or 30 men,— they are a dastardly set of wretches. . . . A few bomb shells thrown into this Town would do damage and cause great alarm. Their Batteries are all in bad order, and they are very bad Gunners."

As early as January 1804, Preble began inquiring whether the squadron might obtain two or three mortar boats and three or four gunboats in Toulon, Leghorn, or Naples. From Leghorn, where he had been sent in search of the needed vessels, Consul James Cathcart sent the commodore a plan of a typical Mediterranean gunboat mounting a 24- or 32- pounder cannon. Such vessels, constructed of oak, elm, and pine, with "Sails, Oars, Anchors, Cables" but not including guns, could be built for an estimated $3,776 per vessel. But the contractor wanted four and a half months to build four vessels, and Preble did not have that much time. Cathcart also wrote the American commercial agent in Marseilles, but armed boats could be built in France only with the permission of the French government, and it was unlikely that France would implicate itself in the conflict with Tripoli. Meanwhile, a Florentine foundry estimated that it would take a year to make four mortars for the American mortar boats.

Preble turned his attention to a cheaper, faster alternative: he would borrow gunboats from the Italians, who were more or less perpetually at war with Tripoli. Working through American commercial agents, Preble put out feelers to several seaports in Sicily and the Italian mainland. There was some indication that the Kingdom of Naples might be willing to oblige the squadron. To make the formal application, Preble and the *Constitution* sailed from Palermo for the Bay of Naples on May 7. Passing between the islands of Ischia and Capri at one o'clock on the afternoon of the ninth, the frigate let go of her best bower anchor that evening shortly after sunset, a mile from the densely populated harborfront. It was a calm and moonless night, with a light breeze from the west southwest. The enormous cone of Mount Vesuvius loomed over the harbor, more dramatic than the view of Etna from Syracuse because it was so much closer.

Midshipman Melancthon Woolsey had been aboard another American frigate, the *Boston*, when she harbored in Naples two years earlier. He recorded his impressions then in his journal:

> We were no sooner anchored than we were serenaded by a band of music who came off in a small boat and laid under our stern. Before night we were surrounded by boats, some loaded with fruit, others containing jugglers who gain their subsistence by performing sleight of hand tricks. One of them I particularly noticed. After performing several tricks with the cups and balls, either to excite our pity or surprise, I cannot say which, [he] tortured himself by running an iron skewer or pin upwards of six inches in length up his nose. He also imitated the notes of different birds in a most surprising manner.

The morning after the *Constitution*'s arrival, Preble called upon Prime Minister John Acton, who received him sympathetically. Acton suggested that Preble submit his request for gunboats in a letter which he would pass on to King Ferdinand. The commodore had the letter delivered to Acton's offices the same day. "I was so much engaged while at Naples that I did not see Pompeii, Herculaneum, or any of the curiosities for which that country is so much celebrated and so much visited," Preble wrote Mary. He was amazed at the size and density of the city: "the city of Naples is perhaps the most populous in the world for the ground it covers. The houses are five and six-story high, and each floor generally inhabited by families that have no acquaintance with each other."

On May 13, Preble received welcome news. The kingdom would provide six gunboats, two bomb ketches (vessels specially designed to throw exploding shells), six long 24-pounder cannon, and a "discreet quantity" of shot, match, shells, gunpowder, and other supplies. All of this would be presented to the Americans without charge, "under the Title of a friendly Loan." The vessels were at Messina, and the Americans were invited to take possession as soon as they could be made ready for sea.

CHAPTER NINE

On July 25, 1804, at two hours after midnight, *Constitution* and her little flotilla of borrowed Italian gunboats and bomb ketches fell in with the blockading vessels *Siren*, *Argus*, *Enterprise*, and *Scourge*. Preble's force now numbered fifteen sail: the flagship, three brigs, three schooners, two bomb ketches, and six gunboats, manned by 1,060 men. In two and a half years of war, it was the largest American naval force that had ever been assembled before Tripoli.

A heavy sea was running on shore, and as anxious as Commodore Preble was to begin his attack on the town, he was forced to admit that conditions were not right. It was, by now, a familiar ordeal. For a week, the squadron was forced to stand off and on the coast while awaiting an improvement in the weather. During intermittent periods of clear air, the men on deck could see the distant shape of Tripoli's walls and harbor fortifications. From the masthead, through a telescope, the lookouts spotted an encampment of troops along the south side of the bay, a flotilla of gunboats that appeared heavily armed and manned, and a total of 115 cannon in the outer batteries.

The morning of July 30, the wind built up to gale force and Preble ordered the squadron to separate so that each vessel could gain a safe offing. The *Constitution* lay to under double-reefed courses. On July 31, with "the wind blowing very heavy, and a rough sea," the foresail and mizzen topsails were torn to shreds. The next night, more of the same: "we split the foresail from clew to Earing." The crew struck the topgallant yards and rigged preventer stays to buttress the masts. All that night, *Constitution* lay head-to-wind "under low sail with a rough sharp sea."

The wind finally subsided to a breeze on the morning of August 3, and the squadron set a course for Tripoli. At the noon observation, *Constitution* was about two miles northeast of the Molehead Battery. Preble signaled for the other vessels to draw in closer to the flagship, so that he could speak directly to their commanders across the water. His plan was simple: The gunboats and ketches would approach the town in two divisions, sailing in a line abreast. They were to engage the enemy gunboats positioned outside the rocks at the entrance to the harbor. *Constitution* and the other cruisers would hover in the offing, firing at long range if necessary.

In fifteen minutes, the small vessels cast loose and began their approach. At half past twelve, *Constitution* tacked and stood inshore behind them.

Yusuf had mobilized his people for the expected attack. "The Bashaw is ready to receive the enemy whatever type of hostility the enemy wishes to attempt," Beaussier had reported to his government in March. "This port bristles with cannon, quite independent of the twelve gunboats that defend the approaches. Now this prince does not rely upon the vigilance of anyone: he shows himself day and night and inspects everything." A gang of fourteen master ship carpenters had been recruited from Spain to build new gunboats. Several dozen of the seamen-prisoners of the *Philadelphia* had been forcibly employed in erecting new batteries. Fearing for the safety of his wives and children, Yusuf had moved them all inland. Tripoli was as prepared as it had ever been for an assault from the sea.

It was a brilliantly clear and sunny day. The city, the harbor, and the fortifications were plainly visible from the flagship's quarterdeck. Preble's spyglass brought the whole scene right up close to his eye—the Tripolitan gunboats, crowded with heavily armed defenders; the imposing sandstone batteries, with their lines of embrasures housing big brass artillery pieces; the huge, white-washed edifice of the castle; the brightly colored banners flying from the masts and towers; the domes and minarets of the mosques; the rooftops and terraces of the houses, teeming with spectators. To the east was the long semicircular curve of the beach, backed by a row of well-tended date palms; and beyond them the Bashaw's verdant gardens, with flowering hibiscus, sweet jasmine, pomegranates, and oleander trees. To the west, beyond the city walls, a sequence of fields cultivated with barley and tobacco—and then, further in the distance, nothing but "a Sandy Desert . . . as far as the eye could reach."

Twenty-two Tripolitan gunboats were arrayed in three divisions just outside the harbor rocks. Each mounted a 24- or 32-pounder brass cannon and was manned by thirty to fifty men.

At 2:30 p.m., *Constitution* made the signal for general battle: a blue flag over a yellow/blue flag over a red/blue flag. As the American flotilla closed with the enemy line, one of the bomb ketches lobbed a shell toward the

Molehead Battery; as it exploded, the Tripolitan boats and batteries opened fire all at once, and "in an Instant the whole Squadron was engaged." Shots fell on every side of the bomb ketches, throwing up high columns of seawater and spray. On the foredeck of the *Constitution*, Richard O'Brien looked down from the starboard rail and saw that the sea under her bow "was kept entirely in a foam from the enemy's shot."

The first American gunboat division, commanded by Stephen Decatur, opened fire with 24-pounder round shot. Each vessel had time to fire and reload three times before the Tripolitan boats began to retreat to within the rock barrier. Decatur's boat pursued, navigating a 12-foot-wide channel through the rocks, taking heavy fire from the artillery in the Bashaw's Castle. From a distance of about 20 yards, she got off a murderous volley of canister shot and musket fire, while keeping her sails filled to attempt a boarding action.

As Decatur's vessel collided with the first enemy boat, he and nineteen other boarders crossed the gunwales and fell on the defenders. Wielding pistols, pikes, axes, and cutlasses, they slashed, thrusted, hacked, shot, and stabbed their way across the enemy deck. It was the most ferocious and bloody engagement the navy had ever fought. In fifteen minutes, the boarders had possession of the boat. The casualty ratios leave the impression that the defenders refused to surrender, or the attackers did not give them much quarter, or both. Out of a crew of thirty-six Tripolitans, sixteen lay dead on the deck, fifteen lay wounded, and just five prisoners had been taken unharmed. The Americans had lost none killed, four wounded. "I find hand-to-hand is not child's play. 'Tis kill or be killed," Decatur remarked. "Some of the Turks died like men, but much the greater number like women."

Gunboat No. 2 was commanded by Decatur's younger brother, James. He steered toward the second boat in the Tripolitan formation. Waiting until the range had closed to 20 or 30 yards, the Americans opened a well-directed volley of muskets and blunderbusses. The Tripolitans who were left standing hauled down the colors, and James Decatur ordered his men to cease fire. As he stepped across the gunwales to take possession of the surrendered boat, one or more muzzles were raised and fired. Decatur took a musket ball in the forehead and fell between the boats. As the Americans rushed to fish their fallen commander from the sea, the surviving Tripolitans took hold of their oars and started pulling for the inner harbor.

As Stephen Decatur's gunboat No. 4 was pulling back to the safety of the flagship, with her captured vessel in tow, she came within hailing distance of No. 2. From Midshipman Thomas Brown, Decatur learned of the sham surrender, and then looked down and saw his younger brother, shot through the head and probably mortally wounded. Most of gunboat No. 4's original crew had been detached to the prize, so Decatur was undermanned—but he nevertheless bore away and chased the fleeing enemy. For the second time that afternoon, Stephen Decatur boarded an enemy vessel. Nine men followed him. It was a rash action—there were twenty-four defenders aboard and they were willing to fight. Again Decatur and his men stabbed, slashed, and hacked their way across the enemy's deck. As Decatur exchanged blows with the boat's Tripolitan commander, his (Decatur's) cutlass broke just above the crossguard, leaving him defenseless. The two men grappled and fell to the deck, sprawling across the gunwale. The Tripolitan drew a *yataghan*—a long, curved Turkish knife—and was on the verge of plunging it into Decatur's exposed chest when the lieutenant found his pistol and fired it into his antagonist's side, mortally wounding him. Four more Tripolitans were advancing on the still-prone Decatur and were about to cut him to pieces when the lieutenant's personal servant and a marine private rushed into the fray, armed with a tomahawk and cutlass. They fell upon the four and killed them all. Again the ratio of killed to wounded defenders was a measure of the savagery of the combat. Twenty-one Tripolitans lay dead; only three had been taken alive.

Gunboat No. 6, commanded by Sailing Master John Trippe, was engaged in an equally desperate battle. Running aboard the third gunboat in the enemy line, Trippe led a party of marines across—but before all the American boarders had crossed, the boats separated. Trippe and a handful of marines found themselves engaged in hand-to-hand combat with the thirty-six-man crew. Trippe grappled with the enemy commander, "a remarkably athletic, gallant man, about twenty-four years of age: his height considerably exceeded six feet. Before he engaged in battle, he swore upon the Koran that he would conquer or die." The two adversaries rolled on the deck; other Tripolitans closed in and slashed and hacked at Trippe as he lay prostrate on the deck, wounding him eleven times. One of the Americans rushed into the melee with a boarding pike and ran it through the Tripolitan commander's body. Before he died, he shouted to his men to avenge him.

The battle was over in fifteen minutes, and "20 Turks lay weltering in their Gore." Trippe prevented his men from massacring the prisoners, and even pulled some of the survivors from the sea. The casualty ratios imply that Trippe showed more mercy than had Decatur: out of a crew of thirty-six, twenty-two Tripolitan prisoners were taken, fifteen of them unwounded. The Americans laid hold of the oars and began pulling out of the harbor, chased by a furious cannonade from the harbor guns. One sailor, Jacob Boston, reported that a cannon ball passed within six inches of his shoulders: the wind of the ball left a deep bruise where it passed. Another shot took the mast down, but Trippe and his prize escaped safely out of range.

From the deck of the *Constitution*, Commodore Preble saw that the advancing line of American gunboats was entering the range of the Molehead Battery, and that two divisions of Tripolitan gunboats were preparing to pass back through the rock barrier. He ordered the signal: "Cover the boats." The *Constitution* stood in for the inner harbor, followed by the brigs and schooners. As her bow chasers and the forward guns of her starboard battery came to bear, the flagship discharged a volley of grape shot that sent the enemy gunboats into confusion. When she had approached to within a few hundred yards of the rocks, she wore and stood to the west. The maneuver brought the *Constitution*'s full larboard battery to bear on the Bashaw's Castle, the enemy flotilla, and the Molehead. She poured out three ear-splitting broadsides, her shots blasting large chunks of masonry out of the fortifications and momentarily obscuring the enemy guns behind a cloud of dust.

As the flagship passed to the west, the shore guns came back to life. It was a dangerous moment. *Constitution* was exposed to heavy fire, at a range of 300 or 400 yards, from weapons that had the advantage of being mounted on a stationary platform. Fortunately for the *Constitution* and her crew, the Tripolitan gunnery was very poor. They had not found the range. Sailing Master Haraden estimated that two hundred shots were fired at the *Constitution*, almost all of which overshot or fell short. Many fell close to the ship, sending high columns of spray over the bulwarks and soaking the men on deck. The commodore himself had a near escape—he was standing in the starboard gangway when an enemy shot hit the 24-pounder cannon nearest to him. The hit blasted fragments of iron shrapnel from the weapon and shattered a marine private's arm "to pieces." Preble's clothing was torn by the blast, but he was otherwise left unscathed.

The prevailing easterly breeze was carrying the flagship away from the fight. Preble had no choice but to bear up and stand to the northward. For the better part of an hour, the *Constitution* was taken out of action as she maneuvered to come in for another pass. As she stood in from the northeast, she again made the signal: "Cover the boats," and again ran right in under the guns of the castle and Molehead. Her first broadside "drove the Tripolitans out of the castle." One shot struck a mosque inside the city walls, and as the men on the deck of the *Constitution* watched in astonishment, its minaret— the tower from which a *muezzin* summoned the faithful to prayer five times each day—trembled and fell crashing to the ground.

At four thirty in the afternoon, the wind was freshening and a heavy sea setting onshore. Preble gave the signal to withdraw, and the gunboats began pulling out to sea. *Constitution* sent her barge and jolly boats to assist in towing the gunboats. At five, the full squadron rendezvoused about two miles north of the town. The mortally wounded James Decatur was brought aboard the flagship, and was shortly thereafter pronounced dead by the surgeon.

The attackers had won a resounding victory. Three Tripolitan gunboats had been captured, fifty-two men taken prisoner, and an estimated forty-four killed. Enemy casualties in the harbor fortifications, castle, and town were unknown, but assumed to be numerous. American losses, by contrast, had been surprisingly light: thirteen men wounded and one killed. No vessels had been lost.

Though she had taken heavy fire from the shore batteries, the *Constitution* had not sustained the sort of damage that would require her to return to a friendly port. Her mainmast had suffered a direct hit from a 24-pounder shot, about 20 feet above the deck, but the mast had not fallen and appeared to be strong enough to carry sail. A dozen or more balls of grape shot were pried out of her hull, but none had done serious damage. The rigging was fairly shot up: the main royal yard and main topgallant yard had been shot away entirely, and various shrouds hung limp and useless. The foredeck jacks could look forward to hours of knotting and splicing to repair the damage.

Fifty-two Tripolitan prisoners were brought aboard the *Constitution*. Half were wounded, and four died before morning. On the fifth, Preble sent fourteen of the most severely wounded into Tripoli under a flag of truce, asking that an equal number of the *Philadelphia* prisoners be sent out. Minister Dghies, however, refused to release any American prisoners.

Dr. Cowdery, the *Philadelphia*'s surgeon, was summoned to the castle and ordered to attend to the Tripolitan casualties. So reluctant was he to assume this new responsibility that he dishonored his Hippocratic oath. "I was ordered to dress the wound of a mameluke who had his hand shattered by the bursting of a blunderbuss," he wrote. "I amputated all his fingers but one, with a dull knife, and dressed them in a bungling manner, in hopes of losing my credit as a surgeon in this part of the country—for I expected to have my hands full of wounded Turks in consequence of the exploits of my brave countrymen."

AUGUST 5 AND 6, the squadron lay in the offing six miles north of Tripoli, "in continual preparation" for a second attack. Some of the hands were set to work altering the captured gunboats from lateen rigs to a more familiar sloop rig. Once again, the Americans were forced to await a change in the weather: "The wind to the Northward of East heaves such a swell on shore as to make it improper to attack," wrote Purser Morris.

There had been a lot of talk about the idea of lobbing exploding shells over the city walls. Writing in lime juice from his prison on June 22, William Bainbridge had assured Preble that the inhabitants of Tripoli "have dreadful Ideas of bombs and their houses [are] slightly built. . . ." A bombing attack on the town, he predicted, would set off an exodus of refugees and bring pressure on Yusuf to end the war. But the bomb ketches had performed poorly in the August 3 engagement. Each of the 26-inch-caliber mortars had fired several shells, but almost all had fallen short of the walls; they had not achieved the promised range. To be effective, the bomb vessels would have to be maneuvered much closer to the city walls, but this would bring them within easy range of the harbor guns.

Lieutenant Charles Stewart believed he had the solution. West of the city, an indentation in the coastline formed a shallow bay with a long, curving beach. Tripoli's harbor guns did not cover this bay. The bomb ketches, he reasoned, could approach unmolested, drop anchor, and heave their mortars over the city's western wall. The Tripolitans might respond by sending their gunboats through the rock barrier into the western bay, but if they did so, they would expose themselves to the *Constitution*'s covering fire. Richard O'Brien objected to the scheme, saying, "I think a blow in the face is better than a kick in the stern," but Preble was inclined to try it. If it did not succeed, he reasoned, there would be every opportunity for a second frontal attack on the town.

On August 7, at ten o'clock in the morning, Commodore Preble ordered the signal: "Advance in a line abreast." The weather was mild, but contrary breezes and currents forced the squadron into confusion. Each vessel had to stay out of range of the harbor batteries, while also avoiding being swept onshore by the wind. Evidently, the Americans had not yet learned the local current patterns. The gunboats and ketches were carried out of position, far to the westward, and their exhausted crews had to row for hours against the current. It was not until after noon that the first bomb ketch dropped anchor about a mile and a half from the city wall. From this range her mortars could hit the western quarter of the city, and they did considerable damage. The explosions echoed through the town and smoke rose above the rooftops.

As the other vessels straggled into the anchorage, they came under unexpected cannon fire. Yusuf, foreseeing the attack, had ordered two small batteries hastily constructed to cover the western bay. An artillery duel ensued.

The larger and more dangerous of the shore batteries was "almost totally destroyed"—big holes were blasted in its newly erected walls and all but one of its guns were dismounted. Each time the gunboats stopped firing at it, however, its one remaining weapon persistently came back to life.

At about three o'clock in the afternoon, a flotilla of fifteen Tripolitan gunboats made a brief foray beyond the safety of the Molehead Battery. They concentrated their guns on the first American bomb ketch, which was anchored closer to the city than any of the other attacking vessels. Shot fell on every side of the little vessel, and (Preble wrote) "the clothes of every man in the Boat were wet through with the spray of sea which the Enemy's shot threw over them." Her commander had no alternative but to cut her cables and withdraw to a safer distance. The Tripolitan gunboats, keeping a wary eye on the *Constitution*, rowed back to the safety of the reef and the harbor fortifications.

At three thirty, every man's head was turned by an ear-splitting explosion. Gunboat No. 9, commanded by Lieutenant James Caldwell, had blown up. Dr. Cowdery witnessed the event from the roof of the Bashaw's Castle: "I saw the mangled bodies of my countrymen precipitated into the air." Preble saw a blinding white flash and a column of smoke. Midshipman Robert Spence, who was commanding the crew of No. 9's bow gun, survived the blast. "I went up some distance in the air and lighted by the gun again," he later wrote. "Around me lay arms, legs, and trunks of bodies in the most mutilated state." Spence recognized Lieutenant Caldwell, who was "without arms, or legs; his face so mutilated that I could not discriminate a feature—by his dress only I recognized him; he was not dead, although he sank instantly."

The event seemed to stun both the attackers and defenders; all guns fell silent for several minutes. As the smoke wafted away, all that was remaining of gunboat No. 9 was the bow section. Spence exhorted the gun crew to load and fire one last shot, but as they were attempting to do so, the bow and the gun sank beneath the surface. With defiant bravado, the survivors gave a cheer as they went down. Spence, who was "ignorant of the art of swimming," hung on to an oar until he could be pulled from the sea. All the men who had not been killed in the explosion were picked up by the other boats.

The explosion of No. 9 was a major blow to the squadron's fortunes. Ten Americans were killed instantly, including James Caldwell and Midshipman John Dorsey. Six others were wounded: four critically and two mortally. Preble attributed the explosion to a direct hit by a red-hot shot from one of the shore batteries, but it is more likely that the magazine was touched off by flaming wad from No. 9's bow gun.

The battle continued for two hours. The Tripolitans fought on with renewed ferocity. Several of the other American gunboats came under heavy fire. No. 6 had her lateen yard shot away, which made it almost impossible for her to maneuver into safer range. No. 4, commanded by Stephen Decatur, was hit by a 24-pound ball that blew a hole in the hull above the waterline. No. 8 was also struck in the hull, and the shrapnel-like splinters thrown off by the impact killed two of her crew.

By about five thirty, Preble had seen enough; *Constitution* flew the signal to disengage. Before dark the small vessels were again under tow and the squadron sailed back into the offing.

During the day's action, the ketches and gunboats threw forty-eight bombshells and more than five hundred round shot into the town and fortifications. The bombs had mostly fallen in the city's Jewish quarter, where an untold number of private homes had been damaged or completely destroyed. The strategic value of the attack was doubtful. So long as his rule was secure, Yusuf did not have to answer for the welfare of his subjects, whether believers or infidels; he was certainly unmoved by the suffering of Tripoli's Jews. What mattered to the Bashaw was that the attack had done nothing to weaken his defenses, while the obliteration of gunboat No. 9 had boosted the morale of his troops and seamen. Tribesmen from the backcountry were streaming into the city to join the fight. They ran through the streets, shaking their weapons in the air and shouting: "I am my father's son!"

The bodies of the dead Americans washed up on shore west of the town, where they were discovered by a Tripolitan patrol on August 17. Lieutenant Caldwell could be identified only by the epaulet on his right shoulder. Dr. Cowdery, who was permitted to go and see the bodies, found them "in a state of putrefaction on the beach. . . . They were scattered on the shore for miles, and torn in pieces by dogs." The Tripolitans would not bury them, nor allow the American prisoners to do so.

As the squadron was withdrawing, the *Argus* made the signal: "Strange ships in sight are friends." Earlier in the day, Commodore Preble had sent her away to the northward to reconnoiter a sail on the horizon. The newcomer joined company shortly after dark: she was the *John Adams*, storeship to Commodore Samuel Barron's relief squadron, now reported en route to Tripoli.

Dispatches from Secretary Smith carried the unwelcome news that Edward Preble would be superseded in command of the squadron. Worse, he would be third in command after John Rodgers. The letters were written in such a way as to soothe Preble's ego, insisting that "no want of confidence in you has been mingled with the considerations which have imposed upon us the necessity of this measure" and adding that "your whole conduct has received the unqualified approbation of the President of the United States and his confidence in you remains unabated." But Preble was bitterly disappointed: "How much my feelings are lacerated at this supersedure at the moment of victory cannot be described and can be felt only by an officer placed in my mortifying situation."

Knowing Barron would shortly arrive to supplant him, Preble elected to try another round of negotiations. On August 9, he wrote to French consul Beaussier and raised his offer for a peace settlement: $80,000 ransom for the crew of the *Philadelphia* and a $10,000 "consular present." The overture was poorly timed. If the first attack had alarmed Yusuf, the second had restored his confidence. The new offer only confirmed Yusuf's impression that he had the upper hand. He declared to the Frenchman that he would not settle for less than $300,000, although Beaussier privately told Preble the figure could probably be haggled down to $150,000.

That day, Yusuf sent for Dr. Cowdery and made a bold speech, which the doctor paraphrased:

> He said that for two dollars he could repair all the damages that the bombardment did to his town; that but one man was hurt by the shells; that what he had been offered for the American prisoners was but fifty dollars per man; that he would make him earn that sum in two months. He asked me what I thought my country would give for me. I told him I did not know. He said he would not take twenty thousand dollars for me; to which I replied, I might then expect to remain in slavery for life. He patted me on the shoulder and said, I must then content myself to stay with him.

Two days later, Preble made his position even worse. Still alert for any appearance on the horizon of the expected frigates, Preble raised his offer yet again: $100,000 ransom and $20,000 in consular bribes. If Beaussier was right, the difference was now just $30,000. A continuation of the war would cost that amount and more on both sides. But on the evening of August 11, when no flag was raised over the French consulate, Preble had his answer: Yusuf had refused the terms.

The squadron began preparations for a third attack, but the weather continued to serve as Tripoli's best defense. For nine days, without intermission, there were high northerly winds and choppy seas. The gunboats, designed for harbor defense, could only be handled safely in calm conditions. Again and again the squadron stood in for the town; again and again—August 12, on August 16, 17, and 22—Preble judged that conditions were unsuitable and cut off the attack. The wear and tear began to tell: abrasions, lost rigging, torn sails, broken blocks. The officers and men were physically and mentally exhausted.

Most critically, provisions and freshwater stores were low. On August 18, Sailing Master Haraden recorded that the *Constitution* had 14,000 gallons of fresh water. At her daily consumption rate of 600 gallons, she was supplied for twenty-three days; but some of the other vessels in the squadron, as Preble observed, "have now been upwards of five months in sight of this dismal coast, without once visiting a friendly port," and they would have to be replenished from the flagship's own stores. Preble ordered a short water ration: 5 pints, including that used for cooking rice and peas and mixing with grog. On the fifteenth he wrote the Navy Agent on Malta in a tone that speaks for itself:

> Our Water is nearly exhausted. I conjure you to charter two or three
> Vessels for fear of the miscarriage of one, and load them with water
> immediately, & send me 300 puncheons at least, as soon as possible.
> If one is not here in 8 days we shall be ruined, as I have only 14 days
> water for the Squadron. Let no price stop you from chartering. Send
> us some fresh stock, Vegetables, Apples, Melons, etc. . . . Hire as
> many boats & men as can work to load the Vessels & for God's Sake
> dispatch a Vessel in 24 hours, and let the rest follow.

On the night of August 18, Lieutenant Stephen Decatur and Isaac Chauncey took two small boats, manned with a few oarsmen, to the outer edge of Tripoli Harbor. Their mission was to reconnoiter the harbor and its defenses. They approached under cover of darkness to within musket-shot range of the sentinels on the Molehead Battery, close enough even to see the soldiers on the walls of the castle. Returning to the *Constitution* after midnight, they reported that the Tripolitan gunboats were moored in a line abreast from the battery to the castle, their bows to the east.

Six days later, weather conditions seemed suitable for a night attack, and the squadron stood in for the town, coming to anchor at eight o'clock in the evening. At midnight the breeze fell off entirely, and Preble ordered the bomb ketches to proceed into the harbor under sweeps (oars). The first mortar was thrown at two o'clock in the morning, and the bombardment continued until dawn. In all, the ketches threw about fifteen to twenty shells. None of the shore batteries fired a gun during the attack. At 6:00 a.m., the bomb ketches withdrew, and the entire squadron fell back to a safe offing about four miles from the town.

Reports on the results of the bombardment were mixed. Sailing Master Haraden thought he had caught a glimpse of a 40-foot-wide breach in the outer wall of the Bashaw's Castle. Midshipman F. Cornelius DeKrafft, whose journal serves as a valuable historical record of the Tripolitan War, wrote that the bombardment did "considerable damage by sinking 2 of the enemies gun boats & 1 of their galliotts." But Dr. Cowdery insisted that every single shell fell short, and added that "such attempts served rather to encourage than to intimidate the Tripolitans; and the Bashaw was in high spirits on the occasion."

After yet another aborted attack two nights later, Preble began to wonder why Barron had not yet arrived. The *John Adams* had arrived fully three weeks earlier, and she should have been much slower than the big frigates.

On August 27, with mild weather and a favorable northeast breeze, the American gunboats anchored near the "western passage"—a gap in the rocks that could only be navigated by smaller vessels. They opened fire on the Tripolitan flotilla at about 3:00 a.m. and continued the bombardment without intermission for two hours. Most of the gunboats fired about forty rounds each, and a few fired more than fifty. Haraden calculated that they threw six hundred rounds of 24-pounder shot and a similar amount of grape shot. A galliot and a three-masted galley were sunk in the attack, and part of the Molehead Battery was leveled.

The harbor guns awakened about an hour before dawn, but none of the American gunboats was hit, except in the rigging. At dawn, a single Tripolitan gunboat emerged through the western passage and closed to a distance of about 50 yards from the easternmost boat in the American line. A round of grape shot fired from the nearest American boat killed four of the Tripolitan crew and wounded two, and she withdrew to within the rocks.

Watching from the quarterdeck of the flagship, well beyond the reach of the harbor guns, Commodore Preble worried that the gunboats might be running low on ammunition. As the dawn's early light rose on the eastern horizon, *Constitution* advanced into the concentrated fire of seventy-two harbor guns. "The Commodore's ship, when standing in and during the engagement, was the most elegant sight that I ever saw," wrote Purser John Darby of the *John Adams*. "She had her tompions out, matches lit, and batteries lighted up, all hands at quarters, standing right in under the fort, and receiving a heavy cannonading from their Battery."

In obedience to Preble's signal, the gunboats began heaving up their anchors to withdraw from action. Their crews cheered the *Constitution* as she ran downwind toward the Molehead. At 400 yards' range, the flagship tacked, put her head into the wind, backed her sails, and poured out nine consecutive broadsides. The barrage sank one Tripolitan gunboat and disabled two more, which ran themselves onto the beach to avoid sinking. The harbor fortifications fell silent as the Tripolitan gun crews ran for their lives. "At every Broadside we gave them, showers of stone & dust would completely cover their batteries," Haraden observed in his journal. The *Constitution* took heavy fire on her approach, with most of the shots passing through her rigging and shredding various shrouds, stays, and running lines. The hull was struck by nineteen round shot and an untold number of grape shot, but all were later pried out of the planks, having done no serious damage. *Constitution*'s live oak scantling was doing her justice.

At nine minutes after seven, *Constitution* hauled off from the attack and stood back out to sea. With several of the gunboats and bomb ketches in tow, she worked to windward until eleven, and then anchored five miles in the offing. The squadron had lost only one vessel, a small boat belonging to the *John Adams*, sunk by a double-headed shot from one of the shore guns. Three of her crew had been killed and one seriously wounded.

Witnesses in Tripoli agreed that the bombardment had done considerable damage. Dr. Cowdery, who was awakened by "a heavy and incessant fire of cannon, and the whistling and rattling of shot all around me," observed that "many men were killed and wounded." Two petty officers of the late *Philadelphia* wrote Preble to report that "you have injured a great many houses, killed several Turks, and drove them entirely out of three of their batteries." In the eastern gardens, a camel was struck and killed by a round shot. Dutch consul Antoine Zuchet rose from his bed just moments before "a cannon hit the wall in my bedroom and skimmed along my bed to the pillow and then embedded itself in the wall opposite causing much damage . . . I would have been cut in half."

The castle came under heavy bombardment. According to one report, a shot pierced the wall of Yusuf's bedchamber about five minutes after he had risen from his bed. William Bainbridge was nearly killed when a 36-pounder ball smashed through the wall of the officers' prison and "passed within a few inches of his body." The captain had to be dug out of a pile of stones and mortar, and for months afterward he walked with a limp.

Four more days of hard gales out of the east, and the squadron again lay to in the offing. During her weeks at sea, the *Constitution* had lost several valuable sails, both to enemy fire and to the weather, and on the last day of August a reefed foresail and double-reefed main topsail blew out of their clewholes. Another commodore would have taken the entire squadron back to Malta or Syracuse for a long rest and refit. Some of the subordinate officers were surprised Preble had not done so much earlier. But Preble, expecting Barron's squadron at any moment, continued to push for a resolution. On August 29, he sent the brig *Argus* into Tripoli Harbor under a white flag of truce with dispatches for Minister Dghies and French consul Beaussier. The avowed purpose of this latest overture was to arrange a prisoner exchange, but Preble also reiterated his willingness to offer ransom in exchange for the balance of the prisoners in Tripoli's possession. Beaussier, showing his frustration with Preble's continual and self-defeating requests for a new parley, responded sharply:

> I cannot but view this Step as most impolitic as well as detrimental to the Interests of your Country, because at this moment it must be construed to your disadvantage & tend to raise the pretensions of this Regency. It [would have] been much better at the beginning to have threatened, and to have followed up your attacks with energy & effect, without entering into any negotiations. . . .
>
> You have therefore Monsieur the Commodore no alternative but to attack the Town & particularly the Castle without intermission, unless you feel yourself authorized to approach nearer to the conditions proposed. If you do not it will be superfluous to reply and you must persevere until the Bashaw, harassed at all points, shall himself ask for a Parley.

PREBLE PLACED HIS LAST HOPES in a plan to destroy the Bashaw's gunboats by sending a "fireship" into Tripoli's inner harbor. A small crew would navigate a vessel crammed with powder and incendiaries into the heart of the enemy's anchorage. Once in position, the men would light slow fuses and then flee to safety in two fast rowboats. When the fireship detonated, the explosion would lay waste to everything within a quarter-mile radius. Or so it was hoped.

The vessel chosen for this mission was the *Intrepid*, the captured Tripolitan ketch that had been employed in Stephen Decatur's successful mission to destroy the *Philadelphia* the previous February. Carpenters from several different vessels in the squadron were detailed to make the necessary alterations. *Intrepid*'s magazine was crammed with fresh gunpowder—nearly one hundred barrels, or 5 tons—and then tightly planked over. One hundred and fifty mortar shells were stacked on a tier above the magazine. Small holes were drilled in the bulkheads for the fuses, and then troughs for trains of gunpowder were run to the bow and stern. Once lit, the trains and fuses were supposed to burn for eleven minutes before touching off the payload.

It was well understood by both the officers and the seamen that the fireship mission would be extremely perilous. The *Intrepid*, literally a floating powder keg, would have to be sailed into the heart of the enemy flotilla, well within range of more than a hundred hostile guns. A direct hit would very likely detonate the magazine and blow the entire crew to kingdom come. Under no circumstances could the *Intrepid* be surrendered, since her 5 tons of gunpowder could in that case be used to resupply the enemy's shore guns. If she were boarded and carried, it would be converted into a suicide mission; the crew would have to touch off the magazine. In spite of these sobering considerations, Preble was inundated with volunteers. Every single officer in the squadron wanted to go, and some lobbied the commodore directly for the assignment. Preble thought it fair to choose officers who had been disappointed not to participate in Decatur's mission to destroy the *Philadelphia*. The fireship mission would be commanded by Decatur's old friend, Richard Somers; he would be accompanied by two other officers and ten enlisted men.

On September 1, the squadron prepared for a fifth attack on the town, and at 11:00 a.m. the next morning, *Constitution* hoisted the signal: "Prepare for battle." The gunboats stood in toward the harbor and opened fire at two in the afternoon; however, the Tripolitan flotilla slipped their cables and withdrew into the safety of the inner harbor. The bomb vessels managed to heave about twenty mortars into the town from a mile away. According to Dr. Cowdery, they did little damage, but terrified the populace: "The men, women and children ran out of the town in the utmost terror and distraction."

The bomb ketches took heavy fire from the Molehead Battery. No. 1 had every shroud shot away, depriving her mast of all support. The recoil of her own mortar ruptured her hull and she began to fill with water. Noting that the bomb vessels "were very much exposed, and in great danger of being sunk," Preble put the *Constitution* on a course to run in close to the batteries. As she advanced, the shore guns opened fire at long range and columns of spray rose to starboard and larboard, soaking the masts and courses to the height of the lower yard. As in the previous engagement, *Constitution* fired several consecutive broadsides on the harbor fortifications and took heavy fire in return. As before, the flagship suffered damage to her spars and rigging but virtually none at all to her hull. At 4:30 p.m., with the wind freshening and veering northward, Preble gave the signal to the squadron to break off the action, and the gunboats and ketches came out and were soon taken in tow.

Final preparations were made for the fireship attack. The volunteers wrote out their last wills, specifying which of their shipmates would inherit a jacket, a tarpaulin hat, or a pair of duck trousers.

At eight o'clock the next evening, *Intrepid* slipped her moorings and sailed in toward the harbor, borne along by a soft northeast breeze. The Tripolitan lookouts saw her enter the western passage, and two shore guns were sounded as an alarm. Then all fell silent, and darkness obscured her next maneuvers. At 9:47 p.m. there was a flash of light, followed by an enormous explosion.

"How awfully grand!" Midshipman Spence exclaimed. "Everything wrapped in dead silence made the explosion loud and terrible. The fuses of the shells, burning in the air, shone like so many planets. A vast stream of fire, which appeared ascending to heaven, portrayed the walls to our view." Several of the mortars detonated late, some at a height of 300 feet. "For a moment, the flash illumined the whole heavens around, while the terrific concussion shook every thing far and near," Midshipman Charles Ridgeley wrote. "Then all was hushed again, and every object veiled in a darkness of double gloom." From the deck of the *Constitution*, men could hear terrified cries from the inhabitants of the town and the low roll of kettledrums beating out an alarm.

The squadron waited for the two rowboats in which the *Intrepid*'s crew were to have made their escape. Hours passed. Preble ordered sky rockets fired at ten-minute intervals. As the first blue glow of dawn broke on the horizon, lookouts at the mastheads scanned the horizon. There was no sign of the *Intrepid* or her boats. Hopes faded.

Preble and the other officers rallied around an explanation that they may or may not have actually believed. In his official letter to Secretary Smith, Commodore Preble wrote that the *Intrepid* had come under attack and Somers, preferring death to capture, had "put a match to the tram leading directly to the magazine, which at once blew the whole into the air, and terminated their existence." The story was echoed by the other officers in the squadron. "What a Noble Death, & truly characteristic of that Noble Somers," wrote Spence to his parents. It was a version of events that allowed the family and friends of the *Intrepid*'s crew to believe they had died a glorious death. It also drew attention away from the likelihood that thirteen American lives had been thrown away to no good purpose.

In fact, no Tripolitan vessels or lives were lost in the attack, and it is almost certain that the *Intrepid* exploded accidentally before reaching the inner harbor. "The explosion caused only a frightful noise and a general shock felt well out into the countryside, without damaging the fort," Beaussier reported to Talleyrand. To Preble, the French consul said the mission "was fatal only to yourselves. . . . The fort was not shaken, and the explosion caused only a general shock in the city and the countryside. In my own case I lost all the windows in my house." Dr. Cowdery was awed by the magnitude of the blast, but agreed that it "did but little damage." The Tripolitans observed a day of thanksgiving for the town's deliverance, filled with prayers and singing, "accompanied with the sound of an instrument made by drawing a skin over a hoop."

Captain William Bainbridge was granted permission to examine the *Intrepid* crew's remains, which had washed up on the beach at the edge of the harbor. He was accompanied by Lieutenant David Porter and an armed guard. In his private journal, Bainbridge described what he found:

> [We] there saw six persons in a most mangled and burnt condition lying on the shore, whom we supposed to have been part of the unfortunate crew of the fire vessel . . . Two of these distressed-looking objects were fished out of the wreck. From the whole of them being so much disfigured it was impossible to recognize any known feature to us, or even to distinguish an officer from a seaman.

Yusuf had the bodies transferred into the arsenal, where they were placed on public display. The Bashaw, reported Consul Zuchet, "amused himself by watching his people hurl curses and insults at the corpses." They were partly eaten by stray dogs. Not until three days later were Dr. Cowdery and a gang of the *Philadelphia*'s enlisted men permitted to bury the bodies in a communal grave east of the town wall.

On the morning of September 5, Preble went up the companionway to the *Constitution*'s quarterdeck and took in a discouraging scene: the wind was shifting to the north northeast, a heavy swell was setting on shore, and "the weather wore a threatening aspect." The summer campaign against Tripoli, he decided, had come to an end. Provisions had not arrived from Malta. Several vessels were badly in need of refitting, and low in stocks of fresh water, provisions, and ammunition. Officers and men were physically exhausted. The commodore ordered the gunboats and bomb ketches to disarm their guns and mortars and transfer them into the holds of the *Constitution* and *John Adams*. The *John Adams*, *Siren*, *Enterprise*, and *Nautilus* took the smaller vessels in tow. That evening at 6:30 p.m., the flagship hoisted the signal that sent most of the squadron back to Syracuse: "Make the best of your way for your intended port." The *Argus* and the *Vixen* would remain on the station with the *Constitution*, keeping up the blockade and awaiting Barron's arrival.

THE FOUR FRIGATES OF SAMUEL BARRON's squadron crept into Gibraltar Bay on August 12, after a thirty-eight-day transatlantic passage. Following seas and a steady southwest wind had delivered them from the Virginia Capes to the Azores in just two weeks. But then the wind had veered directly ahead, and for 1,000 miles the squadron had been obliged to beat tediously to windward, sometimes making scarcely more than 20 miles between noon and noon.

At Gibraltar, Commodore Barron heard rumors that the emperor of Morocco was again threatening to send his cruisers to attack American shipping. The U.S. consul in Tangier, James Simpson, begged the commodore to leave a portion of the squadron in the vicinity of the Straits. Barron agreed. The *President* and *Constellation* would sail up the Mediterranean in search of Preble and the *Constitution*. The *Congress* under Captain Rodgers, and the *Essex*, commanded by the commodore's younger brother, James Barron, would sail for Tangier to make a timely show of force and obtain the emperor's assurances that he was not contemplating a breach of the treaty he had ratified less than a year earlier.

President and *Constellation* sailed from Gibraltar on August 16, but before they had doubled Cape Gata the wind abruptly died, and for five long, languid days the two frigates lay becalmed under a relentless sun. The sea was as clear as gin and "uncommonly smooth." One of the *President*'s civilian passengers fixed a deep-sea line to a cream-colored porcelain plate and sank it over the stern; he was amazed to see it at a depth of 148 feet. The foremast jacks indulged an ancient superstition by whistling and scratching the shrouds and stays with the backs of their knives, convinced that if they whistled and scratched long enough they would summon the wind. The technique invariably worked, eventually. After five days, a little breeze sprang up from the west and the ships spread their sails.

On the afternoon of the twenty-third, an ominous shudder ran through the *President*. From beneath the hull came a sound of rumbling and grinding, and the deck moved violently enough to throw men from their feet. Samuel Barron described it as "a violent shock like striking on an uneven, rocky bottom, which at every stroke seemed to lift and let fall the ship about one foot." He rushed up the companionway to the quarterdeck, assuming (with every other man aboard the ship) that the *President* had run aground. Once on deck, however, he "discovered no appearance of the shoal, nor had the ship lost her way."

The *Constellation* maneuvered to within hailing distance, and her officers reported that she too had grounded. Like the *President*, she had mysteriously passed over the shoal without losing velocity or suffering any damage. A passing Spanish merchantman later gave a similar account.

By eliminating every plausible explanation for the phenomenon, the officers of the two frigates determined that they must have sailed through the seismic effects of an undersea earthquake. Although they had heard of such things, none had imagined how loud or violent such an event could be. The *President*'s common seamen were overcome with superstitious fear. "Their alarm, agitation, and amazement appeared much greater than what had been created, I believe, had the ship been actually aground," Barron remarked.

WITH MOST OF COMMODORE PREBLE'S force having sailed for Syracuse, the blockade of Tripoli was carried on by the *Constitution*, the *Argus*, and the *Vixen*. Though Preble knew the September gale season would soon force him to end the blockade, he wanted the new commodore to find him off Tripoli, and not in port.

About midday on Sunday, September 9, the *Constitution* was cruising about a dozen miles northeast of Tripoli Harbor when the *Argus*, several miles to the east, flew a signal: "Discovering strange ships Northeast." The flagship tacked and stood toward the *Argus*. In an hour, Preble had a visual fix on two big ships, hull-down on the horizon, dead to windward, and standing down on the *Constitution* and her consorts. They appeared to be warships. American? Yes—as the distance closed, some of the *Constitution*'s keener eyes recognized the familiar shapes as the *President* and *Constellation*. Preble ordered his commodore's broad pendant lowered as a gesture of submission to the man who had arrived to take his place.

Secretary Smith had taken pains to emphasize that he and Jefferson were perfectly satisfied with Preble's performance, and regretted seeing him superseded. They hoped he would be willing to stay on in the Mediterranean as a frigate captain, acting under Barron's command. But there was never the slightest chance of that; the proud down-easter had grown accustomed to his role as the supreme American military commander in that part of the world, and he was not the type to suffer demotion with equanimity. "Commodore Barron's arrival to supersede me in the command of the fleet has determined me to return," Preble told his wife, Mary. He would never accept another naval command short of a full squadron, "having served so long a time in that capacity . . . with reputation to myself and honor to my country."

An hour before dawn on Wednesday, with a gentle wind in the northwest, *Constitution* was close-reaching on a larboard tack, in position to cross safely over the bows of the *President*, which was approaching the same point on the opposite tack. The maneuver was routine, and would have come off without incident had it not been for a sudden and untimely wind shift. The *Constitution* was "brought up all standing"—at one moment she had been moving through the water at about 3 knots; at the next she was dead in the water and directly in the course of the rapidly oncoming *President*.

The two 1,500-ton frigates collided, *President*'s larboard bow to *Constitution*'s stem. The former's cathead crashed into the latter's upper cutwater; *Constitution*'s bowsprit ran afoul and her jib booms carried away; fragments of dislocated timber rained into the sea directly beneath the impact. Shrouds and yardarms were intricately engaged; the anchors fell afoul; the frigates helplessly embraced one another. The same wind shift that had backwinded the *Constitution* had simultaneously filled the *President*'s sails, and she sailed on, hauling her sister along with her. The two crews made a hawser fast from bow to bow, and then worked to clear the rigging, using hatchets when necessary. A spring line was run back from *President*'s bow and made taunt to the capstan on *Constitution*'s quarterdeck. After forty-five minutes, the bow hawsers were cast off, and the *Constitution* began to pay off to leeward. At last the spring line was cast off, and the two big frigates were free of each other.

Both Edward Preble and Samuel Barron were silent about the incident; no reference to it appears in their official letters to the Navy Office. Both men must have grasped the uncomfortable symbolic implications of a violent collision between the current and former flagships, and agreed not to report the accident. (Sailing Master Nathaniel Haraden of the *Constitution* described the event in his journal.)

Constitution hove to to lick her wounds, which were considerable. A large section of her cutwater and trailerboards were gone. Her bowsprit was badly sprung and would need to be replaced. Most spectacularly, her original figurehead—a likeness of Hercules dressed in a lion's skin, standing on "the firm rock of Independence" and grasping a scroll of paper representing the U.S. Constitution—was "cut to pieces and thrown aside as useless." The Hercules figurehead would be replaced by a modest billethead, a plain length of timber decorated with flying dragons.

Barron and Preble agreed that the *Constitution* should return to Malta for recaulking and refitting. Preble also asked the new commodore for permission to return to the United States. The *Constitution*, once repaired, could be turned over to Stephen Decatur, whose mission to destroy the *Philadelphia* had since been rewarded with a promotion to captain—a two-rung promotion, bypassing the rank of master commandant. Barron assented. The twenty-five-year-old Decatur was thus transformed, in a little more than six months' time, from an anonymous lieutenant of midlevel seniority into a national celebrity and commander of one of the country's three largest ships of war.

Six weeks later, as the *Constitution* was still undergoing repairs in Valetta, Captain Rodgers and the *Congress* arrived. The Marylander soon fell into a bitter feud with Preble. Though dueling was pervasive among the navy's junior officers, there had not yet been a duel between two captains. Rodgers seemed determined to set the precedent. Preble was strongly opposed to the practice, but he might find it difficult to escape a challenge from a man whose "reputation as a fighting man," in a contemporary's view, was based upon "his black looks, his insufferable arrogance, and the frequent and unmerited assaults he has made on poor and inoffensive citizens."

The details are murky. Rodgers wrote Preble a note, which he may or may not have sent:

> Sir:
> A respect I owe to my country prevented me yesterday from requiring of you to explain the cause of your observations on the comparative good order of the *Constitution* and *Congress* and other incoherent remarks, feeling sensible that any dispute between us (in the situation I am now placed) could not fail to be productive of injury to the service. When we meet in the United States you shall then be explicitly informed of my opinion of your conduct.
>   I am, with consideration, your obedient servant,
>   John Rodgers

Rodgers was soon involved in an even more acrimonious rivalry with the Barron brothers—an escalating dispute that would injure the morale and cohesiveness of the Mediterranean Squadron throughout the winter of 1804–05, and that would lead to a series of threats and near challenges. By the time Rodgers returned to the United States, his conflict with Preble was apparently forgiven, or at least forgotten.

Nine days after Preble's supercession, two midshipmen—both veterans of the actions off Tripoli—fought a duel in Syracuse. One, William Nicholson, was killed. The source of the quarrel is unknown; a trivial insult apparently passed between them. The dead boy was buried in the Latomia dei Cappuccini, an ancient stone quarry that had been transformed into a flourishing garden. Two centuries later, the headstone is intact. It reads, in part:

In memory of William R. Nicholson, a Midshipman in the Navy of the United States, who was cut off from society in the bloom of his youth and health, on the eighteenth day of September, A.D. 1804, aged eighteen years.

His killer was Cornelius DeKrafft, the man whose journal covers the Tripolitan War. DeKrafft was arrested and sent back to the United States in the brig *Scourge*.

Based on the way the navy had handled previous cases, DeKrafft had no reason to be concerned. The duel had been fought according to accepted customs and strictures; it had been a fair fight, a fight in which Nicholson might just as easily have killed DeKrafft. Not only could the young officer expect to escape prosecution, but he could expect to be returned to naval service with no adverse repercussions on his career.

But DeKrafft had not yet heard the news that Alexander Hamilton had been killed by Aaron Burr on July 11 in Weehawken, New Jersey. That duel—the most infamous in American history—took place six days after Barron's squadron had sailed from Norfolk. It had tipped the balance of public opinion. Dueling was denounced in increasingly strident terms in newspaper editorials and from church pulpits. Reverend Nathaniel Bowen expressed a typical sentiment when he urged his South Carolina congregation to hold dueling in "the contempt to which its origins, its principles, and its effects, so deservedly entitle it."

Was DeKrafft to be made the first example in a looming crackdown? When the *Scourge* arrived in Norfolk, he was handed a curt note from Secretary Smith: "Immediately upon Receipt hereof, you will repair to the City of Washington & report yourself at this office."

But there would be no trial. The Nicholson family declined to press charges. Citing the "prevalent Example of older, wiser and more exalted men than himself," Congressman Joseph Nicholson asked the navy to restore William's killer to the service with his rank intact. Dueling, he explained, was reprehensible, and "yet the wisest Legislatures and the most able Magistrates have for some hundred years in vain endeavored to check it. It is one of those Evils which is consequent upon Society. It most frequently proceeds from the noblest feeling of the Heart. Before it can be stopped, the State of Society itself must change, and till then, human Laws and human Punishments will be vain."

PART THREE

England Again

CHAPTER TEN

————◆————

Ex-Commodore Preble came home with the bitter taste of defeat in his mouth. On his watch, the navy had lost one of its finest frigates and seen a crew of more than three hundred American officers and sailors thrown into the enemy's hands. At the height of his squadron's attacks on Tripoli, Preble had learned that he was to suffer the personal humiliation of being superseded by Samuel Barron. The last act of his command had been to send thirteen Americans to their deaths in the premature explosion of the *Intrepid*. He had assured his superiors that he would force Yusuf to capitulate. He had failed to do so. Edward Preble was forty-three years old, the third oldest captain on the active list. His health was less than perfect, and his future in the U.S. Navy seemed uncertain.

But to his surprise and gratification, Preble was greeted by his countrymen as a returning hero. "I cannot but be a little flattered with the reception I have met with Here," he wrote his wife from Manhattan, where he landed in February 1805. "The people are disposed to think that I have rendered some service to my country." In one important respect, Preble had succeeded where his predecessors had failed: He had not won the war, but he had at least carried the fight to the enemy. To a nation eager for any kind of good news from the Mediterranean, the destruction of the *Philadelphia* and the August 1804 attacks on Tripoli had been psychologically rewarding, if nothing else. Preble had fought hard, and honorably. In the eyes of his countrymen, who had been conditioned to expect very little, it was enough.

Letters from the Mediterranean left no doubt that Preble's vigorous prosecution of the war had made its mark. For the first time in years, said William Eaton, "an American is no longer ashamed of an American Uniform here . . . and a Barbary cruiser views an American flag in this sea with as much caution as a skulking debtor does any deputy sheriff in our country." Pope Pius VII, from his seat in Rome, was said to have framed the war as a clash of civilizations. "The American Commander," he was quoted as saying of Preble, "with a small force and in a short space of time, has done more for the cause of Christianity than the most powerful nations of Christendom have done for ages!" And Admiral Nelson—in naval circles a higher authority than the pope—was said to have remarked that Decatur's mission to destroy the *Philadelphia* was "the most bold and daring act of the age."

After three gratifying days in New York, Preble set out on the overland journey to Washington, where he was to debrief the Navy Secretary. He arrived March 4, the day of Jefferson's second inaugural ceremony. When Preble presented himself at the Navy Office, Secretary Smith immediately walked him across to the White House to call on the commander in chief. Jefferson had already forwarded Preble's official dispatches to Congress with a cover message lauding "the energy and judgment displayed by this excellent officer, through the whole course of the service lately confided to him." Congress, in turn, had voted a resolution to award Preble a gold medal, "emblematical of the attacks on the town, batteries, and naval force of Tripoli." Swords would be presented to each of the officers of the squadron, and the enlisted men would be paid a bonus equivalent to one month's pay.

During the two weeks that Preble remained in the capital, he was eagerly sought out by administration officials and members of Congress. He spent several days with Secretary Smith at the Navy Office, poring over maps of the Mediterranean. He dined at the White House with Jefferson on the sixth and at the home of James and Dolley Madison on the twelfth. His return to Maine was a multi-city victory tour: Philadelphia, Trenton, New York, Boston—in each place he was greeted as a national hero. Banquets were given in his honor. In Philadelphia, he stayed with Stephen Decatur's parents and had his portrait painted by Rembrandt Peale. On arriving in Boston, he was invited to Quincy for an audience with former President Adams. Rumors circulated that he was about to be appointed Secretary of the Navy.

From New York, Preble sent a hogshead of Marsala wine by coasting vessel to Washington, in care of Robert Smith, to be presented as a gift to the president. In the course of one of their conversations in Washington, Jefferson had expressed curiosity about this wine, which he thought might be comparable to Madeira. As much as the Marsala suited Jefferson's tastes, however, his sense of probity would not allow him to accept a gift from a military officer. "It is really a painful and embarrassing thing," he told Robert Smith. "To reject may be supposed to imply impure motives in the offer. To receive leads to horrid abuse." The president's tactful solution was to offer Preble a gift of equivalent value. It was a polygraph, or "portable secretary"—a device which made duplicate copies of letters by employing two pens attached to a wooden arm. "I have used one for the last 18 months," Jefferson told Preble in his letter accompanying the device, "and can truly say that it is an inestimable invention." Deeply moved, Preble wrote a note of thanks that would have rankled his fellow Federalists had it ever been made public: "I beg leave to assure you of my ardent wishes that Heaven may preserve your health and long continue your valuable life, an honor to our country and to human nature."

THOUGH YUSUF'S PUBLIC RHETORIC remained defiant, he no longer entertained any doubts about American resolve. With the reinforcements that had crossed the Atlantic under Commodore Barron's command, the American naval presence in the Mediterranean was larger than ever before. Like the other Barbary regencies, Tripoli had prospered by extracting tribute from the second-rate maritime powers. It did Yusuf no good to persist in a war against a nation that blockaded his harbor, seized his cruisers, shelled his city, made common cause with his exiled brother, and raised mercenary armies to march against him. Preferring to see this pugnacious enemy go away and leave him alone, he sent out peace feelers the same month Commodore Preble sailed from the Mediterranean.

Tobias Lear, the U.S. consul designated to negotiate with Tripoli, conveyed the American terms. The United States would pay no money for peace; the peace would have to be permanent; prisoners would be exchanged one for one; ransom would be paid only for the excess number of American prisoners held by Yusuf. On this last point, Lear implicitly agreed to the controversial point that a "token" ransom could be paid to win the safe release of William Bainbridge and the crew of the *Philadelphia*, and in order to provide Yusuf with a face-saving way out of the war. But when the Tripolitan counterterms were presented in April 1805, they were far in excess of what Lear was willing to consider: $200,000 for peace and ransom. The war would go on.

Meanwhile, a bitter and potentially deadly feud was playing out in the uppermost ranks of the Mediterranean Squadron, between John Rodgers and the Barron brothers. Throughout most of the winter of 1804–05, Commodore Samuel Barron had been prostrated with a painful liver disease. He could barely lift a pen to write, and remained ashore in Syracuse, convalescing in bed, for months on end. Thus incapacitated, he was in no condition to manage squadron logistics or plan the coming summer campaign against

Tripoli, and would have been wise to yield command (at least until his health improved) to his second-in-command, John Rodgers. But Barron preferred to rely upon his younger brother, James (the third-ranking officer in the squadron), as a kind of surrogate commander. The commodore issued orders through James, blurring the chain of command and sending Rodgers into as black a rage as this rage-prone officer had ever experienced. The psychodrama raised the specter of gunplay between the second- and third-ranking officers of the U.S. Mediterranean Squadron during a time when the squadron was actively engaged in a war.

The issue came to a head in the summer of 1805, when James Barron conveyed to Rodgers, through an intermediary, that "he had heard that [Rodgers] had spoken in a disrespectful manner of his brother's character, for which aspersion he should call on him to answer in a proper place and time, and that Commodore Barron's illness prevented him from doing it immediately." Rodgers replied by calling James Barron a "two-faced Judas," and said he looked forward to receiving the promised challenge upon returning to America. He added, gratuitously, that if Barron did not follow up with the challenge, "I shall impute it to a want of what no gentleman—one who wears a uniform—should be deficient in," and pledged that if he did not hear from Barron's second, he would issue a challenge of his own.

Fortunately, the antagonists agreed to put off the duel until their responsibilities in the Mediterranean had ended. Later, to get ahead of the story, when both men had returned to America, Rodgers did challenge James Barron. Barron agreed to fight but postponed the encounter because he had himself fallen sick. In the interim, several of their fellow officers intervened and mediated a settlement that would avert the duel. Both men signed a statement agreeing that the matter had been resolved to their mutual honor and satisfaction. For the rest of their lives, however, Rodgers and James Barron continued to share a toxic hatred for each other.

The 1805 campaign against Tripoli would involve a combined assault by sea and land. Former U.S. consul William Eaton would raise an army in Egypt, which would march across the desert to capture Derna and Benghazi, and from there be transported across the Gulf of Sidra by naval vessels to be landed on the coast, where they would launch the final assault on Tripoli. If the audacious plan proved successful, Yusuf would be deposed and Hamet Karamanli restored to the throne.

Eaton's polyglot army comprised eight U.S. Marines, some seventy Greek mercenaries, and about three hundred Arabs and Bedouins. The march from Alexandria was an unruly affair, with the tribesmen repeatedly refusing to carry on unless given additional pay and occasionally threatening to massacre their Christian paymasters. But Eaton was able to hold the army together as far west as Derna, where a small squadron under the command of Master Commandant Isaac Hull, comprising the *Argus, Nautilus,* and *Hornet,* dropped anchor in the bay to take part in the attack. While Hull's squadron shelled Derna, Eaton's troops stormed and captured the town on April 27. The action gave the Marine Corps an important part of its founding mythology and a line in the Marine Hymn: "From the halls of Montezuma to the shores of Tripoli / We will fight our country's battles on the land as on the sea."

While Eaton prepared to push on to the west, Tobias Lear's discussions with Yusuf grew more constructive. Yusuf knew that his brother was at the head of a hostile army, just across the Gulf of Sidra—and he knew that the summer would bring another attack from the sea, this time by five frigates instead of one. As the Bashaw confessed to Lear, he cherished no illusions that Tripoli's defenses could stand against that much force:

> I know that the exertions of your squadron this summer will be suf-
> ficient to reduce my capital; but recollect I have upwards of three
> hundred of your countrymen in my hands; and I candidly tell you
> that, if you persevere in driving me to the last extremity, I shall retire
> with them to a castle about ninety miles in the interior of the coun-
> try, which I have prepared for their confinement and my own secu-
> rity. Money is not my object at present, but a peace on terms that will
> not disgrace me hereafter.

The debate among the Americans now hung on the question of whether to agree to pay some modest sum as ransom for the American prisoners. Eaton and others argued strenuously that Yusuf must be forced to capitulate with no such payment at all, that only a total victory would protect the United States against the aggression of the other Barbary States. Lear's case for a face-saving ransom was bolstered by surreptitious lime juice letters from Bainbridge, reporting that Hamet had no popular following in Tripoli and would be unlikely to hold on to his throne even if the Americans put him on it. Another *coup d'état* in Tripoli would raise the danger of another war; Lear argued that it was in American interests to leave a chastened Yusuf in power.

Commodore Barron, swayed by Lear's reasoning and Bainbridge's let-ters, allowed Lear to land at Tripoli under a flag of truce. Five days of nego-tiations yielded a treaty on June 3, 1805. The United States would make no payment for peace or tribute, but it would pay $60,000 as ransom for the

American prisoners. Hamet would be forced to withdraw from Derna. The treaty was signed a few days later in the greatcabin of the *Constitution*.

After the military and naval successes of 1804, the treaty that brought the Tripolitan War to an end was disappointing to many Americans. It was the $60,000 ransom payment that really stuck in the craw. "I must say I had expected a treaty of a different character," said Secretary Smith, on first receiving the news—"And informed as I now am, I wish that such a peace had not been made." Eaton, Hamet, and the Americans absconded from Derna in the dead of night, escaping to the *Constellation* in small boats before the tribesmen and mercenaries could learn that they had been sold out. An embittered Eaton would publicly castigate "Aunt Lear," the Barron brothers, Rodgers, and everyone else he regarded as having been a party to the treaty, and his allies in Congress campaigned against ratification. Preble did not offer a public opinion on the issue, but privately he agreed that the treaty was "ignominious," and had come at the "sacrifice of national honor."

But the disappointment was not so great as to place ratification in doubt. Complaints were aired on the Senate floor, but the chamber voted to approve the treaty in April 1806. The nation was happy to welcome Bainbridge, his officers, and his crew safely home. The treaty reopened the lucrative Mediterranean trade routes. Neither the war nor the peace with Yusuf had placed any real strain on the American economy. The Tripolitan War had been, in the Jeffersonian view of the world, a perfectly acceptable overseas military adventure. It had been conducted on a scale compatible with Albert Gallatin's severe fiscal limitations; it had given the American people something to celebrate; and it had signaled to the world that the United States was capable of projecting military force in defense of its national interests. Republicans could argue, with some justification, that Jefferson had succeeded where his Federalist predecessors had failed. In his annual message the following December, Jefferson reported: "The states on the coast of Barbary seem generally disposed at present to respect our peace and friendship."

For twenty years, Jefferson had spoken of an enduring, international solution to the problem of Barbary piracy. He envisioned a system in which the maritime trading nations would form a coalition to patrol the Mediterranean sea-lanes, each member contributing warships, men, or money in proportion to the value of its Mediterranean trade. Simultaneously, the Barbary States would be offered new trade opportunities to replace the tribute, ransom, and booty on which they had come to depend. It was a high-minded vision, one that did Jefferson credit. He would continue to press it upon his European and American correspondents for years afterward.

But Jefferson also knew perfectly well that the nations of Europe had never shown much interest in a coalition response to the North African question, even while at peace. There was not the remotest possibility they would do so while at war. America was not a great power, and could not take on, single-handed, a project to transform this distant and culturally alien part of the world. A decade later, in 1815, Stephen Decatur would lead a mission to put an end to Barbary piracy once and for all. But in the interim, and for as long as Jefferson remained in office, the United States would do what other maritime nations had done in the Mediterranean for centuries. Diplomats would seek the best deals they could get, employing a deft combination of threats and bribes. They would keep the sea-lanes open to American ships, while allowing the violence of Barbary to fall on others.

ENTERING THE MIDDLE YEARS of his presidency, Jefferson found himself at the height of his power. The nation was riding a wave of prosperity, created largely by the phenomenal expansion of its shipping and trade. Maritime commerce brought vast private fortunes into the cities, simultaneously benefiting farmers by driving up prices of exported foodstuffs. If there was ever a doubt that America prospered by European misery, it was dispelled by the performance of the American economy between 1801 and 1807. For fourteen months between March 1802 and May 1803, the European war was placed on hold by the abortive Peace of Amiens. As a direct consequence, American exports (including re-exports) fell from $93 million in 1801 to $56 million in 1803. After the resumption of war, exports rose to $78 million in 1804, $96 million in 1805, and peaked at $108 million in 1807. The American shipbuilding industry boomed as it never had before, with more than 100,000 tons of new shipping built and launched in each of three consecutive years—1804, 1805, and 1806.

Booming trade filled the treasury with customs revenue, surpassing Treasury Secretary Gallatin's most sanguine expectations. The windfalls allowed for the elimination of unpopular internal taxes while simultaneously permitting Gallatin to meet his aggressive debt-reduction goals. The unexpected costs of the Tripolitan War were absorbed without difficulty. In 1803, Jefferson executed the largest real estate transaction in American history by acquiring the 800,000-square-mile Louisiana Territory from France. The Louisiana Purchase doubled the territory of the United States while resolving a potential source of instability and conflict on the western border. With the treasury awash in revenue, Gallatin managed to raise the $11.25 million cash payment required to complete the transaction without asking Congress for new taxes.

The opposition Federalists were as bitter and intractable as ever, but their great political and intellectual leader, Alexander Hamilton, was dead, and the party had been so badly routed at the polls that its survival seemed doubtful. Before 1800, the Federalists had controlled both houses of Congress, each with decisive majorities; but after being pulverized consecutively in the elections of 1800, 1802, and 1804, they found themselves outnumbered by a margin of 27–7 in the Senate and 114–28 in the House. In 1804, Jefferson was reelected in one of the most lopsided presidential contests in American history. Running against South Carolinian Charles Cotesworth Pinckney, he polled 162 electoral votes to Pinckney's 14, winning every state but Delaware and Connecticut. Senator William Plumer of New Hampshire, one of a handful of surviving Federalists in Washington, confided in his diary: "I think myself, federalism can never rise again."

In his second inaugural address, Jefferson reminded his countrymen of all the reasons they had supported his party. The Republicans had promised peace, prosperity, and an end to internal taxes. In 1805, the country was at peace, it was prosperous, and "it may be the pleasure and pride of an American to ask, what farmer, what mechanic, what laborer, ever sees a tax-gatherer of the United States?"

Jefferson was often seen riding his horse through the streets of Washington, unaccompanied by servants or guards. (His carriage left the White House stables only when his daughters were visiting.) He rode to church on Sunday, to the Great Falls of the Potomac, to the wooded bluffs above the Anacostia River, and to the shops of the "Center Market" between Seventh and Ninth Streets. His account books show that the president attended scientific lectures, horse races, theater performances, and on one occasion (three days before Christmas 1806) a tightrope act. He was an inveterate shopper. On any given afternoon, a customer in a shop on Capitol Hill or Georgetown might glance out the window and see the president of the United States climbing down from his saddle, and (as one said) "fastening his horse's bridle himself to the shop doors."

Though he was a scion of the Virginian slave-owning aristocracy, Jefferson managed to reinvent himself, in the eyes of the American people, as an icon of neoclassical republican simplicity and modesty. He would later maintain that the Republican electoral victory in 1800 was "as real a revolution in the principles of our government as that of [17]76 was in its form." It was an argument that dated back to the First Congress, when Vice President Adams had proposed that President Washington should be addressed as "His Highness the President of the United States and protector of their liberties." Jefferson had remarked to Madison that the ostentatious title was "the most superlatively ridiculous thing I ever heard of," and Madison had agreed that it threatened to inflict "a deep wound to our infant government." The proposal was defeated, but throughout the decade of the 1790s, during the Washington and Adams administrations, Republican journalists had ridiculed practices that seemed to ape the ceremonies and fashions of a European court. They objected to official celebrations of the president's birthday, to presidential "levees" (weekly receptions, denounced by critics as too similar to an Old World court ritual), to the use of the terms "Lady Washington" and "Lady Adams," and to placing presidential portraits on the national currency. With the benefit of hindsight, many of these criticisms seem tinged with paranoia; but to contemporaries who imagined a threat to America's fledging democratic institutions, it seemed essential to purge the nation's highest office of quasi-royalist pomp.

As president, Jefferson asked the local militias not to fire salutes on his birthday. With the exception of his two inaugural ceremonies, he refused to appear in person before Congress. At White House dinners, all distinctions based on rank were eliminated, and guests were admitted on the basis that "all are perfectly equal, whether foreign or domestic, titled or untitled, in or out of office." Upon taking office, Jefferson told Congressman Nathaniel Macon of North Carolina, "Levees are done away." The president would host just two public receptions each year: one on the Fourth of July and one on New Year's Day. Shortly after Jefferson took the oath of office (according to an account related by his grandson, Thomas Jefferson Randolph), a "crowd of ladies and gentlemen, fashionably dressed for the occasion" arrived unexpectedly at the White House. They had apparently not learned of the cancelation of the weekly levee. Finding the president not at home, they decided to wait. Some time later, Jefferson returned from his daily ride. Though he was dirty and tired, his manners did not fail him—still wearing his boots, still carrying his riding crop, he "greeted them with all the ease and courtesy of expected guests that he had been prepared to receive, exhibiting not the slightest indication of annoyance. They never again tried the experiment."

In response to Federalist criticism of the new protocols, Jefferson arranged to have a defense published in the pro-administration *Aurora General Advertiser*. It was printed without a byline, as if it had been written by the editor. Behind this safe veil of anonymity, Jefferson used unusually sharp language. Referring to the day he had taken office, March 4, 1801, he wrote:

That day buried levees, birthdays, royal parades, and the arrogation of precedence in society by certain self-styled friends of order, but truly styled friends of privileged orders. . . . In social circles all are equal, whether in or out of office, foreign or domestic, & the same equality exists among ladies as among gentlemen. No precedence therefore, of any one over another, exists either in right or practice at dinners, assemblies, or any other occasions. "Pell-mell" and "next the door" form the basis of etiquette in the societies of this country.

Jefferson's predilection for informality was never more apparent than when he was working in his study on the first floor of the White House, where he surrounded himself with books, maps, architectural drawings, musical instruments, mechanical inventions, scientific devices, roses and geraniums, and a mockingbird in a cage suspended from the ceiling. Even when the press of official business was heavy, the president pursued his interests in music, languages, agriculture, law, philosophy, theology, architecture, archeology, horticulture, and paleontology. In his letters during his two terms in office, one finds occasional references to politics and policy amid dissertations on (to pick a few subjects at random) gas lighting, Native American arts and crafts, geology, tooth-extracting instruments, steam engines, sculpture, the calculation of longitude, ventriloquism, heat conduction, mathematics, nailmaking, French wines, and the use of gypsum as a soil dressing.

The president was willing to receive unscheduled visitors during the morning and midday hours, just as he would receive a neighbor at Monticello, but he assumed no obligation to dress for the occasion. Senator Plumer, when accompanied by Congressman Joseph Varnum to meet Jefferson for the first time in 1802, recalled that "a few moments after our arrival, a tall, high-boned man came into the room. He was dressed, or rather undressed, in an old brown coat, red waistcoat, old corduroy small-clothes much soiled, woolen hose, and slippers without heels. I thought him a servant, when General Varnum surprised me by announcing that it was the President." The English chargé d'affaires (later ambassador) John Foster gave a similar description: "He wore a blue coat, a thick grey-coloured hairy waistcoat with a red underwaistcoat lapped over it, green velveteen breeches with pearl buttons, yarn stockings and slippers down at the heel, his appearance being very much like that of a tall, large-boned farmer." The editor of the *Evening Post*, in 1802, found him "dressed in long boots with tops turned down about the ankles like a Virginia Buck; overalls of corduroy faded, by frequent immersions in soap suds, from yellow to a dull white; a red single-breasted waistcoat; a light brown coat with brass buttons, both coat and waistcoat quite threadbare; linen very considerably soiled; hair uncombed and beard unshaven."

Some interpreted Jefferson's "negligent simplicity" as a calculated provocation. Foster said that the president, in ignoring the standards of dress and grooming expected of a head of state, "flattered the low passions of a mere newspaper-taught rabble, and seemed pleased to mortify men of rank and station."

Anthony Merry, the first British ambassador to establish a permanent residence in Washington, was introduced to Jefferson in November 1803. For the occasion, Merry wore formal diplomatic regalia: a dark blue coat, trimmed with gold braid and rich black velvet; immaculate silk breeches and stockings; shoes with highly polished buckles; a plumed hat; and at his belt, a ceremonial sword. Accompanied to the White House by Secretary of State Madison, the two men found the front entrance hall deserted, with no servants within sight or earshot. Undaunted, Madison led Merry directly into the hallway leading to the president's study. "Mr. Jefferson entered the entry at the other end," Merry wrote Lord Hawkesbury, the British foreign minister, "and all three of us were packed in this narrow space, from which to make room, I was obliged to back out. In this awkward position my introduction to the President was made by Mr. Madison."

The accordion effect of this hallway introduction was embarrassing, but it was not nearly so galling as the contrast between the ambassador's magnificent getup and Jefferson, who was "actually standing in slippers down at the heels, and both pantaloons, coat, and underclothes indicative of utter slovenliness and indifference to appearances, and in a state of negligence actually studied."

The gaffe could have been blamed on Madison, whose responsibility it was to explain the relaxed protocols of official Washington. Merry ought to have received a fair warning, and he apparently did not. In any event, the awkward introduction would have been forgotten if not for a second provocation at a White House dinner on December 2. Among the guests was the French chargé d'affaires, Louis-André Pinchon. To invite the ministers of two warring nations to the same table was an error in diplomatic protocol. If Ambassador Merry was offended, he apparently concealed his irritation well. The real scandal occurred when the assembled party moved from the parlor into the dining room. Merry had been led to believe that he was the guest of honor. As such, the diplomatic protocols of a European court would have required Jefferson to offer Elizabeth Merry his arm and escort her to the table, where she would have been seated to his right. Instead, Jefferson escorted Dolley Madison to the table and seated her in the place that Mrs. Merry believed was rightfully hers. The Merrys were forced to scramble for their chairs, and Mr. Merry was elbowed aside by a lowly congressman. All of this occurred, Merry reported to his government, "without Mr. Jefferson's using any means to prevent it or taking care how I might be otherwise placed."

Four days later, Merry and the other ministers were invited to dine at the Madisons' house, and a similar informality was practiced. James Madison offered his arm to Hanna Gallatin, leaving Mrs. Merry to fend for herself and Mr. Merry in a state of "visible indignation." Quietly infuriated, Merry ordered his carriage brought around as soon as the plates had been cleared away. In the weeks that followed, there were various snubs and countersnubs among the diplomats and cabinet heads, the details of which were spelled out in the British, French, and Spanish ambassadors' dispatches to London, Paris, and Madrid. The Merrys declined dinner invitations from both the Smiths and the Dearborns. Merry accepted an invitation to tea from the Gallatins but did not turn up. At the end of December, Merry reported to his government that he had decided to "avoid all occasions where I and my wife might be exposed to a reception of the same want of distinction toward us, until I have received authority from you to acquiesce in it."

Rightly or wrongly, Jefferson blamed Elizabeth Merry as the ultimate source of the continued rancor. She was a "virago," he told James Monroe, the American ambassador in London—"she has already disturbed our harmony extremely. . . . If [she] perseveres she must eat her soup at home, and we shall endeavor to draw [Mr. Merry] into society as if she did not exist."

In January 1804, Secretary Madison provided Merry with an official explanation. American diplomatic protocols adhered to a rule of "pell-mell." Seating at dinners was not determined by rank, but by the same informality that would be observed at a private dinner party among friends. Jefferson had always escorted the wives of his cabinet officers to the table, and that would continue to be his custom. Merry might find these practices objectionable, but it was the right of the host country to establish its own code of diplomatic etiquette, and, as Jefferson told Monroe, "we might as well attempt to force our principle of equality at St. James as [Merry] his principle of precedence here."

When the next set of dispatches arrived from London, Lord Hawkesbury firmly instructed Merry to acquiesce in the American protocols. Insofar as the public diplomacy was concerned, this brought the imbroglio to an end. But the Merrys continued to decline invitations to the White House on the principle that they should first receive an apology. It was an apology Jefferson did not believe he owed, and would not give.

Did the Merry affair have a bearing on the future course of history? Could a pair of slippers come between nations? Could a quarrel over who offered what arm to whose wife end in war? Weighing in Jefferson's favor the fact that "no law of the United States or treaty stipulation forbade Jefferson to receive Merry in heelless slippers, or for that matter in bare feet, if he thought proper to do so," Henry Adams concluded that the slippers and the parlor wars that followed "left distinct marks of acrimony in the diplomacy of America and England, until war wiped out the memory of reciprocal annoyances."

THE LOUISIANA PURCHASE, by resolving a looming conflict with France on the western border, had freed Jefferson and his cabinet to concentrate on the next-ranking items on the nation's foreign policy agenda. Prominent among these were neutral maritime rights and the ongoing harassment of American vessels at sea, a crisis that grew in proportion to the size and success of the American merchant marine. The United States nursed grievances against several European powers on this score, but the ascendancy of the Royal Navy gave England the means to do the most harm. Beginning in late 1803, the Jefferson administration took a newly assertive tone with the British government, and seemed determined to obtain a new treaty that would guarantee American rights at sea.

In a sequence of coldly formal letters to Ambassador Merry, Secretary Madison protested the harassment of American merchant vessels, the violation of American territorial waters by British warships, and the seizure on dubious pretenses of ships and cargoes that should have been protected, in the American view, by the sanctity of the U.S. flag. On Christmas Eve, 1803, Madison wrote Merry to protest that an officer of the HMS *Bellerophon* had boarded an American merchantman in the West Indies and written in the register that "Every port in the Island of St. Domingo being in a state of blockade by his Britannic Majesty's Squadron, you are hereby warned off from that Island, and if seen you will be made a prize of." This rude act of defacing a ship's register, Madison complained, was not as objectionable as the British practice of declaring blockades but failing to enforce them rigorously—so-called paper blockades. Armed with an impressive set of international legal precedents, Madison argued that England had no right to declare under blockade "a whole Island, of vast extent and abounding with ports and places of commerce," unless the Royal Navy was willing and able to station a force adequate to the task off each port.

Merry countered with complaints of his own. Local officials in American seaports, he charged, regularly enticed British seamen to desert British merchant and naval vessels. The problem was especially acute in Jefferson and Madison's home state of Virginia, where desertions occurred virtually every time a British ship put into Norfolk, apparently with the encouragement of local courts and law officers. Several such deserters, Merry said, were known to have enlisted aboard American frigates preparing to sail for the Mediterranean (Samuel Barron's relief squadron). Merry also protested the detention of British warships in New York, when they were suspected of planning to follow a French privateer to sea and attack her in American territorial waters.

The most emotionally charged dispute between the United States and Great Britain was the "impressment," or forcible conscription, of American seamen into the Royal Navy. Throughout the summer of 1804, Madison addressed angry protests to Merry, using terms that the ambassador described as "high language . . . accompanied even with some degree of menace." The impressment of seamen from the decks of American ships, Madison told Merry, could no longer be tolerated by the American people. England must renounce the practice. Several weeks later, the American ambassador in London, James Monroe, protested to the British Foreign Office that more than fifteen hundred Americans had been forced into the Royal Navy since March 1803. Indeed, incidents of impressment were sharply on the rise throughout the summer of 1804, and if the tone of the British government was a guide, they were likely to increase further.

The system of impressment rested upon the English doctrine of "indefeasible allegiance and the recognized prerogative of the crown to require the services of all seamen for defense of the realm." In Britain, it was carried out in the seaports by "press gangs" who patrolled the waterfront neighborhoods and practiced a brutal mode of on-the-spot conscription, putatively aimed at "seafaring men and persons whose occupations and callings are to work in vessels and boats upon Rivers," but often resulting in the detention of any able-bodied adult male unlucky enough to find himself in the gang's path. Impressment was also carried out at sea, as boarding parties detached from British naval vessels seized men from the decks of British and foreign merchantmen. English law never claimed the right to press foreigners into the Royal Navy, and men who had been born in the United States, before or after the American Revolution, were in theory exempted, but all native-born British seamen could be pressed into service, including those who had been naturalized as American citizens. As a practical matter, it was virtually impossible to distinguish between British and American seamen, either by speech or appearance. As a result, large numbers of native-born American seamen were abducted and forced to serve in the Royal Navy between 1792 and 1812.

It is not known exactly how many were taken. Incidents of impressment often went unreported. The British, by definition, regarded all pressed men as their own, so British naval records did not specify how many Americans had been forced to serve. Contemporary estimates ranged as high as 50,000, but this was almost certainly far above the actual number. Lists of pressed men who attempted to obtain release through official channels were compiled by the U.S. State Department and by American agents in London. These lists, adjusted for duplicate names, yield a figure of 9,991 Americans pressed between 1796 and 1812. Of these, the majority—about 6,000—were pressed after 1803, in the period after the failure of the Peace of Amiens and the return to power of Prime Minister William Pitt.

The phenomenon of impressment, as it affected both British and American seamen in this era, is best understood in the context of three related trends. The first was the unprecedented wartime expansion of the Royal Navy. Before the outbreak of war in 1792, the British fleets had employed about 10,000 men; by 1812, the number had grown to 140,000. The second was the equally unprecedented expansion of the American merchant service during the same period. Employment in American merchant vessels rose from fewer than 10,000 seamen before 1792 to about 70,000 in the peak years before 1812. By 1800, the United States was the largest neutral maritime power in the world, and by a considerable margin. The third was a pandemic of desertion from the Royal Navy. Horatio Nelson estimated that 40,000 men had deserted the navy between 1793 and 1801, and C. S. Forester judged that "at least" one half of the hands enlisted aboard the typical British warship between 1803 and 1812 would desert at the first opportunity. Every man who deserted had to be replaced. More often than not, he was replaced by a pressed man. But it was the pressed man who was most likely to desert. It was a vicious cycle, and the longer it continued the more vicious it became.

It was no secret that many British seamen—including both deserters and seamen who, though not deserters themselves, were liable to be pressed by virtue of their British birth—found their way onto American ships. They were lured by better pay, better working conditions, and the certainty they would be released from service at the end of a voyage. Once employed on an American vessel, they could pass themselves off as native-born Americans, often with the active collaboration of their officers and shipmates. Treasury Secretary Gallatin, with typical candor, told Jefferson that the number of British seamen employed in American ships exceeded the number of American seamen impressed into British warships. Total American merchant tonnage, he said, had grown at the rate of about 70,000 tons per year between

1803 and 1807; of the 4,200 seamen needed to man this annual increase, between one half and one third were probably British. Moreover, the British sailors tended to be highly trained and experienced "able seamen." Gallatin estimated that of the 18,000 able seamen employed in American merchant vessels in the two years before 1807, half were British. Admiral Sir George Cranfield Berkeley, commander in chief of the British North America station, said that "high wages given both in their [American] Men of War and trading Ships cannot be withstood by the Men," and estimated "according to the best intelligence I can procure above 10,000 English Seamen under these protections are at present employed in the Service of the Americans." Other estimates ranged as high as 20,000.

To feed its voracious appetite for men, the Royal Navy was determined to reclaim as many of these British-born seamen as possible. Admiralty orders directed commanders to stop and search American merchant vessels and to seize all British sailors they could identify. How to identify which men were British was left to the discretion of the commanders on the scene. Americans carried official citizenship certificates, known as "protections," but British seamen could obtain these documents fraudulently without much difficulty. Regarding the protections as a sham, the English tended to ignore them: "[T]he flagrant and undeniable abuses of the official documents of American Citizenship have obliged their Lordships [the British Admiralty] to look at all such documents with the utmost distrust."

A majority of impressments occurred just off the North American coast, often within the three-mile limits of U.S. territorial waters, in the major sea-lanes off the Virginia Capes, the Delaware Capes, Sandy Hook (New York), Rhode Island, and Boston. In some cases, American ships were stripped of so many men that they were left precariously short-handed, and forced to make their way as best they could to the nearest safe harbor. British commanders, operating at a great distance from London, were allowed broad latitude in carrying out their orders. A common ruse was to impress any man whose name began with the Scottish prefix "Mc" or "Mac." It was useless to point out that Scotsmen had been immigrating to America for nearly two hundred years. Some ignored the niceties of national identity altogether, and openly avowed an intention to press Americans into their ships. As one English captain said, with admirable candor, in 1797: "It is my duty to keep my ship manned, & I will do so wherever I find men that speak the same language with me, & not a small part of them British subjects, & that too producing Certificates of being American Citizens."

Once pressed into the Royal Navy, an American seaman was immediately confronted with a Hobson's choice. He could "enter the books"—that is, enlist formally—in which case he would be eligible to receive wages. In doing so, however, he renounced any right to appeal for his release though official channels. If he refused to enter the books, he would still be forced to serve as any other member of the crew, while receiving no pay. If he refused to obey orders, he would be flogged half to death. If injured or disabled in the line of duty, he would simply be landed on the nearest shore, ineligible to receive a pension or medical care at a naval hospital. His officers might confiscate and destroy his protection certificate and take measures to prevent him from contacting American government officials to petition for his release. Even when a protest was lodged through diplomatic channels, it could be rejected at the Admiralty on any number of flimsy pretexts. If the appeal led to a discharge order, the commanding officer might shelve it indefinitely, on grounds of necessity. In either case, the appeals process could be expected to drag out for years.

By the system's perverse logic, a pressed American seaman was transformed into a subject of the British crown. He could be compelled to fight and die in England's wars. After the outbreak of war between America and Britain in 1812, he could be compelled to fight and kill his own countrymen. If he managed to escape, he was forever labeled a deserter, and would be hunted for the rest of his life on land and sea. If he subsequently served in the U.S. Navy during the War of 1812 and was taken prisoner, he could be condemned as a traitor and executed.

Why was such a travesty permitted to continue for so long, and on such a large scale? The attitudes that countenanced impressment were a product of the extreme pressures on Britain during the middle and later stages of the Napoleonic Wars. Desperate times, it seemed, called for desperate measures. The English people believed they were fighting a just and necessary war on behalf of all civilized nations. The Royal Navy was the last barricade standing between Napoleon and his ambition to conquer the world. A vocal segment of British public opinion despised Americans as unprincipled scavengers, eager to enrich themselves in the wartime carrying trade while England held back the Corsican Tyrant. If Americans were complicit in draining away manpower from the Royal Navy, and if there was no practicable way to stanch the flow, why not dragoon a few Yankee seamen into joining the great campaign?

JEFFERSON AND MADISON WOULD HAVE LIKED to persuade England and the other warring powers of Europe to recognize an expansive version of American maritime rights, summed up in the slogan: "Free ships make free goods." Jefferson chose a metaphor to justify the American position. In a civilized society, "the place occupied by an individual in a highway, a church, a theater, or other public assembly, cannot be intruded on, while its occupant holds it. . . . No nation ever pretended a right to govern by their laws the ship of another nation navigating the ocean. By what law then can it enter that ship while in peaceable and orderly use of the common element?"

The question of neutral maritime rights during wartime was hardly a new one. It was governed by an intricate set of historical and legal precedents. The navy of a belligerent power had the right to stop and search neutral merchant vessels, and to interdict shipments of "contraband"—arms, ammunition, and war materiel—to an enemy port. Belligerent powers, however, tended to favor a broader definition of contraband than neutrals were willing to concede. For example, Britain had provoked the indignation of several neutral maritime powers in 1778–83 by interdicting shipments of naval stores and timber from the Baltic seaports to France. The neutral powers had joined in an "Armed Neutrality," and resolved to declare war on Britain if their rights were not respected. (The threat had influenced the British government's decision to recognize American independence.) Jefferson and Madison did not dispute Britain's right to stop American merchantmen and search them for contraband, nor its right to blockade an enemy port. But they insisted upon a narrow definition of contraband, and objected to "paper" blockades, which gave the Royal Navy a pretext to seize and condemn American vessels even when not laden with contraband.

With the return of the Pitt ministry to power in May 1804, the British government took a less fastidious view of neutral maritime rights. British naval power had virtually swept the French merchant marine from the sea, cutting the ties between France and its remaining overseas colonies. The English were determined not to allow the French economy to continue to prosper by shifting its traditional colonial mercantile trade into neutral ships. By a controversial doctrine known as the "Rule of 1756"—so called because it dated back to Seven Years' War of 1756–63—England denied any nation the right to carry cargo on a route that would be denied to that nation's vessels in a time of peace. For example, if France's peacetime mercantile restrictions barred foreign ships from carrying goods between Guadaloupe and Le Havre (as they generally did), then England would not recognize a third nation's right to trade on the same route during wartime (when the sea was no longer safe for French merchantmen). During the Napoleonic Wars, as in the earlier conflict, the rule had a very specific purpose: to sever all commercial tendons between France and the French West Indies.

American merchants circumvented the Rule of 1756 by purchasing cargoes of sugar and coffee for their own accounts, transporting them back to the United States as if they were to be imported directly into the American domestic market, and then "re-exporting" them to Europe. In order to decontaminate the paper trail, the goods were actually unloaded from the ships and stacked on the wharves in the American seaports. Import duties were paid to the U.S. Treasury Department (and later reimbursed). New bills of lading were drawn up. The "Americanized" goods were subsequently reloaded, often into the same ships that had brought them. This "re-export" trade was a major engine of the American maritime economy, growing from $26 million in 1796 to $53 million in 1805.

For years, England had acquiesced in the re-export trade on the principle that a neutral had the right to carry non-contraband goods on its own account. The party was brought to an end on July 22, 1805, when a Vice Admiralty Court in Nassau, New Providence (the present-day Bahamas), rendered a decision that outlawed the practice in a single stroke. The case concerned an American merchant brig, the *Essex*, which had unloaded a cargo of Spanish-bought goods onto the wharves at Salem, Massachusetts, paid import duties, reloaded the cargo, and sailed for Havana. She was captured by a British privateer, the *Favourite*. The court ruled that the cargo aboard the *Essex* had been brought from Spain and landed in Salem "solely to colour the true purpose . . . that the voyage was in fact to the Havanna, touching at Salem." Because the detour to Salem was solely for the purpose of evading the Rule of 1756, the *Essex* and her cargo were declared rightful prize. The judge, Sir William Scott, justified the ruling by adding: "I cannot hesitate in denying to a fraudulently circuitous voyage those immunities which are withheld from a direct one." The decision was subsequently upheld at Whitehall.

Whatever the legal merits of the *Essex* ruling, it prompted seizures of hundreds of American merchant ships all throughout the Atlantic. The policy served many different British interests at once, not least of all the officers and seamen of the Royal Navy, who enjoyed a unexpected windfall of prize money. Many of the captures occurred before news of the court's decision had reached American seaports. Maritime insurance rates spiked by as much as 400 percent. The Americans protested that the sudden attacks were not much different from piracy, and compared the British to the Barbary corsairs. The *Norfolk Gazette and Ledger* carried an account of the Virginian vessel *Ann Elizabeth*, boarded by the crew of a British 16-gun brig on October 1, 1805, while en route to Norfolk from Malaga. The American captain reported that a heavily armed boarding party, numbering ten or twelve men, "broke open my trunks, took away my wearing apparel, $200 in cash, my watch, hat, shoes, hammock, and sheets, did not leave me one shirt . . . all my navigation books; also my mate's clothes and $20, also . . . destroyed my papers and accounts. They beat the mate and people most dreadfully."

In Britain, where anti-American sentiment ran high, the press generally applauded the *Essex* ruling, or else complained that it did not go far enough. Many wondered why England did not simply seize all American commerce, using the entire weight of its naval power. A vocal minority demanded an outright declaration of war, even an invasion of North America and a campaign to reconquer the ex-colonies. A contemporary English pamphlet described the sources of the animosity:

> Hatred of America seems a prevailing sentiment in this country. Whether it be that they have no crown and nobility, and are on this account not quite a *genteel* Power; or that their manners are less polished than our own; or that we grudge their independence, and hanker after our monopoly of their trade; or that they closely resemble us in language, character, and laws . . . the fact is undeniable that the bulk of the people would fain be at war with them.

In October 1805, a lawyer named James Stephen published a book entitled *War in Disguise; Or the Frauds of Neutral Flags*. It argued that Americans had conspired to circumvent trade restrictions to undermine the British war effort, and should be regarded as Napoleon's collaborators. Widely circulated and hugely influential, *War in Disguise* served to rally public support for the Pitt ministry's aggressive policies. In the same month, Nelson wiped out the combined French and Spanish fleet at the Battle of Trafalgar. If there was any question that England possessed the will to quash American shipping, there was no longer any doubt that it possessed the means. As the *Naval Register* proudly declared: "The winds and seas are Britain's wide domain / And not a sail, but by permission, spreads!"

AMERICANS GREETED THE NEWS of the *Essex* decision with an upwelling of popular anger. Ambassador Merry wrote of the "sensation and clamour excited by this news from England." Memorials and petitions from merchant and seaport communities poured into Washington. Jefferson forwarded these to Congress, adding his opinion that the British policy was "producing the most ruinous effects on our lawful commerce and navigation." In the two-year period between 1805 and 1807, some 469 American ships were forced into British ports for adjudication. Jefferson's 1805 annual message, prepared for the first session of the Ninth Congress in December, alluded to the Royal Navy's "system of hovering on our coasts and harbors . . . to the great annoyance and oppression of our commerce."

Privately, Jefferson worried that the Republicans' well-known hostility to standing armies and navies had invited European aggression. "The love of peace, which we sincerely feel and profess," he wrote Judge Cooper, "has begun to produce an opinion in Europe that our government is entirely in Quaker principles, and will turn the left cheek when the right has been smitten. This opinion must be corrected when just occasion arises, or we shall become the plunder of all nations."

Madison retired to the solitude of his office and composed a 200-page treatise attacking the legality of the *Essex* decision, entitled simply *An Examination of British Doctrine*. Copies were delivered to each member of the House and Senate. Drawing upon centuries of precedent, the *Examination* left no doubt that England had acted in flagrant contravention of settled principles of international maritime law. It was exhaustively researched, tightly reasoned, masterfully argued—and otherwise irrelevant. The most cogent retort was offered by Virginia congressman John Randolph, who acknowledged Madison's lawyerly erudition but dismissed the effort as "a shilling pamphlet against eight hundred ships of war."

Randolph was a distant cousin of Jefferson's, a former friend and ally of Madison, and the chairman of the House Ways and Means Committee. He was a skilled debater and leader of the congressional faction known as the "Old Republicans." Randolph and his followers professed to stand for the party's traditional core principles, and opposed what they regarded as the Jefferson administration's drift away from those principles. The neutral carrying trade, he said, served no vital national interest and was not worth fighting for. American lives, American treasure, and American independence should never be placed at risk to support "this mushroom, this fungus of war." The notion that the United States could or would ever dare to dispute England's command of the sea was preposterous. Randolph asked: "Shall this great mammoth of the American Forest leave his native element and plunge into the water in a mad contest with the shark? Let him stay on shore, and not be excited by the mussels and periwinkles on the strand!" The Virginian had no doubt that American patriots would turn back any invasion of American soil, but as for the sea, "I will never consent to go to war for that which I cannot protect. I deem it no sacrifice of dignity to say to the Leviathan of the deep:

'We are unable to contend with you in your own element; but if you come within our actual limits, we will shed our last drop of blood in their defense.'"

Randolph and his allies pressed for an embargo, forbidding all American ships to leave American seaports. By withdrawing from the sea altogether, they reasoned, America could no longer come into hostile contact with the warring powers. "In six months," Randolph said, "all your mercantile megrims would vanish." As for the economic pain an embargo would cause at home, Randolph allowed that "it would cut deep," but insisted: "we can stand it."

After debating the subject for several weeks, Congress voted instead to impose trade sanctions, a policy with historical roots in the American Revolutionary era. The Non-Importation Act of 1806, passed on March 25 and scheduled to take effect, at the president's discretion, on November 15, generally barred the importation of all "luxuries" and manufactured goods from Great Britain.

IN APRIL 1806, two Royal Navy frigates, *Cambrian* and *Leander,* lay to in the waters just off Sandy Hook, in the sea corridor leading to and from New York Harbor. So long as the weather was fair, these two warships managed to stop and search virtually every merchantman sailing in or out of New York. One of the *Leander*'s midshipmen, Basil Hall, described how it was done:

> Every morning at daybreak, we set about arresting the progress of all the vessels we saw, firing off guns to the right and left to make every ship that was running in heave-to, or wait until we had leisure to send a boat on board "to see," in our lingo, "what she was made of." I have frequently known a dozen, and sometimes a couple of dozen, ships lying a league or two off the port, losing their fair wind, their tide, and worse than all their market, for many hours, sometimes all day, before our search was completed.

Few vessels were tempted to make a run for the safety of the harbor. A direct hit by a single 18-pounder ball could sink a small merchant vessel in minutes. When *Cambrian* or *Leander* fired a warning shot, an interdicted vessel was quick to "let fly the sheets," heave to, and wait for the boarding party to come over the side. An English officer would demand and examine the ship's documents. Any deficiency, real or perceived, was enough to trigger the order that the vessel be detained, navigated to Halifax, and the case adjudicated by a British Admiralty judge. Any one of many different pretexts could then be employed to condemn her—missing documents, a reference to a French port in a private letter found in a crew member's possession, a stamp on a barrel in the hold. Even if the case was decided in the American owner's favor, the long delay often resulted in the decay and spoilage of the cargo, and no claims for delay-related losses were allowed. The boarding parties also made a practice, in Midshipman Hall's words, of pressing any sailor "whom they had reason, or supposed or said they had reason" to believe was a subject of the king of England.

The presence of the *Cambrian* and the *Leander* off New York began to seem more and more, in the spring of 1806, like a peacetime blockade. Among American merchants and seamen, the names of the two ships were notorious. An incident on April 24 ignited a firestorm of public anger. *Leander* fired a warning shot across the bow of an incoming merchantman. The ball skipped off the sea and struck the quarter-rail of another vessel, the *Richard*, a small Delaware coasting sloop. A splinter thrown off by the impact decapitated the *Richard*'s helmsman, John Pierce. Later that afternoon, Pierce's head and body were brought ashore in lower Manhattan and paraded through the streets by an angry mob. Stones were thrown through the windows of the English consul's house, and British officers who happened to be in the city were obliged to go into hiding. The martyr's body was placed in public exhibition outside the Tontine Coffee House. A grand jury indicted Henry Whitby, captain of the *Leander*, on a charge of murder.

In the following weeks, as the news spread north and south, so did the general sense of outrage. "I well remember the sensation excited by the murder of Pierce," Congressman DeWitt Clinton of New York later recalled. "It was a glow of patriotic fire that pervaded the whole community; from Georgia to Maine it was felt like an electrical shock."

On the same day the news reached Washington, Jefferson issued a proclamation. Captain Whitby of the *Leander*, if and when he ever set foot on American territory, was to be arrested and delivered up to the authorities in New York to answer the murder charge. The *Leander*, the *Cambrian*, and a third vessel, the *Driver*, were ordered to "immediately & without any delay depart from the harbours & waters of the U.S." If the banished frigates did not abide by the order, American citizens were forbidden to provide them with provisions, fresh water, pilotage services, or "supplies of any kind."

Privately, Jefferson said the presence of the Royal Navy at Sandy Hook was "an atrocious violation of our territorial rights." He considered sending three American frigates to New York to enforce his order, but decided instead to accept Ambassador Merry's assurances that the British squadron was "not to remain there." Writing Ambassador James Monroe in London on May 4, Jefferson seemed determined to assert American hegemony in the western Atlantic:

> England may, by petty larceny, thwartings, check us on [the sea] a little, but nothing she can do will retard us there one year's growth. We shall be supported there by other nations, & thrown into their scale to make a part of the great counterpoise to her navy. . . . We have the seamen & materials for 50 ships of the line, & half that number of frigates; and were France to give us the money & England the dispositions to equip them, [Americans] would give to England serious proofs of the stock from which they are sprung, & the school in which they have been taught. . . .
>
> We begin to broach the idea that we consider the whole Gulf Stream as of our waters, in which hostilities & cruising are to be frowned on for the present, and prohibited so soon as either consent or force will permit us.

THE END OF THE TRIPOLITAN WAR had been followed by another naval downsizing. Jefferson had ordered the officers furloughed, the enlisted men discharged, and the vessels laid up in ordinary (mothballed). As in 1801, Jefferson insisted that all the frigates be navigated up the Potomac to the Washington Navy Yard, where they would be "under the immediate eye" of the government and would require just "one set of plunderers" to look after them. By mid-December 1805, five of the six original frigates were at the yard, either dismantled or in the process of being dismantled. Only the *Constitution* remained in service, patrolling the Mediterranean against renewed aggression by the Barbary States.

With an eye on the increasing Anglo-American tensions at sea, Navy Secretary Robert Smith began pressing for a large-scale naval buildup in the spring of 1806. He proposed to return all the frigates to service and ask Congress to fund a crash program to build battleships and gunboats. Albert Gallatin, still a fiscal superhawk in spite of the huge revenue surpluses pouring into the treasury, asked whether a large navy, "by encouraging wars and drawing us in the usual vortex of expenses and foreign relations, [would] be the cause of greater evils than those it is intended to prevent. . . ." Gallatin attacked Smith's management of the Navy Department and his frequent "loose demands for Money." The intracabinet debate soon escalated into a feud in which the Smith family's formidable influence in Congress came into play.

For the moment, Congress was more interested in harbor defense than the blue-water navy; and after some debate it appropriated funds for seaport fortifications ($150,000) and gunboats ($250,000) on April 21, 1806. The same legislation limited the number of naval personnel to 13 captains, 9 masters commandant, 72 lieutenants, 150 midshipmen, and 925 sailors. The navy was to sell any vessel that "is so much out of repair that it will not be for the interest of the United States to repair the same."

Officers not actively employed were placed on half pay, and since half pay was rarely sufficient to live comfortably ashore, many found themselves scrambling for berths on merchant vessels. "I have obtained a furlough, and have got a ship for China," Master Commandant Isaac Chauncey wrote Edward Preble. " . . . If I can bring any thing for you from that country, it will afford me pleasure to receive your commands. I see no prospect of Congress doing any thing for the Navy or officers, therefore the sooner we can get good employ in private Ships the better. . . ." Some of the midshipmen were even willing to sail "before the mast"—that is, as common seamen.

Even during periods when most naval vessels were out of service, competition for appointments and promotions was intense. There was never a time in the pre–1815 navy when there were not at least four or five candidates for every one vacancy in the naval officer corps. Robert Smith took the subject of appointments and promotions very seriously, and the result was a material improvement in the overall quality of the officer corps during his eight-year tenure at the Navy Department. Chief Navy Accountant Charles Goldsborough said Smith "was particularly happy in discovering the merits of the most promising young officers of the Navy." Under his administration, new officers entered the service and learned the ropes in early adolescence.

An application for a midshipman's berth included all the same basic elements as a modern-day college admissions application—evidence of prior academic achievement, letters of recommendation, and an essay composed in the young applicant's own hand. A successful campaign was mounted on behalf of sixteen-year-old Charley Boarman of Georgetown. Charley's application arrived at the Navy Office with a letter of recommendation from the mayor of Washington, Robert Brent, who confessed that "The son is not personally known to me" but added that Charley's father "has sustained the best possible character." Also enclosed was Mr. Boarman's letter to the mayor, in which he described his son's academic qualifications: Charley had been enrolled for some years at Georgetown College and "consequently, has studied the languages for a certain space of time and is as well versed in arithmetic as most of his age generally are." Lastly, there was Charley's own letter:

> Though sixteen years old, I already begin to think myself a man! And why not? Alexander, it is said, was a little man, yet fame gives him the credit and honor of possessing a great soul! May not, Sir, great feats be performed by a little David as well as by a Goliath? Methinks I already hear the roaring of the cannons, and my soul, impatient of delay, impetuously hurries me on to the scene of action!

All agreed that naval officers could only be trained and seasoned while serving actively at sea. In the years after the Tripolitan War, when most of the frigates were out of service, such opportunities were limited. If they could not go to sea, however, midshipmen could at least receive schooling and instruction on shore. Between 1805 and 1807, midshipmen attended daily classes in writing, mathematics, and navigation aboard the frigate *Congress* as she lay moored in the East Branch near the Washington Navy Yard. *Congress* was thus the original forebear of the U.S. Naval Academy.

Secretary Smith was equally tenacious in choosing the men who would enter the lists of captain and master commandants, and he sometimes promoted junior officers over the heads of their more senior colleagues. By July 1807, the median age of the captains and master commandants in the navy was thirty-four. Several of the leading figures in the command ranks had been promoted at an early age. Both John Rodgers and William Bainbridge had won promotion to captain at age twenty-six, during the Quasi War. Twenty-five-year-old Stephen Decatur, as a reward for the destruction of the *Philadelphia*, had won a two-rung promotion from midlevel lieutenant to captain, bypassing altogether the rank of master commandant. The men thus leapfrogged were deeply resentful. For Lieutenant Andrew Sterrett, who had not won promotion after capturing a Tripolitan galley while commanding the *Enterprise* in 1801, it was too much to bear. He submitted his resignation, telling Secretary Smith he found it "impossible to be reconciled to the promotion of a junior officer over me, nor is it compatible with correct principles of honor to serve under him." Smith was unmoved. Promotions rewarding extraordinary conduct in action, he said, would stimulate others to "deeds of equal valor." The secretary was sorry to lose Sterrett, but he accepted the resignation rather "than give up a principle believed essential to the good of the service . . . and holding out to all equally the means of obtaining its benefits."

WITH THE DEATH OF WILLIAM PITT in January 1806, his ministry was succeeded by Lord Grenville's "Ministry of All the Talents." The new foreign minister was Charles James Fox, a Whig leader who had argued (among other things) for the rights of Irish Catholics, a negotiated peace with France, British parliamentary reform, and respect for the maritime rights of neutrals. Fox was thought to be a friend of America, and Jefferson greeted the news of his appointment with relief. "In Mr. Fox, personally, I have more confidence than in any man in England," he told Monroe. " . . . While he shall be in the administration, my reliance on that government will be solid." Though the new government did not order an immediate suspension of the *Essex* ruling, the "Fox Blockade" of northern France and Germany implicitly acquiesced in the resumption of an unmolested re-export trade.

Whatever Fox's personal inclinations, however, it was soon clear that there would be no fundamental change in British policy. The press and public opinion, still under the influence of *War in Disguise*, resented America's spectacular rise as a commercial and maritime rival. The English newspapers reprinted excerpts from the debates in the U.S. Congress on defense and naval measures, and it was plain that America was not arming for war. It was not building or launching new warships, it was not recruiting new troops, and it was doing only the bare minimum to fortify its seaports. If the United States was neither willing nor able to fight, why should England, so often compelled to fight for its own survival throughout the centuries, lift a finger to placate this insolent ex-colony?

James Monroe and a second American envoy, William Pinkney, managed to negotiate a new treaty with the British government in the fall of 1806. The Monroe-Pinkney Treaty would have secured for American merchants a specific set of guarantees allowing them to prosper in the wartime neutral trade, and barred British naval cruisers from stopping and searching American shipping within five miles of the American coast. However, the treaty also committed the American government to lift trade sanctions imposed on England, and failed to address basic points demanded by Jefferson and Madison, including a ban on impressment of seamen from American ships and compensation for shipping losses after the *Essex* decision. Jefferson declined to submit the treaty to the Senate for ratification.

In any case, the Monroe-Pinkney treaty was quickly rendered obsolete by new developments in Europe. In the fall of 1805, Napoleon's victories over the Austrians and Russians at the battles of Ulm (October 16–20) and Austerlitz (December 2) had left him the seemingly invincible master of continental Europe, and secured for him a place alongside Alexander the Great, Julius Caesar, and Genghis Khan as one of the greatest conquerors of all time. Interposed chronologically between those two battles was the British victory at Trafalgar (October 21), which had left England the undisputed champion of the world's oceans. With France unable to strike England at sea, and England not yet able to strike France on land, the two belligerents, separated by a 22-mile channel, were like two hostile dogs chained to opposite posts, nose to nose but not close enough to fight.

Earlier restrictions on neutral trade had dealt principally with enemy contraband. After 1806, France and England entered into full-scale economic warfare. In November 1806, Napoleon issued the "Berlin Decree," which purported to place the entire British Isles in a state of blockade. The decree created the infamous "Continental System," which was aimed at starving England by cutting off its trade with continental Europe. Because there was not much of a French navy left afloat, the purported blockade had no real effect, other than as a pretext for condemning neutral ships seized in a European port. The real blow to American commerce came with a British countermeasure, decreed by the Grenville ministry in January 1807. The Order in Council declared that no vessel could sail from one port to another while both ports were under French or French-allied control. Since it was the practice of American ships to sail from port to port seeking out the best prices for their cargoes, the dueling French and British measures of 1806 and early 1807, taken together, rendered most categories of American commerce with continental Europe subject to capture by either Napoleon's coalition or by Britain.

Though Jefferson occasionally took a bellicose tone in private letters, he was not prepared to ask Congress for a military buildup. He continued to hope that the European war might end in a negotiated peace. The president's annual message for 1806 dismissed a proposed mobilization of troops: "Were armies to be raised whenever a speck of war is visible in our horizon, we never should have been without them. Our resources would have been exhausted on dangers which have never happened, instead of being reserved for what is really to take place." He also continued to resist Navy Secretary Smith's calls for frigates and battleships, regarding them as excessively costly and hopelessly overmatched by the Royal Navy. Instead, Jefferson grew infatuated with the idea of building a large fleet of small, shallow-draft gunboats.

Gunboats were 50 to 75 feet in length, 15 to 20 feet in the beam, and armed with a single 24- or 32-pounder long gun on the bow. They were copper-bottomed, rigged with one or two masts, and manned by a crew of twenty to thirty men. They could be sailed in a wind or rowed in a calm. Designed for inland waters and harbor defense, they were not seaworthy enough to be trusted far from shore. Josiah Fox, who supervised the fitting out of some of the first American-built gunboats, compared them to the crafts used by oystermen on the Delaware and Chesapeake Bays. Commodore Preble had employed borrowed Italian gunboats with some success in the 1804 attacks on Tripoli Harbor.

The gunboats were never popular with the Federalists, who regarded them as poor substitutes for frigates and ships of the line. On September 8, 1804, during a "dreadful Storm," the first American-built gunboat was driven from her moorings off Whitemarsh Island, Georgia, and landed high and dry in a corn field. She lay there, stranded, for almost two months. The Federalist newspaper *Connecticut Courant* gleefully commented that the gunboat might, if left in the field, "grow into a ship of the line by the time we go to war with Spain. Should this new experiment in agriculture succeed, we may expect to see the rice-swamps of Carolina and the tobacco fields of Virginia turned by our philosophical Government into dry-docks and gunboat gardens."

The theory of gunboat defense was not ridiculous on its face. Advocates pointed to the long, lightly populated American coastline, impossible to defend at every vulnerable point with fixed fortifications. Gunboat flotillas could serve as floating, mobile batteries to be brought into action wherever the enemy chose to attack. A fleet of large warships concentrated the navy's entire capital into a handful of assets that could be captured in the first few weeks of a war. A fleet of several gunboats could not be taken all at once. Advocates also maintained that gunboats were more economical than larger warships, though that premise was subsequently refuted by cost overruns.

The gunboat navy appealed to the Jeffersonians because it took their cherished archetype of national defense—the local citizens' militia—and transferred it into the realm of naval warfare. Just as the infantry militia was the Republican alternative to a standing army, gunboats offered an alternative to a standing navy. They would be built by local shipwrights and manned by local crews. Like infantry militias, naval militias and their gunboats were unmistakably intended for home defense and not foreign military adventures. Because gunboats were all but useless in the open ocean, Jefferson said, they could never "become an excitement to engage in offensive maritime war, toward which [they] would furnish no means." Posing no threat to the Royal Navy, they were unlikely to provoke the English to a preemptive attack. In peacetime, they could be hauled up on shore to be stored under protective sheds, and their crews returned to their usual livelihoods.

In February 1807, Jefferson sent Congress a special message recommending the construction of a large fleet of gunboats. In addition to those previously authorized, he asked that two hundred additional vessels be constructed at an estimated cost of $1 million. He specified the number of vessels to be stationed in each section of the American coastline, from "the Mississippi and its neighboring waters" to "Boston and the harbors north of Cape Cod." Thomas Paine, author of the American revolutionary pamphlets *Common Sense* and *The American Crisis,* published a series of newspaper editorials supporting the proposal. The Republican majority in Congress, thankful for an excuse not to fund a larger naval mobilization, authorized the construction of 180 of the vessels.

As the first gunboats were launched and placed in service, criticism mounted. They were wet, cramped, and uncomfortable. It was often difficult to recruit full complements of seamen to man them. Officers took the first opportunity to be transferred into a frigate. When a Norfolk gunboat capsized and sank in six fathoms of water, Stephen Decatur dryly asked a fellow officer: "What would be the real national loss if all gunboats were sunk in a hundred fathoms of water?"

An anonymous letter published in the *Washington Federalist,* clipped and carefully filed among Jefferson's personal papers, called the gunboat navy a "wasteful imbecility." The author rejected the argument advanced by Paine and others that fifty gunboats were equivalent in force to a 74-gun battleship. While that might be true in a calm, he wrote, "In a breeze, the 74-gun ship . . . will have no more difficulty in running down a squadron of [gunboats] than a ship of three hundred tons would have in running down a fleet of birch canoes." With cabin headroom of just four feet, the men below "will not only not be able to stand upright under cover, but cannot sit upright, unless they squat upon the floor like puppies in a dog kennel." The author mocked the idea that a volunteer naval militia could provide adequate coastal defense:

> When danger menaces any harbor, or any foreign ship behaves naughty, somebody is to inform the governor, and the governor is to desire the marshal to call upon the militia general or colonel in the neighborhood, to call upon the captains to call upon the drummers (these gentlemen who, we are informed from high military authority, are all important in the day of battle) to beat to arms, and call the militia men together . . . to go on board the gunboats and drive the naughty stranger away, unless he should take himself off during this long ceremonial.

Over time, the critics were proven right. The gunboats were effective only in exceptionally calm conditions. If hit by a heavy cannon ball fired by an enemy frigate or battleship, they were liable to sink. They were nearly impossible to man. Of the 278 gunboats authorized by the Congress between 1805 and 1807, only 176 were actually built, and fewer placed into service. The cost per vessel, originally estimated at $5,000, was actually closer to $10,000. Funds spent on the gunboat program eventually reached $1.5 million, a sum that could have paid for a small squadron of battleships or a large squadron of frigates. The program would be quietly abandoned after the inauguration of James Madison in 1809.

CHAPTER ELEVEN

When coming on deck, a sailor stepped with his left foot first. When his ship was becalmed, he whistled. Pointing to the horizon, he used his whole hand, all fingers extended, because a single pointed finger could act as a lightning rod for evil spirits. The appearance of a petrel normally foretold a gale, unless the petrel was first seen *during* a gale, in which case the gale was on the verge of coming to an end. Cats held significant powers—black cats, especially. It was good luck to have a single black cat on board, but two on the same ship were considered bad luck (and one should be thrown into the sea). Every seabird was believed to carry the soul of a dead sailor, so it was considered very bad luck to kill one. To have one fly alongside the ship was generally lucky (except in the earlier case of a petrel before a gale). Above all, there was no creature luckier than an albatross, and no ship luckier than one with an albatross flying alongside.

Some seafaring superstitions had the potential to cause actual harm, such as the belief that it was dangerous to bathe because the water might wash away one's good luck; or that blood spilled into the sea would cause a storm to abate; or that a man's tattoos protected him against venereal diseases. Even the most gullible sailors conceded that some ancient myths were patently ridiculous, such as the theory that barnacles hatched baby geese, or the belief that seamen's wives should burn their hair and fingernail cuttings lest they be stolen by witches and used to stir up storms. By the early nineteenth century, many officers, surgeons, and chaplains campaigned against superstitions, pointing out that the beliefs in question had been empirically disproven, or were detrimental to a sailor's health, or sacrilegious. But seasoned officers also understood that long-held beliefs, whether true or not, retained a powerful hold over the minds of seamen. Their effects on morale could be controlled, but they should never be wholly ignored, because they sometimes threatened to turn self-fulfilling.

The frigate *Chesapeake* has often been described as "unfortunate," "unlucky," or "unhappy." For the most part, these judgments were rendered after 1807, and especially after 1813. In later years, however, a feeling grew within naval circles that there had been something wrong with the *Chesapeake* from the beginning. Among the original six frigates, she was an oddity in several respects. Hers was the last of the six keels to be laid down on the stocks (in Norfolk). Originally designated as "Frigate D," she was eventually named *Chesapeake* although there was already a sloop of war in commission with that name (the smaller vessel was rechristened *Patapsco*). Unlike each of her sisters, her name did not honor a feature or symbol of the U.S. Constitution. When launched in December 1799, *Chesapeake* was 152 feet in length—13 percent shorter than the three 44-gun frigates and 7 percent shorter than *Constellation* and *Congress*. In proportion to her length, she was heavier and beamier than her sisters, rendering her, by most accounts, a lethargic sailor. She was easily outrun by the *President* in a friendly contest near Guadaloupe in 1800, and Stephen Decatur, eight years later, remarked that "The *Chesapeak* as a Vessel of War Sails uncommonly dull."

Chesapeake was built by Josiah Fox after his bitter falling out with fellow Quaker Joshua Humphreys. Fragmentary records do not make clear whether Fox shortened her keel because of his own design preferences, or because he did not have enough live oak timber on hand to build her to the larger specifications in Humphreys's plan. The timber shortage was probably a factor, since much of the timber originally shipped to Norfolk had been redirected to Baltimore for the completion of the *Constellation*. But Fox, who had never liked Humphreys's design, seems to have seized on the opportunity to throw aside the plans ordered by the Navy Office, and build *Chesapeake* according to his own ideas. As a result, she was the only one of the six original frigates explicitly disowned by Joshua Humphreys.

A reputation for bad luck could work to the detriment of a ship's career as well as a man's. Officers and seamen sensed that a ship was a living being, with a unique personality, and the facility to do evil as well as good. A nineteenth-century captain said his ship "can do anything but talk, and sometimes she can do even that." Another engaged in one-sided conversations with his ship's mizzenmast, asking how much sail she would like to carry. The question of *Chesapeake*'s unluckiness has been addressed more recently by Captain Edward Beach, a World War II and Cold War–era submarine commander who published several distinguished works of naval history before his death in 2002:

"All ships have accidents from time to time, but in some ships every accident is considered the work of a malevolent star, some evil spirit of bad luck hovering over her. Such was the case with the *Chesapeake* . . . and it may have begun because, of the original six ships, she was the runt of the litter."

EARLY IN 1807, Secretary Smith ordered the *Chesapeake* to sail for the Mediterranean to relieve the *Constitution*, which had been cruising without interruption since Preble had taken her out in 1803. Most of the *Constitution*'s enlisted men had served for more than three and a half years, well beyond their two-year enlistment terms. Dispatches suggested that the *Constitution*'s officers had detected symptoms of mutiny on the lower decks. The *Chesapeake* was needed in the Mediterranean, the sooner the better, so that *Constitution* could return from her long tour and discharge her disgruntled crew.

Chesapeake's captain would be James Barron, who would also carry the title of commodore of the much-diminished U.S. Mediterranean Squadron. Barron was to be provided with a flag captain, an officer who would bear day-to-day responsibility for looking after the ship and her crew. This was Master Commandant Charles Gordon, who received his orders on February 22.

At the time of Smith's order, *Chesapeake* lay in ordinary at the Washington Navy Yard, where she was one of a long line of bare hulls in the shallows of the Potomac's Eastern Branch. More than six months were needed to restore her to seaworthy condition. As the delays mounted, the officers accused the management and tradesmen of the Navy Yard of incompetence and even corruption. "I have long known the perverse disposition of the rulers of that establishment," said Barron. Criticism began to appear in the press. "Foreign nations must form a high opinion of our energy and activity," the *Norfolk Gazette and Ledger* of January 26, 1807, remarked with heavy sarcasm, "when they observe the whole attention of the Navy Department directed to one frigate, and she cannot be got to sea in something less than six months."

After a last furious burst of activity in the first week of June, the *Chesapeake* cast loose her moorings and followed the channel buoys down the Eastern Branch and into the Potomac River. Tradition required the ship to fire a salute in honor of George Washington as she passed Mount Vernon on the river's western bank. When the moment came, however, Captain Gordon "was struck with astonishment when the first lieutenant reported to me that neither the sponges nor cartridges would go in the guns." This failure to fire the customary salute should have been construed as a sign that the *Chesapeake* was not yet ready for sea, but the lesson, apparently, was not taken to heart.

June was spawning season, and the *Chesapeake* shared the river with an armada of tiny shad, herring, and sturgeon boats. As she progressed down the Potomac, the banks gradually receded on either side, the stream widened to as much as seven miles, the current diminished and then died, and the water grew increasingly brackish. There was no exact point at which the river could be said to end and the Chesapeake Bay to begin. The average depth of the bay was about 20 feet, and the *Chesapeake* drew nearly that much, so she had to be piloted with care. Passing Windmill Point, she entered the shoal water off the Rappahannock River, where it was essential for the pilot to know the exact position of the notorious shoal known as the Wolf Trap, so named because it had put an end to the *Wolf*, a 300-ton merchantman, more than a century earlier. Most of the lower bay's major shoals had been marked with buoys—a Virginia statute condemned any man caught stealing them to "suffer death without benefit of clergy."

The *Chesapeake* came safely to anchor in Hampton Roads on June 4. The little town of Hampton, visible through the trees on the western shore, was the hometown of Commodore James Barron, and he would remain ashore until the ship was ready to sail. After a cursory inspection of the ship, he wrote Secretary Smith to say that "from the extreme cleanliness and order in which I found her, I am convinced that Captain Gordon and his officers must have used great exertions. Captain Gordon speaks in high terms of his lieutenants. The state of the ship proves the justice of his encomiums." Whether the praise was sincere or just a routine professional courtesy to Gordon would be a subject of later controversy. Barron would regret having written the letter.

For two weeks, the crew worked fitfully to ready the ship for sea. The remaining 18-pounder long guns and 32-pounder carronades were brought on board, fitted into their carriages, and loaded with powder and shot. The men were divided into watches. On June 19, Captain Gordon reported that the ship was ready to sail: "we are unmoored and ready for sea on the first fair wind."

A FEW MILES EAST AS THE CROW FLIES, anchored in Lynnhaven Bay, were several frigates and battleships of the Royal Navy. They had been stationed there throughout the winter, ostensibly to watch a few French warships that had taken refuge in the upper Chesapeake the previous August. In spite of rising Anglo-American tensions, the British squadron had maintained cordial relations with the towns and communities of Tidewater Virginia. They had not obstructed commercial traffic in the manner of the *Cambrian* and *Leander* off New York a year earlier, and British naval officers were frequently seen walking the streets of Norfolk or Hampton, where they purchased most of the squadron's provisions.

But the British officers were incensed at having recently lost a large number of deserters. Sailors were prone to desert British warships wherever they sailed, and this was especially true in American coastal waters, where if a deserter managed to get ashore he was free to begin a new life among people who spoke his own language. Local sheriffs and magistrates were never inclined to cooperate in returning these asylum seekers, and this tendency had been elevated to a high principle in Virginia, where state law imposed penalties on any local official who laid a hand on a British deserter. There was a perpetual shortage of prime seamen in Norfolk, and merchants and shipowners relied on foreign (generally British) sailors to man their outbound vessels. Even when there were enough hands to go around, it was always in the merchant's interest that there should be more, because nothing depressed wages so efficiently as large numbers of unemployed seamen.

In the spring of 1807, every vessel in the British squadron at Lynnhaven Bay had lost a portion of her crew to desertion, including the 74-gun ships of the line *Triumph*, *Bellisle*, and *Bellona*, the storeship *Chichester*, and the frigate *Melamphus*. Only the most trusted seamen in the British squadron were ever permitted to set foot on shore, but as the weather grew warmer, some men had managed to swim to freedom and others had commandeered boats. On the night of March 7, 1807, five members of the crew of the English 16-gun sloop *Halifax* had overpowered a midshipman, ran a jolly boat on shore at Sewell's Point in Hampton Roads, and melted into the local community.

With every reason to fear the lash or the noose if apprehended, a British deserter's safest form of maritime employment was to enlist in a foreign navy. By custom, law, and standing orders, the Royal Navy had no authority to stop and search the naval vessels of a nation at peace with England. To do so could be interpreted as an act of war.* So it was not surprising that a number of deserters from the British squadron—including several men who had fled the *Melamphus* and all five of the men who had made their escape in the *Halifax*'s jolly boat—went to a U.S. Navy recruiting station in Norfolk and entered onto the *Chesapeake*'s books under false names.

---

* There had been two previous cases in which sailors had been removed from an American man-of-war, and in each there had been a mitigating circumstance. North of Cuba, in 1798, a British squadron had taken five men out of the sloop of war *Baltimore*. The *Baltimore*'s officers had been unable to produce papers proving she was a naval vessel. Off Cadiz, in 1805, another British squadron had taken three seamen off of U.S. Gunboat No. 6. The three went willingly, claiming protection as British subjects.

When the British officers got wind of this, they lodged protests with their American counterparts. Stephen Decatur, who now commanded the Gosport Naval Yard, replied he had nothing to do with the manning of the *Chesapeake* and referred the matter to Commodore Barron. Barron suggested that the British take the question up with the civil authorities. The commander of the *Halifax* lodged a complaint with the British consul in Norfolk, the consul referred the matter to the British ambassador in Washington, and the ambassador lodged a formal protest with Secretary of State Madison, who declined to intervene in the case because the issue of British deserters had never been addressed in any Anglo-American treaty. (Madison's transparent objective was to force the British government to negotiate a treaty addressing both desertion and impressment.)

With no recourse though legal or diplomatic channels, the British officers stewed. It was bad enough that known deserters from the squadron could go straight to a Norfolk rendezvous and enlist aboard a Yankee frigate. It was even worse that they could parade through the streets of Norfolk, boasting of their escape to all who would listen. In March, on a street near the Norfolk wharves, Captain James Townsend of the *Halifax* came face-to-face with two of the men who had stolen his jolly boat. Realizing he had no power to coerce them while on American soil, Townsend attempted to coax them into returning to the *Halifax* voluntarily. One, a British-born seaman named Jenkin Ratford, hurled epithets at his ex-commander and declared (according to Townsend) that "he would be damned if he should return to the ship; that he was in the Land of Liberty; and that he would do as he liked, and that I had no business with him."

The infuriating exchange was reported to Admiral Sir George Cranfield Berkeley, commander in chief of the British North American station, headquartered in Halifax. Known deserters from the *Halifax*, wrote Captain Townsend, "were seen by me & several of the Officers . . . patrolling the Streets of Norfolk in triumph." He estimated that no fewer than thirty-five British seamen had enlisted aboard the *Chesapeake*. Admiral Berkeley forwarded the reports to London and asked for instructions. On June 1, 1807, having not yet received a reply, he wrote out a circular order to be distributed to the commanders throughout his station:

Whereas many Seamen, subjects of His Britannic Majesty, and serving in His Ships and Vessels . . . while at Anchor in the Chesapeak, deserted and entered On Board the United States frigate called the *Chesapeak*, and openly paraded the Streets at Norfolk, in sight of their Officers under the American flag, protected by the Magistrates of the Town and the Recruiting Officer belonging to the above mentioned American Frigate. . . .

The Captains & Commander of his Majesty's Ships and Vessels under my Command are therefore hereby required and directed in case of meeting with the American frigate the *Chesapeak* at sea . . . to show to the Captain of her this Order; and to require to search his Ship for the deserters from the before mentioned Ships, and to proceed and search for the same; and if a similar demand should be made by the American, he is to be permitted to search for any Deserters from their Service, according to the Customs and usage of civilized nations on terms of peace and Amity with each other.

These orders were carried from Halifax to the Virginia Capes by Berkeley's flagship, the 52-gun frigate *Leopard*. After a passage of twelve days, in which she pressed seamen from several merchant vessels along the American coast, *Leopard* anchored in Lynnhaven Bay.

MONDAY, JUNE 22, DAWNED with clear skies and a gentle southwest breeze. At 7:00 a.m. *Chesapeake* took aboard her jolly boat and cutter. Fifteen minutes later, all hands were turned out to make sail, and the ship stood down the fairway and out for sea.

Her crew of 381 included 329 officers and seamen and 52 marines. In addition, there were several civilian passengers, including Dr. John Bullus, the newly appointed Mediterranean Navy Agent, with his wife, three children, and two servants; the wife of Marine Captain John Hall; and ten Italian musicians who had performed for some years as the Marine Band, and were being permitted to return, at their request, to Italy.

The logistical challenges of maintaining an active squadron far from American shores, combined with Jeffersonian parsimony, required the *Chesapeake* to ship a large quantity of provisions, stores, baggage, and spare ammunition on her passage to the Mediterranean. The frigate was doing double duty as her own storeship, and in the rush to get to sea various articles had been hastily stowed wherever a vacant corner could be found—spare lumber, casks of water and wine, an armorer's forge and anvil, a horse, a grindstone, furniture and baggage belonging to the officers and civilian passengers. Large coils of thick anchor cable lay on the gun deck, obstructing access to the guns and storerooms—the officers had assumed there would be time to transfer them to the cable tier once the ship was at sea. Thirty-two of the frigate's crew were on the sick list, and by order of the surgeon their hammocks had been strung between the guns on the spar deck, where they could take in the sun and fresh air. *Chesapeake*'s guns were loaded and shotted, but most had been securely lashed up in case of heavy weather during the Atlantic crossing.

No one denied that all this clutter was unseamanlike. But the United States was at peace with the entire world, and neither Barron nor any of his officers, passengers, or crew had any reason to expect a hostile encounter between the Capes of Virginia and the Straits of Gibraltar. Even in the Mediterranean, none of the Barbary States had shown an antagonistic tendency since the end of the Tripolitan War two years earlier. It seemed essential to get the much-delayed frigate underway at last, and to make a safe and comfortable Atlantic crossing. Once they had reached the Mediterranean, the provisions and stores could be landed on shore, the passengers disembarked, and everything made taut in man-of-war fashion. Until then, no one seemed to give the *Chesapeake*'s readiness for action a second thought.

At 9:00 a.m., *Chesapeake* passed by the British squadron at Lynnhaven Bay. Through his telescope, James Barron observed the 74-gun *Bellona* making signals to the other ships of the squadron, but he was unable to read them and thought nothing of them. *Chesapeake* doubled Cape Henry and steered into the offing, dead east on the compass. At noon, with the lighthouse bearing southwest by south, the hands were put to unbending the larboard anchor cable, stowing the anchor, and "clearing Ship for Sea."

The *Leopard* had put to sea just ahead of the *Chesapeake*. Several of the American officers found her maneuvering peculiar. She had "hauled by the wind, close around Cape Henry, and stood to the Southward, under easy sail, thereby showing that it was not her intention to get off the land speedily." If *Leopard* did not intend to sail away from the coast, why was she sailing at all? And why at that particular moment? But the English frigate's maneuvers, quixotic as they were, did not arouse Barron's suspicions.

At three o'clock in the afternoon, when the *Leopard* was three or four miles away to the south, she wore round and stood northward, directly toward the *Chesapeake*. As she closed the distance, several of the *Chesapeake*'s officers noticed that her lower deck gunports were open and the tompions had been taken out of her guns. It seemed likely she was cleared for action. But Barron later testified that he still did not assume there was any cause for concern. It was possible that the *Leopard* merely intended to ask the Americans to carry dispatches to Europe, a courtesy frequently extended between vessels at sea.

At 3:30 p.m., the *Leopard* came within hailing distance. Her captain, Salusbury Pryce Humphreys, hailed Barron across the water and asked permission to send an officer, with dispatches, to go aboard the *Chesapeake*. Barron, through a speaking trumpet, answered that he would heave to and await the *Leopard*'s boat, and he had *Chesapeake*'s main topsail thrown aback to take the way off her.

The *Leopard*'s boat was lowered and rowed across to the *Chesapeake*, and Lieutenant John Meade came aboard. Meade handed Commodore Barron a copy of Admiral Berkeley's circular order. The last clause—"according to the Customs and usage of civilized nations on terms of peace and Amity with each other"—might have been considered by the Americans as a bad joke, but it was clear from the young lieutenant's grave demeanor that the English were serious. The *Leopard* intended to muster the *Chesapeake*'s crew as she would muster the crew of any common merchantman.

Lieutenant Meade remained aboard the *Chesapeake* for about forty minutes, and then returned to the *Leopard* with a note from Commodore Barron to Captain Humphreys. Barron wrote that he did not know of any such man as the circular described, and added, "I am also instructed never to permit the crew of any ship that I command to be mustered by any other but their own officers. It is my disposition to preserve harmony, and I hope this answer to your dispatch will prove satisfactory."

As the British lieutenant was being rowed back to the *Leopard*, Barron observed that "their intentions appear serious" and ordered Captain Gordon to send the crew to quarters. The commodore specified that it be done silently, so as not to provoke the British to a preemptive strike. In the confusion that followed, the drummer began tapping out the traditional roll to bring the men to quarters. Gordon silenced him by knocking him down with the flat of his sword. The truncated drum roll sent the crew into confusion: some assumed that the order to clear for action had been countermanded, and froze.

Nothing was ready; nothing was organized; chaos reigned aboard the *Chesapeake*. Not a single gun was primed and ready to be fired. There were no powder horns on the gun deck, no matches in the match tubs, and not enough rammers, sponges, and handspikes to serve a full broadside. Sick men were still lying in hammocks slung between the spar deck guns. Coils of anchor cable, the armorer's forge, casks, ladders, furniture, lumber, baggage, and various other articles obstructed the lanes leading fore and aft on the gun deck. Orders were shouted and countermanded; men rushed back and forth; and precious minutes continued to slip away.

Captain Humphreys knew perfectly well that the *Chesapeake* was unprepared, and had no intention of giving the Americans time to sort themselves out. He shouted across the water: "Commodore Barron, you must be aware of the necessity I am under of complying with the orders of my commander-in-chief!" Barron played for time, shouting: "I do not understand what you say!"—and then urged Gordon to "hurry" and get the ship ready for action.

Leopard fired a warning shot across *Chesapeake*'s bow. Barron ignored it.

At 4:30 p.m., the *Leopard* opened fire on the *Chesapeake* from pistol-shot range. Most of the balls struck *Chesapeake* amidships, creating secondary explosions of splinters on the interior walls of the bulwarks and gun deck. A few crashed through the rigging, sending down a rain of cordage and fragments of spars. Among the wounded was Commodore Barron himself, who received a splinter in his right thigh. With no priming powder on hand, none of the *Chesapeake*'s guns could be fired in response. The gunner was below, in the magazine, fumbling with the cartridges and powder horns.

On the quarterdeck, Commodore Barron clambered onto a signal locker and attempted to hail the *Leopard*, shouting that he would send his boat on board the English ship to discuss the issue of the deserters. Captain Humphreys, assuming his adversary was attempting to stall for more time, ignored these overtures.

Leopard's guns erupted in a second broadside. More shot crashed into the *Chesapeake*, and splinters exploded in the faces of the men standing at the guns they could not fire. "For God's sake, gentlemen," cried Barron—"will nobody do his duty?" He turned to the sailing master and asked, "Is it possible we can't get any guns to fire?" Recognizing the hopelessness of the *Chesapeake*'s situation, the commodore sent a junior officer forward to deliver a message to Captain Gordon: "For God's sake, fire one gun for the honour of the flag. I mean to strike."

A few of the *Chesapeake*'s 18-pounders were finally primed, but the loggerheads normally used to fire them were not yet heated. Lieutenant William Henry Allen retrieved a red-hot coal from the galley and touched it to the priming hole of one of the guns, causing it to fire. It was the only shot fired by the *Chesapeake* that day. Barron shouted down the hatchway: "Stop firing, stop firing. We have struck, we have struck." At 4:45 p.m., while the American colors were actually on their way down from the mizzen peak, the *Leopard* fired a third broadside.

Three of the *Chesapeake*'s crew lay dead. Eighteen were wounded, ten seriously and eight slightly. One of the wounded men would later die.

Fifteen minutes after the last shot had been fired, two boats were lowered from the *Leopard*. They brought across two lieutenants and a party of seamen. The boarding party ordered the *Chesapeake*'s sailing master to produce the muster books and muster the crew. The English officers studied the faces of the *Chesapeake*'s men and identified three deserters. A fourth, Jenkin Ratford, was dragged out of the coal hole, where he had hidden at the end of the action. The four were taken back to the *Leopard*.

Commodore Barron retired to his cabin and wrote a quick note to Captain Humphreys: "Sir, I consider the Frigate *Chesapeake* as your prize, and am ready to deliver her to an Officer authorized to receive her. By the return of the boat I shall expect your answer." A boat was lowered and Lieutenant Allen was rowed across to deliver the note. Half an hour later he returned with Captain Humphreys's reply:

> His majesty's ship *Leopard*, At sea, June 22, 1807
> Sir,
>   Having to the utmost of my power, fulfilled the instructions of my Commander in Chief, I have nothing more to desire; and must, in consequence, proceed to join the remainder of the Squadron; repeating that I am ready to give you every assistance in my power, and do most sincerely deplore that any lives should have been lost in the execution of a service which might have been adjusted more amicably, not only with respect to ourselves, but to the Nations to which we respectively belong.
>   I have the honour to remain, sir, your obedient humble servant,
>   S. P. Humphreys

A few minutes passed, and the *Leopard* hauled off for the Virginia Capes. After a brief meeting with his officers, Barron decided that the *Chesapeake* must return to Norfolk. The hands were set to work repairing damage, splicing injured rigging, getting the anchors clear, and pumping three feet of water out of the hold. After darkness had fallen, *Chesapeake* got underway in the *Leopard*'s wake. At 8:00 a.m. on June 23, she entered the bay for which she was named, and passed the British squadron, where *Leopard* was anchored between *Bellona* and *Melamphus*. At half past noon, the disgraced American frigate let go of her anchor in Hampton Roads.

THE WAVE OF PUBLIC OUTRAGE raised by the *Chesapeake-Leopard* encounter was unlike any the American people had felt since the Revolution.

Henry Adams identified it as the nation's first "feeling of a true national emotion"—that is, the first to transcend the bitter rift dividing Federalists and Republicans. "The brand seethed and hissed like the glowing olive-stake of Ulysses in the Cyclops' eye," wrote Adams, "until the whole American people, like Cyclops, roared with pain and stood frantic on the shore, hurling abuse at their enemy, who taunted them from his safe ships."

Minutes after the *Chesapeake*'s return to Hampton Roads, angry crowds gathered on the Norfolk and Portsmouth wharves. Even from a distance, an educated eye could study the frigate at her moorings and see she had been shot up. When one of *Chesapeake*'s boats brought eleven injured men to be landed at the hospital, the sight of the wounded transformed the crowd into a mob. They turned their collective fury against two hundred casks of fresh water recently purchased by the British squadron, smashing them to pieces.

Stephen Decatur and Samuel Barron went aboard *Chesapeake* at approximately 4:00 p.m. and remained for two hours. They found James Barron lying in his cabin, his leg wrapped in bloody bandages. By the appearance of the ship, Decatur concluded that the *Chesapeake* had been entirely unprepared to defend herself. He may have been influenced by conversations with the ship's lieutenants. When Captain Gordon was dispatched to Washington to report the encounter, he carried with him a letter to Navy Secretary Smith, signed by all the *Chesapeake*'s lieutenants, recommending that Barron be court-martialed.

Writing to his father from the "Late USS *Chesapeake*," Lieutenant Allen gave some idea of the depths of shame and anguish to which the frigate's officers had sunk:

> Oh! that some one of their murderous balls had deprived me of the power of recollection the moment our colors were struck—I could have greeted it, received it to my bosom, with a kindred smile—nothing could equal so horrible a scene as it was, to see so many brave man standing to their Quarters among the blood of their butchered and wounded countrymen and hear their cries without the means of avenging them. . . . My God is it possible? My country's flag disgraced. You cannot appreciate, you cannot *conceive* of my feeling at this moment . . . to be so *mortified*, *humbled*—cut to the soul. Yes, to have the finger of scorn pointing me out as one of the *Chesapeake*.

A public meeting was called at Norfolk's town hall. The building proved too small to accommodate the crowds, and the meeting was relocated to

Christ Church. A resolution moved that all commerce and communication with the British squadron should be prohibited. Another proposed that all citizens wear mourning clothes for ten days, in honor of the *Chesapeake*'s martyrs. The smashing of the water casks was endorsed as "highly laudable and praiseworthy." The governor was urged to call out the militia, and Commodore Decatur was asked to put Norfolk's gunboats into service. The *Gazette and Public Ledger* noted that war with England would be devastating to America, and to Norfolk in particular, but added, "we look upon it as degrading beneath contempt if we are to submit to such an insult."

On June 27, one of the *Chesapeake*'s casualties, Robert MacDonald, died of his wounds in the hospital at Portsmouth. A boat brought his body across the river to Norfolk. Vessels in the harbor flew their colors at half-mast, and a salute was fired by the shore battery. A crowd estimated at four thousand turned out for the funeral procession, which began at Market Square, proceeded up Catherine Street, turned on Freemason Street, and terminated at Christ Church. The casket was carried by pallbearers chosen from among the captains of merchant vessels at anchor in the harbor. The *Chesapeake*'s officers and crew joined the solemn, angry procession.

Dark rumors intensified the sense of imminent danger. There were reports (later proved false) that a party of Royal Marines was moving to take Norfolk from the undefended inland side. Boatloads of British attackers were expected to advance up the river at any hour. Militiamen poured into the streets of Norfolk—the Richmond Light Infantry Blues, the Petersburg Republican Blues, the cavalry. The young men of the city met at the Exchange Coffee House and resolved to place themselves under Decatur's command. Slave gangs worked to repair Fort Norfolk and fill powder cartridges for her newly mounted 18-pounder guns. Sailors from the *Chesapeake* worked to rig and arm the gunboats.

On June 29, a town ordinance prohibited contact between residents of Norfolk and the British squadron at Lynnhaven Bay. British commodore John E. Douglas had not previously threatened the town, but he now wrote Norfolk mayor Richard E. Lee to demand that the law be "immediately annulled."

> You must be perfectly aware that the British flag never has been, nor will be, insulted with impunity. You must also be aware that it has been, and still is, in my power to obstruct the whole trade of the Chesapeake since the late circumstance. . . . Agreeably to my intentions, I have proceeded to Hampton Roads, with the squadron under

my command, to await your answer, which I trust you will favor me
with without delay.

As if to underscore his sincerity, the British squadron interdicted all outbound merchant traffic. British boats were sent to take soundings in the lower
Roads, which was taken as a signal that Douglas was preparing to advance
with his battleships into the Elizabeth River for an attack on Norfolk itself.

News of *Leopard*'s attack on *Chesapeake* reached Washington the afternoon of June 25. Congress had adjourned in March, and two department
heads—Treasury Secretary Gallatin and War Secretary Dearborn—had left
for the summer. Jefferson had been preparing to saddle up for the four-day
ride to Monticello, where he would remain until early autumn, as he did each
year. ("I consider it as a trying experiment for a person from the mountains
to pass the two bilious months on the tidewater," he had written in 1801.)
Deciding that the crisis required his entire cabinet to be present in the capital, Jefferson wrote Gallatin and Dearborn, asking that they hurry back
"without a moment's avoidable delay."

On July 2, the president issued a proclamation ordering all British naval
vessels "now within the harbors or waters of the U.S. immediately & without
any delay to depart from the same." If the British refused to comply, local
officials were to prohibit any commerce or communication with them, and
punish any citizen who supplied them with fresh water, provisions, or pilot-
ing services.

During the following weeks, the cabinet met almost daily to organize the
national defenses. All gunboats in commission were ordered to rendezvous at
the points on the American coast where a direct attack was thought most
likely. The *Constitution* and other vessels of the Mediterranean Squadron
were ordered to sail for home. Jefferson asked Virginia governor William
Cabell to call up the state militia and prepare for a possible British invasion
of the tidewater region, including a thrust at Norfolk itself. Dispatches were
sent to Ambassador Monroe in London, instructing him to demand an immediate disavowal of the action as well as the recall of Admiral Berkeley and the
return of the men taken from the *Chesapeake*. When Jefferson learned that the
British had asked compensation for the water casks destroyed by the Norfolk
mob, he said he was reminded of the man "who, having broke his cane over
the head of another, demanded payment for his cane."

One of the many remarkable consequences of the *Chesapeake-Leopard*
affair was that Albert Gallatin was brought over to the war party. The
Genevan immigrant who had shot like a rocket into the highest ranks of

American government, and who had always shunned European-style wars of national aggrandizement, now believed it might be necessary to fight England for the "honor of the nation." "Our commerce will be destroyed and our revenue nearly annihilated," he wrote Hanna Gallatin on July 10. "That we must encounter; but our resources in money and men will be sufficient considerably to distress the enemy and defend ourselves everywhere but at sea." A week later, he told Congressman Nicholson that the British government should be given an opportunity to disavow the act and punish the officers responsible; but if the redress was inadequate, as he expected, the nation would have no choice but to declare war. "Nor do I know whether the awakening of nobler feelings and habits than avarice and luxury might not be necessary to prevent our degenerating, like the Hollanders, into a nation of mere calculators."

Gallatin confessed he was troubled by "one subject of considerable uneasiness"—the safety of New York City, where a substantial portion of the nation's wealth was concentrated and "which is now entirely defenceless, and from its situation nearly indefensible." He was not alone. New Yorkers middle-aged or older could remember the long, ruinous occupation of the city from 1776 to 1781. Jefferson asked Secretary of War Henry Dearborn to organize the city's defenses, warning that "the British commanders have their foot on the threshold of war. . . . Blows may be hourly possible."

In Norfolk, the *Chesapeake* was moored broadside to the main channel of the Elizabeth River, with a line of a dozen gunboats at anchor on either side of her. By Secretary Smith's orders, Stephen Decatur took command of the ship. The twenty-eight-year-old captain now commanded all naval forces stationed on the southern half of the Atlantic seaboard. Decatur declared he would welcome the privilege of "burning the first Powder" with the British.

Tensions eased on July 6, when a Norfolk lawyer visited the British squadron under a flag of truce. Commodore Douglas indicated that he had no intention of attacking Norfolk. He actually seemed perplexed that the Americans had interpreted his earlier letter as menacing, and suggested that it was the English who were, in fact, the aggrieved party in the dispute. Soon afterwards, all British vessels withdrew from the lower Roads and returned to their anchorage in Lynnhaven Bay. Jefferson, plainly relieved, observed that the squadron's intentions were for the time being "manifestly pacific" and surmised that they "do not mean an immediate attack on Norfolk, but to retain their present position till further orders from their Admiral." He seized the opportunity to escape Washington for the summer, but arranged to have frequent dispatches brought to Monticello by postal service couriers on fast horses.

JAMES BARRON HAD HOPED HIS JUNIOR OFFICERS would close ranks around him, just as the *Philadelphia*'s lieutenants and midshipmen had closed ranks around William Bainbridge after the loss of that frigate in Tripoli four years earlier. He would have no such luck. The *Chesapeake*'s officers asked that Barron be court-martialed for incompetence, if not cowardice, and Secretary Smith was of the same mind.

Recriminations flew. Barron referred to his lieutenants as "the greatest cowards that ever stood on a ship's deck," and complained that his old rival, John Rodgers, was seeking to eject him from the navy by working through his protégé, Lieutenant Allen, whom Barron called "the most infamous and the most Vindictive Rascal of them all." According to Allen, there were no fewer than seven duels fought over the incident in July and August, including one that wounded Captain Gordon. Under Secretary Smith's strict orders, Commodore Decatur at last put an end to the gunplay, and in November reported that "all differences between the officers & gentlemen of this place I am informed are adjusted."

Among the officers who would sit in judgment were Bainbridge, Decatur, and Rodgers, who had two years earlier called Barron a "two-faced Judas." The court convened in January 1808 and heard evidence for a month. James Barron made a long, eloquent defense, in which he implied that he had been wrongfully scapegoated for a humiliation that any commander in his position might have suffered. When judgment was rendered on February 8, Barron was cleared of three out of four charges, but on the second charge of "neglecting on the probability of an engagement, to clear the ship for action," the court found Barron guilty and voted to suspend him from the navy without pay for a period of five years.

When Stephen Decatur took command of the *Chesapeake*, he employed reverse psychological methods to drill her crew into a state of high readiness. The frigate, while he commanded her, would wear her disgrace publicly. She would not fire or return salutes, because "a ship without honor can render none." In any future close encounter with a vessel of the Royal Navy, Decatur told the crew, the *Chesapeake* would be set on a hair trigger for action. And if she was ever so fortunate as to come upon the *Leopard*, the *Chesapeake* would attack preemptively, whether the two nations were at war or not.

IN INSTRUCTIONS TO THE LONG-SUFFERING James Monroe, who had performed various diplomatic assignments in Paris, London, and Madrid since 1803, and was currently serving as Minister to the Court of St. James's, Madison spelled out the American demands. First, "A formal disavowal of the deed, and restoration of the four seamen to the ship from which they were taken." Second, the recall of Admiral Berkeley. Third, the "exclusion of all armed ships whatever from our waters." Finally, and most controversially, "an entire abolition of impressments from vessels under the flag of the United States."

Lord Grenville's "All Talents" ministry had given way to a Tory ministry headed by the Duke of Portland. (The change in regime had been prompted by the en masse resignations of Grenville's cabinet to protest George III's harsh policy toward Irish Catholics; Henry Adams described the new ministry as "a creature of royal bigotry trembling on the verge of insanity.") George Canning, the new foreign secretary, argued that Napoleon's unscrupulous conduct had released England from any obligation to comply with the strictures and traditions of international maritime law. The Tories were determined, above all, to preserve England's maritime and naval superiority. To this end, they were resolved to suppress the growth of American trade and take back the thousands of British seamen they knew to be employed in it.

Early in September 1807, a British fleet laid the city of Copenhagen under bombardment. Denmark was a neutral power, but threats of a French invasion left the British concerned that the Danish fleet would fall into Napoleon's hands. When the Crown Prince of Denmark refused an ultimatum to deliver the Danish navy into England's "custody," the British fleet opened fire. There was no formal declaration of war. The objective of the shelling was simply to demolish Copenhagen, one neighborhood at a time, until the Danes capitulated. After three days, more than two thousand civilians lay buried under the rubble of their homes, and the Danish fleet surrendered. Simultaneously, the Royal Navy swept what was left of the Danish merchant marine from the seas, adding about $10 million worth of property to English coffers.

When Jefferson and his advisers learned what had happened at Copenhagen, they realized that the *Leopard*'s attack on the *Chesapeake* was the least of their concerns. Copenhagen was better fortified than New York, Philadelphia, or Boston. If England was prepared to terrorize seaports in order to impose its will on neutral powers, Americans had much to fear.

Leading British newspapers applauded the *Leopard*'s attack on the *Chesapeake* and called for more of the same. The *Morning Post* charged that American policies were aimed at "striking at the very vitals of our commercial existence . . . humbling our naval greatness and disputing our supremacy," and added: "It will never be permitted to be said that the *Royal Sovereign* has struck her flag to an American cockboat." The editors called for war: "Three weeks blockade of the Delaware, the Chesapeake, and Boston Harbor would make our presumptuous rivals repent of their puerile conduct." *The Times*, reflecting angrily on the belligerent editorials in the American newspapers, remarked that "If the Government of the United States were to take its tone from what seems to be the habitual pettishness and impetuosity of myriads of adventurers of all nations who have inundated that country, it would be impossible to preserve peace with America for six months together."

A powerful combination of British interests stood to profit by a war with the United States. The capture and condemnation of American vessels in British prize courts subsidized a broad constituency, including every man in the Royal Navy from the admirals down to the humblest ordinary seamen, as well as the entire hierarchy of Admiralty judges and lawyers. Merchants and shipowners would gain by the suppression of a maritime rival. England's pro-war party, Monroe told Madison, was "composed of the ship owners, the navy, the East and West Indian merchants, and certain powerful characters of great consideration in the State. So powerful is this combination that it is most certain that nothing can be obtained of the government on any point but what may be extorted by necessity."

But the Portland ministry did not wish to add the United States to the ranks of England's enemies, at least not at that moment. Days after news of the *Chesapeake-Leopard* incident reached London, Foreign Minister Canning wrote Monroe to "assure you that his Majesty neither does nor has at any time maintained the pretension of a right to search ships of war in the national service of any State for deserters." In subsequent meetings, Canning indicated that the British government planned to recall Admiral Berkeley, as he had acted outside the scope of his authority. This fulfilled one of the American demands, though the foreign minister emphasized that the recall would have occurred in any case. But Canning dismissed as a non-starter Monroe's demand that England renounce its right to press seamen from American merchant ships. Search and impressment, he told Monroe, were rights that had "existed in their fullest force for ages previous to the establishment of the United States of America as an independent government." If Monroe's instructions required him to link settlement of the *Chesapeake-Leopard* affair to the broader subject of impressment, further negotiations were "for the present rendered unavailing."

As if to underline the point, on October 16, King George issued a proclamation "For recalling and prohibiting British seamen from serving foreign Princes and States," which commanded officers of the Royal Navy to "seize upon, take, and bring away" all native-born British seamen found aboard foreign merchant ships. On November 11, a new Order in Council required American merchant vessels to stop at a British seaport and apply for a British license before touching at any continental European port. Because all vessels sailing from a British port had been excluded from Europe by Napoleon's Berlin Decree, the effect of this new policy was to eliminate any safe route of commerce between America and Europe. Under any set of circumstances, American ships would be subject to capture and condemnation by either England or France. In defiance of every principle and tradition of international maritime law, neutral trade, in effect, had ceased to exist.

CONGRESS, RESPONDING TO THE PRESIDENT'S CALL, returned to Washington a month early, convening on October 26. For the first time, the House of Representatives met in its newly completed chamber in the south wing of the Capitol. It was the work of the English-born architect and engineer Benjamin Henry Latrobe, who had earlier collaborated with Jefferson in the abortive plan to build a dry dock capable of sheltering the entire navy. The new oval chamber was framed by fluted sandstone columns, dressed with sumptuous red drapes, and flooded with light from glass panels in the ceiling. Congressmen agreed that their new home was very handsome, but some complained of poor acoustics. In debates, members' voices were liable to be drowned in a sea of echoes.

The Capitol's great dome would not be completed for several decades. For the present, the House and Senate were housed in separate buildings, which were connected by a ramshackle boardwalk. The grounds were still overgrown with brambles and littered with construction materials. From a distance, one contemporary remarked, the complex appeared crumbing and dilapidated, like "the ruins of a castle." The neighborhood had changed very little since Jefferson's first inauguration in 1801. There were a few more boardinghouses, a few more stables, and a few new commercial establishments, including a saddlemaker, a bakery, a notary, a liquor store, and a couple of bookshops. According to Margaret Bayard Smith, the slope west of the Capitol was "covered with grass, shrubs and trees in their wild and uncultivated state." On this hill, close under the walls of the Capitol itself, hunters shot snipe and partridge. In Goose Creek, at the foot of Capitol Hill, John Foster of the British legation found fish so plentiful "that by shooting in among them one may get a good dish-full, for as many will leap on shore from fright probably as can be killed with the shot."

In the four months since the *Chesapeake-Leopard* incident, the public's zeal for war had cooled perceptibly. Jefferson's special message to the Congress on October 27 took a far more moderate tone than his public statements of the previous summer. He cited "injuries and depredations committed on our commerce and navigation upon the high seas for years past" and the "long and fruitless endeavors" of American diplomats to obtain redress. He recited American grievances, but in a weary, almost melancholy tone. In hinting that Congress might eventually be called upon to declare war, Jefferson's phrasing was so roundabout that he seemed embarrassed by his own suggestion: "The love of peace so much cherished in the bosoms of our citizens, which has so long guided the proceedings of their public councils and induced forbearance under so many wrongs, may not insure our continuance in the quiet pursuits of industry."

Fissures within the Republican ranks were more apparent than ever before. The northern, urban wing of the party cried out for federal assistance in fortifying the seaports. Referring to the Royal Navy's frequent incursions into Raritan Bay, Congressman Mumford of New York warned his colleagues that the great city was vulnerable. Whereas other major seaports were protected by "sandbars, shoals, and rocks in our harbors and rivers," New York was "only 27 miles from the sea, almost in a direct line, carrying up twenty-four feet of water and no obstruction. . . . Thus we are exposed Winter and Summer to the insult of the first marauder that chooses to lay us under contribution."

But to a hard core of "old Republicans," chiefly from the southern states, it would be folly to even attempt to defend the seaports against the mighty British navy. "When the enemy comes," said Nelson of Maryland, "let them take our towns, and let us retire into the country." Hadn't this strategy won the American Revolution? Randolph of Virginia predicted that any attempt to defend New York would end in a military debacle, as it had in 1776. Even if the harbor could be fortified against attack by sea, he said, the British could simply land an invasion force elsewhere on the coast and take the city from the north. Holland of North Carolina went further, declaring that the vulnerability of the northern seaports was a *good* thing, because it discouraged their citizens against agitating for war. "Our commercial towns are defenseless, and that is our only safety at present," he said. "I want to see not a single ship, or any preparation for war."

On one point all could agree. After the *Chesapeake*'s humiliating failure to defend herself, there should be no more money wasted on the frigates. Not all would go so far as Congressman Randolph, who was "reluctant to vote large sums for the support of our degraded and disgraced Navy"—but the future of America's oceangoing fleet appeared very much in doubt. *Constitution* arrived in Boston on October 14. She had been away for four years and two months, since Preble had taken her to the Mediterranean in 1803. With all the frigates safe in port, Jefferson issued an order relegating them to the status of receiving ships:

> The *Constitution* is to remain at Boston, having her men discharged . . . the *Chesapeake* to remain at Norfolk; and the sending of the *United States* frigate to New York is reserved for further consideration, inquiring in the meantime how early she could be ready to go. It is considered that in case of war these frigates would serve as receptacles for enlisting seamen, to fill the gunboats occasionally.

Leading authorities, including Edward Preble, told the president what he clearly wanted to hear: that gunboats and shore fortifications could put an end to the Royal Navy's bold incursions into American waters. On November 1, Jefferson told Virginia governor Cabell that Congress "will authorize a complete system of defensive works . . . [and] a considerable enlargement of the force in gunboats. A combination of these will, I think, enable us to defend the Chesapeake at its mouth, and save the vast line of preparation which the defence of all its interior waters would otherwise require." On November 8, Secretary Smith asked Congress to appropriate $850,000 for the construction of 188 additional gunboats, which would bring the total number of vessels in service to 257. He made no mention of the frigates. The Department of the Navy, as one contemporary wag put it, had become the Department of Gunboats.

In his diary, Massachusetts senator John Quincy Adams wrote that his colleagues had no real appetite for war. "I observe among the members great embarrassment, alarm, anxiety, and confusion of mind, but no preparation for any measure of vigor, and an obvious strong disposition to yield all that Great Britain may require, to preserve peace under a thin external show of dignity and bravery."

UNWILLING TO TAKE THE FATEFUL STEP of asking for a declaration of war, Jefferson fell back on the alternative of trade sanctions, or "peaceable coercion." The strategy was deeply woven into the fabric of American revolutionary folklore. Boycotts against imported British goods dated back to the 1760s, and the domestic substitutes, such as "homespun" clothing, had long been celebrated as symbols of patriotic self-denial. The power of trade sanctions as an instrument of U.S. foreign policy was a mainstay of Republican ideology. Writing to French foreign minister Talleyrand two years earlier, Ambassador Louis-Marie Turreau had said of Jefferson and Madison's philosophy: "To conquer without war is the first object of their politics."

Earlier in the year, Congress had passed a Non-Importation Act, but allowed the measure to lie dormant, awaiting the outcome of Monroe's negotiations. On December 14, over the objections of merchant interests, Jefferson signed an authorization placing the measure into effect. Most English imported goods—including clothing, silk, pictures, prints, silver, glassware, and various other household items—were banned from America's domestic market.

Now Jefferson sought to go further. He asked Congress to enact a policy of non-exportation, or embargo. By cutting off exports of American foodstuffs and raw materials, he reasoned, the British West Indian colonies would be starved, portions of the British domestic population would go hungry, and the British merchants who relied on the Americans to carry their goods to overseas markets would be bankrupted. The Senate passed the bill promptly, and after a three-day debate the House followed, by a vote of 82 to 44. On December 22, 1807, Jefferson signed the Embargo Act into law.

Upon taking the oath of office in 1801, Jefferson had promised "a wise and frugal Government, which shall restrain men from injuring one another, shall leave them otherwise free to regulate their own pursuits of industry and improvement, and shall not take from the mouth of labor the bread it has earned." Seven years later, he staked his presidency on a policy of unprecedented federal intrusion into the livelihoods of citizens living in America's maritime communities.

The embargo was a sweeping prohibition of all foreign trade. The law decreed that no American ship could depart for any "foreign port or place." The owners of any coastal trading vessel wishing to transport goods from one American port to another were required to post a bond equivalent to double the value of the ship and her cargo. The initial act was enacted hastily and with little debate, and it was soon obvious that enforcement would require draconian measures. Smuggling and other evasions were rampant. Vessels slipped out of port without clearances. Coastal traders were "accidentally" blown off course and forced to seek refuge in the West Indies or Canada. Some six hundred vessels were permitted to sail on the pretext that they were fetching home American property left abroad. Foreign ships brought goods to market and then illegally carried American cargoes out of port. In Vermont, whose economy depended to a great degree on agricultural exports to Canada, the citizens rose up in a general rebellion. Farmers built huge timber rafts on Lake Champlain, to carry enormous quantities of wheat, pork, beef, and potash. One of these rafts was said to be nearly half a mile long, and on it was erected a timber fortress defended by men with small arms and even cannon. They seemed willing to kill any federal agent who was brave or foolish enough to interfere. Jefferson issued a proclamation declaring the Lake Champlain region to be in a state of general insurrection.

With the longer and warmer days of spring, evasions of the embargo were prevalent all up and down the Atlantic seaboard. Jefferson pushed for increasingly severe enforcement measures. The embargo laws, he said, "have bidden agriculture, commerce, navigation to bow before that object, to be nothing when in competition with that." Jefferson knew, from the outset, that the American people's tolerance would not continue indefinitely. The nation had decided to "take the chance of one year by the embargo," he wrote, and if one year was the term fixed in Jefferson's mind, he was single-minded in his determination to make that year count.

Much of the enforcement responsibility fell to the Treasury Department, and therefore to Albert Gallatin. Though he had opposed the policy, the loyal Gallatin issued some 584 circulars to customs collectors and revenue officers stationed in the various seaports, generally urging more stringent enforcement and authorizing stronger measures. Most of the larger ships of the navy were inactive during the embargo, but a few vessels were deployed to patrol the American coast. Under Secretary Robert Smith's orders, Decatur and the *Chesapeake* got to sea on July 13, 1808, and patrolled the coastline between New York and Passamaquoddy Bay at the northern boundary of modern-day Maine. In early September, off the Maine coast, *Chesapeake* was outrun by two smugglers, prompting Decatur's remark that the frigate was an "uncommonly dull" sailor. Gunboats were deployed to lie to in the offing near the most rebellious harbors, with orders to "seize the Boats and vessels of American Citizens that may be found violating or attempting to violate the embargo Laws."

The American economy was devastated. Exports plunged from $108 million in 1807 to $22 million in 1808. Because the federal government was almost entirely dependent on customs revenues, the fiscal surplus vanished. This, in turn, deprived the nation of the resources needed to mobilize for war, just as Gallatin had warned. Farmers and lumbermen shared in the pain with merchants and seamen, as timber, wheat, tobacco, rice, and cotton piled up to storehouse rafters. Imported and manufactured goods sold at scarcity prices. Wages fell, or were not paid. Debtors were unable to manage their debts, and creditors took them to court or threw them into prison. Gangs of idle sailors loafed on the wharves. An Englishman who visited New York during the height of the embargo described the grim scene:

> The port indeed was full of ships, but they were dismantled and laid up; the decks were cleared, their hatches fastened down, and scarcely a sailor was to be found on board. Not a box, bale, cask, barrel, or package was to be seen on the wharves. Many of the counting houses were shut up, or advertised to be let; and the few solitary merchants, clerks, porters, and laborers that were to be seen were walking about with their hands in their pockets. The coffee houses were almost empty; the streets, near the water side, were almost deserted; the grass had begun to grow upon the wharves.

Opposition to the embargo gave new life to the Federalists, who took pleasure in reversing the spelling of the word—"O-grab-me"—and held Jefferson personally responsible for its economic privations. New England communities submitted petitions calling for an end to the embargo. Some of the testimonials employed the language of civil disobedience and revolution, language very much like that enshrined in the Declaration of Independence. An Essex County petition cited "a season of uncommon publick danger and alarm," and protested that the people had been "deprived of the exercise of invaluable rights." Armed mobs attacked federal collectors on the streets of Newburyport. Referring to Jefferson's interests in philosophy and the natural sciences, Federalists lampooned the president as an irresponsible dreamer whose fanciful theories had brought ruin to the American people. William Cullen Bryant, still in his adolescence, published a popular anti-Jefferson verse:

> *Go, wretch, resign the Presidential chair;*
> *Disclose thy secret measures, foul or fair;*
> *Go, search with curious eyes for horned frogs,*
> *Amid the wild wastes of Louisianan bogs,*
> *Or where the Ohio rolls its turbid stream*
> *Dig for huge bones, thy glory and thy theme.*

In August, Gallatin informed Jefferson that evasions could only be prevented if federal agents were invested with "arbitrary powers" that were "equally dangerous & odious." Enforcement would require a policy forbidding a single vessel in any port of the United States to move except with the "special permission of the Executive," to allow the collectors "the general power of seizing property anywhere," to remove and confiscate the rudder of any suspicious vessel, and to immunize the collectors against civil suits. The president replied that he was willing to authorize whatever measures were necessary to suppress the "sudden and rank growth of fraud and open opposition by force." Any vessel owned by any merchant suspected of prior violations could be seized. Entire communities were barred from sending a single vessel to sea. Justifying such a measure against Buckstown, in Maine's Penobscot Bay, Jefferson said that "a general disobedience to the laws in any place must have weight toward refusing to give them any facilities to evade." As for Nantucket: "Our opinion here is that that place has been so deeply concerned in smuggling, that if it [suffers food shortages] it is because it has illegally sent away what it ought to retain for its own consumption."

The question of the day was whether the people of England—and France—had suffered enough economic pain to force their governments to the negotiating table. Here the evidence was conflicting. Napoleon's response was a mingling of disgust and indifference. He remarked that "the United States have preferred to renounce commerce and the sea rather than recognize their slavery," and ordered the seizure of American ships on the pretext that they must be disguised English vessels. In Britain, the combined effects of non-importation and embargo, conjoined with Napoleon's Continental System, had severely distorted several important sectors of the economy. Market prices of many imported goods—timber, silk, cotton, flour, rice, flax, linseed—doubled or tripled. The coffee and sugar of the British West Indian colonies, which had once been carried to Continental markets by American vessels, glutted the storehouses of the Channel ports. British manufacturers predicted (cogently) that New England merchants would pour their capital into a domestic American manufacturing industry that would grow to rival England's.

But the embargo also benefited a number of powerful European interests, who would not have minded seeing it continued indefinitely. Farmers welcomed the high prices that attended the scarcity of imported foodstuffs. English merchants and shipowners were only too happy to see their American competitors yield the sea lanes, and their voices were strongly represented in Parliament. As one British writer later put it: "The late Jeffersonian Embargo was a Rod which produced no other sensation on the rough hide of John Bull, than the pleasurable one which arises from titillation. The poor Animal was delighted, and not suspecting that this philosophical experiment on his Hide was intended to produce pain, he regretted that weariness had ultimately compelled Mr. Jefferson to cease scratching."

Jefferson's special emissary to London, William Pinkney, had been instructed to offer an end to the embargo in exchange for a lifting of the offensive Orders in Council. Foreign Minister Canning's refusal of this offer, dated September 23, was inscribed in terms of heavy sarcasm: "[I]f it were possible to make any sacrifice for the repeal of the embargo," he wrote Pinkney, the British government "would gladly have facilitated its removal as a measure of inconvenient restriction upon the American people."

When this stinging rebuff arrived in Washington in late October, Jefferson bowed to the inevitable. The embargo had been an abject failure. He admitted as much in his 1808 annual message, forwarded to Congress on November 8. Though the president would have liked to report that the European powers had revoked "their unrighteous edicts," they had not done so. Accordingly, the "candid and liberal experiment" of the embargo had "failed." As to the question of what should be done next, Jefferson offered no direction; it "will rest with the wisdom of Congress to decide on the course best adapted to such a state of things . . . [and to] weigh and compare the painful alternatives out of which a choice is to be made."

THE REPUBLICANS WOULD PAY A PRICE in the 1808 elections. The huge Republican majority in Congress was secure, but the Federalist minority doubled its numbers in the House. In Massachusetts, Federalists came within a whisker of defeating the state's Republican governor, and won a controlling majority in the state legislature. In the presidential campaign, however, the unpopularity of the embargo was not enough to halt a third consecutive Republican landslide. Jefferson having declined to seek a third term, James Madison was elected fourth president of the United States, defeating Federalist Charles Pinckney by an electoral vote of 122 to 47. (Jefferson's vice president, George Clinton, polled 6 votes.)

In contrast to those of his predecessor, Madison's inaugural ceremonies had a distinct military flavor. At dawn on March 4, 1809, the deep baritone reverberations of the big shore guns at the Navy Yard rumbled through the capital. Calvary militia companies from Georgetown and Washington escorted the president-elect's carriage from his house on F Street down Pennsylvania Avenue to Capitol Hill, arriving at exactly noon. An estimated ten thousand people had gathered, easily the largest crowd ever seen in Washington. Stepping down from his carriage, Madison walked past nine companies of uniformed infantry militia in review. In the House chamber, Margaret Bayard Smith told a correspondent, "the sovereign people would not resign their privileges, and the high and low were promiscuously blended on the floor and in the galleries."

The *National Intelligencer* reported that Madison was "dressed in a full suit of cloth of American manufacture, made of the wool of Merinos raised in this country." As was his habit, he dressed all in black from his boots to his neck. He stood all of five feet five inches tall: a shy, wan, uncharismatic man, prone to hypochondria, with his long hair powdered and securely clubbed. Washington Irving, who attended the ceremony, described him as "but a withered little apple-John."

Carrying on the tradition begun by Jefferson, the new president delivered his inaugural address in a voice so soft and faint that the audience could barely hear a word of it. Mrs. Smith, seated near the rostrum, said that Madison was "extremely pale and trembled excessively when he first began to speak, but soon gained confidence and spoke audibly," but John Quincy Adams said definitively that "he could not be heard." There was not much to hear. The speech was moderate, equivocal, and laden with platitudes. At a moment of crisis, when the nation seemed poised on the brink of war, Madison offered barely a hint of the direction he intended to take.

An inaugural ball was hosted that evening at Long's Hotel. The *National Intelligencer* described it as "the most brilliant and crowded ever known in Washington," and John Quincy Adams did not entirely disagree: "The crowd was excessive, the heat oppressive, and the entertainment bad." The windows were thrown open to bring in the air, but the room remained stifling, and someone had the idea to smash the upper panes. Mrs. Smith and her husband stood on a bench with their backs against one of the walls, and "from this situation we had a view of the moving mass; for it was nothing else." Dolley Madison, wearing pearls and a garish turban, was "almost pressed to death, for everyone crowded round her, those behind pressing on those before, and peeping over their shoulders to have a peep of her, and those who were so fortunate as to get near enough to speak to her were happy indeed." The new first lady, seventeen years younger and two inches taller than the president, was "all dignity, grace, and affability." By contrast, her husband struck Mrs. Smith as "spiritless and exhausted."

While he [Madison] was standing by me I said, "I wish with all my heart I had a little bit of seat to offer you." "I wish so too," said he, with a most woe-begone face, and looking as if he could scarcely stand. The managers came up to ask him to stay to supper. He assented, and turning to me, [said] "but I would much rather be in bed."

Jefferson seemed "in high spirits and his countenance beamed with a benevolent joy." In Smith's version of their conversation, she told him: "You have now resigned a heavy burden," and he replied: "Yes indeed, and I am much happier at this moment than my friend."

The embargo had devastated Jefferson's plantations in Virginia, and he had recently learned that his personal financial situation was dire, with debts amounting to about $20,000. But he wore a brave face. "Never did a prisoner released from his chains feel such relief as I shall on shaking off the shackles of power," he wrote du Pont de Nemours on March 2, 1809. "Nature intended me for the tranquil pursuits of science by rendering them my supreme delight." A week after Madison's inauguration, Jefferson climbed into the saddle for the four-day ride to Monticello. He had traveled the same stretch of road at least fifty times before; this would be his last. During the seventeen years remaining in the balance of his long life, Jefferson would never again set foot in the capital.

OF THE NEW PRESIDENT, French consul Beaujour of Philadelphia remarked: "Mr. Madison is an intelligent man but irresolute, who will always see what ought to be done but will not dare do it. . . . He is a weak upstart who . . . will be the slave and not the master of events." The judgment was vicious, but there was a seed of truth in it. As the leading architect of the Constitution, Madison held distinct views concerning the scope of presidential powers and felt obligated to defer to Congress in major decisions of national policy. He did not possess Jefferson's status as an icon of the American Revolution, and had never mastered Jefferson's talent for floating above the factional strife within the Republican camp. The foreign policy crises of 1807–09 had left the Republicans more divided than ever before. A congressional caucus had chosen Madison as the Republican presidential candidate in 1808 (disappointing the other leading contender, James Monroe). Because the Republicans maintained a hammerlock on the electoral college, the decision had, in effect, elevated Madison to the presidency. Having placed him in office, House and Senate leaders were hardly in a mood to be steered by him: Madison had inherited an office with much-diminished powers.

No one expected the embargo to continue through the spring sailing season of 1809, but the question of what policy would replace it posed a conundrum. William Crawford of Georgia said that if Congress repealed the embargo, it was honor-bound to declare war; any other policy would be "mere whipping the devil round the stump." But there was not much enthusiasm for war, either in Congress or among the American people at large. To challenge "the powerful navy of Great Britain on the sea," said Congressman Alston of North Carolina, would bring "a loss of everything dear to the American character—a loss of our liberty and independence as a free people."

The nation was rudderless, unsettled, and unhappy, and its leaders eventually chose to procrastinate. At the outset of the Madison administration, the embargo was repealed and trade reinstated with all nations except England and France. When and if either belligerent power should act to withdraw its objectionable orders, the president was authorized to restore full trading rights with that nation, leaving the restrictions in place for the other. Though American merchant ships were technically not permitted to trade with either England or France, however, all knew that this restriction was unenforceable and would be widely disregarded. American merchantmen were essentially free to seek markets where they could find them, eluding capture or harassment as best they could.

During the embargo, none of the frigates except *Chesapeake* had seen oceangoing service. Early in 1809, a growing pro-navy faction among the Republicans joined with the Federalists to force a change in policy. The House passed a bill to increase naval enlistment from 1,440 to 2,000. In a surprise move, the Senate added an amendment to fit out, man, and deploy "all the frigates and other armed vessels of the United States." Treasury Secretary Gallatin decried the waste of an estimated $6 million at a time when the treasury had been impoverished by the embargo. To mobilize the navy without regard to national purpose, he said, would sacrifice "the Republican cause itself, and the people of the United States, to a system of favoritism, extravagance, parade, and folly." After a lengthy debate in the House—in which the pro- and anti-navalist arguments might as well have been lifted word for word from the debates of 1794, 1798, 1804, and so on—the offending provision was sent to a House-Senate committee. The Senate conferees stood firm, maintaining that the frigates were needed in service to "defend the gunboats and their operation," and to induce seamen to enlist in the navy, since few could be recruited to serve in the gunboats. In the end, the House agreed to a compromise. Four frigates, including *President* and *United States*, would be returned to active service.

After eight years as Treasury Secretary, Gallatin aspired to succeed Madison as Secretary of State, and Madison was willing to nominate him to the office. But Gallatin's enemies in Congress (including William Branch Giles, who wanted the office for himself, and Senator Samuel Smith, brother of Navy Secretary Robert Smith) rounded up enough votes to deny him confirmation, focusing on his foreign birth as a disqualifier. Instead, Robert Smith was nominated and confirmed as the new Secretary of State, and Gallatin remained at Treasury. This ended Smith's long reign as Secretary of the Navy. In his place Madison nominated Paul Hamilton, a little-known former governor of South Carolina. The navy's officers initially regarded the change with anxiety, but most soon took a liking to Hamilton. "You may rest assured of one fact," William Bainbridge told a colleague, after meeting Hamilton, "that we have an excellent secretary and that he is a most zealous friend to the navy."

Bainbridge took command of the USS *President* and got her underway from Hampton Roads in September 1809, with orders to patrol the mid-Atlantic coast. After an eight-day passage from the Virginia Capes, in which the *President* encountered constant headwinds and a three-day gale, she crept into New York Harbor, already in need of a refit. Anchored in the East River, not far from the Brooklyn Navy Yard in which she had been born a decade earlier, the *President*'s sails and rigging were thoroughly overhauled. Her hull received a new coat of paint and her decks a new layer of cork. She took on water and provisions sufficient for a long voyage. Sailing again on September 25, *President* patrolled the New England coast, harbored three days at Newport, and then stretched away to the south as far as Charleston. The big frigate, Bainbridge said, was "as fast a sailing Ship as Swims." The cruise to the south, he told John Rodgers, was a series of "Gales, Shoals, the Shores, rocks, Cape Hatteras . . . the Gulf Stream."

Returning to the Virginia Capes and anchoring in Lynnhaven Bay in late October, the frigate was buffeted by "a most furious snow storm accompanied with hail & rain . . . it blew a perfect storm; we parted one of our best cables about 12 o'clock and expected every moment to go ashore on a very dangerous shoal called the horse shoe." A sailor was lost overboard as he was climbing the rigging to the foretop—his freezing hands had not been able to grip the ratlines. In the *President*'s anchorage that night, one merchant brig was wrecked on the beach and another driven out to sea. Several others limped into the bay, dismasted.

The sailing season had emphatically come to a close, but Bainbridge was determined to force his crew into a state of high efficiency and readiness, and he hurried the *President* back into the offing. "I am growing old and heartily tired of the sea. My constitution is by no means as strong as it was," the thirty-five-year-old captain wrote David Porter, with whom he had shared the long captivity in Tripoli:

> But when I have a ship complete in every respect for action and service, I cannot bear the idea of lying in port. . . . As a strong proof of my declaration, I gave up double lanteens [lanterns] on the Norfolk station where I commanded, to come to sea at this season of the year, to harden and discipline my crew. I am the only ship that is now cruising or has been this winter. I have as fine a ship and as well officered as I could possibly wish, and if opportunity offers, I trust the result will be such as my countrymen would approve and as you, my dear Friend, would have no cause to blush.

Navigating as far south as the St. Mary's River, patrolling for illegal slave ships (the slave trade having been outlawed in 1807), the *President* sighted very few vessels of any sort, and her crew could not see "Sun, Moon, or Stars" for days on end. She chased a 22-gun British sloop of war, the *Squirrel*, out of American territorial waters. According to Midshipman Henry Gilliam, Bainbridge told the crew that if the *President* was obliged to go into action, "he would never surrender while life remained . . . [and vowed] never to strike but to sink alongside."

In June 1810, William Bainbridge was transferred to shore duty, and John Rodgers assumed command of a squadron that included both *President* (his flagship) and *Constitution*, commanded by Isaac Hull. Rodgers planned to take both frigates to Boston, where they would rendezvous with additional vessels and patrol American waters in force. Secretary Hamilton's orders emphasized that the disgrace of the *Chesapeake* must never be repeated:

> You, like every other patriotic American, have observed and deeply feel the injuries and insults heaped on our Country by the two great belligerents of Europe. . . . Amongst these stands most conspicuous the inhuman and dastardly attack on our Frigate the *Chesapeake*—an outrage which prostrated the flag of our Country. . . .
>
> What has been perpetrated may again be attempted. It is therefore our duty to be prepared and determined at every hazard, to vindicate the injured honour of our Navy, and revive the drooping Spirit of the Nation.

After these orders were read aloud to the officers and crews of both frigates, Midshipman Gilliam wrote his uncle to say that "you may expect to hear shortly of a little fighting."

But the *Constitution* was too slow to sail in company with the *President*. She was moving through the water like a barge, and Captain Hull knew why. Seven years had passed since her bottom had been sheathed in Paul Revere's copper, and she was due for a thorough cleaning. On July 26, in Hampton Roads, Hull arranged to have divers examine the frigate's bottom. They found enormous colonies of barnacles, mussels, oysters, and seaweed. To underscore the point, Hull arranged to have samples sent to Washington, where they must have arrived fairly ripe after a week-long journey in high summer. The *Constitution*, Hull told Secretary Hamilton, had "ten waggon loads of them on her bottom . . . you can have no doubts as to the cause of her not sailing."

In August, Hull took the *Constitution* up the Delaware river into fresh water, hoping that the saltwater shellfish hanging from the hull like "bunches of grapes" would perish and fall off. The mussels let go quickly, but the oysters were more stubborn. Two weeks of vigorous scouring with a custom-designed iron scraper were needed to restore the ship to a respectable condition.

NO ONE HELD OUT MUCH HOPE that the complicated diplomacy played out by Madison in 1809, 1810, and 1811 would secure American rights at sea. Hoping for an armistice in Europe, which would render most of the disputed points moot, many American leaders preferred to wait and watch. "While we can procrastinate the miseries of war," Congressman Williams of South Carolina said, "I am for procrastinating." Repeal of the embargo in 1809 had triggered a new boom in shipping and trade, and the nation's economy underwent a rapid recovery. Although the Non-Intercourse Act, which had replaced the embargo, technically prohibited trade with Britain, France, or France's allies, the shrewd Yankee merchants had no trouble evading these restrictions. Trade resumed with neutral ports in the Mediterranean, the Baltic, and Spanish America. Lord Wellington's troops in the Iberian Peninsula subsisted largely on American foodstuffs imported into Lisbon under special licenses granted by the British government. In 1809, the nation's registered tonnage employed in foreign trade leapt to 910,059 tons, a figure larger than any year prior to Jefferson's embargo. The nation was at peace, and prosperity was returning with pleasing speed. Why rock the boat?

A month after Madison took office, a new British minister, David

Erskine, signed a treaty providing for the suspension of both the American and British trade measures. But when the convention arrived in London, Foreign Secretary Canning repudiated it on the grounds that Erskine had exceeded his instructions. Again the prospect of war was debated in Washington, but as Gallatin observed privately, the nation was ill-prepared. "I will only observe that we are not so well prepared for resistance as we were one year ago," he wrote. "Then almost all our mercantile wealth was safe at home, our resources entire, and our finances sufficient to carry us through the first year of the contest." A year of embargo had left the treasury "exhausted," and a mobilization of forces would require heavy borrowing.

Another new British minister, Francis James Jackson, arrived in Washington in the fall of 1809 to succeed the chastened Erskine. His mission would be brief. After an exchange of letters with Secretary of State Robert Smith (Smith's letters were almost certainly ghost-written by Madison), the American government took exception to some of the language in his correspondence and refused any further contact with him. For a second time that year, a British ambassador was forced to withdraw from Washington.

France's bullying and plundering of neutral shipping was no less offensive than Britain's. On Napoleon's orders, American ships and cargoes were seized on negligible pretenses, or on none at all. When shipowners asked compensation, it was a foregone conclusion that they would be rebuffed, no matter how flagrantly they had been looted. Responding to the Non-Intercourse laws, Napoleon issued the Rambouillet Decree, by which American ships and cargoes in French-controlled ports were seized without warning or explanation. When news of the seizures arrived in Washington in May 1810, Madison remarked to Jefferson that "the late confiscations by Bonaparte comprise robbery, theft, and breach of trust, and exceed in turpitude any of his enormities not wasting human blood."

The Non-Intercourse Act had attempted to play England and France against each other by offering to restore trade with whichever power acted first to lift its offensive regulations. Now Congress adopted the mirror image of that policy. "Macon's Bill No. 2" permitted normal trade to resume with both England and France, but allowed the president to reimpose nonintercourse against either of the belligerent powers if and when the *other* accommodated American demands. Napoleon countered with a shrewd maneuver. In August 1810, the French foreign minister, the duc de Cadore, wrote a carefully worded letter vowing to withdraw the Continental Decrees on the condition that the United States "shall cause their rights to be respected by the English." Simultaneously, Napoleon issued a new decree imposing exorbitant tariffs on most products carried by American ships, which had the effect of continuing the previous restrictions in another guise. Madison, however, chose to interpret the "Cadore Letter" as satisfying the condition in Nathaniel Macon's bill, and ordered non-importation reasserted against England in February 1811. The editors of the British *Naval Chronicle* were surprised by this evidence of American pluck. "In North America, they, who ought daily to offer up thanksgivings for being a safe distance from the din of arms, seem madly ambitious of war, with a certain annihilation of their present enviable advantages!"

The British government, charging that the Cadore Letter had been a ruse and that Madison's policy favored France, refused any concessions. Anglo-American relations deteriorated. The American ambassador to the Court of St. James's was withdrawn, leaving only a lowly chargé d'affaires in London. The Royal Navy continued to maintain a powerful presence off the North American coast; impressments and violations of American territorial rights continued unabated. That summer, a new British ambassador, John Foster, arrived in Washington with a rigid set of instructions, leaving no doubt that British restrictions on neutral trade would remain in place. Positions hardened, resentments accumulated, and war seemed increasingly likely.

IN APRIL 1811, JOHN RODGERS took the USS *President* up the Chesapeake Bay to Annapolis, where she would harbor for a few weeks while the thirty-nine-year-old captain visited his family in Havre de Grace, Maryland. While in Havre de Grace, Rodgers received word that an English frigate, HMS *Guerrière*, had interdicted American shipping off New York and had impressed several American seamen into her crew. Rodgers raced back to Annapolis and ordered the *President* readied for sea. Sailing from the Capes of Virginia on May 14, she set a course for New York.

Two days later, shortly after noon, the lookout reported a sail in the east. The stranger hoisted unrecognizable signals; receiving no answer, she wore and ran south. The *President* made all sail in chase. The pursuit continued throughout the afternoon and into the early evening. In the failing light, Rodgers scrutinized the fleeing stranger through his telescope. He could see that she had hoisted her colors but could not make them out, and "although her appearance indicated she was a Frigate, I was unable to determine her actual force." As darkness fell, the two vessels were separated by just a mile and a half. Continuing the chase as best he could, Rodgers took care to maintain the weather gauge (the position to windward). At 8:15 p.m., *President* came to within about 100 yards of the stranger. Rodgers lifted his speaking trumpet and bellowed: "What ship is that?"

What followed was the familiar nocturnal game of nerves, in which each commander demanded to know the name of the unknown ship before giving the name of his own. When Preble had played it, as the *Constitution* entered Gibraltar Straits on a dark night in August 1803, it had nearly climaxed in an exchange of broadsides with the HMS *Maidstone*.

When Rodgers's hail came back, echoed verbatim, in plain English— "What ship is that?"—very little doubt remained that the stranger was a British man-of-war. "Having asked the first question," Rodgers later said, "and of course considering myself entitled by the common rules of politeness to the first answer, after a pause of fifteen or twenty seconds, I reiterated my first enquiry of 'What Ship is that?' "

Before Rodgers could lower his speaking trumpet, a gun was fired. All at once, both vessels opened a furious barrage of cannon and musket fire. The *President* was struck in the mainmast and foremast, and several of her shrouds and stays were cut to ribbons. In the intermittent light of the muzzle flashes, however, Rodgers could see that the other ship had a lower profile and a lighter broadside than the *President*. She was no frigate. Under the *President*'s heavy cannonading, the smaller vessel's main topsail yard came down, her colors were either hauled down or shot away, and most of her battery was silenced. Fifteen minutes after the first gun, Rodgers ordered his crew to cease fire.

With the wind freshening, the two commanders again tried to communicate, but neither could understand the other. The *President* wore, ran under the stranger's lee, and hove to at a safe distance to repair the modest damage she had sustained in her rigging. One of the crew, a boy, was slightly wounded.

At daybreak on May 17, the Americans finally had a good look at their opponent. She was a British 20-gun corvette, the *Lille Belt*, commonly called the *Little Belt*. The *President*, some distance to windward, ran down to the smaller vessel. As the United States and Britain were not at war, Rodgers offered to render whatever assistance the *President* could provide. The English captain, Arthur Bingham, sent word back that he "had on board all the necessary requisites to repair the damages, sufficiently to enable him to return to Halifax."

The *Little Belt* had suffered badly, with her hull pierced in several places between wind and water, her sails and rigging "cut to pieces," and her starboard pump destroyed. Nine of her men were killed and twenty-three wounded, several of them mortally. Captain Bingham's spirited refusal of assistance almost resulted in the loss of his ship. When a gale came up two days later, the sea worked into the *Little Belt* through a dozen different holes in her hull, and she nearly foundered.

In his official letter to the Navy Office, dispatched from New York, Rodgers reported categorically that the *Little Belt* had fired the first shot, but he also expressed regret at having fired upon "a vessel of her inferiour force," and lamented the loss of life among her crew. Any man with a "humane & generous heart," he said, would feel the same way. He asked that a court of inquiry examine his conduct. Secretary Hamilton's response, May 28, took the opposite tone. He was frankly triumphant. Ignoring the request for an inquiry, he ordered Rodgers to hurry the *President* back to sea, urging him to be prepared for "a trial much more serious than that to which you have been invited; for I am certain that the chastisement which you have very properly inflicted will cause you to be marked for British vengeance."

Not until the end of August did the requested court of inquiry take the testimony of Commodore Rodgers and his officers. Stephen Decatur sat as president. Twelve days and fifty witnesses later, the court released its report, which accepted as fact all of the particulars in Rodgers's account: that the engagement had begun with a single cannon shot from the *Little Belt*; that Rodgers had twice attempted to hail the English captain during the exchange, attempting to call a cease-fire; that the British were entirely responsible for the losses they had suffered.

Captain Bingham and his officers were equally adamant in maintaining that the *President* had fired the first shot, and the British inquiry confirmed that version of events. The *Naval Chronicle* made a great deal of the sworn statements of two seamen, recorded in Halifax a month after the engagement, who claimed to have served aboard the *President* during the action and subsequently deserted. One stated that the action had commenced when a gun in the American frigate's second division was fired by accident. His testimony, however, was discredited by his identification of the American lieutenant commanding the division as "Lieutenant Belling," a name that did not appear on the *President*'s muster rolls. It will never be known which vessel fired first.

The *President–Little Belt* affair prompted a new round of editorial fulminating on both sides of the Atlantic. "The blood of our murdered country-men must be revenged," declared the *Morning Courier* in London, choosing words that could have been taken verbatim from an American newspaper four years earlier. To the issue of which ship fired first, the *Gazette* asked: "[W]ho will put the veracity of an American captain in competition with that of an honorable British officer?" The Baltimore-based *Niles' Register* answered that Rodgers was a man "of known reputation and unsullied character, whose honor is as unimpeachable as his courage is unquestioned." Captain Bingham, on the other hand, was "an unknown impertinent fellow," whose testimony was "false and scandalous."

Most Americans seemed to share Secretary Hamilton's view that the rough handling of the *Little Belt* was a just comeuppance. Whether *President* or *Little Belt* had fired the first shot, said *Niles'*, was beside the point. The Royal Navy had invited the punishment by its own misconduct. "Will any man say that *Great Britain* would suffer *our* ships to hover on *her* coasts, impress *her* seamen, murder *her* subjects in the mouths of *her* harbors, and capture *her* ships as they enter or leave *her* ports? Certainly not."

AS THE FIRST SESSION of the Twelfth Congress opened in November 1811, the members sensed that their decisions would have long-lasting and historic consequences. "Never did the American Congress assemble under circumstances of greater interest and responsibility," said the *Boston Chronicle*. Madison's annual message, delivered to Capitol Hill on November 5, protested England's "war on our lawful commerce," and asked Congress to put the nation "into an armor and an attitude demanded by the crisis."

Congress had been transformed by the rise to prominence of a Republican faction known as the "War Hawks." Their leader was a thirty-five-year-old Kentuckian, Henry Clay, who was elected Speaker of the House on the first day of the session. The House Foreign Relations Committee, weighted with Clay's War Hawk allies, reported to the full House on November 29. The report recited grievances against both France and England, dwelling on violations of American maritime rights by the Royal Navy, including "the practice of forcing our mariners into the British navy, in violation of the rights of our flag, carried on with unabated rigor and severity." Resolutions called for filling the ranks of a 10,000-man army, mobilizing the militias, arming merchantmen, and returning the remaining vessels of the navy to active service. Congressman Peter Porter of New York told his colleagues that they should consider the resolutions as precursors to war: "Do not let us raise armies unless we intend to employ them."

Clay and his allies were young, charismatic, strong-willed, intellectually gifted, and well organized. In stirring, well-coordinated speeches, they made skillful use of the rhetoric and mythology of the American Revolution to press the case for a second war against England. They returned again and again to the same line of reasoning. The sole remaining alternative to war was submission to British domination. Submission would be tantamount to a surrender of American independence, betraying the sacrifices of the patriots of 1776. "We must now oppose further encroachments of Great Britain by war," argued Johnson of Kentucky, "or formally annul the Declaration of Independence." "If we submit," agreed Calhoun of South Carolina, "the independence of this nation is lost."

In deference to the naval power of Great Britain, many of the War Hawks argued that the United States should strike at Canada. Seizing Canadian territory, they said, would compensate America for its losses at sea, break the power of British-allied Indian tribes in the Northwest, and force England to the negotiating table. "We shall drive the British from our continent," said Felix Grundy of Tennessee; " . . . I am willing to receive the Canadas as adopted brethren." With an eye to invading Canada, a resolution was passed calling for a 250 percent increase in the authorized size of the permanent army, to 35,000 men.

If the main thrust of an American war effort was to be an invasion of Canada, it would leave little role for the navy. But there were voices among the War Hawks calling for a major naval mobilization. Chief among them was Langdon Cheves of South Carolina, chairman of the Naval Committee, who asked the House for the fantastic sum of $7.5 million to build ten new frigates and twelve 74-gun battleships. Holding the floor for two days in mid-January 1812, Cheves calculated that the United States had spent a cumulative total of $27.2 million on the U.S. Navy since the original "six frigates" bill in 1794, compared with cumulative expenditures of $37.5 million on the U.S. Army. Citing the Quasi War and the Tripolitan War, Cheves said that the navy had been the more "useful" and "honorable" of the two services. In response to objections that American naval forces would be trapped in port by a British blockade, Cheves replied (with impressive foresight) that for every American warship in port, three British warships of equal or greater force would be required to blockade her. Such a heavy strain on the Royal Navy would force the British to the negotiating table. "The God of Nature did not give to the United States a coast of two thousand miles in extent, not to be used."

The debate that followed Cheves's presentation dominated the House's agenda for almost ten full days, filling nearly 200 pages of small print in the *Annals of Congress*. It was the longest and in some ways the most interesting naval debate that had ever been held in Congress. Pro-navalists conjured up the old dread of a standing army and saluted the navy as "less dangerous to your civil institutions." Republican Samuel Mitchell of New York said the war against England should be fought on land and sea: "To employ an army alone would be to fight with one hand tied behind our back. To equip a naval force in aid of the other is to strike with both hands." Federalist Josiah Quincy mocked the strategy of attacking Canada to punish England's behavior at sea. "If you had a field to defend in Georgia," he said, "it would be very strange to put up a fence in Massachusetts. And yet, how does this differ from invading Canada for the purpose of defending our maritime rights?"

As in 1794, 1799, 1803, and every other year in which the question had been debated, the anti-navalists marshaled their traditional arguments, which had changed very little. A large European-style navy, said Samuel McKee of Kentucky, would mean the end of peace in America because it would establish "a class of society who are interested in creating and keeping up wars and contention. Officers in the army and navy are mere cyphers in society in times of peace, and are only respectable in time of war, when wealth and fame may await their exertions." The anti-navalists' favorite argument remained the same—that the navy was an unconscionable waste. The cost of a navy, said Adam Seybert of Pennsylvania, "far exceeds the profit which arises from the commerce which it is intended to protect." Reading from Navy Department reports, Seybert reviewed the total expenditures for maintenance and repairs on a single American frigate, the *Constitution*. He found that she had consumed, between 1800 and 1807, "the enormous sum of $302,582, or upwards of $43,000 per annum for seven years in succession." And what was the likely outcome of a naval war with Great Britain? *Constitution* and the other oceangoing vessels of the U.S. Navy would be swept up by the powerful English fleets. "Shall I be pardoned, sir," asked Seybert, "when I fear our vessels will only tend to swell the present catalog of the British navy?"

On January 10, Treasury Secretary Gallatin threw a hand grenade into the midst of this debate by announcing that a war mobilization would require a loan of $10 million, which in turn would require higher customs duties and new taxes on property. Opposition to internal taxes was written on every page of the Republican Party's history, and many Republicans, even those in the pro-war camp, flatly refused to vote for them. Gallatin's reminder of the fiscal limitations put Congress in a more parsimonious mood, and Cheves's naval program was defeated across the board, though a few of the votes were tantalizingly close. In the end, Congress voted only to fit out the frigates not currently in service, including the *Chesapeake* and *Constellation*, both in ordinary at the Washington Navy Yard.

AT THE START OF APRIL 1812, Congress approved a ninety-day embargo. This was not intended as a measure of economic coercion, like Jefferson's embargo. It was a prelude to a declaration of war, aimed at ensuring the American merchant fleet would be safe in port at the commencement of hostilities. Few merchants or shipowners seemed to take the prospect of war seriously, however, and the seaports were bustling as vessels were readied to sail before the embargo took effect on April 4. Freight costs leapt by 20 percent, seamen's wages doubled, and 140 ships sailed from New York alone. Insurance rates remained low. "We hear from all quarters that the people do not expect war," said Congressman Lowndes.

There was still hope that ongoing diplomatic efforts in Europe would bear fruit. In April and May, the nation's leaders expected dispatches to arrive from London in the brig *Hornet*, commanded by Master Commandant James Lawrence. Week after week went by, and there was no word of her. At last, on May 19, she arrived in New York Harbor. The news was not encouraging. Lord Castlereagh, the foreign secretary, in instructions to Ambassador John Foster dated April 10, had refused to withdraw the offending Orders in Council. Taking this letter as the last word of the British government, Madison prepared to ask the Congress for a declaration of war.

The president faced a dilemma: Should he ask for a declaration of war against Britain, France, or both? Napoleon's violations of American maritime rights had been no less grievous than England's, and it was clear that France, in spite of the soothing words in the Cadore Letter of the previous year, had no intention of relaxing the Continental System. Mailing copies of the *Hornet*'s dispatches to Jefferson at Monticello, Madison wrote in a covering note: "France has done nothing towards adjusting our differences with her . . . the business is become more than ever puzzling." The cabinet had considered a "triangular war," declared against each of the major belligerents simultaneously, but that option presented "a thousand difficulties." Though France was not capable of striking directly at the United States by either land or sea, a declared war between the United States and France would deny American privateers the use of French Channel ports, from which they could otherwise attack British shipping in that nation's home waters.

During a long speech in the House on May 29, John Randolph mocked the War Hawks for talking bravely of war while failing to prepare for it. "Go to war without money, without men, without a navy!" he cried—"Go to war when we have not the courage, while your lips utter war, to lay war taxes! When your whole courage is exhibited in passing Resolutions! The people will not believe it!" The long European war, said Randolph, was none of America's business: "It is a war unexampled in the history of mankind. A war, separated as we are from the theater of it by a wide ocean, from which it behooves us to stand aloof, to set our backs against the wall, and await the coming of the enemy, instead of rushing out at midnight in search of the disturbers of our rest, when a thousand daggers are pointed at our bosoms."

Randolph's objections rang true to an older generation of Americans, who had lived through the devastation of the Revolution. Most of the War Hawks were too young to remember the terror that fell over New York City in June 1776, when a gigantic British fleet appeared suddenly off Staten Island, or the way Washington's army of novices had been driven like a herd of cattle from Brooklyn, to Manhattan, to New Jersey, to Pennsylvania. They were too young to remember the long, ruinous occupations of New York, Philadelphia, Newport, Norfolk, and Charleston, or the quick work made by the British in sweeping the Continental Navy from the sea. Fear of a war's consequences rose in proportion to a community's proximity to the ocean. The citizens of Providence, Rhode Island, enacted resolutions against "this wild spirit of war." Amphibious assaults on the coast would "leave us with our houseless wives and children, amidst the smoking fragments of our habitations." "It is evident that under the circumstances of this country," the *Boston Centinel* editorialized on May 30, "a declaration of war would be in effect a license and booty offered by our government to the British fleet to scour our coasts—to sweep our remaining navigation from the ocean, to annihilate our commerce, and to drive the country, by a rapid declension, into that state of poverty and distress which attended the close of the revolutionary struggle."

In London, America's ninety-day embargo was taken as a prelude to a declaration of war. Admiralty orders were dispatched to Halifax and Newfoundland, alerting local naval commanders to the likelihood of hostilities and instructing them, should war be declared, "to attack, take or sink, burn or destroy, all ships or vessels belonging to the United States or to the citizens thereof." At the same time, however, influential British voices were urging that the government act to avert the war. The various trade sanctions aimed at England—Napoleon's Continental System, the American nonimportation measures, the new American embargo—were blamed for growing internal economic pressures. Unemployment in London and Manchester had doubled in two years. Unemployed textile workers in Nottingham rallied behind the radical leadership of a figure named Ned Ludd, and the "Luddites," as they came to be known, attacked wool and cotton mills and destroyed machinery that was thought to have displaced workers. The movement escalated into a large-scale revolt, requiring the deployment of more than ten thousand British troops. Petitions arrived at the Houses of Parliament, signed by industrial worker groups in Leicester, Birmingham, and Liverpool, asking that the Tory ministry of Spencer Percival repeal the offending Orders in Council.

On May 11, a deranged assassin shot and killed Prime Minister Percival as he entered the House of Commons. His successor, Lord Liverpool, favored a more pragmatic policy toward the Americans, and on June 12, Lord Castlereagh announced the repeal of the offending Orders in Council. Had the news been known immediately in Washington, the War of 1812, in all likelihood, would never have been declared. But the first transatlantic telegraph cable would not be laid until half a century later, and the time lags required for diplomatic communication ensured that the news did not reach the United States until several weeks after the fact.

Ignorant of the encouraging developments on the far side of the Atlantic, President Madison delivered his war message to Congress on June 1. Though the message occasionally veered into the Virginian's habitually dry, courtly prose, it also included a blunt indictment of the entire British policy, which he termed a "series of acts hostile to the United States as an independent and neutral nation." He cited incursions into American territorial waters, impressment of American seamen (a "crying enormity"), confiscations of American ships and property, paper blockades, and alleged incitements of Indians in the Northwest Territories. Reviewing at length the diplomacy surrounding the Orders in Council, Madison concluded that England's policy had little to do with waging war and everything to do with her desire to seize a "monopoly which she covets for her own commerce and navigation."

In the House, a war bill was introduced and debated behind closed doors. Protesting Federalists insisted that the doors be opened to the public; when outvoted, they boycotted the debate. The House took three days to declare war, by a vote of 79–49, with every Federalist and several Republicans voting against. Senate action was delayed by the question of whether the war should be limited to maritime operations, in the tradition of the Quasi War. Such a war could be carried on largely through privateers, requiring no government funding, and leave in Madison's hands the power to end the conflict at any time by executive order. Opponents of the proposal believed Canada to be Britain's Achilles' heel, and argued that an invasion of the north was the key to American victory.

The Senate turned back the "sea war only" bill by the narrowest possible margin: a tie vote, broken by the president pro tempore of the Senate. This allowed the declaration of war to come to a vote on June 18. It passed by a margin of 17–13. In the congressional tally, nearly 40 percent of the members, including every Federalist in each house, had voted in the negative. No other declaration of war has ever passed the U.S. Congress by such a narrow margin.

On the afternoon of June 19, after signing the declaration, Madison paid a visit to the modest two-story brick building, just west of the White House, that served as joint headquarters of the State, War, and Navy Departments. There he circulated among a crowd of officers, functionaries, clerks, and various other well-wishers. Treasury Comptroller Richard Rush, who took part in the festivities, remarked that the president conducted himself "in a manner worthy of a little commander-in-chief, with his little round hat and huge cockade."

CHAPTER TWELVE

"Many nations have gone to war in pure gayety of heart; but perhaps the United States were first to force themselves into a war they dreaded, in the hope that the war itself might create the spirit they lacked." Henry Adams's judgment on the War of 1812—that it was an "experiment of thrusting the country into war to inflame it, as crude ore might be thrown into a furnace"—finds support in a private letter written by James Madison himself, nine months into the conflict. Recalling the war debates, the president admitted that "it had become impossible to avoid or even delay war," even though "we were not prepared for it." It had been necessary to take the fateful plunge because "it was certain that effective preparations would not take place, whilst the question of war was undecided."

For a dozen years, the party in power had championed a policy of minimalism in the armed services, and the results were evident. The small clerical staffs of the War and Navy Departments were buried under mountains of paper—requisitions, warrants, appointments, promotions, and cruising orders. Weapons, uniforms, and provisions were in short supply. The army had seven thousand men enlisted in its ranks, but most were badly equipped and totally untrained. The coastline and the western frontier were unguarded. In New England, where the war was unpopular, virtually nothing was done to mobilize forces, even after the declaration of war. The best-defended American seaport was New York, where there were nine hundred men in uniform, and yet no one had much confidence that the city could withstand a determined attack. An officer told Treasury Secretary Gallatin that the New York troops were "raw & undisciplined, that no officer could risk his life & honour with them."

America's seagoing navy, gunboats excluded, consisted of nineteen vessels, sixteen of which were in service. Seven of the sixteen were frigates; the rest were sloops, brigs, and other unrated vessels. By comparison, the Royal Navy had more than 600 vessels in active service, with an additional 250 in port, either in process of construction or undergoing repairs. Of the British warships in service, about 175 were ships of the line, mounting at least 64 guns on two covered gun decks. Any one of these powerful vessels would overmatch the largest ship in the U.S. fleet. To be sure, the Royal Navy had global commitments, and the full brunt of British naval power would not fall all at once on the North American coast. But even the British North American Station, headquartered at Halifax, consisted of a battleship, nine frigates, and twenty-seven unrated warships. Adding the strength of nearby bases in Newfoundland, Jamaica, and the Leeward Islands, the Royal Navy had four battleships, twenty-three frigates, and seventy-one unrated vessels positioned in the Americas at the outset of the War of 1812, and reinforcements would begin arriving by September.

In January 1812, after eleven years of stony silence, retired ex-Presidents John Adams and Thomas Jefferson had renewed their correspondence. Their conversation ranged across a wide terrain, only occasionally touching on politics or current affairs; in the first year alone, they devoted more space to the theology of the American Indians than to any other subject. But their early letters also happened to coincide with the war crisis, and the two aging revolutionaries could hardly avoid the subject. Adams could not resist taking the Republicans to task for having squandered precious millions on a gigantic fleet of nearly worthless gunboats, while failing to reinforce the oceangoing navy. "I lament . . . the total Neglect and absolute Refusal of all maritime Protection and Defence," he lectured Jefferson in a letter dated June 28. "Money, Mariners, and Soldiers would be at the Public Service, if only a few Frigates had been ordered to be built. Without this our Union will be a brittle China Vase, a house of Ice, or a Palace of Glass. I am, Sir, with an affectionate Respect, yours."

The numerical superiority of the Royal Navy was demoralizing in itself, but to this was added an almost supernatural aura of invincibility. When the *Evening Star* in London declared that England would never yield "the proud preeminence which the blood and treasure of her sons have obtained for her among the nations, by a piece of striped bunting flying at the mastheads of a few fir-built frigates, manned by a handful of bastards and outlaws," most Americans would have agreed with the outlook, even while resenting the insult. President Madison, his cabinet heads, and congressional leaders dreaded the specter of a crushing naval defeat in the opening weeks of the war. Influential voices had argued that the entire American fleet should be kept safe in port for the duration of the conflict. Better to keep the ships out of harm's way, they reasoned, than to see them delivered into the hands of the enemy.

On learning of this intended strategy in February 1812, William Bainbridge felt "infinite regret and mortification." He and a colleague, Captain Charles Stewart, happened to be in Washington at the time, and called at the Navy Office to register their objections. Secretary Paul Hamilton confirmed that the frigates, in the event of war, would probably be ordered to New York, where they would be moored near the Narrows to function as fixed batteries. Appalled, the two commanders asked for and were granted an audience at the White House. They urged Madison to send the American frigates to sea. At the end of the meeting, according to Stewart, Madison announced that he was persuaded. "It is victories we want," said the president. "If you give us [victories] and lose your ships afterwards, they can be replaced by others."

But how should the frigates be deployed? Near the American coast or in distant waters? Should they cruise alone, or in squadrons? Should they seek engagements with the British cruisers? Should they protect American commerce or attack enemy commerce? These questions went to the heart of naval strategy, and Secretary Hamilton, a farmer by profession, was ill-suited to decide them. In late May, Hamilton asked two senior captains—John Rodgers (commanding *President*, in New York) and Stephen Decatur (commanding *United States*, in Norfolk)—to advise the department in choosing a deployment strategy that "will enable our little navy to annoy in the utmost extent the Trade of Gt Britain while it least exposes it to the immense naval force of that Government."

Both officers suggested that the frigates be deployed in commerce-raiding cruises far from American shores. Rodgers, apologizing for his barely intelligible handwriting, which he blamed on a lame finger, recommended that a squadron consisting of two or three of the fastest frigates in the American navy, supplemented with a sloop of war, be dispatched to cruise in the waters surrounding the British home islands. The existence of a strong squadron near Britain would, in Rodgers's view, force the Royal Navy to divert forces away from the American coast, opening the sea-lanes for the return of merchantmen and allowing privateers to sally out of port. Not surprisingly, Rodgers nominated himself as commodore, adding that "I may with propriety pledge myself to make the commerce of that arrogant nation feel its effects to the very quick." Decatur proposed that the frigates should be deployed singly or in pairs, laden with sufficient provisions for a long cruise, and "without giving . . . any specific instructions as to place of cruising, but to rely on the enterprise of the officers." He reasoned that one or two frigates, in preference to a large squadron, would not be easily detected by the British, would cover large distances more quickly, and could attack British convoys. On the other hand, if one or two frigates were unfortunate enough to sail into the midst of a larger British squadron and be captured, "we would not have to regret the whole of our marine crushed at one blow."

Disagreements within Madison's cabinet added another layer of complexity to the debate. Gallatin was anxious about the fate of American merchant vessels caught at sea when war was declared. There were several hundred such vessels thought to be inbound to American ports, with an aggregate value (Gallatin estimated) of between $1 million and $1.5 million per week in the first four weeks of the war. With his eye on the bottom line, the Treasury Secretary wanted the American frigates deployed to guard the sea-lanes near the major American ports until these important assets were safely home.

Hamilton hesitated. Rodgers's and Decatur's letters sat on his desk for two weeks. In the meantime, Madison and his cabinet decided to concentrate the entire navy at New York, under the command of Commodore Rodgers, who was now, at age forty, the senior officer in active sea service. New York was chosen as the point of rendezvous because it was the most securely defended of the major seaports, it was centrally located on the coast, and it was the port to which the largest number of American merchantmen would be returning in the first weeks of the war. Decatur, with the *United States*, the *Congress*, and the brig *Argus*, sailed from Norfolk on June 16, reaching Sandy Hook one day after the declaration of war. Decatur and Rodgers, with *President* and the fine sloop of war *Hornet*, rendezvoused and combined forces.

Both officers were eager to sail immediately. Rodgers hoped to strike a hard blow against local British forces, "to cripple & reduce their force *in detail*," before reinforcements could be deployed to the western Atlantic. The commodore had also learned that a giant convoy of enemy merchantmen, reportedly consisting of 110 sail with an aggregate value of some £12 million, was due to sail from Jamaica for England. It is fair to assume that Rodgers and every other man in the squadron was salivating at the thought of the prize money to be won in a surprise attack on this convoy. But Rodgers was still without orders from Washington, and therefore obliged to wait. The situation was exasperating.

On June 21, three days after the declaration of war, Gallatin complained to the president that Secretary Hamilton still had not sent the needed cruising orders. Those orders, he wrote, "ought to have been sent yesterday, and . . . at all events not one day longer ought to be lost." After a hurried cabinet meeting on Monday, June 22, orders were at last dispatched to New York by an express rider. Rodgers was ordered to divide his force into two squadrons, to cruise in the offing near New York and Norfolk, respectively. The chief objective, reflecting Gallatin's influence, was to "afford to our returning commerce all possible protection—nationally & individually. The safe return of our commercial vessels is obviously of the highest importance."

These orders were never received. Commodore Rodgers and his five-ship squadron sailed from New York the day before they were written. It was not the first time an American commander had sailed without orders, nor would it be the last. The commodore's decision bordered on insubordination, but it also revealed boldness, initiative, and a keenness to be at sea. Rodgers grasped what Hamilton may have only dimly understood—that every hour lost to dithering gave the enemy another hour to react to the American declaration of war.

On the afternoon of the twenty-second, in the offing south of Long Island, the squadron fell in with an American merchant brig inbound to New York from Madeira. Her master told Commodore Rodgers he had been boarded, one day earlier, by the British frigate *Belvidera*. The squadron continued on to the east before gentle westerly breezes.

Shortly after first light the next morning, 100 miles southeast of Nantucket Shoal, the *President*'s lookout sighted a "large Sail" to the northeast, and Rodgers made the signal for a general chase. The stranger hoisted unintelligible signals, and when they were not answered by the Americans, she tacked and made sail to windward. The wind having veered into the north, the American vessels were obliged to sail close-hauled in light breezes, frequently wetting their sails to make them hold the wind better. By a quarter past seven, the stranger was hull-up on the northeast horizon. Rodgers did not doubt she was the *Belvidera*.

The *President* had a well-earned reputation as a fast ship, and she gained rapidly on the chase. She also outsailed the *United States*, the *Congress*, and the rest of the American squadron, which fell behind to leeward. At eleven, the *President* cleared for action. Soon afterward, the *Belvidera* hoisted British colors.

In midafternoon, the breeze subsided to a near calm. The *Belvidera* was near enough for Rodgers to observe her closely through his telescope, but just beyond the extreme range of *President*'s 24-pounder long guns. She was rated as a 36-gun frigate, though she mounted 42. She was significantly smaller and lighter than the *President*. Her captain, Richard Byron, had not yet received word of the American declaration of war, but he had no doubt of the Americans' hostile intentions. As *Belvidera* coasted along with bare steerageway, just out of range of her pursuer, Byron calmly sent the hands to dinner. There was no reason they should fight on empty stomachs.

The first shot of the War of 1812 was fired at 4:20 p.m. on June 23. The *President* having gradually closed to within long range of the *Belvidera*, Commodore Rodgers picked up a slow-match and touched it to the primer of one of the *President*'s bow-mounted chase guns. Before the ball had even reached the British ship, *Belvidera*'s four stern chasers—two long 18-pounders and two 32-pounder carronades—responded. The range diminished as the American ship overtook her adversary. The *President*'s early volleys were well directed. Shots struck the *Belvidera*'s rudder-coat, crashed into Captain Byron's cabin, and dented the muzzle of one of the enemy's larboard chase guns. A British seaman was killed and several other men, including the armorer and the carpenter, were severely wounded.

To win the engagement, *President* needed only to detain the *Belvidera* long enough to allow the rest of the American squadron to sail into range. In that case, Captain Byron would probably be forced to surrender. But at 4:30 p.m, the *President* suffered a devastating accident. One of the chase guns on her main deck burst, tearing a gaping hole in the forecastle and killing or wounding sixteen men. It was a horrific scene, with bodies and parts of bodies strewn along the deck. Rodgers himself was among the casualties—one of his legs was bloodied and broken. The *President*'s larboard guns fell silent while the crew removed the dead and wounded and heaved new weapons into position.

The wounded Rodgers ordered the *President* to yaw to larboard, a maneuver that brought her full starboard broadside into action. He hoped that the concentrated fire of the flagship's starboard guns would knock away one of *Belvidera*'s masts or spars, preventing her escape. There would be no such luck. The British frigate made sail and was soon out of range of the American guns. At sundown, the *Belvidera*'s crew lightened her by cutting away two small bower anchors, throwing two boats over the side, and dumping 14 tons of fresh water into the sea. They knotted and spliced her damaged rigging and repaired her injured main topmast. After nightfall, the *Belvidera* altered her course to the east, unseen by the Americans. By dawn on the twenty-fourth, she was out of danger. She reached Halifax on July 1, and notified the British station chief, Vice-Admiral Herbert Sawyer, that hostilities had commenced.

The damage sustained by the *President* was severe, but not severe enough to induce Rodgers to return to port. The Jamaica convoy remained his main objective. For three days, the American squadron lay to as the flagship licked her wounds and the commodore allowed his fractured leg to be set by the surgeon. Two midshipmen and a marine who had been killed in the action were buried at sea with the customary honors. On June 26, the squadron set sail to the northeast to hunt the convoy.

AT THE OUTSET OF WAR, the Washington Navy Yard was the best-supplied naval shipyard in the country, but its stores were rapidly depleted as requests for powder, armament, and supplies poured in from naval stations to the north and south. On July 9, the commandant, Thomas Tingey, told the Navy Office that the yard did not have a single 18-pounder or 24-pounder cannon ball, and only ten barrels of gunpowder left in the magazine. Softwood timbers for masts and spars were scarce. A shipment of good black spruce logs had arrived from Maine, but several of the longest, including a bowsprit originally intended for the *Constellation*, had been finagled by Captain Isaac Hull for the repairs to the *Constitution*. *Constellation* was therefore obliged to remain moored in the Eastern Branch until new timbers could be brought up the river.

Isaac Hull had been bred to the sea. Born in Derby, Connecticut, he had first shipped out as a common sailor aboard a merchantman at the age of fourteen. He was "rather short and thick-set, with a countenance deeply bronzed by long exposure to sun and weather, he having gone to sea when a boy." He was a man "of plain, unassuming manners, and rather silent than loquacious." Hull had entered the service as sixth lieutenant aboard the ship he now commanded, on her maiden cruise in 1798. Among the enlisted men, he was perhaps the most popular captain in the service. He was also, perhaps, the greatest all-round seaman in the navy, with a genius for ship-handling and navigation that would serve him well in the weeks to come.

In the spring, *Constitution*'s rigging had been almost entirely replaced, her hull recaulked, her masts stripped and partly replaced, her planking replaced, her lower decks thoroughly washed, her ballast rinsed and reseated. She was rigged with new sky poles and a split dolphin striker, allowing her to carry more sail than ever before. At first it was thought that the frigate's bottom might need to be re-coppered, but when she was hove down, a journal entry noted: "bottom better than was Expected." After almost a decade in service, Paul Revere's copper was mostly sound, needing only some local patching along the centerline and starboard side. The officer who oversaw these operations at the Washington Navy Yard was Nathaniel "Jumping Billy" Haraden, who had served under Commodore Preble in the Third Mediterranean Squadron as sailing master of the *Constitution*, and knew the ship as well as any man in the service. During the refitting operations, Secretary Hamilton toured the ship several times. It was the most extensive overhaul the *Constitution* had ever received in her fifteen-year career, and she began the War of 1812 in exceptional condition.

On June 19, as the newly refitted frigate worked her way down the Potomac, the declaration of war was read out to the crew, who answered with three cheers. The *Constitution* sailed up the bay to Annapolis, where she remained at anchor just off the town for two weeks, taking on additional men and equipment and a new battery of 32-pounder carronades. From the moment the new hands came aboard the ship, they drilled constantly at the great guns and small arms. Cannon crews practiced their marksmanship every day by firing live charges at hogsheads anchored several hundred yards away from the ship. The targets were smashed to splinters, and the reverberations of the guns were heard for miles across Chesapeake Bay. "[T]he Crew you will readily conceive, must yet be unacquainted with a Ship of War, as many of them have but lately joined us and never were in an armed Ship before," Hull told Hamilton. "We are doing all that we can to make them acquainted with the duty, and in a few days we shall have nothing to fear from any single deck Ship."

Hull's orders required him to "use the utmost dispatch to reach New York," where the *Constitution* would be attached to Commodore Rodgers's squadron. Secretary Hamilton wrote Hull again on July 3, adding that in the event *Constitution* should fall in with a British cruiser during the passage to New York, "you will be guided in your proceeding by your own judgment, bearing in mind, however, that you are not, voluntarily, to encounter a force superior to your own."

Constitution sailed from Annapolis with the morning tide on July 5. She took a week to work her way down the Chesapeake Bay, during which time the crew continued to drill continuously. On the twelfth, she cleared the Virginia Capes and put to sea.

Light headwinds and a current setting to the southward made for slow sailing. For three days, *Constitution* crept along the coasts of Maryland and Delaware. There was not a single sail visible on the horizon until the afternoon of the fifteenth, when the frigate fell in with a merchant brig inbound to Baltimore and gave her the news that war was declared. The same day, Hull ordered the newly mounted carronades fired five times with double charges and double shot; the experiment proved the guns "to stand very well."

On July 17, when the frigate was just off Barnegat and Egg Harbor on the New Jersey coast (near the modern-day location of Atlantic City), the lookout caught sight of four topsails in the north. Their hulls were still down over the horizon, but judging by the size of their sails they were "apparently Ships of War." An hour later, the lookout sighted a fifth sail further out to sea. Five was the exact number of vessels in Rodgers's squadron, and since Hull had expected to find Rodgers in the waters off nearby Sandy Hook, he naturally assumed that the strangers were friendly. At 4:00 p.m., Hull ordered the *Constitution* to tack and stand to the east, toward the nearest sail. He hoped to get within night-signaling range in order to confirm that the strangers were Americans.

At sunset, the wind veered around into the south, which brought the *Constitution* to windward of the other vessels. Shortly thereafter, as a precaution, the drummer tapped out the call to quarters and the crew went to their battle stations. As darkness fell, *Constitution* drew steadily closer to the nearest of the strangers, which could now be discerned as a frigate. At 10:00 p.m., Hull judged that he was within night-signaling range—about six to eight miles—and the lanterns were hoisted. None of the strangers, not even the nearest frigate, set a signal in response. Hull went forward into the forecastle to have a better look. It was an unusual place for a captain, and according to Able Seaman Moses Smith, the foremast jacks "clustered around him respectfully." Hull was beginning to sense that all was not right. At eleven o'clock, when the signals had remained unanswered for an hour, he gave the order to haul the sheets and make all sail to windward.

That night, the officers and enlisted men remained at their battle stations. Smith, who later published a memoir entitled *Naval Scenes in the Last War* (1846), recalled that "every man on board the *Constitution* was wide awake. There was no sneaking from duty in any part of the brave old ship." He was assigned to act as sponger for gun No. 1, positioned forward on the larboard side of the gun deck, and tried to catch a few hours of sleep by curling up on deck, his ramrod and sheepskin sponger clutched in his hands.

At the first light of dawn, the officers and crew of the *Constitution* took in an appalling sight. Two frigates were positioned just under the *Constitution*'s lee, almost within cannon-shot range. A third was directly astern, about five or six miles away. A few miles further astern, hull-down from the deck but hull-up from the masthead, lay a fourth frigate, a battleship, a brig, and a schooner. All were flying British colors.

The frigates were the *Shannon*, *Belvidera*, *Aeolus*, and *Guerrière*; the battleship was the 64-gun *Africa*; and the squadron commodore was Captain

Philip B. V. Broke of the *Shannon*. Having sailed from Halifax the same day the *Constitution* had sailed from Annapolis, Broke's squadron had swept down the American coast, taking every vessel unlucky enough to be caught in its path. On July 16, it had pounced on the 14-gun brig *Nautilus*, a vessel that had seen extensive duty as part of Edward Preble's Third Mediterranean Squadron in 1803–04.

It was Hull's duty to run from such an overwhelming force, and he ordered the hands to make all sail. But as the sun rose, the breeze abruptly vanished, and it fell a dead calm. The *Constitution* wallowed helplessly on the swell, her sails hanging limp from the yards, and would not answer her helm at all. The ship, wrote First Lieutenant Charles Morris, was "entirely becalmed and unmanageable." With no steerageway, the *Constitution*'s bow began to fall off toward the two frigates to larboard. In so doing, she was in danger of rotating into a position in which she would be vulnerable to a raking broadside.

Shortly after sunrise, one of the British frigates, the *Shannon*, tried a few long-ranging cannon shots. One of the high-arching balls actually passed *over* the *Constitution* and splashed down into the sea to windward—but the range, said Lieutenant Morris, was "too great for accuracy, and their shot did not strike our ship."

There was only one hope of saving the *Constitution*, and that was to lower the boats and take the ship under tow. The first and second cutters were hoisted out. Hawsers were secured to the bowsprit, and a long scope was paid out to the boats, in order to make the angle of the towline nearly horizontal. Pulling hard and in unison, the oarsmen gradually brought the *Constitution*'s head around to the southward. This kept her larboard broadside facing the enemy, who remained just beyond cannon-shot range. With the oarsmen still pulling, the great ship began moving through the sea, at a speed of perhaps half a knot, toward Delaware Bay.

The towing brought the pursuers astern of the *Constitution*, where her main battery would not bear. The frigate had not mounted stern chasers, and Hull now ordered a 24-pounder long gun—a weapon weighing more than 2 tons—hoisted up from the gun deck. An 18-pounder was run aft along the gangway from the forecastle. The carpenters were summoned to cut away the *Constitution*'s taffrail, to allow the guns to fire over the stern. Below, another set of men invaded the sanctity of the captain's cabin in order to run two more 24-pounders through the stern windows.

At seven in the morning, Hull tried a ranging shot from one of the newly mounted guns, with the barrel at maximum elevation. The captain took the match in his own hand to fire the first shot. "I stood within a few feet of Hull at the time," Moses Smith remembered. "He clapped the fire to my gun, No. 1, and such a barking sound as sounded over the sea! It was worth hearing. No sooner had our iron dog opened his mouth in this manner, than the whole enemy opened the whole of theirs. Every one of the ships fired directly toward us. Those nearest kept up their firing for some time; but of course not a shot reached us then, at the distance we were."

Not long after the *Constitution*'s boats began towing ahead, the British imitated the maneuver. Captain Byron of the *Belvidera* ordered his ship's boats hoisted out. Soon afterward, Commodore Broke made a signal ordering his consorts to send all of their boats to tow the *Shannon*. With several boats towing her in unison, wrote Hull, the *Shannon* "came up very fast."

At that moment, about eight o'clock in the morning, the officers and crew of the *Constitution* shared a strong conviction that the ship was doomed. If *Shannon* was brought into cannon-shot range, she could probably detain the *Constitution* long enough to allow the other British warships to close the distance. Hull wrote: "It soon appeared that we must be taken, and that our Escape was impossible." Morris said that "it was supposed that the first steady breeze would bring up such a force as would render resistance of no avail; and our situation seemed hopeless." In his journal, Surgeon Amos Evans spoke of an "inexpressible anxiety" as the men had "given over all expectations of making our escape." Midshipman Henry Gilliam, striving for literary effect, told his uncle that the situation was "pregnant with the most fatal consequences to our gallant ship."

Hull resolved to go down fighting. He told Lieutenant Morris he intended to lay the *Constitution* broadside to the pursuing squadron and trade cannon fire until the frigate was sunk. Moses Smith, speaking for the enlisted men, said: "we resolved to save ourselves from capture, or sink in the conflict . . . we were determined to a man that [the flag] should never go down but with the ship. Captain Hull saw and felt this patriotic feeling, and cherished it to the utmost."

It was at this moment that Lieutenant Morris suggested an unconventional tactic. The *Constitution* could attempt to "kedge" ahead. Kedging (or "warping") was accomplished by running an anchor and long anchor cable ahead in a boat. The anchor was dropped and the cable hauled in by the capstan, thus moving the ship up to the position of the anchor. If two boats with two anchors worked simultaneously, the ship could advance without interruption. Kedging was generally used only in harbors or other inland waterways as a means of maneuvering a large ship through a crowded anchorage, a channel, or a tideway. To kedge at sea was virtually unheard of, because it could only be done in shallow water. But soundings had revealed that the depth of water was only 24 fathoms. With a long enough anchor cable, it might be possible. Why not try it? Hull agreed.

Three or four hundred fathoms of spare rope—"all the spare rigging out of the boatswain's store-room"—were spliced or bent to the anchor cables. In this manner the *Constitution*'s seamen constructed two cables, each nearly a mile long. Two small kedge anchors were lowered into the launch and the first cutter. The first boat dropped a kedge about half a mile ahead, and the men at the frigate's capstan began hauling in the cable. The *Constitution* advanced at more than a knot of speed, and (Hull reported) "we began to gain ahead of the Enemy."

The British soon recognized the "Yankee trick" and imitated it. The *Shannon* kedged ahead smartly, and at one point seemed to gain on the *Constitution*. The *Belvidera* also employed the procedure. But the *Constitution* had an important advantage. If the pursuing frigates sent their boats too far ahead, whether kedging or towing, they came within dangerous range of the *Constitution*'s stern chasers. The British ships hung back, just out of range, waiting for a breeze that would allow them to resume the chase under sail.

At 9:00 a.m., helped by a fleeting breeze, the *Belvidera* came up on the *Constitution*'s lee beam and fired several ranging shots. All the balls fell just short, serving only (said Lieutenant Morris) "to enliven our men and excite their jocular comments." The *Constitution*'s stern guns fired in response. While Dr. Evans watched through a telescope, a cluster of men standing in the British frigate's forecastle broke apart, dodging right and left, as one of the *Constitution*'s high-arching shots fell into "the midst of the group." From that range, however, the force of the shot was spent, and it did no damage.

The breeze again died off entirely, and the crew of the *Constitution* continued their laborious towing and kedging operations. The late morning sun beat down; the oppressive high summer heat and humidity closed around them; and a sickening, oily swell passed under the ship.

The men sweated but they could not rest. The sails, still hanging lifelessly from the masts and yards, were manipulated to take advantage of every waft of air, no matter how feeble. The occasional "cat's paw" of wind required that the boats—leading ahead to either drop the kedge anchors or tow the ship—be hoisted aboard while the *Constitution* was moving through the water. The exercise required flawless timing. Lieutenant Morris later explained that the boats were not hoisted all the way on deck, but rather suspended "to the spars in the chains by temporary tackles, with their crews in them, ready to act again at a moment's notice."

Between ten and noon, Hull gave the order to dump the *Constitution*'s fresh water. As the men worked the chain pumps, some 2,335 gallons poured over the deck and shot through the scuppers. This raised the *Constitution* by approximately one inch. It was a small margin, but even a small margin might prove decisive.

As the long, languid summer afternoon wore on, the officers and seamen of the *Constitution* were pushed to the point of exhaustion. Both watches were called up to work the ship, man the capstan bars, serve the cannon, or take the oars. Men took any opportunity to catch a wink of sleep, sometimes curling up at their battle stations, only to be roused by the call of the bosun's pipe. At sunset, the British squadron was still in determined pursuit, just beyond cannon-shot range. The breeze remained weak and variable until eleven that evening, when a light but steady breeze sprang up from the south. *Constitution* and her pursuers set all sail.

At dawn on July 19, two British frigates were almost on top of the *Constitution*. The *Belvidera* posed the greatest threat. She was abeam of the *Constitution*, to leeward. On *Constitution*'s weather quarter was the *Aeolus*. The three ships were close-hauled to a gentle breeze, still with only bare steerageway. *Constitution* tacked and passed well within range of the *Aeolus*, but the British ship did not fire, possibly because her captain feared that the recoil of the guns would impair the speed of his ship. It was an intense moment. A negligible shift in wind or current could decide the outcome of the race.

Having been freshly overhauled, *Constitution* was surprisingly swift, and she gradually led ahead of her pursuers. As the morning wore on, the breeze grew "tolerably steady, though still light." Hull ordered that the sails be wetted in order to make them hold the wind better. This required heavy buckets of seawater to be hoisted up to the highest parts of the rigging, and more backbreaking work for the exhausted crew.

At nine in the morning, a new sail was seen inshore, to windward. She appeared to be an American merchantman. With hopes of luring the unidentified vessel into a trap, the *Belvidera* hoisted the Stars and Stripes. Hull countered by hoisting British colors. The American merchantman hauled her wind, turned stern-to, and escaped safely to one of the ports along the New Jersey shore.

"At noon we had the wind abeam and as it gradually freshened, we began to leave our fleet pursuer," said Lieutenant Morris. The *Constitution* tore through the sea with gratifying speed, leaving a long, foaming wake behind her. At 2:00 p.m., the log registered a speed of 12.5 knots. "Our hopes began to overcome apprehension, and cheerfulness was more apparent among us."

By six thirty that evening, a heavy rain squall approached from windward. The men raced aloft to take in the studding sails and royals before it hit. As the squall enveloped the ship, the men took in the skysails, topgallant sails, and flying jib, and the mizzen topsail and spanker were reefed. Just as quickly, as the violence of the squall passed over and obscured the *Constitution* from the enemy's view, Hull ordered the men to make all sail and sheet home quickly. The *Constitution* cracked on to windward, extending her lead by about a mile.

The wind moderated during the night. Although the men again slept at their battle stations, they rested easier than they had the night before. At daylight on July 20, it was clear that the *Constitution* was out of danger. The British hauled off to the northeast, giving up the pursuit.

The three-day chase had been one of the longest and most desperate in the entire history of sail. By saving the *Constitution*, Hull had averted a capture that might have dealt a devastating blow to the nation's confidence and morale at the outset of the war. Though it was not a victory, the triumphant escape against heavy odds had revealed that the Royal Navy had no inherent advantage over the Americans in the mastery of seamanship. Afterward, the English officers conceded that the handling of the American frigate had been "elegant."

The *Constitution* had escaped capture after her officers and crew despaired of saving her. The life lesson, as Lieutenant Morris later put it in his *Autobiography*, was to keep faith in "the advantages to be expected from perseverance . . . so long as *any* chance for success may remain."

ON JULY 25, AS THE *CONSTITUTION* beat into a headwind toward Boston Light, Dr. Evans admired the "very romantic and picturesque" hills rising up from the capes and islands of Massachusetts Bay. Even from far down the fairway, the men on deck could see the steeples of several Boston churches and the dome of the Bulfinch State House, which was sheathed in Revere's copper, as was the *Constitution*.

Captain Hull had chosen to take the ship into Boston because the British now commanded the sea-lanes into New York. He was still under orders to rendezvous with Commodore Rodgers. In Boston, perhaps, he could learn of the American squadron's whereabouts. *Constitution* also needed to replenish her depleted supplies, particularly the 10 tons of fresh water that had been dumped into the ocean. On the afternoon of July 26, Purser Thomas J. Chew took one of the frigate's boats up the channel. He carried Hull's dispatches to Secretary Hamilton and Commodore Rodgers, as well as a long list of supplies and provisions needed to prepare the *Constitution* for another cruise. The captain urged the local Navy Agent to "work night and day" to fill the *Constitution*'s stores. He wanted the ship ready to return to sea in three days.

The next morning, *Constitution* was towed up the channel by her cutters. She anchored in President Roads, just below the fort at Castle Island. Almost immediately, a small flotilla of lighters began transferring provisions and casks of fresh water to the ship. Just before noon, Hull went ashore at Boston's Long Wharf. As he walked up State Street, he was cheered by crowds of Bostonians who had heard reports of the *Constitution*'s escape. At the Exchange Coffee House (which served as a combined post office, conference center, newsstand, and social club for Boston's merchants and sea officers), Hull took up a pen and wrote the following message in the public register of shipping news:

> Captain Hull, finding his friends in Boston are correctly informed of his situation when chased by the British squadron off New York . . . takes this opportunity of requesting them to make a transfer of a great part of their good wishes to Lt. Morris, and the other brave officers, and the crew under his command, for their very great exertions and prompt attention to orders while the enemy were in chase.

The Federalist influence was strong in Boston, however, and there was considerable local sentiment against the war. Surgeon Amos Evans browsed in several Boston bookshops, where he found "plenty of sermons in pamphlet form, & pieces against 'Maddison's ruinous war,' as they call it." Writing in his journal, Dr. Evans wondered whether New England could be counted on to provide any support to the war effort. "Judging from present symptoms, I fear not."

Boston was buzzing with rumors about the presence of British naval forces off the New England coast. No one yet knew what Commodore Broke had done after losing the *Constitution*; it was feared that he might move north to blockade Boston. (In fact, Broke's squadron had sailed to the West Indies to intercept and protect the hundred-sail Jamaica convoy.) There were reports that the British frigate *Maidstone* was cruising just off Cape Cod, and had captured several American fishing vessels. Other reports referred to two British frigates operating in Massachusetts Bay itself, or a little eastward of Cape Ann.

Hull had good reasons to hurry the *Constitution* back to sea. Apart from the rule that a ship at sea was a better weapon than a ship in port, there was the constant possibility that a strong British blockading force would arrive to cut off her escape. To these were added a third, unspoken consideration. William Bainbridge, who stood senior to Hull on the captain's list, was stationed in Charlestown as commanding officer of the Navy Yard, where the frigate *Chesapeake* was undergoing repairs. Before the war, Bainbridge had been notified that he would be given the command of the *Constellation*, still fitting out at the Washington Navy Yard. But since *Constitution* was a larger ship than her sisters *Chesapeake* and *Constellation*, Bainbridge, by the iron rule of seniority, should have been entitled to supersede Hull in command of her. It seems that both Hull and Bainbridge expected precisely such orders to arrive from Secretary Hamilton at any moment. If *Constitution* sailed without orders, however, Hull would have the opportunity to make a successful cruise before being obliged to relinquish the ship.

While preparations for sea continued, Hull wrote Secretary Hamilton to justify his imminent departure: "Should I proceed to Sea without your further orders, and it should not meet your approbation, I shall be very unhappy . . . I shall act as at this moment I believe you would order me to do, was it possible for me to receive orders from you." He intended to take the *Constitution* in search of Rodgers. If he did not find Rodgers, he would "continue cruizing where (from information I may collect) I shall be most likely to distress the Enemy." At the same time, Hull was telling his father that "I may not return for some time." Further, he took same spare moments to shop for nautical charts in Boston, and purchased charts covering not only the North Atlantic but also Brazil, the Rio de la Plata, Africa, and the Spanish Main. Was Hull planning a long, unauthorized cruise far from American shores?

On Sunday, August 2, a week after arriving in Boston, Hull wrote a second letter to Hamilton. The wind having "hawled so far to the Westward as to enable us to fetch out," the captain had decided to "take a responsibility on myself." The *Constitution* would depart Boston in order to avoid a blockade that might trap her in port for several months. "These Sir, are the Motives that have led me to take the Steps I have," he concluded, "and should they not meet your approbation I shall truly be unfortunate."

THE CREW SHIPPED THE CAPSTAN BARS and hove up the anchors, and the big frigate went down Boston's long, intricate fairway, threading the channel through the dozens of neatly cultivated islands, passing the lighthouse and putting to sea. In spite of the war, Massachusetts Bay was dotted with small sails; Dr. Evans counted fifty around the horizon. At 11:30 a.m., Hull ordered the sails sheeted in, and the *Constitution* hauled off to the northeast, toward the English shipping lanes off Halifax and the Gulf of St. Lawrence.

In the following two weeks, *Constitution* sailed north and east along the coast of Maine as far as the Bay of Fundy, then crossed to Cape Sable, Nova Scotia. With heavy fog hanging over the sea, the *Constitution*'s lookout saw no ships for days on end. Bearing away to the east, passing near the Isle of Sables and Cape Race in the Gulf of St. Lawrence, the *Constitution* entered the shipping lanes that would carry men and war materiel from England to the maritime provinces for the defense of Canada. Here she had more success, capturing two English merchant brigs on August 10 and August 11. Rather than man these prizes and send them into American ports for prize court adjudication, Hull chose to burn them. In so doing, he eschewed the prize money they offered, revealing that his ultimate purpose was to meet an English man-of-war while the *Constitution* was at full fighting strength.

On August 15, the lookout caught sight of five sail in the southeast, and *Constitution* set all sail in chase. An English sloop of war had captured several American merchantmen. The sloop escaped, but the *Constitution* recaptured the merchantmen and took their prize crews prisoner. From the prisoners, Hull learned that several well-known British frigates of the Halifax station, including *Belvidera*, *Guerrière*, *Shannon*, and *Aeolus*, had turned back toward the North American coast after escorting the Jamaican convoy into the mid-Atlantic. Not wishing for another close encounter with the entire British squadron, Hull stretched away to the south, toward Bermuda.

The night of Sunday, August 16, in rainy and foggy weather, *Constitution* overhauled a 14-gun privateer brig out of Salem, the *Decatur*, named for Hull's colleague, Stephen Decatur. The *Decatur* had been chased by the 44-gun British frigate *Guerrière* about 100 miles to the south. The *Constitution* steered southward in search of her.

At 2:00 p.m. on August 19, in 41° 42′ North by 55° 48′ West—about 750 miles east of Boston—the lookout caught sight of a big, full-rigged ship on the southern horizon. She was on a starboard tack, close-hauled to the wind under easy sail. Captain Hull gave one of the midshipmen his telescope and sent him aloft. The midshipman hailed the deck to report that the stranger was a "tremendous ship." Hull gave the order to beat to quarters, and the crew of the *Constitution*, wrote Able Seaman Moses Smith, came "flocking up like pigeons from a net bed. From the spar deck to the gun deck, and from that to the berth deck, every man was roused and on his feet."

The stranger was indeed the *Guerrière*, commanded by twenty-eight-year-old Captain James R. Dacres. She had been ordered away from Broke's squadron to sail for Halifax on August 6. The two frigates, on opposite tacks, closed rapidly.

As *Guerrière* approached, the Americans could make out four words painted across her foretopsail: "NOT THE LITTLE BELT." She was not, in other words, the 20-gun corvette that John Rodgers (in *President*) had nearly sunk in a night action the previous year, having mistaken her for the *Guerrière*. That incident had left Dacres and the other officers of the *Guerrière* feeling as if they had a personal score to settle with the Americans. Three days earlier, Dacres had written out a challenge in the register of a merchant brig, inbound to New York: "The *Guerrière*, 44 guns, and 300 men, will be happy to see the *President*, Commodore Rodgers, outside the Hook, or any other of the large frigates, to have a sociable *tête-à-tête*." Now, as the *Guerrière* and *Constitution* maneuvered for position, Captain Dacres announced to his crew that he expected to take the *Constitution* in thirty minutes or less and would be "offended with them if they did not do their business in that time." At about the same time, a barrel of molasses was hoisted into the *Guerrière*'s rigging. The British had vowed to make "switchel," a syrupy beverage popular in New England, for the prisoners they soon expected to have locked in the hold.

The taunts were examples of the hubris that had seeped into the culture of the Royal Navy in the later stages of the Napoleonic Wars. Though Dacres was only twenty-eight years old, he was an experienced commander, having won promotion to post rank at twenty-two. A month earlier, during the long chase off the New Jersey shore, he had taken a good look at the *Constitution*. He must have known she was larger and more heavily armed than the *Guerrière*, and he could not have any doubt that she was well handled. It was Captain Dacres's business to know these things, and yet the option of running from the *Constitution* never seems to have entered his mind. The idea that a British frigate could be beaten by an American ship of anything resembling equivalent force was simply beneath serious consideration. To flee the *Constitution* would have exposed Dacres to the calumny of his colleagues, his superiors, and the entire British public. He would have faced a court-martial and very likely been stripped of his rank.

When the two frigates had closed to within about two miles, the *Guerrière* hauled up the English colors and fired a gun. *Constitution* stood on to leeward before the freshening northeast breeze, wearing double-reefed topsails and courses, with her royal yards struck down on deck. The British ship yawed, first to port, then to starboard, and fired two long-range broadsides.

Most of the balls splashed into the sea or passed harmlessly through the *Constitution*'s rigging. An 18-pounder shot hit home near the larboard knighthead; another struck the foremast and cut clean through a fish hoop (one of the bands encircling the lower masts). Midshipman Gilliam said of this long-ranging cannon fire, "we paid very little attention to it."

Dacres bore up to put the wind on the *Guerrière*'s quarter, placing her on the same tack as the *Constitution*. Both ships wore round several times in succession, as Dacres attempted to maneuver to windward of the *Constitution* and Hull maneuvered to keep *Guerrière* under his lee. For the next forty-five minutes the two ships ran on parallel courses, the *Constitution* steadily gaining on her adversary because she had spread more sail.

At 6:00 p.m., the *Constitution* ranged up on the *Guerrière*'s weather quarter, about 200 yards away. As she came abeam of her adversary, the distance closed to about 75 yards. Aboard the *Constitution*, Moses Smith later recalled, there was an eerie, almost preternatural stillness. Occasionally a sound cut through the silence, as an officer shouted a command, or the rigging creaked, or a wave broke against the side of the ship, but there was no talking among the hands, and "Every man stood firm at his post."

One by one, as they came to bear on the *Constitution*, the *Guerrière*'s 18-pounders opened fire. A ball crashed through a gunport and dismounted a long gun, sending a shock through the *Constitution*'s deck that was strong enough to throw a man off his feet. First Lieutenant Morris asked: "Shall we return the fire?" But Captain Hull intended to open with a single, concentrated broadside at close range—one that would give full effect to the *Constitution*'s superior weight of metal—and he told Morris to wait. Slowly the *Constitution* came abeam of the enemy, and when all of the guns would bear, Hull ordered the jib hauled down and the main topsail backed against the mainmast to slow her speed. At 6:05 p.m., he turned to Morris, and said: "Yes sir, you may now fire."

The *Constitution* fired a double-shotted broadside at pistol-shot range. It was, Hull reported, "a very heavy fire from all of our Guns, loaded with round, and grape, which done great Execution." The shock of the broadside sent tremors through the *Constitution*, so that the entire ship "shook from stem to stern. Every spar and yard in her was on a tremble." Immediately after the guns were fired, the *Constitution*'s gun crews gave a triple cheer that was heard on the deck of the *Guerrière*.

As the wind tore away the curtain of smoke, it was obvious that the first broadside had done its work. The *Guerrière*'s mizzenmast had ruptured a few feet above the main deck, and was crashing into the sea over the starboard quarter. Her mainyard had been shot away, taking the sail with it. This wreckage of spars and rigging, wrote Smith, was "hanging in great confusion over her sides, and dashing against her on the waves." The American crew gave another triple cheer—they seized every excuse to give the triple cheer—and an anonymous voice shouted that the *Guerrière* had been converted into a brig, and would soon be converted into a sloop. Captain Hull reportedly split his breeches in climbing up onto the hammock netting to see the enemy. At the sight of the *Guerrière*'s mizzenmast going by the board, he exclaimed: "By God, that ship is ours!"

The *Guerrière*'s fire fell off noticeably, as many of her gun crews had been ravaged. On the *Constitution*, the only damage suffered was in her rigging. Two fore royal halyards were shot away, bringing down one of the American ensigns. An Irish seaman named Dan Hogan picked up the flag, climbed the rigging, and secured it to the topmast. Several of the American boats, lashed upside down on the spar deck, were beaten to splinters. But the *Constitution*'s heavy planks and live oak frame provided good protection to the men who kept their heads down. As one of *Guerrière*'s 18-pounder balls bounced harmlessly back into the sea, a member of the *Constitution*'s crew exclaimed: "Her sides are made of iron!" The remark was later widely reported in the press, and the nickname stuck: "Old Ironsides."

The horrendous scene aboard the heavily outgunned *Guerrière* was later described by Benjamin Hodges, an American prisoner whose merchant vessel had been captured a few days earlier. The effect of the *Constitution*'s first broadside, he wrote, was like "a tremendous explosion . . . as if Heaven and Earth had struck together," causing the *Guerrière* to "reel and tremble as though she had received the shock of an earthquake." Hodges was stationed below, in the surgeon's cockpit, where he had agreed to help cope with the English wounded. Shortly after the *Constitution* opened fire, he said, rivulets of blood began running down the ladders "as freely as if a washtub-full had been turned over." Fifteen or twenty wounded officers and seamen were carried down to the cockpit, some missing an arm or leg. Hodges was impressed by the mordant good humor of the wounded men. A British officer, while the surgeon's saw was actually moving through his arm, called out to another casualty who was being carried down: "Well, shipmate, how goes the battle?"

With her mizzenmast trailing in the sea, *Guerrière*'s helmsman was powerless to prevent the frigate from turning up into the wind, toward the *Constitution*. This allowed the American ship to draw ahead and luff short round the British ship's larboard bow, assuming a raking position from which the marine riflemen in her foretop could sweep the *Guerrière*'s decks. The engagement was rapidly turning into a rout. Surging ahead and wearing round, the *Constitution* brought her larboard battery into action, and poured out a raking broadside.

Dacres realized that his last hope was to run the *Constitution* aboard and send a boarding party over the rail to carry the American frigate in hand-to-hand combat. The *Guerrière* luffed into the wind; her bow came into contact with *Constitution*'s larboard quarter; her bowsprit crossed over the American ship's taffrail and entangled in the mizzen shrouds. Clasped together, the frigates rotated counterclockwise in a lethal waltz. The gun crews serving the Englishman's two bow chasers kept up a vigorous fire, killing two members of one of the *Constitution*'s aftermost gun crews. One of the *Guerrière*'s 18-pounder long guns was run out and fired at point-blank range through a stern window of Captain Hull's cabin. Either the shot or a flaming wad from the cannon ignited a fire, which an American fire crew rushed aft to extinguish.

Dacres and Hull each gave the order to rally a boarding party. On both ships, heavily armed men pressed toward the point where the vessels were in contact. "One might see the whites of the eyes, and count the teeth of the enemy," said Moses Smith. On *Constitution*'s quarterdeck, Marine Lieutenant William S. Bush leaped up onto the taffrail, sword in hand, and was shot in the face. The musket ball entered his left cheek, traveled through his brain, and exited the back of his head. He was killed instantly, and fell back to the deck. First Lieutenant Morris thought an "advantage" might be gained by securing the enemy's bowsprit to the after rigging, so as to lock the *Guerrière* in a position from which she could be raked fore and aft by the *Constitution*'s larboard broadside. Morris climbed up to the same exposed position in which Bush had just been killed, and was reaching up to "pass some turns of the main brace" over the *Guerrière*'s bowsprit when he was shot through the abdomen and fell back to the quarterdeck. At about the same time, *Constitution*'s sailing master, "Jumping Billy" Haraden, was shot in the shoulder.

The British officers also suffered. The *Constitution*'s raking fire cut down the first, second, and third lieutenants, a marine lieutenant, and three midshipmen. The sailing master was shot through the knee. The *Guerrière*'s petty officers rose to the occasion, stepping into the command roles vacated by the wounded commissioned officers. The sailing master's mate and an acting purser assumed command of some of the gun crews. The American stern guns continued to fire and reload in rapid succession, and they wreaked devastation along the full length of the *Guerrière*. The barrel of molasses that had been hoisted on the main stay was shattered, and the contents emptied onto the British deck.

A high sea was running, and both ships were heaving and plunging. The *Guerrière*'s long bowsprit tore free of the *Constitution*'s mizzen rigging and the ships separated. At about the same time, the *Guerrière*'s teetering foremast went by the board, and its weight dragged the mainmast over the side with it. Now there was not a spar left standing in the British ship. Fulfilling the earlier prediction of that prescient sailor aboard the *Constitution*, the *Guerrière* had been transformed from a frigate into a brig, then into a sloop, and finally into a hulk.

The *Constitution* made sail before the wind and hove to a short distance to the east of her adversary. Her crew went to work repairing braces, halyards, and running rigging that had been cut to pieces by the *Guerrière*'s guns, and swaying up new yards to replace those that had been shot away. Then she returned and assumed a raking position on the *Guerrière*'s quarter.

The British ship had been hulled about thirty times on her larboard side. Five sheets of her copper sheathing had been torn from the bottom. Several of her guns had come loose from their breechings and were traveling around the deck, threatening to crush any man caught in their path. None of her remaining guns would bear on the *Constitution*. Nearly a third of her crew was killed or wounded. In the words of one of the English officers, the loss of the masts had left the *Guerrière* "in the trough of the sea, rolling her main deck guns under water. Our opponent, by this time, had refitted and wore round to rake us; and all attempts to get the ship before the wind, or to bring any of our guns to bear, [proved] in vain."

After a hurried conference with his remaining officers, Captain Dacres decided the *Guerrière* had had enough. At 6:30 p.m. on August 19, he ordered the British white ensign removed from the stump of the *Guerrière*'s mizzenmast, and a gun fired to leeward in token of surrender. Captain Hull ordered a gun fired in acknowledgment. A boat was lowered from the *Constitution*, and Third Lieutenant George C. Read and a crew went across to take possession of the surrendered frigate. Coming under *Guerrière*'s stern, Read called out: "Commodore Hull's compliments, and wishes to know if you have struck your flag?" According to Benjamin Hodges, Dacres's dry response was: "Well, I don't know. Our mizzenmast is gone; our mainmast is gone; and, upon the whole, you may say we have struck our flag."

About twenty minutes later, Read's boat brought Dacres across to the *Constitution*. Stepping onto the quarterdeck, Dacres offered his sword in token of surrender. Hull, playing his part in the chivalrous ritual, refused to accept it. Dacres complimented Hull on the performance of the *Constitution*, remarking that the American crew had fought "like tigers."

Dismasted, rolling heavily, and strewn with dead and wounded men, the British frigate presented an awful scene. Dr. Evans would only say that "immense mischief and destruction [was] done by our grape & canister shot," but Midshipman Henry Gilliam's description was more graphic: "pieces of skulls, brains, legs, arms & blood Lay in every direction and the groans of the wounded were enough almost to make me curse the war." The *Guerrière* was in danger of sinking, and it was decided that the prisoners and wounded men should be transferred to the *Constitution* as quickly as possible. It was a dark night, with high seas and strong winds. It would be a difficult operation. All serviceable boats were lowered into the sea and a towing hawser was passed between the two ships. Working together, the two crews helped sixty wounded men into the boats and hauled them across a heaving sea to the *Constitution*, which maneuvered "to keep in the best position to receive the boats."

Dr. Evans of the *Constitution* and Dr. Irwin of the *Guerrière* worked together to save the wounded, making no distinction between Americans and British (though there were many more of the latter). The doctors worked through the night, taking no sleep. Dr. Evans amputated two arms and two legs. First Lieutenant Charles Morris's chances were considered doubtful. (He survived, though he did not regain consciousness for several days.) A British seaman's entire lower jaw had been shot off; despite the doctors' best efforts to stem the bleeding, he soon died. An American sailor, Dick Dunn, cursed the surgeons as a "hard set of butchers" while they were actually sawing through his leg. In the days after the battle, according to Moses Smith, Captain Hull was often seen visiting the sick bay, bending over the hammocks of the wounded men, "tendering the consolations needed in such an hour, and showing his humanity to the best advantage." The bodies of Lieutenant Bush and a British seaman were buried at sea in a joint ceremony. Including those who died of their wounds, American casualties totaled seven killed and seven wounded. The *Guerrière* had lost twenty-three killed and fifty-six wounded.

At 7:30 a.m. on August 20, Lieutenant Read hailed from the *Guerrière* to report that there was five feet of water in the hold, and the water was rising faster than the prize crew could pump it out. After a failed attempt to take the British ship under tow, Hull bowed to the inevitable: *Guerrière* would soon be on her way to the bottom of the Atlantic. There was no hope of bringing the prize back into port. The Americans set charges on a slow match in the *Guerrière*'s storerooms and returned to the *Constitution*. Read and the last few members of his crew came aboard the American ship at 3:00 p.m. The *Constitution* hauled her sheets and sailed east to a safe distance, about three miles away.

All aboard turned to watch the "incomparably grand and magnificent" sight of the British frigate's last moments. Captain Dacres watched silently from the *Constitution*'s taffrail. "It was like waiting for the uncapping of a volcano, or the bursting up of a crater," wrote Moses Smith.

> Scarcely a word was spoken on board the *Constitution*, so breathless was the interest felt in the scene. . . . The first intimation we had that the fire was at work was the discharge of the guns. One after another, as the flame advanced, they came booming toward us. Roar followed roar, flash followed flash, until the whole mass was enveloped in clouds of smoke. We could see but little of the direct progress of the work, and therefore we looked more earnestly for the explosion, not knowing how soon it might occur. Presently there was a dead silence; then followed a vibratory, shuddering motion, and streams of light, like streaks of lightning running along the sides; and the grand crash came! The quarter deck, which was immediately over the magazine, lifted in a mass, broke into fragments, and flew in every direction. The hull, parted in the center by the shock, and loaded with such masses of iron and spars, reeled, staggered, plunged forward a few feet, and sank out of sight.

The *Constitution* set sail to the eastward. During the nine-day passage to Boston, the crew continued to drill frequently at the cannon and small arms. The lookout caught sight of Boston Light at 6:00 p.m. on August 29.

As the frigate beat up the bay, a flotilla of small vessels approached. To the first that came within hailing distance, seamen standing at the frigate's rail shouted: "The *Constitution* has captured the *Guerrière*!" The men in the boat removed their hats, thumped them on the side, "and rising, gave cheers upon cheers. They hailed other boats; and thus the air was rent with cheers; and the victory passed along till it reached the shore, and then spread like wildfire, over the city and country." As the great frigate entered the ship channel in Boston's outer Roads, boats filled with well-wishers came down the narrows to greet her. In the inner harbor, the roar of artillery mingled with the sound of the church bells swinging in their belfries, and as the news passed from mouth to mouth throughout the city and surrounding towns, the self-appointed messengers commanded their neighbors never to forget what had happened in latitude 41° 42′ North and longitude 55° 48′ West, on August 19 in the year 1812. Wherever the amazing news was told, the bells rang and the guns roared; before long they would be ringing and roaring all across America.

CHAPTER THIRTEEN

Vice-Admiral Herbert Sawyer, commander in chief of British naval forces at Halifax, received the shocking news from Captain Dacres in a letter from Boston dated September 7: "Sir, I am sorry to inform you of the Capture of His Majesty's late Ship *Guerrière* by the American Frigate *Constitution*, after a severe action on the 19th of August in Latitude 40.20 N and Longitude 55.00 West."

Sawyer had been slow to react to the American declaration of war. This was due in great part to the limitations of early nineteenth-century communications. After learning of the *Belvidera*'s dustup with the *President* in late June, he had dispatched a sloop of war, the *Colibri*, to sail to New York under a flag of truce and request an explanation. Even after confirming that war had been declared, Sawyer had continued to order captured American merchant vessels released, pending instructions from London. Sawyer was a junior admiral, and he was conscious of his duty to prevent "incidents" at sea from escalating into wider conflicts without the sanction of the British government. There was hope that hostilities would be called off when the American government learned that the offending British Orders in Council had been repealed in early June.

British public opinion was divided over the prospect of an American war. Many of the leading newspapers continued to take a belligerent tone, and the fortunes to be won in capturing American commerce were a powerful enticement to the officers and seamen of the Royal Navy, as well as to the myriad other British interests that held a stake in the prize system. When news of the American declaration of war reached London, the British government commanded that "H.M.'s ships of war and privateers do detain and bring into port all ships and vessels belonging to citizens of the United States of America." American vessels found in British ports were peremptorily seized, American goods were confiscated, and debts owed American merchants were annulled. But there were also many British citizens, including Whig politicians and newspapers, who argued that England could ill afford to take on new enemies. The struggle against Napoleon was at a critical phase. The same week Madison had signed the American declaration of war, the French emperor had crossed the Niemen River into Russia with the largest army assembled in modern times—some 400,000 troops, all told. There was every reason to expect the campaign to succeed, if only because Napoleon had never failed. If Russia was conquered, there would be no other viable threat to France in the east, and Napoleon would be free to turn his full attention to defeating the British armies under Lord Wellington on the Iberian Peninsula, and perhaps to renewing his old dream of invading England.

Wellington's forces in Portugal and Spain were gathering their strength to drive the French beyond the Pyrenees. It was the largest and most important land campaign England had ever mounted against Napoleon, and its success was essential to the overall course of the war. British forces were supplied principally by sea, through the port of Lisbon, by some two thousand ships per year. Any interruption of that supply line posed a serious threat to the British war effort. Moreover, Wellington's troops relied heavily on imported American grain and corn. As recently as April, Admiral Sir David Milne, writing from Lisbon, had told a colleague that "if it was not for the supplies from America, the army here could not be maintained." War with America threatened to cut off this trade, while at the same time unleashing American privateers on the sea routes between England and Portugal.

On August 6, Admiral Sawyer was superseded by the appointment of Admiral Sir John Borlase Warren as "commander in chief of H.M.'s squadron on the Halifax and West India stations, and down the whole Coast of America." The order merged all of the operations of the Royal Navy in the Western Hemisphere, from the northernmost navigable waters of the Atlantic to the Gulf of Mexico and the Spanish Main, under one command. Sailing from Portsmouth in the 80-gun *San Domingo* on August 14, Sir John suffered a wet, nasty crossing. The flagship was beleaguered by fierce, unseasonable gales, and one of her consorts, the sloop of war *Magnet*, went down with the loss of all hands. When *San Domingo* reached Halifax on September 27, Warren learned of the capture of the *Guerrière*.

Warren, fifty-nine years old, had nearly forty years of service in the Royal Navy. He also brought wide-ranging political and diplomatic experience to the job, having served for several years in Parliament and as ambassador extraordinary to Russia in 1802. His appointment was a measure of how seriously

Whitehall took the threat of an American war. The admiral's instructions empowered him to offer an armistice to President Madison. He was to refer to the June repeal of the Orders in Council, but had no authority to offer concessions on the question of impressments. As his first official act, Admiral Warren wrote directly to the American president, offering an immediate cessation of hostilities, with reparations or indemnities to be determined by a bilateral commission. Though Warren's instructions also granted authority to "attack, sink, burn or otherwise destroy" enemy warships, privateers, and merchantmen, the full weight of British naval power would not fall on the American seaboard until the last hope of a peaceful reconciliation had been extinguished.

JUST AS THE VICTORIOUS *CONSTITUTION* entered the outer Roads of Boston, the sails of Commodore Rodgers's squadron—*President, United States*, and *Congress*, in company with the smaller vessels *Hornet* and *Argus*—had appeared in the offing.

After his brush with the *Belvidera* ten weeks earlier, Rodgers had put his powerful squadron on a course to intercept the England-bound Jamaica convoy. Near the Newfoundland Bank, *President* and her consorts had picked up a trail of floating coconut shells and orange peels. Cracking on to the eastward, they had reached the western approaches to the English Channel on August 6. Not wanting to sail into the hands of the Royal Navy's Channel Fleet, Rodgers had given up the pursuit. The squadron stretched away to the south for Madeira and the Azores, then doubled back to the westward, passing south of Cape Sable, and finally to Boston. By that time, "that wretched disease the scurvy, having made its appearance on board of the vessels," many of the hands were losing teeth and hair, and a few had died. That seamen should be made to suffer the effects of a vitamin-deprived diet on a cruise of less than three months, in an era when it was widely known that the disease could be prevented by shipping an adequate store of vegetables and citrus fruits, was indefensible. It was also foolhardy, because it forced Rodgers to return home earlier than he would have liked.

With bitter remorse, Rodgers reported to Secretary Hamilton that the squadron had "only made seven Captures & one recapture." The value of the prizes taken did not equal the cost of keeping five warships at sea for ten weeks. Rodgers blamed heavy fog, which was often so thick that the ships of the squadron could not see one another even when separated by just a few hundred yards.

As shrewd observers understood, however, Commodore Rodgers's cruise had achieved important strategic objectives. It had diverted British naval forces away from the American coast at a time when hundreds of American merchantmen were homeward-bound. "We have been so completely occupied looking for Commodore Rodgers's squadron," said one British officer, "that we have taken very few prizes." The safe return of so many ships and cargoes was a boon to the American economy, and injected badly needed revenues into the treasury. The British failure to impose an early blockade also allowed a swarm of American privateers to sail unmolested into the Atlantic. In July, a Halifax newspaper reported that enemy privateers were "swarming round our coast and in the Bay of Fundy," and advised that it was "imprudent for any vessel to sail from this port unless under convoy." Lloyds of London reported a spike in the insurance rates paid by shipowners and merchants. On September 5, the *Niles' Register* published a list of 136 British prizes sent into American ports by privateers, and that list was probably less than half the actual number. "Prizes are pouring into almost every convenient port; and many privateers are still fitting out . . . a hundred sail are at sea."

With Commodore Rodgers's arrival virtually in the wake of the *Constitution*, the entire U.S. Navy was again safe in port. With the exception of *Constellation*, still undergoing repairs at the Washington Navy Yard, all of the original six frigates were now moored in Boston Harbor, not far from the Charlestown wharves. The triumphant *Constitution* was often surrounded by a flotilla of boats filled with well-wishers. Liquor in bladders was smuggled to the enlisted men. On September 5, five hundred citizens of Boston fêted the ship's officers at a victory banquet in Faneuil Hall. A model of the *Constitution* was placed in the gallery, "with her masts fished and the Colors as they flew during the action." A wreath of flowers was arranged on the wall behind Isaac Hull's seat, and a band played patriotic songs as the dinner was served. The guests drank seventeen toasts, and each was answered in succession by the roar of artillery, positioned just outside the doors and manned by local militia companies. A hastily written play depicting the *Constitution-Guerrière* action was performed at the theater. Dr. Evans saw it and pronounced it "a very foolish, ridiculous thing."

When Hull's report arrived in Washington on September 9, Secretary Hamilton, who was not generally effusive in giving praise, wrote the captain: "In this action, we know not which most to applaud, Your gallantry or Your skill. You, Your officers & Crew are entitled to & will receive the applause & the gratitude of Your gratefull country." Congress voted to award a gold medal to Hull and silver medals to the lieutenants and midshipmen.

The timing of Hull's sensational victory was critical, not only for the nation but for the Hull family. Three days before the capture of the *Guerrière*, an American army commanded by Brigadier General William Hull, Isaac Hull's uncle, had surrendered without a fight to an inferior British and Indian force at Fort Detroit. In the Ohio Valley, where the security of American settlements was immediately placed in jeopardy, General Hull's name was cursed, "and if he was to attempt to pass this way," said John Graham, a resident of the valley, "he would be hunted and shot like a mad dog." Richard Rush dismissed the general as a "gasconading booby" and Dolley Madison asked a correspondent: "Do you not tremble with resentment at this treacherous act?" The surrender was reported in the Boston newspapers on September 2, two days after the return of the *Constitution*. In maritime Boston, a popular quip circulated: "We have a Hull-up and a Hull-down."

Before the war, many Americans had assumed Canada would be conquered without much difficulty ("a mere matter of marching," Jefferson had predicted), while anticipating little success in the war at sea. The humiliation at Detroit and the sensational capture of the *Guerrière* reversed these expectations. Those who had argued for keeping the U.S. Navy safe in port fell abruptly silent. Madison and his advisers quickly settled on a new deployment strategy. The fleet would be divided into three squadrons, to be commanded by the three seniormost captains on active duty: John Rodgers, Stephen Decatur, and William Bainbridge. The 44-gun frigates *President*, *Constitution*, and *United States* would serve as flagships. Each would be accompanied by one of the smaller frigates and a brig. Each commodore was at liberty to choose his own cruising ground, based on his judgment of how best "to afford protection to our trade & to annoy the enemy."

The simultaneous presence of so many needy frigates in Boston Harbor placed tremendous strains on the Charlestown Navy Yard, which was poorly equipped and understaffed. Amos Binney, the newly hired Boston Navy Agent, later recalled being overwhelmed by "the chaos that surrounded me."

> Every ship required complete supplies of provisions and every kind of stores. I was but newly appointed, had no experience, no precedents, no forms, no instructions; was obliged to form a whole system from the chaos that surrounded me, was always short or wholly destitute of funds. I resorted to the banks and to my friends for money on loans and on interest, was soon overwhelmed with requisitions from the public ships in every department—pursers, boatswains, carpenters, gunners, armourers; and frequently had half a dozen midshipmen, with as many boats' crews, calling for stores, etc.

Eager to get the fleet to sea as quickly as possible, Secretary Hamilton was willing to throw money at the problem. On September 8, he authorized a cash warrant of $33,000 to be paid to Binney for repairs, pay, provisions, medicines, and "contingencies." The amount was $6,000 more than Binney had requested. The secretary took it on himself to increase the sum so that "no inconvenience may arise to the public Service. . . . We are extremely anxious to get all our public vessels to Sea, with the least possible delay—and we confidently hope that every assistance on your part will be promptly rendered to effect this desirable object."

Commodores Rodgers and Decatur, with *President* and *United States* as their respective flagships, sailed together from Boston on October 8. Four days later, they parted company. Decatur and the *United States*, accompanied by the brig *Argus*, sailed east toward the Azores and Cape Verde Islands. In the mid-Atlantic, Decatur ordered *Argus* to part ways with the flagship, believing that the two ships could cover more of the sea by cruising alone.

Stephen Decatur's career had been closely intertwined with that of the *United States* since 1796. When the ship was under construction in Joshua Humphreys's Southwark shipyard, Decatur had been employed as a teen-aged captain of one of the building crews. When white oak timbers were needed for the keel of the ship, Decatur had traveled with a cutting expedition into the Catskills and the forests of western New Jersey. In his first active naval assignment, he had served aboard the *United States* under John Barry as a midshipman during the Quasi War. In the two years prior to the War of 1812, he had commanded her as flagship of the U.S. Navy's southern station, based in Norfolk.

After the maiden cruise of the *United States* in the summer of 1798, Captain John Barry had praised her sailing qualities. In the fourteen years since, however, the big Philadelphia-built frigate had earned a reputation as a slow, unwieldy sailor. Among the enlisted men, she was affectionately known as the "Old Wagon," though it was considered a breech of discipline to say those words within earshot of an officer. *United States* may not have been the world's fastest-sailing frigate, but she was one of the most powerful. Like *President* and *Constitution*, she mounted 24-pounder long guns on her gun deck, and she was built with the same heavy live oak scantlings that had earned one of her sisters the more flattering nickname "Old Ironsides."

At dawn on Sunday, October 25, when the *United States* was about 500 miles south of the Azores, the lookout hailed the deck to report a large sail on the weather beam, about 12 miles north. Though the Americans did not yet know it, the strange ship was HMS *Macedonian*, a 38-gun frigate commanded by Captain John Surinam Carden. Coincidentally, both the captain and the ship were well known to Decatur. Carden and *Macedonian* had harbored in Norfolk for several weeks in early 1812, while the British frigate was waiting to receive dispatches from the British ambassador in Washington. During Carden's sojourn in Norfolk, the two men socialized frequently; Carden was a guest of Stephen and Susan Decatur at their home in Norfolk at least twice, and he visited the *United States* at least once. According to Decatur's earliest biographer, the two men jokingly waged a beaver hat on the prospective outcome of a battle between their two ships, though the exchange was probably apocryphal. What is known with greater certainty is that Carden had lectured Decatur on the dangers of overarming. Britain's experience, said Carden, had proven that frigates were more effective when armed with 18-pounder cannon rather than 24-pounders; and Carden added, "When the American officers have had as much experience as we have had, they too will prefer eighteen pounders."

The crew of the *Macedonian* were turned out in their best clothes, as was their custom on the Sabbath, including "black, glossy hats, ornamented with black ribbons, and with the name of our ship painted on them." An easy breeze blew out of the south, inclining into the southeast; the *Macedonian* was steering northwest by west. The British ship's lookout sighted the *United States* at about the same time the American lookout caught sight of the *Macedonian*. Carden ordered his men to make all sail to windward in chase, and the *United States* simultaneously altered course to close with the British ship.

Among the crew of the *Macedonian* were several pressed Americans. When Captain Carden gave the order to clear the ship for action, an American named John Card, not wishing to fight his own countrymen, approached the captain and asked permission to go below. When Captain Dacres of the *Guerrière* had been approached with a similar request by several American seamen before her engagement with the *Constitution*, he had complied (and afterward cited the resulting shortfall in manpower as one of the factors in *Guerrière*'s defeat). Carden was less accommodating. According to a British seaman who claimed to witness the exchange, Carden "very ungenerously ordered [Card] to his quarters, threatening to shoot him if he made the request again."

At 8:30 a.m., as the two frigates were closing, *Macedonian* made the private English signals. *United States*, ignorant of the countercode, answered by hoisting an American ensign at each masthead. A few minutes later, Decatur made an unexpected maneuver. The *United States* wore round and turned away from the wind. It almost seemed as if she was attempting to flee. As the

Macedonian attempted to close the distance between the two ships, the *United States* kept two points off the wind, and as a result, Carden later reported, "I was not enabled to get as close to her as I could have wished." In fact, Decatur chose his tactics deliberately. Knowing that his 24-pounder long guns would be more effective at long range than the Englishman's 18s, he kept the *United States* in a position to rake the *Macedonian* as she steered down on the American frigate's starboard quarter.

At 9:00 a.m., the *United States* fired a ranging broadside. From the *Macedonian*, the flash of the cannon was seen before the sound reached their ears. The balls fell well short, splashing down in the sea in a ragged line of white geysers. A few minutes later, *Macedonian*'s three forwardmost larboard guns fired at extreme range—long, high-arching shots that also fell short of their target. An English officer shouted: "Cease firing—you are throwing away your shot!"

The two frigates were now sailing together toward the east, both under fighting sail, about three quarters of a mile apart and closing gradually. The *United States* was leading ahead, but the British ship was clearly faster. As the range closed, Carden gave the order to open fire, and the *Macedonian*'s larboard battery erupted in a cloud of white smoke. A few of the shots actually passed over the *United States* and splashed into the sea on the far side.

At 9:20 a.m., with the range closing rapidly, the *United States* poured out a second broadside. The sound and shock of the guns was so powerful that some of the seamen aboard the *Macedonian* wrongly concluded that the Americans' powder magazine had detonated, and gave an abortive cheer. The wind of the 24-pounder cannon balls, said a British sailor, sounded like "the tearing of sails, just over our heads." Several of the upper deck carronades on the *Macedonian*'s engaged side were dismounted. The British ship's mizzen topmast and driver gaff were brought down, giving the *United States* a sudden advantage in maneuvering, which Decatur acted quickly to exploit. He backed his main topsail, turned hard into the wind, and took up a raking position on the *Macedonian*'s quarter. The American gun crews reloaded and fired as quickly as they could, hardly pausing to aim the weapons. Several balls passed cleanly "through and through" the *Macedonian*, puncturing both sides of the ship and disappearing into the sea on the far side.

The grisly scene aboard the British ship was described by a literate British seaman, Samuel Leech, in a memoir entitled *Thirty Years from Home: Being the Experience of Samuel Leech, Who Was for Six Years in the British and American Navies* (1843). The literary conventions of that era typically sanitized the graphic details of war violence for the sake of readers' sensitivities.

Leech's account was an exception. He prefaces his narrative with an apology, warning that "the recital may be painful," but insists on recording the carnage aboard the *Macedonian* to "reveal the horrors of war and show at what a fearful price a victory is won or lost."

As the *United States*'s heavy shot smashed through the hull of the *Macedonian*, "torrents of blood" ran on the deck and "the cries of the wounded rang through all parts of the ship." One of the men stationed at Leech's gun was struck in the wrist by a round shot; his hand apparently vanished, with a jet of blood suddenly appearing in its place. A Portuguese boy assigned to carry gunpowder had the bad luck to have a cartridge ignite in his hands. The explosion "burnt the flesh almost off his face. In this pitiable situation, the agonized boy lifted up both hands, as if imploring relief, when a passing shot instantly cut him in two." Men who were killed outright—and at least one who was alive but thought unlikely to survive—were lifted from the deck and thrown overboard. It was deemed essential to keep the area around the guns clear of bodies.

Leech was amazed at the bravery of his shipmates, who fought stripped to the waist, and cheered as they served the guns. "I cheered with them," he wrote, "though I confess I scarcely knew for what. Certainly there was nothing very inspiriting in the aspect of things where I was stationed." Men were falling on every side, including the wardroom steward, the schoolmaster, a midshipman, a lieutenant, and a master's mate. As one wounded man was carried below, Leech recalled hearing "the large blood-drops fall pat, pat, pat, on the deck; his wounds were mortal." The boatswain was attempting to secure the backstay when "his head was smashed to pieces by a cannon-ball." A goat kept by the English officers for milk was struck in the hindquarters—"her hind legs were shot off, and poor Nan was thrown overboard." The carronades on the spar deck of the *United States* had been loaded with grape and canister shot, which came "pouring through our port-holes like leaden rain, carrying death in their trail."

Fifteen minutes after the first American broadside had hit home, the *Macedonian*'s main topmast "went by the cap"—that is to say, it broke near the point where the topmast was joined to the lower mast. It fell forward, into the fore topmast, and both came down together, covering the forecastle in a hopeless thicket of cordage and spars. The British ship's remaining rigging hung uselessly from the shreds of her lower masts. She would no longer answer her helm. Her hull had been punctured nearly a hundred times, and many of her guns lay dismounted on the deck.

The British officers attempted to organize a boarding party. A cluster of men gathered on the gangway, armed with cutlasses and pikes. Other teams were sent with hatchets to clear away the wreckage and heave it overboard. Before much progress could be made in clearing a path to the forecastle, however, the mizzenmast came down "by the board" (just above deck-level), dragging wreckage behind it, and leaving nothing standing except the stumps of the lower foremast and mainmast, and no sails drawing wind except a tattered foresail.

The *United States* crossed the *Macedonian*'s bow and sailed a short distance to windward. She hove to, and the American crew was set to knotting and splicing the minor damage she had sustained in her standing and running rigging. The British officers ordered the gun crews to cease fire. As the silence fell, the "stifled groans" of the wounded suddenly became audible. About fifteen minutes later, the *United States* filled her sails and ran back down to the stricken *Macedonian*, taking up a raking position just off her larboard quarter.

The *Macedonian* was a hulk, wallowing helplessly on the waves, rolling her gunports under the sea. All of her boats but one—the jolly boat, which had been towing astern—had been smashed to splinters. The decks were literally covered with dead and dying men—she had thirty-six killed and sixty-eight wounded. The *Macedonian*, said Carden, was "a perfect wreck, an unmanageable Log."

The surviving officers huddled briefly on the quarterdeck. The first lieutenant recommended that the *Macedonian* fight on and "sink alongside," if necessary, but Captain Carden decided that he had no choice but to surrender. The colors were hauled down. "To me it was a pleasing sight," wrote Leech, "for I had seen fighting enough for one Sabbath; more than I wished to see again on a week day."

A boat was lowered from the *United States* and a prize crew came across to take possession of the surrendered frigate. "Fragments of the dead were distributed in every direction," one of the American officers said; "the decks covered with blood, one continued agonizing yell of the unhappy wounded; a scene so horrible of my fellow-creatures, I assure you, deprived me very much of the pleasure of victory." Below, the *Macedonian*'s surgeon and his mates were doing their best to cope with the wounded. Because the cockpit was too small to accommodate all of the casualties, the long dining table in the officers' wardroom was converted into an operating table, "covered with the bleeding forms of maimed and mutilated seamen." After each amputation, one of the mates would carry the severed limb to a gunport and heave it into the sea. Leech was appalled by the cries of the wounded men: "Some were groaning, others were swearing most bitterly, a few were praying, while those last arrived were begging most piteously to have their wounds dressed next."

There was a near-complete breakdown in discipline aboard the shattered frigate. Several seamen broke into the spirit room and began drinking heavily. Others looted the pursuers' storeroom, or the officers' possessions, or stripped the dead of their clothing and personal possessions. A few threatened to attack members of the American prize crew. Leech was surprised at how differently his surviving shipmates reacted to the trauma of defeat—"some who had lost their messmates appeared to care nothing about it, while others were grieving with all the tenderness of women."

According to a report later published in the *Niles' Register*, one of the pressed Americans among the *Macedonian*'s crew—possibly John Card, the man whose request to be excused from the fight had been denied by Captain Carden—had been struck in the head by a round shot during the battle, "and his brains and blood dashed against a beam and the spar deck of the ship." When the dead man's surviving messmates pointed out his remains, several members of the American prize crew gathered up fragments of his skull "and swore they would preserve the precious relic to the end of their lives, as a stimulus to avenge the death of their brother on the despoilers of the ocean."

As Captain Carden came aboard the *United States*, Captain Decatur was there to greet him. The two captains knew each other well, and each was conscious of the role he was meant to play. Carden offered his sword to Decatur in token of surrender, and Decatur refused it. Thinking himself the first officer to surrender a British frigate to the Americans, Carden remarked, sadly, that he was an "undone man." Decatur eased Carden's mind, or disturbed it further, by advising him of the capture of the *Guerrière* by the *Constitution* two months earlier.

The *United States* was barely scratched. She had suffered superficial damage to her rigging and shrouds, and only nine shots in her hull. She had five men killed and seven wounded. The disparity in casualties was even more dramatic than that of the *Constitution-Guerrière* action, and offered further vindication of Joshua Humphreys's insistence on unconventionally heavy live oak framing.

Decatur was determined to bring the captured frigate safely into an American port. He placed Lieutenant William Allen in command of her. A large contingent of seamen from the *United States*, assisted by a number of the British prisoners, pumped seven feet of water out of her hold and plugged dozens of shot holes in her hull. Decatur vetoed a proposal to throw the

Macedonian's guns overboard. With the hull repaired sufficiently for the voyage back to the North American coast, the *Macedonian* was jury-rigged with new topmasts, spare yards, and cordage removed from the storerooms of the *United States*. The work required a full two weeks.

"One half of the satisfaction arising from this victory is destroyed in seeing the distress of poor Carden," Decatur wrote his wife during the passage back to America. "I do all I can to console him." All of the English officers' personal possessions were saved and returned to them, and to compensate Carden for articles that he did not wish to take with him back to England, including casks of wine and some of the musicians' instruments, Decatur gave him $800. In his memoirs Carden would write: "I must here & always bear testimony to the marked Gentlemanly Conduct of Commodore Decatur."

The nickname "Old Wagon" was confirmed when the jury-rigged and hull-patched *Macedonian* consistently outsailed the *United States*. The prize often had to reduce sail in order to remain in company with her captor. It was thought likely that British frigates and battleships would be patrolling the American coast in force. Samuel Leech said that a majority of the *Macedonian*'s common seamen "sincerely wished to avoid" recapture, but the English officers felt differently, and they studied the horizon eagerly, day after day. "I was always alive to the chance that some of our Cruisers might Cross our Course to the Enemies Port & recapture the *Macedonian*," Captain Carden later wrote, "—But NO!—We were nearly one Month on the American Coast, & never saw a British cruiser."

Choosing to avoid the busiest sea-lanes—those into New York, Boston, the Chesapeake and Delaware Bays—Decatur steered for a landfall near Block Island Sound. On December 3, the *United States* raised Montauk Point, at the eastern end of Long Island, and the next morning came to anchor off New London, Connecticut. Separated from her captor by thick fog and later by adverse winds, the *Macedonian* took refuge in Newport, Rhode Island. The *Newport Mercury* trumpeted the news under the headline ANOTHER BRILLIANT NAVAL VICTORY. Newporters pressed down to the wharves to get a glimpse of the prize. "This day has been a most gratifying sight for us," wrote Master Commandant Oliver Hazard Perry, who commanded the Newport naval station, "this beautiful frigate mooring as a prize in our harbor."

Lieutenant Archibald Hamilton, son of the Navy Secretary, was dispatched to carry Decatur's report to Washington. He reached the capital on the night of December 10, a date that had been previously chosen for a "naval ball" at Tomlinson's Hotel on Capitol Hill. Virtually all of official Washington was there, including members of Congress, cabinet heads, Supreme Court justices, diplomatic ministers, and First Lady Dolley Madison. The captured ensigns of the *Guerrière* and the *Alert*, a British brig captured by the *Essex* on August 13, were displayed on one of the walls of the ballroom. The band played long and loud, and one guest complained that the dancers stepped "as usual upon the toes and trains of those that did not dance."

At about 10:00 p.m., Lieutenant Hamilton appeared at the door, still dirty from his ride. He was escorted into the center of the ballroom "amid the loud acclamations of the Company, and greeted with national music from the band." In a theatrical gesture, Lieutenant Hamilton knelt before Dolley Madison and unfurled the *Macedonian*'s ensign (which he had carried with him from New London) on the floor. The newspapers reported the scene in loving detail, embroidering it with rhetoric about how America had "snatched the Trident of Neptune from the mistress of the ocean," etc. But it was a day not so fondly remembered by the staunch pacifists of the Society of Friends, when a renegade Quaker first lady celebrated the combat victories of warships built by a renegade Quaker shipwright, and blushed approvingly as a trophy of war was flung at her feet. "This was rather overdoing the affair . . . ," wrote Mrs. B. H. Latrobe to a friend; "and I could not look at those colors with pleasure, the taking of which had made so many widows and orphans."

The next morning, President Madison forwarded Decatur's official report to Congress, adding: "too much praise cannot be bestowed on that officer and his companions on board, for the consummate skill and conspicuous valor by which this trophy has been added to the naval arms of the United States." The same week, reports had arrived in Washington of a bloody victory won by the American 18-gun sloop *Wasp* over the British 16-gun *Frolic* on October 18. The victories brought a timely boost to national morale and eased the pain of the humiliating reverses suffered by the army on the Canadian frontier. "Our brilliant naval victories," said an army officer, "serve, in some measure, to wipe out the disgrace brought upon the Nation by the conduct of our generals."

In the last week of December, *United States* and *Macedonian* sailed in company down Long Island Sound and anchored off Frog's Neck. Decatur and most of his officers traveled ahead by boat for a "grand naval dinner" on December 29 at the City Hotel in Manhattan. The four-story red brick building dominated an entire city block on Broadway between Cedar and Thames, just north of Trinity Church. A row of "fashionable shops" faced the avenue, and on the first floor was a vast, airy public hall, the largest in North America. The banquet was the hottest ticket in New York. Five hundred guests crowded into the dining room, and at least three hundred more were turned away at the door. The room was garishly decorated with masts, spars, sails, transparent paintings, and flags entwined with laurel. Each table had as its centerpiece a miniature model of an American frigate, and at the head table, where Mayor DeWitt Clinton presided with Decatur seated on his right, the centerpiece was an artificial lake, with banks made of real grass, and a model of the *United States* floating at her moorings. During the toasts, a sail behind the head table was clewed up like a curtain, exposing an illuminated transparent painting depicting the captures of *Macedonian* and *Guerrière*. The band struck up "Yankee Doodle," a song seldom heard since the days of the Revolution ("We are glad this old tune is coming into fashion," *Niles'* remarked). The guests danced late into the night, and upstairs, in one of the hotel's seventy-eight rooms, a mother gave birth to a baby boy, whom she named Stephen.

On New Year's Day, the *United States* and her prize successfully navigated the difficult "Hell Gate" passage from Long Island Sound into the East River. "We came into New York with the *Macedonian* as a New Year's gift, the starspangled banner proudly waving over the British cross," wrote Able Seaman Elijah Shaw. "We anchored between North Battery and Governor's Island, and fired a number of grand salutes, which were answered by the Battery." Both frigates were soon "thronged with spectators," as members of the crews pocketed payments of admission from civilians.

The enlisted seamen of the *United States* had not been invited to the December 29 banquet, and someone suggested giving a second dinner in their honor. On January 8, 1813, four hundred seamen, immaculately dressed in blue jackets and trousers with red waistcoats, were taken on board a steampowered ferry boat and landed at New Slip pier. They marched in procession up Broadway, trailed by a "crowd of urchins," to the City Hotel. "We found it difficult to elbow our way through the streets, so dense was the throng," wrote Shaw.

At dinner, served in the same hall in which the earlier event had been held, the sailors enjoyed the unfamiliar joys of an unlimited food and liquor ration. The boatswain and his mates hovered over the tables, enforcing discipline. As the plates were cleared away, the boatswain's pipe announced the arrival of Alderman John Vanderbilt, who gave a long, appreciative speech, and of Commodore Decatur, who thanked the men for their "orderly and decorous conduct." All the effects of the earlier banquet were recycled for the sailors—the clewing up of the sails, the revealing of the transparencies, the band striking up the old, patriotic tunes—and "their admiration was expressed by repeated huzzas, and enthusiastic acclamations." The toasts offered on the sailors' behalf (to "America's brave and hardy sons of Nep-

USS *President* setting sail. Engraving by Jean-Jérôme Baugean. National Maritime Museum, London.

James Madison by Gilbert Stuart, c. 1821. Ailsa Mellon Bruce Fund, National Gallery of Art, Washington, D.C.

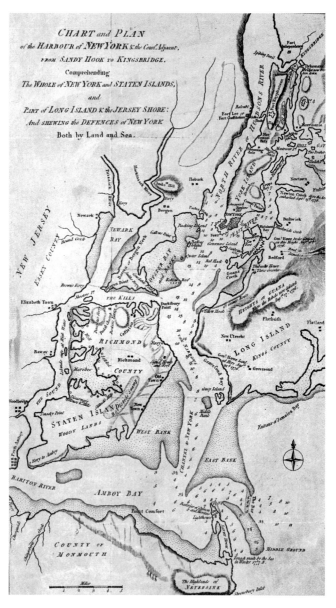

Chart and Plan of the Harbour of New York, 1781. New York Public Library.

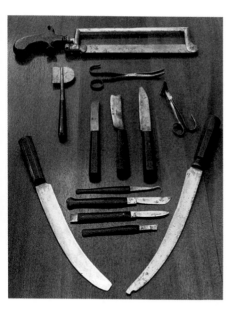

Naval surgical instruments: hacksaw, forceps, bone scraper, knives, artery clamp, suture hook, scalpels. U.S. Naval Historical Center, Washington, D.C.

Cat-o'-nine-tails. Two dozen lashes were said to reduce a man's back to butcher's meat. The Mariners' Museum, Newport News, Virginia.

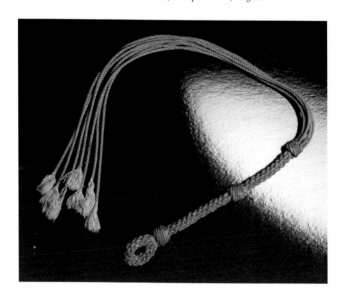

Isaac Hull. Oil on canvas by Orlando S. Lagman (after Gilbert Stuart), 1967. U.S. Naval Historical Center, Washington, D.C.

USS *Constitution* escaping from a British squadron, July 1812. Painting by F. Muller. U.S. Naval Historical Center, Washington, D.C.

USS *Constitution* capturing HMS *Guerrière*. Oil on canvas by Seymour Samuel, c. 1812–15. The Mariners' Museum, Newport News, Virginia.

A Boxing Match, or Another Bloody Nose for John Bull. Etching with watercolor by William Charles, 1813. Library of Congress.

USS *Constitution* capturing HMS *Java*. Hand-colored lithograph by Nathanial Currier, 1846. Library of Congress.

Commodore Philip Broke, HMS *Shannon*, leads boarders onto the deck of USS *Chesapeake*, June 1, 1813. Engraving from *Memoirs of Admiral Broke*. U.S. Naval Historical Center, Washington, D.C.

USS *President*, the morning after her capture by a British squadron off New York, January 1815. Lithograph by Thomas Buttersworth. The Mariners' Museum, Newport News, Virginia.

USS *Constitution* towing HMS *Cyane*, captured February 28, 1815. Artist unknown. Library of Congress.

Boston Harbor from Constitution Wharf. Robert Salmon, 1833. U.S. Naval Academy, Annapolis, Maryland.

USS *Constitution*, 1997. Photograph by Janet Stearns, courtesy of USS Constitution Museum, Boston.

tune," to "the American Eagle—may its claws grab the ships of the King of England") were answered by toasts offered by the sailors themselves (to "plenty of prize money," to "all the pretty girls who like Yankee tars"), and afterward they poured out of the ballroom in high spirits, smashing a number of plates and glasses as they went, and made their way up Broadway to the Park Theater, where the pit had been reserved for their exclusive use. During the performance, which featured a reenactment of the *United States–Macedonian* action, the sailors frequently interrupted the actors to offer praise or criticism.

WHEN THE FIRST REPORTS of the loss of the *Guerrière* arrived in London, the newspapers devoted long, sober columns to the event. "It is more than merely that an English frigate has been taken . . . but that it has been taken by a new enemy, an enemy unaccustomed to such triumphs, and likely to be rendered insolent and confident by them," *The Times* lamented. "Never before in the history of the world did an English frigate strike to an American; and though we cannot say that Captain Dacres, under all circumstances, is punishable for this act, yet we do say there are commanders in the English navy who would a thousand times rather have gone down with their colours flying, then have set their brother officers so fatal an example."

The shock of defeat hit the navy's officers every bit as hard as the civilians. "What an unfortunate business the capture of the *Guerrière* frigate!" exclaimed Admiral David Milne of the HMS *Impetueux*—"It is a thing I could not have expected." Nearly ten years had passed since a British man-of-war had been defeated in a single-ship action, and it had been even longer since a British frigate had struck her flag to an enemy of nominally equal force. It remained an article of faith among naval officers that a 38-gun English frigate, as the *Naval Chronicle* put it, "should undoubtedly (barring extraordinary accidents) cope successfully with a 44-gun ship of any nation." Even Captain Dacres, who knew the capabilities of the American 44s as well as anyone, declared at his court-martial (in which he was acquitted) that if given the opportunity, he would fight the *Constitution* again with another British frigate of the same dimensions and armament as the *Guerrière*.

It was difficult for the British public to keep the naval losses in perspective. The loss of a single frigate was trifling. England's huge fleets were safe, and the strength of the Royal Navy was essentially undiminished. The August 13 capture of a British 20-gun brig and a troop transport by the U.S. frigate *Essex* was shrugged off, given the disparity in force—it was one of those unlucky events that could always happen in war. The bloody victory on October 18 of the American 18-gun sloop *Wasp* over the 16-gun HMS *Frolic* prompted more uneasiness, but the Royal Navy still came out ahead when both victor and prize were recaptured later that same afternoon by one of His Majesty's 74-gun battleships, the *Poictiers*. The overall course of events in both North America and Europe was running very much in England's favor. Three times the Americans had attempted to invade Canada, and three times they had been repulsed. In Spain, Wellington had won a critical victory at Salamanca and entered Madrid. Napoleon had reached Moscow, but with winter fast approaching it was doubtful whether he could hold the city, and his army was beginning to suffer heavy losses.

But in January 1813, when reports of the capture of the *Macedonian* by the *United States* arrived in London, the British people were incredulous. The loss of two frigates seemed to mark the demise of something immensely valuable, though intangible: the Royal Navy's almost mystical aura of qualitative superiority. The news "produced a sensation in the country scarcely to be equalled by the most violent convulsions of nature," said George Canning, the Americans' old *bête noire*, in a speech to the Commons. "[I]t cannot be too deeply felt that the sacred spell of invincibility of the British navy was broken by these unfortunate captures." Referring to Napoleon's defeats in Russia, *The Times* wrote: "The land spell of the French is broken, and so is our sea spell."

If English mastery of the sea was a racial and cultural trait, as some Englishmen had argued, then perhaps the American successes should be attributed to the common ancestry of "our trans-atlantic descendents." No one should be surprised to learn that "men who are bone of our bone, and flesh of our flesh" could fight well at sea, said the editors of the *Québec Mercury*. It was a fashionable opinion, but no less painful to contemplate. "It is a cruel mortification," said one of the British ministers, "to be beat by these second-hand Englishmen upon our own element."

Dissenting voices protested that the public's shock and consternation were all out of proportion. The *Guerrière* and *Macedonian*, they said, were simply overwhelmed by larger and more heavily armed adversaries. Some questioned whether the American 44s even deserved the name of frigates; perhaps they should be considered "disguised ships of the line." Referring to a critic of Captain Dacres, an anonymous correspondent to the *Naval Chronicle* asked: "Has any person informed him that the upper deck of the *Constitution* is flush fore and aft, and that she thereby mounts a double tier of guns like a line-of-battle ship?" The *Chronicle* published a table comparing the dimensions of the American 44s—length on gun deck, beam, and tonnage—

to those of the *Guerrière* and *Macedonian*. "Is not the term frigate most violently perverted," the editors asked, "when applied to such vessels?"

The Times brushed aside these excuses. "Is it true, or is it not, that our navy was accustomed to hold the Americans in utter contempt? Is it true, or is it not, that the *Guerrière* sailed up and down the American coast with her name painted in large characters on her sails, in boyish defiance of Commodore Rodgers? Would any captain, however young, have indulged such a foolish piece of vain-boasting if he had not been carried forward by the almost unanimous feeling of his associates?"

A poem published in *Cobbett's Political Register*, referring to the capture of the *Macedonian*, mocked Captain Carden's assertion that he had been duped into engaging a ship more powerful than his own:

> *When Carden the ship of the Yankee Decatur*
> *Attacked, without doubting to take her or beat her,*
> *A Frigate she seemed to his glass and his eyes;*
> *But when taken himself, how great his surprise*
> *To find her a SEVENTY-FOUR IN DISGUISE!*
>
> *If Jonathan thus has the art of disguising,*
> *That he captures our ships is by no means surprising;*
> *And it can't be disgraceful to strike to an elf*
> *Who is more than a match for the devil himself!*

Lord Liverpool's ministry came in for severe criticism. "The size and force of the American frigates, with the great number of men they carry, were made known to government long before any difference took place between the two countries," wrote "Oceanus" to the editors of the *Naval Chronicle*. "Why, therefore, did they not provide against the chance of our ships falling a prey to the enemy, from inferiority of force?" *The Times* took the government to task for having failed to have a "plan matured and ready, for falling upon the sea-coasts of America, blocking up her ports, hindering her privateers from sailing, and capturing or destroying every frigate she might dare to send to sea." In its defense, the Admiralty pointed out that British naval forces in Halifax, Bermuda, and the West Indies, at the outset of the war, were superior to the entire U.S. Navy in the proportion of eighty-five to fourteen.

Critics also charged that by sending Admiral Warren to North America with orders to negotiate a truce, the government had waged a "war of conciliation and forbearance." In a long speech in the Commons, Canning charged that "the arm which should have launched the thunderbolt was occupied in guiding the pen," and that the Royal Navy had been sent to "attack the American ports with a flag of truce."

The point was rendered moot on October 27, when the offered truce was rejected by the American government. Secretary of State James Monroe, responding to Admiral Warren's offer, stated that peace negotiations must be preceded by a British pledge to cease impressing seamen from American ships. Warren had no authority to make such a concession, and the British government was unwilling to give up what Lord Bathurst termed "a right hitherto exercised without dispute, and of the most essential importance to our maritime superiority." General reprisals were ordered against American shipping, and the Prince Regent published a "Declaration on the Causes of the American War," charging the Madison administration with "palliating and assisting the aggressive tyranny of France."

There was no more talk of peace. Whatever the issues at the bottom of the Anglo-American quarrel, the captures of *Guerrière* and *Macedonian* had revealed a new and more urgent dimension to the war. To restore the charm of British naval supremacy, it was now necessary to "punish the temerity" of America, as a correspondent to the *Naval Chronicle* put it, "in pretending to dispute the command of the ocean with us."

WILLIAM BAINBRIDGE was one of the great survivors of the early American navy. He had been exonerated for every mishap that had occurred under his command, including the surrender of the *Philadelphia* to the Tripolitans in 1803, and he had managed to retain his place on the captain's list despite taking several long furloughs to command merchant voyages in the years before 1812. His reputation as a fine seaman had served him well, as had his political skills, and the reverence for seniority that dominated the culture of the navy.

In August 1812, while Isaac Hull and *Constitution* were at sea on the cruise that would climax in the victory over *Guerrière*, Bainbridge had received orders from Washington directing him to assume command of the *Constitution*. When Hull returned to Boston as a conquering hero, therefore, there was every possibility that the two officers would run afoul of one another. Instead, Hull chose to be accommodating. He carried the guilty knowledge that he had sailed without orders, while knowing that those orders would probably deprive him of his ship. William Bainbridge stood above him on the captain's list and therefore had every right to expect a certain degree of deference. Moreover, Hull had learned, on arriving in Boston, of the untimely death of his brother, and he required time ashore to grieve and to put his family's financial affairs in order. When Bainbridge revealed Secretary Hamilton's orders giving him command of the *Constitution*, Hull readily agreed to the transfer. Bainbridge came aboard the frigate and hoisted his broad commodore's pendant on September 15.

The change in command touched off a near mutiny. Several sailors and at least one petty officer broke ranks and begged the beloved "Capt. H." not to leave the ship. "Many of our crew were not at all pleased with this arrangement," wrote Moses Smith. "We had become personally attached to Captain Hull, and hated to have him leave us. Such was the state of feeling that it almost amounted to a mutiny." Ten years earlier, a younger William Bainbridge might have responded to such an affront by flogging every man on the ship. Now he tried diplomacy, asking: "My men, what do you know about me?" A few replied that they had served under Bainbridge on the *Philadelphia*, and spent a year and a half in Tripoli as prisoners, and would prefer to sail with "any of the other commanders." When informed that the change in command was irreversible, the dissenters "requested to be transferred on board any other vessel."

With Hull gone and Bainbridge in command, the *Constitution* was a tense ship. There was no doubt that several men would seize the first opportunity to desert, and Bainbridge posted eighteen sentries on deck the first night after taking command. When two sailors attempted to steal the frigate's second cutter, they were quickly apprehended. Bainbridge saw an opportunity to turn the incident to his advantage. Mustering the crew the next morning, he offered to pardon the would-be deserters and spare them the flogging they would normally suffer, on the condition that their shipmates accepted Bainbridge as the frigate's rightful commander. "This was appealing to our best feelings," wrote Smith. "It was an argument in favor of our new commander at the very commencement of our acquaintance on the decks of the *Constitution*. The result was that nearly every man consented, to save his brother sailors from punishment."

Throughout September and most of October 1812, *Constitution* underwent repairs in Boston Harbor. Though she had not been seriously damaged in the recent action, Bainbridge was planning a long cruise to the southward, possibly even around Cape Horn and into the Pacific. The ship's log is replete with the tedious details of stepping three new lower masts, setting up "an entire new Gang of Standing Rigging," refitting the tops, mounting the trestletrees, and swaying up the topmasts and topgallant masts. New bridle ports were cut in the hull, just aft of the beakhead; they would allow more convenient handling of the anchor cables. Most of the spars were discarded and replaced with new ones, and what little damage the frigate had sustained in her hull was patched and painted over.

Bainbridge preferred his old command, the *President*, which he called "one of the finest Ships in the World." He offered John Rodgers $5,000 to exchange *President* for *Constitution*. Rodgers refused. Both commodores knew there was a fortune in prize money to be won in capturing British merchantmen, and the faster ship stood a better chance of bringing home more prizes.

Bainbridge's squadron would include the 32-gun frigate *Essex*, commanded by another ex-Tripolitan prisoner of war, Captain David Porter, and the 18-gun sloop of war *Hornet*, commanded by Master Commandant James Lawrence. For advice in choosing the squadron's cruising ground, the commodore wrote William Jones, a Philadelphia merchant and future secretary of the navy, asking where he was most likely to fall in with unprotected British merchantmen. Jones recommended a cruise into the southern Atlantic, along the east coast of Brazil, where inbound and outbound East India convoys often touched for rewatering and reprovisioning. Accepting the advice, Bainbridge recruited a man who knew those waters well, a master navigator from Salem named John Carlton. Though he was not a clergyman, and evidently did not intend to conduct himself as one, Carlton was entered on the payroll as "chaplain." The commodore also purchased Carlton's book of charts, entitled *The Complete East India Pilot; or, Oriental Navigator*.

During the first and second weeks of October, *Constitution* completed her stores. She would carry four to five months' provisions, but only a hundred days' freshwater ration. On October 16, she was warped across the harbor from Charlestown Wharf to Boston's Long Wharf. Five days later she dropped down the fairway to President Roads, in company with *Hornet*, and on the twenty-seventh, with a fair tide and the wind shifting south and west, the two vessels put to sea.*

A six-week passage delivered the *Constitution* and *Hornet* to São Salvador (formerly Bahia), Brazil. Master Commandant Lawrence took the *Hornet* in to reconnoiter the port. In the harbor he found an English sloop of war,

---

* *Essex* was meanwhile refitting in the Delaware River. Bainbridge left instructions for Captain Porter to attempt a rendezvous at the Cape Verde Islands or the island of Fernando de Noronha, north of Brazil. If he did not find the squadron, however, Porter was at liberty to cruise wherever he chose. Failing to locate Bainbridge, Porter navigated *Essex* around the Horn and into the eastern Pacific, where she pillaged the British whaling trade with great success before being captured by two British frigates in March 1813.

Bonne Citoyenne. Lawrence learned that the English ship was taking on board the fantastic sum of $1.2 million in gold bullion, with orders to transport the money to London.

The Americans could not attack the *Bonne Citoyenne* while she remained in São Salvador. Such an attack would infringe upon Portuguese neutrality and trigger a protest at the highest levels of government. Instead, Lawrence (with Bainbridge's approval) sent a direct, written challenge to the English captain, Pitt Barnaby Greene, proposing that the *Hornet* and *Bonne Citoyenne* meet in the offing and fight a ship-to-ship duel. Bainbridge pledged to keep the *Constitution* clear of the battle. If *Bonne Citoyenne* was victorious, he wrote, Captain Greene would be free to take his prize and sail away without further interference.

Greene refused the challenge. He explained that it was his paramount duty to see the bullion safely home. He also doubted whether he could trust in the promised non-participation of the powerful *Constitution*. Angered by the Englishman's reluctance to accept at face value the "sacred pledge I made to him," Bainbridge left Lawrence and the *Hornet* to blockade São Salvador and took the flagship about thirty miles into the offing.

Two days later, at about 8:00 a.m. on December 29, 1812, the lookout caught sight of two sails inshore. As they drew closer to the *Constitution*, it was apparent that one of the strangers was a large warship, either a frigate or a battleship. The other ran for the safety of São Salvador. The *Constitution* flew the American private signals, and the stranger flew unintelligible signals in response. At 11:30 a.m., when the unknown warship was about four miles distant, Bainbridge tacked the *Constitution* and made all sail away from the coast. Bainbridge later said his objective was to get clear of Portuguese territorial waters, but Dr. Evans wrote in his journal that the commodore had concluded that the stranger was a double-deck battleship, an overmatch for the *Constitution*. In any case, the stranger soon altered course and made all sail in chase.

She was the British frigate *Java*, rated for 38 guns but mounting 47. She had been French, originally the *Renommée*; captured in a squadron action off Madagascar in May of the previous year. *Java* had sailed from Portsmouth on November 12, and was bound for the East Indies. She was carrying as a passenger the newly appointed governor of Bombay, Lieutenant-General Sir Thomas Hislop, with his staff of about one hundred, as well as several dozen other military and civilian passengers. Her captain was Henry Lambert, a senior commander with extensive combat experience.

With passengers and crew numbering 397, and a large quantity of baggage and naval stores stowed in the hold (including a quantity of copper-bottom sheathing intended for other British naval vessels in India), the *Java* was crowded and heavily laden. Her complement had been rounded out, just before she had sailed, with a draft of raw landsmen, many of whom "had never smelt salt water." Captain Lambert had neglected the routine of gunnery practice during the passage from England. The crew had drilled at the guns only once, and only with blank cartridges. The British officers would regret the oversight.

The *Java* was the faster ship, by a generous margin, and she soon overhauled the *Constitution*. Shortly after one in the afternoon, Bainbridge tacked the *Constitution* again, shortened sail, and stood back toward the *Java* under a moderate east northeast breeze. By now Bainbridge and his crew could plainly see that the enemy was a frigate.

The *Java* bore down on the *Constitution*, intending to rake her fore and aft. Bainbridge wore the *Constitution* round in response. "Considerable Manoeuvers were made by both Vessels to rake and avoid being raked," Bainbridge wrote in his journal. The commodore set a large amount of sail, hoping to compensate for the superior sailing qualities of the *Java*. Both the English and American officers later testified that the other ship had kept away, at a distance, preferring "long balls" to close action.

A few minutes after 2:00 p.m., with the breeze freshening, and the two ships sailing on parallel southeasterly headings about half a mile apart, *Constitution* opened fire from her larboard broadside. A few of the shots struck the *Java*'s starboard side or passed through her rigging; none did any significant damage. As the distance between them closed, both ships held their fire.

As *Java* was ranging up on the *Constitution*'s weather quarter, Bainbridge observed that she had hauled down her ensign, and ordered the third division to fire a shot "to make him show his Colours." The shot was answered by a broadside, and the battle was joined.

Early in the action, *Java*'s 18-pounder long guns, carronades, and small arms did serious damage. Several American seamen were killed or wounded. Spars and sections of rigging fell to the deck. *Constitution*'s wheel was blasted to splinters. Bainbridge was struck in the left hip by a musket ball fired by a marine sharpshooter in one of the *Java*'s tops. An 18-pounder ball struck the copper railing of the aft hatchway, dislodging a fragment of metal that hit Bainbridge in the right thigh, giving him his second wound in as many minutes.

The loss of *Constitution*'s wheel required Bainbridge to shout orders down through a grating in the deck, to a specially placed crew of men hauling on relieving tackles fixed to the tiller in the wardroom pantry. With two wounds below the waist, the commodore's trousers were visibly bloody on both the right and left sides. He did not leave the quarterdeck, however, until almost seven hours later.

Constitution wore round and the two ships again maneuvered for a raking position. Fifteen minutes later they engaged from the opposite side, the gun crews of each ship crossing to serve the guns on the other side. At 2:35 p.m., the *Java* wore round and crossed close under the *Constitution*'s stern. It was a perfectly timed maneuver, and gave the English frigate an opportunity to fire a raking broadside that might have proved decisive. When the critical moment came, however, only one of the *Java*'s gun crews managed to get off a shot.

The *Constitution*'s heavy broadsides were wreaking devastation on the *Java*'s gun deck, and the American marksmen picked off several British officers on her quarterdeck. With his crew falling at a greater rate, and his ship's fire beginning to slacken noticeably, Lambert's last hope was to carry the *Constitution* by a boarding action.

At 2:50 p.m., *Java*'s helm was put hard to weather; as she turned down into the *Constitution*, her bowsprit passed over the American ship's taffrail and fouled in her mizzen-rigging, and the scene must have looked remarkably similar to the moment when *Guerrière* and *Constitution* had come afoul of each other during their engagement the previous August. As the frigates came into contact, the *Java*'s boatswain, his arm bound in a tourniquet, sounded the pipe—but as the sailors and marines gathered in the gangway and forecastle, pikes and cutlasses in hand, they were cut to pieces by several tightly grouped volleys of grape, canister, and double-headed bar shot from the *Constitution*'s stern chasers. The marksmen stationed in the American mizzentop, meanwhile, took advantage of the close range, firing down at the boarders on the British forecastle and picking several of them off individually.

The second hour of the action saw a steady wearing down of the *Java*'s defenses under the continuous heavy bombardment of the *Constitution*'s 24-pounders. Bainbridge's journal records the dismantling of the *Java* in oddly laconic terms, as if he was describing an ordinary shipyard procedure:

AT 3   The Head of the enemies Bowsprit & Jib boom shot away
            by us
AT 3.5   Shot away the enemies foremast by the board
AT 3.15   Shot away The enemies Main Top mast just above the Cap
AT 3.40   Shot away Gafft and Spunker boom
AT 3.55   Shot his mizen mast nearly by the board

The late historical novelist Patrick O'Brian depicted the *Constitution-Java* action in his novel *The Fortune of War* (1979). O'Brian's rendering is based on a close reading of the relevant documents, and is faithful to the historical record with one exception—he places his main character, Jack Aubrey, in the *Java*'s forecastle at the moment her foremast comes down:

> But then over all the din, cutting clear through, the high shrieking hail from the *Java*'s foretop, "Stand from under," and the mast, the towering great edifice of the foremast with all its spreading yards, its fighting-top, its sails, its countless ropes and blocks, came crashing down, the lower part kicking aft to cover the main deck, the upper covering the forecastle.
>
> There was an immense amount of rigging, of spars over them and over the forward guns; there were some men pinned, others wounded; and for the next few minutes, in the fury of clearing so that the guns could fire, Jack lost all track of the relative position of the ships. When at last the forward battery was to some extent restored he saw the *Constitution* well ahead, and in the act of wearing across the *Java*'s bows. Not a gun could the *Java* fire in this position, and the *Constitution* raked her deliberately from stem to stern, killing a score of men and bringing down her maintopmast.
>
> Once again the wild labour of clearing, slashing at the wreckage with axes, anything that came to hand; and now the *Constitution* lay on their starboard quarter, pouring in a diagonal fire; lay there a moment before bearing up and giving the *Java* her full larboard broadside. . . .
>
> The *Java*s, undismayed, fired like demons, streaming with sweat under the smoky sun, often with blood; and the stabbing flames from almost every shot they fired set light to the tarred wreckage hanging over the side: fire-buckets, powder, fire-buckets, powder, the remaining officers had them running in a continual stream. At one point the ships were side by side again, and the *Java*'s great guns gave as good as they got; or at least did all they could to do so; and she being low in the water now, some of her round shot made cruel wounds. But the *Java* lacked her fighting-tops—fore and mizen were gone and the maintop was a wreck—whereas the American did not. Her tops were filled with marksmen, and it was one of these that brought Jack down. The blow knocked him flat, but he thought nothing of it until on getting up he found that his right arm would

not obey him, that it was hanging at an unnatural angle. He stood, swaying, for with two masts and all but one sail gone the *Java* was rolling very heavily; and as he stood amidst the din, still shouting at the crew of number nine to depress their gun, an oak splinter knocked him down again.

At about 3:30 p.m., Captain Lambert was taken down by one of the American sharpshooters. The ball struck him in the chest, near the heart. He was carried below. The *Java*'s surgeon instantly saw that the wound was mortal. It had shattered the captain's sternum: "I put my finger in the wound, detached and extracted several pieces of bone."

With the loss of Lambert, command of the *Java* passed to First Lieutenant Henry Chads, who was also wounded, but had been treated by the surgeon and returned to action. Chads rallied the remaining men to keep fighting, but with part of her bowsprit and all of her jib boom shot away, and what remained of her headsails tattered and dangling, *Java*'s helm would not answer. The *Constitution* took up a raking position on the enemy's starboard quarter, "pouring in a tremendous galling fire," and maneuvering to prevent the *Java*'s full broadside coming to bear.

At 4:00 p.m., the *Constitution* shot ahead to windward. Bainbridge set the hands to repairing the *Constitution*'s parted braces and shrouds, and re-reeving her damaged running rigging.

The *Java*, according to the court-martial testimony of Lieutenant Chads, was "a perfect wreck, with our main-mast only standing, and main-yard gone in the slings." Most of her starboard guns were hopelessly entangled in a dense thicket of wreckage from the fallen main topmast. During the brief respite provided by the *Constitution*'s withdrawal, the British crew hacked away at the trailing wreckage, and managed to rig a jury sail from the stump of the foremast and bowsprit. As this work was proceeding, however, the *Java* was rolling violently because of the loss of her sails, and seemed on the verge of rolling out the tottering remains of her mainmast. Lieutenant Chads concluded he had no choice but to cut away the weather shrouds and let the mast fall over the lee rail.

When the crew was mustered and counted, 110 men were missing (casualties were later tallied at 22 killed and 102 wounded). *Java*'s hull was pierced in dozens of places, and a great deal of water was entering the ship. Every spar was gone; one of the pumps was shot away; four forecastle guns and six quarterdeck guns were dismounted. It was obvious that the *Java* was no longer capable of making effective resistance. Chads's last remaining hope was that the *Constitution* would come close enough to permit a second boarding attempt.

In his fictional version of the battle, Patrick O'Brian envisions the finish:

Now was the time to profit from a God-sent mistake: now or never. If the *Constitution* would only neglect the weathergage, would only come close enough to allow them to board in a last dash through her fire . . . but the *Constitution* intended nothing of the kind. Deliberately and under perfect control she crossed the *Java*'s bows at rather more than two hundred yards, shivered her main and mizen topsails, and lay there, gently rocking, her whole almost undamaged larboard broadside looking straight at the dismasted *Java*, ready to rake her again and again. . . . Jack could see her captain looking earnestly at them from his quarterdeck.

"No," said Chads in a dead voice. "It will not do." He looked at Jack, who bowed his head: then walked aft, as a resolute man might walk to the gallows, walked between the sparse gun-crews, silent now, and hauled the colours down.

CHAPTER FOURTEEN

"The public will learn, with sentiments which we shall not presume to anticipate, that a *third* British frigate has struck to an American," the *London Pilot* reported on March 20, 1813. One day earlier, Lloyds of London had released similarly distressing news: an estimated five hundred British merchant vessels had fallen into American hands during the first seven months of the war. "*Five hundred merchantmen and three frigates!*" the *Pilot* cried. "Can these statements be true, and can the English people hear them unmoved?"

Anyone who had predicted such a result of an American war this time last year would have been treated as a madman or a traitor. He would have been told, if his opponents had condescended to argue with him, that long ere seven months had elapsed the American flag would be swept from the seas, the contemptible navy of the United States annihilated, and their maritime arsenals rendered a heap of ruins. Yet down to this moment not a single American frigate has struck her flag. They insult and laugh at our want of enterprise and vigour. They leave their ports when they please, and return to them when it suits their convenience. They traverse the Atlantic; they beset the West India Islands; they advance to the very chops of the Channel; they parade along the coasts of South America. Nothing chases, nothing intercepts, nothing engages them but to yield them triumph.

The *Naval Chronicle* declined to elaborate on the details of the *Java*'s loss, confessing: "The subject is too painful for us to dwell upon." But the same issue carried the report of a bloody action between the French frigate

Arethuse and the HMS *Amelia* off Sierra Leone on March 7. *Arethuse* had fought with unexpected ferocity, killing more than half the crew of the *Amelia*, and the Frenchman had subsequently escaped. "Is it not obvious," asked the *Chronicle*, "that they are stimulated by American triumphs?" Englishmen dreaded nothing so much as the resurrection of French naval power. For more than a decade, French officers and sailors had been cowed by the "superstitious terror" that their defeat was inevitable, leaving them "half-conquered" before a single shot was ever fired. The Americans now threatened to supply a jolt of courage to the remnants of Napoleon's navy—perhaps even to arouse a "spirit of emulation and national rivalry."

For the first time in years, there was the kind of sharp public criticism that was the essential first step toward reform—criticism aimed at the distended Admiralty bureaucracy, the politicization of naval promotions and assignments, the corrupting influence of prize money, the neglect of the North American Station. Contemplating the lopsided casualties suffered aboard the British ships in the three recent actions, some speculated that the Americans had discovered some innovation that enhanced the "destructive havoc of their broadsides." Was it their use of lead (instead of cloth) cartridges? Was it some new type of firing lock, or gunsight? A correspondent to the *Chronicle* wondered: "Are their rammers, sponges, worms, wads, shot, crows, handspikes, cartridges, tubes, powder horns, or tackle different?" Others expressed concern that British standards of gunnery had atrophied. "American seamen have been more exercised at firing at a mark than ours," complained an officer. "We are not allowed a sufficient quantity of powder in one year to exercise the people one month."

Admiral Warren was evidently concerned, because he circulated a standing order, on March 6, directing his commanders to give priority to "the good discipline and the proper training of their Ships Companies to the expert management of the Guns." All officers and seamen on the North American station were urged to keep in mind "that the issue of the Battle will greatly depend on the cool, steady and regular manner in which the Guns shall be loaded, pointed & fired." Two weeks later, the Admiralty issued a circular to all the British admirals, discouraging the daily "spit and polish" scouring of the brasswork and directing that "the time thrown away on this unnecessary practice be applied to the really useful and important points of discipline and exercise at Arms."

Gunnery could at least be improved with practice, but there was no ready solution to the poor manning of His Majesty's ships. With more than six hundred ships in service, manned by some 140,000 seamen and marines, the

Royal Navy was stretched to the extreme limits of efficiency. Ship for ship, it could not rival the quality of the crews employed in the small, all-volunteer U.S. Navy, whose recruiting officers enjoyed the luxury of selecting the cleverest, healthiest, and most experienced men. The shock of defeat emboldened domestic critics, who now challenged the Royal Navy's reliance on "the brutal horrors of the press," and the disgraceful treatment of British sailors, who were crammed into overcrowded ships, fed rations that many Englishmen would not force upon their dogs, flogged half to death at the least provocation, and never paid a shilling nor allowed to set foot on shore for years on end. Was it any wonder so many seized the first opportunity to desert? Or were willing to fight under the American flag, against their former shipmates and countrymen? One correspondent wrote of the "mania of apathy and discontent" that predominated in the typical British warship, while another blamed a recruiting system that drew in "good, bad, and indifferent, viz, ordinary seamen, landsmen, foreigners, the sweepings of Newgate, from the hulks, and almost all the prisons in the country."

The superior force and scantlings of the American 44-gun frigates, now denounced as "disguised ships of the line," prompted the Admiralty to issue a "Secret & Confidential" order to all station chiefs prohibiting single-frigate engagements with the *Constitution*, *President*, or *United States*. A lone British frigate was henceforth ordered to flee from the big American frigates, or (if it could be done safely) to shadow them at a prudent distance, remaining out of cannon-shot range, until reinforcements could be brought into action. At the same time, the Admiralty ordered a crash building program to launch ships on lines similar to those produced by Joshua Humphreys in Philadelphia almost twenty years earlier. In response to Admiral Warren's specific request, a number of older British 74-gun ships of the line had their uppermost decks removed or "razeed." These hybrid "razees" were not well liked in the service (officers derided them as "mules"), but the new class would at least match up to the American 44s. What the English people demanded, above all, was a fair victory over one of the big American frigates.

MORE THAN ANY OTHER NATION, Great Britain appreciated and had mastered the art of blockade. When carried out successfully, a naval blockade struck simultaneously at an enemy's freedom of movement, his supply lines, and his economic vitality. It protected commercial shipping by preventing enemy privateers and cruisers from sallying out of port or returning with prizes. It chipped away the foundations of the enemy's seapower by denying him the means to keep his fleet at sea. Britain's ten-year-old commercial and military blockade of continental Europe had largely succeeded in its twin goals of interdicting most seagoing commerce while keeping the French navy imprisoned in its ports. It was not surprising, therefore, that the main thrust of Great Britain's naval strategy in the War of 1812 was a blockade of the American coast.

British policy drew a distinction between a military blockade, designed to prevent American warships from getting to sea, and a commercial blockade, which aimed to cut off all merchant traffic into or out of American seaports. Ostensibly, the entire American coast came under military blockade at the outset of the war. The commercial blockade, on the other hand, was ordered in several stages. The first was a "most complete and vigorous Blockade of the Ports and Harbours of the Bay of the Chesapeake and of the River Delaware," ordered in November 1812. The second, ordered in March 1813, extended the commercial blockade southward and northward, from New Orleans to Rhode Island. First Lord of the Admiralty Melville told Admiral Warren: "We do not intend this as a mere paper blockade, but as a complete stop to all trade & intercourse by Sea with those Ports, as far as the wind & weather, & the continual presence of a sufficient armed Force, will permit & ensure." Considering New England as "friendly," and hoping to negotiate a separate peace with that region, the British did not attempt to interdict American commerce north of Cape Cod until April 1814, when the commercial blockade was extended to include all of New England.

In truth, however, the British blockade was far from perfect, and many parts of the long American coast were left completely unguarded. As the British had learned through generations of experience in Europe, the effectiveness of every blockade relied upon the close proximity of safe naval bases, and the speed at which blockading ships could be refit and reprovisioned at those bases. In Europe, the British relied on the proximity of the huge British Channel ports for resupply and repairs. In America, the main British naval bases were Halifax and Bermuda, and both were several hundred miles away from the theater of operations. Moreover, neither had a well-developed shore establishment or a labor force adequate to service large numbers of warships.

With the force under his command, Admiral Warren was expected to achieve several different objectives simultaneously: hunt the American frigates, patrol the sea-lanes against an armada of American privateers, provide convoys for British merchantmen sailing home from the West Indies, and maintain a commercial blockade. Warren had been asked to do the impossible. Realizing that he did not have enough ships to accomplish these various objectives, he applied for reinforcements. His last letter of 1812, dated December 29, referred to "the Swarms of Privateers and Letters of Marque, their numbers now amounting to 600," that infested the waters of the western Atlantic. Without "a strong addition of Ships," he warned, "trade must inevitably suffer, if not be utterly ruined and destroyed."

The Lords showed little sympathy for Warren's predicament. British naval forces were needed in the English Channel, the Bay of Biscay, and the Mediterranean. England could ill afford major redeployments to the far side of the Atlantic. With heavy reluctance, they consented to withdraw "Ships from other important Services for the purpose of placing under your orders a force with which you cannot fail to bring the Naval War to a termination, either by the capture of the American National Vessels, or by strictly blockading them in their own Waters." Warren's forces would now amount to ten battleships, thirty frigates, and fifty sloops of war. In addition, the Admiralty sent a land force comprising two Royal Marine battalions and an artillery company to be used in coastal raids. Having placed such an enormous force under Warren's command, the Lords expected quick results. He was to maintain the blockade, suppress the privateers, and protect British merchantmen—and in addition, "It is of the highest importance to the character and interests of the country that the naval force of the enemy should be quickly and completely disposed of."

A second letter from London, dated February 10, 1813, took an even harsher tone. If the estimated strength of ninety-seven British warships against fourteen American warships was accurate, asked the Lords, why did the U.S. Navy continue to exist at all? Warren commanded "a force much greater in proportion than the National Navy of the Enemy opposed to you would seem to warrant." He must "strike some decisive blow." As for the privateers, Warren should deal with them through a combination of blockade, convoys, and patrols, and their numbers must be "in a great degree exaggerated; as [their Lordships] cannot suppose that you have left the principal ports of the American Coast so unguarded as to permit such multitudes of Privateers to escape in and out unmolested."

By February 1813, Warren did indeed have a powerful force under his command: In North America, fifteen 74-gun battleships, fifteen frigates, twenty sloops of war, and nearly thirty unrated vessels. In the West Indies, he had another battleship and four frigates; in Newfoundland, a 50-gun ship and two frigates; off Brazil, a battleship, two frigates, and two brigs. The full weight of British naval power was now poised to fall on the North American coast, and Admiral Warren, under intense pressure from his superiors, gathered his strength to carry out the apparent will of the British people as expressed by the *Evening Star*: "All the prating about maritime rights, with which the Americans have recently nauseated the ears of every cabinet minister in Europe, must be silenced by the strong and manly voice of reason . . . and America must be beaten into submission!"

DESPAIRING OF THEIR CHANCES in the presidential election of November 1812, the Federalists nominated an anti-war New York Republican, DeWitt Clinton, to lead the ticket. Clinton and his allies ran an eccentric campaign, opposing the war but occasionally condemning Madison for not fighting it hard enough, and appealing unsuccessfully to anti-Virginia jealousies in the mid-Atlantic states. Clinton carried New York and every New England state except Vermont, but lost in the electoral college by a vote of 128 to 89. With Madison's reelection, the Virginia Republican dynasty entered its twelfth year.

President Madison was only too happy to bask in the reflected glory of the navy that Congressman Madison had once voted not to build. In his second inaugural address, he acknowledged that the disastrous Canadian campaigns had thrown the reputation of the army "under clouds" but rejoiced that the "gallant exploits of our naval heroes proved to the world our inherent capacity to maintain our rights." In rejecting the armistice offered by Admiral Warren, Madison redefined the war as a crusade to end the "arbitrary violence" of impressment. The Republican majority in Congress discovered a new fondness for the navy, and with the passion of the newly converted they moved to expand the fleet. A month of debate ended in a vote, two days before Christmas, for four new 74-gun battleships and six new 44-gun frigates, at a cost of $3.5 million. It was the first major naval construction program, not counting Jefferson's gunboats, since the end of the Adams administration. (Jefferson, living in retirement at Monticello, gave credit where credit was due. "I sincerely congratulate you on the successes of our little navy," he wrote Adams, "which must be more gratifying to you than to most men, as having been the early and constant advocate of wooden walls." Adams replied magnanimously, recalling Jefferson's campaign to send frigates to the Mediterranean in the 1780s: "That you were always for a Navy to compel the Barbary Powers to peace, I distinctly remember in many of our personal Conversations in Europe; and I have carefully preserved very strong Letters from You full of arguments for such a Navy.")

Intoxicated with pride in the navy and its officers, official Washington focused its collective adulation on the one American frigate that remained in the Potomac—the *Constellation*, under the command of Captain Charles Stewart. On November 26, 1812, a "splendid entertainment" was held on board the ship as she lay moored in the Eastern Branch, about half a mile from the Navy Yard wharf. All of Washington society was invited, including the president and first lady. Five hundred guests were rowed out to the ship in colorfully decorated barges. The day was bitterly cold, with a freezing wind, but the *Constellation*'s spar deck was enclosed with flags and awnings, and heated by fires from two galley stoves so "as to make the temperature delightful." A band played and the guests danced until three in the afternoon, when "the boatswain's whistle called us to a magnificent dinner below." The Madisons were seated at the head of a banquet table that extended the entire length of the gun deck. At six, the visitors were rowed back to their waiting carriages at the Navy Yard wharf, and as the president's barge left the *Constellation*, the 18-pounders fired an ear-splitting salute. "We have no doubt but that the *Constellation* will sustain her high reputation," *Niles'* remarked, "and that Captain Stewart will direct better salutes than these to the enemy."

One unpleasant detail of naval business, at the outset of the new administration, was the replacement of Navy Secretary Paul Hamilton. Hamilton had been charged with having spent most of every day drunk, pouring his first glass at midmorning or earlier. Although per capita alcohol consumption was higher than in any subsequent period of American history, alcoholism, somewhat paradoxically, was taboo. Hamilton's drinking may have been a symptom of his problems, rather than the cause of them—his plantations were verging on bankruptcy, with creditors forcing the auctioning of his slaves in groups of ten or twenty. Unlike his two predecessors, he was a planter, not a merchant. He had no prior experience in outfitting ships or overseeing the complex accounts of a large maritime organization. Bookkeeping standards declined; chaos reigned in the Navy Office; anti-navalist Republicans triumphantly pointed out that the administration could not say how vast sums had been spent, and Congressman Nathaniel Macon of North Carolina spoke for many of his colleagues when he said that the hard-drinking South Carolinian was "about as fit for his place as the Indian prophet would be for Emperor of Europe." Madison accepted Hamilton's resignation on the last day of the year.

The man appointed in his place was William Jones, the Philadelphia merchant, shipowner, and former sea captain who had declined the job when Jefferson first pressed it on him twelve years earlier. Jones had served a term in the House of Representatives and was influential in the politics of Pennsylvania. Undaunted by the blizzard of paperwork he found on his arrival in the capital, Jones threw himself into the job, and the intensity of his devotion to work placed him in the same league as Alexander Hamilton, Albert Gallatin, or Benjamin Stoddert. "As to exercise, it is out of the question, except the head and hands," he wrote his wife in Philadelphia. "I rise at seven, breakfast at nine, dine at half-past four, eat nothing afterward . . . I write every night till midnight, and sleep very well when I do not think too much." In his first week on the job, Jones fired the navy's Chief Clerk, who had served since 1801. By January 1814, he had replaced the entire civilian staff of the Navy Office, with the exception of a messenger. He resolved to oppose "the corruption of self-interested men who have taken root in the Establishment . . . like the voracious poplar, nothing can thrive in their shade."

As gratifying as the naval victories of 1812 had been, it was clear that the 1813 campaign would pose a larger set of problems. In embarrassing the Royal Navy, America had seized a tiger by the tail. Remarking on the excesses of the grand naval balls celebrated in Washington, Mrs. B. H. Latrobe told a friend: "We may have reason to laugh out of the other side of our mouths some of these days; and as the English are so much stronger than we are with their navy, there are ten chances to one that we are beaten." The interruption of American commerce had caused a plunge in customs revenues, and Treasury Secretary Gallatin estimated that the federal government would require the colossal sum of $20 million to carry on the war another year. Because most of the nation's disposable private capital was in the hands of anti-war Federalists, Gallatin told the president, "I think a loan to that amount to be altogether unattainable." Negotiating behind closed doors with a small circle of major merchant bankers in New York and Philadelphia, among them John Jacob Astor and Stephen Girard, Gallatin managed to raise a loan of $15.5 million. The funds relieved the immediate financial crisis, but another year of war would exhaust the treasury.

An end to impressment was now the sole American condition to an armistice, but the British government continued to insist that impressment was a right it would never yield. In February 1813, Congress enacted a law designed to ease the way to negotiations on the question, by forbidding the employment of any foreign citizen on board any American vessel, to take effect at the end of the war. There were as many at ten thousand British seamen employed on American merchantmen, privateers, and naval vessels. The law, if enforced, would result in the discharge of these seamen, who would then have little choice but to return to service on British ships. They would almost certainly exceed the number of impressed Americans in the

Royal Navy. On its face, the law seemed to offer England a powerful incentive to negotiate an end to the war.

As early as the fall of 1812, Tsar Alexander of Russia had approached the U.S. minister at St. Petersburg, John Quincy Adams, with an offer to mediate Anglo-American peace talks. The offer reached the American capital about the same time as the first reports of Napoleon's catastrophic defeat in Russia. Madison leapt at the offer, and nominated a three-headed peace commission comprised of Albert Gallatin (who was eager to conclude his twelve-year tenure at the Treasury Department by any means possible), James Bayard of Delaware, and John Quincy Adams, who would await the arrival of his two colleagues in Russia. Only after Gallatin and Bayard had sailed for St. Petersburg did word arrive in America that the British government had rejected the Russian offer. The Admiralty reminded Admiral Warren, on May 17, 1813, that he had no authority "to enter into any Negotiation, or to defer or relax your measures of hostility on the proposition from the Russian Minister, or from the American Government."

CAPTAIN CHARLES STEWART, one of the many veterans of Preble's Mediterranean tour who had risen through the ranks since the end of the Tripolitan War, experienced all the usual difficulties in preparing the *Constellation* for sea—a shortage of adequate supplies and maritime artisans at the Washington Navy Yard, and a dearth of prime seamen, many of whom had shipped out on privateers. Following a time-honored tradition, he sailed from Washington short-handed and only partly provisioned, expecting to find what he needed at ports closer to the sea. Navigating into the Chesapeake and up to Annapolis, *Constellation* completed her manning and stores. On the first day of February 1813, in bitter winter weather, with the ice making fast in the harbor, she hove up her anchor and sailed for Hampton Roads, where she would pause only briefly before putting to sea.

Three days later, doubling Old Point Comfort and Willoughby Bay, just north of Hampton Roads, Stewart and his crew were shocked to come face-to-face with a powerful British squadron, comprising two ships of the line, three frigates, a brig, and a schooner. They were well inside Cape Henry, between the Middle Ground and Horseshoe shoals, just out of cannon-shot range, and beating into a headwind toward Hampton Roads. The route to the open sea was obstructed, and Stewart was forced to decide in an instant how the *Constellation* would make her escape. He could turn into the wind and sail back up the bay, or he could turn into Hampton Roads and run in under the protecting guns of Fort Norfolk. He chose Norfolk. With the wind failing, he ordered the boats hoisted out and kedge anchors run ahead, but as the tide ran out the *Constellation* ran soft aground on the mudflats. To lighten her, Stewart ordered the fresh water pumped out and the hands sent below to turn out the provisions. With the help of small civilian vessels and the evening tide, *Constellation* was lightened, floated, and brought up the narrows to the relative safety of Norfolk. The British squadron, lacking a local pilot and wary of running aground, dropped back down the Roads and anchored in Lynnhaven Bay.

Admiral George Cockburn (pronounced "Coburn"), Admiral Warren's second-in-command on the North American Station, arrived in the 74-gun *Marlborough* with three other vessels to reinforce the advance squadron on March 3. Cockburn was wary of Norfolk's shore defenses, and chose not to attempt an immediate assault on the *Constellation* or the city. Instead, he sent two frigates to anchor off Newport News, near the mouth of the James River, where they could take soundings, buoy the channels, and stage raids into the inland waterways, while also plundering the river traffic. With the exception of scattered resistance by the local militias, Americans had no effective means of repelling these raids. Nineteen days later, Admiral Warren's flagship, the 74-gun *San Domingo*, dropped anchor in Lynnhaven Bay, accompanied by another ship of the line and a frigate. The Royal Navy's local strength now amounted to four battleships, five frigates, two sloops, two brigs, and three tenders, completing the transformation of the lower Chesapeake Bay into a major British naval base.

Chesapeake Bay offered a seemingly infinite number of rich, vulnerable targets; but since English public opinion had demanded, above all, the capture or destruction of the hated American frigates, Captain Stewart assumed an attack on the *Constellation* must come. "I am persuaded they intend something more than a blockade in this quarter," he told Jones. He was concerned by the primitive conditions of Norfolk's defenses. The Gosport Navy Yard did not include enough buildings, barracks, or storehouses, and much of the local weaponry, ammunition, and naval stores were obliged to be left out under the weather. The hospital had originally been set up in a room directly upstairs from the commandant's small office, and Commandant John Cassin complained that "whenever they wash it the water runs all over me, books & everything." Several ancient hulks were sunk in the Elizabeth River's main channel, between Craney Island and Lambert's Point, to obstruct navigation. Stewart found ten of Norfolk's twenty-odd gunboats in service, but they were "so weakly manned and so utterly incompetent to protect themselves" that he ordered them withdrawn up the river, under the guns of Fort Norfolk.

Throughout February and early March, Stewart kept the *Constellation* ready to sail on a moment's notice, hoping for an opportunity to escape past the British squadron into the open sea. On March 9, he maneuvered the ship down the river as far as the bight of Craney Island. The next morning, three British battleships and two frigates kedged up into Hampton Roads, nearly within cannon-shot range. In the face of such an overwhelming force, Stewart took the *Constellation* back upriver and moored her permanently in the channel between Norfolk and Portsmouth. "I am getting out of the Ship all the Stores, Sails, Spars, etc and sending them up the Elizabeth river," he told Jones on March 17, "as it is now reduced to a certainty that this ship will not have an opportunity of getting to sea."

Norfolk's civilians piled their belongings into wagons and fled to the relative safety of inland Virginia. The road from Norfolk to Richmond was jammed with carts, wagons, horses, and people on foot, and committees were formed in Richmond and Petersburg to provide them with food and shelter. Intermingled with the refugees were a considerable number of young men who had deserted from the local militia companies. British raids up the James and Nansemond Rivers resulted in a large number of captures of rivercraft, and navigation became so dangerous that the daily mail boat which normally crossed from Hampton to Norfolk was dragged up onto the beach, and regular deliveries of mail to Norfolk ceased. The newspapers quoted the British commanders as having threatened an attack on *Constellation*, and boasting that no defensive measures would withstand the impending assault.

In response to urgent requests for reinforcements, Navy Secretary Jones candidly replied that Stewart would have to "make the best use of the means you possess, and increase them by all the resources within your vicinity." The entire American coastline was vulnerable, Jones wrote, and there were a "number of places not less exposed than Norfolk, and with much less protection." He urged Stewart to feel consoled by the knowledge that "while a strong squadron of the enemies Ships are employed in watching your little squadron . . . our gallant commanders are scouring the ocean in search of a superior foe."

The battleships and frigates of the British squadron remained, for the most part, in Lynnhaven Bay, exactly where the HMS *Leopard* had lain in wait for the *Chesapeake* in June 1807. They anchored in tight formation, within hailing distance of one another. Coastal raids were carried out by launches, each manned with twenty-five to thirty men and armed with a swivel-mounted howitzer. In fair weather, these launches traveled as far as ten or fifteen miles up the bay or rivers, landing at unprotected points on the shore,

seizing shad boats, oyster boats, skiffs, smacks and river barges, and returning to the squadron by nightfall. The Cape Henry Lighthouse was raided, the
terrified keeper robbed of his hams, mince pies, and sausages, and a nearby
windmill burned to the ground. "Notice Is Hereby Given," proclaimed a
Treasury Department circular signed by Albert Gallatin, "That the lights of
the light-house on Cape Henry, and also of all the other light-houses in the
Chesapeake, will be immediately extinguished."

Local newspapers carried sarcastic reports of the British raids. When a
party of Royal Marines landed at an isolated farm on the Nansemond River,
finding no one but an elderly black woman at home, the *Norfolk Herald* gleefully reported the encounter:

> The marines being most accustomed to that kind of warfare, were
> sent round to the rear of the house by a private avenue, under an offi-
> cer of great experience, to surprize the henhouse; another party
> composed of the most resolute spirits were ordered to storm a neigh-
> boring pig-sty, and the third, being the remaining disposable force,
> headed by the commander in chief, proceeded to sack the dairy and
> smokehouse. The arrangement was excellent, but unfortunately the
> marines, by omitting to send out an advance guard, were surprised
> while defiling through a narrow pass, by a flock of turkeys, who
> charged them furiously in flank and rear. After a sharp engagement
> of near half an hour, however, the assailants were either killed, taken
> prisoner, or put to flight; without the smallest injury to his majesty's
> troops. . . . [The] turkeys having been defeated, the hen-roosts were
> taken possession of; the pig-sty was carried after a slight resistance,
> the storehouses were sacked, and the whole of the forces retreated in
> excellent order, laden with spoil, and without the loss of a man!

In the first week of April, Admirals Warren and Cockburn took the better part of the British fleet up the bay, leaving a small but still superior force
to prevent the escape of the *Constellation*. The Chesapeake and its tributaries
formed a vast inland sea, with hundreds of miles of completely undefended
coastline. Anchoring the large ships at the mouth of the Rappahannock, the
admirals sent a flotilla of launches fifteen miles upriver, where they attacked
and captured four armed schooners. The captured vessels, disguised as common Yankee traders, managed to approach and capture dozens more unsus-
pecting schooners, barges, and pilot boats, and the list of British prizes grew
to more than forty vessels. As the Chesapeake was an essential link in the

internal trade and communication of the United States, the interruption of traffic caused immediate shortages of foodstuffs and other goods in the cities and towns throughout the mid-Atlantic region, including Washington.

Continuing up the bay, the fleet arrived at the mouth of the Patapsco on April 22. Warren remained with the main force, threatening an attack on Baltimore, while Cockburn took two frigates and six smaller vessels to the Chesapeake's shallow northern extremity, with orders to destroy anything resembling an article of war. He anchored at the mouth of the Susquehanna River and dispatched raiding parties on shore to seize provisions. British troops destroyed the Cecil Foundry, near the Elk River, where many of the cannon for the American frigates had been cast. The Maryland militia was unprepared, underarmed, and inexperienced, with command divided between the eastern and western shores of the Chesapeake. With embarrassing regularity, they broke and ran whenever the enemy landed.

When the American townspeople capitulated without resistance, the British raiding parties generally left their houses and barns alone. Admiral Cockburn offered to pay for the cattle and pigs and crops seized in the raids, albeit in bills of exchange which would have to be submitted to the British government at some indefinite point after the end of the war. But when shots were fired at the British raiding parties, Cockburn authorized reprisals. It was on this pretext that the British destroyed Georgetown and Fredericktown on the eastern shore, and to several generations of Tidewater Marylanders, Admiral Cockburn's name would be remembered with the same loathing that General Sherman's name was later remembered by the people of Georgia.

On May 3, before dawn, nineteen barges landed a party of several hundred seamen and marines near Havre de Grace, Maryland, the hometown of Commodore John Rodgers, who was at that moment cruising the North Atlantic in *President*. After the local militia made a halfhearted stand, the civilians of the town paid a heavy price. The British set up a battery of fieldpieces within range of the town and opened up a vicious barrage of shells and rockets, driving the inhabitants in a panic from their homes. *Niles'* reported: "Many fled from their burning houses almost in a state of nudity, carrying in their arms their children, clothing, etc." A party of Royal Marines set torches to the abandoned houses and some of the wagons carrying the personal possessions of the fleeing refugees. Two hours of work leveled almost every building in the area. A detachment was sent with special orders to pillage Commodore Rodgers's house. Brushing aside the tearful pleas of his family, they carried away several of his personal possessions, including a carriage and a pianoforte, but left the manorhouse standing as a professional courtesy to the commodore. Having completed the mission, they retreated to their barges.

Rejoining Warren and the main squadron in the first week of May, Cockburn reported that most of the remaining towns in the upper Chesapeake had capitulated, and that the raids had left "neither public property, vessels, not warlike stores remaining in this neighborhood." In a little over a week, without losing a man, Cockburn's small force had spread terror throughout the entire region. The British had made an important point: with their overwhelming naval superiority, they could descend on any cape, spit, beach, or riverbank they chose, looting and destroying as they pleased, and there was very little the Americans could do to stop them.

The greatest problem faced by the British in carrying out these coastal raids arose within their own ranks. Many of the enlisted men attempted to desert as soon as they set foot on American soil. They were generally welcomed by the local inhabitants as English-speaking cousins escaping the tyranny of a common enemy. Early in April, according to a Baltimore newspaper, thirty to fifty seamen had recently escaped the British squadron, and six weeks later Captain Stewart reported that deserters were still "coming up to Norfolk almost daily." When the seamen and marines were not permitted to go ashore, they sometimes escaped by stealing a boat, and many British launches went over to the enemy. As the weather grew warmer in late spring, men took the risk of swimming to freedom. British sailors' "naked bodies are frequently fished up on the bay shore," Stewart told the Navy Office, "where they must have been drowned on attempting to swim."

Admirals Warren and Cockburn brought the squadron back down the bay on May 12. Fifteen warships anchored in a formidable line extending from Willoughby's Point to Cape Henry, and Norfolk braced itself for an attack. But on the seventeenth, Admiral Warren sailed for Halifax with forty prizes, and Captain Robert Barrie in the *Dragon* sailed for Bermuda with thirty more. The safe disposition of these captured vessels was a priority that every man in the fleet could agree upon, since every man in the fleet would receive a share, however small, of the prize money. (One of Warren's fellow admirals, Sir David Milne, told a correspondent that Warren had taken John Rodgers's looted pianoforte to his house in Bermuda, and had been seen riding around Halifax in Rodgers's carriage. "What do you think of a British Admiral and Commander-in-Chief?" asked Admiral Milne, in disgust. "This is not the way to conquer America.") Cockburn, left in command of the remaining ships at Lynnhaven Bay, maintained the blockade and kept his forces busy in sounding and buoying the channel up to Norfolk.

Captain Stewart had orders from the Navy Office to travel overland to Boston, where he would assume command of the *Constitution*, but he was reluctant to leave at such a critical moment, and Secretary Jones agreed to allow him to delay his departure. At last, substantial numbers of militia reinforcements were streaming into Norfolk from the inland country: the "Henrico Rifles," the Albemarle cavalry, and the "Petersburg Blues," united under the command of Brigadier General Robert Taylor. Defensive breastworks were thrown up at Lambert's Point, Tanner's Creek, and Princess Anne Road. Taylor and Stewart agreed that the essential point of defense was Craney Island, a low-lying scrap of scrub and dune at the mouth of the Elizabeth River, connected to the western shore by a footbridge. General Taylor sent five hundred troops to the island to erect a blockhouse and two redoubts, and Stewart stationed seven gun boats in the mouth of the river. *Constellation* remained five miles upriver, moored in the river off the Gosport Navy Yard, with boarding netting rigged above her bulwarks. A large portion of her crew, about 150 seamen and marines, were sent to man the guns on Craney Island. A resident of Norfolk observed that "the utmost vigilance pervaded this body of men; they scarcely closed an eye during the night." The army and navy were for once working in harmony—officers of both services agreed that if the island fell, so would the *Constellation*, so would the Navy Yard, and so would Norfolk.

Admiral Warren and the *San Domingo* returned to Lynnhaven Bay on June 19, escorting six troop transports carrying an expeditionary force of about 2,200 infantrymen and Royal Marines. Lord Bathurst had dispatched this force to America "to effect a diversion on the Coasts of the United States of America," in the hope of forcing Madison to transfer American troops from the thinly defended Canadian border to the south. Colonel Sir Thomas Sidney Beckwith, who had served with distinction under Wellington in Spain and Portugal, commanded the troops. Among them were two companies of *Chasseurs Britanniques*, comprising about 250 French prisoners who had agreed to join the British army rather than sit out the rest of the war in prison. These Frenchmen were less than happy to be serving in the British Army, and among them were a number of very dangerous men—Beckwith would later describe them as "a desperate Banditti, impossible to control."

On the afternoon of June 19, three British frigates sailed up the channel to Hampton Roads with orders to attack shipping in the James River. In the evening the wind subsided, and the frigates were left becalmed, with one, the 38-gun *Junon*, about three miles away from her consorts. At 11:00 p.m., fifteen American gunboats in two divisions dropped down the Elizabeth and took up a crescent formation around the lone British ship. The Second Division was manned with officers and crew of the *Constellation*. Half an hour before dawn, they began (according to Captain John Cassin's report) a "heavy, galling fire on [the *Junon*] at about three quarters of a mile distance." The barrage continued for forty-five minutes. It ended when a breeze came up that allowed the *Junon*'s consorts to be brought up into action, and the gunboats prudently withdrew. Cassin was sure the *Junon* must have suffered badly in the attack, but in fact she had lost only one marine killed and three seamen wounded, with "several shot in our hull and some of the standing and running rigging cut." The Americans lost a petty officer aboard gunboat No. 139 when an 18-pounder shot fired from the *Junon* "passed through him & lodged in the mast."

As this indecisive action was coming to a close, British reinforcements moved up to the Roads—thirteen sail in all, including four ships of the line, four frigates, two sloops and three transports. They anchored north of Craney Island, safely out of range of the shore guns, and prepared their boats—about fifteen altogether—for a frontal attack on the island. At the first light of dawn, the Americans saw British troops disembarking on the western shore, near Pig's Point, two miles north of the island. The *Constellation*'s crew hauled several of the 18-pounders across the island, to a breastwork closest to the landward side where they could be brought to bear on the troops advancing along the shore. Ammunition and powder was brought in boats from the *Constellation*.

The engagement began as the men of the Royal Marine Artillery fired a series of Congreve rockets from a farmhouse on shore. All fell onto the sand. Two of the American cannon soon destroyed the farmhouse and drove the attackers back. Colonel Beckwith, commanding the British troops advancing along the shore, withdrew out of range of the American guns. Several of his men were killed or wounded by the artillery fire, and about twenty-five deserters melted away into the surrounding pine forest.

During these rocket and artillery exchanges, one of the British boats advanced to the northern shore of Craney Island to take soundings, while the others hung back, awaiting a signal. An American witness admired the "extreme daring" of the men in that first boat. "A brisk fire was kept upon his boat, and a shower of shot fell close to and around her, yet none appear to strike her." She returned to the British flagship, and soon afterward all fifteen boats set sail, advancing in a line abreast on the island. The British crews cheered loudly and repeatedly, and were answered by the American defenders. The lead boat was the *Centipede*, Admiral Warren's magnificent personal barge, a 50-foot vessel rowed by twenty-four immaculately dressed oarsmen and armed with a bow-mounted brass 3-pounder known as a "grasshopper." During the attack, *Centipede* was commanded by Captain John Hanchett of HMS *Diadem*, who held an umbrella over his head in a gesture of contempt for the Americans. A small terrier, apparently belonging to one of the officers, sat in the bow.

The gun crews on the island waited patiently, until the barges were well within range. When the order came to open fire, their concentrated volleys of grape and canister shot cut the attackers to pieces. "[T]he Officers of the *Constellation* fired their 18 pounder more like riflemen than Artillerists," Cassin reported. "I never saw such shooting and seriously believe they saved the Island yesterday." Most of the British boats grounded on the shoals, about 300 yards from the beach. The *Centipede* was cut in half by a direct hit from a heavy round shot. One of the crew, a Frenchman, had both his legs shot off; Captain Hanchett was hit by a canister shot in the thigh, and "kept on his legs as long as possible, but sunk at last from the loss of blood." Some of the Virginia militiamen waded out into the water and shot at the swimmers, including (according to later British reports) men who were unarmed and attempting to surrender. Dozens were taken prisoner, and dozens more swam toward the mainland and the safety of the woods in the hope of deserting. The dog was saved.

Watching at a distance from the deck of the *San Domingo*, Warren decided to call off the attack. In his official report, the admiral reported none killed, ten wounded, and ten missing, but the British *Naval Chronicle* later estimated the combined losses at ninety men. As many as forty British deserters—sailors, soldiers, and marines—crossed the lines. Both sides agreed that the American guns had sunk two British barges. Lieutenant-Colonel Charles Napier of the British 102nd Regiment attributed the defeat to overconfidence: "we despise the Yankees too much."

Infuriated by the bloody repulse, the British troops landed on the opposite shore of the bay, near the village of Hampton, eighteen miles from Norfolk. It was a place of no military significance, defended by about 440 Virginia militiamen. The British boats shelled the town with artillery and rockets while the main body of troops marched on the town from the south. The militiamen killed five and wounded thirty-three of the attackers, but then broke ranks and ran for their lives.

Once the defenders were driven away, the British officers were either unwilling or unable to prevent the troops from running wild. Private homes were looted; the communion plate was stolen from the Episcopal church; several soldiers found a stash of liquor and were soon blind drunk. At least one American soldier was executed after having surrendered. The French *Chasseurs* committed an unknown number of civilian atrocities. In two isolated farmhouses north of the village, between five and seven women were apparently raped by the Frenchmen, although reports suggested that at least one British soldier was involved, as one of the victims asserted that he was "dressed in red" and "spoke correctly the English language." A sixty-five-year-old man who attempted to intervene to stop one of the assaults was striped naked and stabbed. Another, who was sick and unable to rise from his bed, was summarily executed. When the British re-embarked into their ships two days later, and the Virginia militia returned, they found corpses strewn on the ground, stripped of clothing and valuables. Only "the shells of houses" remained standing.

Brigadier General Taylor, commanding the Virginia militia at Norfolk, dispatched a severely worded protest to his British counterparts. "It is important to us and the world to know what species of warfare the arms of Great Britain mean to wage," he told Colonel Beckwith, and closed with a ringing denunciation: "Worthless is the laurel steeped in female tears."

Beckwith responded elusively, at first refusing to admit that any such events had occurred; next representing them as reprisals for the shooting of British swimmers off Craney Island; and finally blaming them on the *Chasseurs*—as if the French soldiers under his command, being French, were not his responsibility. Although Beckwith arranged to have the *Chasseurs* withdrawn from the North American theater, none were punished, and the British never acknowledged that crimes had been committed. Lieutenant-Colonel Napier, who served under Beckwith, confessed in his memoirs that he had been repelled by the behavior of the army at Hampton: "Every horror was perpetrated with impunity—rape, murder, pillage—and not a man was punished."

NEW YORKERS AGED FORTY or older had not forgotten the long, ruinous occupation of Manhattan Island by the British Army in 1776–81, when the wharves had been taken to pieces for firewood, half the population had fled into the backcountry, and two great fires ('76 and '78) laid waste to a quarter of the city. With a strong squadron of British battleships and frigates lying to off Sandy Hook, it seemed likely that history was destined to repeat itself. There was a seemingly infinite number of vulnerable terrain features on Staten Island, Long Island, Manhattan, and New Jersey. Engineers, militiamen, sailors, and laborers worked around the clock to dig trenches, erect barricades, mount gun emplacements, and haul stones to redoubts. Eight companies of New Jersey militia camped on the Highlands, near the beach, and were provisioned by potatoes, cider, and apples purchased from the farmers on the mainland and transported across Raritan Bay in shallow-draft skiffs. While working furiously to complete a new fort, with barracks and blockhouses, they also kept watch over the British ships and communicated their movements to New York via an optical telegraph.

In spite of the seemingly dire threat to the city, it proved impossible to mobilize New York's entire flotilla of gunboats, because Master Commandant Jacob Lewis could not recruit enough seamen to man them. "Although invited not one appeared," he told Secretary Jones. The failed recruiting drive, he said, "served to prove incontrovertibly that volunteers cannot be depended on." Having received similar reports from Baltimore, Norfolk, and Delaware Bay, Jones informed Congress a few weeks later that the gunboats could not be manned because of "the preference which Seamen naturally give to Vessels better adapted to their habits and Comfort."

By contrast, Commodore Stephen Decatur had no difficulty in filling the complements of the USS *United States* and the USS *Macedonian*, the latter having been repaired, overhauled, and brought into the U.S. Navy with her original name. Decatur planned to sortie through lower New York Bay with the two frigates and a sloop of war, the *Hornet*. Evading the British blockade, he would cruise east to Bermuda, north to the Grand Bank, and finally to Ushant, at the gateway to the English Channel, in the hope of intercepting returning East and West Indian convoys. In April and May, the British force off New York consisted of two battleships, *Valiant* and *Ramillies*, and two frigates, *Acasta* and *Orpheus*. With British topsails just off the Hook, Decatur determined to escape New York by the same route he had entered, five months earlier—through the Hell Gate passage into Long Island Sound. From there he would make a dash for the open sea by Montauk Point, the easternmost extremity of Long Island.

On Tuesday, May 18, the three ships of Decatur's squadron raised their anchors and sailed up the East River. On the approach to Hell Gate, *United States* ran aground. Though she suffered no damage in the accident, she was stranded until the next high tide. The next morning, the squadron got underway once again and stood north for the straits, passing beneath the modern-day site of the Triborough Bridge.

The difficulty at Hell Gate was not the depth of water in the channel—there was enough, even at low tide, for the *United States* or any other big ship to pass safely through the straits. The danger arose from the violence of the tide and the numerous rocks and shoals lying hidden just beneath the surface. The margins of the channel were strewn with 150 years' worth of shipwrecks. From long experience, New York pilots had learned that the best time to try the Gate was at low-water slack, because the reduced depth of water was a reasonable price to pay for the absence of current, and the most treacherous rocks were exposed to view. A contemporary pilot's guide spelled out the instructions:

> As you run up between Flood Rock, which is steep-to, and the Point of Long Island, bear up more Easterly, keeping Mid Channel. The last Drain of Tide will show the *Hogsback-dangers* on your Larboard, and the *Pot-Rock* on your Starboard, by the uncommon Ripple and the boiling Appearance of the Water. There is sufficient Depth for large ships until you come up with Marsh Isle, where it Shoals and forms a Bar across the Channel, with only four Fathoms at the Top of High Water; and about a third of the Way over from the Isle there is a single Rock with no more than ten Feet Water.

The squadron passed through safely, and the pilots disembarked into their boats for the return passage to New York. East of Marsh Island (not far from the modern-day site of La Guardia Airport), the *United States* and her consorts skirted the shoals known as the Stepping Stones and Executioner's Rocks, and entered the safer waters of Long Island Sound, with its regular and predictable soundings. Even so, the night of the twenty-sixth brought thunder and hard rain, and a bolt of lightning struck the mainpeak of the *United States*, bringing down Decatur's broad pendant. The electrical charge shot down the mast, leapt across the spar deck to one of the 24-pounder guns, traveled through the wardroom and the surgeon's quarters (where it put out a candle and demolished a cot), tore away a few panels of the frigate's copper bottom sheathing, and finally passed into the Sound. Twenty or thirty men stationed in the tops or on deck received a painful jolt, but none was injured. The *Macedonian* was following a half cable's length astern—her watch officer, fearing the flagship's magazine would detonate, shouted for all sails to be thrown aback. The incident did no serious harm, but it was precisely the kind of dark omen that put the sailors on edge.

Five days after sailing from New York, the squadron anchored in the lee of Fishers Island, pausing there for five days in order to complete victualling and watering and waiting for a heavy fog to lift. Decatur had received "various information of the force of the Enemy off Montaug but were only certain of his having a line of battle ship & a frigate there." Wary of sailing blind into the arms of a superior force, Decatur waited several days for the weather to clear, finally getting the squadron underway at dawn on June 1. At 9:00 a.m., as they were rounding Montauk Point, they came into contact with the 74-gun *Valiant* and the frigate *Acasta* about seven or eight miles to leeward.

Even with the advantage of the wind, Decatur's odds of evading the blockading force were diminished by the agonizing sluggishness of the *United States*. He might have chanced an engagement if the *Valiant* and *Acasta* were the only enemy vessels in sight, but southward progress soon revealed two more strange sails in the lee of Block Island, apparently maneuvering to cut off a potential escape into Newport. With presumed enemies closing from two directions, Decatur gave the order to haul the wind and beat back through the "Race" to New London. The chasing *Acasta* got within long cannon-shot range of the fleeing Americans, and fired a high-arching ball that splashed just short of the *United States*, but the slow-sailing flagship and her consorts (which could have outsailed her handily had they wished) put into the Thames River at two in the afternoon. Neither *Valiant* nor *Acasta* had a local pilot aboard, and neither had ever navigated through the Race. Captain Dudley Oliver of the *Valiant*, fearing for the safety of his ships, called off the chase and returned to the anchorage at Gardiners Island.

Connecticut's Thames River (it rhymes with "games," unlike the English river for which it was named) was not an impregnable refuge. There were fortresses on each side of the river, Forts Griswold and Trumbull, but it was doubtful whether either was strong enough to withstand an attack by a 74-gun ship. Decatur took the *United States*, *Macedonian*, and *Hornet* above New London, and detached boatloads of seamen and marines to return down the river and strengthen the forts. Stores, guns, provisions, and water were hoisted out to lighten the frigates, enabling them to be navigated four miles further up the river to a place called Dragon Hill. On June 9, HMS *Ramillies* (74 guns) and HMS *Orpheus* (36 guns) reinforced *Valiant* and *Acasta*. The blockaders took soundings of Long Island and Block Island Sounds, plundered the coast for provisions, and moved their permanent anchorage to Fishers Island, within sight of the mouth of the Thames. Decatur expected the English to risk everything to recapture the *Macedonian*, "even if they followed her into a cornfield."

FOUR FRIGATES LAY IN BOSTON HARBOR that spring. Commodore John Rodgers, with *President* and *Congress*, had returned to Boston on the last day of 1812 from a three-month cruise in which they had encountered no enemy warships and taken only two prizes. The *Constitution* had returned from her victory over *Java* on February 27 (the sinking condition of the *Java*, following the battle, had obliged Captain William Bainbridge to take the prisoners on board the *Constitution* and burn the captured ship to the waterline). Bainbridge had been appointed commandant of the Charlestown Navy Yard, leaving the most famous frigate in the American service temporarily without a commander. *Chesapeake* had arrived on April 10, after a 115-day cruise in which she had passed through some of England's busiest shipping lanes but taken only three prizes, enhancing her reputation as a star-crossed ship.

With so many ships in port, all competing for attention, the Charlestown shore establishment was once again overwhelmed. Although neither *President* nor *Congress* required major repairs, three months were consumed in refitting and reprovisioning them. Explaining the delays to the Navy Office on March 8, 1813, Commodore Rodgers blamed the weather, which "has been so intollerably cold, and the Country so covered with Ice and Snow, that we have been able to do but very little towards the Ship's completion for sea. The mercury in the Thermometer stands today Six degrees above zero—a degree of cold scarcely ever known here at this Season." Despite generous cash disbursements from Washington, there seemed to be a permanent shortage of money. A large proportion of the *Chesapeake*'s seamen had reached the end of their two-year enlistments and wanted to be paid off, but there was not enough cash on hand to pay them the wages and prize money they were owed. Captain Samuel Evans believed *Chesapeake* needed a new mainmast and perhaps a new mizzenmast, but Secretary Jones was absolutely determined that "not a moment should be lost" in preparing her for another cruise, and urged that she sail with her existing masts, if at all possible.

The British squadron off Boston included the 74-gun *La Hogue* and the frigates *Shannon*, 38 guns, and *Tenedos*, 38. In early April, *La Hogue* returned to Halifax for provisions. Commodore Philip Broke of *Shannon* hoped to lure *President* and *Congress* out to engage *Shannon* and *Tenedos*, and conveyed verbal challenges to that effect to Rodgers by various fishing smacks and pilot boats. Either because he was determined to obey his orders to concentrate on commerce raiding, or because he suspected *La Hogue* was still in the bay, Rodgers would not take the bait.

In the last week of April, *President* and *Congress* made ready to escape to sea. Firing a thunderous salute to the town, which brought thousands of cheering Bostonians down to the wharves to see them off, the two frigates weighed and sailed down the fairway, dropping their hooks again in the lower Roads to await a chance to slip past *Shannon* and *Tenedos*. The weather was on the side of the Americans. Springtime temperature inversions had laid the entire bay under a heavy fog. Lieutenant Henry Edward Napier of HMS *Nymphe* wrote of the challenge of watching Boston in that part of the year:

> In most climates we may expect fine weather after thunderstorms, but on this coast an almost constant fog, still and damp, reigns paramount throughout the months of April, May and June, with longer intervals of fine weather, as it approaches July, when its visits become less frequent and its continuance shorter. The only interruption to this detestable weather is storms and hard rain with now and then a gleam of sunshine, which seldom continues more than a few hours. I have been assured by several people that they have known these fogs to last three weeks, without the slightest intermission.

On the morning of May 1, aided by a favorable combination of wind and tide, and well-concealed by the obsidian murk, the two big frigates pushed out to sea and vanished beyond the eastern horizon. When the news arrived in London, maritime insurance premiums would spike and every merchant in the empire would pay for it out of his own pocket. Captain Thomas Bladen Capel of *La Hogue* reported the news to Admiral Warren in a tone that speaks for itself: "It is with great mortification I am to acquaint you, that . . . two of the Enemy's Frigates (the *President* and *Congress*) have escaped from Boston. I deeply lament the circumstance, but trust you will be satisfied that every exertion was made by the Ships under my orders to prevent the Enemy putting to Sea . . . the long continued Fogs that prevail on this part of the Coast at this Season of the year give the Enemy great advantage."

Late that April, Captain Evans and several of the *Chesapeake*'s lieutenants fell ill, and either for this or for other reasons Secretary Jones assigned the newest officer on the captain's list to take command of her. This was thirty-two year-old James Lawrence, a New Jersey native and (like so many of his colleagues) a combat veteran of Preble's 1803–04 tour in the Mediterranean. Lawrence had earned his recent promotion during his cruise to South America, in Commodore Bainbridge's squadron, as commander of *Hornet*. After Bainbridge and *Constitution* had left San Salvador on December 27, 1812 (going on to capture and destroy the *Java* two days later), Lawrence and *Hornet* were left lying off the harbor to watch the *Bonne Citoyenne*. The *Citoyenne*'s captain, Pitt B. Greene, had refused Lawrence's challenge to a prearranged ship-to-ship duel on the basis that his orders to transport a large quantity of specie home to England must take precedence. Applying the principles of the *code duello*, Lawrence concluded that Greene was a coward for refusing a fair fight, and implied as much in conversations with San Salvador's American consul, knowing the man was likely to circulate the damning allegation in English naval circles. The incident was destined to weigh heavily on Lawrence's mind in a forthcoming encounter, in which the roles would be exactly reversed.

After a fruitless, month-long blockade of San Salvador, *Hornet* was chased away by the arrival of the British 74-gun battleship *Montague*. Sailing alone up the Brazilian coast as far as the mouth of the Demerara River, *Hornet* chanced upon a British 18-gun brig, the *Peacock*. The two vessels fought a short, bloody action. Fifteen minutes after the first gun, the *Peacock* surrendered and soon afterward sank, taking several hands with her to the bottom. Returning to New York, the victorious Lawrence was promoted to captain and swiftly received orders to assume command of the *Chesapeake*.

Lawrence welcomed the promotion but did not much care for his new assignment. He had hoped for the *Constitution*, but she had been promised to Charles Stewart, who stood senior to him on the list. In any case, *Constitution* was undergoing repairs and months away from being ready for sea. If he could have chosen between *Chesapeake* and *Hornet*, Lawrence would have preferred to keep the *Hornet*, despite the fact that she was an unrated vessel, unsuitable to his new rank. He was apparently wary of *Chesapeake*'s reputation as an unlucky ship. But Secretary Jones's letter placing him in command of *Chesapeake* came in the form of an order, not an offer, and Lawrence dutifully set out on the four-day overland journey to Boston, arriving the night of May 18, 1813.

He found the frigate in good order, nearly ready for sea, needing only a few additional provisions and slops (seamen's clothing). She was almost fully manned, awaiting only the arrival of a few new recruits from Maine. This assessment of her readiness was reaffirmed by First Lieutenant Augustus Ludlow, who told his brother Charles on May 28, "The ship is in better order for battle than ever I saw her before." Lawrence's orders were to get clear to sea, evading the watchdogs as Rodgers had done a month earlier, and attack enemy shipping in the Gulf of St. Lawrence, with hopes of taking a few troop transports and checking the buildup of British military forces on the Canadian border. He prepared to sail on the first fair wind.

Outside the harbor, meanwhile, HMS *Shannon* was close inshore, backing and filling within a few cable lengths of Boston Lighthouse. From her masthead, a lookout could plainly see the top yards of the *Chesapeake*, and it was obvious to Captain Broke that she was ready for sea. Would she escape in the fog, as Rodgers had? Or was there any hope of drawing her out for a single-ship duel on equal terms? Hoping fervently for the latter, Broke sent the *Tenedos* away to cruise south of Cape Sable and ordered her not to return to Boston before June 14. *Shannon* continued to capture American merchant vessels in the sea-lanes leading into Boston, but Broke burned them to the waterline rather than send them into Halifax, because (as Lieutenant Ludlow explained) the English commander "does not intend to weaken his crew by manning prizes." Broke was willing to relinquish the wealth offered by prize-taking in order to conserve his ship's strength for a meeting with the *Chesapeake*.

Lawrence and the other officers of the U.S. Navy did not know much about Philip Broke, or about the *Shannon*, other than the fact that she had been operating in American waters since the earliest days of the war, and was one of the enemy frigates that had come within a whisker of capturing the *Constitution* off the New Jersey coast in July 1812. Having commanded the *Shannon* for seven years, Broke was one of the most experienced and efficient frigate captains in the British service. In the post-Nelson, post-Trafalgar era of unquestioned naval supremacy, when the remnants of France's navy were mostly caged in its harbors, and occasions to fire a shot in anger were few and far between, the Royal Navy's overall standards of gunnery and readiness had declined. The *Shannon* was an exception. Captain Broke was a zealous advocate of daily gun drills. Anyone who doubted it could have taken a telescope and climbed to a hilltop of one of Boston Harbor's outer islands on any clear afternoon and watched the *Shannon*'s boats towing empty barrels into a practice range, and heard her 18-pounder batteries let rip their deafening broadsides, discharging huge columns of thick white smoke into the sky, and afterward scanned the surface of the bay in vain for any sign of the barrels. Broke was even more adamant in his insistence on small arms drills, and every day the *Shannon*'s topmen and marines perfected their mastery of grenades, rifles, blunderbusses, and swivel guns.

Shannon was as ready for battle as any frigate had ever been, and Captain Broke wanted the opportunity to prove it. "All fog and rain these days, and chance sight of strangers through the gloom," he wrote his wife on Monday, May 31. "Fog again, so no prospect at all; however, we hope better fortunes. *Chesapeake* is not gone."

On Sunday morning, *Chesapeake* cast off her moorings and sailed from Long Wharf down to President Roads. Climbing aloft into the main rigging of the *Shannon* to have a look into Boston Harbor for himself, Broke saw that the American frigate had her royal yards crossed and was ready for sea. The last day of May was unseasonably clear, and the *Chesapeake* would not have the option of sneaking out through the fog, as her sisters had done a month earlier. Would she await a turn in the weather? Or could she be coaxed to come out and fight? Broke elected to communicate his feelings on the subject to Lawrence directly, and his challenge is worth quoting in its entirety:

Sir,

As the *Chesapeake* appears now ready for Sea, I request you will do me the favor to meet the *Shannon* with her, Ship to Ship, to try the fortune of our respective Flags. To an Officer of your character, it requires some apology for proceeding to further particulars. Be assured, Sir, that it is not from any doubt that I can entertain of your wishing to close with my proposal, but merely to provide an Answer to any objection which might be made, and very reasonably, upon the chance of our receiving an unfair support.

After the diligent attention which we had paid to Commodore Rodgers, the pains I took to detach all force but *Shannon* and *Tenedos* to such a distance that they could not possibly join in any Action fought in sight of the Capes, and the various Verbal messages which had been sent into Boston to that effect, we were much disappointed to find that the Commodore had eluded us, by sailing on the first change, after the prevailing Easterly winds had obliged us to keep an offing from the Coast. He, perhaps, wished for some stronger assurance of a fair meeting. I am therefore induced to address you more particularly, and to assure you that what I write I pledge my honor to perform to the utmost of my power.

The *Shannon* mounts twenty four Guns upon her broadside, and one light Boat-Gun, Eighteen pounders on her Main deck, and Thirty two pound Carronades on her Quarter deck and Forecastle; and is manned with a Complement of Three Hundred Men and Boys, (a large proportion of the latter), besides Thirty Seamen, Boys, and Passengers which were taken out of recaptured Vessels lately. I am thus minute, because a report has prevailed in some of the Boston papers, that we had one Hundred and Fifty Men additional lent us from *La Hogue*, which really never was the case. *La Hogue* is now gone to Halifax for Provisions, and I will send all other Ships beyond the power of interfering with us, and meet you wherever is most agreeable to you, within the limits of the undermentioned Rendezvous, viz: from Six to Ten leagues east of Cape Cod light House, from Eight to Ten Leagues East of Cape Ann lights, on Cashe's ledge in Lat. 43° N. or, at any bearing and distance you please to fix; off the South breaker of Nantucket, or the Shoal on St George's bank.

If you will favor me with any plan of Signals, or Telegraph, I will warn you (if sailing under this promise), should any of my Friends be too nigh, or any where in sight, until I can detach them out of our way—or I would sail with you, under a truce Flag, to any place you think safest from our Cruisers, hauling it down when fair to begin Hostilities.

You must, Sir, be aware that my proposals are highly advantageous to you, as you cannot proceed to Sea singly in *Chesapeake* without imminent risk of being crushed by the superior force of the numerous British squadrons which are now abroad, where all your efforts, in case of a *rencontre*, would, however gallant, be perfectly hopeless.

I entreat you, Sir, not to imagine that I am urged by mere personal vanity to the wish of meeting the *Chesapeake*, or that I depend only upon your personal ambition for your acceding to this Invitation: we have both nobler motives. You will feel it as a compliment if I say that the result of our meeting may be the most grateful Service I can render to my Country; and I doubt not that you, equally confident of success, will feel convinced that it is only by continued triumphs in even combats, that your little Navy can now hope to console your Country for the loss of that Trade it can no longer protect. Favor me with a speedy reply. We are short of Provisions and Water, and cannot stay long here. I have the honor to be, Sir, Your obedient humble Servant,

> P. B. V. Broke,
> Captain of His Britannic Majesty's Ship
> *Shannon*

There was a postscript indicating that the letter had been written in a hurry, and the author, on reading over his first draft, had wanted to clarify a few minor points. Broke promised to keep the challenge a secret if Lawrence was under particular orders not to accept it, concluding: "Choose your terms, but let us meet." The letter was signed, sealed, and entrusted to a discharged American prisoner, who was permitted to take his boat into Marblehead with the promise that he would ride south to Boston and deliver it directly into Lawrence's hands.

By this stage of the war, it was clear that single-ship duels ran against America's strategic interests. The frigate victories of 1812 had been electrifying in their effects on American national morale and self-confidence, and devastating to British public perceptions in a similar magnitude. Apart from these intangible effects, however, they had done nothing to alter the balance of power, which still weighed heavily in favor of the Royal Navy. In the American view, the war could be called off at any moment if the British government would only soften its stand on the abduction of seamen from foreign ships, while the British ministers continued to regard the American war as a unwelcome distraction from their long struggle against Napoleon. By the spring of 1813, the American naval strategy was not to defeat individual enemy warships, but to force England to the negotiating table by inflicting a severe economic penalty on its politically influential merchant interests. Ship-to-ship duels, whether they were won or lost, could no longer serve American objectives in the war. A single lost ship represented a significant diminution of America's navy and an insignificant diminution of England's navy. Even if victorious, an American frigate, following an action, was likely to be removed from active service for several months while undergoing repairs. The greatest impact any American frigate could have in the course of the war—as President Madison, Secretary Jones, and the rest of the cabinet in Washington understood and had decreed—was to get loose in the Atlantic and prey upon British shipping.

Whatever dry calculations occupied the minds of statesmen and diplomats in Washington and London, however, the war had developed into a monstrous affair of honor between the two navies. Even if James Lawrence had not issued a similar challenge to the captain of the HMS *Bonne Citoyenne* in San Salvador six months earlier, and been rebuffed in a manner that gave him grounds to question his adversary's courage, he would have found it difficult to refuse or ignore Captain Broke's challenge. "To an Officer of your character, it requires some apology for proceeding to further particulars." There was not the remotest trace of a taunt or insult in Broke's challenge; he took it as given that Lawrence shared his desire for battle on equal terms. "I entreat you, Sir, not to imagine that I am urged by mere personal vanity to the wish of meeting the *Chesapeake*, or that I depend only upon your personal ambition for your acceding to this Invitation: we have both nobler motives." In a sense that jars modern sensibilities, Broke and Lawrence were brother officers, more deeply beholden to one another than to the civilian statesmen they served. "Favor me with a speedy reply. We are short of Provisions and Water, and cannot stay long here." To transmit such valuable intelligence to an enemy, under different circumstances, would be traitorous. "Choose your terms, but let us meet." Broke guaranteed any arrangement that would prevent other British warships from providing "unfair support" to the *Shannon*, and he assumed, in turn, that Lawrence would accept that pledge as sacred.

As it happened, Lawrence never received Broke's letter, nor would it have made any difference if he had. The first day of June brought clear skies and a mild southwest breeze, and the watch officer woke Lawrence to report that the *Shannon* was still in the offing. The captain came on deck, spyglass in hand, and went aloft into the main rigging to have a look. After a few minutes he climbed back down the ratlines and ordered the *Chesapeake* to sea.

Even without knowing the *Shannon* was short of provisions and fresh water, Lawrence must have known it was in his power to slip past her without a fight, simply by waiting a few days for a change in the weather. He had commanded the *Chesapeake* less than two weeks, hardly enough time to grasp her idiosyncrasies. Half of his officers and probably a quarter of his crew were new to the ship, and many had not yet even stowed their dunnage (baggage). Many of the new hands had not yet been exercised at small arms and the great guns. Finally, he had peremptory orders to get his ship out to sea, avoiding an engagement if possible. None of it caused him a moment's hesitation. Lawrence chose to take the *Chesapeake* out at once, apparently not doubting that she would achieve a sixth consecutive American victory in a single-ship action.

Returning to his greatcabin, he wrote a quick note to Secretary Jones, informing him of his intention to fight the *Shannon*, and another to his brother-in-law, James Montaudevert, asking him to look after his wife and children in the event of his death, concluding: "The frigate is plain in sight from our deck and we are now getting under way." It was the last letter he would ever write.

At noon, the wind and tide were right, and the hands shipped the capstan bars to heave up the anchor. The *Chesapeake* loosed her topsails, sheeted them home, and sailed down the Narrows amid a small flotilla of spectator boats whose passengers boisterously cheered the ship and her crew. At half past one she rounded the lighthouse and bore away to the northeast, following in the wake of the *Shannon*, which was leading ahead under staysails and royals. Broke intended to fight well out to sea, in the offing between Cape Ann and Cape Cod, far enough from Boston that he would have no reason to fear being attacked by shore craft. He kept *Shannon* on her course until five, when she had arrived at a position about twelve miles south southwest of Cape Ann. Then he hove to the wind and waited for his adversary to close.

Lawrence kept the deck as the *Chesapeake* sailed out into the bay. He wore his freshly brushed blue uniform coat, with epaulets, lapels, and high standing collar trimmed with glittering gold lace, white trousers, top boots, a black cocked hat, and a polished sword in scabbard at his belt. His long hair was braided tightly in a queue and tied with a black ribbon. With Lieutenant George Budd at his side, he circulated among the gun crews, inspecting their preparations, and ordered canister and bar shot loaded on top of the round and grape. In a custom borrowed from the Royal Navy, each of the *Chesapeake*'s great guns had been given a name, painted in large white letters above the gunports: *Wilful Murder, Dreadnought, United Tars, Pocahontas, Bunker's Hill, Liberty for Ever, Washington, Raging Eagle,* etc. On the principle that men should not be sent into battle with empty stomachs, Lawrence ordered the hands piped to dinner, and they messed as usual, on tables slung between the guns. "Bear a hand, boys, and get your dinner," Lawrence told them as they ate—"you will have blood for supper."

Spreading a huge expanse of canvas in the mild breeze, *Chesapeake* out-sailed the yachts, schooners, and sloops, filled with civilian well-wishers, that had followed her into the bay. Her sides were gleaming with a fresh coat of paint, and she was dressed for the occasion, with three ensigns flying in the main and mizzen rigging, and at the forepeak a long white banner embla-zoned with the words "FREE TRADE AND SAILORS' RIGHTS." In Boston, a grand victory banquet was being prepared in honor of Captain Lawrence and his soon-to-be victorious officers, and a length of wharf was kept clear for the soon-to-be captured *Shannon.* Crowds of spectators climbed the hills and headlands of Cape Ann and Cape Cod and were "striving to catch a glimpse of the capture of the British frigate."

The two ships were a near-perfect match. Their length on deck was vir-tually the same; each carried a gun deck battery of twenty-eight long 18-pounders; and their armament on the upper decks was about the same. The *Chesapeake*'s only advantage was in her number of crew—379 men against the *Shannon*'s 330.

Aboard the *Shannon,* Commodore Broke wore a black top hat and a heavy Scottish broadsword, which hung from a shoulder strap. When asked if the *Shannon* should hoist more flags and bunting to match the colorfully decorated appearance of the *Chesapeake,* he answered: "No, sir. We have always been a modest ship; one flag is enough for us, but as I know you never intend it to come down, it shall be lashed to the peak." It was an audacious order, one that might cost many lives if the *Shannon* found herself beaten and incapable of asking for quarter. Calling his crew back to the waist, Broke made a terse speech:

> Shannons, you know that from various causes the Americans have lately triumphed on several occasions over the British Flag in our frigates . . . they have said, and they have published in their papers, that the English have forgotten the way to fight. You will let them know today that there are Englishmen in the *Shannon* who still know how to fight.
>
> Don't try to dismast her. Fire into her quarters; main-deck into the main-deck; quarter-deck into the quarter-deck. Kill the men and the ship is yours. Don't hit them about the head for they wear steel caps, but give it to them through the body. Don't cheer. Go quietly to your quarters. I feel sure you will all do your duty, and remember that you now have the blood of your countrymen to avenge.

At 4:50 p.m., the adversaries were separated by about two miles. Lawrence ordered the *Chesapeake*'s light sails taken in and her royal yards struck down on deck. Broke decided to leave the *Shannon*'s royals crossed, guessing that the breeze would die off at sunset. *Chesapeake* was closing with *Shannon* from windward, so Lawrence had the potentially decisive advantage of the weather gauge. Broke made no effort to maneuver the *Shannon* into a better position. Lawrence recognized that his opponent was deliberately conceding a valuable advantage, and he refused to accept it. Communicating by means of a seaman's unspoken language, the commanders agreed to dispense with all pre-combat maneuvers. *Shannon* would not fire on the *Chesapeake* as she came downwind, and *Chesapeake* would not exploit the weather gauge in order to rake the *Shannon*. It could have been a medieval jousting match. Afterward, the English officers praised Lawrence for his gallantry, but as Midshipman Raymond of the *Shannon* later wrote, "He certainly came down in a most brave and officer-like manner, but he was too confident."

At five forty-five, *Chesapeake* closed to a distance of 50 yards on the *Shannon*'s weather quarter. Lawrence shouted to the helmsman: "Luff her!" and the *Chesapeake* immediately threw her head into the wind and ranged up abeam of her enemy. The crew of the *Shannon* could hear the order given on the American ship, and they were ready at the starboard guns. The action did not commence with a single dramatic broadside on either side, but with the deep concussive thuds of the great guns keying in individually, as each came to bear on its target, accompanied by the high-pitched crackle of the muskets and swivel guns. After the first few seconds, there was only a wall of sound: a continuous, earsplitting roar.

Shot crashed through the *Chesapeake*'s rigging, cutting many of her forward shrouds and braces to ribbons; shrapnel-like clouds of splinters were blasted out of the interior walls of her bulwarks, where the Englishman's round shot struck. A swath of grape and canister shot swept across the quarterdeck, killing or wounding many of the American officers in the first two minutes of action. The sailing master was killed outright; the helmsman was killed; Lieutenant White's head was blown off; Captain Lawrence took a musket ball under his right knee and clutched the binnacle to keep his feet. A man stepped forward to replace the fallen helmsman, and was killed. A third stepped forward, and a direct hit from one of the *Shannon*'s 9-pounder pivot guns killed him and also smashed the *Chesapeake*'s wheel to pieces. Out of the 150 men stationed on the *Chesapeake*'s spar deck, 100 were killed or wounded in the first two minutes of the action. Among the fallen were nearly all the American officers.

The *Shannon* suffered as well, particularly from the rapid, well-aimed fire of the *Chesapeake*'s 18-pounders and the marine sharpshooters stationed in the tops. A round shot struck the chocking quoin of one of *Shannon*'s quarterdeck carronades and launched it toward Broke, missing him by inches and shattering the gun captain's knee. Another man stationed on the main deck was struck in the midsection by a round of grape—he refused to be carried down to the surgeon, but invited his mates to reach into the wound and pull out the shot. The *Shannon*'s helmsman, a Trafalgar veteran, was struck in the wrist and nearly lost his arm, but stayed at the wheel. A dozen or more dead men were thrown from the gunports into the sea. But the *Shannon*, unlike the *Chesapeake*, had not yet lost any of her senior officers, and her internal command structure remained intact.

From the moment she had luffed up, the *Chesapeake* had kept more speed through the water than the *Shannon*, and she continued to range ahead, until her forward guns could no longer bear on her adversary. The damage to her fore rigging made her headsails unmanageable, and they flapped uselessly in the breeze. This, combined with the loss of the helm and helmsmen, left the *Chesapeake* at the mercy of events. She turned her quarter to the *Shannon*, flew up into the wind, lost her headway, was taken aback, and began to gather stern way. That is to say, *Chesapeake* actually began to travel backward through the water, directly toward the British ship. As the distance closed, the *Shannon*'s gun crews and topmen kept up a relentless fire, and the unprotected quarterdeck of the *Chesapeake* became as inhospitable to human life as the surface of the moon. First Lieutenant Ludlow was killed; the lieutenant of marines was killed; Lawrence was wounded but still on his feet when he received a second, more deadly wound in his groin, fell to the deck, and was yanked through the after hatch by his third lieutenant. Every officer, seaman, or marine stationed aft of the mizzenmast was soon taken down by the marksmen firing from the *Shannon*'s fore and maintops. A witness compared the combined effect of the English grape shot, canister shot, and musketry to a "pelting gale."

Drifting helplessly, the *Chesapeake*'s stern came into contact with the *Shannon* amidships, and her mizzenyard fouled in the British frigate's fore rigging. *Shannon* had a sheet anchor stowed in her mainchains, and the fluke of this anchor smashed the *Chesapeake*'s quarter-gallery window, entered Lawrence's cabin, and temporarily locked the ships together. Captain Broke, stationed on the *Shannon*'s gangway near the point of impact, and seeing the American quarterdeck strewn with bodies and otherwise abandoned, called for boarders. The boatswain attempted to lash the ships together, passing a brace over the *Chesapeake*'s taffrail, but one of the Americans in the greatcabin saw what he was doing, reached up through the quarter gallery with a cutlass, and began hacking ferociously at the man's arm. The limb was severed completely, and splashed into the sea between the two ships. Still the *Chesapeake* could not get clear; the wind kept her stern pressed firmly against the *Shannon*.

As the mortally wounded Lawrence was carried to the surgeon's cockpit, he called for boarders—but the bugler, whose responsibility it was to sound the call, had fled his station in terror. The order passed haphazardly through the gun deck, by word of mouth, and the remaining lieutenants and midshipmen did their best to rally a boarding party. But there was not enough time. Not a single living officer was left on the spar deck, and confusion reigned throughout the *Chesapeake*. The men crowded forward or fled belowdecks, and any man brave enough to charge up through the *Chesapeake*'s main or after hatches was cut down instantly in a hailstorm of enemy fire.

A grenade lobbed from the *Shannon*—by some reports, thrown by Broke himself—landed in an open chest of musket cartridges, which blew up and enveloped the quarterdeck in a cloud of thick, white, billowing smoke. A party of boarders, armed with pikes, pistols, and cutlasses, had collected on the *Shannon*'s gangway. Broke shouted, "Follow me, who can!" and climbed over the hammock nettings; he reached his foot across to the roof of the *Chesapeake*'s quarter gallery, shifted his weight across; stepped on the muzzle of the American ship's aftermost carronade, pulled himself over her bulwark, drew his service sword, and dropped to her deserted quarterdeck. He was the first of the *Shannon*'s crew to board, followed close behind by his first lieutenant and about thirty others.

The *Chesapeake*'s chaplain, Samuel Livermore, fired a pistol at Broke from close range, but missed. Broke slashed at him, gouging a deep wound in the clergyman's arm, and charged forward along the gangway, slashing and hacking at the few seamen and marines he met, his men following close behind. The boarders drove the remaining defenders forward into the forecastle. With no officers to rally them, most of the Americans succumbed to panic, crowding down the forward hatch or vaulting over the rail and through the bridle ports to the relative safety of the gun deck.

Below, Captain Lawrence lay mortally wounded in the cockpit. He refused medical treatment, and continued to demand that his officers rally a boarding party. But when we saw the rush of panicked seamen coming down the ladders, Lawrence realized all was lost. "Don't give up the ship," he cried, to anyone who would listen: "Fight her till she sinks." He repeated the order again and again; and finally: "Don't give up the ship. Blow her up." The order, which no seaman could fail to understand, was to strike a match and throw it into the *Chesapeake*'s magazine. *Don't give up the ship*. It was strange that these dying words, comprising an order (not obeyed) to commit mass suicide, were subsequently adopted as the navy's unofficial motto. They were not the kind of words that were spoken with posterity in mind; they were never intended to be quoted or even remembered. *Don't give up the ship*. This was the final, despairing roar of a man who was bleeding to death, a man who had fought gallantly but ineffectively, losing a valuable ship to a thirty-man boarding party in an action lasting less than fifteen minutes.

While the British took control of the *Chesapeake*'s upper deck, the marines and swivel men in the American frigate's fighting tops continued to fire down on Broke and his men. Broke shouted up to the midshipmen commanding the *Shannon*'s tops to silence this deadly fire from their American counterparts, and the *Shannon*'s topmen showed extraordinary courage in carrying out the order. The captain of the English ship's maintop, finding his view of the enemy veiled by the *Shannon*'s topsail, crawled out to the end of the main yardarm, and from that vantage point picked off three men in the American mizzentop. The captain of the *Shannon*'s foretop, Midshipman Smith, actually led a boarding party of five men across her foreyard, and with a heaving sea 50 feet beneath his feet leaped across to the end of the *Chesapeake*'s foreyard. Sword in hand, Smith stormed the *Chesapeake*'s foretop, killed several of the Americans he found there, and drove the rest down on deck, where they surrendered to Broke and his party.

A melee continued in the forecastle, as a few Americans managed to force themselves up the fore hatch. Broke found himself fending off the combined assault of three American sailors. One thrust at him with a pike; he parried the blow with his sword, but could not get out of the way of a musket swung at his head. The blow sent him reeling, and in his daze he could do nothing to defend himself against the third man, who struck him hard in the forehead with a cutlass. A long flap of scalp was peeled back from Broke's skull, and about three inches of his brain cavity were exposed to view. A British marine rushed into the fray and bayoneted the American armed with the cutlass; the others were driven back and surrendered. At the same moment that Lawrence, below, was exhorting his men not to give up the ship, the British boarders were herding the surrendered prisoners down the hatches and securing the gratings over them.

The boarding party had paid a heavy price, with more than two thirds of the British seamen and marines who followed Broke onto the *Chesapeake* killed or wounded. The battle ended messily, as boarding actions often did. Some of the Americans fired their weapons up the hatches, killing a British marine; Broke told his men to fire down the hatches until the Americans called for quarter, and by some reports the British continued firing even after repeated cries of surrender, and even aimed shots into the surgeon's cockpit where dozens of helpless men lay wounded. There were reports of wounded Americans being executed outright while lying on deck. One of the American midshipmen stationed in the rigging later testified that a British lieutenant ordered his men to throw him overboard, though he was unarmed and had surrendered. Lieutenant Watt, first lieutenant of the *Shannon*, had hauled down the American ensign and was attempting to hoist the British colors when he was accidentally killed by a grape shot fired by one of the *Shannon*'s carronades. Four or five other British seamen were similarly killed by friendly fire in the closing minutes of the action.

When the flotilla of spectator boats, some as close as a mile and a half away, saw the British ensign raised to the *Chesapeake*'s mizzen peak, they hauled their wind and hurried back into Boston Harbor.

It had been the bloodiest naval action of the war, one of the bloodiest of any war up to that date. Two hundred and twenty-eight men lay dead or wounded, and many of the wounds were mortal. *Shannon* had suffered twenty-three killed and fifty-eight wounded; *Chesapeake* recorded forty-eight killed and ninety-nine wounded, and another twenty-three of the combined wounded would die in the following days and weeks. Among the *Chesapeake*'s casualties were most of her officers, including her captain; her first, second, third, and fourth lieutenants; her lieutenant of marines; seven midshipmen; her sailing master; and more than twenty petty officers. A witness described the appearance of the *Chesapeake*'s spar deck: "the coils and folds of rope were steeped in gore as if in a slaughter house. . . . Pieces of skin, with pendant hair, were adhering to the sides of the ship, and in one place I noticed portions of fingers protruding, as if thrust through the outer wall of the frigate."

Most of the casualties on both sides had been killed or wounded by small arms fire. As a result, neither ship suffered severe damage. No spars had been shot away in either frigate; and although each had taken several round shots in the hull, the punctures in each case were above the waterline, and neither was leaking badly. "Both Ships came out of Action in the most beautiful order," said the British battle report, "their Rigging appearing as perfect as if they had only been Exchanging a Salute."

The *Shannon* was the better ship, and Broke the better commander. The British deserved to prevail, and they did. But the *Chesapeake-Shannon* action also demonstrated the principle that a single stroke of bad luck can quickly turn decisive. Had the *Chesapeake* not lost her headsails at the outset of the action, causing her to luff up into the wind and exposing her quarterdeck to a savage, raking fire, the result might have been very different. Similarly, if Lawrence had maneuvered to his full advantage in the early part of the action, Broke's boarding action might never have been possible. The casualties inflicted on the *Shannon* by the *Chesapeake*'s early cannonade were severe enough to suggest a battle of running broadsides might have been decided in the American ship's favor.

Two hours after the last gun had been fired, the *Shannon* and her prize were ready to sail for Halifax. They remained in close company during the five-day passage, the *Shannon* making a fair amount of water on the larboard tack but no more than usual on the starboard tack. Lawrence's wound was bound up as tightly as possible, but he continued to lose blood, and died on June 5. The British wrapped his body in the *Chesapeake*'s ensign. At Halifax he would be buried with full military honors, with six officers of the Royal Navy serving as his pallbearers. Broke's gruesome head wound was pronounced mortal by the surgeon, but he continued to hang on, immobilized on a stretcher in his cabin. He even managed to speak, though only in monosyllables.

The two frigates reached Halifax on June 6, a Sunday morning, when many of the town's residents were at religious services. At St. Paul's Church, according to a contemporary account, a man entered and whispered loudly to an acquaintance sitting near the back. The news "flew from pew to pew," and a moment later, ignoring the pastor, the worshippers poured out of the church and ran down to the harbor. As *Chesapeake* came into view, making her way down the long harbor toward the Navy Yard on the western shore, her American colors were plainly visible and above them the white ensign of St. George. Every wharf and housetop "was crowded with groups of excited people, and as the ships successively passed, they were greeted with vociferous cheers." Bells were rung in every belfry in Halifax; before long, they would be ringing all over England. Broke had done it; the doubts could be laughed away; the Royal Navy's honor was saved, and the world that had been turned upside down, in those few disturbing months of 1812, had at last rotated back to its right side up.

CHAPTER FIFTEEN

In the early weeks of the war, ex-President Jefferson had assured the Republican editor William Duane that an invasion of Canada, with a population about one tenth that of the United States, would be "a mere matter of marching." General Hull's abject surrender at Detroit had followed nine days later. Two subsequent invasion attempts had been turned back in the fall; and by the spring of 1813, Americans had reason to fear being invaded in turn. John Adams, observing events from his retirement in Quincy, had given Jefferson his opinion that the only sure means of securing the northern frontier was to win naval supremacy on the Great Lakes, particularly Ontario and Erie: "We must have a Navy now to command The Lakes, if it costs Us 100 Ships of the Line; whatever becomes of the Ocean."

Men, money, ordnance, munitions, shipwrights, and naval stores flowed north. Blockaded American frigates, including the *Constellation* at Norfolk, *Macedonian* and *United States* at New London, and *Constitution* at Boston, were stripped of much of their crews, and the men sent to report for duty at Sackets' Harbor, on Lake Ontario. Captain Isaac Chauncey was removed from his command of the New York Navy Yard and placed in command of America's freshwater naval forces on Lakes Ontario and Erie. Commodore Oliver Hazard Perry supervised a crash shipbuilding program in the remote wilderness of Presque Isle, Pennsylvania (present-day Erie), and with this hastily constructed array of small brigs and schooners, he engaged and annihilated the British Lake Erie Squadron on September 10. His flagship, the *Lawrence*, sailed into action flying a banner inscribed with the fallen captain's last words: "Don't Give Up the Ship." In his official letter reporting the result of the battle, Perry coined an equally memorable phrase, destined to be taken up as another of the navy's slogans: "We have met the enemy and they are ours." A month later, American militia and army forces defeated a combined British and Indian army at the Battle of Thames, in which Tecumseh, the great Shawnee chief, was killed in action. The battles of Lake Erie and the Thames ruled out any British invasion from that part of Canada. Equally important was the effect on the American people's perceptions and morale. The victories rallied public support for the war at a moment when it had seemed on the verge of unraveling.

The tightening grip of the British blockade was beginning to take a severe economic toll on communities throughout the country. The drain on the treasury remained a pressing concern, and the Republican-dominated Congress finally recognized the need for more tax revenue; a new levy fell on licenses, carriages, auctions, sugar refineries, and salt. Admiral Warren's forces, unfazed by the bloody repulse at Craney Island, continued to roam the Chesapeake at will. "Strong is my dislike to what is perhaps a necessary part of our job: namely, plundering and ruining the peasantry," Lieutenant-Colonel Charles Napier wrote in his diary. "We drive all their cattle, and of course ruin them. My hands are clean; but it is hateful to see the poor Yankees robbed, and to be the robber." In mid-July, reports arrived in Washington that a squadron of enemy battleships and frigates was steering a course up the Potomac River, threatening to attack the capital itself. The city prepared to flee. For a month, Madison had been bedridden at the White House with a dangerous bout of influenza. His doctors could not say whether the commander in chief would survive, and he was in no condition to be moved. As it happened, the British ships did not ascend the river beyond the Kettle Bottoms, but they sent boats ahead to take soundings and learn the channel for a potential future operation. After it was confirmed that the enemy had returned to the bay, Secretary of War John Armstrong reassured the capital's flustered inhabitants that his defensive preparations were sufficient to repel any future British attack.

On September 26, 1813, Commodore Rodgers and USS *President* returned safely from a five month cruise, putting in at Newport, Rhode Island. Parting ways with *Congress* shortly after escaping Boston in early May, *President* had probed as far south as the Azores, turned back to the north and harassed British whalers through the North Sea (where the sun appeared "at midnight several degrees above the Horrison"), replenished her fresh water at Bergen on the Norwegian coast, cruised with impunity in the waters around the Shetlands, the Orkneys, and the northern Irish Channel, and then passed through the crowded sea-lanes of the western approaches before shaping a course for home. Returning to the North American coast, *President*

eluded the British cordon by threading the shoals of the rarely used Tucker-
nuck passage between Nantucket and Martha's Vineyard. She had taken
twelve enemy prizes, including the schooner HMS *High Flyer*, Admiral Warren's personal tender (some had been destroyed, others sent into port earlier
manned by prize crews). In the final weeks of her long cruise, the frigate's
large crew subsisted on reduced rations "of the roughest fare." Though the
sailors were "in better health than might be expected," Rodgers told Jones,
"you may well suppose that their scanty allowance has not been of any advantage to their Strength or appearance."

Rodgers expressed disappointment at not having fallen in with an enemy
warship, but in fact the *President* had accomplished a great deal. Reports of
her whereabouts—often conflicting—filled the British newspapers, and her
presence in the offing spread fear and uncertainty. The Admiralty was subjected to withering criticism for its failure to hunt down the "successful
marauder" (*Naval Chronicle*), and the specter of an American frigate cruising
openly in Britain's home waters dramatized the threat to British commerce.
The cruise won John Rodgers a notoriety among Englishmen greater than
that enjoyed by any of his colleagues—even those, like Hull, Decatur, and
Bainbridge, who had taken a British frigate. Secretary Jones congratulated
Rodgers on an "active, vigilant, and useful Cruize." The Admiralty had been
forced to deploy a great deal of force in the search for *President*, while the cost
to British shipping would be felt, once again, in the all-important calculation
of maritime insurance. Jones had asked for a war against British commerce,
and Rodgers had delivered it.

On December 14, the *Congress* came to anchor in the outer harbor of
Portsmouth, New Hampshire. She had been out nearly eight months, one of
the longest cruises of the war. Captain John Smith was embarrassed to report
that the *Congress* had managed to capture only four enemy vessels in all her
time at sea. The value of these four prizes would not equal the cost of keeping the *Congress* at sea for such a great length of time. It had been the least
profitable cruise of the war. Secretary Jones wanted the frigate refitted and
reprovisioned for another cruise as soon as possible, but close inspection
revealed that her timbers were decayed, her bowsprit was shot, her lower rigging required a complete overhaul, and the entire deck and hull need recaulking. As *Congress* was dismantled at the Portsmouth Navy Yard wharf, a short
distance from the stocks on which she had been built, the shipwrights grew
increasingly pessimistic about her condition. With the instinctive parsimony
of a veteran shipowner, Jones ordered the *Congress* laid up in ordinary and her
guns hauled overland to Lake Ontario.

"Here we are," wrote Stephen Decatur from New London, "John Bull and us, all of a lump." Captain Thomas Masterman Hardy, the HMS *Ramillies*, and the rest of the British blockaders seemed content to remain anchored in the lee of Fishers Island indefinitely, keeping the frigates *United States* and *Macedonian* imprisoned in the Thames River. To Decatur's chagrin, the people of New London did not seem inclined to rally to the defense of the blockaded American squadron. Connecticut was Federalist territory, and "Mr. Madison's War" was deeply unpopular. There was growing pro-British sentiment in the region, and Decatur suspected that disloyal locals were passing vital intelligence to the British. The presence of the *United States*, with *Macedonian* and *Hornet*, ensured that the port would remain closely blockaded, interrupting the coastal trade and severely penalizing New London's maritime economy. It was generally believed that the British planned to attack upriver and would probably destroy the town. "A desperate engagement may be hourly looked for," reported a local paper.

Reports of the behavior of Admiral Cockburn's forces in the Chesapeake had terrified local civilians, but Captain Hardy, who had served as Nelson's flag captain at Trafalgar, did not intend to allow the kind of pillaging that had occurred to the south. He conveyed a message to the people of New London, through the local customs inspector, "to assure the ladies that they may rely on his honor, that not a shot should be fired at any dwelling (at least while he had the command) unless he should receive very positive orders for that purpose, which he had not the most distant idea would be received." The message calmed fears considerably, and also did a great deal to confirm and enhance pro-British sentiment in Connecticut. Hardy's candid promises to the civilians of New London stood in welcome contrast to the evasive answers given by Colonel Beckwith after the sack of Hampton. "On the whole," observed the *Niles' Register*, a newspaper hardly known for pro-British sentiment, "Hardy must be a noble fellow."

With several American seaports now strongly blockaded, leaders in Washington took an interest in weapons innovations that might alter the balance of power. In March 1813, Congress passed the so-called Torpedo Act, which made it lawful for "any person or persons to burn, sink or destroy any British armed vessels of war . . . and for that purpose to use torpedoes, submarine instruments, or any other destructive machines whatever." (At that time, the term "torpedo" referred to a wide array of spar-mounted weapons, undersea devices, and both fixed and floating mines.) Any American, civilian or military, who managed to sink an enemy warship by such means would be paid a federal bounty equivalent to half the value of the vessel destroyed. In the case of a frigate or battleship, the bounty could easily exceed $100,000, a fantastic sum. All up and down the Atlantic seaboard, entrepreneurs and inventers turned their minds to the challenge.

One of the best-known weapons innovators of the day was Robert Fulton, a failed portrait artist whose work in steam engine propulsion was only one of many interests. Fulton had hawked his inventions in London, Paris, and other European capitals before returning to the United States in 1805. In lobbying the Navy Office to fund his torpedo experiments, Fulton avowed that "every Physical operation which is not contrary or at Varience with the laws of nature is practicable for man to perform . . . [and] torpedoes with practice must succeed, for there is no Physical impossibility to prevent it." When Fulton dismissed objections that his torpedoes were dishonorable, his opinions, like his inventions, foreshadowed a very different kind of future:

> [I]s war confined within the limits of honor? The British, by pressing American Citizens and compelling them to fight against their Brethren, have not consulted Honor, the Laws of Nations, or humanity, but simply their own convenience or caprice. Everything in these times to weaken the enemy and defeat them on our coast is Right, and for War sufficiently Honorable.

In April 1813, Secretary Jones agreed to lend Fulton a fireship for torpedo experiments in New York, on the condition that the navy would "incur no expense whatever on account of these experiments." Fulton demonstrated that a 100-pound projectile could be fired underwater with enough force to pass through a three-foot oak plank at a range of six feet. Master Commandant Jacob Lewis, charged with monitoring Fulton's experiments in New York, was enthusiastic. If a submerged weapon could be maneuvered to within point-blank range of an anchored British warship, it seemed possible she could be sunk. "I think submarine Batteries can be turned to a good Account," he concluded.

In the Chesapeake, a naval petty officer named Elijah Mix conceived a plan to destroy some of the vessels of Admiral Warren's fleet by towing a floating mine or "powder machine" to the enemy's anchorage and cutting it loose. The mine would be allowed to drift down on an anchored vessel, where it would explode on impact. On June 5, in Lynnhaven Bay, the boats of the HMS *Victorious* picked up one of these "infernal Machines," crammed with 500 pounds of gunpowder, as it was drifting down on the British ship with the ebb tide. Admiral Cockburn, who had already demonstrated that he had limited scruples in interpreting the rules of war, was nevertheless outraged by this attempt to "dispose of us by wholesale Six Hundred at a time," and warned the other British commanders to watch for unidentified floating objects. On July 24, another of Mix's floating mines approached the HMS *Plantagenet*, but detonated prematurely at a range of 100 yards, throwing up "an immense column of flame" and raining a cascade of water down on the battleship's deck. No one was injured. The *Naval Chronicle* reported: "Our blockading ships on the coast have kept the most sharp look-out, in their guard-boats, since this infernal attempt was made."

A group of New York merchants devised a more insidious attack. Why not booby-trap a coasting vessel with explosives, allow her to be captured, and rig her to explode when brought alongside an enemy warship? A schooner, the *Eagle*, was crammed with black powder and "a great Quantity of Combustibles," hidden under a cargo of provisions and naval stores. A trip line was secured to the bottom of one of the casks, so that when it was lifted from the hold it would trigger a gun-lock and set off an explosion large enough to destroy both the booby-trapped schooner and any large ship lying alongside.

On the morning of June 25, the *Eagle*, appearing like any number of other common coasting schooners, was seen approaching New London in a failing breeze. Captain Hardy sent a master's mate with a party of seamen in the *Ramillies*'s barges to go after her. The *Eagle*'s crew fired a few shots at their pursuers and then fled for shore in a small boat. Hardy, perhaps suspecting something was amiss, ordered the captured vessel anchored some distance from the *Ramillies*, and sent a boarding crew under the command of a lieutenant to unload her provisions into the *Ramillies*'s boats. At 2:00 p.m., one of the boarding party tripped the lock-line and the *Eagle* "blew up with a most tremendous explosion." The lieutenant and ten seamen were killed instantly, and three others were "Much Scorched in the Face, Arms, & Legs."

The British were enraged. Admiral Warren called it "a Diabolical and Cowardly contrivance of the Enemy." The *Naval Chronicle* said the men responsible for the scheme were "held in detestation by every friend of humanity." But there were also expressions of relief that the explosion had not killed Hardy, who was held in special reverence by the British public because of his connection to Nelson. Orders went out from Halifax requiring every British man-of-war on the American coast to search every strange vessel at a distance before bringing her alongside.

Two months later, an American operating a primitive, one-man submarine attempted to attach an explosive device directly to the hull of the *Ramillies*. The attempt failed, but served to elevate tensions even further. Now Hardy was reluctant to keep the *Ramillies* at anchor anywhere near the shore, and had her bottom swept with a cable at regular intervals. He took American prisoners aboard, ensuring that they would share the ship's fate should any of the American attacks succeed. He also let it be known that, notwithstanding his earlier pledge, he would retaliate against any coastal town suspected of planning such attacks against the British squadron. When he received warning that a new attempt was being planned by a civilian resident of East Hampton, New York, Hardy sent a party of armed men to seize the man in his home and bring him aboard the *Ramillies*, where he was kept in iron manacles. Upon learning what Hardy had done, President Madison ordered a British prisoner of war selected at random to be put into "the same state of degradation & suffering."

The "Torpedo War" never fulfilled its sponsors' hopes, but it did serve to embitter the conflict considerably. The British charged the Americans with practicing an unprecedented, inhumane, and cowardly mode of warfare; the Americans retorted that the British had no right to take a tone of moral superiority while forcing abducted American seamen to serve in their ships. The case of Hiram Thayer dramatized the injustice of impressment in a way that resonated powerfully with the public. Thayer was a U.S. citizen, born and raised in Massachusetts, who had been pressed into the Royal Navy in 1802. In the summer of 1813 he was serving as a boatswain's mate aboard one of the ships of Hardy's squadron, the 46-gun frigate *Statira*. Upon first learning of the American declaration of war, Thayer had approached the *Statira*'s captain, Hassard Stackpoole, and asked to be relieved of duty. Stackpoole refused, reportedly telling him: "If we fall in with an American man-of-war, and you do not do your duty, you shall be tied to the mast to be shot at like a dog."

Thayer's father was John Thayer, a Massachusetts farmer. When he heard that the *Statira* was off New London, the elder Thayer asked Commodore Decatur to provide him with a vessel under a flag of truce. Decatur assented. As the boat approached the *Statira*, the long-separated father and son caught sight of each other and both burst into tears of joy. In Decatur's words: "The son descried his father at a distance in the boat, and told the first lieutenant of the *Statira* that it was his father; and I understand the feelings manifested by the old man, on receiving the hand of his son, proved, beyond all other evidence, the property he had in him." The tearful reunion left no doubt that Hiram Thayer was, as he had always claimed, a Massachusetts-born citizen of the United States—but Captain Stackpoole would not release him, or even treat him as a prisoner of war. (Thayer eventually won his release, after the case was elevated to diplomatic channels.)

Month after month, the *United States* and her consorts swung uselessly on their moorings in the Thames. Decatur had hoped that Hardy's squadron would withdraw from Long Island Sound as winter approached, but there was every sign that the British were planning to remain through the season. The American squadron dropped downriver to a new anchorage just off New London and began taking on provisions and water for a long cruise, hoping to make a dash for the open sea on a dark, dirty night when the wind was blowing hard offshore. But Decatur's first attempt to sail, a week before Christmas, was apparently foiled by local spies. Two blue lights were burned, one on either side of the river, appearing to broadcast signals to the British squadron in the Sound. In a letter to the Navy Office on December 20, afterward distributed to the newspapers, Decatur charged that traitors living in and around New London were conspiring to deliver the *United States*, *Macedonian*, and *Hornet* into enemy hands.

The accusation placed a further strain on relations between the town and the American squadron, and served as a harsh reminder of how sharply the War of 1812 had divided the nation. Federalists everywhere detested the war, but Connecticut Federalists were especially adamant in their loathing for Madison and the Virginia Republican dynasty he represented. In a town called New London, on a river called the Thames, in a region called New England, many felt sympathy for the British in their long struggle to defeat Napoleon, and some believed (or professed to believe) that Madison had entered into a secret alliance with the French. There were even those who entertained the idea, at least in private, that if losing the war promised to drive the Republicans from power, then losing the war might not be a bad result.

Trapped by a superior enemy force, Decatur offered Hardy a prearranged meeting between ships of comparable force. The challenge was a violation of his orders. After the loss of the *Chesapeake*, Secretary Jones had forbidden American commanders from "giving or receiving a Challenge, to, or from, an Enemy's Vessel." But since his squadron was unlikely to get to sea by any other means, Decatur, on January 17, 1814, wrote to Hardy under a flag of truce. He offered a two-on-two engagement between the *United States* and *Macedonian* and two of the frigates in the British squadron, *Endymion* (Captain Hope) and *Statira* (Captain Stackpoole). In Decatur's judgment, the *Macedonian* was an equal match for the *Statira*, and the *United States* for the *Endymion* (which also carried a main battery of 24-pounders). Decatur's note closed with the thought that "we beg you will assure Captains Hope and

Stackpoole, that no personal feeling towards them, induces me to make this communication. They are solicitous to add to the renown of their country: we honor their motives."

Hardy replied the following day, agreeing to a duel between *Statira* and *Macedonian*, "as they are sister-ships, carrying the same number of guns, and weight of metal." But he would not countenance a meeting between the two larger frigates, "as it is my opinion, the *Endymion* is not equal to the *United States*." Hardy justified his view with a long technical discussion of the force of the two ships, pointing out that the *Endymion* was slightly smaller and less powerfully armed than her proposed adversary, and concluded: "The captains of H.B.M. frigates under my orders, as well as myself, cannot too highly appreciate the gallant spirit that has led to the communication from you, sir."

Decatur would not allow the *Macedonian* to sail alone. He suspected the *Statira*'s complement would be reinforced from the rest of the British squadron, and if he reinforced the *Macedonian* in similar fashion he would leave the *United States* undermanned and unable to put to sea. He added that "the guarantee against recapture, in case the *Macedonian* should prove successful, is very far from satisfactory." There the exchange ended. No one called anyone else a coward—Hardy expressed his hope for an "amicable adjustment of the differences between the two nations," and Decatur reciprocated the sentiment. But the American commodore could not resist scoring one last rhetorical point. Captain Stackpoole, in a separate response to the challenge, had expressed his opinion that England was "engaged in a just and unprovoked war." Decatur might have replied that Stackpoole, having recently refused to allow a proven American to leave his crew, could hardly pretend not to know what had provoked the war. Instead, he took up the mantle of the professional: "Whether the war we are engaged in be just and unprovoked on the part of Great Britain, as Captain Stackpoole has been pleased to suggest, is considered by us as a question exclusively with the civilians; and I am perfectly ready to admit both my incompetence and unwillingness to confront Captain Stackpoole in its discussion."

WITH *UNITED STATES* and her consorts bottled up at New London, *Constellation* at Norfolk, *Constitution* at Boston, and *President* at Newport, the navy's offensive commerce-raiding strategy was, at least for the moment, effectively thwarted. By concentrating his blockading forces off ports known to be harboring the American frigates, however, Admiral Warren left gaping holes in other parts of the British cordon. Again and again, the pattern reasserted itself, as the British fixation on the U.S. Navy's frigates allowed other American vessels to get safely to sea. In the drive to capture or destroy the *Constellation*, the British neglected the southern and Gulf coasts, which became a haven for American privateers stalking the Caribbean sea-lanes. "We are here, three sail of the line, viz. *Marlborough*, *Victorious*, & *Dragon*," wrote Captain Robert Barrie, who had been left in command at Lynnhaven Bay, "literally doing nothing but blocking up a Yankee Frigate and almost twenty gunboats." When Decatur's squadron sailed from New York into Long Island Sound, the blockading warships withdrew to Montauk to cut him off, and allowed an untold number of merchantmen and privateers to break out via Sandy Hook. Broke's decision to send the *Shannon*'s consorts away from Massachusetts Bay succeeded in bringing Lawrence and the *Chesapeake* out to fight (and lose) a ship duel, but it also allowed a small armada of Yankee vessels to escape Boston during a two-week window, at the height of the sailing season, when the port was left totally unwatched.

To the growing frustration of British merchants, American privateers were sallying out of port by the hundreds. "Jonathan's privateers have roved with impunity and success to all corners of the earth," a correspondent to the *Naval Chronicle* complained. An editorial in the same paper appeared under the headline: "Success of American Trade War Unprecedented." By the fall of 1813, the British were losing as many as forty-five merchant vessels per month. Privateers swarmed in the Bay of Fundy, in the West Indies, off the coast of Portugal, in the North Sea, and in the western approaches to the English Channel. They stalked the big East India convoys and pounced on the stragglers. With the French welcoming American vessels into the Channel ports, they staged daring raids into the heart of Britain's home waters. The *True Blooded Yankee* descended on a remote Irish island and occupied it for six days, then crossed the Irish Sea and terrorized a remote Scottish harbor, burned half a dozen merchantmen, and vanished back to sea before the Royal Navy could respond. The *Lion* captured some twenty merchantmen in November alone, and made off with the fantastic sum of $400,000 in specie taken from a vessel bound to Lisbon for the support of Wellington's troops.

Wellington complained directly to Lord Melville, First Lord of the Admiralty: "Surely the British navy cannot be so hard run as not to be able to keep up the communication with Lisbon for this army!" Later: "If they only take the ship with our shoes, we must halt for six weeks." And then: "I am certain that it will not be denied, that since Great Britain has been a naval power, a British army has never been left in such a situation." When Melville referred to political constraints on the government, Wellington responded in a tone that must have made the First Lord wince:

> What I have written has been founded upon my own sense of a want of naval assistance on this coast. . . and I assure you that I neither know nor care what has passed, or may pass, in Parliament or in the newspapers on the subject.
>
> I complain of an actual want of naval assistance and cooperation with the army. I know nothing about the cause of the evil, I state the fact, which nobody will deny; and leave it to government to apply a remedy or not as they think proper.

In London, a peace faction was beginning to make itself heard. The *Naval Chronicle* purported to speak for the Royal Navy, but its editors had never liked the American war, regarding it as a costly diversion of military forces from the European theater. Beginning in the summer of 1813, the editors pressed the point in nearly every issue: "Peace Needed With America," "America—The Need for Peace is Apparent," "Peace With America Must Be Negotiated." The *Chronicle* grasped England's dilemma. To wage the war more ruthlessly, as many in the press and public were demanding, would only weaken America's pro-British domestic opposition and cause the American people to "rally round the executive." The editors likened the situation to that of 1778. A long, bitter, open-ended war could gain nothing for England—it could only create "an inextinguishable spirit of hatred and revenge . . . Let us rather secure the respect of America, by our justice and moderation—and accept of her proffered amity, whenever we can do it on terms compatible with our honour and our safety."

In Parliament, members of the opposition calmly proved that the cost of the war was not justified by its purported objective. The war was costing Britain about £10 million a year. The entire enlisted payroll of the Royal Navy was only £3 million. Why not double or even triple the pay of every seaman in the navy? It would be cheaper than fighting for the right to impress men from foreign ships, while probably eliminating the need to do so. Lord Erskine pressed an even more fundamental point. Where was this endless Anglo-American feud going? How was it all supposed to end? "It has been said that this war, if the Americans persist in their claims, must be eternal," he said. "If so, our prospects are disheartening. America is a growing country, increasing every day in numbers, in strength, in resources of every kind. In a lengthened contest all the advantages are on her side, and against this country."

When Tsar Alexander of Russia had first offered to serve as a diplomatic mediator, in the fall of 1812, the British government had rejected the proposal. The American peace commissioners—Gallatin, Bayard, and John Quincy Adams—had rendezvoused at St. Petersburg before learning of the refusal. After six idle months in the Russian capital, word came that the British foreign secretary, Robert Castlereagh, prompted by Perry's victory on Lake Erie, had proposed direct negotiations with the American government. Madison accepted the offer without hesitation. The American team was reinforced by two additional commissioners, one of whom was Henry Clay, Speaker of the House of Representatives and leader of the congressional "War Hawk" faction (he resigned his seat to accept the diplomatic assignment). Peace talks were originally to take place in Gothenburg, Sweden, but were subsequently moved to the charming little canal town of Ghent in Belgium.

Initially, the American negotiators remained under strict instructions not to offer concessions on the issue of impressment. But the progress of the war, both in Europe and America, gradually undermined the American negotiating position. Cockburn's punitive expeditions in the Chesapeake had demonstrated the vulnerability of the long American coastline. Every attempted American invasion of Canada had been turned back. The cost of the war to the United States was enormous and growing. American privateers were enjoying success, but the American merchant marine had been all but annihilated. British cruisers had sent hundreds of prizes into Bermuda and Halifax, and between 1812 and 1814, both imports and exports fell by more than 80 percent. The blockade had interrupted the all-important coastal trade: a gallon of wine cost $25 in New York, more than ten times its peacetime cost, and Rhode Island suffered dangerous shortages of imported grain and corn. The treasury was exhausted; customs revenues had diminished to an imperceptible trickle; there was a danger of default on upcoming federal interest payments, which would lead to bank failures across the country, and it was difficult to imagine how American merchants could be persuaded to accommodate any new government borrowing. Throughout New England, trading with the enemy had become so widespread and systematic that Madison turned to the old Republican remedy of an embargo, but the further injury to trade threatened to activate an open revolt, perhaps even a dissolution of the Union.

In Europe, events were ominous. Napoleon's October 1813 defeat at Leipzig allowed the allied armies to mass on the Rhine, apparently preparing to drive into the heart of France. In April 1814, Napoleon abdicated his throne and was exiled to the Mediterranean island of Elba. Ex-President Adams grasped the American dilemma. The Corsican Freebooter had never been an American ally, and his overthrow deserved to be celebrated through-out the civilized world. But who, in his absence, would keep England in check? "Though France has been humbled, Britain is not," he wrote Jefferson. "Though Bona is banished, a greater Tyrant and wider Usurper still domineers. John Bull is quite as unfeeling, as unprincipled, more powerful, [and] has shed more blood, then Bona. . . . How shall the Tyrant of Tyrants be brought low? Aye! there's the rub."

With England free to turn the full weight of its military power against the United States, Madison made the painful decision to drop his one *sine qua non*, the point on which two years of war had been fought. The capitulation came on June 27, 1814, in a secret letter to the American negotiating team. "On mature consideration," Secretary of State Monroe wrote, "it has been decided that . . . you may omit any stipulation on the subject of impressment, if found indispensably necessary to terminate [the war]. You will of course not recur to this expedient until all your efforts to adjust the controversy in a more satisfactory manner have failed." From this day forward, Madison's sole remaining objective was to end the war without sacrifice of American independence, territory, or national honor.

ADMIRAL WARREN'S REPORTS to London remained pessimistic throughout 1813. The Admiralty had demanded that he accomplish several things at once: maintain a rigorous blockade of the entire American coast; provide convoys to the West India merchant fleets, patrol the sea-lanes for privateers; and capture or destroy the remaining American frigates, so that a portion of his forces could be redeployed. The Lords had little sympathy for the admiral's repeated pleas for reinforcements, informing him that the force at his disposal "exceeds very much what on a mere comparison with the means of the Enemy would appear necessary."

On November 12, 1813, Halifax was struck by a devastating hurricane. Though it lasted only an hour and a half, the storm drove more than fifty ships onto the beach, including Warren's flagship, the 74-gun *San Domingo*. A large portion of the British North American fleet was "materially crippled by this event." The combination of hurricane damage and winter weather significantly weakened the blockade, and when *President* and *Constitution* escaped safely back to sea in the last month of the year, Warren grumbled, "the good Fortune of these Rascally privateer Frigates makes me almost Despair of ever seeing them." Writing the Admiralty from his winter head-quarters at Bermuda two days before the New Year, Warren expressed concern about the growth of the privateering threat. "The rapidity with which the Americans build and fit out their Ships is scarcely credible, and I am very apprehensive of the mischief their Cruizers will do to our Trade." Not only did he need reinforcements, he told the Lords, but he needed to be reinforced with faster ships, because "all the American Men of War, Privateers and even Traders, are particularly good Sailing Vessels."

Warren had every right to complain. He had been made the victim of unrealistic expectations. The Admiralty had consistently underestimated the challenge of blockading the long American coast, the audacity and skill of the American privateers, and the armament and efficiency of the American frigates. The Lords had sent Warren to North America with instructions to arrange a truce, and then faulted him for not inflicting enough punishment on the enemy. Whether he deserved it or not, however, Warren was finished. The Admiralty sent orders by fast-sailing packet to Bermuda, informing him that his eighteen-month command was terminated. His replacement would be Vice-Admiral Sir Alexander Cochrane, a fifty-six-year-old veteran officer who had served with distinction in the Mediterranean, the Leeward Islands, and the English Channel.* Admiral Cockburn was retained as Cochrane's second-in-command, and the North American station was heavily reinforced with ships released from blockade duty in Europe.

Even as the first direct peace talks were beginning in Europe, the British gathered their strength to strike the kind of mortal blow that would hasten the end of the war. During the summer of 1814, relentless, punitive, amphibious raids in the South would be combined with invasion from the North. The planned offensive was a concession, at least in part, to domestic political pressures—a large segment of the British public continued to demand that America be bludgeoned into submission, and a vocal minority was agitating to restore hegemony over the former colonies. The papers were full of exhortations to "let havock, with all its horrors and devastations, be carried into her interior. Bombard her towns—abolish her works—burn her shipping." The editors of the furiously pro-war *Times* never failed to find the words to express their feelings on the subject. May 24: "They are struck to the heart with terror for their impending punishment; and oh may no false liberality, no mistaken lenity, no weak and cowardly policy, interpose to save them from the blow! Strike! Chastise the savages, for such they are!" The *Naval Chroni-*

---

* Admiral Cochrane's nephew, Thomas Cochrane, was the famed fighting captain whose Mediterranean cruises in the HMS *Speedy* would be the inspiration for Patrick O'Brian's novel *Master and Commander* (1970).

cle's campaign for a truce was rebutted by anonymous letters to the editor. "I am of opinion that a peace with America would at this time be hurtful to us," wrote "C.H." in July; "how often would our disasters be thrown in our teeth, and the loss of our ships be a subject for their triumph? . . . [T]hey have shown to other nations that the British navy is not invincible—these nations will not inquire the difference of force, but believe the Americans, and we cannot deny it, that THEIR FRIGATES *have* CAPTURED OURS."

But the British were frustrated by all the old, familiar problems of the American Revolutionary War. How to strike a decisive blow against a sprawling, pastoral republic with no vital center? Cities could be occupied, or even destroyed, but resistance forces could retire to the backcountry, as Washington and the Continental Army had done in 1776–81. When the cabinet consulted General Wellington on the question, he gave them little encouragement: "In such countries as America, very extensive, thinly peopled, and producing but little food in proportion to their extent, military operations are impracticable without river or land transport." Regarding the planned offensive: "I do not know where you could carry on such an operation which would be so injurious to the Americans as to force them to sue for peace."

Admiral Cochrane seemed to harbor a deep personal enmity toward the Americans, possibly dating back to the combat death of his brother, Charles, at Yorktown in 1781. From the outset of his command, he left no doubt that he would wage a ruthless war. As retribution for the destruction of British shipping and the burning of several Canadian towns, he authorized Cockburn "to act with the utmost hostility against the shores of the United States." In February 1814, Cockburn arrived in the Chesapeake and carried out an effective campaign of terror and harassment throughout the bay region. On July 18, Cochrane circulated an order directing his commanders to burn all American towns, houses, and private property that came within their reach. The commercial blockade was extended to include all of New England. In the early spring of 1814, a British force penetrated eight miles up the Connecticut River and burned all the shipping it could find. Another expedition conducted hit-and-run attacks against the small, largely undefended seaports of Buzzards Bay in southern Massachusetts. For four days in August, Commodore Hardy's Long Island Squadron bombarded the town of Stonington, Connecticut, with rockets, incendiary missiles, and exploding bombshells. British troops occupied coastal Maine between the Penobscot and the Passamaquoddy, requiring the inhabitants to swear an oath of allegiance to George III.

In July, four battalions of British troops under the command of Major-General Robert Ross sailed from the Gironde River in France. After six years of hard campaigning, these battle-seasoned veterans of Wellington's Peninsular Campaign might have liked to be sent home rather than across the ocean to fight (and possibly die) in a conflict they could only regard as a sideshow to the war they had just won; but they had no say in the matter, and would do as they were ordered. Joined at Bermuda by additional reinforcements from the Mediterranean, they sailed in a fleet of fifty-one sail, including twenty troop transports, reaching the Virginia Capes in mid-August. Had they attacked Norfolk immediately, they would have almost certainly taken both the town and the long-blockaded *Constellation*, which had been stripped of most of her remaining crew the previous April; but instead, they sailed up the bay to rendezvous with Admiral Cockburn's squadron at Tangier Island. An additional battalion of Royal Marines was assembled from all the ships of the British fleet, bringing the total invasion force to four thousand.

The entire region was critically underdefended. Although recruiting had increased the U.S. Army's total strength to more than forty thousand, the administration had continued to deploy most new recruits to the Canadian frontier, leaving the south heavily dependent on local militias. The only active American naval force on the bay was a small flotilla of row galleys, gunboats, and armed barges under the command of Joshua Barney, which had been bottled up in the Patuxent River by Cockburn's huge fleet. On August 17, Cockburn sent a strong force up the river, followed the next day by General Ross and several troop transports. Faced with inevitable defeat, Barney scuttled the flotilla and marched his sailors overland from Nottingham to Washington to assist in the defense of the capital. Cockburn, Ross, and the British invasion force landed at Benedict, Maryland, on the nineteenth and marched east at a frightening pace. With terrible suddenness, the nation's capital was in jeopardy.

Assuming the British would not or could not advance that far inland, Secretary of War Armstrong had neglected the city's defenses. But Ross's veterans had won the Peninsular Campaign by outmarching their enemies, and they could cover twenty miles a day on decent roads. The British could attack Washington from any direction they chose, and the local American commander, Brigadier General William Winder, was suddenly faced with the problem of defending several places at once. Covering fifty miles in four days, including feints to the west and north, the British troops advanced south along the Bladensburg Road toward Washington. Winder hurried his army of several thousand regulars and militia to cut off the British advance and was reinforced at the last minute by Barney's sailors and marines; but the Americans reached the field too late to prepare strong fortifications, and when the

British appeared at midday on August 24, they charged, flanked, and quickly routed the defenders.

The Battle of Bladensburg, also known as the Bladensburg Races, was by far the most ignominious defeat ever suffered by an American army in the field, up to that time and ever since. In fairness, however, it should be said that the retreat highlighted the distinctive traits of Yankee ingenuity and self-reliance. Realizing there was no time, in all the confusion, to check in with their commanding officers, the soldiers and militia did not wait to be told to run for their lives. They knew a man could move faster when not burdened with weapons, ammunition, and extra gear, so they left most of it behind. Sensing that if they all ran away in the same direction, the British would follow and attempt to renew the battle, they split up into small groups and took different routes of escape—north to Baltimore, south to Virginia, west through the capital, over the Rock Creek bridges into Georgetown, and a few even doubled back to the east. Nor could it be said that the Americans were not physically fit. "Never did men with arms make better use of their legs," a British lieutenant later wrote, and even Admiral Cockburn was impressed by the "Swiftness with which the Enemy went off." Some hardly stopped running until they had reached their homes and farms, 50 or 100 miles away.

Only the sailors and marines, acting as artillerists under the command of Commodore Barney, stuck to their guns. When about five hundred American soldiers broke and ran from the high ground behind them on the right, the British were able to take up a position on their flank, and their situation became hopeless. Barney's horse was shot out from under him; he got back to his feet, and was shot in the thigh. The sailors and marines fought on, with replacements stepping forward as the men serving the guns were killed; but after a stubborn defense, finding the British infantry closing from every direction, Barney gave the order to surrender. General Ross and Admiral Cockburn advanced and spoke personally to Barney, treating him (in the commodore's words) with "the most marked Attention, respect, and Politeness."

With the road to Washington now completely undefended, the tired British troops rested for two hours and then resumed marching, reaching Capitol Hill at 8:00 p.m. Cockburn and Ross had already reached their controversial decision to burn all the public buildings in the city, an act of vandalism that even Napoleon had not practiced in the many foreign capitals he had occupied. Apologists later linked the act to the burning of buildings in York (modern-day Toronto) by American troops, but the British commanders did not refer to that precedent as a justification at the time. Flames devoured both the House and Senate wings of the Capitol, the White House, the Treasury, the War and Navy Office buildings, and the great bridge across the Potomac. The Library of Congress, a collection that had been largely assembled by Jefferson, was a total loss. The offices of the *National Intelligencer* were smashed up as punishment for all the invective the paper had hurled at the British over the years, and Cockburn ordered that the C's be removed from the lettertypes and destroyed, "so that the rascals cannot any longer abuse my name." Before setting fire to the White House, Cockburn and his officers, famished after a long day of marching, fighting, and burning (marching and burning, especially), sat down to eat a dinner that had been left behind by the Madisons in their haste to evacuate. As a souvenir, Cockburn took a seat cushion from Dolley Madison's chair. Fortunately for the capital's inhabitants, the well-disciplined British troops committed no civilian atrocities, and only one private home was destroyed, after shots were reportedly fired from it.

Secretary Jones had left orders that the Washington Navy Yard, with all its ammunition and naval stores, must be destroyed rather than permitted to fall into the hands of the enemy. As news arrived of the British advance, the staff of the yard scrambled to obtain horses and wagons to transport as much of the movable supplies as possible to safety, but the rout at Bladensburg had been so swift and unexpected that there was hardly any time. Captain's Clerk Mordecai Booth learned of the defeat when he saw the retreating American army passing the Capitol. "Oh! My Country! But I blush Sir! to tell you," he later told Navy Yard Commandant Thomas Tingey, "I saw the Commons Covered with the fugitive Soldiery of our Army—running, hobbling, Creeping, & apparently pannick struck."

Riding at full gallop through the woods and past the marine barracks, Booth heard the whistling of musket balls overhead. He raced through the Navy Yard gates and informed Tingey that the city would soon be in the hands of the enemy. Working quickly, the two men set matches to trains of gunpowder leading into all the administrative buildings, tradesmen's shops, sail loft, timber sheds, arsenal, and storehouses on the property, and all were soon engulfed "in irresistible flame." Rushing down to the river, they set fire to a new frigate, the *Columbia*, still on the stocks but caulked and nearly ready for launch; and to the new sloop of war *Argus*, which lay alongside the wharf, virtually ready for sea. Both vessels were "immediately enveloped in a sheet of inextinguishable fire."

The inferno quickly spread through the entire complex: the ground was covered with "Chips, Timber, Pitch, Tar, and other combustible matter, [and] to set fire to any one object must produce the successive conflagration of the whole." An inventory of the destroyed naval stores, taken afterward, included (in part): "about 100 Tons of Cordage, some Canvas, a considerable quantity of Salt petre, Copper, Iron, Lead, Block Tin, Blocks, Ship Chandlery, Naval and Ordnance Stores, implements and fixed ammunition, with a variety of manufactured articles in all the Branches; 1743 barrels of Beef and Pork, 279 barrels of Whiskey, and a moderate Stock of Plank and Timber." The Tripoli Monument, a 30-foot-high marble column erected in honor of the officers killed in the Mediterranean, escaped with only minor damage, and can be seen today on the grounds of the Naval Academy in Annapolis.

The following morning, a British party arrived at the Navy Yard to make certain that the devastation was complete. Less than an hour was needed to finish the job, which they did by setting fire to the ropewalk and arsenal, which had escaped the previous evening's conflagration. Then Cockburn, Ross, and the British invasion force retreated from the capital, maintaining their remarkable pace over the ground, and re-embarked into their ships and transports on the Patuxent on August 29.

It had been a daring and crushingly successful foray. In eleven days, the British had penetrated fifty miles inland, trounced an army twice the size of their own, occupied and wrecked the American capital, and escaped to the safety of their fleet, having suffered casualties of only 64 killed and 185 wounded.

At the same time, a British squadron under the command of Captain James A. Gordon had warped up the Potomac River against contrary winds, grounding repeatedly on the Kettle Bottom shoals, and engaged Fort Washington in a brief artillery duel that ended when the American garrison spiked their guns and fled. The squadron, which comprised two frigates, three bomb vessels, and a rocket ship, took up position at Alexandria and prepared to bombard the town. The Americans unloaded provisions from all the merchant shipping, and several vessels were sunk to prevent capture. Captain Gordon offered to spare the town, but his conditions were humiliating: all vessels must be immediately surrendered; the Alexandrians must themselves reload all the provisions and cargoes that had been removed during the squadron's approach, including all that had been sent inland in wagons; and the vessels that had been sunk to prevent capture must be raised from the bottom of the river, restored to sailing condition, and handed over to the British. The town council acceded to Gordon's terms the same afternoon. The squadron dropped back down the river with twenty-two prize vessels in company, fought its way past a series of newly erected shore batteries, and rejoined Admiral Cochrane's fleet on September 9.

Gordon's delay allowed Baltimore to fortify its defenses by erecting new redoubts and earthworks, reinforcing the militia garrisons, and sinking block-ships off Lazaretto Point. Admiral Cochrane was determined to occupy the city, which was notorious as a hub of the American privateering industry. The British fleet did not take up position in the Patapsco until September 12. Troops were landed at North Point at dawn, but they failed to break through the American lines, and General Ross was killed by a sniper. That night, Cochrane brought his fleet up the river and anchored within cannon-shot range of Fort McHenry, the bedrock of the city's defense. A Georgetown lawyer and militia officer, Francis Scott Key, witnessed the night bombardment from the deck of a truce ship, a few miles down the Patapsco. Moved by the sight of the American flag flying over the ramparts, illuminated in the glare of the Congreve rockets and in seeming defiance of the mortar shells bursting all around it, Key, who wrote verse on the side, reached for his pen and jotted down a few lines. The following day he reworked them into a poem, later set to music, which he entitled "The Star-Spangled Banner."

Baltimore refused to fall, and Cochrane, loathe to admit defeat in his official dispatches to the Admiralty, characterized the operation as a "demonstration" rather than an actual attempt to take the city. The fleet sailed down the bay to the Capes. A small force was left at Lynnhaven; Cockburn was dispatched to Bermuda for a refit; and Cochrane sailed for Bermuda with the main force and a small armada of prizes.

When news of Admiral Cockburn's successful attack on Washington reached Monticello, Jefferson was incensed. Having taken a direct hand in designing the public edifices that had gone up in flames, and having personally collected and catalogued most of the books in the Library of Congress, the ex-president deplored "the Vandalism and brutal character of the English government." He predicted that the event would arouse public sympathy for the Americans and anger against Britain, especially in Europe. "This will be worth the million of dollars the repairs of their conflagration will cost us," he told Monroe.

Jefferson would be proven right. Humiliating as it was, the fall of Washington did not substantially interrupt the progress of the war. The young, underpopulated capital had not yet attained any real economic or strategic importance. Madison and his cabinet returned and took up leases in new buildings. Records were reconstructed, and dispatches were still sent and received from commanders at sea and in the field. Federalists who had clamored for accommodation to British demands found themselves weakened and discredited. Public opinion rallied around President Madison. The fate of Washington stiffened the defenses at Baltimore, and may have saved the city.

Then came news of a major American naval victory in the north. On the morning of September 11, in Plattsburgh Bay on Lake Champlain, a freshwater squadron under the command of Master Commandant Thomas Macdonough had engaged and defeated a British squadron of superior force. The two-hour battle was fought at anchor and at close range, with heavy casualties suffered on both sides. The British commodore, Captain George Downie, was killed early in the action, and Macdonough was twice knocked to the deck by flying debris, the first time by the decapitated head of one of his own midshipmen. The American vessels had set multiple anchors with springs on their cables, allowing them to "wind ship" (that is, to rotate 180 degrees and present fresh broadsides to the enemy) at a critical moment in the action. The contest ended with the capture of all the British ships, amounting to a frigate, a brig, and two sloops of war.

The Battle of Plattsburgh averted a threatened invasion of New York State. A British army of ten thousand men under the command of General Sir George Prevost, including more of Wellington's feared veterans, had marched down the eastern shore of Lake Champlain, brushing aside several American infantry attacks, and would undoubtedly have continued into the Hudson River Valley if Downie had prevailed. Once the Americans had established control of the lake, however, General Prevost decided on a quick retreat to friendly territory, leaving his sick and wounded behind. The withdrawal, according to Downie's first lieutenant, was carried out "in the most precipitate and disgraceful manner." Prevost became a pariah among his officers, his soldiers, and the entire British people. Recalled to England to face a court-martial, he died before he could make his defense.

IN GHENT, NEGOTIATIONS DRAGGED on through the late summer and early fall. The British government was represented by a veteran officer of the Royal Navy, Lord Gambier; an Admiralty lawyer, William Adams; and an undersecretary in the Colonial Office, Henry Goulburn. Taking a high tone from the outset, even after Madison's major concession on impressment, they demanded that England's Indian allies be provided with a buffer state in the Northwest, and that additional territories along the border be ceded to Canada. The Americans rejected both demands. "A Treaty concluded upon such terms would be but an armistice," they replied in a note signed August 24. "It cannot be supposed that America would long submit to conditions so injurious and degrading."

A rupture seemed inevitable, and the American envoys prepared to sail for home. This brought the issue to a head. If the American delegation left Europe, England would be forced to carry on the war for another year, at least. As this uncomfortable truth sank in, Lord Liverpool and his ministers began counting up the high economic, political, and diplomatic costs of the war. Napoleon's downfall had seemed to free up military resources for deployment in America, but dissent among the allies now threatened a renewal of the war, and England's ships and troops were needed in Europe. The new assertiveness of Russia was a major subject of discussion in London. The nations of continental Europe were jealous of England's power, and their people (said Gallatin) openly "rejoiced at anything which might occupy and eventually weaken our enemy." Post-Napoleonic France was sympathetic to the American cause, and allowed American privateers to outfit in its Channel ports. The repulse at Baltimore gave the lie to the British government's assurances that an American capitulation was at hand. In Paris, crowds in the Palais-Royal gardens erupted into cheers at the announcement of Macdonough's victory on Lake Champlain.

The English public's enthusiasm for the war was declining. When it was announced that another year's campaign would require a prolongation of the detested wartime property tax, the news, according to the *Morning Chronicle*, was greeted with "a sense of horror and indignation." Losses at sea were growing. On September 9, a caucus of Liverpool merchants announced that the city had lost a combined total of eight hundred vessels to the Americans since the beginning of the war. At the end of September, Lloyd's of London reported that 108 British merchantmen had been snapped up in that month alone. Maritime insurance rates for vessels sailing from Liverpool to Halifax were 30 percent; between Liverpool and Ireland, 13 percent—the latter represented a 300 percent increase over the rate charged when all of Europe had been at war. Captain Thomas Boyle of the Baltimore privateer *Chasseur*—an allusion to the troops responsible for the rape of Hampton the previous year—sailed into a British port and issued a tongue-in-cheek notice of blockade, extended to "all the ports, harbours, bays, creeks, rivers, inlets, outlets, islands and sea coast of the united kingdom of G. Britain and Ireland." The opposition Whigs launched a parliamentary investigation of the Admiralty's failure to deal with the American privateers. Headlines in the *Naval Chronicle* told the story of that influential newspaper's continuing skepticism: "The War with America Britain Cannot Win"; "On the Remarkable Success of the Young American Navy"; "America—The Need for Peace is Apparent"; "Desertion to the Enemy a Growing Problem"; "The Poverty of British Naval Leadership"; "Why is America So Powerful at Sea?"

President Madison allowed the correspondence from Ghent to be published in the American newspapers. In doing so, he advertised to the world that the United States had already dropped its condition on impressment, and that the British negotiators were demanding territorial concessions as the price of peace. As a result, Lord Liverpool's government was obliged to answer the charge, both at home and abroad, that Britain was waging a Bonaparte-style war of conquest on the North American continent. The major issues of postwar Europe were being sorted out at the grand, multilateral Congress of Vienna, and British leaders were keen to preserve England's prestige and moral authority. The British team at Ghent had been maneuvered into an untenable position, from which their only option was retreat. Liverpool was aggravated: "Our Commissioners have certainly taken a very erroneous view of our policy." Aggressive territorial demands, he said, were unwise because they failed to take account of "the inconvenience of the continuance of the war."

To avert the collapse of the talks, the British envoys gave up their demand for an Indian state, which they had earlier presented as non-negotiable, and consented instead to a vague (and therefore unenforceable) provision returning the Indians to their 1811 status. For the ensuing month, negotiations hinged on the issue of whether the war should be concluded on the basis of *uti possidetis*—that is, each side to keep the territory it held at the cessation of hostilities. Under this arrangement, the British would retain control of occupied territory in northern Maine, which would open a secure corridor between Québec and Nova Scotia, and fortresses on the Great Lakes and the St. Lawrence taken in the course of the war. But on October 24, with their position immeasurably strengthened by the news of Baltimore and Plattsburgh, the Americans rejected *uti possidetis* and declared that they would negotiate only on the basis of *status quo ante bellum*—that is, "status before the war," or a restoration of all occupied territories.

At first, the British cabinet assumed that the American delegation's intransigence must bring a rupture in the negotiations. Lord Liverpool wrote Castlereagh, who was representing Great Britain at the Congress of Vienna, to warn that the American war "will probably now be of some duration." The cost of another season of campaigning was projected at £10 million. "We must expect, therefore, to hear it said that the property tax is continued for the purpose of securing a better frontier for Canada."

On November 3, the British government asked Lord Wellington, then serving as ambassador in Paris, to take command of the army in Canada. Wellington did not refuse the assignment outright, but he reiterated the objections he had voiced since the beginning of the War of 1812—that it was a wasteful diversion, that England would encounter all the same problems of 1775–81, and that no invasion from Canada could succeed without naval supremacy on the Great Lakes, a prediction borne out in the fiasco at Plattsburgh. But he reserved his most devastating remarks for the progress of the talks at Ghent. "In regard to your present negotiations," he told Castlereagh on November 9,

> I confess that I think you have no right, from the state of the war, to demand any concession of territory from America. . . . You have not been able to carry it into the enemy's territory, notwithstanding your military success and now undoubted military superiority, and have not even cleared your own territory on the point of attack. You cannot on any principle of equality in negotiation claim a cessation of territory excepting in exchange for other advantages which you have in your power. . . . Then if this reasoning be true, why stipulate for the *uti possidetis*? You can get no territory; indeed, the state of your military operations, however creditable, does not entitle you to demand any.

The Iron Duke's blunt assessment proved decisive. The British envoys were instructed to offer another humiliating concession. *Uti possidetis* was dropped, and peace offered on the basis of *status quo ante bellum*.

The final obstacle was an internal rift among the American delegates. John Quincy Adams was adamant that the coastal fishing rights negotiated by his father in the 1783 Treaty of Paris must be reasserted in the new treaty. (The senior Adams had lobbied both Madison and his own son not to surrender them.) The British considered the fishing rights as annulled by the war, but seemed willing to restore them in exchange for navigation rights on the Mississippi River. But Henry Clay, representing the western interest, was adamantly opposed to the latter. When it seemed as if the American consensus might founder on this issue, Albert Gallatin acted as a mediator, and at length persuaded Adams and Clay to shelve both issues. The treaty would include no mention of either, with the understanding that they would be settled in future negotiations. John Quincy Adams generously credited Gallatin with "the largest and most important share to the conclusion of the peace," and added, "It would have been an irreparable loss if our country had been deprived of the benefit of his talents in this negotiation."

The Treaty of Ghent, signed on Christmas Eve, 1814, was essentially nothing more than an agreement to stop fighting. It did not address any of the issues that had prompted the American declaration of war. Pending ratification by the U.S. Senate, however, the war was over.

RAPID COMMUNICATION between Europe and America did not become possible until 1858, when the first greeting was transmitted from Queen Victoria to President James Buchanan by a transatlantic telegraph cable. In 1815, news traveled as it always had in the past—in a ragged, gradually widening circle over land and sea. Outside that circle, the Anglo-American war continued to rage, and in the more distant theaters the fighting would go on for months.

In April 1814, after almost a year of cooling his heels in New London, where the *United States* and her consorts remained closely blockaded, Stephen Decatur had accepted command of the *President*, then lying at New York. The *United States* and the *Macedonian* were taken about five miles up the Thames and dismantled. Decatur, his officers, and much of the crew of the *United States* traveled overland through Connecticut to New York Harbor and took possession of the *President*. His orders were to sail to the far side of the world to prey on the enemy's East India commerce. Months of refitting followed, while the Americans waited for the kind of nasty weather that would blow the British squadron off their station at Sandy Hook.

The opportunity did not come until January 14, 1815—three weeks after the treaty had been signed in Ghent—when an icy blast out of the northwest forced the blockaders to run about fifty miles out to sea. *President* had anchored in a shallow bay northeast of Staten Island. About eight o'clock at night, in pitch-blackness, with a driving snowstorm and freezing winds, the crew shipped the capstan bars and heaved the anchor out of the mud. It was the worst possible time to navigate a heavily laden, deep-draft frigate out of New York, but it was also the only chance of evading the British cordon. *President* ran down the Narrows on the wings of the gale, taking care to steer clear of the shoals off Great Kills and Vandeventer's Point on Staten Island, and skirting Middle Bank to the east, then put her helm down and aimed for the five-fathom channel over "the bar," a submerged barrier dividing the bay from the open sea. The channel was supposedly marked by anchored boats, but they were difficult to see in the storm, and the frightened pilot was reduced to guesswork. He guessed wrong and drove the *President* hard aground.

For almost two hours, the big frigate thumped helplessly on the bar. She suffered severe injuries. Her keel was mangled and hogged, with part of the copper and the false keel torn off; her masts were unseated; and several of her rudder braces were broken. If it had been possible to return to New York for repairs, Decatur would have done so, but there was no hope of making progress into the teeth of the gale. There was nothing to do but try to force the *President* over the bar, little by little, shoved along by the combined force of wind and waves, and eventually out to sea. The hands were called to heel the ship from side to side by running in unison from larboard to starboard and back again. She made progress, bit by bit, but the repeated violent shocks of the hull striking the ground exacerbated the damages she had already suffered.

Finally, at about 10:00 p.m., *President* was free. Decatur shaped a course along the southern coast of Long Island, sailing large before the gale. At about three in the morning, off Fire Island, he adjusted course slightly to the southward. At first light, with the gale diminishing, the lookout at the masthead caught sight of four ships dead to east, the nearest only two miles away. They could only be the British squadron, and they were—the razeed battleship *Majestic*, the familiar heavy frigate *Endymion*, and the 38-gun frigates *Pomone* and *Tenedos*. Commodore John Hayes had guessed which course Decatur would take from Sandy Hook, and his guess had been perfect. The *President* had sailed right into his arms.

Decatur hauled up and ran north toward Montauk under a press of sail, but the damage to *President*'s hull had taken a few knots of speed out of her, and she was making enough water to require men to work her pumps constantly. By midday, the wind fell to a breeze, and then nearly a calm. The *Endymion* was the fastest ship in the British squadron, and she was gaining perceptibly. Decatur ordered the *President* lightened, and everything not essential to battle went over the side: boats, cables, extra spars, casks of provisions. The fresh water was started from the hold, the anchors cut away, and buckets of water hauled aloft to wet the sails, "but notwithstanding all that," wrote Midshipman George Hollins, "they steadily gained on us."

At twilight, *Endymion* got within cannon-shot range and opened fire with her bow chasers. At 5:30 p.m., she was able to being her forwardmost 24-pounder long guns to bear on *President*'s starboard quarter. Decatur was running out of alternatives. He could steer off the wind and fight, but that would only allow the other enemy ships to come up and join the action. He could continue fleeing, but in that case *Endymion* could continue to peck away at *President*'s vulnerable quarter. Decatur called the crew back to the mizzenmast and announced his intention to put his helm down, run the enemy aboard, and take her by boarding. If the attempt was successful, the Americans would scuttle the damaged *President* and take the captured *Endymion* into New York.

It was a bold notion, but impossible to carry out in the light and baffling breezes. Captain Hope skillfully kept his ship away, and the two big frigates ran to the south, trading broadsides. The *President* suffered heavy casualties. First Lieutenant F. H. Babbitt's right leg was shot off as he stood on the quarterdeck; he bled to death two hours later, after dictating a letter to his sweetheart. Lieutenant Archibald Hamilton, son of former Navy Secretary Paul Hamilton, was struck by a round of grape shot, and as he fell to the deck, mortally wounded, he shouted to the men of his division, "Carry on! Carry on!" Stephen Decatur was hit in the chest by a splinter and knocked to the deck. He was temporarily stunned, but soon returned to his feet. A few minutes later he was hit by another splinter, this time in his forehead. Blood streamed down his face, but he remained on his feet, insisting the wound was not serious. Altogether, the *President* suffered twenty-five killed and sixty wounded, and among the dead were five lieutenants.

Hoping to disable his antagonist, Decatur had the gun crews load the *President*'s guns with dismantling shot—chain and bar shot designed to hack away the enemy's rigging. The *Endymion* did not lose a spar, but her rigging and sails were badly cut up. *President* hauled her wind, turned her stern to the *Endymion*, and attempted to run from the other ships, fast approaching, but this maneuver allowed *Endymion* to fire two raking broadsides into the American frigate's unprotected stern, to great effect. Midshipman Hollins walked back to the quarterdeck and became transfixed by the sight of a dead sailor, illuminated in the glow of the binnacle light. The body had been "cut in two by a shot." Decatur approached from behind, placed his hand on Hollins's shoulder, and asked: "Young gentleman, have you nothing else to do than to be looking at such things as that? Go and attend to your duty."

As the night wore on, *Pomone* and *Tenedos* continued in hot pursuit, and at about ten o'clock *Pomone* closed to within cannon-shot range. She fired a broadside, perhaps two, and Decatur gave the fateful order to haul down the light at the mizzen peak, which substituted for the *President*'s ensign in the darkness. When hailed by the *Pomone*, Decatur called out: "I surrender to the squadron."

For three years the British had wanted to take one of the American 44-gun frigates in single combat, and some of the early newspaper reports flatly asserted that the *President* had been beaten and captured by the *Endymion* alone. Decatur always maintained that he had surrendered to the entire British squadron, rather than to any one ship. Later, there would be some controversy over how many broadsides the *Pomone* fired at the *President* prior to her surrender, and to what effect, and whether the *Tenedos* was also within range. Decatur's own reports are contradictory. It is known that he told his wife, Susan, that he had decided in advance that if the British pursuers came within range of the *President* a second time, he would surrender in order to avoid spilling more American blood in an impossible fight. Decatur was exonerated in his subsequent court-martial, but the surrender of the *President* struck many as oddly tame for an officer with his ferocious reputation. It is likely that physical exhaustion played a role in the outcome: the *President*'s officers and crew had been on their feet, exposed to the raw winter weather, for thirty consecutive hours.

The *President* was navigated into Bermuda, and subsequently taken into the Royal Navy as the HMS *President*. Decatur, his officers, and his crew were soon paroled and allowed to return to the United States, where they learned of the peace upon arriving in mid-March 1815.

THE LAST MAJOR BRITISH AMPHIBIOUS operation of the war was directed against the Gulf Coast and New Orleans. The army that had occupied Washington and been repulsed at Baltimore sailed from the Chesapeake to Jamaica. With additional reinforcements from Europe and the West Indies, their numbers exceeded ten thousand men. As General Robert Ross had been killed at Baltimore, command of the army was transferred to General Sir Edward Pakenham, brother-in-law to the Duke of Wellington. The officers and troops of this formidable invasion force included several thousand veterans of the Peninsular Campaign, including some of the most elite companies in the British Army.

Pakenham's objective was New Orleans, a polyglot city of 25,000 inhabitants located on the north bank of the Mississippi River, about 100 miles from the Gulf. Apart from the rich plunder the city offered, its conquest and occupation would enable the British to interdict navigation of the Mississippi, and thus force the American delegation at Ghent to assume a more submissive attitude.

Sailing from Jamaica in late November, in a fleet commanded by Admiral Cochrane, the invaders landed at Cat Island on December 13, attacked through Lake Borgne, captured or destroyed a small American gunboat squadron, and landed on the mainland east of New Orleans. An advance party marched through bayous and cypress swamps to a plantation on the eastern bank of the Mississippi, about eight miles downriver of New Orleans. One by one, the British regiments were brought up into position, their numbers eventually approaching six thousand. With the recent experience of Bladensburg in mind, the British commanding officers assumed that a frontal attack on the American lines would quickly rout the defenders.

The American forces were commanded by Major General Andrew Jackson, a native of South Carolina who had commanded the entire Gulf Coast region since May 1814. Having arrived in New Orleans only a month earlier, Jackson had found the city critically unprepared for the British invasion, and his engineers worked at a furious pace to throw up earthworks and redoubts. At first the defenders were badly outnumbered, but they were gradually reinforced as militiamen streamed into the city from the surrounding region. A small force of U.S. Army regulars were joined by crack riflemen from Kentucky and Tennessee, free black regiments raised over the objections of local politicians, a handful of Choctaw Indian scouts, and a gang of pirates under the leadership of Jean Lafitte. Lafitte's pirates were wanted men, but they were motivated to join Jackson's army by a combination of patriotism, hatred of the British, and the hope of a future pardon. The New Orleans French naturally took up arms against their hereditary enemies; "Yankee Doodle" and the "Marseillaise" were the tunes most often heard on the streets of the city.

Jackson established his lines about two miles upriver from the British encampment. His works extended across the Chalmette plain, from the river about one quarter of a mile to the edge of a nearly impenetrable cypress swamp. A strong parapet was built to a height of five feet, abutted by a ditch about ten feet wide and four feet deep. Batteries of heavy artillery were constructed at regular intervals. By January 8, 1815, the American lines were manned with about 3,500 men, with another 1,000 in reserve.

On the morning of January 8, with a thick mist rising from the plain, the British army advanced along the river in two columns under the command of Major Generals Samuel Gibbs and John Keane. The American cannon opened fire when the enemy were at 500 yards, the riflemen at 300 yards, and the muskets at 100 yards. The fire from the American lines was devastating, but the disciplined British troops refused to break and run. They advanced into the maelstrom with suicidal courage. General Gibbs was killed and General Keane severely wounded; General Pakenham rode forward to rally the 44th and was promptly eviscerated by a volley of grape shot. Many of the British veterans later said that it was the most murderous fire they had ever seen. "The vibration seemed as if the earth was cracking and tumbling to pieces, or if the heavens were rent asunder by the most terrific peals of thunder that ever rumbled," one witness wrote; "it was the most awful and the grandest mixture of sounds . . . the woods seemed to crack to an interminable distance, each cannon report was answered a hundredfold and produced an intermingled roar surpassing strange. . . . the flashes of fire looked as if coming out of the bowels of the earth . . . the reverberation was so intense towards the great wood, that anyone would have thought the fighting was going on there."

As the guns fell silent and the smoke cleared, the ground in front of the American lines was strewn with 1,500 dead and wounded British soldiers. A truce was arranged, and throughout the afternoon, unarmed men from both armies worked side by side to remove the wounded from the field. About three hundred were taken to the American camp and then transported back to the hospitals at New Orleans. The bodies of Pakenham and Gibb were disemboweled and sealed in casks of liquor to be returned to England. British burial details heaved the dead into shallow mass graves, but several days of rain over the following week brought many of the bodies to the surface, exposing heads and limbs.

The British had lost 291 dead, 1,262 wounded, and 484 captured. Among the casualties were three generals, seven colonels, and seventy-five field officers. The 4th regiment alone had lost twenty-four officers, including its colonel and twelve sergeants. The 93rd Scottish Highlanders, one of the most celebrated regiments in the British Army, had lost two of every three men. The Americans, well protected behind their parapet, had suffered only six killed and seven wounded. It had been the most lopsided defeat ever suffered by a British army in the field, all the more tragic for having been fought two weeks after the war was over.

General John Lambert, succeeding to command upon Pakenham's death, rejected Admiral Cochrane's proposal to launch a second assault. The British survivors, many now starving, retreated to Lake Borgne by the same route they had come, re-embarked on their ships, and sailed away. Lieutenant George Robert Gleig wrote: "We, who only seven weeks ago had set out in the surest confidence of glory . . . were brought back dispirited and dejected. Our ranks were woefully thinned, our chiefs slain, our clothing tattered and filthy, and even our discipline in some degree injured."

CAPTAIN CHARLES STEWART had commanded the *Constitution* for eighteen months, more than half the war. It was an unusually long command, but Stewart and the ship passed fourteen of those months in Boston Harbor as prisoners of the British blockade. A four-month cruise in the winter and early spring of 1814 had ended prematurely when a long crack was discovered in the mainmast and the frigate was forced to return to port for a refit, eluding the cordon and racing into Marblehead Harbor on April 3. The British ships gave chase, and the *Constitution* entered the harbor with several enemy frigates in close pursuit. It was a Sunday morning, and many of the local inhabitants of Marblehead and Salem were in church. According to one contemporary's account, Reverend Bentley of the South Church in Salem, upon hearing the news, closed his prayer book and announced to the congregation that the service was over, adding: "We can serve God no better than by defending our country." He put on his hat, ran out of the church, and led the parishioners to the beach, where the militia was setting up cannon to repel the hostile squadron. The pursuing ships hauled off and gave up the chase. Two weeks later, *Constitution* slipped back into Boston.

Passing the summer and fall in Boston, closely blockaded by a heavily reinforced British squadron, *Constitution* was again forced to wait for winter weather. The opportunity to escape finally came on December 18, when Stewart learned that Massachusetts Bay had been momentarily abandoned by the enemy. The *Constitution* went down the Roads, cheered by a crowd at Long Wharf, and pushed into the open sea. She rounded Cape Cod, sailing large on a "fine smart breeze," and shaped a course for Bermuda. She took one prize, then sailed east to Madeira and the Portuguese coast, where she seized a deeply laden Indiaman. Raising Cape Finisterre, in northwest Spain, and then doubling back to the south, *Constitution* was about 100 miles north northeast of Madeira on February 20, 1815, when the lookout hailed to report a strange sail two points on the weather bow. A few minutes later, word came down from the masthead that another sail was discovered on the lee bow, and at the same time the first ship altered course to intercept the *Constitution*.

They were the British warships *Cyane* and *Levant*, three days out of Gibraltar, sailing as a rearguard to a convoy of merchantmen bound for the West Indies. The former was a 24-gun light frigate, the latter an 18-gun corvette. In combined broadsides, they threw a similar weight of metal to the *Constitution*, but each ship was armed principally with 32-pounder carronades, which were effective only to a range of about 400 yards, whereas the *Constitution*'s 24-pounder long guns could hit an enemy from a range of 1,200 yards.

When *Constitution* failed to respond to the English private signal, the British captains resolved to engage her, hoping either to capture her or at least to lead her away from the convoy that was just over the western horizon. Passing within hail of one another, they planned to try to seize the advantage of the weather gauge, but soon abandoned the effort.

The *Constitution* "Set every rag in chase," but as the wind rose through the afternoon, her main royal mast cracked and gave way. Men raced aloft to cut away the wreckage and rig a new spar, and within an hour the *Constitution* was again cracking on toward the strangers at a speed approaching 10 knots. At 5:00 p.m. she fired on the nearest British ship with her two larboard bow chasers, but the shot splashed into the sea, well short of the target. As the *Constitution* came down on the wind, *Cyane* and *Levant* formed into a line ahead, about half a cable's length apart, and hoisted English ensigns. *Constitution* hoisted the American colors, and the three ships, as if by unspoken agreement, closed for battle.

Five minutes after six, *Constitution* ranged up on the starboard quarter of the *Cyane*, at a range of 600 yards, and opened fire. The three ships fought a battle of running broadsides for fifteen minutes. A ball fired by a British carronade crashed through the *Constitution*'s waist, killing two men and smashing one of her boats to fragments. A thick curtain of smoke obscured the view to leeward, so Stewart ordered the guns to rest for a few minutes. When the smoke cleared, the Americans could see that *Levant* was luffing up to cross the stern. Stewart ordered the main and mizzen topsails thrown aback to take the way off their ship, and her larboard broadside and the musketry of her marines in the tops came into action at short range. *Levant*, badly hit by the *Constitution*'s heavier guns, tried to wear round, but the Englishman's deck was already "a perfect slaughterhouse" and his rigging shot to ribbons.

Meanwhile, the *Cyane* was bearing up, apparently in the attempt to cross the *Constitution*'s bows and rake her. Stewart ordered the topsails sheeted home and filled, the ship responded beautifully, and the tables were turned. The *Constitution* crossed *Cyane*'s wake and poured two raking broadsides into her stern at a range of about 100 yards. Coming up into the wind, *Constitution* ranged up on the crippled *Cyane*'s larboard quarter, and was on the verge of showing her the fresh starboard broadside when the Englishman hauled down his colors and fired a lee gun in submission. It was 6:45 p.m. Second Lieutenant Beekman Hoffman was sent aboard with a party of fifteen marines to take possession of the prize. The British officers were brought aboard the *Constitution*.

Levant, meanwhile, had sheered away to leeward to repair the damage to her rigging. Captain Douglas had bravely carried his ship back into action, and at 8:40 p.m., with the moon rising in the east, the antagonists passed within 50 yards' range of each other on opposite tacks, and exchanged starboard broadsides. The *Constitution* quickly wore round and got off a raking broadside across the smaller ship's stern, smashing her wheel to pieces, piercing her lower main- and mizzenmasts, and killing perhaps a dozen men on the quarterdeck. Many of *Levant*'s surviving sailors decided they had seen enough. Ignoring their officers, they crowded down the hatches to the relative safety of the lower deck. Captain Douglas, correctly assuming the *Cyane* was no longer under English colors, now attempted to escape to windward, but *Constitution*'s speed was superior, and she needed only an hour to run her quarry down. Ranging up on the *Levant*'s larboard quarter, her bow chasers opened fire, and the American gun crew could hear the sound of the planking ripped from the enemy's side. Shortly after 10:00 p.m., Douglas realized the game was up. *Levant* luffed up into the wind and fired a gun from her disengaged side.

An American prize crew was sent across in a boat to take possession. One of the officers later described the macabre scene he found on *Levant*'s quarterdeck: "The mizzenmast for several feet was covered with brains and blood; teeth, pieces of bones, fingers and large pieces of flesh were picked up from off the deck. It was a long time before I could familiarize myself to these . . . more horrid scenes than I had witnessed." Out of a crew of 159, *Levant* had suffered 23 killed and 16 wounded.

Both captured ships were in a sorry state. The *Cyane* had five feet of water in the hold, her masts were teetering, and her rigging was trailing in the sea. *Levant*'s masts and spars were in better shape, but her hull had been riddled between wind and water. The *Constitution*'s damages were negligible. Three hours of hard work by the prize crews put the captured ships in a condition to make sail, and by dawn on Sunday morning they were standing into the west. Some of the British officers engaged in loud arguments over which ship was to blame for the defeat, and a few of the British seamen became unruly enough that they had to be placed in irons.

Stewart navigated the prizes into the Portuguese harbor of Porto Praia in the Cape Verde Islands. At dawn the next day, the topsails of three large men-of-war were seen above the morning fog. They were three British frigates—*Leander*, *Newcastle*, and *Acasta*—the first two of similar force to the *Constitution*, having been built especially to deal with the American 44s. The squadron, which was under the command of Commodore Sir George Collier (captain of *Leander*), was clearly standing in for the Porto Praia roadstead. Though Porto Praia was a neutral port, Stewart did not take any chances. *Constitution* and her consorts cut their anchor cables and got to sea with remarkable speed, clearing East Point, at the northern end of the harbor's mouth, just as the hostile squadron reached extreme cannon range. The British frigates tacked and set all sail in chase.

For a time it looked as if Collier's superior force must overhaul the *Constitution*. Stewart gave the order to cut away the gig and first cutter, which were towing astern. At 1:00 p.m., he gave the signal for *Cyane* to tack. She did, and none of the British ships pursued her, allowing her to escape. As the afternoon wore on, *Levant* fell behind and looked certain to be snapped up. A few minutes after three o'clock, Stewart signaled her to tack to the northwest, just as the *Cyane* had. She did so, and this time the entire British squadron tacked with her, giving up any hope of catching the *Constitution*. *Levant* managed to run back into Porto Praia, but Collier's ships, in an affront to Portuguese sovereignty, chased her into the harbor and bombarded her at close range until she surrendered.

Cyane made New York on April 9, three and a half months after the Treaty of Ghent had been signed. *Constitution* arrived at Sandy Hook on May 14, and sailed for Boston ten days later. Upon her arrival at President Roads, the guns at Castle Island fired a thunderous salute, and the city erupted in joyous celebration. The *Constitution*, her immortality secure, moored alongside the Charlestown waterfront. Stewart was rowed across the harbor in his barge. Following the tradition begun by Isaac Hull in 1812, he went ashore at Boston's Long Wharf and walked up State Street to the Exchange, cheered by a huge crowd and trailed by a band playing patriotic tunes.

HAVING CLAMORED LONG AND LOUD for a punitive war against America, *The Times* bitterly resented the Treaty of Ghent. "We have retired from the combat with the stripes yet bleeding on our back, with the recent defeats at Plattsburgh and on Lake Champlain unavenged," an editorial exclaimed—"With the bravest seamen and the most powerful navy in the world, we retire from the contest when the balance of defeat is heavy against us." The *Morning Chronicle* abused Liverpool and his cabinet for having "humbled themselves in the dust" by accepting a peace with America that neither severed any territory nor forced the Americans to pay indemnities. The complaints were somewhat muffled by the abrupt surge in economic confidence brought about by the end of the war, accompanied by plunging maritime insurance rates, the rapid fitting out of merchantmen, the return of workers to the factories, and soaring markets—"the greatest Bull Account which has been known for years," as the *Morning Chronicle* reported. But critics worried that Britain had erred in allowing America to keep its small navy, which threatened to grow over time into a large navy. "[I]t must be allowed the Americans have fought us bravely at sea," wrote "Albion" to the *Naval Chronicle* on February 6; "they have almost in every instance been successful; and there cannot be a doubt they will speedily become a respectable, and ere long, a truly formidable naval power." Admiral Sir David Milne, like many British naval officers, believed England should have invested more money and men in the war: "I most sincerely wish to see their naval power nipt in the bud, for if they ever get it to any extent they will give us trouble enough."

In March 1815, however, two bulletins effectively silenced criticism of the American treaty. The first was the crushing defeat at New Orleans. The second was the appalling news that Napoleon had left Elba and was returning in triumph to Paris. The "Hundred Days" had begun, and Britons, weary but dogged, mobilized for yet another campaign. America was generally forgotten in all the excitement, but "Albion," whose letters to the *Naval Chronicle* often told hard, unpopular truths, saw the bloody repulse at New Orleans for what it was—the beginning of a new phase in transatlantic relations:

> Thus has ended in defeat all our attempts on the American coast, and thus have the measures and inadequate force provided by our government brought disgrace . . . for assuredly we have now done our worst against this infant enemy, which is already shown a *giant's* power. Soon will the rising greatness of this distant empire (and its distance is, perhaps, fortunate for Europe) astonish the nations who have looked on with wonder, and seen the mightiest efforts of Britain, at the era of her greatest power, so easily parried, so completely foiled. Lamenting the fallen fortunes of my country, and the unavailing loss of so many brave men, I now take my leave of the American contest. It is to all appearance over, but history will record our defeats, and posterity will see and appreciate their consequences. *Sic transit Gloria mundi.**

---

* "Thus passes the glory of the world."

EPILOGUE

Many Americans had assumed the negotiations in Ghent would inevitably fail, while also fearing that the British army would take New Orleans as easily as it had taken Washington the previous September. Federalist leaders, having recently gathered at a convention in Hartford, Connecticut, were threatening to declare New England independent of the Union unless the war was brought to an immediate end. The island of Nantucket had already issued a formal declaration of neutrality. Trading with the enemy was widespread and apparently growing, especially in the northern seaports. The nation's fiscal credit had collapsed. With customs revenue having slowed to a trickle, and little hope of borrowing additional funds from either domestic or foreign lenders, it was doubtful whether the federal government could continue to function through another year's campaign.

On February 4, 1815, the electrifying news of Andrew Jackson's victory in New Orleans arrived in the capital. Exactly a week later, on February 11, the British sloop of war *Favourite* arrived in New York under a flag of truce, bearing news of the Treaty of Ghent. A special messenger carried the dispatches overland to Washington, delivering them into the hands of Secretary of State Monroe on the thirteenth. Madison submitted the treaty to the Senate without suggested amendments; unanimous ratification followed on February 16. Madison sent Congress a message, with the ratified treaty, on February 20, in which he congratulated the country on a war "waged with the success which is the natural result of the wisdom of the legislative councils, of the patriotism of the people, of the public spirit of the militia, and of the valor of the military and naval forces of this country." Throughout the nation the news was met with the traditional rituals of rejoicing—ringing bells, thundering cannon, nighttime illuminations, and bands of music. Even hard-core

Federalists were jubilant, and the northern secessionist movement was stopped dead in its path. In Hartford, the *American Mercury* reported on February 14, "It is impossible to describe the sensations which this glorious event excited among all classes of our citizens—the ringing of bells, the beating of drums, and shouts of joy . . . which were heard through the night . . . best describe the public feeling."

The postwar economic surge was immediate and gratifying. Prices of stocks and government bonds shot up. Exportable produce, which had been all but worthless in the closing stages of the war, was suddenly in demand, and prices rose accordingly. Ships were fitted out in the harbors, preparing to sail for foreign markets. Imported manufactured goods and commodities, which had been scarce and expensive during the war, were suddenly cheap and abundant. Cotton and tea fell by more than 50 percent; tin by more than 60 percent. From a near standstill in the last year of the war, trade was quickly restored to levels approaching those of 1811, the last year of peace. The total net tonnage capacity of vessels entering American ports rose from 108,000 tons in 1814 to 918,000 tons in 1815; exports rose more than sevenfold, from $7 million in 1814 to $53 million in 1815. British forces withdrew from occupied territories on the northern border and from Tangier Island, in the Chesapeake. The British officers had the honor and good sense to disregard that part of the treaty requiring them to return runaway slaves to their American masters: many were allowed to settle as free citizens of the Maritime Provinces.

Federalist newspapers attacked the Republicans for having plunged the nation into a ludicrous and costly war. The *Boston Gazette* admitted that the "whole population devoted itself to expressions of joy," but a week later printed the names of all the congressmen who had voted for war in 1812, adding, "they must stand condemned as weak, ignorant, and impolitic men." During the treaty deliberations in the Senate, Federalist senator Rufus King of New York, though he supported ratification, "poured forty minutes of sarcastic oratory on the war and its backers." Hopeful Federalists assumed that the Republicans, having been forced to accept a treaty that did not secure the nation's stated objectives in the war, would be punished at the polls. "The treaty must be deemed disgraceful to the Government who made the war and the peace," said Federalist senator Christopher Gore of Massachusetts, "and will be so adjudged by all, after the first effusions of joy and relief have subsided."

It was not to be. The American public was in no mood to be told that the War of 1812 had been futile and unnecessary. They much preferred the story line offered by the Republicans—that Americans had prevailed in a great patriotic campaign. "*We have triumphed*," announced the Worcester *National Aegis*—"let snarling malcontents say what they will, *we have gloriously triumphed*." The humiliating reverses in Canada, the near secession of New England, the widespread trading with the enemy, the collapse of the national finances, the near-total destruction of trade, and the hard fact that none of the war's formal objectives were achieved in the treaty—all of these considerations were quickly wiped from the public memory, and the War of 1812 was proclaimed a "Second War of Independence." The mood of the country was ebullient: so much so that the period of American history that began in 1815 would be remembered as the "Era of Good Feelings."

Henry Clay, who had been both a leading advocate of the war and a principal architect of the peace, asked his House colleagues in January 1816: "Have we gained nothing by the war?"

> Let any man look at the degraded condition of this country before the war; the scorn of the universe, the contempt of ourselves; and tell me if we have gained nothing by the war? What is our present situation? Respectability and character abroad—security and confidence at home. If we have not obtained in the opinion of some the full measure of retribution, our character and our Constitution are placed on a solid basis, never to be shaken.

Responding to criticism that the Treaty of Ghent was silent on impressment and neutral trading rights, Republicans maintained that these issues had been rendered moot by the pacification of Europe. "Peace, at all time a blessing," Madison said in his message accompanying ratification, "is peculiarly welcome, therefore, at a period when the causes for the war have ceased to operate." Retired ex-President Jefferson told a correspondent that the peace was "in fact but an armistice, to be terminated by the first act of impressment committed on an American Citizen." Clay's ally in the House, South Carolinian John Calhoun, argued that persisting in the war only to obtain a British concession on impressment "would have been fighting to resist a speculative claim, on the part of the British government, which in practice had ceased."

Opponents of the war were vilified for years afterward. "Hartford Convention" became a watchword for treachery and disloyalty, and the anti-war Federalists, as one Republican editor wrote, had only brought "Disappointment!—Disgrace!—Detection!—Despair!" upon themselves. The Federalists had been outmaneuvered yet again, and this time the mistake would prove fatal. The party's candidates would be routed in the 1816 election, and the long Virginian Republican dynasty would continue with the two-term presidency of James Monroe (1817–25).

What was remembered and cherished about the War of 1812, above all, was the fact that America's tiny fleet had shocked and humbled the mightiest navy the world had ever known. Decatur, Hull, Bainbridge, Lawrence, Perry, and Macdonough were among the most exalted heroes of nineteenth-century America: their names were as widely known as the names of Hollywood stars or professional athletes are today. Towns, cities, and counties were named for them. Homes were decorated with engraved prints, pewter cups, platters, punch bowls, urns, and woodcarvings with the images of America's first ships or their commanders. As early as 1816, enterprising English manufacturers in Staffordshire began decorating ceramic pitchers and plates with scenes of American naval victories, and found plenty of eager buyers in the lucrative U.S. market. Sailors kept fragments of wood said to have come from one of the navy's victorious ships, as if they were relics of the true cross. Naval mythology aroused a new feeling of national unity after the partisan bitterness of the Federalist and Jeffersonian periods, and it was only after the War of 1812 that Americans began speaking of the United States in the singular rather than in the plural.

The last vestiges of Republican anti-navalism were abandoned. No sooner was the Treaty of Ghent ratified than Madison asked Congress for a declaration of war against Algiers, which had seized the opportunity afforded by the Anglo-American war to resume attacks on U.S. shipping. Two separate squadrons were prepared to sail for the Mediterranean—one in Boston, under William Bainbridge, and one in New York, under Stephen Decatur. As Bainbridge was the senior officer, he would command the newly launched 74-gun battleship *Independence*. Decatur's nine-ship squadron (which included the *Constellation*) sailed on May 20, 1815. Decatur's force captured the Algerian frigate *Mashuda*, and on July 3, with the guns of the squadron trained on his city, the Dey of Algiers signed a treaty forswearing future tribute and releasing American prisoners with no payment of ransom. Decatur then sailed to Tunis and Tripoli, extracting similar concessions, as well as cash payments to compensate American shipowners for their recent losses. The United States would never again encounter problems with the Barbary powers. Bainbridge, detained in Boston by delays in the outfitting of the *Independence*, arrived in the Mediterranean too late to share any of the glory, and was resentful toward Decatur for years afterward. Decatur, now the most prominent naval hero in American history, returned to the United States and proposed a famously double-edged toast at a banquet in his honor: "To our country! In her intercourse with foreign nations may she always be in the right—but our country, right or wrong."

Congress had ordered a new ship construction program late in 1812, and several vessels were launched and fitted out in the immediate aftermath of the war. These included, in addition to the *Independence*, the 74-gun battleships *Washington* and *Franklin*, as well as the new 44-gun frigates *Guerrière* and *Java*, whose names were intended to annoy the British. A sixth was the 30-gun *Fulton*, the world's first steam-powered frigate, propelled by a single paddle wheel that was enclosed within two pontoon hulls in order to protect it from enemy shot. The *Fulton* was an unwieldy vessel, and the internal-wheel design was soon abandoned. More than half a century would pass before the last sailing warships were rendered obsolete.

The nation's new enthusiasm for naval power continued into the postwar years. Madison, allowing that "a certain degree of preparation for war is not only indispensable to avert disasters in the onset, but affords also security for the continuance of the peace," asked Congress to enact a long-term building program. Passage of an Act for the Gradual Increase of the Navy followed in April 1816. This law authorized the construction of nine battleships and twelve heavy frigates at a projected cost of $1 million per year for a period of eight years. Jefferson, commenting privately to Monroe in a letter of January 1815, recognized that a complete repudiation of the principles of 1801 was inevitable, given the performance of the navy in the war: "Frigates and seventy fours are a sacrifice we must make, heavy as it is, to the prejudices of a part of our citizens."

The navy of the early nineteenth century was chiefly occupied in suppressing piracy and the slave trade, but confidence in the long-term potential of American naval power was a factor in the so-called Monroe Doctrine, articulated by President Monroe (though largely formulated by Secretary of State John Quincy Adams) in his annual message of December 1823. The president declared that North and South America "are henceforth not to be considered as subjects for future colonization by any European powers . . . that we should consider any attempt on their part to extend their system to any portion of this hemisphere as dangerous to our peace and safety . . . we could not view any interposition for the purpose of oppressing [the Latin American republics], or controlling in any other manner their destiny, by any European power, in any other light than as the manifestation of an unfriendly disposition toward the United States."

———

NEARLY TWO CENTURIES after the fact, the causes and effects of the War of 1812 remain a subject of spirited debate among historians. The war lacked the historical significance of the American Revolution, and it never approached the scale of the Civil War or the major wars of the twentieth century. From England's point of view, it was a sideshow in the long contest with Napoleon. It was a war ostensibly declared in defense of American maritime rights, but it was deeply unpopular among the inhabitants of the northern seaports. It was a conflict between sovereign nations, but it was imbued with the intimate personal bitterness of a civil war. It might have been avoided if not for bad luck and bungling diplomacy on both sides. Had a telegraph cable linked London and Washington in 1812, the war would not have been fought; had such a cable existed in 1815, General Pakenham's troops would have returned to their families in England and not been slaughtered on a battlefield south of New Orleans two weeks after the treaty had been signed. No other foreign war has ever divided the American people so bitterly, and if it had lasted one year longer it might have caused a dissolution of the Union. At the close of hostilities, neither side could point to any tangible gains, and the Americans were forced to admit they had been fortunate not to have lost territory on the Canadian border.

Winston Churchill, in his *History of the English-Speaking Peoples*, pronounces the War of 1812 a "futile and unnecessary war"—but adds, almost in the same breath, that "the results of the peace were solid and enduring." This is an essential point. There were many cases after 1815 in which British and American interests clashed, but diplomacy somehow prevailed in resolving every dispute, and there was never a third Anglo-American war. Not many contemporaries on either side of the Atlantic, in 1815, would have believed such a result was possible. British and American newspapers frequently spoke of the likelihood of a renewed war. In 1816, Henry Clay told his colleagues in the House: "That man must be blind to the indications of the future, who cannot see that we are destined to have war after war with Great Britain, until, if one of the two nations be not crushed, all grounds of collision shall have ceased between us."

But the lessons of the war were taken to heart. "Anti-American sentiment in Great Britain ran high for several years, but the United States was never again refused proper treatment as an independent Power," wrote Churchill. "The British Army and Navy had learned to respect their former colonials." The point was echoed in private correspondence from the postwar period. The U.S. Army had done poorly, on the whole, in several attempts to invade

Canada, and the Canadians had shown that they would fight bravely to defend their country. But the British did not doubt that the thinly populated territory would be vulnerable in a third war. Admiral Sir David Milne told a correspondent, in 1817, "we cannot keep Canada if the Americans declare war against us."

Although the Treaty of Ghent did not provide any security against the impressment of seamen from American ships, the practice ended. Even during the naval remobilization of the "Hundred Days" in 1815, the Royal Navy took the utmost pains not to permit the impressment of seamen from American ships. In population, in economic production, and in territorial extent, the United States was growing more rapidly than Britain. With these demographic trends in mind, Henry Adams passed his judgment on the Treaty of Ghent: "Perhaps at that moment the Americans were the chief losers; but they gained their greatest triumph in referring all their disputes to be settled by time, the final negotiator, whose decision they could safely trust."

A FLOURISHING LITERARY TRADITION grew up around the U.S. Navy in the first half of the nineteenth century, but the early writers and historians, with a few exceptions, did the subject little justice. Modeled after the "heroic style" of the classical historians, particularly Livy and Virgil, these early works were generally full of errors, overwrought, and shot through with national bias. Their authors adopted a swaggering, romantic tone: frigate actions were depicted as a kind of latter-day contact sport, fought with good-humored bravado by dashing young officers and cheerful roughneck sailors. One such work, published in 1816, was entitled *Naval Monument, containing official and other accounts of the battles fought between the navies of the United States and Great Britain during the late war*. The cover illustration depicts a regal female figure, "America," riding across the surface of the sea in a chariot formed of waves. The god Neptune, her charioteer, points his trident to the top of an immense stone pedestal, rising somehow from the sea, upon which stand several of the victorious American officers of the War of 1812.

Among the authors who wrote on the early navy were several of the giants of nineteenth-century American literature. Washington Irving published a series of biographies of American naval officers in the *Analectic Review*. Nathaniel Hawthorne wrote about Captain "Mad Jack" Percival, who commanded the *Constitution* in the 1840s, in his *American Note-Books*. Herman Melville served as an ordinary seaman aboard the frigate *United States* in 1843–44 and published a thinly fictionalized account of his experience in the

1850 novel *White-Jacket*. James Fenimore Cooper served briefly in the navy as a midshipman in 1808, and later published several sea novels, including *The Pilot* (1824), *The Two Admirals* (1842), and *The Sea Lions* (1849). In 1839, Cooper published his *History of the Navy of the United States of America*, a poorly written panegyric that is nevertheless deemed required reading for modern naval historians, because the author enjoyed direct access to living witnesses and participants in the events described in his book. None of these works is well remembered today, but they tended to sell briskly at the time they were published, providing a lucrative source of income to authors who were often living hand-to-mouth. Though *White-Jacket* is ranked as one of Melville's lesser works, for example, it sold far better than did *Moby-Dick* during the author's lifetime.

Not many British writers were inclined to linger over the War of 1812, and Wellington's great victory over Napoleon at Waterloo on June 18, 1815, made it that much easier to put the entire episode out of mind. In contrast to the postwar publishing boom in the United States, very few works were written or published in England on either the land or naval operations of the War of 1812.* An exception was *Naval Occurrences of the War of 1812: A Full and Correct Account of the Naval War Between Great Britain and the United States of America, 1812–1815*, first published in 1817 by an English Admiralty lawyer named William James. *Naval Occurrences* was widely read and hugely influential, so much so that it became the standard British text on the naval war of 1812–15, and was largely accepted by later generations of British naval historians as the last word on the subject. James subsequently published a magisterial six-volume *Naval History of Great Britain*, covering the period from 1793 to 1827. Based on the latter work, especially, James has been nominated by his admirers as "the father of modern naval history."

Having practiced for many years in the Admiralty Courts of Jamaica, James had happened to be passing through the United States when the War of 1812 was declared. Arrested in Philadelphia as an enemy alien, James was still in the city in August, when news arrived that the *Guerrière* had been captured by the *Constitution*. Shaken by the event, but suspecting that the *Guerrière* had been overmatched by the American frigate, James began to gather data on the U.S. Navy in preparation to write a book correcting the record. In October 1813, James escaped from Philadelphia and made his way to Halifax the

---

* To this day, the overwhelming majority of scholarly work on the War of 1812 has been produced by Americans and Canadians. A larger contribution by British scholars would enrich the field.

following month. There he wrote several articles for the *Naval Chronicle*. Returning to England after the Treaty of Ghent, James persuaded several of the officers who had fought in the American war to provide him with information and assistance. He worked at a breakneck pace, completing *Naval Occurrences of the War of 1812*, a full seven hundred pages long, in the spring of 1817.

The accounts of individual battles in *Naval Occurrences* are written with great attention to detail, and in many respects the book set a new standard for research methodology in naval history. James's legal training is apparent throughout the book. Documentary evidence is often examined with impressive thoroughness, statistics are cited authoritatively and marshaled effectively in support of the book's thesis, and inconsistencies are exposed in the penetrating style of a lawyer's cross-examination of a witness. Official letters and excerpts from court proceedings are helpfully published in a long appendix, altogether comprising over one hundred documents. On the whole, James demonstrated, convincingly, that many of the American successes in the naval war were due in large part to the superior size and armament of the American ships. Since none of the "instant histories" appearing in the United States after the war had acknowledged this important point, while many had actually asserted that the reverse was true, James's book served as a useful corrective.

On the other hand, *Naval Occurrences* is a bitterly sarcastic and deeply malevolent work. Nearly every page is sprinkled with gratuitous insults aimed at American officers and seamen, with the occasional *ad hominem* whack at the entire American people or the American "character" ("It may suit the Americans to invent any falsehood, no matter how barefaced, to foist a valiant character on themselves"). James wrote with the high passion of a man possessed by his hatred for England's recent enemy, and he never managed to achieve the detachment and composure required of a great historian. Nor was he an especially trustworthy arbiter when evidence was contradictory or lacking. As an attorney, James assumed the familiar role of a courtroom advocate presenting a case on behalf of a client. In every instance in which the particulars of the British and American accounts disagree, he accepts those of the former at face value. He often makes sweeping assertions without even attempting to support his facts, and when he errs, as he often does, his errors always manage to work in favor of the British officers and ships. In failing to achieve his potential as a great historian, James failed even to be a good one.

For six and a half decades, James's book stood unrefuted. It fell to Theodore Roosevelt, as a twenty-two-year-old law student, to produce an effective response. Roosevelt began researching the subject as an undergraduate at Harvard College in 1879, somehow finding time for the work despite carrying a heavy schedule of classes, sports, social engagements, and extracurricular activities. He wrote the early chapters of the book that would eventually be published as *The Naval War of 1812* (for which he received no academic credit at Harvard) while simultaneously churning out his senior thesis. Graduating with high honors in 1880, Roosevelt moved back into his mother's house on West Fifty-Seventh Street in New York, married Alice Hathaway Lee, and enrolled at Columbia Law School. In the afternoons, after his law classes, he often did research for his naval history at the Astor Library on Lafayette Place. In the evenings, at home, he would work on the book for an hour or so before dinner.

A friend, Owen Wister, recalled that Roosevelt "finished his naval history of 1812 mostly standing on one leg at the bookcases in his New York house, the other leg crossed behind, toe touching the floor, heedless of dinner engagements and the flight of time." Wister continued:

> A slide drew out from the bookcase. On this he had open the leading authorities on navigation, of which he knew nothing. He knew that when a ship's course was one way, with the wind another, the ship had to sail at angles, and this was called tacking or beating. By exhaustive study and drawing of models, he pertinaciously got it all right, whatever of it came into the naval engagements he was writing about.
>
> His wife used to look in at his oblivious back, and exclaim in a plaintive drawl: "We're dining out in twenty minutes, and Teedy's drawing little ships!"
>
> Then there would be a scurry, and he would cut himself shaving, and it wouldn't stop bleeding, and they would have to surround him and take measures to save his collar from getting stained.

Roosevelt was no seaman, and did not easily master the details of ship-handling and maneuvering, or the finer points of early nineteenth-century naval armament and relative force. It was an enormous task, particularly since much of the original historical documentation remained in its raw form, not yet transcribed and published as it is today. "I have plenty of information now, but I can't get it into words; I'm afraid it is too big a task for me," he told his sister. "I wonder if I won't find everything in life too big for my abilities." But he managed to push through to the end, and *The Naval War of 1812* was published by G. P. Putnam's Sons in 1882. Reviews were favorable, and for many years the book was required reading for midshipmen at the U.S. Naval Academy in Annapolis.

Much of *The Naval War* is fairly dry and technical, structured largely as a point-by-point rebuttal of James's book (Roosevelt actually used the relevant chapters from James's *Naval History of Great Britain*, an abridged version of *Naval Occurrences*). Roosevelt does not dismiss James's main thesis out of hand; indeed, he concedes the truth of many of the Englishman's claims, and praises his book as "an invaluable work, written with fullness and care," while in the same breath condemning it as "a piece of special pleading by a bitter and not over-scrupulous partisan." There are outcroppings of humor in Roosevelt's prose, as when he quotes James as noting a "similarity" of language between Americans and Britons, calling the remark "an interesting philological discovery that but few will attempt to controvert." After quoting James's long-winded justification of the British practice of impressing seamen from American ships, Roosevelt dismisses it as a "euphemistic way of saying that whenever a British commander short of men came across an American vessel he impressed all of her crew that he wanted, whether they were citizens of the United States or not."

Occasionally, Roosevelt seizes upon one of James's unsupported assertions and shows how, if carried to logical extremes, it would lead to a perverse conclusion. For example, when James estimates that of the crews of the American ships, "one third in number and one half in point of effectiveness" were in fact British seamen, Roosevelt challenges the truth of the claim, but for the sake of argument applies the rule to the *Constitution-Java* action (in which the crews numbered 450 and 400, respectively):

> That is, of the 450 men the *Constitution* had when she fought the *Java*, 150 were British, and the remaining 300 could have been as effectively replaced by 150 more British. So a very little logic works out a result that James certainly did not intend to arrive at; namely, that 300 British led by American officers could beat, with ease and comparative impunity, 400 British led by their own officers.

To the same point, in discussing the *Constitution-Guerrière* action, Roosevelt quotes court-martial testimony in which the British captain had claimed his ship was "very much weakened by permitting the Americans on board to quit their quarters." Roosevelt adds:

> Coupling this with the assertion made by James . . . that the *Constitution* was largely manned by Englishmen, we reach the somewhat

remarkable conclusion that the British ship was defeated because the Americans on board would *not* fight against their country, and that the American was victorious because the British on board *would*.

Roosevelt's book exposed enough of James's distortions and fabrications to leave no doubt that the latter was, in spite of his talents, guilty of "every known form of willful misstatement, from the suppression of the truth and the suggestion of the false to the lie direct." But Roosevelt's purpose was not only to refute James, but to show that James's American contemporaries were equally culpable. When the American ships were better manned and more heavily armed than their adversaries, Roosevelt states the case clearly, and admits that many of the American naval victories of the War of 1812 were "magnified absurdly by most of our writers at the time." There was no reason not to "tell the truth" about the relative force of British and American ships in the War of 1812, said Roosevelt, for the American victories would not have been possible if not for the courage and skill of both officers and crew:

> And it must always be remembered that a victory, honorably won, if even over a weaker foe, *does* reflect credit on the nation by whom it is gained. It was creditable to us as a nation that our ships were better made and better armed than the British frigates. . . . Some of my countrymen will consider this but scant approbation, to which the answer must be that a history is not a panegyric.

Of course, what was most interesting about *The Naval War of 1812* was not the book itself but the identity of its author, and the lessons he would draw from naval history in the course of his remarkable career as an American statesman and a devoted imperialist. During the next several years of Roosevelt's whirlwind of a life, he was elected to the New York State Assembly, rising to the rank of minority leader at age twenty-five; suffered the tragedy of having his wife and mother die (of different illnesses) on the same day; took up cattle ranching in the remote Dakota Territory on the western frontier; and published his second book, *Hunting Trips of a Ranchman* (1885). Roosevelt was invited to speak at the Naval War College in Newport, Rhode Island, in June 1887. To an audience of naval officers and professors, Roosevelt delivered a speech laced with stunningly bellicose rhetoric. He was beginning to develop the high-voltage speaking style that would make him such an iconic figure in American public life: his high raspy voice sometimes breaking into falsetto, his arm-waving, his fist-shaking, his practice of smacking his right fist into his left palm, and his way of leaning far over the rostrum as if trying to get his face closer to the audience.

> We ask for a great navy, partly because we think that the possession of such a navy is the surest guaranty of peace, and partly because we feel that no national life is worth having if the nation is not willing, when the need shall arise, to stake everything on the supreme arbitrament of war, and to pour out its blood, its treasure, and its tears like water, rather than submit to the loss of honor and renown. . . . No triumph of peace is quite so great as the supreme triumphs of war.

At the Naval War College, Roosevelt was introduced to Alfred Thayer Mahan, a naval officer turned historian who would shortly publish *The Influence of Sea Power Upon History*, destined to become one of the most influential naval works ever written. When it was published two years later, Roosevelt wrote the captain: "During the last two days I have spent half my time, busy as I am, in reading your book, and that I found it interesting is shown by the fact that having taken it up I have gone straight through and finished it. . . . It is a *very* good book—admirable; and I am greatly in error if it does not become a naval classic." Roosevelt wrote an admiring review in the *Atlantic Monthly*, reserving special praise for Mahan's conclusion that the War of 1812 had shown that the United States needed a fleet of capital ships, or battleships, of the heaviest class. Captain Mahan would join an inner circle of Roosevelt's advisers, allies, and fellow imperialists that would include John Hay, Elihu Root, and Massachusetts Senator Henry Cabot Lodge.

After stints as a member of the U.S. Civil Service Commission and New York City Board of Police Commissioners, Roosevelt was appointed, in 1897, Assistant Secretary of the Navy in the administration of William McKinley. Roosevelt agitated in favor of a naval buildup, the cutting of a canal across the Central American isthmus, the annexation of Hawaii, and intervention in Cuba on the side of anti-Spanish revolutionaries. He openly hoped for a war with one of the European imperial powers, "by preference Germany—but I am not particular, and I'd take even Spain if nothing better offered." After the explosion of the USS *Maine* in Havana Harbor, Roosevelt cabled Admiral George Dewey, commander of the Asiatic Squadron at Hong Kong, and ordered him to prepare to attack the Spanish fleet in the Philippines. When McKinley was slow to ask for a declaration of war, Roosevelt privately remarked that the president had "the backbone of a chocolate éclair." Six days after the American declaration of war against Spain on April 25, 1898, Dewey's fleet surprised and destroyed the Spanish fleet at Manila Bay, and the Philippines came under American control.

A week later, Roosevelt quit the Navy Department. He obtained an army commission, led the "Rough Riders" regiment in a famous charge up San Juan Hill in Cuba, returned to the United States as a war hero, and was elected governor of New York State in 1898. In 1900, he was elected vice president in the second McKinley administration. When McKinley was shot and killed by an assassin in Buffalo, New York, the following year, Roosevelt, at age forty-two, suddenly found himself the twenty-sixth president of the United States.

Using the "bully pulpit" of the presidency (a term he coined), President Roosevelt campaigned for a major naval building program. He delivered his famous "Big Stick" speech in Chicago in April 1903. "There is a homely old adage which runs, *Speak softly and carry a big stick: you will go far*," he told the audience. "If the American nation will speak softly, and yet build, and keep at a pitch of the highest training, a thoroughly efficient navy, the Monroe Doctrine will go far." The next morning, the *Chicago Tribune* ran a headline: SPEAK SOFTLY AND CARRY A BIG STICK, SAYS ROOSEVELT. In the following days, people who came out to see the president carried baseball bats and makeshift clubs, brandishing them above their heads.

During his first term, Roosevelt convinced Congress to build ten first-class battleships, four armored cruisers, and seventeen smaller vessels. Naval spending rose nearly 40 percent, surpassing $100 million for the first time. It was the largest peacetime naval expansion in American history. By 1906, the United States had more battleships afloat than any other naval power except Great Britain.

Early in his career, Roosevelt had believed that the United States might find itself in a third war with England. After the peaceful settlement of an Alaska-Yukon boundary dispute in 1903, he wrote: "There is no danger to us from England now in any way. I think there never will be." Roosevelt regarded Germany, with its territorial ambitions in South America, as America's most dangerous rival; and he believed Japan, recent victor of the Russo-Japanese War of 1904–05, posed a longer-term threat in the Pacific. Roosevelt told Cecil Spring-Rice, an English friend who would later serve as British ambassador to Washington: "In a dozen years the English, Americans and Germans, who now dread one another as rivals in the trade of the Pacific, will have each to dread the Japanese more than they do any other nation."

In 1906, Roosevelt traveled to Panama aboard the USS *Louisiana* to inspect the progress of construction of the Panama Canal—a project he regarded as essential to enable the United States to maintain a credible naval presence in both the Atlantic and Pacific Oceans. It was the first time a sitting president had traveled outside the United States. (The canal would be completed and opened in 1914.) In 1907, Roosevelt proposed that the main battle fleet of the U.S. Navy—sixteen first-class battleships known as the "Great White Fleet," so named because they were painted white—should sail on a "goodwill" circumnavigation of the world, both in order to advertise American naval power and to drill the officers and men in a technically demanding exercise. No fleet of capital ships had ever made such a voyage. When Congress balked at the expense, Roosevelt ordered the ships to sail for the Pacific using existing resources, and then dared Congress not to appropriate funds for the fleet's return. Roosevelt later remarked, "There was no further difficulty about the money."

Roosevelt saw the White Fleet off from Hampton Roads in December 1907. The column of ships stretched for seven miles across the sea. Watching from the presidential yacht, the *Mayflower*, Roosevelt asked: "Did you ever see such a fleet? Isn't it magnificent? Oughtn't we all feel proud?" The fleet traversed 43,000 miles, making twenty port calls on six continents over a period of fourteen months, and returned to Hampton Roads in February 1909, just days before Roosevelt was due to retire from office. Again the president watched from the deck of the *Mayflower*. As each ship passed, she fired a 21-gun salute in honor of the commander in chief. Roosevelt was, as he often said, "deeee-lighted."

Almost a century had passed since the Anglo-American war of 1812–15. Theodore Roosevelt, whose career had begun with an exhaustive study of the naval operations of that war, had almost single-handedly persuaded his countrymen to recognize and adopt, as he had put it to the midshipmen of the Naval Academy a few years earlier, "the lessons which should be learned by the study of the War of 1812."

CHRONOLOGY OF LATER EVENTS: 1815–2005

1815

Stephen Decatur leads a naval expedition to the Mediterranean and obtains highly favorable treaties with the Barbary powers.

1816

USS *Constitution* laid up in ordinary (mothballed) at the Charlestown Navy Yard.

1817

Former USS *President*, now HMS *President*, has seen only two years' active service in the Royal Navy after her capture off New York in January 1815. Cumulative damages sustained in her grounding at Sandy Hook, her battle with *Endymion*, and a gale during the return passage from Bermuda to England have rendered her unfit for repair. In 1817 she is broken up at Portsmouth, England.

1818

An act of the U.S. Congress, passed in April, empowers the president to deploy naval vessels to suppress the illegal slave trade.

1819–20

USS *Constellation* serves as flagship to Commodore Charles Morris (formerly first lieutenant of the *Constitution* under Isaac Hull) on the Brazil station, patrolling against illegal slavers.

Stephen Decatur, having won more prize money than any other commander in the U.S. Navy, is now a wealthy man. He and his wife, Susan, live in a mansion designed by Benjamin Henry Latrobe, on the northwest corner of President's Square (present-day Lafayette Park), a stone's throw from the White House.

James Barron, who commanded the *Chesapeake* when she was attacked by the *Leopard* in 1807 and was suspended from the navy, returns to the United States after an absence of six years, seeking reinstatement. Decatur opposes the reinstatement, and is openly critical of Barron in conversations with other naval officers and government officials in Washington. Barron, from Norfolk, writes Decatur on June 12, 1819: "Sir: I have been informed, in Norfolk, that you have said you could insult me with impunity, or words to that effect. If you have said so, you will no doubt disavow it, and I shall expect to hear from you." Decatur replies June 17: "Whatever I may have *thought*, or *said*, in the very frequent and free conversation I have had respecting you and your conduct, I feel a thorough conviction that I never could have been guilty of so much egoism as to say that 'I could insult you' (or any other man) 'with impunity.' I am, sir, your obedient servant, Stephen Decatur."

Here the quarrel might have ended, but a long correspondence, escalating in tone, passes between them. Decatur to Barron, December 29, 1819: "If we fight, it must be of your seeking. I have now to inform you that I shall pay no further attention to any communication you may make to me, other than a direct call to the field." Barron to Decatur, January 16, 1820: "Whenever you will consent to meet me on fair and equal grounds, that is, such as two honorable men may consider just and proper, you are to view this as that call." The seconds are chosen: Decatur chooses William Bainbridge; Barron, Captain Jesse Elliot. Bainbridge and Elliot agree that the duel will be fought in Bladensburg, Maryland, at the murderous range of eight paces.

The meeting takes place early on the morning of March 22, 1820. Witnesses include John Rodgers and David Porter. Immediately before the duel, Barron says: "Now, Decatur, if we meet in another world, let us hope that we may be better friends." Decatur answers: "I was never your enemy." The duelists seem prepared to conciliate, but Bainbridge and Elliot urge them into their places.

As Bainbridge begins the count, both men fire, both are hit, and both sink to the ground. As they lie bleeding, Barron says, "Decatur, I forgive you from the bottom of my Heart," and "God bless you, Decatur." Decatur, bleeding from his abdomen, certain that his wound is mortal, replies: "Farewell, farewell, Barron."

Decatur is taken back to Washington by John Rodgers (Bainbridge having fled to escape prosecution). He delivers the dying officer to his home on President's Square. Susan Decatur, not told that the duel was to take place, is shocked and grief-stricken. Louisa Adams, wife of Secretary of State John Quincy Adams, visits Susan in the last hours before Decatur's death. "Oh what an agonizing scene," she writes. "What irreparable mischief in a few short hours. The very thought makes me shudder."

Decatur dies early the morning of the twenty-third. His funeral is attended by some ten thousand Americans, including President Monroe, members of Congress, Supreme Court justices, and members of the diplomatic corps.

James Barron recovers from his wound. Though he is nationally reviled as Decatur's killer, he nonetheless wins reinstatement to the navy. Upon the death of John Rodgers in 1838, Barron becomes the senior ranking officer in the service.

1820

Former USS *Chesapeake*, now HMS *Chesapeake*, is sold to a private buyer in Plymouth, England. She is subsequently broken up, and a portion of her gun deck timbers used to build the Chesapeake Mill, a commercial flour mill on the River Meon in Wickham, Hampshire.

1820

In July, *Constellation* sails round the Horn, where she is attached to the Pacific Squadron under Commodore Charles Stewart, patrolling off the coast of Peru.

1821–28

Constitution is returned to service and operates in the Mediterranean, often as flagship of the Mediterranean Squadron. She is visited by the English poet Lord Byron.

1822

Ex-presidents John Adams and Thomas Jefferson, advancing into old age, continue a regular correspondence. For several years after the War of 1812 they do not touch on the subject of the navy. In October 1822, Adams is attempting to organize his files pertaining to the origin of the navy and requests Jefferson's assistance. Adams's memory is faulty: he recalls that the March 1794 legislation had called for four (not six) frigates. He asks if Jefferson can remember details of the debate, now nearly thirty years in the past.

"I have racked my memory and ransacked my papers to enable myself to answer the inquiries of your favor of October 15, but to little purpose," Jefferson replies two weeks later. "My papers furnish me nothing, my memory generalities only." Lingering briefly on the topic, the Virginian explains his reasons for having opposed an expansion of the navy: namely, that "a navy is a very expensive engine." He allows that the performance of the navy in the War of 1812 "certainly raised our rank and character among nations." He apologizes for remembering so little about the events of 1794: "This is all I recollect about the origin and progress of our navy."

The two old friends, seventy-nine (Jefferson) and eighty-seven (Adams), search their fading memories for bits and pieces of thirty-year-old conversations, rummaging through voluminous files with fumbling, arthritic hands; squinting with failing eyes at old letters and journals; trying in vain to reconstruct historical events in which they had participated directly. Almost two centuries later, the answers to many of Adams's questions are literally at the fingertips of any person with an Internet connection and a few hours of spare time.

1822–23

USS *Congress*, Captain James Biddle, patrols the West Indies against piracy, then carries ambassadors to Spain and Argentina.

1826

On July 4, the fiftieth anniversary of the signing ceremony of the Declaration of Independence, Adams and Jefferson both lie on their deathbeds. Adams's last words are: "Thomas Jefferson survives." But Jefferson had died at Monticello a few hours earlier.

The nation mourns. It is believed that the near-simultaneous death of the two revolutionary statesmen on such an important anniversary is a signal of divine providence. When the news reaches the Mediterranean, the flagship *Constitution* "cockbills" her yards. This traditional sign of mourning involves tilting the lower yards at extreme angles, giving the ship a "slovenly appearance as a sign of bereavement."

1827

The dormant feud between Joshua Humphreys and Josiah Fox flares up again after thirty years. Letters are published in newspapers and submitted to the Navy Department by relatives and partisans of the two shipwrights, who disagree over the apportionment of credit for the design of the nation's first frigates. Fox insists that he drew the original drafts; Humphreys insists that Fox only drew copies. Humphreys does concede that Fox is responsible for the *Chesapeake*, having built her to a design that had been altered, against instructions, from the original draft. "She spoke his talents," Humphreys writes, "which I leave the Commanders of that ship to estimate by her qualifications."

Humphreys claims credit for the success of the frigates in 1812. "Had our frigates been less powerful, 'tis probable they might not have been successful, and if they had been taken, the ardor and spirits of our navy would have been very different this day. The first victory gave a tone and led to all the rest; it raised our own spirits and lowered those of the British." He reiterates his case for large, powerful frigates. "A wise general will never send 1000 men to take another thousand (if he can avoid it). He will always send a greater force . . . by making our ships large, it [was] the only plan by which this country [could] in any wise be formidable with a small comparative number of ships."

1828–30

United States puts into the Philadelphia Navy Yard for major repairs. In 1830, she is transferred to New York, where she is rebuilt and made ready for service again in 1832.

1830–33

Constitution is laid up in ordinary in Boston. A rumor circulates that the Secretary of the Navy has recommended that she be broken up. A young Oliver Wendell Holmes writes a poem decrying the alleged plan, which he entitles "Old Ironsides." The final stanza proposes that the revered frigate, rather than face the indignities of the wrecker's yard, should be abandoned at sea, her "holy flag" nailed to the mast, her sails all set, "And give her to the god of storms / The lightning and the gale!" The poem stirs public outrage, and the Navy Department announces that *Constitution* will be repaired and returned to service. The episode is one of America's earliest historic preservation campaigns. She enters the huge Dry Dock No. 1, specially built in Charlestown, in 1833.

1834

A new figurehead, depicting U.S. President Andrew Jackson, is installed on the bow of the *Constitution*. Jackson's political opponents, who are numerous in Boston, are outraged. The commandant of the Navy Yard receives death threats. On July 2, under cover of darkness and rain, the frigate's Jackson figurehead is decapitated and the wooden head stolen. It is later recovered and the figurehead repaired.

A survey of the *Congress* finds the thirty-four-year-old frigate unfit for repair. She is broken up at the Gosport Navy Yard in Norfolk.

1835

In October, *Constellation* sails to Florida to assist in suppressing the Seminole uprising. She carries an army invasion force to land ashore, and deploys her boats on river raids.

1835–38

The newly restored *Constitution* serves once again as flagship of the Mediterranean Squadron.

1838

Henry Adams born in Boston. As a young child, he is a frequent visitor to the home of his grandfather, former President John Quincy Adams.

1839–41

Constitution serves as flagship of the Pacific Squadron.

1841–43

Constellation, as flagship of the East India Squadron, circumnavigates the world. First deployed to waters off southern China (by way of the Cape of Good Hope) during the Opium War, she crosses the Pacific, calling at Hawaii and several South American ports, and rounds Cape Horn to return to the United States.

1842–43

United States serves as flagship of the Pacific Squadron. When the ship calls at Honolulu in 1843, Herman Melville, seeking passage back to the United States, enlists as an ordinary seaman. He serves aboard her for fourteen months, during which there are 163 reported floggings. Melville is appalled by a system of naval discipline that allows a man to be "scourged worse than a hound . . . for things not essentially criminal." His novel *White-Jacket* (published several years later) is a thinly fictionalized account of his service aboard the *United States*. He would later write *Billy Budd*, a short novel about a miscarriage of justice aboard an American warship.

1844

United States returns to Boston in the fall. Melville and the rest of the crew are paid off, and the frigate is taken out of commission.

James K. Polk campaigns for president on the slogan: "Fifty-four Forty or Fight!" The slogan refers to the latitude of the southern border of Russian Alaska, which Polk demands as the northern boundary of the Oregon Territory. A third Anglo-American war looms. After Polk's election, his administration finds itself preoccupied with hostilities with Mexico to the south, and negotiates with England to fix the northwest border at the 49th parallel.

1844–51

Constitution circumnavigates the world under the command of Captain John "Mad Jack" Percival. In 1849, at Gaeta, Italy, the frigate is visited by Pope Pius IX.

1845

On October 10, the U.S. Naval Academy is established on the grounds of Fort Severn in Annapolis, MD. The initial class of fifty midshipmen begins work under a faculty of seven professors.

1846–49

United States is recommissioned and deployed to Africa, the Mediterranean, and Europe; she returns to Norfolk and is again placed in ordinary in February 1849.

1853

Constellation is broken up at the Gosport Navy Yard in Norfolk. Some of her timbers may have been incorporated into a new sloop of war, also christened the *Constellation*. (The latter remains afloat in Baltimore Harbor.)

1853–55

Constitution serves as flagship of the African Squadron, patrolling the "Guinea coast" against slavers.

1858

Theodore Roosevelt is born in New York on October 27.

1860

Constitution, now more than sixty years old, is converted into a training ship at the Naval Academy in Annapolis.

1861–65

Constitution, still in Annapolis at the outbreak of the Civil War, is threatened with destruction by pro-Confederate militias in Maryland. She is transferred to Newport, RI, with the faculty, staff, and students of the Naval Academy, where she remains for the duration of the war, serving as a dormitory and classroom for 200 midshipmen.

During the Civil War, vital exports of cotton to Britain are interrupted by the Union blockade of the southern coast. Before Abraham Lincoln's Emancipation Proclamation of 1863 freeing the slaves in the Confederate states, British public opinion largely favors the rebels. The British provide aid, weapons, and materiel to the southern states by running the Union blockade. Confederate commerce-raiding vessels are built and launched in English seaports.

United States remains in ordinary at Norfolk at the outbreak of the war. In April 1861, the Norfolk Navy Yard is captured by rebel troops. The Confederates repair the frigate and commission her as CSS *United States*. Because of her poor condition, she is fitted with cannon and moored permanently in the harbor as a floating battery.

On November 8, Captain Charles Wilkes of the USS *San Jacinto* stops and boards the British mail packet *Trent* at sea, near Cuba. The Americans arrest and remove two Confederate envoys. In England, the news is greeted with outrage, and Lord Palmerston's government threatens war. President Abraham Lincoln, declaring that he wishes to fight only "one war at a time," disavows Captain Wilkes's action and hands the prisoners over to the British.

In May 1862, the CSS *United States* is sunk in the Elizabeth River to obstruct attacking Union vessels. When the rebel shipwrights first attempt to scuttle the ship, an entire box of axes is worn out attempting to chop through her live oak frame. Eventually, they succeed in boring through the hull with drills. When Union troops recapture the yard later that month, *United States* is raised from the riverbed and towed back to the Navy Wharf.

1865

Constitution returns to Annapolis at war's end. The *United States* is broken up at the Navy Yard in Norfolk, and her timbers sold to private buyers.

1878–79

Constitution carries American exhibits to the Paris Exposition, docking in Le Havre for nine months. She runs aground under the White Cliffs of Dover off the English coast on her return passage, but is eventually rescued by a local tugboat.

1882

TR publishes *The Naval War of 1812*.

1882–97

Constitution serves as a receiving ship and barracks for navy recruits in Portsmouth, NH. A roof is built over her decks, giving her the look of a large, dilapidated houseboat.

1887

TR delivers his "Supreme Triumphs of War" speech at the Naval War College in Newport, RI, and is introduced to Alfred Thayer Mahan.

1889

The first two volumes of Henry Adams's *History of the United States* published by Charles Scribner's Sons. TR, a friend of Adams's, reads the advance copies and recommends them to Captain Mahan and others.

1890

Alfred Thayer Mahan publishes *The Influence of Sea Power Upon History, 1660–1783*.

1897

Largely through the efforts of Massachusetts congressman John F. Fitzgerald (grandfather of JFK), the *Constitution* is placed on public exhibition in Boston Harbor.

1897–98

TR serves as Assistant Secretary of the Navy under Secretary John Long in the first administration of William McKinley. He campaigns for a naval buildup and prepares for a coming war against Spain. After reviewing naval maneuvers and gunnery practice off Hampton Roads in September 1897, TR writes: "Oh, Lord! If only the people who are ignorant about our Navy could see those great warships in all their majesty and beauty, and could realize how well they are handled, and how well fitted to uphold the honor of America, I don't think we would encounter such opposition in building up the Navy to its proper standard."

That same month, hearing a rumor that the British have offered to return the frigate *President*, captured off New York in January 1815, TR writes John Hay, former ambassador to Great Britain and recently named Secretary of State: "I earnestly hope that you will refuse to have anything to do with so preposterous and undignified an effort. How any man with any self-respect can ask you to do such a thing I don't see. To beg to be given back, as a favor, what was taken from us by superior prowess, would be to put us in a position of intolerable humiliation. When the British ask us to give back the flags and guns of the frigates and sloops which we took in the War of 1812, then it will be quite time enough for us to ask to get the *President* back. . . . She is of no more value to us than the *Macedonian* or *Guerrière* or *Java* would be to the British if we were able to return them." TR later learns there is no truth in the rumor. (The *President* was broken up in Portsmouth in 1817.)

1898

USS *Maine* explodes in Havana Harbor on February 15. The ship sinks to the floor of the harbor, though a portion remains above water. Nearly 300 American sailors perish. There is no evidence of a Spanish attack, but the United States declares war on Spain and quickly gains control of the Philippines, Hawaii, Guam, the Samoan Islands, Cuba, and Puerto Rico. TR obtains an army commission to lead an expeditionary force to Cuba (the "Rough Riders"). TR explains his decision to William Sturgis Bigelow: "I have consistently preached what our opponents are pleased to call 'jingo doctrines' for a good many years . . . it seems to me that it would be a good deal more important from the standpoint of the nation as a whole that men like myself should go to war than that we should stay comfortably in offices at home and let others carry on the war that we have urged."

1900

TR elected vice president in the second administration of William McKinley.

. 1901

TR has promised not to voice public dissent to the policies of the McKinley administration. However, he tells Cecil Spring-Rice there is one exception. The Monroe Doctrine is "a doctrine about which I feel so deeply that I should take my stand on it even without regard to the attitude of the administration."

   In September, President McKinley is shot and killed by a deranged assassin in Buffalo, NY. TR becomes president.

1903

TR tells the French ambassador, Jules Jusserand, that he intends to expand American naval power until it is capable of dealing with "foes more formidable than Spain ever was." In April, he delivers his "Big Stick" speech in Chicago. That same month, the House of Representatives passes legislation to build four new battleships and armored cruisers.

1905

Navy Secretary Charles Joseph Bonaparte (grandson of Jérôme Bonaparte, grand nephew of Napoleon Bonaparte) proposes that the *Constitution*, now over a century old and a rotting hulk, should be "used as a target for some of the ships of our North Atlantic fleet and sunk by their fire." Reported in the newspapers, the proposal meets with a chorus of disapproval from the public. Congress moves to appropriate $100,000 to repair the ship, though not for active service.

1906

In November, TR sails to Panama aboard the USS *Louisiana* to inspect the progress of the construction of the Panama Canal. It is the first time a sitting U.S. president has traveled abroad.

1907

TR argues for the "Great White Fleet's" circumnavigation of the world: "I think a cruise from one ocean to the other, or around the world, is mighty good practice for a fleet." When the Republican chairman of the Senate Naval Affairs Committee opposes the plan, TR calls him a "conscienceless voluptuary."

1909

Return of the Great White Fleet to Hampton Roads, and the retirement of TR from office.

1914

Franklin D. Roosevelt, Assistant Secretary of the Navy in the Woodrow Wilson administration, gives a speech to the Society of Naval Architects and Marine Engineers on the subject of "Our First Frigates: Some Unpublished Facts About Their Construction." The speech is published along with drawings of the original frigate plans.

1914–18

During World War I, the government of President Woodrow Wilson protests that neutral maritime rights are routinely violated both by the Allies and by Germany. The British government goes to great lengths to avoid antagonizing America. Sir Edward Grey, British foreign secretary during the conflict, later writes: "There was one mistake in diplomacy that, if it had been made, would have been fatal to the cause of the allies. It was carefully avoided. This cardinal mistake would have been a breach with the United States, not necessarily a rupture, but a state of things which would have provoked American interference with the blockade [of Germany], or led to a ban on exports of munitions from the United States." German submarine warfare, the sinking of American ships, and the killing of American citizens on board the *Lusitania* and other vessels brings the United States into the war in April 1917 on the side of the Allies.

1918

Death of Henry Adams in Washington at age eighty.

1919

Death of TR in New York at age sixty.

1924–29

Constitution's hull is in extremely poor condition: her crew must pump it out each day. Surveys estimate repairs will cost $400,000. A national fund-raising campaign, sponsored by Secretary of the Navy Curtis Wilbur, eventually raises $660,000. A significant share of the total is denominated in pennies collected and donated by schoolchildren.

Release in 1926 of the silent screen classic *Old Ironsides* (*Sons of the Sea* in the UK) starring Charles Farrell, Esther Ralston, George Bancroft, and Nicholas De Ruiz, helps build support for the *Constitution*. She is restored (1927–30) in Dry Dock No. 1, Boston Navy Yard, at more than twice the original estimate.

1931–34

Constitution, towed by a minesweeper, tours the east and west coasts of the United States. She traverses 22,000 miles, passes through the Panama Canal, calls at ninety ports, and accommodates 4.6 million civilian visitors.

1941

Japanese aircraft attack Pearl Harbor on December 7. The United States declares war on Germany and Japan.

1945

Surrender of Germany and Japan.

1946

Winston Churchill delivers his "Iron Curtain" speech at Westminster College, in Fulton, MO.

1963

President John F. Kennedy declares Winston Churchill an Honorary Citizen of the United States—the first foreign citizen ever to receive the honor.

1976

During celebrations of the U.S. Bicentennial on July 11, the *Constitution* exchanges salutes with the Royal Yacht *Britannia* in Boston Harbor. The latter flashes a signal: "Your salute was magnificent—*Britannia* sends." Queen Elizabeth II and Prince Philip are conducted on a tour of the frigate by Captain Tyrone G. Martin and Navy Secretary William Middendorf. When the queen is shown one of the *Constitution*'s 24-pounders, which bears a monogram of George III, she turns to Prince Phillip and says: "We really must talk to the Secretary about these foreign arms sales when we get home."

1992–95

Constitution again enters Dry Dock No. 1. During another complex three-year restoration, she is returned to her appearance in the era of the War of 1812. *Constitution* lies today at the wharf in Charlestown, just across the harbor from Boston's North End, where she was built and launched more than two centuries ago. She is the oldest commissioned naval vessel in the world to remain afloat. (Nelson's HMS *Victory* is the world's oldest warship in commission, but is permanently dry-docked.)

2000

In a June 10 ceremony in Portsmouth, NH, militia leaders from Portsmouth, England, dressed in period uniforms, return a fragment of timber from the *Chesapeake*. The timber comes from the same Chesapeake Mill in Wickham, Hampshire, that was built in 1820 from gun deck timbers extracted from the captured American frigate.

2005

In June, an international fleet, representing thirty-five nations, gathers off Portsmouth, England to mark the bicentennial of the Battle of Trafalgar. The event includes a fleet review presided over by Queen Elizabeth II, and a re-enactment of the battle. A quarter of a million spectators are on hand. To spare French and Spanish feelings, the re-enactment divides the ships into red and blue fleets, with neither identified by nationality. Anna Tribe, seventy-five, great-great-great granddaughter of Lord Nelson and Emma Hamilton, objects to the "red-blue" concept. "I am sure the French and Spaniards are adult enough to appreciate we did win that battle," she tells a reporter of *The Times*.

NOTES

ABBREVIATIONS

AA   Abigail Adams

Annals   *Annals of Congress* (formally known as *The Debates and Proceedings in the Congress of the United States*). New York: D. Appleton, 1857–61. Online at http://memory.loc.gov/ammem/amlaw/lwac.html

ASP   *American State Papers: Documents, Legislative and Executive, of the Congress of the United States.* 38 vols. Washington, DC: Gales & Seaton, 1832–61. I. Foreign Relations; III. Finance, IV. Commerce and Navigation; V. Military Affairs; VI. Naval Affairs. Online at http://memory.loc.gov/ammem/amlaw/lwsp.html

BW   *Naval Documents Related to the United States Wars with the Barbary Powers: Naval Operations Including Diplomatic Background from 1785 Through 1807.* 6 vols. Washington, DC: U.S. Office of Naval Records and Library, Government Printing Office, 1939–44

HUSJ   Henry Adams. *History of the United States During the Administrations of Thomas Jefferson* (1889–91). New York: Literary Classics of the United States, 1986

HUSM   Henry Adams. *History of the United States During the Administrations of James Madison* (1889–91). New York: Literary Classics of the United States, 1986

JA   John Adams

JH   Joshua Humphreys

JM   James Madison

LOC   Library of Congress

NW1812   Dudley, William S., and Michael J. Crawford, eds. *The Naval War of 1812, A Documentary History.* 3 vols. Washington, DC: Naval Historical Center, 1985–2004

NYHS   New-York Historical Society

PHS   Historical Society of Pennsylvania

QW   *Naval Documents Related to the Quasi-War Between the United States and France.* 7 vols. Washington, DC: U.S. Office of Naval Records and Library, Government Printing Office, 1935

RG 45   Navy Documents, Record Group 45, U.S. National Archives

TJ   Thomas Jefferson

TJP   Thomas Jefferson Papers. Series 1: General Correspondence, 1651–1827, at www.loc.gov. In many cases, transcriptions are provided by Paul Leicester Ford's *The Works of Thomas Jefferson in Twelve Volumes*

TR   Theodore Roosevelt

WTJ   *The Works of Thomas Jefferson in Twelve Volumes.* Federal Edition, ed. Paul Leicester Ford. New York and London: G. P. Putnam's Sons, 1904.

PART ONE: TO PROVIDE AND MAINTAIN

5   "Your memorialist has been": Nelson quoted in Pope, *England Expects*, 89.

6   "The best and only mode": Horatio Nelson to a British officer, August 21, 1801, from Downs. Recipient not identified; photostat in U.S. National Archives (NA), RG 45, Box 139.

6   "In case signals can": King and Hattendorf, eds., *Every Man Will Do His Duty*, p. xxiii.

6   "like some awfully tremendous": Ibid., Samuel Leech account, p. 307.

7   One example of such a rout: See Rodger, *The Wooden World*, p. 58.

9   "Sail; do not lose": Bonaparte quoted in Pocock, *The Terror Before Trafalgar*, p. 185.

9   "There was fire": Whipple, *The Seafarers: Fighting Sail*, p. 157.

10   "How my fingers got knocked": "Sam," a sailor on the *Royal Sovereign*, in Lewis, ed., *The Mammoth Book of Life Before the Mast*, p. 170.

10   the outpouring of mass grieving: See Whipple, *The Seafarers: Fighting Sail*, p. 170.

10   For three days, Nelson's body: Herman, *To Rule the Waves: How the British Navy Shaped the Modern World*, p. 396.

11   The *Ann Alexander*: Albion and Pope, *Sea Lanes in Wartime: The American Experience, 1775–1942*, p. 88.

13   "When I see our numerous": Captain Alexander Murray to Navy Secretary Benjamin Stoddert, February 20, 1799, QW II:374.

14   A 250-ton merchantman: Albion and Pope, *Sea Lanes in Wartime*, p. 19.

14   "Should a war": Ibid, p. 17

14   From the outbreak of war in 1792: *Historical Statistics of the United States, Colonial Times to 1970*, U.S. Department of Commerce, Bureau of the Census, Part 2, 1976, series Q 518–523, "Value of Waterborne Imports and Exports of Merchandise," p. 761.

14   In the same fifteen-year period: Ibid., series Q 417–432, "Documented Merchant Vessels," p. 750; 69,000 seamen in 1807 from "Blodget's Economica," figures published in *Niles' Register*, vol. 1, p. 79.

15   "the pleasantest part of my Labours": Anderson, "John Adams, the Navy, and the Quasi-War with France," *American Neptune*, 30(2) (1970):117.

15   "It is very odd": John Adams to Elbridge Gerry, November 5, 1775, *Naval Documents of the American Revolution*, II:896.

16   "scrambling for rank and pay": McCullough, *John Adams*, p. 169.

17   to "insult the coasts of the Lords": Franklin quoted in Powell, *American Navies of the Revolutionary War*, p. 54.

17   "Paul Jones resembles": Morison, *John Paul Jones: A Sailor's Biography*, p. 246.

17   He was branded: Quoted in Thomas, *John Paul Jones: Sailor, Hero, Father of the American Navy*, p. 200.

17   the "flesh of several of them": Ibid., p. 197.

18   "This ship is now a mere": Quoted in Fowler, *Jack Tars and Commodores*, p. 2.

18   "In looking over the long list": JA to President of the Congress, July 6, 1780, in Francis Wharton, ed., *The Revolutionary Diplomatic Correspondence of the United States* (Washington, 1889), III:833.

18   "Until Revenues for the Purpose": Robert Morris quoted in Nuxoll, "The Naval Movement of the Confederation Era," in Dudley and Crawford, eds., *The Early Republic and the Sea*, p. 6.

19   would "no longer be confined": David Ramsey, *Oration on Advantages of Independence* (1778), quoted in McCoy, *The Elusive Republic: Political Economy in Jeffersonian America*, pp. 93–94.

19   "Our plan is commerce": Paine, *Common Sense* online at http://www.classicallibra ry.org/paine.

19   The cover of a popular 1782 almanac: American print in Weatherwise's *Town and Country Almanac*, reprinted in Tuchman, *The First Salute* (illus. insert).

19   Cut off from their traditional markets: See Morris, *The Forging of the Union, 1781–1789*, pp. 136–41.

19   By 1788, ship arrivals: Ibid., pp. 136–38.

20   "suffered more by the Act of Independence": Ibid., pp. 131–48.

20   "Our West Indies business": Szatmary, *Shays' Rebellion: The Making of an Agrarian Insurrection*, p. 25.

20   A French traveler reported: Brissot quoted in Morris, *The Forging of the Union, 1781–1789*, pp. 141–42.

20   "a numerous body of citizens": "Petition No. 4": ASP, Finance, vol. 1, p. 10.

20   In 1785, the *Empress of China*: Morris, *The Forging of the Union, 1781–1789*, p. 160.

21   "well formed, indicating strength": Edmund Bacon, Overseer, quoted in Rosenberger, ed., *The Jefferson Reader, A Treasury of Writings About Thomas Jefferson*, pp. 67–70.

22   "The Ministry are disposed": Quoted in Malone, *Jefferson and the Rights of Man*, p. 50.

22   "An Ambassador from America!": Quoted in McCullough, *John Adams*, p. 337.

22   "false—if it was not too rough": AA to TJ, London, October 19, 1785, in Cappon, ed., *The Adams-Jefferson Letters*, I:84.

22   she had been "repeatedly shocked": AA to TJ, London, October 7, 1785, in ibid., I:79.

22   "I would not give": TJ to AA, Paris, June 21, 1785, in ibid., I:33–35.

23   "I fancy it must be": TJ to AA, Paris, September 25, 1785, in ibid., I:69–71.

23   declaring it a "distinguished honor": McCullough, *John Adams*, p. 336.

23   "as gracious and agreeable": AA to TJ, June 6, 1785, in Cappon, ed., *The Adams-Jefferson Letters*, I:28–29.

23   "There is a strong propensity": JA to Richard Henry Lee, August 26, 1785, quoted in McCullough, *John Adams*, p. 348.

23   "basis of our great power": Elkins and McKitrick, *The Age of Federalism*, pp. 69–70.

24   "The defence of Great Britain": Adam Smith, *Inquiry into the Nature and Causes of the Wealth of Nations* (1880), pp. 35–38.

24   "The words 'Ship and Sailor'": JA to TJ, August 4, 1785, in Cappon, ed., *The Adams-Jefferson Letters*, I:48.

24   "Seamen, the navy": JA to James Bowdoin, Governor of Massachusetts, May 9, 1786, quoted in Malone, *Jefferson and the Rights of Man*, p. 58n.

25   By the mid-1780s, 100 American ships: See Whipple, *To the Shores of Tripoli: The Birth of the U.S. Navy and Marines*, p. 25.

25   "Our sufferings is beyond": Richard O'Brien to TJ, August 24, 1785, quoted in Malone, *Jefferson and the Rights of Man*, p. 27.

26   "absolutely suspended": Jefferson quoted in ibid, p. 27.

26   "Money and fear": Vergennes quoted in TJ to JA, May 30, 1786, in Cappon, ed., *The Adams-Jefferson Letters*, I:132–33.

26   "the Ridicule of it": JA to TJ, February 17, 1786, in ibid., I:121–22.

27   "Sorry to hear that": Ibid., I:121–22

27   "it to be wisest for Us": Ibid., pp. 138–39.

27   "it would be best": TJ to JA, July 11, 1786, in ibid., I:142–43.

28   "great and weighty": Ibid., I:146–47.

28   "The mutual influence": John Quincy Adams quoted in James Morton Smith, *Liberty and Power: Thomas Jefferson, James Madison, and "the Mutual Influence of These Two Mighty Minds."* An "Evening Conversation" at Monticello, sponsored by the Jefferson Legacy Foundation, May 23, 2001, www.jeffersonlegacy.org.

28   Known to his family: Ellis, *Founding Brothers*, p. 53.

28   Late in life: Morris, *Witnesses at the Creation*, p. 99.

29   "against every form of tyranny": Lipscomb, ed., *The Writings of Thomas Jefferson*, X:175.

29   "We are not living": Kaut quoted in Gay, *The Enlightenment: The Rise of Modern Paganism*, p. 20.

29   "such books as may be": JM to TJ, April 27, 1785, in Smith, ed., *Republic of Letters*, I:367.

29   "turning over every book": Quoted in McCullough, *John Adams*, p. 321.

29   "whatever may throw light": JM to TJ, March 16, 1784, in Smith, ed., *Republic of Letters*, I:299–304.

29   He would be happy to have: JM to TJ, April 27, 1785, in ibid., I:367.

29   In a typical letter: TJ to JM, January 12, 1789, in ibid., I:278.

30   "animal curiosities": JM to TJ, May 12, 1786, in ibid., I: 419–23.

30   "For want of something": JM to TJ, June 19, 1786, in ibid., I. 423–28.

30   "with respect to every thing": TJ to JM, February 6, 1786, in ibid., I:410.

30   "interior government is what": TJ to JM, September 1, 1785, in ibid., I: 380–83.

31   "for the purpose of forming": Quoted in Morris, *Witnesses at the Creation*, p. 163.

31   "plaited, clubbed up": Chernow, *Alexander Hamilton*, p. 187.

31   "might have been tracked": Quoted in Tuchman, *The First Salute: A View of the American Revolution*, p. 189.

32   "frequently to temporary want": Hamilton quoted in Flexner, *Young Hamilton*, pp. 207–8.

33   "they cannot bring their ships": Smelser, *Congress Founds the Navy*, p. 8.

33   "No, sir," said: James Jackson and William Grayson quoted in ibid., p. 24.

34   The procession was led: Morris, *Witnesses at the Creation*, pp. 249–50.

34   A scroll hung: Hecht, *Odd Destiny*, p. 163.

34   The most impressive feature of the parade: Morris, *Witnesses at the Creation*, pp. 249–50.

35   addressed a circular letter: Circular by David Humphreys, U.S. Minister to Portugal, October 8, 1793, BW I:47.

35   "four frigates, three Xebecks": David Humphreys to Michael Morphy, October 6, 1793, BW I:46.

35   "I have not slept": Edward Church to Secretary of State, October 12, 1793, BW I:47–50.

36   "the Algerine Cruisers": BW I:56.

36   "On our landing": Letter from David Pierce, December 4, 1793, BW I:57.

37   "all manner of eatables": Smelser, *Congress Founds the Navy*, p. 48.

37   "England and Spain": Edward Church to Secretary of State, September 22, 1793, BW I:44–46.

40   "to register all actual seamen": Smelser, *Congress Founds the Navy*, pp. 29–30.

40   "a naval force": Ibid., p. 30.

40   "By the best information": Committee report to the House of Representatives, January 20, 1794, ASP, Naval Affairs, vol. 1, p. 5.

42   The French Revolution had been preceded: Smelser, *Congress Founds the Navy*, p. 49.

42   "This thing of a fleet": *Journal of William Maclay, United States Senator from Pennsylvania*, pp. 383–84.

43   Take the case of salt: Smelser, *Congress Founds the Navy*, p. 49.

44   "deep as a thunder-growl": Ferguson, *Truxtun of the Constellation*, p. 92.

45   More than a quarter of the nation's total: See Lippincott, *Early Philadelphia*, pp. 275–77. Total American exports in 1793 were $26 million—*Historical Statistics of the United States, Colonial Times to 1970*, U.S. Census Bureau, Part 2, 1776, series Q 518–23, "Value of Waterborne Imports and Exports," p. 716.

45   In 1793, more than 8,000 tons: See Fairburn, *Merchant Sail*, p. 2759.

46   "We took each other": Richard Norton Smith, *Patriarch*, p. xvii.

46   "They are not Men of Arms": Tolles, *Meeting House and Counting House*, p. 47.

46   included an address: See Thomas Paine, *To the Representatives of the Religious Society of the People called Quakers*, at www.classicallibrary.org/paine.

48   During the Revolution, American shipwrights: Chappelle, *American Sailing Ships*, pp. 44–49.

49   "They are superior": Quoted in Magoun, *Constitution and Other Historic Ships*, p. 63.

49   "such frigates": Joshua Humphreys letter book, 1797–1800 (undated), PHS.

51   The professional shipwright: Chapelle, *American Sailing Navy*, pp. 4–5.

51   "rejected by the unanimous voice": "Data copied from papers in the Handwriting of Josiah Fox, Navy Constructor, in his old chest, by his granddaughter Sarah C. Fox, concealed in the garret at her home in Ohio." Josiah Fox Papers; copy in the possession of the American Philosophical Society, Philadelphia.

52   were "extravagant, and that the ships": Joshua Humphreys to Secretary of the Navy William Jones, August 20, 1827, PHS.

52   "who had served his apprenticeship:" "Data copied . . ."

53   "Whether the model has": Secretary of War Knox to John Wharton, May 12, 1794, Naval Historical Center, Washington, DC (microfilm collection).

53   "It is determined of importance": Humphreys quoted in Grant, *Isaac Hull, Captain of Old Ironsides*, p. 25.

53   "a first rate draftsman": Humphreys quoted in Dorwart and Wolf, *The Philadelphia Navy Yard: From the Birth of the U.S. Navy to the Nuclear Age*, p. 35.

54   "I cannot receive hereafter": Joshua Humphreys to Josiah Fox, July 27, 1797, JH letter book, PHS.

55   to "be going great lengths": Ferguson, *Truxtun of the Constellation*, p. 111.

55   The master builders in each city received: Circular letter from Henry Knox to the Naval Constructors dated July 1794, ASP, Naval Affairs, vol. 1, p. 7.

56   "It is impossible he can": George Washington to Alexander Spotswood, March 15, 1794, in Fitzpatrick, ed., *The Writings of George Washington from the Original Manuscript Sources, 1745–1799*, vol. 33, at http://etext.virginia.edu.

57   "powerful interest made here": John Barry to Samuel Nicholson, June 24, 1794, NYHS.

57   The question of seniority: See Fowler, *Jack Tars and Commodores*, p. 23.

57   "no choice of Artificers": Ferguson, *Truxtun of the Constellation*, pp. 113–14.

59   "the most magnificent planted": Muir quoted in Wood, *Live Oaking*, p. 6.

59   "the appearance of a large": Ibid., pp. 7–10.

59   A mature tree: Ibid., p. 61.

59   A nail driven into it: John Lawson, Surveyor-General of North Carolina, in *A New Voyage to Carolina* (1709) quoted in ibid., p. 10.

60   "I have received the moulds": John T. Morgan to Joshua Humphreys, August 30, 1794, JH letter book, PHS.

60   "sober and Industrious Axe-men": From a recruiting advertisement reproduced in Wood, *Live Oaking*, pp. 26–28.

60   A visitor compared their camp: Fowler, *Jack Tars and Commodores*, pp. 24–25.

60   "I have been all but dead": John T. Morgan to Joshua Humphreys, October 21, 1794, JH letter book, PHS.

61   In late October, Captain John Barry: Clark, *Gallant John Barry*, p. 372.

61   "These moulds frighten me": John T. Morgan to Joshua Humphreys, October 21, 1794, JH letter book, PHS.

61   "all but four": John T. Morgan to John Barry, December 29, 1794, NYHS.

61   "Your letter and box of oranges": Joshua Humphreys to John T. Morgan, December 29, 1795, JH letter book, PHS.

62   "few or no materials of any sort": War Office report to the House of Representatives, December 29, 1794, ASP, Naval Affairs, vol. 1, p. 6.

62   The final dimensions: War Office report to the House of Representatives, December 12, 1795, ASP, Naval Affairs, vol. 1, pp. 17–18.

62   The cost of the treaty: *Historical Statistics of the United States, Colonial Times to 1970,* U.S. Department of Commerce, Bureau of the Census, Part 2, 1976, series Y 335–338, "Summary of Federal Government Finances—Administrative Budget," p. 1104 ($1 million settlement divided by $7.54 million 1795 budget expenditures).

62   The president now asked Congress: Message to Congress, March 15, 1796, ASP, Naval Affairs, vol. 1, p. 25.

63   The carriage, he told Abigail: JA to AA, March 5, 1797, quoted in Peabody, ed., *John Adams: A Biography in His Own Words*, p. 359.

63   "as serene and unclouded": McCullough, *John Adams*, p. 469.

63   "Everybody talks of the tears": JA, March 9, 1797, quoted in Page Smith, *John Adams*, vol. 2, p. 918.

63   the "sight of the sun": JA to AA, March 9, 1797, quoted in Ferling, *John Adams: A Life*, p. 335.

64   He had not slept well: JA to AA, March 5, 1797, quoted in Peabody, ed., *John Adams: A Biography in His Own Words*, p. 359.

64   "the profligacy of corruption": Adams, "Inaugural Address," March 4, 1797, U.S. Government Printing Office, 1989.

65   "My entrance into office": JA to John Quincy Adams, March 31, 1797, quoted in McCullough, *John Adams*, p. 476 (emphasis in the original).

66   "He snatched lightning": Turgot quoted in Isaacson, *Benjamin Franklin: An American Life*, p. 145.

66   "It is a tribute": Elkins and McKitrick, *The Age of Federalism*, p. 309.

67   "every hat was in the air": Henry Edgeworth De Firmont in *The French Revolution as Told by Contemporaries*, ed. Higgins, pp. 272–73.

67   if Louis "was a Traytor": Elkins and McKitrick, *The Age of Federalism*, p. 357.

67   Philadelphians lined up . . . In Boston: Minnigerode, *Jefferson, Friend of France*, p. 166.

67   "the cruel and unjust war": Elkins and McKitrick, *The Age of Federalism*, p. 457.

68   "Upon her coming into sight": TJ to James Monroe, May 5, 1793, TJP.

69   On one occasion, thirty-two heads: Schama, *Citizens*, p. 782.

69   "Danton, Robespierre, Marak, etc.": Quoted in McCullough, *John Adams*, p. 443.

69   "We might have seen": Minnigerode, *Jefferson, Friend of France*, p. 167.

69   a "monument of venality": McCullough, *John Adams*, p. 457.

69   "the exertions . . . the Banks": JM quoted in Ellis, *Founding Brothers*, p. 138.

71   "This ball of liberty": TJ to Tench Coxe, January 1, 1795, TJP.

71   "The French are no more capable": JA to Elbridge Gerry, quoted in Ellis, *Founding Brothers*, pp. 188–89.

71   "I know well that no man": TJ to Rutledge, December 27, 1796, WTJ, VII: 93–94.

71   "The next president of the United States": TJ quoted in Ellis, *Founding Brothers*, p. 182.

74   "It is with great regret": Joshua Humphreys to Secretary of War, March 26, 1797, JH letter book, PHS.

74   "pompous carriages, splendid feasts": Quoted in Rosenfeld, *American Aurora*, p. 29.

74   "sesquipedality of belly": McCullough, *John Adams*, p. 462.

74   an "infamous scoundrel": Quoted in Rosenfeld, *American Aurora*, pp. 29–30.

75   "I was thus standing": B. F. Bache, *Aurora General Advertiser*, April 6, 1797, quoted in ibid., p. 5.

76   "for the purpose of securing": JH account books, PHS.

76   "It will be absolutely necessary": Joshua Humphreys to Secretary of War, May 6, 1797, JH letter book, PHS.

76   He informed the War Office: Joshua Humphreys to Secretary of War, May (date uncertain), 1797, JH letter book, PHS.

76   Launching a hull: Guttridge and Smith, *The Commodores: The U.S. Navy in the Age of Sail*, p. 16.

77   he found, to his "unspeakable satisfaction": Ibid.

79   had "inflicted a wound": *Annals*, House of Representatives, 5th Congr., 1st Sess., May 16, 1797.

79   "Our seacoasts": Ibid.

79   "a man divested": Quoted in McCullough, *John Adams*, p. 485.

79   "fed upon pepperpot": *Aurora*, May 18, 1797, quoted in Page Smith, *John Adams*, vol. 2, p. 931.

80   "His Rotundity": McCullough, *John Adams*, p. 485.

80   "As to going to war with France": Quoted in DeConde, *The Quasi War: The Politics and Diplomacy of the Undeclared War with France, 1797–1801*, p. 23.

80   "they could, therefore, be of little use": *Annals*, House of Representatives, June 1797.

81   "every measure of warlike preparation": DeConde, *The Quasi War*, p. 31.

81   "It is evidence of a mind soured": JA to Uriah Foster, June 20, 1797, quoted in Dauer, *The Adams Federalists*, p. 130.

81   "Men who have been": TJ quoted in McCullough, *John Adams*, p. 493.

81   "consult on the best Method": War Office to Joshua Humphreys, July 25, 1797, QW I:9.

82   "it is important to a Nation": JH letter book, PHS.

82   "as many hands": Joshua Humphreys to Thomas Truxtun, June 11, 1797, JH letter book, PHS.

82   "Wind, weather and tide": Quoted in Ferguson, *Truxtun of the Constellation*, p. 130.

83   "with as much exactness": An "observer" quoted in ibid., p. 134.

83   "A Better Launch I never Saw": Captain Thomas Truxtun to Joshua Humphreys, September 1, 1797, QW I:17.

83   "Nothing could surpass": A "Witness" quoted in Ferguson, *Truxtun of the Constellation*, p. 134.

84   Eighteenth-century physicians imagined: See Powell, *Bring Out Your Dead*, and Arnebeck, *Destroying Angel: Benjamin Rush, Yellow Fever and the Birth of Modern Medicine*, online at http://www.geocities.com/bobarnebeck/fever1793.html.

85   could be "left at the Buck Tavern": JH letter book, PHS.

85   "I was in hopes": Joshua Humphreys to Timothy Pickering, September 25, 1797, JH letter book, PHS.

86   "I cannot help feeling": Joshua Humphreys to Secretary of War, October 4, 1797, JH letter book, PHS.

86   Not surprisingly, he suggested: Dorwart and Wolf, *The Philadelphia Navy Yard*, p. 40.

87   "in the shortest possible time": Secretary of War to David Stodder, Naval Constructor, October 6, 1797, QW I:18.

87   "during heavy Squalls": Secretary of War to Tench Francis, Purveyor, September 18, 1797, QW I:17.

87   "To find the length of the main mast": Ferguson, *Truxtun of the Constellation*, pp. 110–11.

88   his "worthy friend's": Humphreys quoted in ibid., p. 117.

88   "pride, ambition, avarice": "President's Speech," *Annals*, 5th Congr., 2nd Sess., November 23, 1797, pp. 630–34.

89   "When we came to calculate": Joshua Humphreys to Thomas Truxtun, July 29, 1796, JH letter book, PHS.

89   Horace Walpole: Walpole and Napoleon quoted in Schama, *Citizens*, p. 678.

89   "his passionless, immovable countenance": Gulian C. Verplanck quoted in Batterberry, *On the Town in New York*, p. 33.

90   "I will not disguise": Bellamy quoted in DeConde, *The Quasi War*, p. 48.

91   "struck dumb": AA quoted in McCullough, *John Adams*, p. 497.

91   "like the shock": Quoted in Rosenfeld, *American Aurora*, p. 72.

91   "The President . . . has chosen": Jefferson, *Anas*, WTJ, I, p. 345, quoted in ibid., p. 73.

91   "the case of Humphreys": Callender quoted in ibid., p. 145.

91   "To John Adams": Quoted in Ellis, *Founding Brothers*, p. 190.

91   would "exhibit to the world": Smelser, *Congress Founds*, p. 143.

91   "branded with the usual": January 11, 1798, quoted in Adams, *The Life of Albert Gallatin*, p. 189.

92   "a commerce can be protected": *Annals*, pp. 2823–32, quoted in Sprout and Sprout, *Rise of American Seapower*, p. 45.

92   to "increase their power": Quoted in McCullough, *John Adams*, p. 499.

92   "The question of war": TJ to JM, March 29, 1798, TJP.

92   "repair with all due Speed": Secretary of War to Captain Thomas Truxtun, March 16, 1798, QW I:16.

92   "Does any man": Ferguson, *Truxtun of the Constellation*, p. 103.

93   "Without officers, what can be": Captain Thomas Truxtun to Secretary of War James McHenry, 1797, quoted in McKee, *A Gentlemanly and Honorable Profession: The Creation of the U.S. Naval Officer Corps, 1794–1815*, p. 153.

93   "If the dunces who are": Quoted in ibid., p. 169.

94   "five feet six Inches": Secretary of War to Captain Thomas Truxtun, March 16, 1798, QW I:16.

94   A sailor could be paid: Captain Thomas Truxtun to Lieutenant John Rodgers, April 1798, QW I:49–50.

94   "It being important": Recruiting instructions from the Secretary of the Navy, September 11, 1798, QW I:388–89.

94   "Every expence attending": Captain Thomas Truxtun to Lieutenant John Rodgers, April 1798, QW I:49–50.

95   she "ran ahead of everything": Quoted in Smelser, *Congress Founds*, p. 144.

95   "incommodes in her present Station": March 31, 1798, QW I:49.

96   "the Decks, topsides": Secretary of War to Joshua Humphreys, March 23, 1798, QW I:45.

96   Barry was overseeing: Captain John Barry to Secretary McHenry, May 26, 1796, NYHS.

96   "Her hair escaped": Griffin, *Commodore John Barry, "The Father of the American Navy": The Records of His Services for Our Country*, p. 112.

96   "in the least suspected": Captain John Barry to Secretary McHenry, September 20, 1796, NYHS.

97   "against the inveterate": Secretary of State Pickering to Robert Liston, British Ambassador, June 22, 1798, QWI:129–30.

97   "the brave and hardy seamen": Recruiting poster, May 12, 1798, QW I:73.

98   "a rough, blustering": Stephen Higginson to Secretary of War, June 6, 1798, QW I:106.

98   "Till there is some system": T. Williams to Secretary of State Timothy Pickering, May 31, 1798, QW I:97 (emphasis in the original).

98   "there ought to be some allowance": Barry quoted in Palmer, *Stoddert's War*, p. 7.

98   urged him "to deliberate": President George Washington to Secretary of War, July 13, 1796, BW I:165–66.

99   "roared like a hundred bulls": Smelser, *Congress Founds*, p. 137.

99   "These hundred staunch": Philadelphia *United States Recorder*, May 3, 1798, quoted in ibid.

99   Gilbert Fox sang: McCullough, *John Adams*, p. 500.

99   "created some alarm": April 12, 1798, quoted in Rosenfeld, *American Aurora*, p. 83.

99   "COCKADEROPHOBIA" and "violently plucks": DeConde, *The Quasi War*, pp. 82–83.

99   The ranks of the Blues: Rosenfeld, *American Aurora*, p. 153.

100   "This city": AA to John Quincy Adams, McCullough, *John Adams*, p. 504.

100   "To arms, then": Smelser, *Congress Founds*, p. 161.

100   one such "Band of Brothers": *Aurora General Advertiser*, May 9, 1798, quoted in Rosenfeld, *American Aurora*, p. 114.

100   "Friendships were dissolved": Deborah Logan quoted in ibid., p. 81.

100   "dogged and watched": Jefferson quoted in Adams, *The Life of Albert Gallatin*, p. 31.

101   "Your country, my boys": Quoted in Rosenfeld, *American Aurora*, pp. 201, 80.

101 "false, scandalous and malicious": Quoted in McCullough, *John Adams*, p. 505.

101 "the good citizens": Quoted in Rosenfeld, *American Aurora*, p. 188.

101 produced "such a shock": TJ to JM, April 6, 1798, TJP.

101 "All, therefore": TJ to JM, April 12, 1798, ibid.

102 "Perhaps it is a universal": JM to TJ, May 13, 1798, in Rakove, ed., *James Madison: Writings*, p. 588.

103 "blowing a violent Hurricane": Captain Thomas Truxtun's Journal, July 4, 1798, QW I:163–64.

103 "the Sea running very Cross": Captain Thomas Truxtun's Journal, July 5, 1798, QW I:169.

103 Truxtun gave the order: Captain Thomas Truxtun's Journal, July 5–7, 1798, QW I:169, 172, 180.

104 "every Article": Captain Thomas Truxtun to Mr. Morgan, June 19, 1798, QW I:124–25.

104 "Whenever a Sail": Captain Thomas Truxtun to the Sea Lieutenants and Master, *Constellation*, June 27, 1798, QW I:144.

104 She was to hunt: Secretary of War to Captain Thomas Truxtun, May 30, 1798, QW I:92–93.

105 "a tremendous Water Spout": Captain Thomas Truxtun's Journal, August 5, 1798, QW I:274.

105 "a Flood of Rain": Captain Thomas Truxtun's Journal, August 6, 1798, QW I:276.

105 "behaved exceeding ill": Captain Thomas Truxtun's Journal, August 15, 1798, QW I:300.

106 Arriving in Philadelphia on June 12: Palmer, *Stoddert's War*, pp. 233–41.

106 He asked Congress for authorization: Secretary of the Navy to Secretary of the Treasury, July 31, 1798, QW I:261–62.

106 to "buy the whole": Secretary of the Navy to Tench Francis, Purveyor, August 25, 1798, QW I:338–39.

106 "How come the Bread & Fish": Secretary of the Navy to Tench Francis, Purveyor, September 22, 1798, QW I:438.

106 Different techniques, styles, and design: See Dorwart and Wolf, *The Philadelphia Navy Yard*, p. 37.

107 "It is the opinion": Joshua Humphreys to Forman Cheesman, July 8, 1799, JH letter book, PHS.

107 "No ship ever went to Sea": Captain John Barry to Joshua Humphreys, July 22, 1798, QW, I:232.

107 The sailing master, James Morris: James Morris to Joshua Humphreys, July 23, 1798, QW, I:233.

108 "Three or four months' full allowance": Quoted in Palmer, *Stoddert's War*, p. 29.

108 He told Stoddert not to believe: Captain Thomas Truxtun to Secretary of the Navy, August 16, 1798, QW I:300–02.

109 "It is the opinion": Joshua Humphreys to Forman Cheesman, July 8, 1799, JH letter book, PHS.

109 Truxtun lectured the Baltimore: Captain Thomas Truxtun to Jeremiah Yellott, Navy Agent, October 26, 1798, QW I:563–64.

109 had "neither seen or heard": Captain Thomas Truxtun to Secretary of the Navy, October 27, 1798, QW I:566–68.

109 Although the earliest naval patrols: Albion and Pope, *Sea Lanes in Wartime: The American Experience, 1775–1942*, p. 70.

110 "It seems in vain": Secretary of the Navy to President Adams, August 25, 1798, QW I:336.

110 "By keeping up": Secretary of the Navy to President Adams, July 30, 1798, QW I:255.

110 "From information which cannot": Captain Thomas Truxtun to Secretary of the Navy, October 27, 1798, QW I:566–68.

110   If Truxtun could confirm: Secretary of the Navy to Captain Thomas Truxtun, January 16, 1799, QW II:243.

111   "as far Leeward as": Secretary of the Navy to Captain Thomas Truxtun, December 8, 1798, QW II:73.

111   "Nothing is said": Palmer, *Stoddert's War*, p. 84.

111   "We bade farewell": Shaw, *Short sketch of the life of Elijah Shaw, who served 21 years in the United States Navy*, p. 7.

111   "gave Directions": Captain Thomas Truxtun's Journal, January 10, 1799, QW II:228.

111   Thirteen days out of Norfolk: Captain Thomas Truxtun's Journal, January 13–17, 1799, QW II:237–53.

112   The *Retaliation* had been commanded: "The United States Naval Chronicle," 1824, pp. 127–29, in QW II:42.

113   "You have paid": Captain Thomas Truxtun to Midshipman John Dent, January 29, 1799, QW II:291–92.

114   "set up the most lamentable": Letter from an officer on board the *United States*, QW II:304.

114   "Very squally": Captain Thomas Truxtun's Journal, February 8, 1799, QW II:322.

114   "I take her": Captain Thomas Truxtun's Journal, February 9, 1799, QW II:328.

115   Truxtun ordered his signal officers: Ferguson, *Truxtun of the Constellation*, p. 161.

116   "such a cracking": John Hoxse quoted in Palmer, *Stoddert's War*, p. 99.

116   "like a race horse": Ibid.

117   the "sole source": Captain Barreaut to General Desfourneaux, February 17, 1799, NA RG 45.

118   "One fellow I was obliged": "Extract of a Letter from Mr. Andrew Sterrett," QW II:334 (emphasis in the original)

118   According to an account: *Claypoole's American Daily Advertiser*, March 26, 1799, in NA RG 45.

118   "should certainly have sent": Rodgers quoted in Palmer, *Stoddert's War*, p. 100.

118   Barreaut had to admit: Captain Barreaut to General Desfourneaux, February 17, 1799, NA RG 45.

119   "Although I would not": Lieutenant John Rodgers to Secretary of the Navy, February 15, 1799, QW II:336–37.

119   Barreaut and his first lieutenant were sent: Palmer, *Stoddert's War*, p. 101.

120   "I send you a list": Letter from David Porter to his father, reprinted in *Claypoole's American Daily Advertiser*, March 16, 1799, NA RG 45.

120   It was deemed too dangerous: "The United States Naval Chronicle," QW II: 327–28.

120   "The french Captain": Captain Thomas Truxtun to Secretary of the Navy, February 9, 1799, QW II:326–27.

121   "untill ordered to the contrary": Captain Truxtun to General Desfourneaux, February 19, 1799, QW II:378–79.

121   "You have united": Captain Barreaut to Captain Thomas Truxtun, February 14, 1799, QW II:354.

122   Truxtun ordered Rodgers: Captain Thomas Truxtun to Lieutenant John Rodgers, May 20, 1799, QW III:217.

122   "brave Truxtun cock'd": Ferguson, *Truxtun of the Constellation*, p. 171.

122   "Captain Truxtun": Department of the Navy, "The Reestablishment of the Navy, 1787–1801," Naval Historical Center Web site: http://www.history.navy.mil.

122   "I wish all the other officers": President John Adams to Secretary of the Navy, April 22, 1799, QW III:84.

123   "who shall execute": Rules and Regulations for the Government of the U.S. Navy, QW VII:462–73.

123   "There is one thing": Captain Alexander Murray to Secretary Stoddert, July 27, 1799, QW III: 551–52.

124   "The sum fixed on": Secretary Stoddert to Captain Truxtun, July 2, 1799, QW III:453–54.

124   an estimate of $84,500: Joshua Humphreys to Secretary Stoddert, July 4, 1799, JH letter book, PHS.

124   Stoddert also considered: Secretary Stoddert to Captain Truxtun, July 9, 1799, QW III:480.

124   His share: See McKee, *A Gentlemanly and Honorable Profession*, Table 32, p. 493.

124   "one of those strokes": AA quoted in McCullough, *John Adams*, p. 507.

124   "Floating Batteries": Anderson, "John Adams, the Navy, and the Quasi-War with France," *American Neptune* 30(2) (1970): 120.

125   "At present there is no": McCullough, *John Adams*, p. 513.

125   Adams said he "thought Hamilton": Ibid, p. 522.

125   "I have always cried Ships!": JA to Francis Adrian Van der Kemp, April 25, 1808, quoted in Anderson, "John Adams, the Navy, and the Quasi-War with France," p. 119.

126   "Always disposed": Senate Journal, 5th Cong., 3rd Sess., February 18, 1799.

126   "Had the foulest heart": Ellis, *Founding Brothers*, p. 192.

127   "like a flock of frightened": AA to JA, ibid., p. 192.

127   "The only negociation": Ferguson, *Truxtun of the Constellation*, p. 170.

127   "Nor do I think": John Adams, *Works*, VIII:651.

127   "Mr. Stoddert is a man": Wolcott quoted in Palmer, *Stoddert's War*, p. 125.

127   by "zeal & spirit": Ibid., p. 128.

128   "I think it will be best": Secretary of the Navy to Captain John Barry, May 13, 1799, QW III:177.

128   The success of the navy: Palmer, *Stoddert's War*, pp. 130–31.

129   "This avarice of Rank": Secretary Stoddert to Alexander Hamilton, July 19, 1799, QW III:516.

129   "We shall never get": JA to Secretary Stoddert, July 5, 1799, QW III:466.

129   "After a detention": JA to Secretary Stoddert, July 23, 1799, QW III:528–32.

129   Stoddert urged him: Ferguson, *Truxtun of the Constellation*, p. 179.

129   "It as little becomes": Captain Truxtun to Officers of *Constellation*, August 9, 1799, QW IV:51.

130   "I must confess": Ferguson, *Truxtun of the Constellation*, p. 185.

130   "On the ocean is our field": Address of Captain Truxtun to ship's company, June 19, 1799, QW III:366–67.

131   "You cannot be too": Secretary Stoddert to Captain Truxtun, November 11, 1800, QW IV:377–80.

131   He ordered the *Constellation*'s carpenter: Palmer, *Stoddert's War*, p. 183.

131   "in excellent trim": Captain Truxtun to Secretary of the Navy, February 3, 1800, QW V:159.

132   "she was a heavy": Captain Thomas Truxtun's Journal, February 1, 1800, QW V:160.

132   "every inch of canvas": Captain Thomas Truxtun's Journal, February 2, 1800, QW V:160–61.

132   Evening came on: "Letter from a gentleman on board the frigate *Constellation*," February 7, 1800, QW V:164–66.

132   "to demand the surrender": Captain Thomas Truxtun's Journal, February 2, 1800, QW V:160–61.

133   At a critical point in the action: "Letter from a gentleman on board the frigate *Constellation*," February 7, 1800, QW V:164–66.

133   "the most perfect wreck": Surgeon Isaac Henry to Hugh Henry, February 1–2, 1800, QW V:162.

134   six "Amputations of Limbs": Isaac Henry to Hugh Henry, February 11, 1800, QW V:208.

134   "It is hard to conjecture": Captain Truxtun to Secretary Stoddert, February 12, 1800, QW V:209–10.

134   she had made for: Account of Captain Pitot, February 1–2, 1800, QW V:166–68.

134   "in a most distressed": Benjamin Hammell Phillips to Captain Truxtun, February 6, 1800, QW V:197.

135   ratlines "were cut up so": Captain Thomas Baker to Secretary of the Navy, February 8, 1800, QW V:196–97.

135   "perforated with round": "Letter from a gentleman in Curacao," February 6, 1800, QW V:198.

135   "hideous transaction": Quoted in DeConde, *The Quasi War*, p. 210.

135   "Whence comes": Quoted in Ferguson, *Truxtun of the Constellation*, p. 200.

136   "laying in the trough": Captain James Sever to Secretary Stoddert, January 11, 1800, QW, V:62–63.

137   "I, sir, am the best": Ibid.

137   "we should have reserved": Lieutenant John Cordis to Secretary Stoddert, April 2, 1800, QW, V:65–66.

137   "The Service is to me": First Lieutenant Benjamin Strother to Major Commandant William Burrows, February 24, 1800, QW, V:64–65.

137   "You soon shall be separated": Secretary Stoddert to Midshipman John Duboise, April 25, 1800, QW V:449.

138   "shot his antagonist": Second Lieutenant Samuel Llewellyn to Major Commandant William W. Burrows, April 25, 1800, QW V:450.

138   "The *Congress* is full": Secretary Stoddert to Josiah Fox, March 20, 1800, QW V:334–35.

138   "You will proceed": Captain Truxtun to Josiah Fox, April 2, 1800, QW V:373–74.

138   "assume all the authority": Secretary Stoddert to Captain Truxtun, April 16, 1800, QW V:421.

138   a "tyrant": Palmer, *Stoddert's War*, p. 211.

138   signed an order: Sentence of Court-Martial in the case of Mutineers on board the frigate *Congress*, May 15, 1800, QW V:520–21.

139   "to put an End": Captain Truxtun to Secretary Stoddert, April 27, 1800, QW V:451–52.

139   "We unanimously acquit": Court of Inquiry, April 29, 1800, QW V:452–54.

139   "flogged with a cat": Sentence of Court-Martial in the case of Mutineers on board the frigate *Congress*, May 15, 1800, QW V:520–21.

139   "As her sails": *Norfolk Herald*, May 24, 1800, QW V:545.

139   "I fear some difficulty": Truxtun to Charles Biddle, May 22, 1800, QW V:544.

140   "sorry to say": Captain Murray to Secretary Stoddert, October 12, 1800, QW VI:468–69.

140   "Regiments are costly": Quoted in Ellis, *Founding Brothers*, p. 193.

140   "artful designing men": McCullough, *John Adams*, p. 529.

140   "eloquence and vehemence": Ibid., p. 531.

141   "I heard him": Chernow, *Alexander Hamilton*, p. 598.

141   "The President has resolved": McCullough, *John Adams*, p. 531.

141   "Let me therefore": Secretary Stoddert to Captain Barry, June 17, 1799, QW III:349.

141   "it will be proper": Secretary Stoddert to Captain Barry, September 20, 1799, QW IV:211.

142   "the most ample and satisfactory": Oliver Ellsworth and W. R. Davie to the Secretary of State, November 1, 1799, QW IV:346.

142   "the terrible and Mortiferous": Thomas Bulkeley, U.S. Consul, Portugal, to Captain Barry, December 18, 1799, QW IV:553.

142   but on Christmas Eve: William Smith, U.S. Minister to Portugal, to Secretary of State, February 1, 1800, QW V:178.

142   the *United States* made landfall: Palmer, *Stoddert's War*, p. 221.

142   a small fishing vessel: William Smith to Secretary of State, February 1, 1800, QW V:178.

142   "the most splendid occasion": Elkins and McKitrick, *The Age of Federalism*, p. 689.

142   a "family quarrel": McCullough, *John Adams*, p.552.

143   "steered the vessel": Ellis, *Founding Brothers*, p. 205.

143   "The counsel which Themistocles": JA to Captain Truxtun, November 30, 1802, QW V:174–75.

PART TWO: TO THE SHORES OF TRIPOLI

147   "The Bible would be cast": Quoted at http://www.hfac.uh.edu/gl/us9.htm.

147   "the refuse of Europe": McCullough, *John Adams*, p. 543.

148   "a true estimate": Ellis, *American Sphinx*, p. 180.

149   "mud, shavings, boards": Margaret Bayard Smith to "her sister," October 5, 1800, quoted at http://www.geocities.com/bobarnebeck/swamp1800.html.

149   the room "was so crowded": Margaret Bayard Smith to Miss Susan B. Smith, March 4, 1801, Smith, *The First Forty Years of Washington Society in the Family Letters of Margaret Bayard Smith*, pp. 25–27.

150   He would continue: Margaret Bayard Smith to "her sister," October 5, 1800, quoted at http://www.geocities.com/bobarnebeck/swamp1800.html.

150   "straight as a gun-barrel": Edmund Bacon in *The Jefferson Reader*, ed. Rosenberger, p. 67.

151   "an ambitious and violent demagogue": Margaret Bayard Smith in her notebook, *The First Forty Years*, pp. 5–7.

152   "in a dark night": Quoted in Young, *The Washington Community 1800–1828*, p. 46.

152   treasured "scientific instruments": Bernard Mayo in The *Jefferson Reader*, ed. Rosenberger, p. 308.

152   "We find this a very agreeable": TJ to T. M. Randolph, June 4, 1801, quoted in Malone, *Jefferson: The President*, p. 42.

152   "got to a steady": TJ to T. M. Randolph, November 16, 1801, quoted in Cunningham, *The Process of Government Under Jefferson*, p. 35.

153   "You saw at a glance": Thomas Jefferson Randolph in *The Jefferson Reader*, ed. Rosenberger, pp. 65–66.

153   a "system of larger and lesser": Young, *The Washington Community*, p. 3.

154   Visitors compared the District: Ibid., pp. 41–53.

154   there were only 109 houses: Ibid., p. 41.

154   "Figure to yourself": John Randolph quoted in ibid., p. 75.

154   "The gentlemen in the rear": T. J. Randolph in *The Jefferson Reader*, ed. Rosenberger, p. 65.

155   "Republicanism is so rare": TJ to Robert R. Livingston, December 14, 1800, TJP.

155   "we shall have to advertise": Ellis, *American Sphinx*, p. 188.

155   a "moral duty": TJ to General Samuel Smith, March 9, 1801, TJP.

156   "To fill that office": Quoted in Adams, *The Life of Albert Gallatin*, p. 300.

156   "the English career": TJ to Gallatin, October 11, 1809, WTJ, IX:264.

156   In his first report: Adams, *The Life of Albert Gallatin*, pp. 292–93.

156   "hostile to the genius": Balinky, *Albert Gallatin: Fiscal Theories and Policies*, p. 55.

157   "if this Administration": Adams, *The Life of Albert Gallatin*, pp. 294–95.

157   "reform the waste": TJ to Walter Jones, March 31, 1801, TJ Miscellany, Manuscript Division, LOC, quoted in Cunningham, *The Process of Government Under Jefferson*, p. 316.

157   "We are hunting out": TJ to T. M. Randolph, June 18, 1801, quoted in ibid., p. 22.

157   "agencies upon agencies": TJ to James Monroe, June 20, 1801, quoted in ibid.

157   In the first full year: ASP, Mis. vol. 1, p. 260, transmitted to Congress by President; Register of Employees for 1802. See also Young, *The Washington Community*, p. 29.

157   At the height of the Quasi War: See McKee, *A Gentlemanly and Honorable Profession*, pp. 413–18.

158   "a most painful Duty": Secretary of the Navy to Captain Alexander Murray, March 27, 1801, QW VII:158.

158 "It directs him": Samuel Smith for acting Secretary of the Navy Dearborn to Captain Sever, June 18, 1801, QW VII:255.

158 "Permit me here": Samuel Smith for acting Secretary of Dearborn the Navy to Lieutenant William Flagg, April 15, 1801, QW VII:195.

158 "I shall be really chagrined": TJ to Samuel Smith, April 17, 1801, TJP.

159 "Besides the safety": Message of the President of the United States to Congress, December 8, 1801, ASP, Naval Affairs, vol. 1, p. 78.

160 The annual cost to maintain each ship: Secretary of the Navy, "Naval establishment and its expenses," to the House of Representatives, January 15, 1801, ASP, Naval Affairs, vol. 1, p. 6.

160 "I have frequently": William Whitehead quoted in letter to Secretary of the Navy from Captain Thomas Tingey, December 5, 1801, QW VII:306.

160 "no unnecessary expence": General Samuel Smith for acting Secretary of the Navy to Captain Alexander Murray, April 11, 1801, QW VII:186.

160 "before timely assistance": Captain Alexander Murray to Secretary of the Navy, April 12, 1801, QW VII:189.

161 Murray wrote Smith to say: Captain Alexander Murray to General Samuel Smith, May 18, 1801, QW VII:227.

161 might "be entirely rotten": TJ to Caesar A. Rodney, December 31, 1802, TJP.

162 "Almost every other": Quoted in Mapp, *TJ: A Strange Case of Mistaken Identity*, p. 2.

162 "If I could not go": TJ quoted in Ellis, *Founding Brothers*, p. 67.

162 "How is it that we hear": Samuel Johnson, "Taxation Not Tyranny," in *The Yale Edition of the Works of Samuel Johnson* (1775; New Haven: Yale University Press, 1977).

162 "1. Justice is in favor": TJ to JA, July 11, 1786, in Cappon, ed., *The Adams-Jefferson Letters*, I:142–43.

162 "such a naval force": TJ to Elbridge Gerry, January 26, in Cunningham, *The Process of Government Under Jefferson*, p. 128.

163 "running navigation mad": TJ to Dr. Joseph Priestley, January 18, 1800, TJP.

163 "Merchants have no country": TJ Jefferson to Horatio C. Spafford , March 17, 1814, TJP.

163 "The cultivators of the earth": "Answers to questions propounded by M. De Meunier," January 24, 1786, WTJ, vol. V, p. 11.

164 "to preserve an equality of right": TJ to John Jay, August 23, 1785, TJP.

165 "no pretence of any periodical": "Treaty of Peace and Friendship between the United States of America and the Bey and Subjects of Tripoli of Barbary," BW I:177.

165 "for the Peace we had paid him": James L. Cathcart, U.S. Consul, Tripoli, to Secretary of State Pro Tempore, October 18, 1800, BW I:382.

165 "the meanest of our Citizens": Ibid.

166 "We were shown to": William Eaton quoted in Whipple, *To the Shores of Tripoli*, p. 55.

167 "A most Superb Gun": "Presents to Tunis," BW II:86.

167 "all the military and naval": Bey of Tunis to President Thomas Jefferson, September 8, 1802, BW II:269.

167 Pleading lack of funds: Richard O'Brien to William Smith, January 10, 1801, BW I:410.

168 "You pay me tribute": Whipple, *To the Shores of Tripoli*, p. 56.

168 "I hope I shall never": Bainbridge to Secretary Stoddert, quoted in Lossing, *Pictorial Field-Book of the War of 1812*, chap. VI.

168 "I am an enemy": TJ to JM, August 28, 1801, TJP.

169 Jefferson put two questions: Jefferson notes quoted in Cunningham, *The Process of Government Under Jefferson*, pp. 48–49.

169 "to superintend the safety": Tucker, *Dawn Like Thunder: The Barbary Wars and the Birth of the U.S. Navy*, p. 135.

169 "an authority equally competent": Ferguson, *Truxtun of the Constellation*, p. 215.

169 "peace can afford": Ibid., p. 216.

169 "the finest frigate": Ibid., p. 217.

171   In a three-hour battle: Whipple, *To the Shores of Tripoli*, p. 80.

171   to "subdue, seize": "An act for the protection of the commerce and seamen of the United States, against the Tripolitan cruisers," passed by the seventh Congress, February 6, 1802, BW II:51–52.

172   "I have a reputation": Captain Thomas Truxtun to Secretary of the Navy, March 3, 1802, BW II:76.

172   "I cannot but consider": Ferguson, *Truxtun of the Constellation*, p. 224.

172   "I never was at sea": Whipple, *To the Shores of Tripoli*, p. 86.

172   to "place all our naval": Secretary of the Navy, Instructions to Captain Richard D. Morris, April 20, 1802, BW II:130.

173   "I have for some time": TJ to Albert Gallatin, March 28, 1803, TJP.

173   "though a fly": William Eaton, U.S. Consul, Tripoli, to James Leander Cathcart, April 26, 1802, BW II:134.

173   "Our operations of the last": William Eaton to Secretary of State, August 23, 1802, BW II:248.

174   "I sincerely wish": Albert Gallatin to TJ, August 16, 1802, quoted in Adams, *The Life of Albert Gallatin*, p. 307.

174   "Shall we buy peace": Cabinet Meeting Notes, May 8, 1803, in Cunningham, *The Process of Government Under Jefferson*, pp. 49–50.

174   "a steady course": TJ to JM, March 22, 1803, TJP.

174   On the morning of: Logbook of Sailing Master Nathaniel Haraden, May 21, 1803, BW II:413.

175   but in 1781 she was a blackened and rotting: Thomas Dring account, *Recollections of the Jersey Prison-Ship* (1829), p. 7.

175   "The hardest battle": *Niles' Register*, vol. 1, p. 350.

176   "ragged and full of small holes": Logbook of Sailing Master Nathaniel Haraden, May 22, 1803, BW II:416.

176   "good, and of proper thickness": Captain Edward Preble to Secretary of the Navy, May 22, 1803, BW II:414.

176   Revere was respected: Triber, *A True Republican: The Life of Paul Revere*, pp. 180–86.

177   "Stripped off Ships": Revere to Smith quoted in ibid.

177   "The mast did not complain": Logbook of Sailing Master Nathaniel Haraden, June 25, 1803, BW II:462.

178   that he could not recruit: Captain Edward Preble to Secretary of the Navy, June 26, 1803, BW II:463.

178   "We are lumbered": Logbook of Sailing Master Nathaniel Haraden, August 4, 1803, BW II:506.

178   "The ship sails well": Captain Edward Preble to Secretary of the Navy, August 19, 1803, BW II:515.

178   Preble wrote out 107 standing orders: "Internal Rules and Regulations for the U.S. Frigate *Constitution*, 1803 to 1804, by Captain Edward Preble," September 6, 1803, BW III:6.

179   "The crew were immediately" . . . and the quotes that follow: Charles Morris, *Autobiography*, quoted in Magoun, *The Frigate Constitution and Other Historic Ships*, pp. 68–69.

182   "I find it hard": Captain Edward Preble to James Simpson, U.S. Consul, Tangier, September 22, 1803, BW III:71.

182   "on Goat Skins": James Simpson to Captain Edward Preble, October 2, 1803, BW III:97.

182   "after this they messed": Logbook of Sailing Master Nathaniel Haraden, October 3, 1803, BW III:101.

183   "invites me (after the War)": Midshipman Henry Wadsworth to Nancy Doane, September 24, 1803, BW III:75.

183   "were trembling in their shoes": Midshipman Ralph Izard to Mrs. Ralph Izard, Sr., October 11, 1803, BW III:126.

183   As a gesture of goodwill: James Simpson to Captain Edward Preble, October 7, 1803, BW III:110.

183   The morning of October 10: Tobias Lear, U.S. Consul General, Algiers, to Secretary of State, October 18, 1803, BW III:146.

183   "I had connected": Midshipman Ralph Izard to Mrs. Ralph Izard, Sr., October 11, 1803, BW III:126.

184   Moroccan governors and ship captains: Declaration of peace between United States and the Emperor of Morocco, October 9, 1803; Captain Edward Preble to James Simpson, October 8, 1803, BW III:118–19.

184   "such a miserable piece": Captain Edward Preble to Secretary of the Navy, October 1, 1803, BW III:95.

185   wrote a formal protest: Lieutenant Charles Stewart to Captain John Gore, Royal Navy, October 7, 1803, BW III:112.

185   "subjects of his Britannic Majesty": Captain John Gore to Lieutenant Charles Stewart, October 8, 1803, BW III:113.

185   "having again placed themselves": Letters between John Gore and Charles Stewart dated October 9, 1803, BW III:120–21.

185   "you will perceive": Lieutenant Charles Stewart to Captain Edward Preble, October 9, 1803, BW III:121.

186   "The Officers of our Navy": Captain Edward Preble to Captain John Gore, October 17, 1803, BW III:143.

186   "many of our men": Lieutenant Charles Stewart to Captain Edward Preble, October 9, 1803, BW III:121.

186   "I know of no such person": Captain Edward Preble to Captain John Gore, October 17, 1803, BW III:143 (emphasis in the original).

186   with "a like number": Captain George Hart, Royal Navy, to Captain Edward Preble, October 21, 1803, BW III:156.

186   "The British make a practice": Captain Edward Preble to Secretary of the Navy, November 9, 1803, BW III:209.

187   to "afford protection": Captain Edward Preble to Captain George Hart, October 22, 1803, BW III:158.

187   "Some misunderstanding" occurred: Surgeon Samuel Marshall to Lieutenant Charles Stewart, October 21, 1803, BW III:157.

187   "at Malta the Ships lay": Captain Edward Preble to Secretary of the Navy, October 23, 1803, BW III:160.

189   "I believe there never was": Zacks, *The Private Coast*, p. 3.

189   "a man destitute of reason": John Rea, *A Letter to William Bainbridge* . . . , quoted in McKee, *A Gentlemanly and Honorable Profession*, pp. 262–63.

190   "as unexpected to me": Captain William Bainbridge to Captain Edward Preble, November 12, 1803, BW III:174.

191   "one man tied to a stake": Captain William Bainbridge to Tobias Lear, February 8, 1804, BW III:176.

191   "to an enemy whom chance": Captain William Bainbridge to Secretary of the Navy, November 1, 1803, BW III:171.

191   by "turning the cock": Court inquiring into the loss of U.S. frigate *Philadelphia*, June 29, 1805, BW III:189.

192   "cut off the hands": Cowdery, *American Captives in Tripoli; or, Dr. Cowdery's Journal in Miniature. Kept during his late captivity in Tripoli*, quoted in Baepler, ed., *White Slaves, African Masters: An Anthology of American Barbary Captivity Narratives*, pp. 161–62. Note that Ray disputes the claim of mutilation, but agrees that there was a melee between the Tripolitans.

192   "The treatment we received": Recipient not indicated, presumably from Captain William Bainbridge, February 18, 1804, BW, III:432.

192   "amidst the shouts": Ibid.

192   "lined with terrific janissaries": William Ray, *Horrors of Slavery, or the American Tars in Tripoli*, in Baepler, ed., *White Slaves, African Masters*, p. 190.

193   "a gracious smile": Recipient not indicated, presumably from Captain William Bainbridge, February 18, 1804, BW, III:432.

193   "set in the European style": Cowdery, *American Captives in Tripoli*, in Baepler, ed., *White Slaves, African Masters*, p. 162.

193   "mats and blankets": Ibid., pp. 162–63.

193   "everything but what we had": Captain William Bainbridge to Secretary of the Navy, November 1, 1803, BW III:171.

193   He introduced Bainbridge: Captain William Bainbridge to Captain Edward Preble, December 13, 1803, BW III: 269.

194   "commanded a handsome prospect": Cowdery in Baepler, ed., *White Slaves, African Masters*, p. 163.

194   "our full approbation": Officers of *Philadelphia* to Captain William Bainbridge, October 31, 1803, BW, III:169.

194   "Misfortune necessitates": Captain William Bainbridge to Secretary of the Navy, November 1, 1803, BW, III:171.

194   "Some Fanatics": Captain William Bainbridge to Captain Edward Preble, November 12, 1803, BW III:174.

194   "We were not Gods": Captain William Bainbridge to Captain Edward Preble, November 25, 1803, BW III:175.

195   "These are the mere reveries": Captain William Bainbridge to Susan Bainbridge, November 1, 1803, BW III:178.

195   "Not a morsel of food" . . . and the account that follows: Ray, *Horrors of Slavery*, in Baepler, ed., *White Slaves, African Masters*, pp. 192–95.

197   grounds of "Interest and Humanity": Captain William Bainbridge to Captain Edward Preble, December 5, 1803, BW III:253.

198   "melancholy and distressing Intelligence": Diary of Captain Edward Preble, November 24, 1803, BW III:175.

198   "I most sincerely pity": Captain Edward Preble to Mary Preble, December 12, 1803, quoted in McKee, *Edward Preble*, 182.

198   "tremendous seas in the channel": Captain Edward Preble to Secretary of the Navy, December 10, 1803, BW III:256.

199   "and very excellent Magazines": Ibid.

199   "Your men on shore": Captain Edward Preble to Lieutenant Stephen Decatur, Jr., December 1, 1803, BW III:245.

199   "distresses me": Captain Edward Preble to Secretary of the Navy, December 10, 1803, BW III:256.

200   "How glorious": James Leander Cathcart to Secretary of State, December 15, 1803, BW III:272.

200   "one of our Finest Frigates": Presumably from Midshipman Henry Wadsworth, January 10, 1804, BW III:322.

200   "I feel most sensibly": Captain Edward Preble to Captain William Bainbridge, December 19, 1803, BW III:280.

200   "I shall not hazard": Captain Edward Preble to Secretary of the Navy, December 10, 1803, BW III:256.

201   "the People on board": Logbook of Sailing Master Nathaniel Haraden, December 23, 1803, BW III:288.

201   "strong breezes from the north": Ibid., III:295.

202   swearing "that one of them": Diary of Captain Edward Preble, December 24, 1803, BW III:294, 371.

202   "If a Tripoline": Captain Edward Preble to Tobias Lear, January 31, 1804, BW III:377.

203   "if government concludes": James Leander Cathcart to Secretary of State, December 15, 1803, BW III:272.

203 Tobias Lear . . . weighed in: Tobias Lear to Secretary of State, December 24, 1803, BW III:291.

203 "A pretty good asking price": Captain Edward Preble to James Leander Cathcart, January 4, 1804, BW III:311.

203 "how to rank us": James Leander Cathcart to Captain Edward Preble, November 18, 1803, BW III:228.

204 "after they bowed": Richard O'Brien to Captain Edward Preble, December 21, 1803, BW III:283–85.

204 "Nature has strongly": Captain William Bainbridge to Tobias Lear, January 14, 1804, BW III:329.

204 "fire on the Town": Richard O'Brien to Captain Edward Preble, December 21, 1803, BW III:283–85.

205 "I shall hazard much": Captain Edward Preble to Secretary of the Navy, December 10, 1803, BW III:256.

205 "could be easily effected": Captain William Bainbridge to Captain Edward Preble, February 15, 1804, BW III:408.

205 "In Decatur I was struck": MacKenzie, *Life of Stephen Decatur*, p. 47.

206 "I was well informed": Captain Edward Preble to the Secretary of the Navy, February 19, 1804, BW III:438–41.

206 "our frigates and schooners": Captain Edward Preble to Secretary of the Navy, February 3, 1804, BW III:384.

207 "Board the Frigate": Captain Edward Preble to Lieutenant Stephen Decatur, January 31, 1804, BW III:376.

207 "were pleased to express": Journal of Midshipman F. Cornelius DeKrafft, *Siren*, February 3, 1804, BW III:388.

207 every man on board: Affidavit of Midshipman Edmund P. Kennedy, BW III:420–21.

207 "dark & hazy": DeKrafft, Journal, *Siren*, February 8, 1804, BW III:399.

207 "if we attempted to go": Midshipman Ralph Izard to Mrs. Ralph Izard, Sr., February 20, 1804, BW III:416–17.

207 and "much injured": Lieutenant Charles Stewart to Captain Edward Preble, February 19, 1804, BW III:415–16.

208 "an accidental supply": Affidavit of Surgeon's Mate Lewis Heermann, Given April 26, 1828, BW III:417–20.

209 "The effect was truly electric": Lewis Heermann quoted in McKee, *Edward Preble: A Naval Biography*, p. 197.

210 "whooping and screaming": Affidavit of Surgeon's Mate Lewis Heermann, BW III:417–20.

210 "enveloped in a dense cloud": Ibid.

210 "in volumes, as large": Lewis Heermann quoted in McKee, *Edward Preble: A Naval Biography*, p. 197.

211 The enemy cannonade: Lieutenant Stephen Decatur to Captain Edward Preble, February 17, 1804, BW III:414–15.

211 "presented a column of fire": Lewis Heermann quoted in McKee, *Edward Preble: A Naval Biography*, p. 197.

211 By six the next morning: Lieutenant Charles Stewart to Captain Edward Preble, February 19, 1804, BW III:415–16.

212 "the most hideous yelling": Cowdery, *American Captives in Tripoli*, in Baepler, ed., *White Slaves, African Masters*, p. 168.

212 "an additional portion of labor": Thomas Appleton, U.S. Consul, Leghorn, to Robert R. Livingston, U.S. Minister to Paris, March 16, 1804, BW, III:494.

213 "prevent the Commodore's acting": Captain William Bainbridge to Minister of Foreign Affairs, Tripoli, February 20, 1804, BW III:445.

213 "very dark and smoky": Cowdery in Baepler, ed., *White Slaves, African Masters*, p. 168.

213 "noxious reptiles": Surgeon John Ridgely to Susan Decatur, November 10, 1826, BW III:425.

213 "our situation is not": Captain William Bainbridge to Captain Edward Preble, March 5, 1804, BW III:474.

213 "Our cruisers should examine": Captain William Bainbridge to Captain Edward Preble, February 17, 1804, BW III:431.

213 "How long has it been": Minister of Foreign Affairs of the Bashaw of Tripoli to Captain William Bainbridge, March 5, 1804, BW III:474.

213 "not merit the appellation": Captain William Bainbridge to Minister of Foreign Affairs of the Bashaw of Tripoli, March 5, 1804, BW III:475.

214 "in quick succession": Affidavit of Surgeon's Mate Lewis Heermann, BW III:417–20 (emphasis added).

214 "a right to expect": Captain Edward Preble to Captain William Bainbridge, March 12, 1804, BW III:489.

214 "but from the kindness": Captain Edward Preble to the Prime Minister to the Bashaw of Tripoli, March 27, 1804, BW III:535–36.

214 "I hope before the end": Captain Edward Preble to Secretary of the Navy, February 19, 1804, BW III:438.

214 "Streets gloomy and ill-built": Irving quoted in McKee, *Edward Preble: A Naval Biography*, pp. 227–28.

215 "full of engravings": Edward Preble to Mary Preble, December 12, 1803, quoted in ibid., pp. 182–83.

215 "It is truly melancholy": Purser John Darby quoted in ibid., pp. 227, 229.

215 "a breach of the marriage vow": Darby quoted in ibid., p. 229.

215 Officers frequented the opera . . . and the quotes that follow: Ibid., pp. 230–33.

217 thirty-six naval officers killed: See Stevens, *Pistols at Ten Paces*. The figure of eighteen deaths before 1815 is cited in McKee, *A Gentlemanly and Honorable Profession*, p. 403.

217 the "Clonmel Code," a set: See "Code Duello: The Rules of Dueling," reprinted from *American Duels and Hostile Encounters* (New York: Chilton Books, 1963).

218 "the most barbarous": TJ to T. M. Randolph, June 23, 1806, quoted in Malone, *Jefferson the President: First Term*, p. 427.

218 "strongly opposed to the practice": Freeman, *Affairs of Honor: National Politics in the New Republic*, p. 159.

218 "one of those imperious cases": Captain Arthur Sinclair quoted in McKee, *A Gentlemanly and Honorable Profession*, p. 405.

218 Among the eighteen dueling fatalities: Ibid., p. 113.

219 "They are young men": Captain Samuel Barron quoted in ibid.

219 "I can't omit": James Barron to Samuel Barron, January 28, 1803, quoted in ibid., p. 403.

220 "I at present am unable": Quoted in ibid., p. 404.

220 "proved the famous duellist" and the paragraph that follows: Captain Daniel Carmack, U.S. Marine Corps, to Lieutenant Colonel Commandant William W. Burrows, October 15, 1802, BW II:293.

221 "The envy & jealousy": Midshipman Henry Wadsworth to Nancy Doane, March 17, 1804, BW III:495.

221 "have given every assurance": Captain Edward Preble to Secretary of the Navy, January 17, 1804, BW III:339.

221 Midshipman Melancthon Woolsey recalled: Melancthon Woolsey Journal, quoted in McKee, *A Gentlemanly and Honorable Profession*, p. 128.

222 "Those Yankees": MacKenzie, *Life of Stephen Decatur*, p. 56.

222 The stranger proved to be: In MacKenzie's 1846 biography of Decatur, Bainbridge's antagonist was erroneously identified as a "Mr. Cochran," private secretary to Governor Ball. The trouble may have started with Midshipman Wadsworth's identification of the man as "Mr. Cochran," though Wadsworth said only that he was "an Englishmen residing at Valletta." Donald Sultana, with the help of Maltese records, corrected the error in 1993—Sultana, "Samuel Taylor Coleridge, An American Naval Hero and a Mysterious Duellist in Malta," *Melita Historica New Series* 11 (1993).

222 Bainbridge chose Stephen Decatur: MacKenzie, *Life of Stephen Decatur*, p. 58; and the eyewitness account of a Maltese sergeant named Salvatore Piott, cited in Sultana, "Samuel Taylor Coleridge, An American Naval Hero and a Mysterious Duellist in Malta."

222 "this morning a duel": Journal of Midshipman Henry Wadsworth, February 14, 1803, BW II:362.

223 "[T]his accident renders": President Thomas Jefferson's message to Congress, March 20, 1804, BW III:506.

224 "I have never been so mortified": TJ to Robert Smith, April 27, 1804, TJP.

224 "thwarting the negotiations": JM to Thomas Fitzsimons, April 13, 1804, BW IV:23.

224 It required: "An Act Further to protect the commerce and seamen of the United States against the Barbary Powers," BW III:522.

224 A storeship, the *John Adams:* Secretary Smith to Lieutenant John Cassin, April 19, 1804, BW IV:39–40.

224 "all that a sound mind": Secretary Smith to Samuel Barron, June 6, 1804, BW IV:152–54.

225 "the Frigates *President* and *Congress*": Secretary of the Navy to Lieutenant John Cassin, March 21, 1804, BW III:509.

226 "a most awful sight": William Couper, April 29, 1804, quoted in Wertenbaker, *Norfolk: Historic Southern Port*, p. 128.

226 "in the place of that Number": Captain John Rodgers to Secretary Smith, June 8, 1804, BW IV:164.

226 missing "many Articles": Captain John Rodgers to Benjamin King, June 15, 1804, BW IV:193.

226 "can be made ready": Captain John Rodgers to Secretary Smith, June 8, 1804, BW IV:164.

227 "drummed on shore": McKee, *A Gentlemanly and Honorable Profession*, p. 256.

227 a "solid Peace": Captain Edward Preble to Robert Livingston, March 18, 1804, BW III:498–99.

227 "If it was not for the situation": Captain Edward Preble to Secretary of the Navy, February 3, 1804, BW III:384.

228 "the ardent desire": Talleyrand, French Minister of Exterior Relations, to Robert Livingston, January 17, 1804, BW III:335.

228 "The Bashaw's pretension": Captain Edward Preble to M. Beaussier, June 12, 1804, BW IV:180–81.

228 "Through these instruments": William Eaton to Secretary of the Navy, September 6, 1804, BW IV:525–26.

229 five hundred barrels: Captain Edward Preble to Secretary of the Navy, January 17, 1804, BW III:337.

229 "Although it does not accord": Secretary of State to William Eaton, August 22, 1802, BW II:245 (emphasis in the original).

229 "without means": M. Beaussier to Captain Edward Preble, March 28, 1803, BW III:542.

229 "constructed and rigged": Captain Edward Preble to Secretary of the Navy, July 16, 1803, BW II:488.

229 "If you will allow": Captain Edward Preble to Secretary of the Navy, January 17, 1804, BW III:337.

230 "I am clearly of Opinion": Captain William Bainbridge to Captain Edward Preble, March 26, 1804, BW III:525.

230 "Sails, Oars, Anchors": James Cathcart to Captain Edward Preble, January 30, 1804, BW III:373.

231 "We were no sooner": Melancthon Woolsey Journal quoted in McKee, *A Gentlemanly and Honorable Profession*, p. 128.

231 "I was so much engaged": Preble quoted in ibid., p. 238.

231   The kingdom would provide: Lord Acton to Captain Edward Preble, May 13, 1804, BW, IV:97.

232   Preble's force now numbered: Captain Edward Preble to Secretary of the Navy, September 18, 1804, BW IV:293–310.

232   "the wind blowing . . . rough sharp sea": McKee, *Edward Preble*, pp. 250–65.

233   "The Bashaw is ready": M. Beaussier to Talleyrand, March 1, 1804, quoted in ibid., p. 206.

233   "a Sandy Desert": Logbook of Sailing Master Nathaniel Haraden, March 27, 1804, BW III:539.

234   "in an Instant": Captain Edward Preble's Journal, August 4, 1804, BW IV:336–38.

234   "was kept entirely": Narrative of Attacks on Tripoli by Richard O'Brien, BW IV:341–43.

234   As Decatur's vessel collided: McKee, *Edward Preble*, p. 257.

234   "I find hand-to-hand": Decatur quoted in ibid., p. 259.

235   "a remarkably athletic": Captain Edward Preble to Secretary of the Navy, September 18, 1804, BW IV:296.

235   "20 Turks lay weltering": Midshipman Robert T. Spence to Mrs. Keith Spence, November 12, 1804, BW IV:351–53.

236   From the deck of the *Constitution:* McKee, *Edward Preble*, p. 260.

236   As the flagship passed to the west: Captain Edward Preble to Secretary of the Navy, September 18, 1804, BW IV:297.

237   "I was ordered": Cowdery, *American Captives in Tripoli*, in Baepler, ed., *White Slaves, African Masters*, p. 171.

238   "The wind to the Northward": Purser Noadiah Morris to unknown recipient, September 7, 1804, BW IV:353–59.

238   "have dreadful Ideas": Captain William Bainbridge to Captain Edward Preble, June 22, 1804, BW IV:213–14.

238   But the bomb ketches: See McKee, *Edward Preble*, pp. 250–65.

238   "I think a blow": O'Brien quoted in ibid., p. 272.

238   "Advance in a line": Ibid.

239   "almost totally destroyed": Captain Edward Preble's Journal, August 8, 1804, BW IV:376–77.

239   "I saw the mangled bodies": Cowdery, *American Captives in Tripoli*, in Baepler, ed., *White Slaves, African Masters*, p. 171.

239   "I went up some distance": Midshipman Robert T. Spence to Mrs. Keith Spence, November 12, 1804, BW IV:351–53.

239   "ignorant of the art": Captain Edward Preble to Secretary of the Navy, September 18, 1804, BW IV:299n.

239   but it is more likely: Nathaniel Haraden and Richard O'Brien each advanced the "flaming wad" theory. See McKee, *Edward Preble*, pp. 271–77.

240   During the day's action: Captain Edward Preble to Secretary of the Navy, September 18, 1804, BW IV:300.

240   Tribesmen from the backcountry: Cowdery, *American Captives in Tripoli*, in Baepler, ed., *White Slaves, African Masters*, p. 173.

240   "in a state of putrefaction": Ibid., p. 175.

240   "Strange ships in sight": McKee, *Edward Preble*, p. 276.

240   The letters were written: See Smith to Preble, May 7, 1804, BW IV:88, and Smith to Preble, May 22, 1804, BW IV:114.

241   "How much my feelings": McKee, *Edward Preble*, p. 282.

241   Preble elected to try: Ibid., pp. 284–85.

241   "He said that for two dollars": Cowdery, in Baepler, ed., *White Slaves, African Masters*, p. 172.

242   the *Constitution* had 14,000 gallons: Logbook of Sailing Master Nathaniel Haraden, August 18, 1804, BW IV:430.

242   Preble ordered a short water ration: Captain Edward Preble to the Commanding Officer of each Ship of War in the Mediterranean Squadron, August 20, 1804, BW IV:438.

242   "Our Water is nearly exhausted": Captain Edward Preble to William Higgins, U.S. Navy Agent, Malta, August 15, 1804, BW IV:417.

242   On the night of August 18: Captain Edward Preble's Journal, August 18, 1804, BW IV:429.

243   "considerable damage": Journal of Midshipman F. Cornelius DeKrafft, August 24, 1804, BW IV:456.

243   "such attempts served": Cowdery in Baepler, ed., *White Slaves, African Masters*, p. 173.

243   "The Commodore's ship": Purser John Darby's Journal, August 28, 1804, BW IV:475–76.

244   "At every Broadside": Logbook of Sailing Master Nathaniel Haraden, August 28, 1804, BW IV:472–74.

244   The *Constitution* took heavy fire: McKee, *Edward Preble*, pp. 289–94.

244   "a heavy and incessant fire": Cowdery in Baepler, ed., *White Slaves, African Masters*, p. 174.

244   "you have injured": Sailmaker Joseph Douglass and Carpenter William Godby to Captain Edward Preble, August 29, 1804, BW IV:479–80.

244   "a cannon hit": Zuchet quoted in Zacks, *The Pirate Coast*, p. 105.

244   "passed within a few inches": *Naval Chronicle*, vol. 1., footnoted in letter from Captain Edward Preble to Secretary of the Navy, September 18, 1804, BW IV:302.

245   "I cannot but view": M. Beaussier to Captain Edward Preble, August 29, 1804, BW IV:481–83.

245   Carpenters from several different vessels: Captain Edward Preble to Secretary of the Navy, September 18, 1804, BW IV:305.

246   "The men, women and children": Cowdery in Baepler, ed., *White Slaves, African Masters*, p. 175.

247   At eight o'clock the next evening: The blowing up of the U.S. ketch *Intrepid* as described by Midshipman Charles G. Ridgeley, BW IV:507–10.

247   "How awfully grand!": Midshipman Robert T. Spence to Mrs. Keith Spence, November 12, 1804, BW IV:351–53.

247   Several of the mortars detonated late: Logbook of Sailing Master Nathaniel Haraden, September 4, 1804, BW IV:506–7.

247   had "put a match": Captain Edward Preble to Secretary of the Navy, September 18, 1804, BW IV:306.

247   "What a Noble Death": Midshipman Robert T. Spence to Mrs. Keith Spence, November 12, 1804, BW IV:351–53.

247   "The explosion caused": Beaussier quoted in McKee, *Edward Preble*, p. 306.

248   "was fatal only to yourselves": Ibid.

248   it "did but little damage": Cowdery in Baepler, ed., *White Slaves, African Masters*, pp. 175–76.

248   "[We] there saw six persons": Bainbridge quoted in McKee, *Edward Preble*, p. 306. Original quote from James Fenimore Cooper, *History of the Navy*, I:411–12.

248   "amused himself": Zacks, *The Pirate Coast*, p. 105.

248   "the weather wore": Captain Edward Preble, to Secretary of the Navy, September 18, 1804, BW IV:307.

248   The commodore ordered the gunboats: McKee, *Edward Preble*, pp. 306–8.

249   The four frigates: Captain John Rodgers to Secretary of the Navy, August 12, 1804, BW IV:402.

249   "uncommonly smooth": Journal of William Eaton, U.S. Navy Agent for the Barbary regencies, August 20, 1804, BW IV:440.

249   "a violent shock": Captain Samuel Barron to Sir Alexander John Ball, Governor of Malta, September 7, 1804, BW V:1.

250   "Discovering strange ships": McKee, *Edward Preble*, p. 307.

250   "Commodore Barron's arrival": Quoted in ibid., p. 308.

252   whose "reputation as a fighting man": Noadiah Morris quoted in McKee, *Edward Preble*, pp. 309–10.

252   "Sir: A respect I owe": Rodgers papers quoted in ibid., p. 310.

253   "In memory of": Lovette, *Naval Customs, Traditions, and Usage*, p. 58.

253   in "the contempt": Nathaniel Bowen, sermon preached in Charleston, 1807, quoted in Williams, *Dueling in the Old South: Vignettes of Social History*, p. 130.

253   "Immediately upon Receipt hereof": Secretary of the Navy to F. Cornelius DeKrafft, February 28, 1805, BW V:377.

253   Citing the "prevalent Example": Honorable Joseph Hopper Nicholson, Representative from Maryland, to Secretary of the Navy, February 28, 1805, BW, V:376.

PART THREE: ENGLAND AGAIN

257   "I cannot but be": McKee, *Edward Preble*, p. 312.

257   "an American is no longer": William Eaton to Colonel Dwight, September 20, 1804, BW V:42.

258   "the most bold and daring": Tucker, *Dawn Like Thunder*, p. 283.

258   "the energy and judgment": President Thomas Jefferson, Message to Congress, February 20, 1805, BW IV:293.

258   During the two weeks: McKee, *Edward Preble*, pp. 314–15.

258   Preble sent a hogshead: Edward Preble to Robert Smith, May 18, 1805, TJP.

258   "It is really a painful": TJ to Robert Smith, May 31, 1805, TJP.

259   a polygraph, or "portable secretary": Malone, *Jefferson the President: Second Term*, pp. 38–44.

259   "I have used one": TJ to Edward Preble, July 6, 1805, TJP.

259   "I beg leave to assure": Edward Preble to TJ, July 30, 1805, TJP.

259   With the reinforcements: McKee, *Edward Preble*, p. 329.

260   "he had heard that [Rodgers]": William Bainbridge to David Porter, July 10, 1805, NYHS.

260   "I shall impute": William Bainbridge to David Porter, July 10, 1805, NYHS.

260   The 1805 campaign: The material that follows is based on McKee, *Edward Preble: A Naval Biography*, pp. 329–35.

262   "I must say I had expected": McKee, *Edward Preble*, p. 329.

262   "ignominious . . . sacrifice of national honor": Ibid.

263   American exports (including re-exports): *Historical Statistics of the United States, Colonial Times to 1970*, U.S. Department of Commerce, Bureau of the Census, Part 2, 1976, series Q 518–523, "Value of Waterborne Imports and Exports," pp. 761, 751. See also Hickey, *War of 1812*, p. 297.

263   Booming traded filled the treasury: See Adams, HUSJ, pp. 393–98.

264   "I think myself": William Plumer's Memorandum of Proceedings in the U.S. Senate, 1803–1807, ed. Everett Brown (New York: The Macmillan Company, 1923), pp. 198–99.

264   Jefferson was seen: Sir Augustus John Foster, "Notes on the United States, 1804–1812," *William and Mary Quarterly*, 3rd ser., 8(1) (January 1951):72.

264   "as real a revolution": TJ to Spencer Roane, September 6, 1819, TJP.

265   "His Highness the President": Koch, *Jefferson and Madison*, pp. 101–2.

265   "all are perfectly equal": Adams, HUSJ, p. 549.

265   "Levees are done away": TJ to Nathaniel Macon, May 14, 1801, TJP.

265   a "crowd of ladies and gentlemen": T. J. Randolph quoted in Rosenberger, ed., *The Jefferson Reader*, pp. 64–65.

266   "That day buried leaves": TJ, February 1804, Response to Etiquette of the Court of the U.S., TJP.

266   "a few moments after": Senator William Plumer, *Life of William Plumer*, p. 242.

266   "He wore a blue coat": Foster, "Notes on the United States," p. 72.

266   "dressed in long boots": Quoted in Adams, HUSJ, p. 550.

267   "flattered the low passions": Foster, "Notes on the United States," pp. 78–79

267   "Mr. Jefferson entered": Larus, "Pell-Mell Along the Potomac," *William and Mary Quarterly*, 3rd ser., 17(B) (1960): 349–57.

267   "actually standing in slippers": Edmund Quincy, *Life of Josiah Quincy*, p. 92.

268   "without Mr. Jefferson's using": Anthony Merry to Lord Hawkesbury, December 6, 1803, Foreign Office 5/41.

268   a "virago": TJ to James Monroe, January 8, 1804, TJP.

268   American diplomatic protocols: Adams, HUSJ, p. 558.

268   "we might as well attempt": TJ to James Monroe, January 8, 1804, TJP.

269   "no law of the United States": Adams, HUSJ, p. 567.

269   "Every port in the island": Secretary of State to Anthony Merry, December 24, 1803, BW III:290.

269   Merry countered with complaints: Adams, HUSJ, pp. 569–73; Secretary of State to Anthony Merry, June 25, 1804, BW IV:224.

270   "impressment": See Tucker and Reuter, *Injured Honor: The Chesapeake-Leopard Affair*, pp. 62–66.

270   "indefeasible allegiance": James Biddle letter book, vol. 2: Analusia Foundation collection.

270   Impressment was also carried out: NW1812 I:61–62 (editorial note); see also Zimmerman, *Impressment of American Seamen*, pp. 246–75.

272   Gallatin estimated: See Tucker and Reuter, *Injured Honor*, pp. 62–66.

272   "[T]he flagrant and undeniable": Hickey, *The War of 1812*, p. 11.

272   "It is my duty": Spencer and Reuter, *Injured Honor*, p. 63.

274   "the place occupied": TJ to Robert R. Livingston, September 9, 1801, TJP.

275   This "re-export" trade: Albion and Pope, *Sea Lanes in Wartime*, p. 70.

275   "solely to colour": Text of the *Essex* decision, rendered by the Vice Admiralty Court of Nassau, New Providence, June 22, 1805, NW1812, I:17–20.

275   "broke open my trunks": *Norfolk Gazette and Ledger*, October 23, 1805, quoted in Wertenbaker, *Norfolk: Historic Southern Port*, p. 98.

276   "Hatred of America": *Orders in Council; or, An Examination of the Justice, Legality, and Policy of the New System, etc.* (London, 1808), quoted in Adams, HUSJ, p. 977.

276   "The winds and seas": Quoted in *Niles' Register*, vol. 2, p. 219.

276   "sensation and clamour": Anthony Merry to Lord Mulgrave, September 30, 1805, quoted in Adams, HUSJ, p. 666.

276   "producing the most ruinous": TJ to House and Senate, January 17, 1806, ASP, Foreign Affairs, vol. 2, p. 727.

277   "The love of peace": TJ to Judge Cooper, February 18, 1806, quoted in Adams, HUSJ, pp. 679–80.

277   "a shilling pamphlet" . . . and the quotes that follow: John Randolph quoted in ibid., pp. 679, 712, 714.

278   "Every morning at daybreak": Midshipman Basil Hall quoted in Albion and Pope, *Sea Lanes in Wartime*, p. 91.

279   Even if the case was decided: Adams, HUSJ, pp. 665–67.

279   An incident on April 24: See Albion and Pope, *Sea Lanes in Wartime*, p. 92.

279   "I well remember": Clinton speech in Congress, January, 1807, *Annals*, House of Representatives, 9th Congr., 2nd Sess., p. 386.

279   Jefferson issued: TJ, May 3, 1806, Henry Whitby Proclamation, TJP.

279   "an atrocious violation": TJ to Jacob Crowninshield, May 13, 1806, TJP.

280   "England may": TJ to James Monroe, May 4, 1806, TJP.

280   "under the immediate eye": TJ to Samuel Smith, April 17, 1801, TJP.

280   By mid-December 1805: Secretary of the Navy to Chairman of Committee on Naval Peace Establishment, December 16, 1805, NW1812 I:7.

280 He proposed to return: Albert Gallatin to TJ, May 30, 1805, quoted in Adams, HUSJ, p. 649.

280 "by encouraging wars": Adams, *The Life of Albert Gallatin*, p. 335.

280 "loose demands": Cunningham, *The Process of Government Under Jefferson*, pp. 61–62.

281 funds for seaport fortifications: NW1812, I:2.

281 The navy was to sell: Fowler, *Jar Tars and Commodores*, pp. 142–43.

281 "I have obtained": Chauncey to Preble, March 25, 1806, NYHS, Isaac Chauncey Letterbooks; NW1812 I:1iii.

281 Even during periods: See McKee, *A Gentlemanly and Honorable Profession*, pp. 40–53.

281 "was particularly happy": Quoted in Cunningham, *The Process of Government Under Jefferson*, p. 133.

281 A successful campaign was mounted: McKee, *A Gentlemanly and Honorable Profession*, pp. 40–41.

282 "Though sixteen years old": Charles Boarman to Robert Brent, August 13, 1811, quoted in ibid., p. 41.

282 the median age: Ibid., p. 179.

282 Several of the leading figures: Ibid., pp. 288–89.

282 For Lieutenant Andrew Sterrett: Sterrett to Smith and Smith to Sterrett, quoted in ibid., p. 298.

283 "In Mr. Fox": TJ to James Monroe, May 4, 1806, TJP.

283 the "Fox Blockade": See Hickey, *The War of 1812*, p. 10.

284 no vessel could sail: Order in Council dated January 7, 1807, quoted in Adams, HUSJ, p. 889.

285 On September 8, 1804: Résumé, presumably prepared in Navy Department ca. 1806–07, concerning U.S. Gunboat No. 1, BW IV:279.

285 "grow into a ship of the line": *Connecticut Courant* quoted in Tucker, "The Jeffersonian Gunboats in Service, 1804–1825," *American Neptune* 55(2) (1995):97.

285 "become an excitement": President Thomas Jefferson, Special Message to Congress on Gun-Boats, February 10, 1807, NW1812 I:13–15.

286 The Republican majority in Congress: See Silverstone, *The Sailing Navy, 1775–1854*, pp. 57–60.

286 "What would be": Decatur quoted in Gene Smith, "A Means to an End: Gunboats and Thomas Jefferson's Theory of Defense," *American Neptune*, 55(2) (1995): 118.

286 a "wasteful imbecility": *Washington Federalist*, March 11, 1807, in TJP.

287 Over time, the critics: See Silverstone, *The Sailing Navy, 1775–1854*, pp. 57–60.

287 The cost per vessel: Editor's Note, NW1812 I:12–13.

289 "The *Chesapeak* as a Vessel": Captain Stephen Decatur to Secretary Smith, September 6, 1808, NA RG 45, Captains' Letters.

290 "All ships have accidents": Beach, *The United States Navy: A 200-Year History*, p. 32.

290 "I have long known": Quotations from James Barron court-martial, a letter from Barron to Charles Gordon dated May 1, 1807, and court-martial documents, all quoted in Adams, HUSJ, p. 932.

290 "was struck with astonishment": Captain Charles Gordon to the Secretary of the Navy, June 22, 1807, quoted in ibid., p. 933.

291 to "suffer death": De Gast, *The Lighthouses of the Chesapeake*, p. 41.

291 "from the extreme cleanliness": James Barron to Secretary of the Navy, June 6, 1807, and Charles Gordon to Barron, June 19, 1807, quoted in Adams, HUSJ, p. 933.

293 The commander of the *Halifax* . . . and the story and quotes that follow: Tucker and Reuter, *Injured Honor*, pp. 64, 68–79.

293 "Whereas many Seamen": Quoted in Adams, HUSJ, p. 930.

294 Monday, June 22, dawned: For details of the account that follows, and all quotations, see Tucker and Reuter, *Injured Honor: The Chesapeake-Leopard Affair*, pp. 1–12.

295 and "clearing Ship for Sea": Log of U.S. frigate *Chesapeake*, NW1812 I:27–28.

298   "Sir, I consider the Frigate" and Humphreys's reply: Messages exchanged between the *Chesapeake* and the *Leopard*, June 22, 1807, from Mariners' Museum Web site at http://www.mariner.org/usnavy.

298   At 8:00 a.m.: Log of U.S. frigate *Chesapeake*, NW1812 I:27–28.

299   "feeling of a true": Adams, HUSJ, p. 946.

299   Stephen Decatur and Samuel Barron: See Tucker and Reuter, *Injured Honor*, pp. 99–100.

299   "Oh! that some one": Lieutenant William Allen to General William Allen, June 24, 1807, quoted in ibid., pp. 100–1 (emphasis in the original).

300   "highly laudable": Ibid., p. 101.

300   "You must be perfectly": Quoted in Adams, HUSJ, p. 946.

301   Jefferson had been preparing: Ibid., pp. 965.

301   all British naval vessels: TJ, July 2, 1807, Proclamation and Draft on Armed Vessels, TJP.

301   "who, having broke": TJ to JM, August 18, 1807, TJP.

302   "Our commerce": Albert Gallatin to Hanna Gallatin, July 10, 1807, in Adams, *The Life of Albert Gallatin*, pp. 357–59.

302   "Nor do I know": Albert Gallatin to Joseph H. Nicholson, July 17, 1807, in ibid., pp. 361–62.

302   "one subject of considerable": Albert Gallatin to Hanna Gallatin, July 10, 1807, in ibid., p. 357.

302   "the British commanders": TJ to Henry Dearborn, July 7, 1807, TJP.

302   "burning the first Powder": Quoted in Dunne and Leiner, "An 'Appearance of Menace': The Royal Navy's Incursion into New York Bay, September 1807," *Log of Mystic Seaport* 44(4) (1993):86–92.

302   "manifestly pacific": TJ to Henry Dearborn, July 13, 1807, and TJ to Governor of Virginia, July 27, 1807, September 7, 1807, all in TJP.

303   Recriminations flew: See Tucker and Reuter, *Injured Honor*, pp. 140–44.

303   "a ship without honor": Beach, *The United States Navy*, p. 69.

304   "A formal disavowal": Secretary of State Madison to James Monroe, American Minister to the Court of St. James's, July 6, 1807, in *James Madison Writings*, ed. Rakove, pp. 673–79.

304   "a creature of royal": Adams, HUSJ, p. 966.

304   Early in September: See ibid., pp. 970–73.

304   "striking at the very vitals": *Morning Post*, August 6, 1807, quoted in ibid., p. 957.

305   "If the Government": *The Times* quoted in Tucker and Reuter, *Injured Honor*, p. 125.

305   "composed of the ship owners": James Monroe to JM, August 4, 1807, ASP, Foreign Affairs, vol. 3, p. 186.

305   to "assure you that": Lord Canning to James Monroe, August 3, 1807, ASP, Foreign Affairs, vol. 3, p. 188.

305   had "existed in their fullest": Lord Canning to James Monroe, September 23, 1807, ASP, Foreign Affairs, vol. 3, p. 199.

305   were "for the present": Ibid.

306   to "seize upon": ASP, Foreign Affairs, vol. 3, pp. 25–26.

306   For the first time: Adams, HUSJ, p. 1031.

306   "the ruins of a castle": Foster, "Notes on the United States," p. 78.

307   Fissures within the Republican ranks: *Annals*, House of Representatives, 9th Congr., 2nd Sess., pp. 387–88, 389–90, also quoted in Adams, HUSJ, p. 844.

308   "reluctant to vote": *Annals*, House of Representatives, November 1807, 10th Congr., 1st Sess., pp. 823–24.

308   "The *Constitution* is to remain": WTJ, I: 330.

308   "will authorize a complete": TJ to William H. Cabell, November 1, 1807, TJP.

308   Secretary Smith asked Congress: Secretary Smith to Samuel Mitchell, November 8, 1807, *Annals*, 10th Congr., 1st Sess., pp. 31–32.

308   "I observe among": John Quincy Adams, *Memoirs*, November 17, 1807, entry.

309   "To conquer": Louis-Marie Turreau to Talleyrand, July 9, 1805, quoted in Adams, HUSJ, p. 661.

309   for any "foreign port or place": Knox, *A History of the United States Navy*, pp. 171–72.

310   "have bidden agriculture": TJ to Albert Gallatin, May 6, 1808, quoted in Adams, HUSJ, p. 1100.

310   to "take the chance": TJ to Benjamin Smith, May 20, 1808, TJP.

310   Much of the enforcement: See Cunningham, *The Process of Government Under Jefferson*, p. 119.

310   "uncommonly dull": Captain Stephen Decatur to Secretary Smith, September 6, 1808, NA # RG 45, Captains' Letters.

310   to "seize the Boats": Secretary of the Navy Smith to Lieutenant Samuel Elbert, May 2, 1808, NW1812 I:35–36.

311   "The port indeed": *Lambert's Travels*, quoted in Albion and Pope, *Sea Lanes in Wartime*, p. 95.

311   "O-grab-me": Hickey, *The War of 1812*, p. 21.

311   "a season of uncommon": Quoted in Cunningham, *The Process of Government Under Jefferson*, pp. 310–14.

311   "Go, wretch": Bryant quoted in Lippincott, *Early Philadelphia*, p. 138.

311   "arbitrary powers": Hickey, *The War of 1812*, p. 21.

312   "special permission" and the quotes that follow: Albert Gallatin to TJ, July 19, 1808, TJ to Albert Gallatin, August 11, 1808, TJ to Albert Gallatin, November 13, 1808, and TJ to Levi Lincoln, November 13, 1808, all quoted in Adams, HUSJ, pp. 1104–7.

312   "the United States have preferred": Napoleon quoted in ibid., p. 22.

312   "The late Jeffersonian": Hickey, *The War of 1812*, p. 21.

313   "[I]f it were possible": Lord Canning to William Pinkney, September 23, 1808, ASP, Foreign Relations, vol. 3, pp. 231–32.

313   An estimated ten thousand: *National Intelligencer*, March 5, 1809.

314   "the sovereign people": Margaret Bayard Smith to Susan B Smith, March 1809, in *The First Forty Years of Washington Society in the Family Letters of Margaret Bayard Smith*, p. 58.

314   "dressed in a full suit": Brant, *James Madison: The President, 1809–1812*, p. 13.

314   "but a withered": James Madison online biography at http://www.whitehouse.gov/history/presidents/jm4.html.

314   "extremely pale": Margaret Bayard Smith to Susan B. Smith, March 1809, in *The First Forty Years of Washington Society*, p. 58.

314   "could not be heard": John Quincy Adams, *Memoirs*, March 4, 1809, entry.

314   "the most brilliant": Quoted in Brant, *James Madison: The President, 1809–1812*, p. 13.

314   "The crowd": John Quincy Adams, *Memoirs*, March 4, 1809, entry.

314   "from this situation" . . . and the quotes that follow: Margaret Bayard Smith to Susan B. Smith, March 1809, in *The First Forty Years of Washington Society*, pp. 58–64.

315   "Nature intended": TJ to du Pont de Nemours, March 2, 1809, WTJ, XII:259.

315   "Mr. Madison is": Beaujour to Champagny, January 25, 1809, quoted in Brant, *James Madison: The President, 1809–1812*, p. 20.

316   "mere whipping": William Crawford quoted in Brown, *The Republic in Peril: 1812*, p. 48.

316   "a loss of": *Annals*, 1808–09, p. 556, quoted in Adams, HUSJ, p. 1185.

316   deploy "all the frigates": Quoted in Symonds, *Navalists and Anti-Navalists*, pp. 137–44.

316   "the Republican cause": Adams, *The Life of Albert Gallatin*, p. 387.

316   to "defend the gunboats": *Annals*, 1808–09, p. 1185.

317   "You may rest assured": William Bainbridge to D. Porter quoted in McKee, *A Gentlemanly and Honorable Profession*, p. 9.

317   After an eight-day passage: Henry Gilliam to William Jones, September 23, 1809,

"Letters of Henry Gilliam, 1809–1817," *Georgia Historical Quarterly* 38 (March 1954): 56–66.

317 "as fast a sailing Ship": Bainbridge quoted in Long, *Ready to Hazard: A Biography of Commodore William Bainbridge, 1774–1833*, p. 116.

317 "a most furious": Henry Gilliam to William Jones, December 29, 1809, "Letters of Henry Gilliam, 1809–1817," p. 52.

318 "I am growing old": William Bainbridge to David Porter, January 29, 1810, from USS *President* off Charlestown, SC, NYHS.

318 "he would never surrender": Henry Gilliam to William Jones, July 28, 1809, "Letters of Henry Gilliam, 1809–1817," p. 49.

318 "You, like every other": Hamilton quoted in Commodore John Rodgers to Captain Isaac Hull, June 19, 1810, NW1812 I:39–40.

319 "you may expect": Henry Gilliam to William Jones, June 25, 1810; "Letters of Henry Gilliam, 1809–1817," p. 54.

319 "ten waggon loads": Quoted in Martin, *A Most Fortunate Ship: A Narrative History of Old Ironsides*, p. 91.

319 "bunches of grapes": Ibid.

319 "While we can procrastinate": *Annals*, 1808–09, p. 657, quoted in Adams, HUSJ, p. 1187.

319 the nation's registered tonnage: ASP, Commerce and Navigation, vol. 1, p. 897.

320 "I will only": Albert Gallatin to. . . . Montgomery, July 27, 1809, quoted in HUSM, p. 79.

320 "the late confiscations": Quoted in ibid., p. 205.

321 "In North America": *The Naval Chronicle: The Contemporary Record of the Royal Navy at War*, vol. V: 1811–1815, p. 7.

321 "although her appearance" . . . and the quotes that follow: Commodore John Rodgers to Secretary of the Navy Paul Hamilton, May 23, 1811, NW1812 I:44–49.

323 Secretary Hamilton's response: Secretary of the Navy Paul Hamilton to Commodore John Rodgers, May 28, 1811, NW1812 I:49–50.

323 One stated that the action: Testimony of William Burket, Halifax, June 22, 1811, in *The Naval Chronicle*, vol. V, pp. 31–35. See also *London Courier* reprinted in *Niles' Register*, I:39, and *London Gazette* reprinted in *Niles' Register*, I:38.

324 "Will any man": *Niles' Register*, I:38 (emphasis in the original). This quotation corrects an erroneously interposed "or" and "to" in the original.

324 "Never did the American Congress": Quoted in Hickey, *The War of 1812*, p. 29.

324 "war on our lawful commerce": ASP, Foreign Relations, vol. 1, pp. 78–80.

324 "the practice of forcing": Adams, HUSM, p. 388.

324 "Do not let us": Quoted in Hickey, *The War of 1812*, p. 32.

325 "We must now oppose": Quoted in Adams, HUSM, p. 393.

325 "If we submit": Quoted in Hickey, *The War of 1812*, p. 26.

325 "We shall drive": Quoted in Adams, HUSM, p. 392.

325 a resolution was passed: Hickey, *The War of 1812*, p. 33.

325 who asked the House: Editorial note, NW1812 I:50–52.

325 Holding the floor . . . and the discussion that follows: *Annals*, House of Representatives, 12th Congr., 1st Sess., pp. 803–25, 871–72.

326 "If you had a field": Josiah Quincy quoted in Hickey, *The War of 1812*, p. 34.

326 "a class of society": Quoted in Symonds, *Navalists and Anti-Navalists*, p. 156.

326 The anti-navalists' argument: See *Annals*, House of Representatives, 12th Congr., 1st Sess., pp. 825–26.

326 a war mobilization would require: ASP, Finance, vol. 2, pp. 523–24.

326 Cheves's naval program: Secretary of the Navy Hamilton to Langdon Cheves, Chairman of Naval Committee, House of Representatives, December 3, 1811, NW1812 I:53–56.

327 Freight costs leapt: Hickey, *The War of 1812*, p. 40.

327   "France has done nothing": President James Madison to TJ, May 25, 1812, *Madison: Writings*, ed. Rakove, p. 684.

327   "Go to war": Quoted in Adams, HUSM, p. 440.

327   "It is a war": Congressman Randolph's anti-war speech, Friday, May 29, 1812, quoted in *Niles' Register*.

328   "this wild spirit of war": "Providence Resolutions," April 7, 1812, NW1812 I:69.

328   "It is evident": *Boston Centinel* quoted in *Niles' Register*, May 30, 1812, NW1812 II: 207.

328   "to attack": Dudley, *Splintering the Wooden Wall: The British Blockade of the United States, 1812–1815*, pp. 64–65.

329   a "series of acts": President James Madison, "War Message to Congress," June 1, 1812, in *Writings*, ed. Rakove, pp. 685–92.

330   "in a manner worthy": Richard Rush to Benjamin Rush, June 20, 1812, in Adams, HUSM, p. 452.

331   "Many nations": Ibid., p. 439.

331   "it had become impossible": JM to John Nicholas. April 2, 1813, in *Writings*, ed. Rakove, pp. 696–97.

331   The army had seven thousand: Brown, *Republic in Peril*, pp. 102–3.

331   America's seagoing navy: NW1812 I:179–82, See also Dudley, *Splintering the Wooden Wall*, pp. 38–40.

332   "I lament": JA to TJ, June 28, 1812, in Cappon, ed., *The Adams-Jefferson Letters*, II:308–10.

332   "the proud preeminence": *Evening Star* (London), reprinted in New York *National Advocate*, December 16, 1812.

333   "infinite regret and mortification": Bainbridge quoted in Long, *Ready to Hazard*, p. 130.

333   "It is victories": Charles Stewart to New York *Courier and Enquirer*, October 10, 1845, reprinted in *United States Nautical Magazine* (November 1845). Stewart's aging memory mistook the chronology; he recalled the meeting as occurring on June 21, after the declaration of war. See Brant, *James Madison, Commander-in-Chief, 1812–1836*, pp. 38–39.

333   "will enable our little navy": Secretary Hamilton to Captain John Rodgers, May 21, 1812, NW1812 I:118–19.

333   Rodgers, apologizing: Captain John Rodgers to Secretary Hamilton, June 3, 1812, NW1812 I:119–22.

333   Decatur proposed: Captain Stephen Decatur to Secretary Hamilton, June 8, 1812, NW1812 I:122–24.

334   Disagreements within Madison's cabinet: See Brant, *James Madison, Commander-in-Chief*, p. 37.

334   "to cripple & reduce": Captain John Rodgers to Secretary Hamilton, June 19, 1812, NW1812 I:138 (emphasis in original).

335   "ought to have been sent": Brant, *James Madison, Commander-in-Chief*, p. 37.

335   "afford to our returning commerce": Secretary Hamilton to Captain Rodgers, June 22, 1812, NW1812 I:148–49.

335   sighted a "large Sail": Captain John Rodgers' Journal, USS *President*, June 23, 1812, NW1812 I:154–57.

335   At eleven, the *President* cleared: Ibid.

336   The *President* having gradually closed: "An account of the proceedings of his majesty's ship *Belvidera*, Richard Byron, Esq. captain, 23d day of June, 1812," in the appendices of William James, *Naval Occurrences of the War of 1812: A Full and Correct Account of the Naval War Between Great Britain and the United States of America, 1812–1815*.

336   But at 4:30 p.m.: Captain John Rodgers' Journal, June 23, 1812, NW1812 I:154–57.

336   The wounded Rodgers: Ibid.

336   At sundown: "An account of the proceedings of his majesty's ship *Belvidera*," in James, *Naval Occurrences of the War of 1812*, appendices.

337   Tingey . . . told the Navy Office: Commodore Thomas Tingey to Secretary Hamilton, July 9, 1812, NW1812 I:188–89.

337   "rather short and thick-set": Drake, *Historic Mansions*, p. 31.

337   "bottom better": Martin, *A Most Fortunate Ship: A Narrative History of Old Ironsides*, pp. 99–101.

338   From the moment the new hands: Smith, *Naval Scenes in the Last War*, pp. 22–23.

338   "[T]he Crew you will readily": Captain Isaac Hull to Secretary Hamilton, July 2, 1812, NW1812 I:160–61.

338   "use the utmost dispatch": Secretary Hamilton to Hull, June 18, 1812, NW1812 I:135–36.

338   "you will be guided": Quoted in Martin, *A Most Fortunate Ship*, pp. 103–4.

338   "to stand very well": Ibid., p. 104.

339   "apparently Ships of War": Captain Isaac Hull to Secretary Hamilton, July 21, 1812, NW1812 I:161.

339   At 10:00 p.m., Hull judged: Ibid., I:161.

339   "clustered around him": Smith, *Naval Scenes in the Last War*, p. 25.

339   "every man on board": Evans, "Journal Kept on Board the United States Frigate *Constitution*, 1812," *Pennsylvania Magazine of History and Biography* 19 (1895), No. 1, p. 154.

339   He was assigned: Smith, *Naval Scenes in the Last War*, p. 25.

340   The *Constitution* wallowed: Captain Isaac Hull to Secretary Hamilton, July 21, 1812, NW1812, I:162.

340   "entirely becalmed": Morris, *Autobiography*, p. 52.

341   "I stood within": Smith, *Naval Scenes in the Last War*, p. 26.

341   "came up very fast": Captain Isaac Hull to Secretary Hamilton, July 21, 1812, NW1812, I:162.

341   "it was supposed": Morris, *Autobiography*, p. 52.

341   an "inexpressible anxiety": Evans, "Journal Kept on Board the United States Frigate *Constitution*, 1812," No. 1, p. 156.

341   "pregnant with": Henry Gilliam to William Jones, September 7, 1812, "Letters of Henry Gilliam, 1809–1817," *Georgia Historical Quarterly* 38 (March 1954): 60.

341   "we resolved to save": Smith, *Naval Scenes in The Last War*, pp. 26–27.

342   "all the spare rigging": Ibid., p. 27.

342   "we began to gain": Captain Isaac Hull to Secretary Hamilton, July 21, 1812, NW1812, I:162.

342   "to enliven our men": Morris, *Autobiography*, p. 53.

342   fell into "the midst of the group": Evans, "Journal Kept on Board the United States Frigate *Constitution*, 1812," No. 1, p. 154n.

342   suspended "to the spars": Morris, *Autobiography*, p. 53.

343   the men worked the chain pumps: Evans, "Journal Kept on Board the United States Frigate *Constitution*, 1812," No. 1, p. 154.

343   This raised the *Constitution*: Captain Isaac Hull to Secretary Hamilton, July 21, 1812, NW1812 I:163.

343   the officers and seamen: Martin, *A Most Fortunate Ship*, p. 108.

343   *Constitution* and her pursuers: Captain Isaac Hull to Secretary Hamilton, July 21, 1812, NW1812 I:163.

343   "tolerably steady": Morris, *Autobiography*, p. 53.

344   "Our hopes began": Ibid., p. 54.

344   the handling of the American frigate: Master Commandant Oliver Perry to Secretary Hamilton, July 26, 1812, NW1812 I:200.

344   "the advantages to be": Morris, *Autobiography*, p. 55.

344   "very romantic": Evans, "Journal Kept on Board the United States Frigate *Constitution*, 1812," No. 1, p. 158.

345   to "work night and day": Captain Isaac Hull to Secretary Hamilton, July 28, 1812, NW1812 I:206–7.

345   Hull went ashore: Evans, "Journal Kept on Board the United States Frigate *Constitution*, 1812," No. 1, p. 159.

345   "Captain Hull": *Niles' Register*, vol. 2, p. 381.

345   "plenty of sermons": Evans, "Journal Kept on Board the United States Frigate *Constitution*, 1812," No. 1, p. 161.

346   "Should I proceed": Captain Isaac Hull to Secretary Hamilton, July 28, 1812, NW1812 I:206–7.

346   he took some spare moments: McKee, *A Gentlemanly and Honorable Profession*, p. 471.

346   "hawled so far": Captain Isaac Hull to Secretary Hamilton, August 2, 1812, NW1812 I:207–9.

347   "flocking up like pigeons": Smith, *Naval Scenes in the Last War*, p. 30.

348   "Not The Little Belt": Ibid., p. 31.

348   Dacres had written out: "Correct copy of Captain Dacres' challenge, on the register of the brig *John Adams*, arrived at New York," in Palmer, *Victories of Hull, Jones, Decatur, Bainbridge* (Philadelphia, 1813), NYHS.

348   "offended with them": *Niles' Register*, vol. 3, p. 31.

349   Most of the balls: Smith, *Naval Scenes of the Last War*, p. 31.

349   "we paid very little attention": Henry Gilliam to William Jones, September 7, 1812, "Letters of Henry Gilliam, 1809–1817," p. 60.

349   "Every man stood": Smith, *Naval Scenes of the Last War*, p. 31.

349   First Lieutenant Morris asked: *Niles' Register*, vol. 3, p. 159.

349   "a very heavy fire": Captain Isaac Hull to Secretary of the Navy Hamilton, August 28, 1812, NW1812 I:231–33.

349   "shook from stem to stern": Smith, *Naval Scenes of the Last War*, p. 32.

350   "hanging in great confusion": Ibid.

350   "By God": *Niles' Register*, vol. 3, p. 159.

350   An Irish seaman: Smith, *Naval Scenes of the Last War*, p. 33.

350   As one of *Guerrière*'s 18-pounders: Martin, *A Most Fortunate Ship*, p. 117.

350   "a tremendous explosion": "Octogenarian" [an American prisoner aboard the *Guerrière*]. This account was originally written in a letter to the *New York Evening Post*, December 3, 1868; reprinted as "Reminiscences of the Last War with England," *Historical Magazine* (January 1870): 31–33. Moses Smith in *Naval Scenes of the Last War*, p. 33, identifies "Octogenarian" as Benjamin Hodges.

351   "One might see": Smith, *Naval Scenes of the Last War*, p. 33.

351   to "pass some turns": Morris, *Autobiography*, p. 56.

352   "in the trough of the sea": Extract from the logbook of a British officer aboard the *Guerrière* during the action with the *Constitution*, in *Niles' Register*, vol. 2, p. 109.

352   "Commodore Hull's compliments": "Octogenarian," "Reminiscences of the Last War with England," p. 83.

352   fought "like tigers": Henry Gilliam to William Jones, September 7, 1812, "Letters of Henry Gilliam, 1809–1817," p. 60.

353   "immense mischief": Evans, "Journal Kept on Board the United States Frigate *Constitution*, 1812," No. 3, p. 374.

353   "pieces of skulls": Henry Gilliam to William Jones, September 7, 1812, "Letters of Henry Gilliam, 1809–1817," p. 61.

353   "to keep in the best position": Captain Isaac Hull to Secretary of the Navy Hamilton, August 28, 1812, NW1812 I:241.

353   a "hard set of butchers": Smith, *Naval Scenes of the Last War*, p. 35.

354   "Scarcely a word": Ibid., p. 36.

354   "The *Constitution* has captured": "Octogenarian," "Reminiscences of the Last War with England," p. 83.

355   "Sir, I am sorry to inform you": Captain James R. Dacres to Vice-Admiral Herbert Sawyer, Royal Navy, September 7, 1812, NW1812 I:243–45.

355   "H.M.'s ships of war": Forester, *The Age of Fighting Sail: The Story of the Naval War of 1812*, p. 19.

356   Wellington's forces in Portugal: See ibid., pp. 80–85.

356   "if it was not for the supplies": Sir David Milne to George Hume, April 9, 1812, "Letters Written During the War of 1812 by the British Naval Commander in American Waters (Admiral Sir David Milne)," *William and Mary College Quarterly Historical Magazine*, 2nd ser., 10(4) (October 1930): 286.

356   as "commander in chief": Forester, *The Age of Fighting Sail*, p. 78.

356   Sailing from Portsmouth, Dudley, *Splintering the Wooden Wall*, pp. 73–74.

356   Warren . . . had nearly forty years: Ibid., p. 69.

357   As his first official act: NW1812 I:236 (editor's note).

357   "that wretched disease": Commodore John Rodgers to Secretary of the Navy Hamilton, September 1, 1812, NW1812 I:264.

358   "We have been so completely": "Letter from a British officer at Halifax, Oct. 15, 1812, to *Naval Chronicle*," quoted in Hickey, *The War of 1812*, p. 93.

358   "swarming round": Ibid., pp. 96–97.

358   "Prizes are pouring into": *Niles' Register*, editorial, vol. 3, p. 14.

358   "with her masts fished": Martin, *A Most Fortunate Ship*, p. 127.

358   "a very foolish": Evans, "Journal Kept on Board the United States Frigate *Constitution*, 1812," No. 3, p. 385.

358   "In this action": Secretary of the Navy Hamilton to Captain Hull, September 9, 1812, NW1812 I:472–73.

359   "and if he was": Graham, et al., quoted in Brant, *James Madison: Commander-in-Chief*, p. 75.

359   "We have a Hull-up": Evans, "Journal Kept on Board the United States Frigate *Constitution*, 1812," September 6, 1812, entry, No. 3, p. 379.

359   "a mere matter": TJ to William Duane, August 4, 1812, TJP.

359   "to afford protection": Secretary of the Navy Hamilton to Commodore John Rodgers, September 9, 1812, NW1812 I:470–72.

359   "the chaos that surrounded": Boston Navy Agent Amos Binney in an account published 1822, NW1812 I:466.

360   he authorized a cash warrant: Secretary of the Navy Hamilton to Navy Agent Amos Binney, September 8, 1812, NW1812 I:467.

360   At dawn on Sunday, October 25: NW1812 I:548–49 (editor's note).

361   "When the American officers": Carden quoted in Palmer, *Victories of Hull, Jones, Decatur, Bainbridge*, NYHS.

361   "black, glossy hats": Samuel Leech account in *Every Man Will Do His Duty: An Anthology of Firsthand Accounts from the Age of Nelson*, ed. King and Hattendorf, p. 305.

361   "very ungenerously ordered": Ibid., p. 306.

362   "I was not enabled": Captain John S. Carden, Royal Navy, to Secretary of the Admiralty John W. Croker, October 28, 1812, NW1812 I:549–52.

362   "Cease firing" . . . and the account that follows: Samuel Leech, *Thirty Years from Home* (1843), in *Every Man Will Do His Duty*, pp. 307–10.

364   "a perfect wreck": Captain John S. Carden, Royal Navy, to Secretary of the Admiralty John W. Croker, October 28, 1812, NW1812 I:551.

364   "To me it was": Samuel Leech account, *Every Man Will Do His Duty*, p. 311.

364   "Fragments of the dead": Unnamed officer quoted in Mackenzie, *Life of Stephen Decatur*, p. 176.

364   "covered with the bleeding forms" . . . and the quotes that follow: Samuel Leech account, *Every Man Will Do His Duty*, pp. 313–16.

365   "and his brains and blood": *Niles' Register*, vol. 3, p. 318.

365   an "undone man": Samuel Leech account, *Every Man Will Do His Duty*, p. 316.

365   The *United States* was barely scratched: Commodore Decatur to Secretary Hamilton, October 30, 1812, NW1812 I:552–53.

366   "One half of the satisfaction": Quoted in Mackenzie, *Life of Stephen Decatur*, p. 179n.

366   to compensate Carden: Palmer, *Victories of Hull, Jones, Decatur, Bainbridge*, NYHS.

366   "I must here & always": Carden, *A Curtail'd Memoir*, p. 265.

366   "I was always alive": Ibid.

366   The *Newport Mercury*: NW1812 I:615 (editor's note).

366   "This day has been": Perry quoted in De Kay, *Chronicles of the Frigate Macedonian, 1809–1922*, p. 98.

366   a "naval ball": *National Intelligencer*, December 10, 1812, quoted in *Niles' Register*, vol. 3, p. 238.

367   stepped "as usual": Mrs. B. H. Latrobe to Mrs. Juliana Miller, December 14, 1812, NYHS.

367   "amid the loud acclamations": *National Intelligencer*, December 10, 1812, quoted in *Niles' Register*, vol. 3, p. 238.

367   "This was rather over doing": Mrs. B. H. Latrobe to Mrs. Juliana Miller, December 14, 1812, NYHS.

367   "too much praise": ASP, Naval Affairs, vol. 1, p. 280.

367   "Our brilliant naval victories": Hickey, *The War of 1812*, p. 97.

367   a "grand naval dinner": Palmer, *Victories of Hull, Jones, Decatur, Bainbridge*, NYHS.

367   The four-story red brick building: Batterberry, *On the Town in New York*, pp. 39–40.

367   Five hundred guests: *Niles' Register*, vol. 3, p. 301, and Palmer, *Victories of Hull, Jones, Decatur, Bainbridge*, NYHS.

368   Each table had: Mackenzie, *Life of Stephen Decatur*, p. 185.

368   The band struck up: *Niles' Register*, vol. 3, pp. 301, 318.

368   "We came into New York": Shaw, *Short sketch of the life of Elijah Shaw, who served 21 years in the United States Navy* (1843), p. 46.

368   four hundred seamen: Mackenzie, *Life of Stephen Decatur*, p. 187.

368   "We found it difficult": Shaw, *Short sketch of the life of Elijah Shaw*, p. 46.

368   "orderly and decorous conduct" and "their admiration": Palmer, *Victories of Hull, Jones, Decatur, Bainbridge*, NYHS.

368   The toasts: Ibid., and Shaw, *Short sketch of the life of Elijah Shaw*, p. 46.

369   "It is more than merely": *The Times* (London) editorial reprinted in *Niles' Register*, vol. 3, pp. 271–72.

369   "What an unfortunate": Sir David Milne to George Hume, October 15, 1812, "Letters Written During the War of 1812," *William and Mary College Quarterly Historical Magazine*, 2nd ser., 10(4) (October 1930):287.

369   "should undoubtedly" *The Naval Chronicle*, vol. V, p. 104.

369   The August 13 capture: Gardner, ed., *The Naval War of 1812*, p. 45.

370   "produced a sensation": Canning quoted in Adams, HUSM, p. 624.

370   "The land spell": *The Times* quoted in ibid., p. 629.

370   "our trans-atlantic descendents": *Québec Mercury* quoted in *Niles' Register*, vol. 3, p. 157.

370   "It is a cruel": Hickey, *The War of 1812*, p. 98.

370   "disguised ships of the line": See Forester, *The Age of Fighting Sail*, pp. 134–36.

370   "Has any person": "R." to the Editor, October 13, 1812, *The Naval Chronicle*, vol. V, p. 114.

371   "Is not the term": Ibid., p. 125.

371   "Is it true": *The Times* quoted in Adams, HUSM, p. 629.

371   "When Carden the ship": Reprinted in Lossing, *The Pictorial Field Book of the War of 1812*, chap. VII.

371   "The size and force": "Oceanus" to the editor of the *Naval Chronicle*, December 1812, in *The Naval Chronicle*, vol. V, p. 115.

371   a "plan matured": *The Times* quoted in Hickey, *The War of 1812*, p. 98.

371   "In its defense": Adams, HUSM, p. 629.

371   a "war of conciliation": *The Times* quoted in ibid., p. 626.

372   "the arm which should": Canning's Speech, November 30, 1812, quoted in ibid., p. 627.

372   "a right hitherto": Lord Bathurst quoted in ibid., p. 631.

372   the Prince Regent published: "The Prince Regent's Declaration on the Causes of the American War," in *The Naval Chronicle*, vol. V, pp. 132–40.

372   to "punish the temerity": "Albion" to the *Naval Chronicle*, The Mariners' Museum, online at http://www.mariner.org/usnavy/

373   "Many of our crew": Smith, *Naval Scenes in the Last War*, p. 38.

373   A few replied: Evans, "Journal Kept on Board the United States Frigate *Constitution*, 1812," No. 3, p. 382.

373   "This was appealing": Smith, *Naval Scenes in the Last War*, p. 39.

373   Throughout September and most of October: William Bainbridge to William Jones, October 5, 1812, NW1812 I:510–12, and Martin, *A Most Fortunate Ship*, pp. 128–30.

374   "one of the finest Ships": William Bainbridge to William Jones, October 5, 1812, NW1812 I:510.

374   He offered John Rodgers: Ibid.

374   Jones recommended a cruise: William Jones to William Bainbridge, October 11, 1812, NW1812 I:512–15.

374   Carlton's book of charts: See McKee, *A Gentlemanly and Honorable Profession*, p. 197.

374   A six-week passage: See Long, *Ready to Hazard: A Biography of Commodore William Bainbridge*, pp. 142–66.

375   the "sacred pledge": Bainbridge quoted in ibid., pp. 142–66.

375   Two days later: Ibid.

375   With passengers and crew: Forester, *The Age of Fighting Sail*, pp. 116–17.

376   Shortly after one in the afternoon . . . and the account that follows: Journal of Commodore William Bainbridge, December 29, 1812, NW1812 I:640–44.

376   Early in the action: Lieutenant Henry D. Chads to Secretary of the Admiralty John W. Croker, December 31, 1812, NW1812 I:646–48.

376   *Constitution*'s wheel: *Niles' Register*, vol. 3, pp. 397–98.

376   Bainbridge was struck: Martin, *A Most Fortunate Ship*, pp. 132–34.

376   An 18-pounder ball: Long, *Ready to Hazard: A Biography of Commodore William Bainbridge*, pp. 142–66.

376   required Bainbridge to shout: Martin, *A Most Fortunate Ship*, p. 132.

376   With two wounds: Long, *Ready to Hazard*, pp. 142–66.

377   At 2:50 p.m., *Java*'s helm: Minutes of a court-martial assembled on board HMS *Gladiator*, at Portsmouth, April 23, 1813, to try the surviving officers and crew of the *Java*, in appendices, James, *Naval Occurrences of the War of 1812*.

377   "At 3 The Head": Journal of Commodore William Bainbridge, December 29, 1812, NW1812 I:641.

378   "But then over all the din": O'Brian, *The Fortune of War*, pp. 119–21.

379   "I put my finger in": Surgeon quoted in Long, *Ready to Hazard*, pp. 142–66.

379   "pouring in a tremendous": "Lieutenant Chads's journal," in James, *Naval Occurrences of the War of 1812*, appendices.

379   "a perfect wreck": Lieutenant Henry Chads's testimony, Minutes of court-martial assembled on board HMS *Gladiator* April 23, 1813, in ibid.

380   "Now was the time": O'Brian, *The Fortune of War*, pp. 123–24.

381   "The public will learn": *London Pilot*, March 20, 1813, reprinted in *Niles' Register*, May 8, 1813, vol. 4, p. 163.

381   "The subject is too painful": *The Naval Chronicle*, vol. V, pp. 150–51.

382   For the first time in years: See Forester, *The Age of Fighting Sail*, p. 128.

382   "destructive havoc": *The Naval Chronicle*, vol. V, p. 154.

382   "Are their rammers": Quoted in Forester, *The Age of Fighting Sail*, p. 130.

382   Others expressed concern: Reprinted in *Niles' Register*, March 27, 1813, vol. 4, p. 64.

382   "American seaman have been": Quoted in Forester, *The Age of Fighting Sail*, p. 130.

382   "The good discipline": Admiral Warren, "Standing Orders on the North American Station," NW1812 II:59.

382 daily "spit and polish": First Secretary of the Admiralty John W. Croker "To Admirals," March 23, 1813, NW1812 II:60 (footnote).

383 "the brutal horrors": Forester, *The Age of Fighting Sail*, p. 128.

383 the "mania of apathy": Ibid.

383 a "Secret & Confidential" order: First Secretary of the Admiralty John W. Croker to Station Commanders in Chief, July 10, 1813, NW1812 II:183–84.

383 officers derided them as "mules": Forester, *The Age of Fighting Sail*, p. 135.

384 a "most complete and vigorous": Lords Commissioners of the Admiralty to Admiral Sir John B. Warren, NW1812 I:633–34.

384 "We do not intend": First Lord of the Admiralty to Admiral Sir John B. Warren, March 26, 1813, NW1812 II:78–79.

384 Considering New England: Dudley, *Splintering the Wooden Wall*, pp. 79–90.

384 In truth, however: Ibid., pp. 60–62.

385 "the Swarms of Privateers": Admiral Warren to First Secretary of the Admiralty John W. Croker, December 29, 1812, NW1812 I:649–51.

385 "Ships from other important Services": First Secretary of the Admiralty John W. Croker to Admiral Sir John B. Warren, January 9, 1813, NW1812 II:14–15.

385 "a force much greater": First Secretary of the Admiralty John W. Croker to Admiral Sir John B. Warren, February 10, 1813, NW1812 II:16–19.

385 By February 1813, Warren did indeed: Forester, *The Age of Fighting Sail*, p. 132.

386 "All the prating": *Evening Star* (London), March editorial, quoted in *Niles' Register*, April 24, 1813, vol. 4, p. 136.

386 In rejecting the armistice: ASP, Naval Affairs, vol. 1, p. 280.

386 "I sincerely congratulate": TJ to JA, May 27, 1813, in Cappon, ed., *The Adams-Jefferson Letters*, II:323–24.

386 "That you were always": JA to TJ, June 11, 1813, in ibid., II:328.

387 a "splendid entertainment": *Niles' Register*, vol. 2, p. 217.

387 so "as to make the temperature": Mrs. B. H. Latrobe to Mrs. Juliana Miller, December 14, 1812, NYHS.

387 "We have no doubt": *Niles' Register*, vol. 2, p. 217.

387 One unpleasant detail: McKee, *A Gentlemanly and Honorable Profession*, pp. 9–12.

387 "about as fit for his place": Quoted in Hickey, *The War of 1812*, p. 90.

388 "As to exercise": McKee, *A Gentlemanly and Honorable Profession*, pp. 9–12.

388 "the corruption of self-interested": Secretary of the Navy Jones to Eleanor Jones, January 23, 1813, NW1812 II:34.

388 "We may have reason": Mrs. B. H. Latrobe to Mrs. Juliana Miller, December 14, 1812, NYHS.

388 Negotiating behind closed doors: Adams, HUSM, p. 650.

389 "to enter into any Negotiation": First Secretary of the Admiralty John W. Croker to Admiral Sir John B. Warren, May 17, 1813, NW1812 II:356.

389 Three days later: Captain Charles Stewart to Secretary of the Navy Jones, February 5, 1813, NW1812 II:311–12.

390 Admiral George Cockburn: Dudley, *Splintering the Wooden Wall*, p. 87.

390 "I am persuaded": Captain Charles Stewart to Secretary of the Navy Jones, April 4, 1813, NW1812 II:346.

390 "whenever they wash": Captain John Cassin to Secretary of the Navy Hamilton, August 25, 1812, NW1812 I:222–23.

390 "so weakly manned" and "I am getting out": Captain Charles Stewart to Secretary of the Navy Jones, March 17, 1813, NW1812 II:315.

391 Norfolk's civilians: *Niles' Register*, March 15, 1813, vol. 4, p. 119.

391 to "make the best use": Secretary of the Navy Jones to Captain Charles Stewart, April 8, 1813, NW1812 II:346.

391 "while a strong squadron": Secretary of the Navy Jones to Captain Charles Stewart, March 27, 1813, NW1812 II:317.

392   The Cape Henry Lighthouse: *Niles' Register,* vol. 3, p. 398, and Treasury Department notice, March 16, 1813, printed in ibid., vol. 4, p. 51.

392   "The marines being": *Norfolk Herald* reprinted in ibid., April 3, 1813, vol. 4, p. 87.

393   "Many fled": *Niles' Register,* May 8, 1813, vol. 4, p. 164.

393   A party of Royal Marines: Admiral Cockburn to Admiral Warren, May 3, 1813, NW1812 II:341–44; see also Sir David Milne to George Hume, January 2, 1814, "Letters Written During the War of 1812 by the British Naval Commander in American Waters (Admiral Sir David Milne)," p. 290.

394   "neither public property": Admiral Cockburn to Admiral Warren, May 6, 1813, NW1812 II:344–46.

394   "coming up to Norfolk": Captain Stewart to Secretary Jones, May 21, 1813, quoted in Dudley, *Splintering the Wooden Wall,* p. 92.

394   "What do you think": Sir David Milne to George Hume, January 2, 1814, "Letters Written During the War of 1812," p. 290.

395   At last, substantial numbers: See Wertenbaker, *Norfolk: Historic Southern Port,* pp. 121–24.

395   Stewart stationed seven gunboats: Captain Charles Stewart to Secretary of the Navy, May 13, 1813, NW1812 II:347.

395   "the utmost vigilance": Anonymous, "Reminiscence of the Last War," *United States Nautical Magazine* 2 (February 1846): 341–44.

395   "to effect a diversion": Lord Bathurst to Colonel Sir Thomas Sidney Beckwith, March 20, 1813, NW1812 II:325.

395   "a desperate Banditti": Colonel Sir Thomas Sidney Beckwith to Admiral Warren, July 5, 1813, NW1812 II:364.

396   a "heavy, galling fire": Captain John Cassin to Secretary Jones, June 21, 1813, NW1812 II:358.

396   "A brisk fire was kept": Anonymous, "Reminiscence of the Last War," p. 343.

396   The lead boat was the *Centipede:* Lossing, *The Pictorial Field Book of the War of 1812,* chap. 30.

397   The gun crews on the island: Captain John Cassin to Secretary Jones, June 23, 1813, ND1812 II:359.

397   Most of the British boats: *The Naval Chronicle,* vol. V, pp. 181–84.

397   "we despise the Yankees": Graves, "Worthless is the Laurel Steeped in Female Tears," *Journal of the War of 1812* (Winter 2002): 9.

398   "dressed in red": Ibid., p. 11.

398   "It is important": Quoted in ibid., pp. 12–13.

398   "Every horror": Napier quoted in Adams, HUSM, p. 812.

399   Eight Companies of New Jersey militia: *Niles' Register,* April 10, 1813, vol. 4, p. 101.

399   "Although invited": Master Commandant Jacob Lewis to Secretary of the Navy, May 23, 1813, NW1812 II:108–11.

399   "the preference which Seamen": Secretary of the Navy Jones to Senator Samuel Smith, June 17, 1813, NW1812 II:148–51.

399   Decatur planned to sortie: Commodore Decatur to Secretary Jones, March 10, 1813, NW1812 II:51.

399   In April and May: NW1812 II:134 (editor's note).

399   On Tuesday, May 18: Commodore Decatur to Secretary Jones, June 2, 1813, NW1812 II:135.

400   "As you run up": "A Chart of New York Harbour with the Soundings, Views of Landmarks, and Nautical Directions for the Use of Pilotage," May 19, 1779.

400   The squadron passed through: *Niles' Register,* June 5, 1813, vol. 4, p. 245.

400   "various information": Captain Robert Dudley Oliver to Admiral Warren, June 13, 1813, NW1812 II:137; Commodore Decatur to Secretary Jones, June 2, 1813, NW1812 II:135.

401   Captain Dudley Oliver: Captain Robert Dudley Oliver to Admiral Warren, June 13, 1813, NW1812 II:137.

401   Decatur took the *United States*: Mackenzie, *Life of Stephen Decatur*, p. 196.

401   Four frigates lay in Boston Harbor: *Niles' Register*, April 17, 1813, vol. 4, p. 118.

402   "has been so intollerably": Commodore John Rodgers to Secretary of the Navy Jones, March 8, 1813, NW1812 II:50.

402   "not a moment": Secretary Jones to Captain Samuel Evans, April 19, 1813, NW1812 II:101–2.

403   "In most climates": Napier quoted in Dudley, *Splintering the Wooden Wall*, p. 52.

403   "It is with great mortification": Captain Capel to Admiral Warren, May 11, 1813, NW1812 II:105.

404   "The ship is in better order": Augustus Ludlow to Charles Ludlow, May 28, 1813, in "The *Chesapeake* and Lieutenant Ludlow," *Magazine of American History* 25(4) (April 1891).

405   "does not intend": Ibid.

405   "All the fog": Broke quoted in Gleaves, *James Lawrence, Captain, United States Navy, Commander of the Chesapeake*, p. 177.

406   "Sir, As the *Chesapeake*": Captain Philip B. V. Broke to Captain James Lawrence (undated, probably May 31, 1813), NW1812 II:126–29.

409   "The frigate is plain in sight": James Lawrence to James Montaudevert, June 1, 1813, in Gleaves, *James Lawrence, Captain, United States Navy, Commander of the Chesapeake*, pp. 173–74.

410   In a custom borrowed: James, *Naval Occurrences of the War of 1812*, p. 115.

410   "Bear a hand": "Affidavit of Benjamin Trefethan," quoted in Gleaves, *James Lawrence*, p. 178.

410   Her sides were gleaming: Ibid.

410   "striving to catch": Thomas C. Haliburton to Admiral Sir George Broke-Middleton, July 1, 1864, in "The Arrival of the *Chesapeake* in Halifax in 1813," *American Neptune* 57 (1997): 161–65; see also *The Naval Chronicle*, vol. V, pp. 161–63.

410   "No sir. We have always": Broke quoted in Gleaves, *James Lawrence*, pp. 185–86.

411   Lawrence ordered the *Chesapeake*'s: Lieutenant George Budd to Secretary of the Navy Jones, June 15, 1813, NW1812 II:133–34.

411   "He certainly came down": Quoted in Gleaves, *James Lawrence*, p. 179.

411   At five forty-five: Lieutenant George Budd to Secretary of the Navy Jones, June 15, 1813, NW1812 II:133–34.

411   Lawrence shouted . . . and the account that follows: Gleaves, *James Lawrence*, pp. 187–196.

416   "the coils and folds of rope": Thomas C. Haliburton to Admiral Sir George Broke-Middleton, July 1, 1864, "The Arrival of the *Chesapeake* in Halifax in 1813," p. 165.

416   "Both Ships came out": Thomas Bladen Capel, "An Account of the *Chesapeake-Shannon* Action," June 6, 1813, NW1812 II:129–33.

416   "flew from pew to pew": Thomas C. Haliburton to Admiral Sir George Broke-Middleton, July 1, 1864, "The Arrival of the *Chesapeake* in Halifax in 1813," p. 161.

418   "We must have a Navy": JA to TJ, June 11, 1813, in Cappon, ed., *The Adams-Jefferson Letters*, II:328–29.

418   "We have met the enemy": Captain Oliver H. Perry to Major General William Henry Harrison, September 10, 1813, NW1812 II:553–54.

419   "Strong is my dislike": Napier quoted in Adams, HUSM, p. 813.

419   Commodore Rodgers and USS *President* returned: Commodore Rodgers to Secretary Jones, September 27, 1813, NW1812 II:251–53.

420   Jones congratulated Rodgers: Secretary Jones to Commodore Rodgers, October 4, 1813, NW1812 II:254–55.

420   On December 14, the *Congress*: Captain John Smith to Secretary Jones, December 14, 1813, NW1812, II:300–2.

421   "Here we are": Decatur quoted in De Kay, *The Battle of Stonington: Torpedoes, Submarines, and Rockets in the War of 1812*, p. 29.

421   "A desperate engagement": Quoted in ibid., p. 31.

421 "to assure the ladies": Quoted in ibid., p. 26.

421 "any person or persons": NW1812 II:160.

422 "every Physical operation": Fulton's Ordnance Experiments (editorial note), NW1812 II:111.

422 "[I]s war confined": Robert Fulton to Secretary of the Navy Hamilton, June 22, 1812, NW1812 I:146–47.

422 would "incur no expense": Robert Fulton to Secretary of the Navy Jones, April 27, 1813 (n), NW1812 II:111–12.

422 Jacob Lewis . . . was enthusiastic: Master Commandant Jacob Lewis to Secretary of the Navy Jones, June 20, 1813, and June 28, 1813, NW1812 II:113–14.

422 a floating mine or "powder machine": "Fulton's Torpedo" (editorial note), NW1812 II:354.

423 Admiral Cockburn . . . was nevertheless outraged: Rear Admiral George Cockburn to Admiral Sir John B. Warren, June 16, 1813, NW1812 II:355–56.

423 "Our blockading ships": "An American Infernal Machine," *The Naval Chronicle*, vol. V, pp. 170–71.

423 "great Quantity of Combustibles": Master Commandant Jacob Lewis to Secretary of the Navy Jones, June 28, 1813, NW1812 II:161.

423 Hardy, perhaps suspecting: Captain Hardy to Admiral Warren, June 26, 1813, NW1812 II:162–64.

423 "a Diabolical and Cowardly": Admiral Warren to First Secretary of the Admiralty John W. Croker, July 22, 1813, NW1812 II:162–64.

423 "held in detestation": *The Naval Chronicle*, vol. V, pp. 168–69.

423 Orders went out: Admiral Sir John B. Warren, General Order No. 87, July 19, 1813, NW1812 II:164.

423 Two months later: Dudley, *Splintering the Wooden Wall*, p. 106.

424 "the same state of degradation": President James Madison to Commissary General of Prisoners John Mason, September 23, 1813, NW1812 II:248.

424 "If we fall in": Stackpoole quoted in Mackenzie, *Life of Stephen Decatur*, p. 205.

424 "The son descried": Decatur quoted in ibid., p. 206.

425 Month after month: Adams, HUSM, pp. 813–14.

425 from "giving or receiving": Dudley, *Splintering the Wooden Wall*, p. 96.

425 Decatur . . . wrote to Hardy: Commodore Decatur to Sir Thomas M. Hardy, January 17, 1814, in James, *Naval Occurrences of the War of 1812*, appendices.

426 Hardy replied the following day: Sir T. M. Hardy to Commodore Decatur, January 18, 1814, in ibid.

426 "the guarantee against recapture": Commodore Decatur to Sir Thomas M. Hardy, January 19, 1814, in ibid.

427 "We are here": Captain Robert Barrie to Eliza Clayton, March 14, 1814, NW1812 III:18–19.

427 "Jonathan's privateers": Hickey, *The War of 1812*, p. 97, and *The Naval Chronicle*, vol. V, p. 237.

427 Privateers swarmed: Dudley, *Splintering the Wooden Wall*, p. 107.

427 "Surely the British navy": Forester, *The Age of Fighting Sail*, p. 90.

428 "What I have written": Wellington quoted in Dudley, *Splintering the Wooden Wall*, p. 107.

428 "Peace Needed": *The Naval Chronicle*, vol. V, pp. 231–32.

428 In Parliament, members: Adams, HUSM, pp. 1208–13 and 632.

429 between 1812 and 1814, both imports and exports: *Historical Statistics of the United States, Colonial Times to 1970*, U.S. Census Bureau, Part 2, 1776, series Q 518–23, "Value of Waterborne Imports and Exports," p. 716. In 1812: imports, $77 million, exports, $39 million, in 1814: imports, $13 million, exports, $7 million.

430 "Though France has been": JA to TJ, July 16, 1814, in Cappon, ed., *The Adams-Jefferson Letters*, II:434–39.

430   "it has been decided": Secretary of State James Monroe to Peace Commissioners, June 27, 1814, ASP, Foreign Affairs, vol. 3, p. 704.

430   The Admiralty had demanded: First Lord of the Admiralty Viscount Robert Saunders Dundas Melville to Admiral Warren, March 26, 1813, NW1812 II:78–79.

430   "exceeds very much": First Secretary of the Admiralty John W. Croker to Admiral Warren, March 20, 1813, NW1812 II:75–77.

430   "materially crippled": Admiral Warren to First Secretary of the Admiralty John W. Croker, November 13, 1813, NW1812 II:284.

430   "the good Fortune": Admiral Warren to Captain Robert Barrie, January 19, 1814, NW1812 III:16.

431   "The rapidity with which": Admiral Warren to First Secretary of the Admiralty John W. Croker, December 30, 1813, NW1812 II:307–8.

431   The Admiralty sent orders: Forester, *The Age of Fighting Sail*, p. 201.

431   to "let havock": Ibid., p. 194.

431   "They are struck": Adams, HUSM, p. 1187.

432   "I am of opinion": "C.H." to the editor of the *Naval Chronicle*, July 16, 1814, *The Naval Chronicle*, vol. V, pp. 232–33.

432   "In such countries": Wellington quoted in Forester, *The Age of Fighting Sail*, p. 195.

432   "to act with the utmost": Vice-Admiral Cochrane to Rear-Admiral Cockburn, April 24, 1814, in Dudley, *Splintering the Wooden Wall*, p. 117.

432   In February 1814, Cockburn arrived: Ibid., pp. 120–21.

433   The entire region was critically: "The Chesapeake Bay Theater, January 1814–May 1815," NW1812 III:1–3.

433   the local American commander: "Naval Preparations for the Defense of Washington," NW1812 III:198.

434   "Never did men": Lieutenant George Gleig quoted in Boileau, *Half-Hearted Enemies: Nova Scotia, New England and the War of 1812*, p. 113.

434   the "Swiftness with which": Rear-Admiral Cockburn to Vice-Admiral Cochrane, August 27, 1814, NW1812 III:220–22.

434   with "the most marked": Captain Joshua Barney, Flotilla Service, to Secretary of the Navy Jones, August 29, 1814, NW1812 III:207.

435   "so that the rascals": Adams, HUSM, p. 1015.

435   "Oh! My Country!": Captain's Clerk Mordecai Booth to Commodore Thomas Tingey, August 24, 1814, NW1812 III:208–14.

435   and informed Tingey: Commodore Thomas Tingey to Secretary of the Navy Jones, October 18, 1814, NW1812 III:318–20.

435   "Chips, Timber": Secretary of the Navy Jones to Congressman Richard M. Johnson, October 3, 1814, NW1812 III:315.

436   The town council acceded: The Alexandria Common Council's answer, in appendices, James, *Naval Occurrences of the War of 1812*.

437   The fleet sailed down the bay: Dudley, *Splintering the Wooden Wall*, pp. 123–24.

437   "the Vandalism": TJ to Marie-Joseph-Paul-Yves Roch Gilbert du Motier, Marquis de Lafayette, February 14, 1815, with Postscript dated February 26, TJP.

437   "This will be worth": TJ to James Monroe, January 1, 1815, WTJ, VI:400.

438   "in the most precipitate": Quoted in Hickey, *The War of 1812*, p. 193.

438   "A Treaty concluded": "The American to the British Ministers," August 24, 1814, ASP, Foreign Relations, vol. 3, pp. 711–13.

439   "a sense of horror": *Morning Chronicle* quoted in Hickey, *The War of 1812*, p. 295.

439   a caucus of Liverpool merchants: Dudley, *Splintering the Wooden Wall*, pp. 138–42.

439   Maritime insurance rates: *The Naval Chronicle* quoted in Hickey, *The War of 1812*, p. 218.

439   "all the ports": *Niles' Register*, January 17, 1815.

440   Liverpool was aggravated: Adams, HUSM, p. 1201, and *The War of 1812*, Hickey, p. 293.

440   the Americans rejected: "The American to the British Ministers," October 24, 1814, ASP, Foreign Relations, vol. 3, p. 725.

440   "will probably now be": Liverpool to Castlereagh, October 28, 1814, quoted in Adams, HUSM, p. 1209.

441   "In regard to your present": Lord Wellington to Castlereagh, November 9, 1814, quoted in ibid., pp. 1211–12.

441   "the largest and most important": John Quincy Adams to Louisa Catherine Adams, January 13, 1815, in Ford, ed., *Writings of John Quincy Adams*, vol. 5, p. 267.

443   "but notwithstanding all that": Hollins, "Autobiography of Commodore George Nicholas Hollins," *Maryland Historical Magazine* 34 (September 1939): 229.

444   "Carry on!": Quoted in MacKenzie, *Life of Stephen Decatur*, p. 218.

444   The body had been: Hollins, "Autobiography of Commodore George Nicholas Hollins," p. 230.

446   The American forces were commanded: Horseman, *The War of 1812*, p. 244.

446   "The vibration seemed": Quoted in de Grummond, *The Baratarians and the Battle of New Orleans*, p. 136.

447   "We, who only seven weeks ago": Gleig, *Campaigns of the British Army*, p. 357.

448   "We can serve God": "Octogenarian," "Reminiscences of the Last War with England," *Historical Magazine* (January 1870): 31–32.

448   "fine smart breeze": Journal of Acting Chaplain Assheton Humphreys in Martin, *The U.S.S. Constitution's Finest Fight, 1815*, pp. 5, 27.

448   They were the British warships: American Minutes of the action, in appendices of James, *Naval Occurrences of the War of 1812*.

448   "Set every rag in chase": Assheton Humphreys's Journal in Martin, *The U.S.S. Constitution's Finest Fight, 1815*, p. 28.

449   "a perfect slaughter house": Ibid., p. 30.

449   Stewart ordered the topsails: American Minutes of the action in James, *Naval Occurrences of the War of 1812*, appendices.

450   "The mizzenmast for several feet": Pardon Mawney Whipple, "Letters from Old Ironsides, 1813–1815," quoted in Martin, *The U.S.S. Constitution's Finest Fight, 1815*, p. 62.

450   Out of a crew of 159: Captain Stewart to the Secretary of the Navy, May 1815, appendices of James, *Naval Occurrences of the War of 1812*.

450   The *Constitution*'s damages: Assheton Humphreys's Journal in Martin, *The U.S.S. Constitution's Finest Fight, 1815*, p. 30.

451   "We have retired": *The Times* quoted in Dudley, *Splintering the Wooden Wall*, p. 4.

451   "the greatest Bull": *Morning Chronicle* quoted in Hickey, *The War of 1812*, p. 297.

451   "[I]t must be allowed": Letter from "Albion" to the editor of the *Naval Chronicle*, February 6, 1815, *The Naval Chronicle*, vol. V, pp. 233–34.

452   "I most sincerely": Sir David Milne to George Hume, May 31, 1815, "Letters Written During the War of 1812," p. 296.

452   "Thus has ended": Letter from "Albion" to the editor of the *Naval Chronicle*, March 12, 1815, *The Naval Chronicle*, vol. V, pp. 281–82.

EPILOGUE

453   "waged with the success": Adams, HUSM, p. 1238.

454   "It is impossible to describe": *American Mercury* quoted in Palmer, "Peace Upon Honorable Terms," *Early American Review* 4(1) (Winter–Spring 2002).

454   Cotton and tea fell: *Historical Statistics of the United States, Colonial Times to 1970*, U.S. Department of Commerce, Bureau of the Census, Part 2, 1976, series Q 506–17, "Net Tonnage Capacity of Vessels Entered and Cleared," p. 760; series Q 518–23, "Value of Waterborne Imports and Exports of Merchandise," p. 761.

454   the "whole population": Palmer, "Peace Upon Honorable Terms: The United States

Ratification of the Treaty of Ghent," *Early American Review* 4(1) (Winter–Spring 2002).

454   During the treaty deliberations: Ibid.

454   "The treaty must" and "*We have triumphed*": Hickey, *The War of 1812*, pp. 298–99.

455   "Have we gained nothing": *Annals*, 14th Congr., 1st Sess., p. 783.

455   "in fact but an armistice": TJ to William H. Crawford, February 14, 1815, with Postscript dated February 26, in TJP.

455   "would have been fighting": Calhoun quoted in Palmer, "Peace Upon Honorable Terms: The United States Ratification of the Treaty of Ghent."

455   "Disappointment!": Hickey, *The War of 1812*, p. 308.

457   "To our country!": American National Biography Online, www.anb.org.

457   "a certain degree of preparation": See Symonds, *Navalists and Anti-Navalists*, pp. 198–200.

457   "Frigates and seventy fours": TJ to James Monroe, January 1, 1815, in WTJ, VI:400.

458   "That man must be blind": *Annals*, 14th Congr., 1st Sess., 1815–16, p. 787.

458   "Anti-American sentiment": Churchill, *A History of the English-Speaking People*, vol. 3: *The Age of Revolution*, p. 324.

459   "we cannot keep Canada": Sir David Milne to George Hume, January 29, 1817, "Letters Written During the War of 1812," p. 297.

459   "Perhaps at that moment": Adams, HUSM, p. 1219.

460   James had happened to be passing: Introduction to James, *Naval Occurrences of the War of 1812*.

462   Roosevelt began researching: McCullough, *Mornings on Horseback*, pp. 204–8, 232–35.

462   "finished his naval history": Owen Wister quoted in Brands, *TR: The Last Romantic*, p. 117.

463   "I have plenty of information": Letter quoted in ibid.

465   "We ask for a great navy": TR quoted in ibid., pp. 316–17.

465   "During the last two days": TR to Alfred Thayer Mahan, May 12, 1890, in Auchincloss, ed., *Theodore Roosevelt: Letters and Speeches*, pp. 45–46.

465   Roosevelt wrote: TR review of Mahan book in *Atlantic Monthly* (October 1890) in Brands, *TR: The Last Romantic*, pp. 237–38.

466   "by preference Germany": Brands, *TR: The Last Romantic*, pp. 322–23.

466   Roosevelt cabled: TR, "Orders to the Asiatic Squadron," to George Dewey, February 25, 1898, in Auchincloss, ed., *Theodore Roosevelt: Letters and Speeches*, p. 141.

466   "There is a homely" . . . and the quotes that follow: Morris, *Theodore Rex*, pp. 215–16.

466   "There is no danger": Brands, *TR: The Last Romantic*, p. 466.

467   "In a dozen years": TR to Cecil Spring-Rice, June 16, 1905, in Auchincloss, ed., *Theodore Roosevelt: Letters and Speeches*, p. 391.

467   "There was no further difficulty": Brands, *TR: The Last Romantic*, p. 612.

467   "Did you ever": Ibid., p. 613.

467   "the lessons which should": TR at the John Paul Jones ceremony, U.S. Naval Academy, Annapolis, MD, April 1907.

NOTES TO CHRONOLOGY OF LATER EVENTS

469   Barron, from Norfolk, writes . . . and the account that follows: See "Memorandum of Samuel Hambleton," in MacKenzie, *Life of Stephen Decatur*, appendix, and Williamson, "The Court of Last Resort," *American History* 33(6) (February 1999):34.

470   "Oh what an agonizing scene": Quoted in Long, *Ready to Hazard*, pp. 227–46.

471   "I have racked": TJ to JA, November 1, 1822, in Cappon, ed., *The Adams-Jefferson Letters*, pp. 584–85.

471   This traditional sign of mourning: Online at "Sea Flags," http://mysite.verizon .net/vzeohzt4/Seaflags/customs/customs.html.

472   "She spoke his talents": Joshua Humphreys to Secretary of the Navy William Jones, August 20, 1827, Joshua Humphreys Papers, PHS.

472   "Had our frigates been": Joshua Humphreys to Secretary of the Navy William Jones, August 20, 1827, Joshua Humphreys Papers, PHS.

477   "Oh, Lord!" TR quoted in Brands, *TR: The Last Romantic*, p. 321.

477   "I earnestly hope": TR to John Hay, September 21, 1897, in Auchincloss, ed., *Theodore Roosevelt: Letters and Speeches*, p. 119.

478   "I have consistently": TR to William Sturgis Bigelow, March 29, 1898, in ibid., pp. 142–44.

478   "a doctrine about which": TR to Cecil Spring-Rice, July 3, 1901, in ibid., pp. 230–33.

478   Details on TR, 1900–03: See Morris, *Theodore Rex*, pp. 127–28, 205, 207.

478   "used as a target": Martin, *A Most Fortunate Ship*, p. 298.

479   "I think a cruise": Quoted in Brands, *TR: The Last Romantic*, p. 609.

479   "There was one mistake": Grey quoted in Massie, *Castles of Steel: Britain, Germany and the Winning of the Great War at Sea*, p. 694.

481   "We really must talk": Quoted in Martin, *A Most Fortunate Ship*, p. 335.

BIBLIOGRAPHY

NAVAL RECORDS, GOVERNMENT DOCUMENTS, JOURNALS, CONTEMPORARY ACCOUNTS

Adams, John. *The Works of John Adams*, ed. C. F. Adams. 10 vols. Boston, 1950–56.

Adams, John Quincy. *Memoirs*, ed. Charles Francis Adams. Philadelphia, 1874.

———. *Writings of John Quincy Adams*, ed., Worthington Chauncey Ford. 3 vols. New York: The Macmillan Company, 1913–17.

American State Papers: Documents, Legislative and Executive, of the Congress of the United States (ASP). 38 vols. Washington, DC: Gales & Seaton, 1832–61. I: Foreign Relations; III: Finance; IV: Commerce and Navigation; V: Military Affairs; VI: Naval Affairs. Online at http://memory.loc.gov/ammem/amlaw/lwsp.html.

Annals of Congress (formally known as *The Debates and Proceedings in the Congress of the United States*). New York: D. Appleton, 1857–61. Online at http://memory .loc.gov/ammem/amlaw/lwac.html.

Anonymous, "Reminiscence of the Last War," *United States Nautical Magazine* 2 (February 1846):341–44.

Baepler, Paul, ed. *White Slaves, African Masters: An Anthology of American Barbary Captivity Narratives.* Chicago: University of Chicago Press, 1999.

Cappon, Lester J., ed. *The Adams-Jefferson Letters.* Chapel Hill, NC: University of North Carolina Press, 1959.

Carden, John Surman. *A curtail'd memoir of incidents and occurrences in the life of John Surman Carden: Vice admiral in the British navy.* London: Oxford University Press, 1912.

Cobbett, William. *Peter Porcupine in America, Pamphlets on Republicanism and Revolution*, David Wilson, ed. Ithaca, NY: Cornell University Press, 1994.

Cowdery, Jonathan. *American Captives in Tripoli* (1806) in Baepler, ed., *White Slaves, African Masters.*

Dring, Thomas. *Recollections of the Jersey Prison-Ship, H. H. Brown.* Providence RI, 1829.

Dudley, William S., and Michael J. Crawford, eds. *The Naval War of 1812, A Doc-*

umentary History (NW1812). 3 vols. Washington, DC: Naval Historical Center, 1985–2004.

Durand, James R. *James Durand, an Able Seaman of 1812: His Adventures on "Old Ironsides," and as an Impressed Sailor in the British Navy.* New Haven: Yale University Press, 1926.

Evans, Amos. "The Journal of the Constitution, 1812," *Pennsylvania Magazine of History and Biography* nos. 1, 3, 4 (1895).

Foster, Sir Augustus John. "Notes on the United States, 1804–1812," *William and Mary Quarterly*, 3rd ser., 8(1) (January 1951).

Haliburton, Thomas C., letter to Admiral Sir George Broke-Middleton, July 1, 1864, reprinted in "The Arrival of the *Chesapeake* in Halifax in 1813," *American Neptune* 57 (1997):161–65.

Hamilton, Alexander, James Madison, and John Jay. *The Federalist Papers.* New York: Mentor, 1961.

Hawes, Lilla M., ed. "Letters of Henry Gilliam, 1809–1817," *Georgia Historical Quarterly* 38 (March 1954):56–66.

Historical Statistics of the United States, Colonial Times to 1970. 2 vols. Washington, DC: U.S. Department of Commerce, Bureau of the Census, 1976.

Hollins, George Nicholas. "Autobiography of Commodore George Nicholas Hollins," *Maryland Historical Magazine* 34 (September 1939).

Hoxse, John. *The Yankee Tar: An Authentic Narrative of the Voyages and Hardships of John Hoxse and the Cruises of the U.S. Frigate Constellation.* Northampton, MA: John Metcalf, 1840.

Hume, Edgar Erskine, ed. "Letters Written During the War of 1812 by the British Naval Commander in American Waters (Admiral Sir David Milne)," *William and Mary College Quarterly Historical Magazine*, 2nd ser., 10(4) (October 1930):279–301.

Humphreys, Joshua. "Letters from the Joshua Humphreys Collection of the Historical Society of Pennsylvania," *Pennsylvania Magazine of History and Biography* 30 (1906):376–78, 503.

———. Letters and Accounts Books, 1794–1801. Historical Society of Pennsylvania.

Jefferson, Thomas. *Memorandum Books*, ed. James A. Bear, Jr., and Lucia C. Stanton. Princeton: Princeton University Press, 1997.

———. *The Works of Thomas Jefferson in Twelve Volumes*, ed. Paul Leicester Ford. New York and London: G. P. Putnam's Sons, 1904.

———. *The Writings of Thomas Jefferson*, ed. Andrew A. Lipscomb and Albert E. Bergh. 20 vols. Washington, DC: Thomas Jefferson Memorial Association, 1903–04.

———. *The Writings of Thomas Jefferson*, ed. H. A. Washington. New York: J. C. Riker, 1853–55.

King, Dean, and John B. Hattendorf, eds. *Every Man Will Do His Duty: An Anthology of Firsthand Accounts from the Age of Nelson, 1793–1815.* New York: Henry Holt, 1998.

Leech, Samuel. *Thirty Years from Home* (1843). Boston: J. M. Whittemore, 1847.

Lewis, Jon E., ed. *The Mammoth Book of Life Before the Mast: An Anthology of Eye-Witness Accounts from the Age of Fighting Sail.* New York: Carroll & Graf, 2001.

Ludlow, Augustus. "The Chesapeake and Lieutenant Ludlow," *Magazine of American History* 25 (April 1891):269–92.

Maclay, William. *Journal of William Maclay, United States Senator from Pennsylvania, 1789–1791*, ed. Edgar S. Maclay. New York: Appleton & Co., 1890.

Madison, James. *Writings*, ed. Jack N. Rakove. New York: Library of America, 1999.

Martin, Tyrone G., ed. *The USS Constitution's Finest Fight, 1815. The Journal of Acting Chaplain Assheton Humphreys*. Mt. Pleasant, SC: Nautical and Aviation Publishing Co., 2000.

McKee, Christopher, ed. "*Constitution* in the Quasi-War with France: The Letters of John Roche, Jr., 1798–1801," *American Neptune* 27 (April 1967): 135–49.

Melville, Herman. *White-Jacket*. New York: Oxford University Press, 1990.

Morris, Charles. *The Autobiography of Commodore Charles Morris, U.S. Navy, with portrait and explanatory notes*. Boston: A. Williams, 1880.

Naval Documents of the American Revolution, ed. William Bell Clark. 10 vols. Washington, DC: Government Printing Office, 1964–69.

Naval Documents Related to the Quasi-War Between the United States and France (QW). 7 vols. Washington, DC: U.S. Office of Naval Records and Library, Government Printing Office, 1935.

Naval Documents Related to the United States Wars with the Barbary Powers: Naval Operations Including Diplomatic Background from 1785 Through 1807 (BW). 6 vols. Washington, DC: U.S. Office of Naval Records and Library, Government Printing Office, 1939–44.

Niles' National Register, containing political, historical, geographical, scientifical, statistical, economical, and biographical documents, essays and facts: together with notices of the arts and manufactures, and a record of the events of the times. Philadelphia, 1811–49.

"Octogenarian," "Reminiscences of the Last War with England," *Historical Magazine* 7 (January 1870): 31–37.

Paine, Thomas. *Common Sense*. Philadelphia: W. & T. Bradford, 1776.

———. *To the Representatives of the Religious Society of the People Called Quakers* (1776). Online at http://www.classicallibrary.org/paine.

Palmer, Thomas. *Victories of Hull, Jones, Decatur, Bainbridge*. Philadelphia, 1813.

Peabody, James Bishop, ed. *John Adams: A Biography in His Own Words*. New York: Newsweek, 1973.

Plumer, William. *William Plumer's Memorandum of Proceedings in the U.S. Senate 1803–1807*, ed. Everett Brown. New York: The Macmillan Company, 1923.

Price, Norma A., ed. "Letters from Old Ironsides, 1813–1815, Written by Pardon Mawney Whipple." Tempe, AZ: Beverly/Merriam Press, 1984.

Ray, William. *Horrors of Slavery, or the American Tars in Tripoli* (1808) in Baepler, ed., *White Slaves, African Masters*.

Raymond, G. "The Shannon and the Chesapeake," *United Service Magazine* 2 (October 1890): 9–16.

Robinson, William. *Jack Nastyface: Memoirs of an English Seaman*. Annapolis: Naval Institute Press, 2002.

Roosevelt, Theodore. *Theodore Roosevelt: Letters and Speeches*, ed. Louis Auchincloss. New York: Library of America, 2004.

Rosenberger, Francis C., ed. *The Jefferson Reader, A Treasury of Writings About Thomas Jefferson.* New York: E. P. Dutton, 1953.

Rosenfeld, Richard N. *American Aurora.* New York: St. Martin's Press, 1997.

Shaw, Elijah. *Short sketch of the life of Elijah Shaw, who served 21 years in the United States Navy.* Rochester, NY: Strong, Dawson, 1843.

Smith, Adam. *Inquiry into the Nature and Causes of the Wealth of Nations.* Oxford, 1880.

Smith, James Morton, ed. *The Republic of Letters: The Correspondence Between Thomas Jefferson and James Madison 1776–1826.* New York: W. W. Norton, 1995.

Smith, Margaret Bayard. *The First Forty Years of Washington Society in the Family Letters of Margaret Bayard Smith.* New York: Frederick Ungar, 1965.

Smith, Moses. *Naval Scenes in the Last War.* Boston: Gleason's Publishing House, 1846.

Snow, Elliot, ed. *Adventures at Sea in the Great Age of Sail.* New York: Dover Publications, 1986.

Stoddert, Benjamin. "Letters of Benjamin Stoddert, First Secretary of the Navy, to Nicholas Johnson of Newburyport, 1798–1799," *Essex Institute Historical Collections* 74 (1938): 350–60.

Strangeways, Alfred. "What It Was Like to Be Shot Up by Old Ironsides," *American Heritage* 34 (April to May 1983): 65–67.

Tracy, Nicholas, ed. *The Naval Chronicle: The Contemporary Record of the Royal Navy at War.* Vol. V: *1811–1815.* London: Chatham Publishing, 1999.

Truxtun, Thomas. *Instructions, Signals, and Explanations, Offered for the United States Fleet.* Baltimore: John Hayes, 1797.

The Writings of George Washington from the Original Manuscript Sources, 1745–1799, ed. John C. Fitzpatrick. 39 vols. Washington, DC: Government Printing Office, 1931–44.

Wharton, Francis, ed.: *The Revolutionary Diplomatic Correspondence of the United States.* 6 vols. Washington, DC: Government Printing Office, 1889.

SECONDARY SOURCES: BOOKS

Adams, Henry. *History of the United States During the Administrations of Thomas Jefferson* (1889–91). New York: Literary Classics of the United States, 1986.

———. *History of the United States During the Administrations of James Madison* (1889–91). New York: Literary Classics of the United States, 1986.

———. *John Randolph.* New York: Houghton Mifflin, 1882.

———. *The Life of Albert Gallatin.* Philadelphia: J. B. Lippincott, 1879.

Albion, Robert G. *Forests and Seapower* (1926). Annapolis: Naval Institute Press, 1970.

———. *Makers of Naval Policy, 1798–1947.* Annapolis: Naval Institute Press, 1980.

———, and Jennie Barnes Pope. *Sea Lanes in Wartime: The American Experience, 1775–1942.* New York: W. W. Norton, 1942.

Allison, Robert J. *The Crescent Obscured: The United States and the Muslim World, 1776–1815*. New York: Oxford University Press, 1995.

Altoff, Gerald. *Amongst My Best Men, African Americans and the War of 1812*. Toledo, OH: The Perry Group, 1996.

Anthony, Irvin. *Decatur*. New York: Charles Scribner's Sons, 1931.

Arnebeck, Bob. *Destroying Angel: Benjamin Rush, Yellow Fever and the Birth of Modern Medicine*, online at http://www.geocities.com/bobarnebeck/fever1793.html.

Balinky, Alexander. *Albert Gallatin, Fiscal Theory and Policies*. New Brunswick, NJ: Rutgers University Press, 1958.

Barrow, Clayton R., Jr. *America Spreads Her Sails; U.S. Seapower in the 19th Century*. Annapolis: Naval Institute Press, 1973.

Batterberry, Michael, and Ariane. *On the Town in New York*. New York: Routledge, 1999.

Beach, Edward L. *The United States Navy: A 200-Year History*. Boston: Houghton Mifflin, 1986.

Boileau, John. *Half-Hearted Enemies: Nova Scotia, New England and the War of 1812*. Halifax: Formac Publishing Co., 2005.

Bolster, Jeffrey. *Black Jacks: African American Seaman in the Age of Sail*. Cambridge, MA: Harvard University Press, 1997.

Bradford, James, ed. *Command Under Sail: Makers of the American Naval Tradition 1775–1950*. Annapolis: Naval Institute Press, 1985.

Brands, H.W. *TR: The Last Romantic*. New York: Basic Books, 1997.

Brant, Irving. *The Fourth President: A Life of James Madison*. Indianapolis: Bobbs-Merrill, 1970.

———. *James Madison, Commander-in-Chief, 1812–1836*. Indianapolis: Bobbs-Merrill, 1961.

———. *James Madison: The President, 1809–1812*. Indianapolis: Bobbs-Merrill, 1956.

Brodie, Fawn M. *Thomas Jefferson: An Intimate History*. New York: W. W. Norton, 1974.

Brown, Roger Hamilton. *The Republic in Peril: 1812*. New York: Columbia University Press, 1964.

Carse, Robert. *Ports of Call*. New York: Charles Scribner's Sons, 1967.

Chapelle, Howard Irving. *The Constellation Question*. Washington, DC: Smithsonian Institution Press, 1970.

———. *The History of American Sailing Ships*. New York: W. W. Norton, 1935.

———. *The History of the American Sailing Navy: The Ships and Their Development*. New York: W. W. Norton, 1949.

———. *The Search for Speed Under Sail, 1700–1855*. New York: W. W. Norton, 1967.

Chernow, Ron. *Alexander Hamilton*. New York: Penguin Press, 2004.

Chidsey, Donald B. *The Wars in Barbary: Arab Piracy and the Birth of the United States Navy*. New York: Crown, 1971.

Churchill, Winston. *A History of the English-Speaking Peoples*. Vol. 3: *The Age of Revolution*. London: Cassell, 1957.

Clark, William Bell. *Gallant John Barry, 1745–1803: The Story of a Naval Hero of Two Wars.* New York: The Macmillan Company, 1938.

Clissold, Stephen. *The Barbary Slaves.* New York: Barnes & Noble Books, 1992.

Coles, Harry Lewis. *The War of 1812.* Chicago: University of Chicago Press, 1965.

Cooper, James Fenimore. *The History of the Navy of the United States of America.* Philadelphia: Lea & Blanchard, 1839.

———. *Lives of Distinguished American Naval Officers.* Philadelphia: Carey & Hart, 1846.

Cunningham, Noble E., Jr. *In Pursuit of Reason: The Life of Thomas Jefferson.* New York: Ballantine Books, 1987.

———. *The Process of Government Under Jefferson.* Princeton: Princeton University Press, 1978.

Dana, Richard Henry, Jr. *Two Years Before the Mast* (1840). New York: Signet Classic, 1964.

Dauer, Manning J. *The Adams Federalists.* Baltimore: Johns Hopkins University Press, 1953.

Davies, David. *A Brief History of Fighting Ships.* New York: Carroll & Graf, 2002.

De Gast, Robert. *The Lighthouses of the Chesapeake.* Baltimore: Johns Hopkins University Press, 1973.

de Grummond, Jane Lucas. *The Baratarians and the Battle of New Orleans.* Baton Rouge, LA: Legacy Publishing Co., 1979.

De Kay, James Tertius. *The Battle of Stonington: Torpedoes, Submarines, and Rockets in the War of 1812.* Annapolis: Naval Institute Press, 1990.

———. *The Chronicles of the Frigate Macedonian, 1809–1922.* New York: W. W. Norton, 1995.

———. *A Rage for Glory: The Life of Commodore Stephen Decatur.* New York: Free Press, 2004.

DeConde, Alexander. *The Quasi-War: The Politics and Diplomacy of the Undeclared War with France, 1797–1801.* New York: Charles Scribner's Sons, 1966.

Donovan, Frank R. *The Tall Frigates.* New York: Dodd, Mead & Co., 1962.

Dorwart, Jeffery M., and Jean K. Wolf. *The Philadelphia Navy Yard: From the Birth of the U.S. Navy to the Nuclear Age.* Philadelphia: University of Pennsylvania Press, 2000.

Drake, Samuel Adams. *Historic Mansions and Highways Around Boston.* Boston: Little, Brown, 1899.

Dudley, Wade. *Splintering the Wooden Wall: The British Blockade of the United States, 1812–1815.* Annapolis: Naval Institute Press, 2003.

Eckert, Edward K. *The Navy Department in the War of 1812.* Gainesville: University of Florida Press, 1973.

Elkins, Stanley M., and Eric McKitrick. *The Age of Federalism: The Early American Republic, 1788–1800.* New York: Oxford University Press, 1994.

Ellis, Joseph J. *After the Revolution: Profiles of Early American Culture.* New York: W. W. Norton, 1979.

———. *American Sphinx: The Character of Thomas Jefferson.* New York: Alfred A. Knopf, 1996.

———. *Founding Brothers.* New York: Alfred A. Knopf, 2000.

————. *His Excellency: George Washington*. New York: Alfred A. Knopf, 2004.

————. *Passionate Sage: The Character and Legacy of John Adams*. New York: W. W. Norton, 1993.

Emmons, George Foster. *The Navy of the United States, from the Commencement, 1775 to 1853*. Washington, DC: Gideon & Co., 1853.

Fairburn, William Armstrong. *Merchant Sail*. 6 vols. Center Lovell, ME: Fairburn Marine Educational Foundation, 1945–55.

Faris, John Thomson. *The Romance of Old Philadelphia*. Philadelphia: J. B. Lippincott, 1918.

Ferguson, Eugene S. *Truxtun of the Constellation: The Life of Commodore Thomas Truxtun, U.S. Navy, 1755–1822*. Baltimore: Johns Hopkins University Press, 1959.

Ferling, John. *John Adams: A Life*. New York: Henry Holt, 1992.

Field, James A. *America and the Mediterranean World, 1776–1882*, Princeton: Princeton University Press, 1969.

Fleming, Thomas J. *Duel: Alexander Hamilton, Aaron Burr, and the Future of America*. New York: Basic Books, 1999.

Flexner, James Thomas. *George Washington and the New Nation*. Boston: Little, Brown, 1969.

————. *The Young Hamilton: A Biography*. Boston: Little, Brown, 1978.

Forester, C. S. *The Age of Fighting Sail: The Story of the Naval War of 1812*. Garden City, NY: Doubleday & Co., 1956.

Fowler, William M., Jr. *Jack Tars and Commodores: The American Navy, 1783–1815*. Boston: Houghton Mifflin, 1984.

————. *Rebels Under Sail*. New York: Charles Scribner's Sons, 1976.

Freeman, Joanne B. *Affairs of Honor: National Politics in the New Republic*. New Haven: Yale University Press, 2001.

Gardiner, Robert. *Frigates of the Napoleonic Wars*. Annapolis: Naval Institute Press, 2000.

————, ed. *The Naval War of 1812*. London: Caxton Publishing, 2001.

Gay, Peter. *The Enlightenment: The Rise of Modern Paganism*. New York: W. W. Norton, 1966.

Gilkerson, William. *Boarders Away: With Steel; The Edged Weapons and Polearms of the Classical Age of Fighting Sail, 1626–1826*. Lincoln, RI: Andrew Mowbray, 1991.

————. *Boarders Away II: With Fire; The Small Firearms and Combustibles of the Classical Age of Fighting Sail, 1626–1826*. Lincoln, RI: Andrew Mowbray, 1993.

Gillmer, Thomas. *Old Ironsides: The Rise, Decline, and Resurrection of USS Constitution*. New York: McGraw-Hill, 1996.

Gleaves, Albert. *James Lawrence, Captain, United States Navy, Commander of the Chesapeake*. New York: G. P. Putnam's Sons, 1904.

Gowans, Alan. *Styles and Types of North American Architecture*. New York: HarperCollins, 1992.

Grant, Bruce. *Isaac Hull, Captain of Old Ironsides: The Life and Fighting Times of Isaac Hull and the U.S. Frigate Constitution*. Chicago: Pellegrini, 1947.

Griffin, Martin I. J. *Commodore John Barry, "The Father of the American Navy": The Record of His Services for Our Country*. Philadelphia, 1903.

Gruppe, Henry E. *The Seafarers: The Frigates*. Alexandria, VA: Time-Life Books, 1979.

Guttridge, Leonard F., and Jay D. Smith. *The Commodores*. Annapolis: Naval Institute Press, 1984.

Harland, John. *Seamanship in the Age of Sail: An Account of the Ship-handling of the Sailing Man-of-War, 1600–1860, Based on Contemporary Sources*. Annapolis: Naval Institute Press, 1984.

Hawes, Alexander Boyd. *Off Soundings: Aspects of the Maritime History of Rhode Island*. Chevy Chase, MD: Posterity Press, 1999.

Hecht, Marie B. *Odd Destiny: The Life of Alexander Hamilton*. New York: Macmillan Publishing Co., 1982.

Henderson, James. *The Frigates: An Account of the Lesser Warships of the Wars from 1793 to 1815*. London: Adlard Coles, 1970.

Herman, Arthur. *To Rule the Waves: How the British Navy Shaped the Modern World*. New York: HarperCollins, 2004.

Hickey, Donald, R. *The War of 1812: A Forgotten Conflict*. Chicago: University of Illinois Press, 1989.

Hill, J.R., ed. *The Oxford Illustrated History of the Royal Navy*. New York: Oxford University Press, 1995.

Hollis, Ira N. *The Frigate Constitution: The Central Figure of the Navy Under Sail*. Boston: Houghton Mifflin, 1900.

Horseman, Reginald. *The War of 1812*. New York: Alfred A. Knopf, 1969.

Howarth, David, and Stephen. *Lord Nelson: The Immortal Memory*. London: Conway Maritime Press, 2004.

Howarth, Stephen. *To Shining Sea: A History of the United States Navy*. New York: Random House, 1991.

Ireland, Bernard. *Naval Warfare in the Age of Sail: War at Sea, 1756–1815*. New York: W. W. Norton, 2000.

Irwin, Ray W. *The Diplomatic Relations of the United States with the Barbary Powers, 1776–1816*. Chapel Hill, NC: University of North Carolina Press, 1931.

Isaacson, Walter. *Benjamin Franklin: An American Life*. New York: Simon & Schuster, 2003.

James, William. *Naval Occurrences of the War of 1812: A Full and Correct Account of the Naval War Between Great Britain and the United States of America, 1812–1815* (1817). London: Conway Maritime Press, 2004.

Keane, John. *Tom Paine: A Political Life*. Boston: Little, Brown, 1995.

King, Dean. *Harbors and High Seas: An Atlas and Geographical Guide to the Complete Aubrey-Maturin Novels of Patrick O'Brian*. New York: Owl Books, 2000.

———. *A Sea of Words: A Lexicon and Companion for Patrick O'Brian's Seafaring Tales*. New York: Henry Holt, 1995.

Kitzen, Michael L. S. *Tripoli and the United States at War: A History of American Relations with the Barbary States, 1785–1805*. Jefferson, NC: McFarland, 1993.

Koch, Adrienne. *Jefferson and Madison: The Great Collaboration*. New York: Alfred A. Knopf, 1950.

Lambert, Andrew. *War at Sea in the Age of Sail: 1650–1850*, London: Cassell, 2000.

Langley, Harold D. *A History of Medicine in the Early U.S. Navy.* Baltimore: Johns Hopkins University Press, 1995.

——. *Social Reform in the United States Navy, 1798–1862.* Urbana: University of Illinois Press, 1967.

Larkin, Jack. *The Reshaping of Everyday Life, 1790–1840.* New York: Harper-Collins, 1988.

Lavery, Brian. *Arming and Fitting of English Ships of War, 1600–1815.* Annapolis: Naval Institute Press, 1989.

——. *Nelson's Navy: The Ships, Men and Organization, 1793–1815.* Annapolis: Naval Institute Press, 2000.

——, ed. *Shipboard Life and Organization, 1731–1815.* London: Navy Records Society, 1998.

Leiner, Frederick. *Millions for Defense, The Subscription Warships of 1798.* Annapolis: Naval Institute Press, 2000.

Lever, Darcy. *The Young Sea Officer's Sheet Anchor.* New York: Dover Publications, 1998.

Lewis, Charles L. *The Romantic Decatur.* Freeport, NY: Books for Libraries Press, 1937.

Lippincott, Horace Mather. *Early Philadelphia.* Philadelphia: J. B. Lippincott, 1917.

Long, David F. *Gold Braid and Foreign Relations: Diplomatic Activities of U.S. Naval Officers, 1798–1883.* Annapolis: Naval Institute Press, 1988.

——. *Ready to Hazard: A Biography of Commodore William Bainbridge, 1774–1833.* Hanover, NH: University Press of New England, 1981.

Longridge, C. Nepean. *The Anatomy of Nelson's Ships.* Annapolis: Naval Institute Press, 1985.

Lossing, Benton J. *The Pictorial Field Book of the War of 1812.* New York: Harper & Bros., 1868.

Lovette, Leland P. *Naval Customs: Tradition and Usage.* Annapolis: Naval Institute Press, 1939.

Lyon, David. *Sea Battles in Close-Up: The Age of Nelson.* Annapolis: Naval Institute Press, 1996.

MacKenzie, Alexander Slidell. *Life of Stephen Decatur, Commodore in the Navy of the United States.* Boston: Little, Brown, 1846.

Magoun, F. Alexander. *The Frigate Constitution and Other Historic Ships.* New York: Dover Publications, 1987.

Mahan, Alfred T. *The Influence of Sea Power Upon the French Revolution and Empire, 1793–1815.* Westport, CT: Greenwood Press, 1968.

——. *The Influence of Sea Power Upon History: 1660–1793.* Boston: Little, Brown, 1890.

——. *Mahan on Naval Warfare.* London: S. Low, Marston & Co., 1919.

——. *Sea Power in Its Relation to the War of 1812.* Boston: Little, Brown, 1905.

Mahon, John K. *The War of 1812.* Gainesville: University of Florida Press, 1972.

Mahoney, Linda. *Captain from Connecticut: The Life and Naval Times of Isaac Hull.* Boston: Northeastern University Press, 1986.

Malone, Dumas. *Jefferson and His Time*. 6 vols. Boston: Little, Brown, 1948–70.

Mapp, Alf J., Jr. *Thomas Jefferson: A Strange Case of Mistaken Identity*. New York: Madison Books, 1989.

Marolda, Edward J. *The Washington Navy Yard: An Illustrated History*. Washington, DC: Naval Historical Center, 1999.

Martin, Tyrone G. *Creating a Legend*. Chapel Hill, NC: Tyron Publishing Co., 1997.

———. *A Most Fortunate Ship*. Annapolis: Naval Institute Press, 1997.

———. *Undefeated: Old Ironsides in the War of 1812*. Chapel Hill, NC: Tyron Publishing Co., 1997.

———. *The U.S.S. Constitution's Finest Fight, 1815*. Mount Pleasant, SC: Nautical & Aviation Publishing Company, 2000.

Massie, Robert K. *Castles of Steel: Britain, Germany and the Winning of the Great War at Sea*. New York: Ballantine Books, 2003.

McCoy, Drew R. *The Elusive Republic: Political Economy in Jeffersonian America*. New York: W. W. Norton, 1980.

McCullough, David. *John Adams*. New York: Simon & Schuster, 2001.

———. *Mornings on Horseback*. New York: Simon & Schuster, 1981.

McKay, Richard C. *South Street: A Maritime History of New York*. New York: G. P. Putnam's Sons, 1934.

McKee, Christopher. *Edward Preble: A Naval Biography 1761–1867*. Annapolis: Naval Institute Press, 1991.

———. *A Gentlemanly and Honorable Profession*. Annapolis: Naval Institute Press, 1991.

Menig, D. W. *The Shaping of America*. Vol. 1. New Haven: Yale University Press, 1986.

Miller, John F. *American Ships of the Colonial and Revolutionary Periods*. New York: W. W. Norton, 1978.

Miller, Nathan. *Broadsides: The Age of Fighting Sail, 1775–1815*. Hoboken, NJ: John Wiley, 2000.

———. *The United States Navy: An Illustrated History*. Annapolis: Naval Institute Press, 1977.

Minnigerode, Meade. *Jefferson, Friend of France*. New York and London: G. P. Putnam's Sons, 1928.

Morison, Samuel Eliot. *John Paul Jones: A Sailor's Biography*. Boston: Little, Brown, 1959.

Morris, Edmund. *Theodore Rex*. New York: Random House, 2001.

Morris, Richard B. *The Forging of the Union, 1781–1789*. New York: Harper-Collins, 1988.

———. *The Peacemakers: The Great Powers and European Independence*. New York: Harper & Row, 1965.

———. *Witnesses at the Creation*. New York: New American Library, 1985.

Nash, Howard P. *The Forgotten Wars. The Role of the U.S. Navy in the Quasi War with France and the Barbary Wars 1798–1805*. London: A. S. Barnes & Co., 1968.

Neill, Peter, ed. *Maritime America*. New York: Balsam Press, 1988.

Nuxoll, Elizabeth M. "The Naval Movement of the Confederation Era," in

William S. Dudley and Michael J. Crawford, eds., *The Early Republic and the Sea.* Washington, DC: Brassey's, 2001.

O'Brian, Patrick. *The Fortune of War.* New York: W. W. Norton, 1991.

———. *Men-of-War: Life in Nelson's Navy.* New York: W. W. Norton, 1974.

O'Brien, Conor Cruise. *The Long Affair: Thomas Jefferson and the French Revolution, 1785–1800.* Chicago: University of Chicago Press, 1996.

O'Neill, Richard, ed. *Patrick O'Brian's Navy.* Philadelphia: Running Press, 2003.

Padfield, Peter. *Broke and the Shannon.* London: Hodder & Stoughton, 1968.

Palmer, Michael A. *Stoddert's War: Naval Operations During the Quasi-War with France 1798–1801.* Columbia, SC: University of South Carolina Press, 1987.

Palmer, Thomas. *Victories of Hull, Jones, Decatur, Bainbridge.* Philadelphia, 1813.

Paullin, Charles Oscar. *Commodore John Rodgers, Captain, Commodore, and Senior Officer of the American Navy, 1773–1838.* Cleveland: A. H. Clark Co., 1910.

Peck, Taylor. *Round-Shot to Rockets: A History of the Washington Navy Yard and U.S. Naval Gun Factory.* Annapolis: Naval Institute Press, 1949.

Petrie, Donald. *The Prize Game: Lawful Looting on the High Seas in the Days of Fighting Sail.* Annapolis: Naval Institute Press, 1999.

Platt, Richard, and Stephen Biesty. *Cross Sections: Man of War.* London: Dorling Kindersley, 1993.

Pocock, Tom. *The Terror Before Trafalgar: Nelson, Napoleon, and the Secret War.* New York: W. W. Norton, 2003.

Poolman, Kenneth. *Guns Off Cape Ann: The Story of the Shannon and the Chesapeake.* Chicago: Rand McNally, 1962.

Pope, Dudley. *England Expects: Nelson and the Trafalgar Campaign.* Kent: Chatham, 1959.

———. *Life in Nelson's Navy.* Annapolis: Naval Institute Press, 1996.

Powell, J. H. *Bring Out Your Dead.* Philadelphia: University of Pennsylvania Press, 1949.

Powell, Nowland Van. *American Navies of the Revolutionary War.* New York: G. P. Putnam's Sons, 1974.

Pratt, Fletcher. *Preble's Boys: Commodore Preble and the Birth of American Sea Power.* New York: W. Sloane, 1950.

Price, Anthony. *The Eyes of the Fleet: A Popular History of Frigates and Frigate Captains 1793–1815.* New York: W. W. Norton, 1996.

Quincy, Edmund. *Life of Josiah Quincy.* Boston, 1868.

Randall, Willard Stern. *Thomas Jefferson: A Life.* New York: Henry Holt, 1993.

Robotti, Frances Diane, and James Vescovi. *The USS Essex and the Birth of the American Navy.* Holbrook, MA: Adams Media Corp., 1999.

Rodger, N. A. M. *The Command of the Ocean: A Naval History of Britain, 1649–1815.* New York: W. W. Norton, 2004.

———. *The Safeguard of the Sea: A Naval History of Britain, 1660–1649.* New York: W. W. Norton, 1998.

———. *The Wooden World: An Anatomy of the Georgian Navy.* London: William Collins, 1986.

Roosevelt, Theodore. *The Naval War of 1812; Or, The History of the United States*

Navy During the Last War with Great Britain, to Which Is Appended an Account of the Battle of New Orleans. New York: G. P. Putnam's Sons, 1882.

Schama, Simon. *Citizens: A Chronicle of the French Revolution*. New York: Alfred A. Knopf, 1989.

Sears, Louis Martin. *Jefferson and the Embargo*. New York: Octagon Books, 1966.

Shellenberger, William H. *Cruising the Chesapeake: A Gunkholer's Guide*. Camden, ME: International Marine Publishing Co., 1990.

Silverstone, Paul H. *The Sailing Navy 1775–1854*. Annapolis: Naval Institute Press, 2001.

Smelser, Marshall. *Congress Founds the Navy*. South Bend, IN: University of Notre Dame Press, 1959.

———. *The Democratic Republic, 1801–1815*. New York: Harper & Row, 1968.

Smith, Edgar Newbold. *American Naval Broadsides: A Collection of Early Naval Prints (1745–1815)*. Philadelphia: Philadelphia Maritime Museum, 1974.

Smith, Page. *John Adams*. Garden City, NY: Doubleday & Co., 1962.

Smith, Richard Norton. *Patriarch: George Washington and the New American Nation*. Boston: Houghton Mifflin, 1993.

Sobel, Dava. *Longitude: The True Story of a Lone Genius Who Solved the Greatest Scientific Problem of His Time*. New York: Walker, 1995.

Sprout, Harold, and Margaret. *The Rise of American Naval Power, 1776–1918*. Annapolis: Naval Institute Press, 1939.

Stevens, William Oliver. *An Affair of Honor: The Biography of Commodore James Barron, U.S.N.* Norfolk, VA: Norfolk County Historical Society, 1969.

———. *Pistols at Ten Paces: The Story of the Code of Honor in America*. Boston: Houghton Mifflin, 1940.

Symonds, Craig L. *The Naval Institute Historical Atlas of the U.S. Navy*. Annapolis: Naval Institute Press, 1995.

———. *Navalists and Antinavalists: The Naval Policy Debate in the United States, 1785–1827*. Newark, DE: University of Delaware Press, 1980.

Szatmary, David P. *Shays' Rebellion: The Making of an Agrarian Insurrection*. Amherst: University of Massachusetts Press, 1980.

Thomas, Evan. *John Paul Jones: Sailor, Hero, Father of the American Navy*. New York: Simon & Schuster, 2003.

Tolles, Frederick B. *Meeting House and Counting House: The Quaker Merchants of Colonial Philadelphia, 1682–1763*. Chapel Hill, NC: University of North Carolina Press, 1948.

Triber, Joyce E. *A True Republican: The Life of Paul Revere*. Amherst: University of Massachusetts Press, 1998.

Tuchman, Barbara W. *The First Salute: A View of the American Revolution*. New York: Alfred A. Knopf, 1988.

Tucker, Glenn. *Dawn Like Thunder: The Barbary Wars and the Birth of the U.S. Navy*. Indianapolis: Bobbs-Merrill, 1963.

Tucker, Spencer C. *Arming the Fleet: U.S. Navy Ordnance in the Muzzle-Loading Era*. Annapolis: Naval Institute Press, 1989.

———. *Stephen Decatur: A Life Most Bold and Daring*. Annapolis: Naval Institute Press, 2004.

————, and Frank T. Reuter. *Injured Honor: The Chesapeake-Leopard Affair.* Annapolis: Naval Institute Press, 1996.

Valle, James E. *Rocks and Shoals: Punishment in the Age of Fighting Sail 1800–1861.* Annapolis: Naval Institute Press, 1980.

Walters, Raymond, Jr. *Albert Gallatin, Jeffersonian Financier and Diplomat.* New York: The Macmillan Company, 1957.

Watson, Paul Barron. *The Tragic Career of Commodore James Barron, U.S. Navy.* New York: Coward-McCann, 1942.

Wertenbaker, Thomas J. *Norfolk: Historic Southern Port.* Durham, NC: Duke University Press, 1931.

Whipple, A. B. C. *The Seafarers: Fighting Sail.* Alexandria, VA: Time-Life Books, 1978.

————. *To the Shores of Tripoli: The Birth of the U.S. Navy and Marines.* New York: William Morrow, 1991.

Williams, Jack K. *Dueling in the Old South: Vignettes of Social History.* College Station: Texas A&M University Press, 1980.

Wills, Garry. *James Madison.* New York: Times Books, 2002.

Wolf, John Baptist. *The Barbary Coast: Algiers Under the Turks, 1500 to 1830.* New York: W. W. Norton, 1979.

Wood, Virginia Steele. *Live Oaking, Southern Timber for Tall Ships.* Annapolis: Naval Institute Press, 1981.

Wright, Esmond. *Fabric of Freedom: 1763–1800.* New York: Hill & Wang, 1961.

Wright, Louis B. *The First Americans in North Africa: William Eaton's Struggle for a Vigorous Policy Against the Barbary Pirates, 1799–1805.* Princeton: Princeton University Press, 1945.

Young, James Sterling. *The Washington Community 1800–1828.* New York: Columbia University Press, 1966.

Zacks, Richard. *The Pirate Coast: Thomas Jefferson, the First Marines, and the Secret Mission of 1805.* New York: Hyperion, 2005.

Zimmerman, James Fulton. *Impressment of American Seamen.* Port Washington, NY: Kennikat Press, 1925.

SECONDARY SOURCES: ARTICLES

Adamiak, Stanley J. "Benjamin Stoddert and the Quasi-War with France," *Naval History* 13(1) (1999):34–38.

Albion, Robert G. "The First Days of the Navy Department," *Military Affairs* 22 (Spring 1948): 1–11.

Allison, Robert J. "Sailing to Algiers: American Sailors Encounter the Muslim World," *American Neptune* 57(1) (1997):5–17.

Anderson, William G. "John Adams, the Navy, and the Quasi-War with France," *American Neptune* 30(2) (1970):117–32.

Baker, Maury. "Cost Overrun, An Early Naval Precedent: Building the First U.S. Warships, 1794–98," *Maryland Historical Magazine* 72(3) (1977):361–72.

Balinky, Alexander S. "Albert Gallatin, Naval Foe," *Pennsylvania Magazine of History and Biography* 82(3) (1958):293–304.

———. "Gallatin's Theory of War Finance," *William and Mary Quarterly*, 16(1) (1959):73–82.

Bass, William P. "Who Did Design the First U.S. Frigates?," *Naval History* 5(2) (1991):49–54.

Bauer, K. Jack. "Naval Shipbuilding Programs, 1794–1860," *Military Affairs* 29 (Spring 1965): 29–40.

Bolander, L. H. "An Incident in the Founding of the American Navy," *United States Naval Institute Proceedings* 55 (June 1929): 491–94.

Calderhead, William L. "U.S.F. Constellation in the War of 1812–An Accidental Fleet-in-Being," *Military Affairs* 40(2) (1976):79–83.

Calkins, Carlos Gilman. "The American Navy and the Opinions of One of Its Founders, John Adams, 1735–1826," *United States Naval Institute Proceedings* 37 (June 1911):453–83.

Carr, James A. "John Adams and the Barbary Problem: The Myth and the Record," *American Neptune* 26(4) (1966): 231–57.

Dunne, William M. P., and Frederick C. Leiner. "An 'Appearance of Menace': The Royal Navy's Incursion in New York Bay, September 1807," *Log of Mystic Seaport* 44(4) (1993):86–92.

Eddy, Richard. "Defended by an Adequate Power: Joshua Humphreys and the 74-Gun Ships of 1799," *American Neptune* 51 (Summer 1991): 173–94.

Emery, William M. "Colonel George Claghorn, Builder of Constitution," *Old Dartmouth Historical Sketches*, no. 56. New Bedford, MA: Old Dartmouth Historical Society, January 1931.

Ferguson, Eugene S. "The Figure-head of the United States Frigate *Constellation*," *American Neptune* 7 (October 1947): 255–60.

———. "The Launch of the United States Frigate *Constellation*," *United States Naval Institute Proceedings* 73 (September 1947): 1090–95.

Fisher, Charles R. "The Great Guns of the Navy, 1797–1843," *American Neptune* 36(4) (1976):276–95.

Fowler, William M. "America's Super Frigates," *Mariner's Mirror* 59(1) (1973): 49–56.

Graves, Donald E. "Worthless is the Laurel Steeped in Female Tears," *Journal of the War of 1812* (Winter 2002).

Hayes, Frederic H. "John Adams and American Sea Power," *American Neptune* 15(1) (1965): 35–45.

Humphreys, Henry H. "Who Built the First United States Navy?," *Journal of American History* 10 (first quarter 1916): 49–89.

Hunt, Livingston. "Bainbridge Under the Turkish Flag," *United States Naval Institute Proceedings* 52 (June 1926): 1147–62.

Jones, Robert F. "The Naval Thought and Policy of Benjamin Stoddert, First Secretary of the Navy, 1798–1801," *American Neptune* 24 (January 1964): 61–69.

Kaplan, L. S. "France and Madison's Decision for War, 1812," *Mississippi Valley Historical Review* 50 (1964): 652–71.

Kastor, Peter J. "Toward 'The Maritime War Only': The Question of Naval Mobilization, 1811–1812," *Journal of Military History* 61(3) (1997):455–80.

Larus, Joel. "Pell-Mell Along the Potomac," *William and Mary Quarterly*, 3rd ser. 17 (1960): 349–57.

Leiner, Frederick C. "Decatur and Naval Leadership," *Naval History* 15(5) (2001):30–34.

———. "The Norfolk War Scare," *Naval History* 7(2) (1993):36–38.

———. "The Subscription Warships of 1798," *American Neptune* 46(3) (1986):141–58.

Maps, James M. "A Long-Forgotten American Naval Cemetery," *American Neptune* 25(3) (1965):157–67.

Marden, Luis. "Restoring Old Ironsides," *National Geographic* (June 1997).

Martello, Robert. "Paul Revere's Last Ride: The Road to Rolling Copper," *Journal of the Early Republic* 20(2) (2000):219–39.

Martin, Tyrone G., and John C. Roach. "Humphreys's Real Innovation," *Naval History* 8 (March–April 1994): 32–37.

Mayhew, Dean R. "Jeffersonian Gunboats in the War of 1812," *American Neptune* 42(2) (1982):101–17.

McCullough, David. "Champion of the Navy," *Naval History* 15(5) (2001): 40–43.

McKee, Christopher. "Fantasies of Mutiny and Murder: A Suggested Psycho-History of the Seaman in the United States Navy, 1798–1815," *Armed Forces and Society* 4 (Winter 1978): 293–304.

Norton, Paul F. "Jefferson's Plans for Mothballing the Frigates," *United States Naval Institute Proceedings* 82(7) (1956):737–41.

Palmer, Aaron J. "Peace Upon Honorable Terms: The United States Ratification of the Treaty of Ghent," *Early American Review* IV(1) (Winter–Spring 2002): http://www.earlyamerica.com/review/2002_winter_spring.

Paullin, Charles O. "Dueling in the Old Navy," *United States Naval Institute Proceedings* 35 (December 1909): 1155–97.

Pistell, Lawrence. "Benjamin Stoddert: Visionary Merchant Patriot," *Financial History* 68 (2000): 23–26.

Rohr, John A. "Constitutional Foundations of the United States Navy: Text and Context," *Naval War College Review* 45 (Winter 1992): 68–84.

Roosevelt, Franklin D. "Our First Frigates: Some Unpublished Facts About Their Construction," *Transactions of the Society of Naval Architects and Marine Engineers* 22 (1914): 139–53.

Savageau, David LePere. "The United States Navy and Its 'Half War' Prisoners, 1798–1801," *American Neptune* 31 (July 1971): 159–76.

Scheina, Robert L. "Benjamin Stoddert, Politics, and the Navy," *American Neptune* 36(1) (1976):54–68.

Smith, Gene A. "A Means to an End: Gunboats and Thomas Jefferson's Theory of Defense," *American Neptune* 55(2) (1995):111–21.

———. "A Perfect State of Preservation: Thomas Jefferson's Dry Dock Proposal," *Virginia Cavalcade* 39(3) (1989):118–29.

Sofka, James R. "The Jeffersonian Idea of National Security: Commerce, the Atlantic Balance of Power, and the Barbary War, 1786–1805," *Diplomatic History* 21(4) (1997):519–44.

Sultana, Donald. "Samuel Taylor Coleridge, An American Naval Hero and a Mysterious Duellist in Malta," *Melita Historica* 11 (1993): 113–27.

Tucker, Spencer C. "American Naval Ordnance of the Revolution," *Nautical Research Journal* 22(1) (1976):21–30.

Westlake, Merle. "The American Sailing Navy: Josiah Fox, Joshua Humphreys and Thomas Tingey," *American Neptune* 59(1) (1999):21–41.

Williamson, Gene. "The Court of Last Resort," *American History* 33(6) (February 1999):3.

Wilson, Gary E. "The First American Hostages in Moslem Nations, 1784–1789," *American Neptune* 41 (July 1981): 208–23.

Wood, Daniel N. "The All-Volunteer Force in 1798," *United States Naval Institute Proceedings* 105 (June 1979): 45–48.

INDEX